Brief Contents

Contents

Supply and Demand: Theory 65

Supply and Demand: Practice 96

MICROECONOMICS

PART 2 Microeconomic Fundamentals

FEATURES

Economics in Everyday Life: Can a Drug Bust Increase Drug-Related Crime? 138
Economics in Popular Culture: Why Did Burger King Hire Shaq? 142
Economics in Everyday Life: Will High Taxes on Cigarettes Reduce Smoking? 144
Economics in Everyday Life: Are Children Substitutes or Complements? 146

FEATURES

Economics in The World: Cuban Cigars 162
Economics in Everyday Life: How You Pay for Good Weather 167

FEATURES

Economics in Everyday Life: "He Never Showed Up" 189
Economics in Everyday Life: Do Secretaries Who Work for Investment Banks Earn More Than Secretaries Who Work for Hotels? 192
Economics in Technology: The First Killer App 194
Economics in Everyday Life: Saying One Thing and Doing Another 196

PART 5   Market Failure and Public Choice

THE WORLD ECONOMY

PART 6 International Economics: Theory And Policy

Nobel laureate James Buchanan once wrote, "a natural economist is one who more or less unconsciously thinks like an economist."[1] But how does an economist think? Buchanan said "an economist . . . views human beings as self interested, utility-maximizing agents, basically independent one from another, and for whom social interchange is initiated and exists simply as a preferred alternative to isolated action."[2] In other words, if we were to tell a natural economist that "human beings are self interested, utility-maximizing agents, basically independent one from another, and for whom social interchange is initiated and exists simply as a preferred alternative to isolated action," we would expect to hear back, "But I never thought things were any different."

Buchanan went on to say that there aren't many natural economists in the world. (Three that he mentioned were Gordon Tullock, Gary Becker, and Armen Alchian.) Those of us who have spent years in the economics profession know that Buchanan is right: there aren't many natural economists. Natural economists are probably no more common than natural-born singers, natural-born baseball players, or natural-born mathematicians.

But just because there are not many natural economists, it doesn't follow that people can't learn how to think about economics naturally. What the phrase "thinking about economics naturally" means to me is to think about economics in an easy, flowing, even effortless way.

To explain what I mean here, consider the difference between Jones and Smith. Jones is a natural-born baseball player. When he is up at bat, he holds the bat correctly, swings correctly, even has just the right snap in his hips. No one had to teach him how to do this, he just does it. Go figure.

On the other hand, Smith is not a natural-born baseball player. It has taken him hours of work to learn how to hold the bat and to swing correctly. But, alas, he has practiced long enough, and he has come to understand the "logic" and "science" of hitting, such that now it comes fairly easily (flowingly) to him. If one didn't know better, one might even say it comes rather "naturally" to him.

Batting coaches can't take individuals who aren't natural born baseball players and turn them into ones. But they can take individuals who aren't natural-born baseball players and teach them how to play baseball naturally. (Not every Major Leaguer is a natural-born baseball player, but all Major Leaguers play baseball naturally.)

UNDERSTANDING THE LOGIC OF ECONOMICS

If we teach economics as a list of topics (unemployment today, theory of the firm tomorrow), we aren't teaching economics. What we are doing is taking our students on a journey through the "encyclopedia of economics." The best they will ever be able to do is spout back the facts and figures of certain topics—and some of them can do this quite well. But this isn't economics. Economics is a "way of thinking," as as almost everyone has been saying for 50 years now. But it is more than just a way of thinking: it is a way of thinking that is built upon a certain logic. Understand the logic, and you understand how economists think, and you will do economics naturally; don't understand the logic, and you don't understand how economists think, and any economics you do will be forced; it will be hit and miss.

Every economics principles book you pick up today looks like an encyclopedia. Each topic has its "15 minutes of fame" before the next topic arrives on the scene. But if we are to teach economics (and not just take the student on an encyclopedic journey), we have to make sure we say certain things as we pass from one topic to another. We have to take all 101 economic topics and show students how each of the 101 topics can be unraveled—and ultimately understood—using just a few simple economic concepts.

1. James M. Buchanan, "The Qualities of a Natural Economist," *Democracy and Public Choice*, ed. Charles Rowley (Oxford: Basil Blackwell Ltd., 1987), p. 9.
2. Ibid.

GETTING A LOT WITH A LITTLE

It has been said that good science is concerned with explaining or predicting behavior as economically as possible. What "economically as possible" means in this context is "with as little as possible." In good science we get a lot from a little.

Getting a lot from a little also holds for the Chinese language. To paraphrase Rudolf Flesch, it is a simple language that conveys a lot.[3] Roughly, whereas English speakers might say, "A dog is an animal," Chinese speakers are much more likely to say something tantamount to "Dog: animal." According to Flesch, Chinese is a language of "full words" (words that have a lot of meaning) and not many "empty words" (words that only connect words that have a lot of meaning) whereas English has many more empty words.

If you think of good science and the Chinese language, there is a similarity. Both are concerned with "getting a lot from a little."

To me, some economics principles books come closer to the "good science–Chinese language" end of the spectrum than others—and that is the part of the spectrum I think one ought to aim for. In other words, while some economics principles books keep to the basics, emphasize the concepts, and develop a reasonable and memorable theme, others do a little of everything, too often take detours, and leave their readers with a feeling of "What just happened here?"

FIVE THEMES

My objective in writing this book was to get as close to the "good science–Chinese language" end of the spectrum as possible. I wanted to keep things simple (without losing meaning), focus on key concepts that can be used repeatedly, and help students learn the logic of economics. If I could do this, I knew students would then have a chance at doing economics naturally.

How did I set out to meet my objective? First, by focusing on theory or model building. Economists use theories or models to organize their thoughts and study the world. The sooner the student learns this, and then goes on to learn how and why it is done, the better.

Second, by focusing on, and repeating as often as possible, the key concepts in economics. The key concepts are the "full words" of the language we call economics.

Third, by emphasizing what Henry Hazlitt thought was one of the key points in economics: the difference between primary and secondary consequences. In other words, by showing, repeatedly, that economic actions have consequences—some further removed from the initial action than others.

Fourth, by pointing out that economists have a certain "model of human behavior" that is implicit in almost all their theories.

Fifth, by softly playing a common tune throughout the text: that economics is about gifts, exchanges, and transfers. Stated differently, there are only three ways to gain in multi-person relationships: by giving or getting a gift (both the gift-giver and gift-recipient gain utility), by exchanging something of lesser value for something of greater value, or by transferring something from others to yourself.

---

3. Rudolf Flesch, *How to Write, Speak, and Think More Effectively* (New York: Penguin Books, 1951).

WHAT PROFESSORS AND STUDENTS HAVE TO SAY

Over the past five editions of this book I have heard from many economics professors and students. Overwhelmingly, they tell me that "the book works." Professors will sometimes add, "Of course, students don't always read as much as we would like them to, but, for the most part, they like reading your book and they read more of it than many other books we have assigned in the past."

Students will often say, "I thought economics was going to be boring. I learned differently. I liked all the applications in the book and, believe it or not, I now look at the world differently than I did before."

It is the last part of this statement—"I now look at the world differently than I did before"—that tells me the student is beginning to understand that economics is more than a list of topics, that it is a "way of thinking" that she is beginning to understand and utilize.

Let me end with a question that I once put to Gary Becker. I once asked him what one or two questions he would ask someone if he wanted to know whether or not the person thinks like an economist. Here is what he had to say:

> *I was recently in Moscow and I was asked by the Vice Dean of Moscow State University to interview some of their students who would come to the University of Chicago to do graduate work. I only had an hour to interview six students so I had to be very quick. I was told what courses they had had, and so I decided to ask them one or two microeconomic questions. My questions were simple economic questions: First, What determines a shortage in a competitive market? Second, What does your answer imply about black market prices? The answers are that a shortage is caused by preventing prices from equilibrating, and black market prices would tend to exceed what market prices would be in a competitive market because supply is restricted. Some [of the students] did quite well and some did not do well. But those would be two of the questions I would ask and there is nothing fancy about them. But the way they answered told me if someone had learned by rote, or had learned to think like an economist.[4]*

As I wrote this book, I always tried to keep Gary Becker's words in mind. Whenever I had written something that I thought the student could only "learn" by memorizing, I decided to delete it and start again. I'd ask myself, "How would a natural economist process the material at hand? What is it that the natural economist thinks that makes this material easy for him?" Then, I'd start to write again. Usually, what followed was some simple economic concept, some example, or some obvious link between the topic before me and some earlier topic. I hope I have asked the right questions and rewritten enough times so that your students will find the economics before them clear, simple, and appealing—almost natural.

---

4. This comes from an interview I conducted with Gary Becker in 1992. The full interview was published in Roger A. Arnold, *Economics*, 2nd ed. (St. Paul, Minnesota: West Publishing Company, 1992).

KEY CONTENT CHANGES

Here are some of the major things that are new to the Sixth Edition of *Economics*.

General Updates and Changes

- Chapter Road Maps at the beginning of each chapter
- Discussion of behavioral economics
- Discussion of corporate scandals
- Discussion of the politics of fiscal policy
- More applications in the *Supply and Demand: Practice* chapter
- Discussion of the Taylor rule in monetary policy
- A new feature, *A Reader Asks*
- More applications of game theory
- More graphs and tables within text
- Cleaner, easier discussion of elasticity
- Better organization of production and costs
- More emphasis on economic thinking and greater discussion of key economic concepts
- New and updated material in the four applications features—*Economics in Everyday Life, Economics in the World, Economics in Popular Culture,* and *Economics in Technology*

ORGANIZATION OF THE SIXTH EDITION

Section I: An Introduction to Economics

Section I presents the "economic way of thinking" to students. Specifically, it introduces key concepts in economics (opportunity cost, efficiency, costs and benefits, deciding at the margin, unintended effects, and more), explains the uses and abuses of theory and theorizing, focuses on two key economic activities—producing and trading—and generally develops one of the key economic frameworks of analysis in economics—supply and demand.

Section II: Macroeconomics

Students start off learning about macroeconomic measurements, then proceed to discuss various schools of macroeconomic thought (Classical, Keynesian, New Classical, Monetarist, New Keynesian) within the context of key economic phenomena—business cycles, inflation, deflation, economic growth, and more. Both fiscal and monetary policy are extensively discussed, as is expectations theory.

Section III: Microeconomics

The theme of the microeconomics part of the book, from the first edition to the sixth, is that microeconomics is about objectives, constraints, and choices. What is the objective of the individual consumer? What constraints does she face? How does she make her choices? What is the objective of the firm? What constraints does it face? How does it make its choices?

Specifically, students start off learning about marginal utility analysis and elasticity, proceed to a discussion of the firm and various market structures, and then turn to a thorough discussion of resource markets and microeconomic policies.

Section IV: The World Economy

In this section of the book students learn the details of international trade theory and international finance theory. Specifically, they learn why countries trade, how exchange rates are established, the effects of tariffs and quotas, and more.

THE STRUCTURE OF EACH CHAPTER

Each chapter of *Economics* contains the following features and pedagogical devices:
- ▶ Opening photo and vignette
- ▶ Chapter Road Map
- ▶ Margin Definitions
- ▶ http:// margin links
- ▶ Interspersed Questions and Answers
- ▶ Thinking Like an Economist
- ▶ Applications Features (*Economics in Everyday Life, Economics in Popular Culture, Economics in the World,* and *Economics in Technology*)
- ▶ Self-Tests
- ▶ A Reader Asks
- ▶ Chapter Summary
- ▶ Questions and Problems
- ▶ Working with Numbers and Graphs
- ▶ Internet Activities
- ▶ Economic Connections to You

Each of these features and pedagogical devices is described in words and visually in the *Student Learning Guide* that follows this preface.

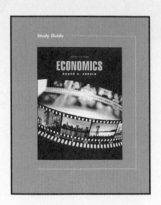

Study Guide

Each chapter explains, reviews, and tests for the important facts, concepts, and diagrams found in corresponding chapters of this book. Chapter parts include a chapter outline, multiple-choice questions, problems and exercises, and a self-test. The Study Guide is also available in microeconomic and macroeconomic splits.

Economics Study Guide   ISBN: 0-324-16364-9
Macroeconomics Study Guide   ISBN: 0-324-16360-6
Microeconomics Study Guide   ISBN: 0-324-16361-4

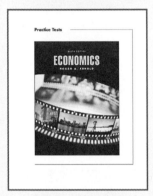

Practice Tests

Each practice test allows students to test their knowledge of the chapter material before they take the assigned test in class. ISBN: 0-324-16366-5

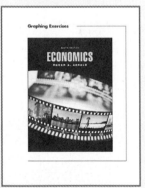

Graphing Exercises in *Economics*

For the introductory economics student, the many graphs in economics may initially seem overwhelming. It takes time and practice to master the "language" of graphs. Graphing Exercises in *Economics* provides you with the practice you need to shorten the time it takes for you to master this language. There are graphing exercises for 17 different topics, including supply and demand, the production possibilities frontier, perfect competition, monopoly, factor markets, and aggregate demand and aggregate supply. ISBN: 0-324-26119-5

Arnold Xtra!

Complimentary access to the Arnold Xtra! Web Site (**http://arnoldxtra.swcollege.com**) is included with every new copy of the textbook.* This site offers a robust set of online multimedia learning tools, including the following.

▣ Diagnostic Pretests

These innovative quizzes offer students diagnostic self-assessment of their comprehension of each chapter and an individualized plan for directed study based on the areas in which they are found to have a weaker understanding.

▣ Technology Road Map

Each chapter's Technology Road Map gives step-by-step instructions associated with each learning objective to guide students systematically through all the activities that will deepen their understanding of that particular concept.

▣ The Graphing Workshop

The Graphing Workshop is a one-stop learning resource for help in mastering the language of graphs, which is one of the more difficult aspects of an economics course for many students. It enables students to explore important economic concepts through a unique learning system made up of tutorials, interactive drawing tools, and exercises that teach how to interpret, reproduce, and explain graphs.

▣ CNN Online

CNN video segments bring the "real world" right to students' desktops. The accompanying CNN video exercises help to illustrate how economics is an important part of their daily lives, and help them learn the material by applying it to current events.

▣ Xtra! Quizzing

Students can create and take randomly generated quizzes on whichever chapters they wish to test themselves, offering them endless practice for exams.

▣ Economic Applications

(e-con @pps) EconNews Online, EconDebate Online, EconData Online, and EconLinks Online features help to deepen students' understanding of theoretical concepts through hands-on exploration and analysis of the latest economic news stories, policy debates, and data.

---

*Students with a used textbook can purchase access to Xtra! online at *http://arnold.swcollege.com*.

SUPPLEMENTS FOR THE INSTRUCTOR

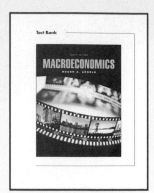

Test Bank

The Test Bank has been revised by Peggy Crane of Southwestern College in San Diego. The Test Bank consists of multiple-choice, true-false, and essay questions. There are more than 4,500 questions in the test bank.

Macroeconomics Test Bank   ISBN: 0-324-16372-X
Microeconomics Test Bank   ISBN: 0-324-16373-8

ExamView Testing Software

ExamView—Computerized Testing Software contains all of the questions in the printed test banks. ExamView is an easy-to-use test creation software compatible with Microsoft Windows. Instructors can add or edit questions, instructions, and answers, and select questions by previewing them on the screen, selecting them randomly, or selecting them by number. Instructors can also create and administer quizzes online, whether over the Internet, a local area network (LAN), or a wide area network (WAN).

ExamView for *Macroeconomics*   ISBN: 0-324-16355-X
ExamView for *Microeconomics*   ISBN: 0-324-16352-5

Instructor's Manual

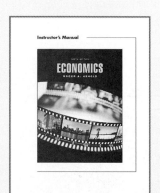

The Instructor's Manual has been revised by Philip Sprunger of Lycoming College. The Instructor's Manual offers detailed lecture assistance, including an overview of each chapter, a list of chapter objectives, key terms, a detailed chapter outline with lecture notes, answers to end-of-chapter questions, and more. ISBN: 0-324-16374-6

Transparency Acetates

More than 150 full color transparencies of key exhibits in the text are available for classroom use.

Macroeconomics Acetates ISBN: 0-324-16299-5
Microeconomics Acetates ISBN: 0-324-16298-7

Microsoft PowerPoint® Presentation Slides

These slides include all exhibits from the textbook. They are available for downloading under "Teaching Resources" at the Arnold Web site **http://arnold.swcollege.com**. ISBN: 0-324-14778-3

Turner Learning/CNN Economics Video with Integration Guide

Professors can bring the real world into the classroom by using the Turner Learning/CNN Economics Video. This video provides current stories of economic interest. The accompanying integration guide provides a summary and discussion questions for each clip. The video is produced in cooperation with Turner Learning Inc. Contact your South-Western/Thomson Learning sales representative for ordering information. ISBN: 0-324-14778-3

Instructor's Resource CD-ROM

Get quick access to all instructor ancillaries from your desktop. This easy-to-use CD lets you review, edit, and copy exactly what you need in the format you want. ISBN: 0-324-16297-9

FOR STUDENTS AND INSTRUCTORS

The Wall Street Journal Edition

The Wall Street Journal is synonymous with the latest word on business, economics, and public policy. *Economics, 6e* makes it easy for students to apply economic concepts to this authoritative publication, and for you to bring the most up-to-date, real world events into your classroom. For a nominal additional cost, *Economics, 6e* can be packaged with a card entitling students to a 15-week subscription to both the print and online versions of *The Wall Street Journal*. Instructors who have at least seven students activate their subscriptions will automatically receive their own free subscription. Contact your South-Western/Thomson Learning sales representative for package pricing and ordering information.

InfoTrac College Edition

An InfoTrac College Edition 4-month subscription card is automatically packaged free with new copies of this text. With InfoTrac College Edition, journals like *Business Week, Fortune,* and *Forbes* are just a click away! InfoTrac College Edition provides students with anytime, anywhere access to 20 years' worth of full-text articles (*more than 10 million!*) from nearly *4,000* scholarly and popular sources! In addition to receiving the latest business news as reported in the popular business press, students also have access to many other journals, among them those that are particularly valuable to the economics discipline—including the *Economist (US), American Economist, Economic Review,* and *Quarterly Journal of Economics.* For more information on InfoTrac College Edition, visit **http://infotrac/thomsonlearning.com/index.html**.

TextChoice: Economic Issues and Activities

TextChoice is the home of Thomson Learning's online digital content. TextChoice provides the fastest, easiest way for you to create your own learning materials. South-Western's Economic Issues and Activities content database includes a wide variety of high-interest, current event/policy applications as well as classroom activities that are designed specifically to enhance introductory economics courses. Choose just one reading, or many—even add your own material—to create an accompaniment to the textbook that is perfectly customized to your course. Contact your South-Western/Thomson Learning sales representative for more information.

The Arnold *Economics* Web Site

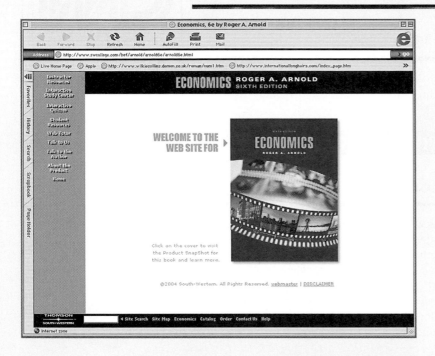

http://arnold.swcollege.com provides instructors and students with updates to the text, teaching and learning resources, and the opportunity to communicate with the author. All Internet addresses in the text are found at this site and are updated regularly.

South-Western Economics Resource Center

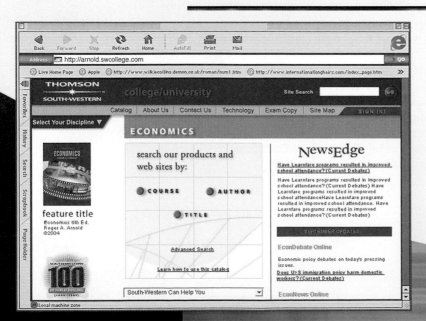

A unique, rich and robust online resource for economics instructors and students. **http://economics.swcollege.com** provides customer service and product information, teaching and learning tips and tools, information about careers in economics, access to all of our text-supporting Web sites, and other cutting-edge educational resources such as our highly regarded EconNews, EconDebate, EconData, and EconLinks Online features.

WebTutor™ on WebCT and on Blackboard

Online learning is growing at a rapid pace. Whether instructors are looking to offer courses at a distance, or to offer a web-enhanced classroom, WebTutor provides instructors with text-specific content that interacts in the two leading higher education course management systems—WebCT and Blackboard. WebTutor is a turnkey solution for instructors who want to begin using technology like WebCT or Blackboard, but do not have web-ready content available or do not want to be burdened with developing their own content. South-Western offers two levels of WebTutor—WebTutor and WebTutor Advantage.

WebTutor—An interactive study guide, WebTutor uses the Internet to turn everyone in your class into a front-row student. WebTutor offers quizzing, concept concept review, flashcards, discussion forums, and more. Instructor tools are also provided to assist communication between students and faculty.

WebTutor Advantage—WebTutor Advantage is more than just an interactive study guide because it delivers innovative learning aids that actively engage students. Its benefits include automatic and immediate feedback from quizzes; interactive, multimedia-rich explanation of concepts, such as Flash-animated graphing tutorials and graphing exercises that use an online graph-drawing tool; streaming video applications; online exercises; flashcards; and greater interaction and involvement through online discussion forums. Powerful instructor tools are also provided to assist communication and collaboration between students and faculty.

For more information and a demo of what WebTutor can do for your classes, visit **http://webtutor.swcollege.com**.

IN APPRECIATION

First Edition Reviewers

Paul Seidenstat
Temple University, Pennsylvania

Shahram Shafiee
North Harris County College, Texas

Alan Sleeman
Western Washington University

John Sondey
University of Idaho

Robert W. Thomas
Iowa State University

Richard L. Tontz
California State University, Northridge

Roger Trenary
Kansas State University

Bruce Vanderporten
Loyola University, Illinois

Thomas Weiss
University of Kansas

Richard O. Welch
University of Texas at San Antonio

Donald A. Wells
University of Arizona

John Wight
University of Richmond, Virginia

Thomas Wyrick
Southwest Missouri State University

Second Edition Reviewers

Scott Bloom
North Dakota State University

Thomas Carroll
University of Nevada, Las Vegas

Larry Cox
Southwest Missouri State University

Diane Cunningham
Los Angeles Valley College

Emit Deal
Macon College

Michael Fabritius
University of Mary Hardin Baylor

Frederick Fagal
Marywood College

Ralph Fowler
Diablo Valley College

Bob Gilette
Texas A&M University

Lynn Gillette
Indiana University, Indianapolis

Simon Hakim
Temple University

Lewis Karstensson
University of Nevada, Las Vegas

Abraham Kidane
California State University, Dominguez Hills

W. Barbara Killen
University of Minnesota

J. David Lages
Southwest Missouri State University

Anthony Lee
Austin Community College

Marjory Mabery
Delaware County Community College

Bernard Malamud
University of Nevada, Las Vegas

Michael Marlow
California Polytechnic State University, San Luis Obispo

Phil J. McLewin
Ramapo College of New Jersey

Tina Quinn
Arkansas State University

Terry Ridgway
University of Nevada, Las Vegas

Paul Snoonian
University of Lowell

Paul Taube
Pan American University

Roger Trenary
Kansas State University

Charles Van Eaton
Hillsdale College

Mark Wheeler
Bowling Green State University

Thomas Wyrick
Southwest Missouri State University

Third Edition Reviewers

Carlos Aguilar
University of Texas, El Paso

Rebecca Ann Benakis
New Mexico State University

Scott Bloom
North Dakota State University

Howard Erdman
Southwest Texas Junior College

Arthur Friedberg
Mohawk Valley Community College

Nancy A. Jianakoplos
Colorado State University

Lewis Karstensson
University of Nevada, Las Vegas

Rose Kilburn
Modesto Junior College

Ruby P. Kishan
Southeastern Community College

Duane Kline
Southeastern Community College

Charles A. Roberts
Western Kentucky University

Bill Robinson
University of Nevada, Las Vegas

Susan C. Stephenson
Drake University

Charles Van Eaton
Hillsdale College

Richard O. Welch
The University of Texas at San Antonio

Calla Wiemer
University of Hawaii at Manoa

I would like to thank Peggy Crane of Southwestern College, who revised the Test Bank, Philip Sprunger of Lycoming College, who revised the Instructor's Manual, and Guillermo Cruz of the College of the Canyons who revised the Internet Activities and http:// links that are in each chapter.

I would also like to thank Robert W. Brown, a friend and colleague in the Economics Department at California State University San Marcos. Our long and detailed talks have helped focus my thinking, some of the benefits of which I hope have spilled over into this book.

I owe a deep debt of gratitude to all the fine and creative people I worked with at South-Western College Publishing. These persons include Jack Calhoun, Editor-in-Chief; Mike Roche, Vice-President/Publisher; Mike Worls, Acquisitions Editor; Jennifer Baker, Developmental Editor; Starratt Alexander, Production Editor; Lisa Lysne, Executive Marketing Manager for Economics; Michelle Kunkler, Senior Design Project Manager; and Sandee Milewski, Manufacturing Coordinator. I would also like to thank Barbara Sheridan, copyeditor, of Sheridan Publications Services, who not only did a masterful job of copyediting the book but also made numerous suggestions on how to improve the presentation.

My deepest debt of gratitude goes to my wife, Sheila, and to my two sons, David, twelve years old, and Daniel, fifteen years old. They make all my days happy ones.

Roger A. Arnold

Student Learning Guide

TO THE STUDENT

Before you begin your study of economics, it is important to know something about the road you are about to travel. That's what this preface is about. Let me suggest how you should read and study this book to get the most out of it. You will find the road to learning economics less bumpy if you know something about the structure of each chapter and about the pedagogical devices used throughout the text.

Chapter Structure and Pedagogy

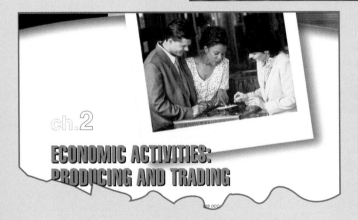

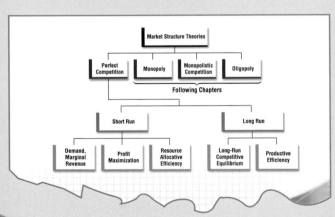

☐ Opening Photo and Vignette

Each chapter opens with a photo and short vignette. Look at the photo and read the vignette (it will take no more than 15 seconds to do both) to get an idea of what the chapter is about.

☐ Chapter Road Map

Reading an economics textbook for the first time is similar to driving to a place you haven't been before: It's easy to get lost. Sometimes a simple road map helps. Each chapter of this book opens with a chapter road map. By reading the opening paragraphs and consulting the chapter road map, you will have a good idea of where your journey through the chapter will take you.

Besides looking at the road map before you start to read the chapter, take another look at it when you have completed the chapter, and also here and there along the way. Referring back to it now and again will help you put the material you are reading into usable form. You will see how what you are currently reading relates to something you read earlier in the chapter, and you will realize how what you are reading now will be connected with something you will soon read about.

☐ Interspersed Questions and Answers

As you are reading, you may have some questions. This feature tries to anticipate the questions you might have. It then answers those questions. These questions and answers are placed at natural stopping places in each chapter.

☐ Self-Tests

Frequent feedback plays an important role in learning new material, so Self-Tests are included throughout the chapters. The answers to the Self-Tests are at the end of the book. Don't skip over a Self-Test because you are in a hurry. Stop, take the test, and then check your answers. If you don't answer a question correctly, go back and reread the relevant material so that you can answer it correctly.

▣ Margin Definitions

The first time you study economics, you have a lot to learn: language, concepts, theories, and ways of thinking. This feature helps you learn the language of economics. All key economics terms and their definitions are in the margins of the text. To more effectively learn and understand these definitions, you may find it useful to first read them and then to re-state them in your own words.

▣ http://

This Internet feature is placed in the margins of the text. It points you to a Web site address where you can find information that relates to the discussion of the material in the text. You can use this feature to enhance your understanding of the chapter, as a starting point for research, or just to check out some interesting, real-world applications of economics.

▣ Thinking Like an Economist

Most economics instructors believe that a primary goal of this course is to teach you how economists think. There's more to thinking like an economist than knowing the concepts and technical tools of analysis. There's a special way of looking at situations, events, decisions, and behavior. Pay attention to this feature—it will give you unique insight into the economist's mind, allowing you to see how interesting issues are approached from an economic perspective.

Budget Deficit
Government expenditures greater than tax revenues.

Budget Surplus
Tax revenues greater than government expenditures.

Balanced Budget
Government expenditures equal to tax revenues.

Expansionary Fiscal Policy
Increases in government expenditures and/or decreases in taxes to achieve particular economic goals.

Contractionary Fiscal Policy
Decreases in government expenditures and/or increases in taxes to achieve particular economic goals.

Discretionary Fiscal Policy
Deliberate changes of government expenditures and/or taxes to achieve particular economic goals.

Automatic Fiscal Policy
[government expendi]... that [...]

expenditures and tax revenues. If expenditures are greater than tax revenues, a **budget deficit** exists. If tax revenues are greater than expenditures, a **budget surplus** exists. If expenditures equal tax revenues, a **balanced budget** exists.

SOME RELEVANT FISCAL POLICY TERMS

Notice in our definition of fiscal policy that we use the term *government expenditures* instead of *government purchases*, the term you are familiar with from earlier chapters. Government expenditure—which is sometimes simply called *government spending*—is not the same as *government purchases*. Government expenditures is the sum of government purchases and (government) transfer payments.[1]

Expansionary fiscal policy refers to increases in government expenditures and/or decreases in taxes to achieve macroeconomic goals. **Contractionary fiscal policy** refers to decreases in government expenditures and/or increases in taxes to achieve these goals.

Expansionary fiscal policy: Government expenditures up and/or taxes down
Contractionary fiscal policy: Government expenditures down and/or taxes up

When changes in government expenditures and taxes are brought about deliberately through government actions, fiscal policy is said to be *discretionary.* For example, if Congress decides to increase government spending by, say, $10 billion in an attempt to lower the unemployment rate, this is an act of **discretionary fiscal policy**. In contrast, a change in either government expenditures or taxes that occurs automatically in response to economic events is referred to as **automatic fiscal policy**. To illustrate, suppose Real GDP in the economy turns down, causing more people to become unemployed. As a result, more people automatically receive unemployment benefits. These added unemployment benefits automatically boost government spending.

---

around the existing quantity of money between various individuals and firms but do not change the total.

Self-Test *(Answers to Self-Test questions are in the Self-Test Appendix.)*

1. Why (not how) did money evolve out of a barter economy?
2. If individuals remove funds from their checkable deposits and transfer them to their money market accounts, will M1 fall and M2 rise? Explain your answer.
3. How does money reduce the transaction costs of making trades?

HOW BANKING DEVELOPED

Just as money evolved, so did banking. This section discusses the origins of banking. The discussion will shed some light on and aid in understanding modern banking.

THE EARLY BANKERS

Our money today is easy to carry and transport. But money was not always so portable. For example, when money was principally gold coins, carrying it about was neither easy nor safe. First, gold is heavy. Second, a person transporting thousands of gold coins can easily draw the attention of thieves. But storing gold [...] to be risky. Most individuals turned to their local goldsmith for [...] was already equipped with safe storage facilities. Goldsmiths [...]nkers. They took in other people's gold and stored it for them. [...]that th[...]ld deposited gold, goldsmiths issued receipts called [...]

http://

Go to *http://www.frbsf.org/currency/civilwar/index.html.* Why aren't living persons portrayed on U.S. money? What do you think explains the reason postage stamps were used as a substitute for coins during the Civil War? What is a greenback?

http://

Go to *http://www.jpmchase.com.* Under the "About the firm" menu, select "History" and then "JPMorgan." When was J. P. Morgan founded? Who were the customers of J. P. Morgan? What effect did the Glass-Steagall Act have on J. P. Morgan? Do you think large companies use banks the same way today as they did 100 years ago?

---

of labor. You will see in the next chapter that the flexible wages and prices position taken by these economists has not gone unchallenged.

The following table summarizes how a self-regulating economy works for three possible states of the economy.

State of the Economy	What Happens If the Economy Is Self-Regulating?
Recessionary gap (Real GDP < Natural Real GDP)	Wages fall and *SRAS* curve shifts to the right until Real GDP = Natural Real GDP.
Inflationary gap (Real GDP > Natural Real GDP)	Wages rise and *SRAS* curve shifts to the left until Real GDP = Natural Real GDP.
Long-run equilibrium (Real GDP = Natural Real GDP)	No change in wages and no change in SRAS.

THINKING LIKE AN ECONOMIST

Like other scientists, economists are often interested in knowing whether the phenomena they are studying have a natural resting place. For example, the natural resting place for a ball thrown high into the air is the ground. Gravity pulls the ball downward. Where is the natural resting place for a competitive market? It is where the quantity demanded of a good equals the quantity supplied of the good. Markets are "at rest" when they are in equilibrium.

Macroeconomists want to know if the economy has a natural resting place. Some economists think it does. They think the natural resting place for the economy is where Natural Real GDP is being produced and the natural unemployment rate exists. Economists who believe that the economy can eliminate both recessionary and inflationary gaps smoothly and quickly by itself, and thus return to its natural state, use the analogy of a person's normal body temperature, which is 98.6 degrees.

THINKING LIKE AN ECONOMIST

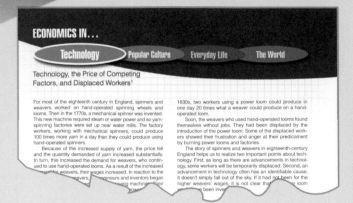

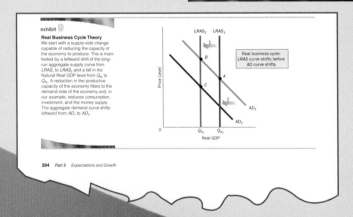

■ Applications Features

Read the features in each chapter titled *Economics in Everyday Life, Economics in Popular Culture, Economics in the World,* and *Economics in Technology.* Often, students gloss over these features because they think they are irrelevant to the discussion in the main body of the text. Nothing could be further from the truth. These features often apply the tools, concepts, and theories discussed in the main body of the text. Without these applications, economics may initially seem dry and abstract. To dispel the notion that economics is simply about inflation, unemployment, costs of production, profit, economic growth, monetary and fiscal policy, and so on, I have included these applications features to show you some of the interesting, everyday things that economics is about. Economics, as I hope you will soon learn, is about many more things than you have ever imagined.

■ A Reader Asks

Have you ever wanted to ask an instructor a question you thought you might get into trouble for asking? Suppose you're learning about supply and demand in economics and you really want to ask, "How will supply and demand help me?" But you don't ask the question because you think the professor will take offense.

Or suppose you want to ask a very practical question, such as, "How much do economists earn?" or "Is an economics degree respected in the marketplace?" Here, you may not ask the question because you think it isn't quite academic enough.

In the feature *A Reader Asks*, I answer some of the pointed and basic questions that real readers have on their minds.

Graphs and Exhibits

Take your time with the diagrams. An introductory course in economics is full of diagrams, and they are central to communicating economic material. The sooner you learn to "think diagrammatically," the more quickly and thoroughly you will learn economics. The way you learn to think in diagrams is to work with them. Read the caption, identify the curves that are mentioned in the text, explain to yourself what they mean when they shift right and left, and so on. Every diagram tells a story; you need to find out what the story is.

■ Graphs

I've carefully used consistent colors, shaded arrows to show movement, multistep formats, and boxed explanations to make it easy for you to visually interpret important economic concepts at a glance.

■ A Closer Look

For many students, the difficult part of economics is seeing how all the topics and concepts fit together. Use these special diagrams to more easily understand how the separate pieces of the puzzle fit together to form a cohesive picture of complex interrelationships. Flow diagrams and other unifying devices are used to help you identify cause-effect relationships and clarify the connections between concepts.

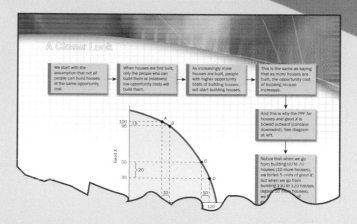

Chapter Summary

■ Chapter Summary

Each chapter ends with a detailed and categorized summary of the main topics in the chapter. The summary is a useful refresher before class and a good starting point for studying.

■ Questions and Problems

Each chapter ends with numerous questions and problems. Be sure to answer all the questions at the end of each chapter. You never really know how well you have learned economics until someone calls upon you to answer a question. If we can't use what we have read and studied to answer a question, we have to wonder if we learned anything in the first place.

■ Working with Numbers and Graphs

Each chapter ends with a few numerical and graphical problems. When you are able to numerically and graphically analyze economic ideas, you will solidify your conceptual understanding.

■ Key Terms and Concepts

A list of key terms concludes each chapter. If you can define all these terms, you have a good head start on studying.

■ Economic Connections to You

Economic Connections to You is a short feature at the end of the chapter. Economic Connections to You requires you to identify how economic facts, actions, and changes (discussed in the chapter) affect you. This feature challenges you to apply your newly acquired economic analysis skills.

■ Internet Activities

Each chapter ends with Web activities, helping you broaden your understanding of the chapter by applying what you've learned to interpreting economic data on the Internet.

Arnold Xtra!

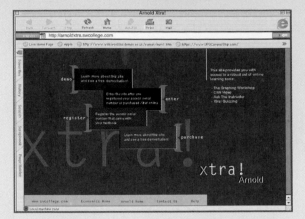

You are probably already aware that you have your own unique learning style—the way you digest information the best. You may learn by reading information, hearing it, seeing it, having hands-on experiences, and so on. Each of these learning styles requires different tools for the most effective delivery of information, and so a textbook alone may not offer you the optimal way to learn. Luckily, today's technology can offer an exciting array of tools to support and extend the textbook in order to reach out to a variety of students like yourself, each of whom has different needs in terms of how they learn best.

To this end, you'll find that complimentary access to the Arnold Xtra! Web site (**http://arnoldxtra.swcollege.com**) is included with every new copy of this textbook. Arnold Xtra! provides you with a comprehensive set of online multimedia learning tools that will help you gain a deeper and richer understanding of the material on many different levels—not just reading the text, but also seeing, hearing, and doing.

Here is a tour through some of the features that you will find in Arnold Xtra!

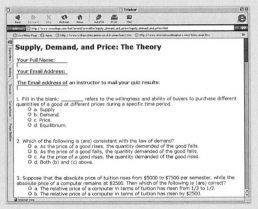

DIAGNOSTIC PRETESTS

These innovative quizzes offer diagnostic self-assessment and an individualized plan for directed study of each chapter. Start each chapter by taking the pretest to assess your understanding of key chapter learning objectives. If you answer a question incorrectly, Xtra! will link you to a Technology Road Map (see below) that will guide you systematically through a variety of learning tools to eliminate confusion and solidify your understanding.

TECHNOLOGY ROAD MAPS

You can also begin studying each chapter by using the Technology Road Map feature. Each chapter's Technology Road Map functions as a central navigational tool and complete e-learning guide to all the Xtra! resources that are available to enhance comprehension of the chapter's main ideas. Step-by-step instructions associated with each chapter learning objective guide you systematically through all available text and multimedia tools to deepen your understanding of that particular concept.

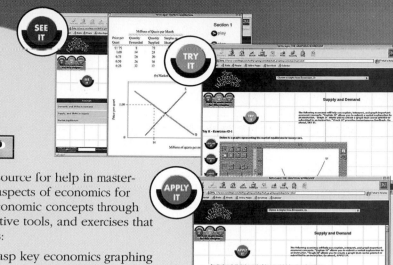

THE GRAPHING WORKSHOP

The Graphing Workshop is your one-stop learning resource for help in mastering the language of graphs, one of the more difficult aspects of economics for many students. It enables you to explore important economic concepts through a unique learning system made up of tutorials, interactive tools, and exercises that teach how to interpret, reproduce, and explain graphs:

- ▶ **Grasp It!** Java-powered graphs allow you to grasp key economics graphing concepts through hands-on interaction with a "live" graph.
- ▶ **See It!** Animated graphing tutorials provide step-by-step graphical presentations and audio explanations.
- ▶ **Try It!** Interactive graphing exercises encourage you to practice manipulating and interpreting graphs with hands-on Java graphing tools. You can check your work online.
- ▶ **Apply It!** Interactive graphing assignments challenge you to apply what you have learned by creating your own graphs from scratch to analyze a specific scenario. Answers can be printed and/or e-mailed to your instructor for grading.

CNN ONLINE

CNN video segments bring the "real world" to your desktop. The accompanying CNN Video exercises help to illustrate how economics is an important part of your daily life and help you learn the material by applying it to current events.

ASK THE INSTRUCTOR

Via streaming video, difficult concepts from each chapter are explained and illustrated. These video clips are extremely helpful review and clarification tools if you have trouble understanding an in-class lecture or are a visual learner.

XTRA! QUIZZING

You can practice for tests, midterms, and finals by creating and taking as many randomly generated quizzes as you like on whichever chapters you wish to test yourself.

ECONOMIC APPLICATIONS (E-CON @PPS)

EconNews Online, EconDebate Online, EconData Online and EconLinks Online features help to deepen your understanding of theoretical concepts through hands-on exploration and analysis of the latest economic news stories, policy debates, and data.

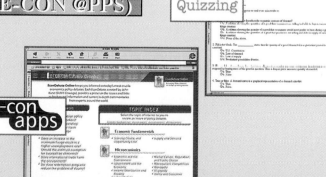

ch.1

WHAT ECONOMICS IS ABOUT

Economists look at the world and ask questions. Their questions give us insights into the economic way of thinking. For example, an economist might look at a college student and ask: What are the benefits and costs to this student of attending college? Thus, the economic way of thinking considers both benefits and costs, and not only one or the other. You will learn much more about the economic way of thinking in this chapter and throughout the book.

Reading an economics textbook for the first time is similar

to driving to a place you haven't been to before: it's easy to get lost.

Following a simple road map makes it less likely you will get lost driving; referring

to an economics road map makes it less likely you will get lost studying economics.

    Each chapter in this text begins with a road map. By reading these opening paragraphs and

consulting the chapter road map, you will have a good idea of where your journey through the chapter will

take you.

    This chapter starts with a basic question: What is economics? *An economist might answer this question by giving*

a formal dictionary-like definition of economics or by discussing the economic way of thinking. *In this chapter, we both*

define economics and outline the details of the economic way of thinking—thinking in terms of (1) various categories of

economics, (2) key concepts in economics, and (3) building and testing theories.

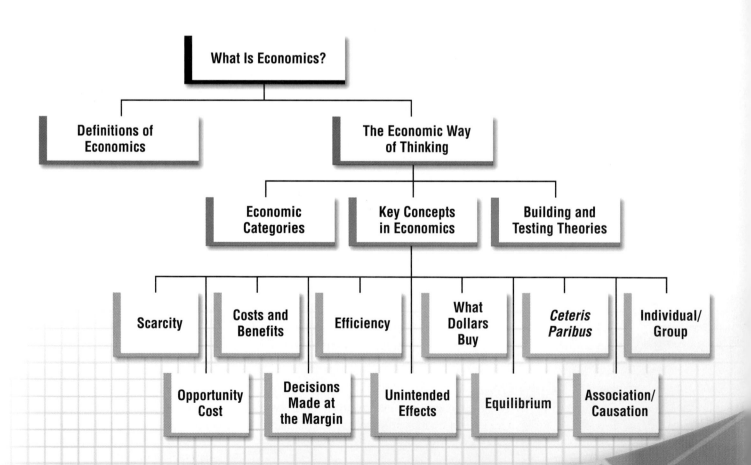

DEFINITIONS OF ECONOMICS

Economics has been defined in various ways in its more than 200 year history. However, some definitions of economics are familiar to almost all economists. We identify three of these definitions in this section, and then give the definition of economics that we use in this text.

The economist Alfred Marshall (1824–1924) was Professor of Political Economy at the University of Cambridge (in England) from 1885 to 1908. Marshall's major work, *Principles of Economics* (first published in 1890), was the most influential economics treatise of its time and has been called the "Bible of British Economics." In the first few lines of the book, Marshall wrote: "Political economy or economics is a study of mankind in the ordinary business of life; it examines that part of individual and social action which is most closely connected with the attainment and with the use of the material requisites of well being." He then said that economics is "on the one side a study of wealth; and on the other, and more important side, a part of the study of man." In short, according to Marshall, economics is the study of mankind in the ordinary business of life; it is the study of wealth and of man.

Lionel Robbins (1898–1984), who taught economics at both Oxford University and the London School of Economics, put forth one of the most widely cited definitions of economics. In his book *The Nature and Significance of Economic Science,* Robbins wrote, "Economics is the science which studies human behavior as a relationship between ends and scarce means which have alternative uses."

Milton Friedman (b. 1912), the 1976 winner of the Nobel Prize in Economics, proposed a similar definition of economics in his work *Price Theory.* Friedman wrote, "Economics is the science of how a particular society solves its economic problems." He then said, "an economic problem exists whenever scarce means are used to satisfy alternative ends."

Ask a noneconomist what economics is and he or she will probably answer that it has something to do with business and wealth. So Marshall's definition of economics accords most closely with the a noneconomist's concept of economics. The Robbins and Friedman definitions both stress the relationship between *ends* and *means*. This relationship naturally leads us to a discussion of scarcity.

Scarcity is the condition in which our wants are greater than the limited resources available to satisfy them. Our wants are *infinite;* our resources are *finite.* That's scarcity. To define scarcity in terms of ends and means, we can say that our ends are *infinite* and the means available to satisfy those ends are *finite.*

Many economists say that if scarcity didn't exist, neither would economics. In other words, if our wants weren't greater than the limited resources available to satisfy them, there would be no field of study called economics. This is similar to saying that if matter and motion didn't exist, neither would physics, or that if living things didn't exist, neither would biology. For this reason, we define **economics** in this text as the *science of scarcity.* More completely, *economics is the science of how individuals and societies deal with the fact that wants (or ends) are greater than the limited resources (or means) available to satisfy those wants.*

Scarcity
The condition in which our wants are greater than the limited resources available to satisfy those wants.

Economics
The science of scarcity: the science of how individuals and societies deal with the fact that wants are greater than the limited resources available to satisfy those wants.

ECONOMIC CATEGORIES

Economics is sometimes broken down into different categories, according to the type of questions economists ask. Four common economic categories are positive economics, normative economics, microeconomics, and macroeconomics.

POSITIVE AND NORMATIVE ECONOMICS

Positive economics attempts to determine *what is.* **Normative economics** addresses *what should be.* Essentially, positive economics deals with cause-effect relationships that can be tested. Normative economics deals with value judgments and opinions that cannot be tested.

Positive Economics
The study of "what is" in economic matters.

Normative Economics
The study of "what should be" in economic matters.

Many topics in economics can be discussed within both a positive and a normative framework. Consider a proposed cut in federal income taxes. An economist practicing positive economics would want to know the *effect* of a cut in income taxes. For example, she may want to know how a tax cut will affect the unemployment rate, economic growth, inflation, and so on. An economist practicing normative economics would address issues that directly or indirectly relate to whether the federal income tax *should* be cut. For example, she may say that federal income taxes should be cut because the income tax burden on many taxpayers is currently high.

This book mainly deals with positive economics. For the most part, we discuss the economic world as it is, not the way someone might think it should be. As you read, you should keep two points in mind. First, although we have taken pains to keep our discussion within the boundaries of positive economics, at times we may operate perilously close to the normative border. If, here and there, we drop a value judgment into the discussion, recognize it for what it is. You should not accept as true something that we simply state as an opinion.

Second, keep in mind that no matter what your normative objectives are, positive economics can shed some light on how they might be accomplished. For example, suppose you believe that absolute poverty should be eliminated and the unemployment rate should be lowered. No doubt you have ideas as to how these goals can be accomplished. But are they correct? For example, will a greater redistribution of income eliminate absolute poverty? Will lowering taxes lower the unemployment rate? There is no guarantee that the means you think will bring about certain ends will do so. This is where sound positive economics can help. It helps us see what is. As someone once said: It is not enough to want to do good, it is important also to know how to do good.

MICROECONOMICS AND MACROECONOMICS

It has been said that the tools of microeconomics are microscopes, and the tools of macroeconomics are telescopes. Macroeconomics stands back from the trees in order to see the forest. Microeconomics gets up close and examines the tree itself, its bark, its limbs, and the soil in which it grows. **Microeconomics** is the branch of economics that deals with human behavior and choices as they relate to relatively small units—an individual, a firm, an industry, a single market. **Macroeconomics** is the branch of economics that deals with human behavior and choices as they relate to an entire economy. In microeconomics, economists discuss a single price; in macroeconomics, they discuss the price level. Microeconomics deals with the demand for a particular good or service; macroeconomics deals with aggregate, or total, demand for goods and services. Microeconomics examines how a tax change affects a single firm's output; macroeconomics looks at how a tax change affects an entire economy's output.

Microeconomists and macroeconomists ask different types of questions. A microeconomist might be interested in answering such questions as:

- How does a market work?
- What level of output does a firm produce?
- What price does a firm charge for the good it produces?
- How does a consumer determine how much of a good he will buy?
- Can government policy affect business behavior?
- Can government policy affect consumer behavior?

On the other hand, a macroeconomist might be interested in answering such questions as:

- How does the economy work?
- Why is the unemployment rate sometimes high and sometimes low?
- What causes inflation?
- Why do some national economies grow faster than other national economies?

http://

Go to *http://www.dismal.com*. On the left side of the home page are recent economic statistics. Can you tell which statistics are macroeconomic and which are microeconomic? Under "Today's Economy" are daily articles on economic topics. Look at the last few topics. Which are microeconomic topics? Which are macroeconomic topics? Which include elements of both?

Microeconomics
The branch of economics that deals with human behavior and choices as they relate to relatively small units—an individual, a firm, an industry, a single market.

Macroeconomics
The branch of economics that deals with human behavior and choices as they relate to highly aggregate markets (such as the goods and services market) or to the entire economy.

- What might cause interest rates to be low one year and high the next?
- How do changes in the money supply affect the economy?
- How do changes in government spending and taxes affect the economy?

Self-Test *(Answers to Self-Test questions are in the Self-Test Appendix.)*

1. Scarcity is the condition of finite resources. True or false? Explain your answer.
2. How are the Friedman and Robbins definitions of economics similar?
3. What is the difference between positive and normative economics? What is the difference between macroeconomics and microeconomics?

KEY CONCEPTS IN ECONOMICS

You can think of the key concepts in economics as tools that the economist keeps in a tool bag. Just as a carpenter uses tools (saw, hammer, screwdriver) to build a house, an economist uses tools to analyze or discuss something of interest. Most of the tools in the economist's tool bag are unique to economics—you won't find them in the sociologist's, historian's, or psychologist's tool bags. A few tools, though, are not unique to economics. The first nine concepts we discuss in this section are used principally by economists; the last two concepts are used by both economists and others.

THINKING IN TERMS OF SCARCITY AND ITS EFFECTS

Recall that *scarcity* is the condition in which our wants are greater than the limited resources available to satisfy them. But what are our wants? Our wants include anything that provides **utility** or satisfaction. In economics, something that provides utility or satisfaction is called a **good.** Something that provides **disutility** or dissatisfaction is called a **bad.** For example, for most people pollution is a bad. Basically, people want goods and they don't want bads.

A good can be either tangible or intangible. For example, a car is a tangible good; friendship is an intangible good. Goods do not just appear before us when we snap our fingers. It takes resources to produce goods. (Sometimes resources are referred to as *inputs* or *factors of production.*)

Generally, economists divide resources into four broad categories: land, labor, capital, and entrepreneurship. **Land** includes natural resources, such as minerals, forests, water, and unimproved land. For example, oil, wood, and animals fall into this category. (Sometimes economists refer to this category simply as *natural resources.*)

Labor consists of the physical and mental talents people contribute to the production process. For example, a person building a house is using his or her own labor.

Capital consists of produced goods that can be used as inputs for further production. Factories, machinery, tools, computers, and buildings are examples of capital. One country might have more capital than another. This means that it has more factories, machinery, tools, and so on.

Entrepreneurship refers to the particular talent that some people have for organizing the resources of land, labor, and capital to produce goods, seek new business opportunities, and develop new ways of doing things.

Scarcity and the Need for a Rationing Device

How does scarcity affect your life? Imagine you are considering buying a T-shirt for $10 at the university bookstore. The T-shirt has a price of $10 because of scarcity. There is a scarcity of T-shirts because people want more T-shirts than there are T-shirts available. And as long as there is a scarcity of anything, there is a need for a rationing device. Dollar price is a **rationing device.** If you are

Utility
The satisfaction one receives from a good.

Good
Anything from which individuals receive utility or satisfaction.

Disutility
The dissatisfaction one receives from a bad.

Bad
Anything from which individuals receive disutility or dissatisfaction.

Land
All natural resources, such as minerals, forests, water, and unimproved land.

Labor
The physical and mental talents people contribute to the production process.

Capital
Produced goods that can be used as inputs for further production, such as factories, machinery, tools, computers, and buildings.

Entrepreneurship
The particular talent that some people have for organizing the resources of land, labor, and capital to produce goods, seek new business opportunities, and develop new ways of doing things.

Rationing Device
A means for deciding who gets what of available resources and goods.

willing and able to pay the price, the T-shirt is yours. If you are either unwilling or unable to pay the price, the T-shirt will not become yours.

If scarcity didn't exist, there would be no need for a rationing device and people wouldn't pay dollar prices for resources and goods. In every transaction—buying a T-shirt at the university bookstore, buying food in a grocery store, or buying a new computer—scarcity plays a role.

Scarcity and Competition

Do you see much competition in the world today? Are people competing for jobs? Are states and cities competing for businesses? Are students competing for grades? The answer to all these questions is yes. The economist wants to know why this competition exists and what form it takes. First, the economist concludes, *competition exists because of scarcity*. If there were enough resources to satisfy all our seemingly unlimited wants, people would not have to compete for the available but limited resources.

Second, the economist sees that competition takes the form of people trying to get more of the rationing device. If dollar price is the rationing device, people will compete to earn dollars. Look at your own case. You are a college student working for a degree. One reason (but perhaps not the only reason) you are attending college is to earn a higher income after graduation. But why do you want a higher income? You want it because it will allow you to satisfy more of your wants.

Suppose muscular strength (measured by lifting weights) were the rationing device instead of dollar price. People with more muscular strength would receive more resources and goods than people with less muscular strength would receive. In this situation, people would compete for muscular strength. The lesson is simple: *Whatever the rationing device, people will compete for it.*

THINKING IN TERMS OF OPPORTUNITY COST

Opportunity Cost
The most highly valued opportunity or alternative forfeited when a choice is made.

As noted earlier, people have to make choices because scarcity exists. Because our seemingly unlimited wants push up against limited resources, some wants must go unsatisfied. We must therefore choose which wants we will satisfy and which we will not. The most highly valued opportunity or alternative forfeited when a choice is made is known as **opportunity cost.** Every time you make a choice, you incur an opportunity cost. For example, you have chosen to read this chapter. In making this choice, you denied yourself the benefits of doing something else. You could have watched television, e-mailed a friend, taken a nap, eaten a pizza, read a novel, shopped for a new computer, and so on. Whatever you would have chosen to do had you decided not to read this chapter is the opportunity cost of your reading this chapter. For example, if you would have watched television had you chosen not to read this chapter—if this was your next best alternative—then the opportunity cost of reading this chapter is watching television.

Opportunity Cost and Behavior

Economists think about people's behavior in terms of opportunity cost. Specifically, they believe that a change in opportunity cost will change a person's behavior. For example, consider Bill, who is a sophomore at the University of Kansas. He attends classes Monday through Thursday of every week. Every time he chooses to go to class he gives up the opportunity to do something else, such as the opportunity to earn $8 an hour working at a job. The opportunity cost of Bill spending an hour in class is $8.

Now let's raise the opportunity cost of attending class. On Tuesday, we offer Bill $70 to cut his economics class. He knows that if he attends his economics class he will forfeit $70. What will Bill do? An economist would predict that as the opportunity cost of attending class increases relative to the benefits of attending class, Bill is less likely to attend class.

This is how economists think about behavior, whether it is Bill's or your own. *The higher the opportunity cost of doing something, the less likely it will be done.* This is part of the economic way of thinking.

Before you continue, look at Exhibit 1, which summarizes some of the things about scarcity, choice, and opportunity cost up to this point.

There Is No Such Thing as a Free Lunch

Economists are fond of saying that *there is no such thing as a free lunch*. This catchy phrase expresses the idea that opportunity costs are incurred when choices are made. Perhaps this is an obvious point, but consider how often people mistakenly assume there *is* a free lunch. For example, some parents think education is free because they do not pay tuition for their children to attend public elementary school. Sorry, but there is no such thing as a free lunch. Free implies no sacrifice, no opportunities forfeited, which is not true in regard to elementary school education. Resources that could be used for other things are used to provide elementary school education.

Consider the people who speak about free medical care, free housing, free bridges ("there is no charge to cross it"), and free parks. None of these are actually free. The resources that provide medical care, housing, bridges, and parks could have been used in other ways.

THINKING IN TERMS OF COSTS AND BENEFITS

If it is possible to eliminate air pollution completely, should all air pollution be eliminated? If your answer is yes, then you are probably focusing on the *benefits* of eliminating air pollution. For example, one benefit might be healthier individuals. Certainly individuals who do not breathe polluted air have fewer lung disorders than people who do breathe polluted air.

But benefits rarely come without costs. The economist reminds us that while there are benefits to eliminating pollution, there are costs too. To illustrate, one way to eliminate all car pollution tomorrow is to pass a law stating that anyone caught driving a car will go to prison for 40 years. With such a law in place, and enforced, very few people would drive cars and all car pollution would be a thing of the past. Presto! Cleaner air! However, many people would think that the cost of obtaining that cleaner air is too high. Someone might say, "I want cleaner air, but not if I have to completely give up driving my car. How will I get to work?"

What distinguishes the economist from the noneconomist is that the economist thinks in terms of *both* costs and benefits. Often, the noneconomist thinks

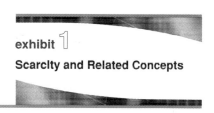

exhibit 1

Scarcity and Related Concepts

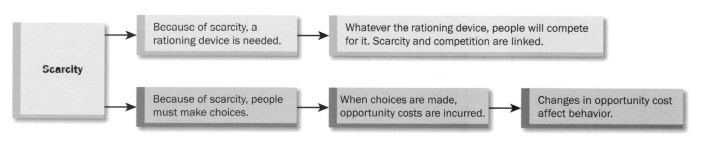

in terms of either one or the other. There are benefits from studying, but there are costs too. There are benefits to coming to class, but there are costs too. There are costs to getting up early each morning and exercising, but let's not forget that there are benefits too.

THINKING IN TERMS OF DECISIONS MADE AT THE MARGIN

It is late at night and you have already studied three hours for your biology test tomorrow. You look at the clock and wonder if you should study another hour. How would you summarize your thinking process? What question or questions do you ask yourself to decide whether or not to study another hour?

Perhaps without knowing it, you think in terms of the costs and benefits of further study. You probably realize that there are certain benefits from studying an additional hour (you may be able to raise your grade a few points), but that there are costs too (you will get less sleep or have less time to watch television or talk on the phone with a friend). Thinking in terms of costs and benefits, though, doesn't tell us *how* you think in terms of costs and benefits. For example, when deciding what to do, do you look at the total costs and total benefits of the proposed action or do you look at something less than the total costs and benefits? According to economists, for most decisions you think in terms of *additional,* or *marginal,* costs and benefits, not *total* costs and benefits. That's because most decisions deal with making a small, or additional, change.

To illustrate, suppose you just finished eating a hamburger and drinking a soda for lunch. You are still a little hungry and are considering whether or not to order another hamburger. An economist would say that in deciding whether or not to order another hamburger, you will compare the additional benefits of the additional hamburger to the additional costs of the additional hamburger. In economics, the word "marginal" is a synonym for "additional." So we say that you will compare the marginal benefits of the (next) hamburger to the marginal costs of the (next) hamburger. If the marginal benefits are greater than the marginal costs, you obviously expect a net (marginal) benefit to ordering the next hamburger, and therefore you order the next hamburger. If, however, the marginal costs of the hamburger are greater than the marginal benefits, you obviously expect a net (marginal) cost to ordering the next hamburger, and therefore you do not order the next hamburger.

What you don't consider when making this decision are the total benefits and total costs of hamburgers. That's because the benefits and costs connected with the first hamburger (the one you have already eaten) are no longer relevant to the current decision. You are not deciding between eating two hamburgers and eating no hamburgers; your decision is whether to eat a second hamburger after you have already eaten a first hamburger.

According to economists, when individuals make decisions by comparing marginal benefits to marginal costs, they are making **decisions at the margin.** The President of the United States makes a decision at the margin when deciding whether or not to talk another 10 minutes with the Speaker of the House of Representatives, the employee makes a decision at the margin when deciding whether or not to work two hours overtime, and the college professor makes a decision at the margin when deciding whether or not to add an additional question to the final exam.

THINKING IN TERMS OF EFFICIENCY

Suppose you are studying for an economics test. What is the right amount of time to study? In economics, the "right amount" of anything is the "optimal" or "efficient" amount and the efficient amount is the amount for which the marginal benefits equal the marginal costs. Stated differently, you have achieved **efficiency** when the marginal benefits equal the marginal costs.

To illustrate, suppose for the first hour of studying, the marginal benefits (*MB*) are greater than the marginal costs (*MC*):

Decisions at the Margin
Decision making characterized by weighing additional (marginal) benefits of a change against the additional (marginal) costs of a change with respect to current conditions.

Efficiency
Exists when marginal benefits equal marginal costs.

Why Anna Kournikova and Venus Williams Are Not in College

Anna Kournikova and Venus Williams are well-known tennis players. Kournikova was born in 1981; Williams, in 1980. Many of the persons who were born in 1980 and 1981 are today sitting in college classrooms learning accounting, biology, economics, or history. But Anna Kournikova and Venus Williams are not sitting in college classrooms. Instead, they are playing tennis on courts around the world.

Why aren't Anna and Venus in college? Not because they can't pay the tuition; both tennis stars have more than enough money to pay the tuition charged at most colleges. Also, either tennis player would likely be admitted to one or more colleges. Anna and Venus are not in college because it is more expensive for them to attend college than it is for most 18 to 25 year olds to attend college.

To understand, think of what it costs you to attend college. If you pay $1,000 tuition a semester for eight semesters, the full tuition amounts to $8,000. However, $8,000 is not the full cost of your attending college because if you were not a student, you could be earning income working at a job. For example, you could be working at a full-time job earning $25,000 annually. Certainly this $25,000, or at least part of it if you are currently working part-time, is forfeited because you attend college. It is part of the cost of your attending college.

Thus, the *tuition cost* may be the same for everyone who attends your college, but the *opportunity cost* is not. Some people have higher opportunity costs of attending college than others do. Both Anna Kournikova and Venus Williams have extremely high opportunity costs of attending college.

Each would have to give up hundreds of thousands of dollars in tennis prize money, endorsements, and so on if she were to attend college on a full-time basis.

This discussion illustrates two related points made in this chapter. First, *the higher the opportunity cost of doing something, the less likely it will be done.* The opportunity cost of attending college is higher for Anna and Venus than it (probably) is for you, and that is why you are in college and Anna and Venus are not.

Second, according to economists, *individuals think and act in terms of costs and benefits and only undertake actions if they expect the benefits to outweigh the costs.* Both Anna and Venus likely see certain benefits to attending college—just as you see certain benefits to attending college. However, those benefits are insufficient for Anna and Venus to attend college because benefits are not all that matter. Costs matter too. For Anna and Venus, the costs of attending college are much higher than the benefits, and so they choose not to attend college. In your case, the benefits are higher than the costs, and so you have decided to attend college.

$$MB \text{ studying first hour} > MC \text{ studying first hour}$$

Given this condition, you will certainly study for the first hour. After all, it is worthwhile. the additional benefits are greater than the additional costs, so there is a net benefit to studying.

Suppose for the second hour of studying, the marginal benefits are still greater than the marginal costs:

$$MB \text{ studying second hour} > MC \text{ studying second hour}$$

You will study for the second hour because the additional benefits are still greater than the additional costs. In other words, it is worthwhile studying the second hour. In fact, you will continue to study as long as the marginal benefits are greater than the marginal costs. Exhibit 2 graphically illustrates this discussion.

The marginal benefit (*MB*) curve of studying is downward sloping because we have assumed that the benefits of studying for the first hour are greater than the benefits of studying for the second hour and so on. The marginal cost (*MC*)

exhibit 2

Efficiency
MB = marginal benefits and *MC* = marginal costs. In the exhibit, the *MB* curve of studying is downward sloping and the *MC* curve of studying is upward sloping. As long as *MB* > *MC*, the person will study. The person stops studying when *MB* = *MC*. This is where efficiency is achieved.

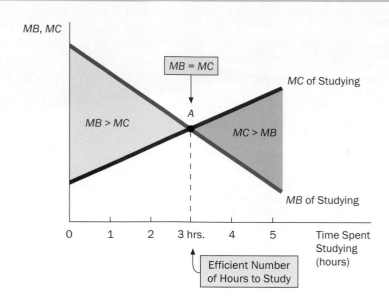

curve of studying is upward sloping because we assume that it costs a person more (in terms of goods forfeited) to study the second hour than the first, more to study the third than the second, and so on. (If we assume the additional costs of studying are constant over time, the *MC* curve is horizontal.)

In the exhibit, the marginal benefits of studying equal the marginal costs at three hours. So three hours is the efficient length of time to study in this situation. At less than three hours, the marginal benefits of studying are greater than the marginal costs, and so at all these hours there are net benefits from studying. At more than three hours, the marginal costs of studying are greater than the marginal benefits, and so it wouldn't be worthwhile to study beyond three hours.

THINKING IN TERMS OF UNINTENDED EFFECTS

Has anything turned out different from what you intended? No doubt, you can provide numerous examples. Economists think in terms of unintended effects. Consider an example. Andres, 16 years old, currently works after school at a grocery store. He earns $5.50 an hour. Suppose the state legislature passes a law specifying that the minimum dollar wage a person can be paid to do a job is $6.50 an hour. The legislators' intention in passing the law is to help people like Andres earn more income.

Will the $6.50 an hour legislation have the intended effect? Perhaps not. The manager of the grocery store may not find it worthwhile to continue employing Andres if she has to pay him $6.50 an hour. In other words, Andres may have a job at $5.50 an hour, but not at $6.50 an hour. If the law specifies that no one will earn less than $6.50 an hour and the manager of the grocery store decides to fire Andres rather than pay this amount, then an unintended effect of the $6.50 an hour legislation is Andres losing his job.

As another example, let's analyze mandatory seatbelt laws to see if they have any unintended effects. Many states have laws that require drivers to wear seatbelts. The intended effect is to reduce the number of car fatalities by making it more likely drivers will survive an accident.

Could these laws have an unintended effect? Some economists think so. They look at accident fatalities in terms of this equation:

Total number of fatalities = Number of accidents × Fatalities per accident

For example, if there are 200,000 accidents and 0.10 fatalities per accident, the total number of fatalities is 20,000.

The objective of a mandatory seatbelt program is to reduce the total number of fatalities by reducing the fatalities per accident. Many studies have found that wearing seatbelts does just this. If you are in an accident, you have a better chance of not being killed if you are wearing a seatbelt.

Let's assume that with seatbelts, there are 0.08 instead of 0.10 fatalities per accident. If there are still 200,000 accidents, this means that the total number of fatalities falls from 20,000 to 16,000. Thus, there is a drop in the total number of fatalities if fatalities per accident are reduced and the number of accidents is constant.

Number of Accidents	Fatalities per Accident	Total Number of Fatalities
200,000	0.10	20,000
200,000	0.08	16,000

However, some economists wonder if the number of accidents stays constant. Specifically, they suggest that seatbelts may have an unintended effect: *The number of accidents may increase.* This happens because wearing seatbelts may make drivers feel safer. Feeling safer may cause them to take chances that they wouldn't ordinarily take—such as driving faster or more aggressively or concentrating less on their driving and more on the music on the radio. For example, if the number of accidents rises to 250,000, then the total number of fatalities is 20,000.

Number of Accidents	Fatalities per Accident	Total Number of Fatalities
200,000	0.10	20,000
250,000	0.08	20,000

We conclude the following: If a mandatory seatbelt law reduces the number of fatalities (intended effect) but increases the number of accidents (unintended effect), it may, contrary to popular belief, not reduce the total number of fatalities. In fact, some economic studies show just this.

What does all this mean for you? You may be safer if you know that this unintended effect exists and you adjust accordingly. To be specific, when you wear your seatbelt, your chances of getting hurt in a car accident are less than if you don't wear your seatbelt. But if this added sense of protection causes you to drive less carefully than you would otherwise, then you could unintentionally offset the measure of protection your seatbelt provides. To reduce the probability of hurting yourself and others in a car accident, *the best policy is to wear a seatbelt and to drive as carefully as you would if you weren't wearing a seatbelt.* Knowing about the unintended effect of wearing your seatbelt could save your life.

THINKING IN TERMS OF WHAT DOLLARS BUY

Alexis, who just graduated from college, tells her grandfather, Bud, that she will earn $36,000 a year in her new job. Bud is both shocked and delighted. He says, "When I first went to work, back in 1924, I earned only $2,000 a year. Alexis, you're rich earning $36,000 a year. That's 18 times more than I earned."

Bud compares Alexis's income ($36,000) to his own ($2,000) and concludes that Alexis is rich because she will earn 18 times more than he earned. But something is amiss here. Intuitively, we know that $36,000 today is much different than $36,000 in 1924. What makes it different, of course, is that prices are higher today than they were in 1924.

According to economists, dollar income is not as important as what the dollar income buys. Although $36,000 is 18 times greater than $2,000, does it buy 18 times as many goods and services? It could, but only if prices are the same for the person with the $36,000 income as for the person with the $2,000 income. It doesn't buy 18 times as many goods and services if prices are different.

http://

Go to *http://www.nhtsa.dot.gov*, and select "Traffic Safety/Occupant Issues." Under "Crash Information," select "Economics of Crashes." Then, click "the Economic Impact of Motor Vehicle Crashes, 2000" and, finally, "Summary." What is the average cost to society of a fatality? of a critical injury accident? How is the cost of a fatality estimated? Seatbelts and other safety devices can protect drivers and passengers enough to change a fatal crash into a critical injury accident. Are these forms of protection economically justifiable according to the NHTSA?

ECONOMICS IN...

Why Is the Extended Family Customary in India and Not in the United States?

People in different countries have different customs and traditions. In India, the extended family is customary. When a man and woman marry, they move in with one or the other's parents. Later, should they have children, they continue to live with the parents. Often, three generations live together under one roof. In contrast, the extended family is not customary in the United States today.

Why is the extended family customary in India and not in the United States? Some people may answer that it is because Indians are more "family oriented" than Americans or because Indians have a longer tradition of the extended family than Americans do. But these are not answers. "Family oriented" simply describes the extended family; it does not explain it. And saying that Indians have a longer tradition of the extended family than Americans does not answer the question of *why* they have a longer tradition.

Let's look at the issue from an economic perspective. An economist would say that several generations of a family are more likely to live together under one roof if it is more costly for the average family member to be independent of the others. Stated differently, the more costly it is to "go it alone," the less likely one will live alone and the more likely one will live with family members.

The per capita income (total income divided by population) is lower in India than in the United States. The average American is more than 18 times richer than the average Indian. In 1999, the per capita income in India was $1,800 and the per capita income in the United States was $33,900.[1]

Now the poorer a person is, the less likely he or she can make it alone. The average newlywed couple in India cannot afford to rent an apartment or buy a home. In fact, it has been estimated that nearly 40 percent of the Indian population is too poor to even afford an adequate diet. Given the poverty in India, the extended family may simply be a means of survival. After all, it is cheaper to house and feed four people under one roof than four people living separately.

In addition, the Indian government does not provide a retirement program comparable to Social Security. Company retirement benefits are also much less common in India than in the United States. Not having Social Security and retirement benefits forces an old person to be more dependent on others than he or she would be otherwise. Adult children in their forties and fifties are more likely to live with their aged parents if their aged parents cannot survive on their own.

In some ways, the extended family in India is simply the Indian form of Social Security. In the United States, Social Security works by having the working generation pay for the retired generation, in return for having the upcoming working generation pay for them when they retire. In India, adult children take care of their aged parents in return for having their children take care of them when they become aged.

In summary, people often talk about customs and traditions as if they cannot be explained. It's always been this way; who knows why? To an economist, there is often an economic explanation for a custom or tradition.

To illustrate, let's suppose the same goods were produced in 1924 as today, but the average price of these goods in 1924 was $40 and the average price of these goods today is $1,000. With an income of $2,000 in 1924, Bud would have been able to buy 50 units of goods in a year ($2,000 income ÷ $40 average price = 50 units of goods). With an income of $36,000 today, Alexis would be able to buy 36 units of goods ($36,000 income ÷ $1,000 average price = 36 units of goods). In other words, although Bud earned a smaller dollar income than Alexis will earn, he was able to buy more units of goods than Alexis will be able to buy with her larger dollar income.

THINKING IN TERMS OF EQUILIBRIUM

People sometimes think in terms of natural resting places. For example, suppose you call up a friend and ask him how he is doing today. He tells you he is sick. "Do you have a fever?" you ask. He says that he has a fever; his temperature is 103.4 degrees.

---

1. The dollar amounts are based on purchasing power parity exchange rates.

Now suppose someone asks you to assign a probability to your friend's body temperature staying at 103.4 degrees for the next two weeks. Would you assign a 100 percent probability, a 75 percent probability, or some much smaller probability? Most people would assign a very tiny probability of your friend's temperature remaining at 103.4 degrees for the next two weeks. Most people would think one of the following two options is more likely: (1) The temperature will rise so high that it kills the person (and therefore it no longer makes much sense to speak of a body temperature) or (2) the temperature will fall until it is close to the normal body temperature of 98.6 degrees.

The normal body temperature of 98.6 degrees is often thought of as a natural resting place in that for living human beings, any temperature higher or lower than 98.6 degrees is a temporary temperature. A person's temperature always seems to settle back down or back up to 98.6 degrees.

Economists tend to think that many economic phenomena have natural resting places. These natural resting places are often called **equilibrium.** One way to think of equilibrium is as a place where economic forces are driving things. To illustrate, let's consider an example.

Equilibrium
Equilibrium means "at rest"; it is descriptive of a natural resting place.

Suppose Smith has a single painting that he wants to sell. He suggests a price of $5,000 for the painting, and at that price, three people say they are willing to buy it. How does he decide to whom he will sell the painting? Will he draw names out of a hat? Will he have the three people draw straws? Most likely he will ask the three people to offer him a higher price for the painting. At $6,000, two people still want to buy the painting, but at $6,500, only one person wants to buy the painting. In other words, the bidding activity of the buyers has moved the price of the painting to its natural resting place or to an equilibrium price of $6,500.

Economists are well known for analyzing economic phenomena in terms of equilibrium. First, they will try to identify whether or not equilibrium exists. Second, if equilibrium exists, they will then proceed to determine how that equilibrium should be specified. They then sometimes proceed to ask, What can change equilibrium? We will have much more to say about this latter question in Chapter 3.

THINKING IN TERMS OF THE *CETERIS PARIBUS* ASSUMPTION

Wilson has eaten regular ice cream for years, and for years his weight has been 170 pounds. One day Wilson decides he wants to lose some weight. With this in mind, he buys a new fat-free ice cream at the grocery store. The fat-free ice cream has half the calories of regular ice cream.

Wilson eats the fat-free ice cream for the next few months. He then weighs himself and finds that he has gained two pounds. Does this mean that fat-free ice cream causes people to gain weight and regular ice cream does not? The answer is no. But why, then, did Wilson gain weight when he substituted fat-free ice cream for regular ice cream? Perhaps Wilson ate three times as much fat-free ice cream as regular ice cream. Or perhaps during the time he was eating fat-free ice cream, he wasn't exercising, and during the time he was eating regular ice cream, he was exercising. In other words, a number of factors—such as eating more ice cream or exercising less—may have offset the weight loss that Wilson would have experienced had these factors not changed.

Now suppose you want to make the point that Wilson would have lost weight by substituting fat-free ice cream for regular ice cream had these other factors not changed. What would you say? A scientist would say, "If Wilson has been eating regular ice cream and his weight has stabilized at 170 pounds, then substituting fat-free ice cream for regular ice cream will lead to a decline in weight, *ceteris paribus.*"

The term **ceteris paribus** means *all other things held constant* or *nothing else changes.* In our ice cream example, if nothing else changes—such as how much ice cream Wilson eats, how much exercise he gets, and so on—then substituting fat-free ice cream for regular ice cream will result in weight loss. This is

Ceteris Paribus
A Latin term meaning "all other things held constant."

based on the theory that a reduction in calorie consumption will result in weight loss and an increase in calorie consumption will result in weight gain.

Using the *ceteris paribus* assumption is important because, with it, we can clearly designate what we believe is the correct relationship between two variables. In the ice cream example, we can designate the correct relationship between calorie intake and weight gain.

Economists don't often talk about ice cream, but they will often make use of the *ceteris paribus* assumption. An economist might say, "If the price of a good decreases, the quantity demanded or consumed of that good increases, *ceteris paribus*." For example, if the price of Pepsi-Cola decreases, people will buy more Pepsi-Cola, assuming that nothing else changes.

The use of the *ceteris paribus* assumption is so prevalent in economics it has even inspired humor: How many economists does it take to change a light bulb? Eight. One to change the bulb and seven to hold everything else constant.

At *http://cnn.com*, you will find a number of news articles. How many of these articles are related to economics? Read carefully.

Q & A

Q: Why would economists want to assume that when the price of Pepsi-Cola falls, nothing else changes? Don't other things change in the real world? Why assume things that we know are not true?

A: Economists do not specify *ceteris paribus* because they want to say something false about the world. They specify it because they want to clearly define what they believe to be the real-world relationship between two variables. Look at it this way. If you drop a ball off the roof of a house, it will fall to the ground unless someone catches it. This statement is true, and probably everyone would willingly accept it as true. But here is another true statement: If you drop a ball off the roof of a house, it will fall to the ground, *ceteris paribus*. In fact, the two statements are identical in meaning. This is because adding the phrase "unless someone catches it" in the first sentence is the same as saying "*ceteris paribus*" in the second sentence. If one statement is acceptable to us, the other should be too.

THINKING IN TERMS OF THE DIFFERENCE BETWEEN ASSOCIATION AND CAUSATION

Association is one thing, causation is another. A problem arises when we confuse the two. Two events are associated if they are linked or connected in some way. For example, suppose you wash your car at 10:00 A.M. and at 10:30 A.M. it starts to rain. Because it rains shortly after you wash your car, the two events are associated (linked, connected) in time. Does it follow that the first event (your washing the car) caused the second event (the rain)? The answer is no. Association is not causation. If *A* occurs before *B,* it does not necessarily follow that *A* is the cause and *B* the effect.

In the car-rain example, it is obvious that association was not causation. But consider a case where this is not so apparent. Suppose Jones tells you that the U.S. trade deficit grew larger in January and 11 months later economic activity had turned down. She then states that the first event (the growing trade deficit) caused the second event (the downturn in economic activity). You may be tempted to accept this as truth. But, of course, a simple statement of cause and effect is not enough to establish cause and effect. Without any evidence, we can't be certain that we haven't stumbled onto a disguised version of the car-rain example.

Q & A

Q: James broke a mirror on Wednesday and has been having bad luck ever since. He thinks that breaking the mirror caused his bad luck. Is this an example where association is not causation?

A: Yes, it is. In fact, most superstitions are nothing more than people incorrectly assuming that association is (necessarily) causation.

THINKING IN TERMS OF THE DIFFERENCE BETWEEN THE GROUP AND THE INDIVIDUAL

Some people will say that what is good or true for the individual is necessarily good or true for the group. Fact is, what is good for the individual may be good for the group, but not necessarily. For example, John stands up at a soccer game and sees the game better. Does it follow that if everyone stands up at the soccer game, everyone will see better? No. Mary moves to the suburbs because she dislikes crowds in the city. Does it follow that if everyone moves from the city to the suburbs for the same reason as Mary, everyone will be better off? No. Andres does his holiday shopping early so he can beat the crowds. Does it follow that if everyone does his holiday shopping early, everyone can beat the crowds? No.

People who believe that what is good for the individual is also good for the group are said to believe in the **fallacy of composition.** Economists do not believe in the fallacy of composition.

Consider two economic examples where the fallacy may appear. Some people argue that tariffs benefit certain industries by protecting them from foreign competition. They then conclude that because tariffs benefit some industries, the economy as a whole benefits from tariffs. This is not true though.

Or consider the fact that some people have limited wants for particular goods. Does it follow that society has limited wants for all goods? Not at all. To argue otherwise is to commit the fallacy of composition.

Fallacy of Composition
The erroneous view that what is good or true for the individual is necessarily good or true for the group.

Self-Test

1. How does competition arise out of scarcity?

2. Give an example to illustrate how a change in opportunity cost can affect behavior.

3. There are both costs and benefits of studying. If you continue to study (say, for a test) as long as the marginal benefits of studying are greater than the marginal costs and stop studying when the two are equal, will your action be consistent with having maximized the net benefits of studying? Explain your answer.

4. Give an example to illustrate how a politician running for office can mislead the electorate by implying that association is causation.

5. Your economics instructor says, "If the price of going to the movies goes down, people will go to the movies more often." A student in class says, "Not if the quality of the movies goes down." Who is right, the economics instructor or the student?

ECONOMISTS BUILD AND TEST THEORIES

An important component of the economic way of thinking is theorizing or building theories or models to explain and predict real-world events. This section discusses the nature and uses of theory.

WHAT IS A THEORY?

Almost everyone, including you, builds and tests theories or models on a regular basis. (In this text, the words *theory* and *model* are used interchangeably.) Perhaps you thought only scientists and other people who have high-level mathematics at their fingertips built and tested theories. However, theory building and testing is not the domain of only the highly educated and mathematically proficient. Almost everyone builds and test theories.

People build theories any time they do not know the answer to a question. Someone asks, "Why is the crime rate higher in the United States than in Belgium?" Or, "Why did Aaron's girlfriend break up with him?" Or, "Why does Professor Avalos give easier final exams than Professor Shaw even though they teach the same subject?" If you don't know the answer to a question, you are likely to build a theory so you can provide an answer.

A Small Private College in Boston Goes Coed

Economics is not just found in the boardrooms of companies, in the government buildings in Washington, D.C., or in a textbook. Economics is all around you—every day. You can find economics in a college class or a local coffee bar or while driving on a freeway or doing your homework.

To find economics in everyday places, you have to look below the surface. Let's consider Emmanuel College, a small private college in Boston, Massachusetts. As you read about Emmanuel, look for some of the topics discussed in this chapter—scarcity, rationing devices, costs and benefits, and so on. See if you can find any economics below the surface.

Emmanuel College was founded in 1919 by the Sisters of Notre Dame de Namur. From its founding in 1919 through the year 2000, Emmanuel College admitted only women. Like many women's colleges founded in the eighteenth, nineteenth, and early twentieth centuries, Emmanuel College was founded to give women the education that was being denied to them by men-only schools.

In 2000, Emmanuel decided to change its women-only policy. Beginning in fall 2001, it would begin to admit men to the college. Emmanuel decided to admit men partly because of the declining number of applicants. In 1999, only 572 women applied to the college and 160 were admitted.

As soon as Emmanuel College went coed, the number of applicants increased. In 2002, 1,607 students applied and 320 students were admitted. Certainly some of the increase in applicants (from 572 to 1,607) was due to men becoming part of the applicant pool. However, the number of women applicants also increased.

Where's the economics in this story about Emmanuel College? Did you notice any economic concepts lying below the surface? If you didn't, think about it for a few minutes, then read on.

First, let's consider scarcity and its effects. Because scarcity exists, a rationing device is needed. The rationing device used by Emmanuel College prior to 2001 was that a person had to (1) have certain grades, (2) be able to pay the tuition, and (3) be a woman. In 2001, the rationing device changed: it was no longer necessary to be a woman. Thus,

for a large subset of the population, the male population, the rationing device used by Emmanuel became less restrictive. (We assume that as Emmanuel changed from a women-only college to a coed college, it did not raise tuition or change the grade point average or SAT scores necessary for admission.)

The question is: *Why* did Emmanuel make its rationing device less restrictive? Might the *restrictiveness* of a rationing device have something to do with the *degree* of scarcity? Think of goods lying along a spectrum, with some of the goods being relatively more scarce than others. An economist would predict that the rationing device used to allocate relatively more scarce goods would be more restrictive than the rationing device used to allocate relatively less scarce goods. Does this prediction apply to Emmanuel? Yes. The declining applicant pool signaled to the college that it was becoming a relatively less scarce (albeit still scarce) good. In response, its rationing device (for purposes of admission) became less restrictive.

Now, let's consider the fact that more women applied to Emmanuel after it became coed. Does this fact have anything to do with the costs and benefits of attending Emmanuel? A quick, and perhaps wrong, answer is that the benefits to women of attending Emmanuel increased after the college became coed. This might be a wrong answer because it is an incomplete answer. While it is certainly possible that the benefits of Emmanuel increased for *some* women after the college became coed, the costs probably increased for other women. In fact, this is exactly what happened. Some women were angry with Emmanuel for changing its women-only policy. Their preference was to attend a women-only college.

So as a result of Emmanuel's change in policy, we surmise that the benefits of attending Emmanuel increased for some women and that the costs increased for other women. Do we know the overall result? Because the number of women applicants increased with the change to the coed policy, we conclude that women who received higher benefits outnumbered those who incurred higher costs.

Theory
An abstract representation of the real world designed with the intent to better understand that world.

Abstract
The process (used in building a theory) of focusing on a limited number of variables to explain or predict an event.

What exactly is a theory? To an economist, a **theory** is an abstract representation of the world. In this context, **abstract** means to omit certain variables or factors when trying to explain or understand something. For example, suppose you were to draw a map for a friend, showing him how to get from his house to your house. Would you draw a map that showed every single thing your friend would see on the trip from his house to yours, or would you simply draw the main roads and one or two landmarks? If you'd do the latter, you would be abstracting from reality; you would be omitting certain things.

You would abstract for two reasons. First, to get your friend from his house to yours, you don't need to include everything on your map. Simply noting main roads may be enough. Second, if you did note everything on your map, your friend might get confused. Giving too much detail could be as bad as giving too little.

When economists build a theory or model, they do the same thing you do when you draw a map. They abstract from reality; they leave out certain things. They focus on the major factors or variables that they believe will explain the phenomenon they are trying to understand.

Suppose a criminologist's objective is to explain why some people turn to crime. Before actually building the theory, he considers a number of variables that may explain why some people become criminals. These variables include (1) the ease of getting a gun, (2) parental childrearing practices, (3) the neighborhood a person grew up in, (4) whether a person was abused as a child, (5) family education, (6) the type of friends a person has, (7) a person's IQ, (8) climate, and (9) a person's diet.

The criminologist may think that some of these variables greatly affect the chance that a person will become a criminal, some affect it only slightly, and others do not affect it at all. For example, a person's diet may have only a 0.0001 percent effect on the person becoming a criminal. But whether or not a person was abused as a child may have a 30 percent effect.

A theory emphasizes only those variables that the theorist believes are the main or critical variables that explain an activity or event. Thus, if the criminologist in our example thinks that parental childrearing practices and family education are likely to explain much more about criminal behavior than the other variables, then his (abstract) theory will focus on these two variables and will ignore the other variables.

All theories are abstractions from reality. But it doesn't follow that (abstract) theories cannot explain reality. The objective in theory building is to ignore those variables that are essentially irrelevant to the case at hand, so that it becomes easier to isolate the important variables that the untrained observer would probably miss.

In the course of reading this text, you will come across numerous theories. Some of these theories are explained in words, and others are graphically represented. For example, Chapter 3 presents the theory of supply and demand. First, the parts of the theory are explained. Then the theory is represented graphically in terms of a supply curve and a demand curve.

BUILDING AND TESTING A THEORY

The same basic procedure for building and testing a theory is used in all scientific work, whether the discipline is biology, chemistry, or economics. Exhibit 3 summarizes the approach outlined next.

1. **Decide what it is you want to explain or predict.** For example, you may want to explain or predict interest rates, the exchange rate between the U.S. dollar and the Japanese yen, or another concept.
2. **Identify the variables that you believe are important to what you want to explain or predict.** Variables are magnitudes that can change. For example, price is a variable. One day the price of a good may be $10, and a week later it may be $12. An economist who wants to explain or predict the buying behavior of consumers may build his "theory of buying behavior" on the variable price.
3. **State the assumptions of the theory.** An assumption is a critical or key element of a theory. It is a statement that one supposes to be true. The difference between an assumption and a fact is that a fact represents objective truth. It is a fact that you are reading this book at this moment; no one doubts

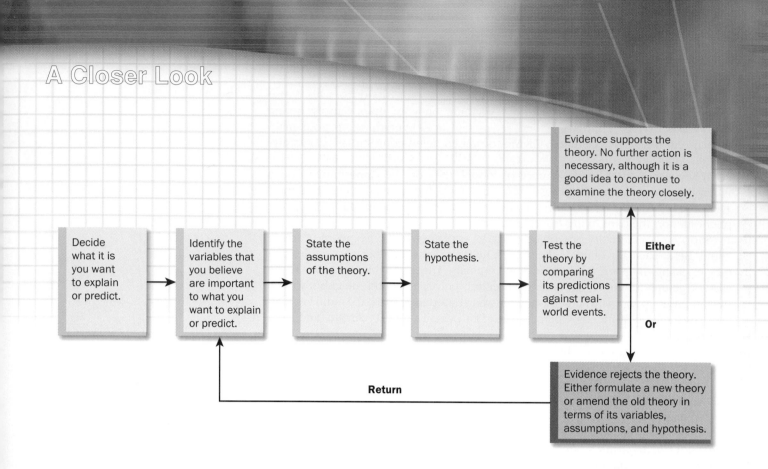

exhibit 3

Building and Testing a Theory

this. With an assumption, objective truth does not necessarily exist; there is room for doubt. An economist may make the assumption that the owners of business firms have only one motive—to earn as much profit as possible. But, of course, this may not be the truth. The owners of business firms may not be motivated only by profits, or they may not be motivated by profits at all. The next section discusses the importance of realistic assumptions in building and testing a theory.

4. **State the hypothesis.** A hypothesis is a conditional statement specifying how two variables are related. Typically, hypotheses follow the "if-then" form. For example, if you smoke cigarettes, then you will increase your probability of getting lung cancer. In effect, the hypothesis is a prediction of what will happen to one thing (e.g., to your lungs) when something else changes (you smoke cigarettes).

5. **Test the theory by comparing its predictions against real-world events.** Suppose an economist's theory predicts that as taxes are raised, there will be less saving in the economy. To test this theory, we look at the data on saving to see if the evidence *supports* the theory that produced that specific prediction.

6. **If the evidence supports the theory, then no further action is necessary, although it is a good idea to continue to examine the theory closely.** Suppose a theory predicts that orange prices will rise within two weeks of a cold snap in Florida. If this actually happens, then the evidence supports the theory.

7. **If the evidence rejects the theory, then either formulate a new theory or amend the old theory in terms of its variables, assumptions, and hypothesis.** For example, suppose a theory predicts that interest rates will

rise within two months of an increase in the amount of money in circulation. If this does not happen, then it is time to either formulate a new theory or amend the old theory.

Q & A

Q: In the preceding point 5, the phrase "supports the theory" was used instead of "proves the theory." Why not say "we look at the data to see if the evidence proves the theory" instead of "we look at the data to see if the evidence supports the theory"?

A: The following example explains why. Suppose a theory predicts that all swans are white. Researchers go out into the field and record the color of all the swans they see. Every swan they see is white. The evidence does not prove the theory is correct because there may be swans that are not white that the researchers did not see. How can the researchers be certain they saw all the swans? Thus, it is more accurate to say that the evidence supports the theory than to say it proves the theory.

HOW DO WE JUDGE THEORIES?

We judge theories by how well they predict. Some people forget this and try to judge a theory by its assumptions. They say that some economic theories are based on unrealistic assumptions. For example, economists assume that business firms try to maximize profits. Do all business firms try to do this every second of every day? Probably not; yet they might do it often enough to make it seem as if they do it all the time.

Economist Milton Friedman argues that the relevant question to ask about the assumptions of a theory is not whether they are descriptively "realistic," for they never are, but whether they are "sufficiently good approximations for the purpose in hand." And this question can be answered only by seeing whether the theory works, which means whether it yields sufficiently accurate predictions.

To illustrate, Friedman cites Newton's law of falling bodies, which assumes, unrealistically, that bodies fall in a vacuum. Does the theory predict well, even though it is based on an unrealistic assumption? For many falling bodies, such as a rubber ball dropped off a roof, it does. Friedman would argue that the theory is useful because it predicts well for numerous falling bodies, even though in the real world bodies do not always fall in a vacuum. We could say that for many falling bodies it is *as if* they were falling in a vacuum. Friedman would say that the assumption of a vacuum is a "sufficiently good approximation for the purpose in hand."

Friedman's position can be summarized as follows: If the theory works, if the evidence supports the theory, then it is a good and useful theory and the assumptions of the theory, no matter what anyone might think of them, are a sufficiently good approximation for the purpose in hand. Some economists accept Friedman's position, along with all its implications. Other economists, many of them well respected, do not. As you will soon find out, there are not only numerous theories in economics but also numerous debates.

WHAT TO ASK A THEORIST

Physicists, chemists, and economists aren't the only persons who build and test theories. Historians, sociologists, anthropologists, and many others build and test theories. In fact, as suggested earlier in this section, almost everyone builds theories (although not everyone tests theories).

Any time you listen to someone expound upon his or her theory, you should always ask a key question: *If your theory is correct, what do you predict we will see in the world?*

To illustrate, let's consider a very simple example. Suppose your history professor comes to class each day clean-shaven and dressed in slacks, shirt, tie, and sports jacket. One day he comes to class unshaven and dressed in jeans and a somewhat wrinkled T-shirt. The difference in appearance is obvious. You turn to your friend who sits next to you in class and ask, "What do you think explains the difference in appearance and dress?"

Notice what you have asked: a question that does not have an obvious answer. Such questions are ripe for theory building. Your friend proposes an explanation. He says, "I think the professor forgot to set his alarm clock last night. He got up late this morning and didn't have time to shave or to dress the way he usually does. He just threw on the first clothes he found and rushed to class."

Your friend has advanced a theory of sorts. He has implicitly assumed that the professor wants to shave and dress in slacks, shirt, tie, and sports jacket but that some unusual event prevented him from doing so today.

Somehow, you don't think your friend's theory is correct. Instead, you think your history professor has decided to make a life change of some sort. He has decided to look more casual, to take life a little easier, to be less formal. You tell your friend what you think explains your professor's new behavior.

You, like your friend, have advanced a theory of sorts. Whose theory, if either, is correct? Now is the time for you to ask your friend, and your friend to ask you, *If your theory is correct, what do you predict we will see in the world?*

Your friend's answer should be, "If my theory is correct, then the next time the professor comes to class, he will be clean shaven and dressed in his old way—slacks, shirt, tie, and sports jacket."

Your answer should be, "If my theory is correct, then the next time the professor comes to class, he will be unshaven and dressed as he is today—in jeans, T-shirt, and so on."

The question—If your theory is correct, what do you predict we will see in the world?—gives us a way to figure out who might be closer to the truth when people disagree. It minimizes talk and maximizes the chances of establishing who is correct and who is incorrect.

Self-Test

1. What is the purpose of building a theory?
2. How might a theory of the economy differ from a description of the economy?
3. Why is it important to test a theory? Why not simply accept a theory if it "sounds right"?

A Reader Asks...

What's in Store for an Economics Major?

This is my first course in economics. The material is interesting and I have given some thought to majoring in economics. Please tell me something about the major and about job prospects for an economics graduate. What courses do economics majors take? What is the starting salary of economics majors? Do the people who run large companies think highly of people who have majored in economics?

If you major in economics, you will certainly not be alone. Economics is one of the top three majors at Harvard, Brown, Yale, University of California at Berkeley, Princeton, Columbia, Cornell, Dartmouth, and Stanford. The popularity of economics is probably based on two major reasons. First, many people find economics an interesting course of study. Second, what you learn in an economics course is relevant and applicable to the real world.

Do executives who run successful companies think highly of economics majors? Well, a *BusinessWeek* survey found that economics was the second favorite undergraduate major of chief executive officers (CEOs) of major corporations. Engineering was their favorite undergraduate major.

An economics major usually takes a wide variety of economic courses, starting with introductory courses—principles of microeconomics and principles of macroeconomics—and then studying intermediate microeconomics and intermediate macroeconomics. Upper-division electives usually include such courses as public finance, international economics, law and economics, managerial economics, labor economics, health economics, money and banking, environmental economics, and more.

According to a College Placement Council survey, the average starting salary for economics majors exceeded all other majors within the business and social sciences. It was $40,776 in 2001. Also, according to the Economics and Statistics Administration of the U.S. Department of Justice, economics undergraduates have relatively higher average annual salaries than students who have majored in other fields. Specifically, of 14 different majors, economics majors ranked third. Only persons with bachelor's degrees in engineering or agriculture/forestry had higher average annual salaries.

Chapter Summary

Definitions of Economics

- Alfred Marshall said, "Political economy or economics is a study of mankind in the ordinary business of life."
- Lionel Robbins said, "Economics is the science which studies human behavior as a relationship between ends and scarce means which have alternative uses."
- Milton Friedman said, "Economics is the science of how a particular society solves its economic problems." He added, "an economic problem exists whenever scarce means are used to satisfy alternative ends."
- In this book, economics is defined as the science of scarcity. More completely, economics is the science of how individuals and societies deal with the fact that wants are greater than the limited resources available to satisfy those wants.

Economic Categories

- Positive economics attempts to determine what is; normative economics addresses what should be.
- Microeconomics deals with human behavior and choices as they relate to relatively small units—an individual, a firm, an industry, a single market. Macroeconomics deals with human behavior and choices as they relate to an entire economy.

Goods, Bads, and Resources

- A good is anything that gives a person utility or satisfaction.
- A bad is anything that gives a person disutility or dissatisfaction.
- Economists divide resources into four categories: land, labor, capital, and entrepreneurship.
- Land includes natural resources, such as minerals, forests, water, and unimproved land.
- Labor refers to the physical and mental talents that people contribute to the production process.
- Capital consists of produced goods that can be used as inputs for further production, such as machinery, tools, computers, trucks, buildings, and factories.

- Entrepreneurship refers to the particular talent that some people have for organizing the resources of land, labor, and capital to produce goods, seek new business opportunities, and develop new ways of doing things.

Scarcity

- Scarcity is the condition in which our wants are greater than the limited resources available to satisfy them. Scarcity implies choice. In a world of limited resources, we must choose which wants will be satisfied and which will go unsatisfied.
- Because of scarcity, there is a need for a rationing device. A rationing device is a means of deciding who gets what quantities of the available resources and goods.
- Scarcity implies competition. If there were enough resources to satisfy all our seemingly unlimited wants, people would not have to compete for the available but limited resources.

Opportunity Cost

- Every time a person makes a choice, he or she incurs an opportunity cost. Opportunity cost is the most highly valued opportunity or alternative forfeited when a choice is made. The higher the opportunity cost of doing something, the less likely it will be done.

Costs and Benefits

- What distinguishes the economist from the noneconomist is that the economist thinks in terms of both costs and benefits. Asked what the benefits of taking a walk may be, an economist will also mention the costs to taking a walk. Asked what the costs of studying are, an economist will also point out the benefits of studying.

Decisions Made at the Margin

- Marginal benefits and costs are not the same as total benefits and costs. When deciding whether to talk on the phone one more minute, an individual would not consider the total benefits and total costs of speaking on the phone. Instead, the individual would compare only the marginal benefits (additional benefits) of talking on the phone one more minute to the marginal costs (additional costs) of talking on the phone one more minute.

Efficiency

- As long as the marginal benefits of an activity are greater than its marginal costs, a person gains by continuing to do the activity—whether the activity is studying, running, eating, or watching television. All the net benefits possible from an activity are achieved when the marginal benefits of the activity equal its marginal costs. Efficiency exists at this point.

Unintended Effects

- Economists often think in terms of causes and effects. Effects may include both intended effects and unintended effects. Economists want to denote both types of effects when speaking of effects in general.

Dollar Income and What Dollars Buy

- According to economists, you have more information when you know what a specific dollar income can buy in terms of goods and services than if you simply know the dollar income. A $4,000 annual income may sound like a low income today, but was it always a low income? Was it a low income in 1936? To answer this question, we need some idea of what prices were in 1936 relative to what they are today. Lower prices in 1936 can make a $4,000 income in 1936 comparable to a much higher dollar income today.

Equilibrium

- Equilibrium means "at rest." Many natural and economic phenomena move toward equilibrium. Economists will often ask if equilibrium exists for a given phenomenon. If equilibrium does not exist, then the economist will try to identify the condition that must exist before equilibrium ("at rest") is achieved.

Ceteris Paribus

- *Ceteris paribus* is a Latin term that means "all other things held constant." *Ceteris paribus* is used to designate what we believe is the correct relationship between two variables.

Association and Causation

- Association is one thing, causation is another. Simply because two events are associated (in time, for example), it does not necessarily follow that one is the cause and the other is the effect.

The Fallacy of Composition

- The fallacy of composition is the erroneous view that what is good or true for the individual is necessarily good or true for the group.

Theory

- Economists build theories in order to explain and predict real-world events. Theories are necessarily abstractions from, as opposed to descriptions of, the real world.
- All theories abstract from reality; they focus on the critical variables that the theorist believes explain and predict the phenomenon at hand.
- The steps in building and testing a theory are:
    1. Decide what it is you want to explain or predict.
    2. Identify the variables that you believe are important to what you want to explain or predict.
    3. State the assumptions of the theory.
    4. State the hypothesis.
    5. Test the theory by comparing its predictions against real-world events.
    6. If the evidence supports the theory, then no further action is necessary, although it is a good idea to continue to examine the theory closely.
    7. If the evidence rejects the theory, then either formulate an entirely new theory or amend the old theory in terms of its variables, assumptions, and hypothesis.
- Economists commonly judge a theory according to how well it predicts, not according to the degree of realism of its assumptions.

Key Terms and Concepts

Scarcity	Disutility	Decisions at the Margin
Economics	Bad	Efficiency
Positive Economics	Land	Equilibrium
Normative Economics	Labor	*Ceteris Paribus*
Microeconomics	Capital	Fallacy of Composition
Macroeconomics	Entrepreneurship	Theory
Utility	Rationing Device	Abstract
Good	Opportunity Cost	

A stone, thrown into a lake, creates ripples. The ripples move away from where the stone entered the lake. Similarly, economic facts, actions, and changes create ripples that move away from their point of origin. Eventually, these ripples can intersect your life and have an effect on you. Consider the following example.

Scarcity, an economic fact, creates a need for a rationing device. The major rationing device in our society is money, or dollar, price. This means that you need money before you can satisfy many of your wants. Attending college helps you obtain money because college students, on average, earn higher dollar incomes than people who do not attend college. Thus, there is a connection between scarcity and your attending college—an economic connection to you.

Based on the material in this chapter, identify other ways in which economic facts, actions, and changes create ripples that eventually affect you.

1. What is the similarity between the Robbins and Friedman definitions of economics?
2. The United States is considered a rich country because Americans can choose from an abundance of goods and services. How can there be scarcity in a land of abundance?
3. Give two examples for each of the following: (a) an intangible good, (b) a tangible good, (c) a bad.
4. What is the difference between the resource labor and the resource entrepreneurship?
5. Explain the link between scarcity and each of the following: (a) choice, (b) opportunity cost, (c) the need for a rationing device, (d) competition.
6. Is it possible for a person to incur an opportunity cost without spending any money? Explain.
7. Discuss the opportunity costs of attending college for four years. Is college more or less costly than you thought it was? Explain.
8. Explain the relationship between changes in opportunity cost and changes in behavior.
9. Smith says that we should eliminate all pollution in the world. Jones disagrees. Who is more likely to be an economist, Smith or Jones? Explain your answer.
10. A layperson says that a proposed government project simply costs too much and therefore shouldn't be undertaken. How might an economist's evaluation be different?
11. Economists say that individuals make decisions at the margin. What does this mean?
12. How would an economist go about defining the efficient amount of time spent playing tennis?
13. A change in X will lead to a change in Y; the predicted change is desirable, so we should change X. Do you agree or disagree? Explain.
14. Smith lives in country A and earns $40,000 a year; Jones lives in country B and earns $50,000 a year. Will Jones be able to buy more goods and services than Smith?
15. Suppose the price of an ounce of gold is $300 in New York and $375 in London. Do you think the difference in gold prices is indicative of equilibrium? Explain your answer.
16. Why would economists assume "all other things are constant," or "nothing else changes," when, in reality, some other things may change?
17. Give three examples that illustrate that association is not causation.
18. Give three examples that illustrate the fallacy of composition.
19. Which of the following statements would Milton Friedman agree with and why?

    Statement 1: The theory does not work because its assumptions are false.

    Statement 2: The assumptions are false because the theory does not work.
20. Why do economists prefer to say that the evidence supports the theory instead of that the evidence proves the theory is correct?
21. Theories are abstractions from reality. What does this mean?

Internet Activities

1. Go to *http://www.whitehouse.gov*. Under West Wing connections, Policies in Focus, select "Economy & Budget." Select and read a press briefing or release that has something to do with the economy. What is the content of the briefing or release?

2. Go to *http://www.yahoo.com*. Click on "advanced search" and then key "sci.econ" in the Search box. Select Usenet in the adjacent box and click "Search." A list of titles will appear. These are writings submitted to a group that discusses economics. Select one of the submissions with an interesting title.

   a. What is the author discussing? Is it a microeconomic or a macroeconomic issue?

   b. Does the author state a hypothesis and then test his or her case scientifically? Or does the author just present an opinion?

   c. Is the author writing from the perspective of positive or normative economics?

   d. Based on what you know so far, do you agree or disagree with the author?

3. Go to *http://netec.wustl.edu/JokEc.html*. Pick a joke that doesn't make sense to you and write it down so you won't forget it. At the end of the class, reread the joke and see if you get it now. How many of the jokes are based on economists always having more than one answer or having answers that are not usable in the real world?

Log on to the Arnold Xtra! Web site now (*http://arnoldxtra.swcollege.com*) for additional learning resources such as practice quizzes, help with graphing, video clips, and current event applications.

Appendix A

WORKING WITH DIAGRAMS

A picture is worth a thousand words. With this familiar saying in mind, economists construct their diagrams or graphs. With a few lines and a few points, much can be conveyed.

TWO-VARIABLE DIAGRAMS

Most of the diagrams in this book represent the relationship between two variables. For example, suppose our two variables of interest are *consumption* and *income*. We want to show how consumption changes as income changes. Suppose we collect the data in Table 1. By simply looking at the data in the first two columns, we can see that as income rises (column 1), consumption rises (column 2). Suppose we want to show the relationship between income and consumption on a graph. We could place *income* on the horizontal axis, as in Exhibit 1, and *consumption* on the vertical axis. Point *A* represents income of $0 and consumption of $60, point *B* represents income of $100 and consumption of $120, and so on. If we draw a straight line through the various points we have plotted, we have a picture of the relationship between income and consumption, based on the data we collected.

Notice that our line in Exhibit 1 slopes upward from left to right. Thus, as income rises, so does consumption. For example, as you move from point *A* to *B*, income rises from $0 to $100 and consumption rises from $60 to $120. The line in Exhibit 1 also shows that as income falls, so does consumption. For example, as you move from point *C* to *B*, income falls from $200 to $100 and consumption falls from $180 to $120. When two variables—such as consumption and income—change in the same way, they are said to be **directly related.**

Now let's take a look at the data in Table 2. Our two variables are *price of compact discs (CDs)* and *quantity demanded of CDs*. By simply looking at the data in the first two columns, we see that as price falls (column 1), quantity demanded rises (column 2). Suppose we want to plot these data. We could place *price* (of CDs) on the vertical axis, as in Exhibit 2, and *quantity demanded* (of CDs) on the horizontal axis. Point *A* represents a price of $20 and a quantity demanded of 100, point *B* represents a price of $18 and a quantity demanded of

exhibit 1

A Two-Variable Diagram Representing a Direct Relationship
In this exhibit, we have plotted the data in Table 1 and then connected the points with a straight line. The data represent a direct relationship: as one variable (say, income) rises, the other variable (consumption) rises too.

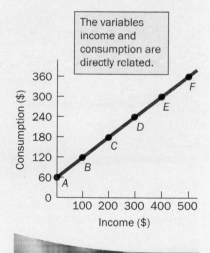

The variables income and consumption are directly related.

table 1

(1) When Income Is:	(2) Consumption Is:	(3) Point
$ 0	$ 60	A
100	120	B
200	180	C
300	240	D
400	300	E
500	360	F

table 2

(1) When the Price of CDs Is:	(2) Quantity Demanded of CDs Is:	(3) Point
$20	100	A
18	120	B
16	140	C
14	160	D
12	180	E

exhibit 2

A Two-Variable Diagram Representing an Inverse Relationship
In this exhibit, we have plotted the data in Table 2 and then connected the points with a straight line. The data represent an inverse relationship: as one variable (price) falls, the other variable (quantity demanded) rises.

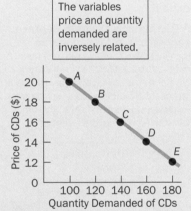

The variables price and quantity demanded are inversely related.

120, and so on. If we draw a straight line through the various points we have plotted, we have a picture of the relationship between price and quantity demanded, based on the data in Table 2.

Notice that as price falls, quantity demanded rises. For example, as price falls from $20 to $18, quantity demanded rises from 100 to 120. Also as price rises, quantity demanded falls. For example, when price rises from $12 to $14, quantity demanded falls from 180 to 160.

When two variables—such as price and quantity demanded—change in opposite ways, they are said to be **inversely related.**

As you have seen so far, variables may be directly related (when one increases, the other also increases), or they may be inversely related (when one increases, the other decreases). Variables can also be **independent** of each other. This condition exists if as one variable changes, the other does not.

In Exhibit 3a, as the X variable rises, the Y variable remains the same (at 20). Obviously, the X and Y variables are independent of each other: as one changes, the other does not.

In Exhibit 3b, as the Y variable rises, the X variable remains the same (at 30). Again, we conclude that the X and Y variables are independent of each other: as one changes, the other does not.

SLOPE OF A LINE

It is often important not only to know *how* two variables are related but also to know *how much* one variable changes as the other variables changes. To find

exhibit 3

Two Diagrams Representing Independence between Two Variables
In (a) and (b), the variables X and Y are independent: as one changes, the other does not.

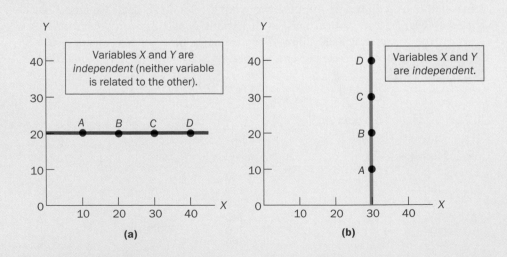

Variables X and Y are *independent* (neither variable is related to the other).

Variables X and Y are *independent.*

(a)　　　(b)

out, we need only calculate the slope of the line. The **slope** is the ratio of the change in the variable on the vertical axis to the change in the variable on the horizontal axis. For example, if Y is on the vertical axis and X on the horizontal axis, the slope is equal to $\Delta Y/\Delta X$. (The symbol "Δ" means "change in.")

$$\text{Slope} = \frac{\Delta Y}{\Delta X}$$

Exhibit 4 shows four lines. In each case we have calculated the slope. After studying (a)–(d), see if you can calculate the slope in each case.

THE SLOPE OF A CURVE

Economic graphs use both straight lines and curves. The slope of a curve is not constant throughout as it is for a straight line. The slope of a curve varies from one point to another.

Calculating the slope of a curve at a given point requires two steps, as illustrated for point A in Exhibit 5. First, draw a line tangent to the curve at the point (a tangent line is one that just touches the curve but does not cross it). Second,

Directly Related
Two variables are directly related if they change in the same way.

Inversely Related
Two variables are inversely related if they change in opposite ways.

Independent
Two variables are independent if as one changes, the other does not.

Slope
The ratio of the change in the variable on the vertical axis to the change in the variable on the horizontal axis.

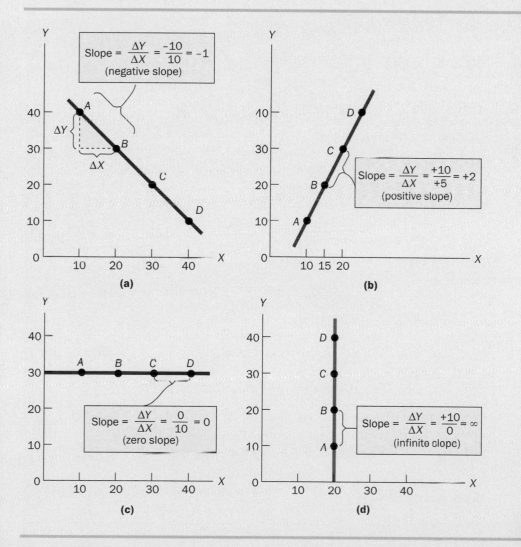

exhibit 4

Calculating Slopes
The slope of a line is the ratio of the change in the variable on the vertical axis to the change in the variable on the horizontal axis. In (a)–(d), we have calculated the slope.

exhibit 5

Calculating the Slope of a Curve at a Particular Point
The slope of the curve at point *A* is +0.67. This is calculated by drawing a line tangent to the curve at point *A* and then determining the slope of the line.

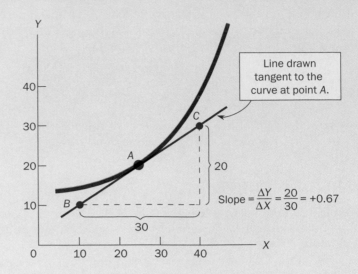

exhibit 6

The 45° Line
Any point on the 45° line is equidistant from both axes. For example, point *A* is the same distance from the vertical axis as it is from the horizontal axis.

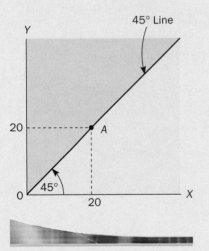

pick any two points on the tangent line and determine the slope. In Exhibit 5 the slope of the line between points *B* and *C* is +0.67. It follows that the slope of the curve at point *A* (and only at point *A*) is +0.67.

THE 45° LINE

Economists sometimes use a *45° line* to represent data. This is a straight line that bisects the right angle formed by the intersection of the vertical and horizontal axes (see Exhibit 6). As a result, the 45° line divides the space enclosed by the two axes into *two equal parts*. We have illustrated this by shading the two equal parts in different colors. The major characteristic of the 45° line is that any point that lies on it is equidistant from both the horizontal and vertical axes. For example, point *A* is exactly as far from the horizontal axis as it is from the vertical axis. It follows that point *A* represents as much *X* as it does *Y*. Specifically, in the exhibit, point *A* represents 20 units of *X* and 20 units of *Y*.

PIE CHARTS

In numerous places in this text, you will come across a *pie chart*. A pie chart is a convenient way to represent the different parts of something that when added together equal the whole. Suppose we consider a typical 24-hour weekday for Charles Myers. On a typical weekday, Charles spends 8 hours sleeping, 4 hours taking classes at the university, 4 hours working at his part-time job, 2 hours doing homework, 1 hour eating, 2 hours watching television, and 3 hours doing nothing in particular (we'll call it "hanging around"). It is easy to represent the breakdown of a typical weekday for Charles in pie chart form, as shown in Exhibit 7. Pie charts give a quick visual message as to rough percentage breakdowns and relative relationships. For example, in Exhibit 7 it is easy to see that Charles spends twice as much time working as doing homework.

BAR GRAPHS

The *bar graph* is another visual aid that economists use to convey relative relationships. For example, suppose we wanted to represent the gross domestic

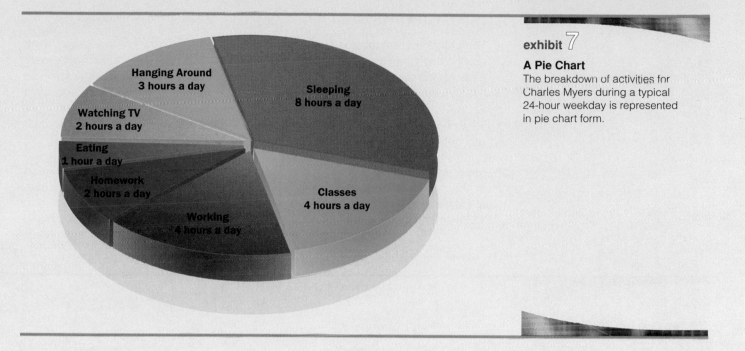

exhibit 7

A Pie Chart
The breakdown of activities for
Charles Myers during a typical
24-hour weekday is represented
in pie chart form.

Hanging Around
3 hours a day

Sleeping
8 hours a day

Watching TV
2 hours a day

Eating
1 hour a day

Homework
2 hours a day

Classes
4 hours a day

Working
4 hours a day

product for the United States in different years. The **gross domestic product (GDP)** is the value of the entire output produced annually within a country's borders. A bar graph can show the actual GDP for each year and can also provide a quick picture of the relative relationships between the GDP in different years. For example, it is easy to see in Exhibit 8 that the GDP in 1990 was more than double what it was in 1980.

Gross Domestic Product (GDP)
The value of the entire output produced annually within a country's borders.

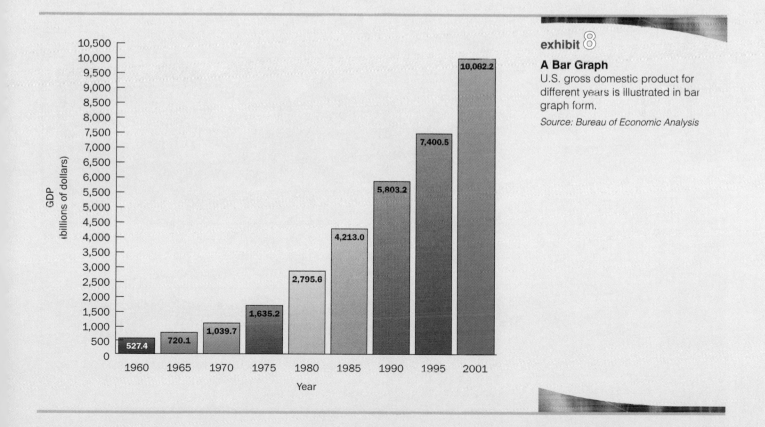

exhibit 8

A Bar Graph
U.S. gross domestic product for
different years is illustrated in bar
graph form.
Source: Bureau of Economic Analysis

GDP (billions of dollars) vs Year

- 1960: 527.4
- 1965: 720.1
- 1970: 1,039.7
- 1975: 1,635.2
- 1980: 2,795.6
- 1985: 4,213.0
- 1990: 5,803.2
- 1995: 7,400.5
- 2001: 10,082.2

LINE GRAPHS

Sometimes information is best and most easily displayed in a *line graph*. Line graphs are particularly useful for illustrating changes in a variable over some time period. Suppose we want to illustrate the variations in average points per game for a college basketball team in different years. As you can see from Exhibit 9a, the basketball team has been on a roller coaster during the years 1989–2002. Perhaps the message transmitted here is that the team's performance has not been consistent from one year to the next.

Suppose we plot the data in Exhibit 9a again, except this time we use a different measurement scale on the vertical axis. As you can see in (b), the variation in the performance of the basketball team appears much less pronounced than in (a). In fact, we could choose some scale such that if we were to plot the data, we would end up with close to a straight line. Our point is simple: Data plotted

exhibit 9

The Two Line Graphs Plot the Same Data

In (a) we plotted the average number of points per game for a college basketball team in different years. The variation between the years is pronounced. In (b) we plotted the same data as in (a), but the variation in the performance of the team appears much less pronounced than in (a).

Year	Average Number of Points per Game
1989	50
1990	40
1991	59
1992	51
1993	60
1994	50
1995	75
1996	63
1997	60
1998	71
1999	61
2000	55
2001	70
2002	64

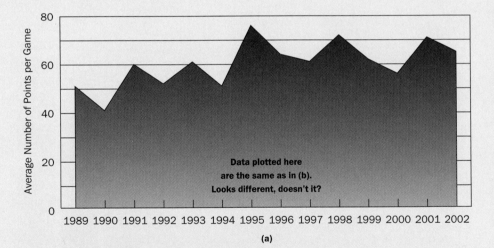

(a)

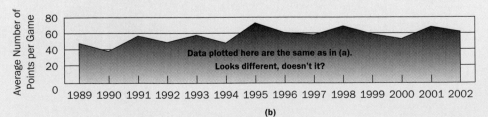

(b)

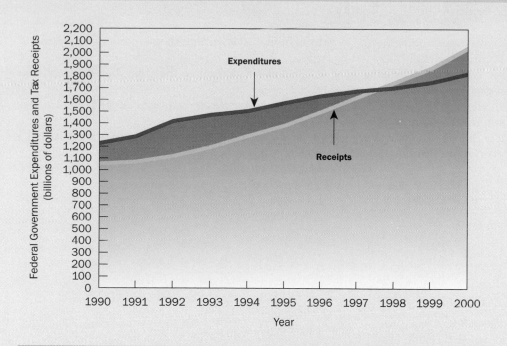

exhibit 10

Federal Government Expenditures and Tax Receipts, 1990–2000
Federal government expenditures and tax receipts are shown in line graph form for the period 1990–2000.

Source: Bureau of Economic Analysis

in line graph form may convey different messages depending on the measurement scale used.

Sometimes economists show two line graphs on the same axes. Usually, they do this to draw attention to either (1) the *relationship* between the two variables or (2) the *difference* between the two variables. In Exhibit 10, the line graphs show the variation and trend in federal government outlays and tax receipts for the years 1990–2000 and draw attention to what has been happening to the "gap" between the two.

Appendix Summary

- Two variables are directly related if one variable rises as the other rises.
- An upward-sloping line (left to right) represents two variables that are directly related.
- Two variables are inversely related if one variable rises as the other falls.
- A downward-sloping line (left to right) represents two variables that are inversely related.
- Two variables are independent if one variable rises as the other remains constant.
- The slope of a line is the ratio of the change in the variable on the vertical axis to the change in the variable on the horizontal axis.

- To determine the slope of a curve at a point, draw a line tangent to the curve at the point and then determine the slope of the tangent line.
- Any point on a 45° line is equidistant from the two axes.
- A pie chart is a convenient way to represent the different parts of something that when added together equal the whole. A pie chart visually shows rough percentage breakdowns and relative relationships.
- A bar graph is a convenient way to represent relative relationships.
- Line graphs are particularly useful for illustrating changes in a variable over some time period.

1. What type of relationship would you expect between the following: (a) sales of hot dogs and sales of hot dog buns, (b) the price of winter coats and sales of winter coats, (c) the price of personal computers and the production of personal computers, (d) sales of toothbrushes and sales of cat food, (e) the number of children in a family and the number of toys in a family.

2. Represent the following data in bar graph form.

Year	U.S. Money Supply (billions of dollars)
1997	1,067
1998	1,075
1999	1,097
2000	1,103
2001	1,135

3. Plot the following data and specify the type of relationship between the two variables. (Place "price" on the vertical axis and "quantity demanded" on the horizontal axis.)

Price of Apples ($)	Quantity Demanded of Apples
0.25	1,000
0.50	800
0.70	700
0.95	500
1.00	400
1.10	350

4. In Exhibit 4a, determine the slope between points *B* and *C*.
5. In Exhibit 4b, determine the slope between points *A* and *B*.
6. What is the special characteristic of a 45° line?
7. What is the slope of a 45° line?
8. When would it be preferable to illustrate data using a pie chart instead of a bar graph?
9. Plot the following data and specify the type of relationship between the two variables. (Place "price" on the vertical axis and "quantity supplied" on the horizontal axis.)

Price of Apples ($)	Quantity Supplied of Apples
0.25	350
0.50	400
0.70	500
0.95	700
1.00	800
1.10	1,000

Log on to the Arnold Xtra! Web site now (*http://arnoldxtra.swcollege.com*) for additional learning resources such as practice quizzes, help with graphing, video clips, and current event applications.

Appendix B

SHOULD YOU MAJOR IN ECONOMICS?

You are probably reading this textbook as part of your first college course in economics. You may be taking this course because you need it to satisfy the requirements in your major. For example, economics courses are sometimes required for students who plan to major in business, history, liberal studies, social science, or computer science. Of course, you may also be taking this course because you plan to major in economics.

If you are like many college students, you may complain that there is just not enough information available to students about the various majors at a college or university. For example, students who major in business sometimes say they are not quite certain what a business major is all about, but then they go on to add that majoring in business is a safe bet. "After all," they comment, "you are pretty sure of getting a job if you have a business degree. That's not always the case with other degrees."

Many college students choose their majors based on their high school courses. History majors sometimes say that they decided to major in history because they "liked history in high school." Similarly, chemistry, biology, and math majors say they chose chemistry, biology, or math as a college major because they liked studying chemistry, biology, or math in high school. In addition, if a student had a hard time with chemistry in high school and found it boring, then he doesn't usually want to major in chemistry in college. If a student found both math and economics easy and interesting in high school, then she is likely to major in math or economics.

Students also often look to the dollars at the end of the college degree. A student may enjoy history and want to learn more history in college but tell herself that she will earn a higher starting salary after graduation if she majors in computer science or engineering.

Thus, when choosing a major, students often consider (1) how much they enjoy studying a particular subject, (2) what they would like to see themselves doing in the future, and (3) income prospects.

Different people may weight these three factors differently. But no matter what weights you put on each of the factors, it is always better to have more information than less information, *ceteris paribus*. (We note *"ceteris paribus"* because it is not necessarily better having more information than less information if you have to pay more for the additional information than the additional information is worth. Who wants to pay $10 for a piece of information that only provides $1 in benefits?)

We believe this appendix is a fairly low-cost way of providing you with more information about an economics major than you currently have. We start by dispelling some of the misinformation you might possess about an economics major. Stated bluntly, some things that people think about an economics major and about a career in economics are just not true. For example, some people think that economics majors almost never study social relationships; instead, they only study such things as inflation, interest rates, and unemployment. Not true.

Economics majors study some of the same things that sociologists, historians, psychologists, and political scientists study. We also provide you with some information about the major that you may not have.

Next, we tell you the specifics of the economics major—what courses you study if you are an economics major, how many courses you are likely to have to take, and more.

Finally, we tell you something about a career in economics. Okay, so you have opted to become an economics major. But the day will come when you have your degree in hand. What's next? What is your starting salary likely to be? What will you be doing? Are you going to be happy doing what economists do? (If you never thought economics was about happiness, you already have some misinformation about economics. Contrary to what most laypeople think, economics is not just about money. It is about happiness too.)

FIVE MYTHS ABOUT ECONOMICS AND AN ECONOMICS MAJOR

Myth 1: Economics is all mathematics and statistics. Some students choose not to major in economics because they think economics is all mathematics and statistics. Math and statistics are used in economics, but at the undergraduate degree level, the math and statistics are certainly not overwhelming. Economics majors are usually required to take one statistics course and one math course (usually an introductory calculus course). Even students who say, "Math isn't my subject" are sometimes happy with the amount of math they need in economics. Fact is, at the undergraduate level at many colleges and universities, economics is not a very math-intensive course of study. There are many diagrams in economics, but there is not a large amount of math.

A proviso: The amount of math in the economics curriculum varies across colleges and universities. Some economics departments do not require their students to learn much math or statistics, but others do. Speaking for the majority of departments, we still hold to our original point that there isn't really that much math or statistics in economics at the undergraduate level. The graduate level is a different story.

Myth 2: Economics is only about inflation, interest rates, unemployment and other such things. If you study economics at college and then go on to become a practicing economist, no doubt people will ask you certain questions when they learn your chosen profession. Here are some of the questions they ask:

- Do you think the economy is going to pick up?
- Do you think the economy is going to slow down?
- What stocks would you recommend?
- Do you think interest rates are going to fall?
- Do you think interest rates are going to rise?
- What do you think about buying bonds right now? Is it a good idea?

People ask these kinds of questions because most people believe that economists only study stocks, bonds, interest rates, inflation, unemployment, and so on. Well, economists do study these things. But these topics are only a tiny part of what economists study. It is not hard to find many economists today, both inside and outside academia, who spend most of their time studying anything but inflation, unemployment, stocks, bonds, and so on.

As we hinted at earlier, much of what economists study may surprise you. There are economists who use their economic tools and methods to study crime, marriage, divorce, sex, obesity, addiction, sports, voting behavior, bureaucracies, presidential elections, and much more. In short, today's economics is not your grandfather's economics. Many more topics are studied today in economics than were studied in your grandfather's time.

Myth 3: People become economists only if they want to "make money."
Awhile back we asked a few well-respected and well-known economists what got them interested in economics. Here is what some of them had to say:[1]

Gary Becker, the 1992 winner of the Nobel Prize in Economics, said: "I got interested [in economics] when I was an undergraduate in college. I came into college with a strong interest in mathematics, and at the same time with a strong commitment to do something to help society. I learned in the first economics course I took that economics could deal rigorously, à la mathematics, with social problems. That stimulated me because in economics I saw that I could combine both the mathematics and my desire to do something to help society."

Vernon Smith, the 2002 winner of the Nobel Prize in Economics, said: "My father's influence started me in science and engineering at Cal Tech, but my mother, who was active in socialist politics, probably accounts for the great interest I found in economics when I took my first introductory course."

Alice Rivlin, an economist and former member of the Federal Reserve Board, said: "My interest in economics grew out of concern for improving public policy, both domestic and international. I was a teenager in the tremendously idealistic period after World War II when it seemed terribly important to get nations working together to solve the world's problems peacefully."

Allan Meltzer said: "Economics is a social science. At its best it is concerned with ways (1) to improve well being by allowing individuals the freedom to achieve their personal aims or goals and (2) to harmonize their individual interests. I find working on such issues challenging, and progress is personally rewarding."

Robert Solow, the 1987 winner of the Nobel Prize in Economics, said: "I grew up in the 1930s and it was very hard not to be interested in economics. If you were a high school student in the 1930s, you were conscious of the fact that our economy was in deep trouble and no one knew what to do about it."

Charles Plosser said: "I was an engineer as an undergraduate with little knowledge of economics. I went to the University of Chicago Graduate School of Business to get an MBA and there became fascinated with economics. I was impressed with the seriousness with which economics was viewed as a way of organizing one's thoughts about the world to address interesting questions and problems."

Walter Williams said: "I was a major in sociology in 1963 and I concluded that it was not very rigorous. Over the summer I was reading a book by W.E.B. DuBois, *Black Reconstruction,* and somewhere in the book it said something along the lines that blacks could not melt into the mainstream of American society until they understood economics, and that was something that got me interested in economics."

Murray Weidenbaum said: "A specific professor got me interested in economics. He was very prescient: He correctly noted that while lawyers dominated the policy-making process up until then (the 1940s), in the future economics would be an important tool for developing public policy. And he was right."

Irma Adelman said: "I hesitate to say because it sounds arrogant. My reason [for getting into economics] was that I wanted to benefit humanity. And my perception at the time was that economic problems were the most important problems that humanity has to face. That is what got me into economics and into economic development."

Lester Thurow said: "[I got interested in economics because of] the belief, some would see it as naïve belief, that economics was a profession where it would be possible to help make the world better."

Myth 4: Economics wasn't very interesting in high school, so it's not going to be very interesting in college. A typical high school economics course emphasizes consumer economics and spends much time discussing this topic. Students learn about credit cards, mortgage loans, budgets, buying insurance,

---

1. See various interviews in Roger A. Arnold, *Economics, 2d edition* (St. Paul, Minnesota: West Publishing Company, 1992).

renting an apartment, and other such things. These are important topics because not knowing the "ins and outs" of such things can make your life much harder. Still, many students come away from a high school economics course thinking that economics is always and everywhere about consumer topics.

However, a high school economics course and a college economics course are usually as different as day and night. Simply leaf through this book and look at the variety of topics covered compared to the topics you might have covered in your high school economics course. Go on to look at texts used in other economics courses—courses that range from law and economics to history of economic thought to international economics to sports economics—and you will see what we mean.

Myth 5: Economics is a lot like business, but business is more marketable. Although business and economics have some common topics, much that one learns in economics is not taught in business and much that one learns in business is not taught in economics. The area of intersection between business and economics is not large.

Still, many people think otherwise. And so thinking that business and economics are "pretty much the same thing," they often choose to major in the subject they believe has greater marketability—which they believe is business.

Well, consider the following:

1. A few years ago *BusinessWeek* magazine asked the chief executive officers (CEOs) of major companies what they thought was the best undergraduate degree. Their first choice was engineering. Their second choice was economics. Economics scored higher than business administration.
2. The National Association of Colleges and Employers undertook a survey in the summer of 2001 in which they identified the starting salary offers in different disciplines. The starting salary in economics/finance was $40,776. The starting salary in business administration was 7.7 percent lower at $37,844.

WHAT AWAITS YOU AS AN ECONOMICS MAJOR?

If you become an economics major, what courses will you take? What are you going to study?

At the lower-division level, economics majors must take both the principles of macroeconomics course and the principles of microeconomics course. They usually also take a statistics course and a math course (usually calculus).

At the upper-division level, they must take intermediate microeconomics and intermediate macroeconomics, along with a certain number of electives. Some of the elective courses include: (1) money and banking, (2) law and economics, (3) history of economic thought, (4) public finance, (5) labor economics, (6) international economics, (7) antitrust and regulation, (8) health economics, (9) economics of development, (10) urban and regional economics, (11) econometrics, (12) mathematical economics, (13) environmental economics, (14) public choice, (15) global managerial economics, (16) economic approach to politics and sociology, (17) sports economics, and many more courses. Most economics majors take between 12 and 15 economics courses.

One of the attractive things about studying economics is that you will acquire many of the skills employers highly value. First, you will have the quantitative skills that are important in many business and government positions. Second, you will acquire the writing skills necessary in almost all lines of work. Third, and perhaps most importantly, you will develop the thinking skills that almost all employers agree are critical to success.

A study published in the 1998 edition of the *Journal of Economic Education* ranked economics majors as having the highest average scores on the Law School

Admission Test (LSAT). Also, consider the words of the Royal Economic Society: "One of the things that makes economics graduates so employable is that the subject teaches you to think in a careful and precise way. The fundamental economic issue is how society decides to allocate its resources: how the costs and benefits of a course of action can be evaluated and compared, and how appropriate choices can be made. A degree in economics gives a training in decision making principles, providing a skill applicable in a very wide range of careers."

Keep in mind, too, that economics is one of the most popular majors at some of the most respected universities in the country. As of this writing, economics is the top major at Harvard, Princeton, Columbia, Stanford, University of Pennsylvania, and University of Chicago. It is the second most popular major at Brown, Yale, and the University of California at Berkeley. It is the third most popular major at Cornell and Dartmouth.

WHAT DO ECONOMISTS DO?

Employment for economists is projected to grow between 21 and 35 percent between 2000 and 2010. According to the *Occupational Outlook Handbook:*

Opportunities for economists should be best in private industry, especially in research, testing, and consulting firms, as more companies contract out for economic research services. The growing complexity of the global economy, competition, and increased reliance on quantitative methods for analyzing the current value of future funds, business trends, sales, and purchasing should spur demand for economists. The growing need for economic analyses in virtually every industry should result in additional jobs for economists.

Today, economists work in many varied fields. Here are some of the fields and some of the positions economists hold in those fields:

Education
College Professor
Researcher
High School Teacher

Journalism
Researcher
Industry Analyst
Economic Analyst

Accounting
Analyst
Auditor
Researcher
Consultant

General Business
Chief Executive Officer
Business Analyst
Marketing Analyst
Business Forecaster
Competitive Analyst

Government
Researcher
Analyst
Speechwriter
Forecaster

Financial Services
Business Journalist
International Analyst
Newsletter Editor
Broker
Investment Banker

Banking
Credit Analyst
Loan Officer
Investment Analyst
Financial Manager

Other
Business Consultant
Independent Forecaster
Freelance Analyst
Think Tank Analyst
Entrepreneur

Economists do a myriad of things. For example, in business, economists often analyze economic conditions, make forecasts, offer strategic planning initiatives, collect and analyze data, predict exchange rate movements, and review regulatory policies, among other things. In government, economists collect and analyze data, analyze international economic situations, research monetary conditions, advise on policy, and much more. As private consultants, economists work with accountants, business executives, government officials, educators, financial firms, labor unions, state and local governments, and others.

Median annual earnings of economists were $64,830 in 2000. The middle 50 percent earned between $47,370 and $87,890. The lowest 10 percent earned less than $35,690, and the highest 10 percent earned more than $114,580.

PLACES TO FIND MORE INFORMATION

If you are interested in an economics major and perhaps a career in economics, here are some places where you can go and some people you can speak with to acquire more information:

- To learn about the economics curriculum, we urge you to speak with the economics professors at your college or university. Ask them what courses you would have to take as an economics major. Ask them what elective courses are available. In addition, ask them why they chose to study economics. What is it about economics that interested them?
- For more information about salaries and what economists do, you may want to visit the *Occupational Outlook Handbook* Web site at *http://www.bls.gov/oco/*.
- For starting salary information, you may want to visit the National Association of Colleges and Employers Web site at *http://www.naceweb.org/*.
- To see a list of famous people who have majored in economics, go to *http://www.marietta.edu/~ema/econ/famous.html*.

CONCLUDING REMARKS

Choosing a major is a big decision and therefore should not be made too quickly and without much thought. In this short appendix, we have provided you with some information about an economics major and a career in economics. Economics may not be for everyone (in fact, economists would say that if it were, many of the benefits of specialization would be lost), but it may be right for you. It is a major where many of today's most marketable skills are acquired—the skills of good writing, quantitative analysis, and thinking. It is a major in which professors and students daily ask and answer some very interesting and relevant questions. It is a major that is highly regarded by employers. It may just be the right major for you. Give it some thought.

Log on to the Arnold Xtra! Web site now (*http://arnoldxtra.swcollege.com*) for additional learning resources such as practice quizzes, help with graphing, video clips, and current event applications.

ECONOMIC ACTIVITIES: PRODUCING AND TRADING

Producing and trading activities occur frequently in everyone's life. People produce goods and services—books, cars, houses, sociology lectures, and so on. People trade money for goods and trade their labor services for money. Most people take their producing and trading activities for granted and rarely study them carefully. In this chapter, we put these two major economic activities—producing and trading— under the microscope. You may be surprised to see what pops up.

Chapter Road Map

Most of our activities involve giving, producing, trading, and transferring. Although economists are interested in all these activities, their primary concerns are producing and trading, the subject matter of this chapter. In analyzing various aspects of production, economists look at (1) individuals and firms producing goods and (2) economies producing goods. In analyzing trade, economists look at (1) trades that affect only the traders and (2) trades that affect the traders and third parties too. Economists also examine some general trade topics—the reason for trading, how the benefits of trade are measured, and how potential trades can be turned into actual trades.

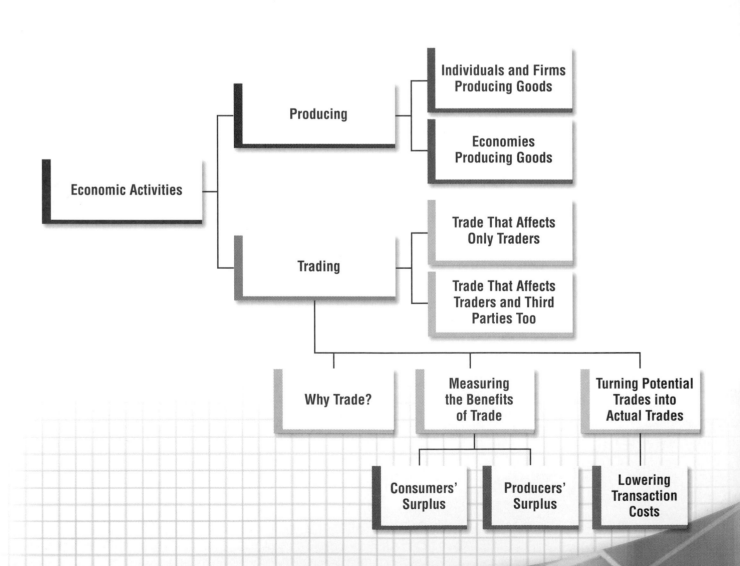

THE PRODUCTION POSSIBILITIES FRONTIER

In order to analyze the various aspects of production, economists find it helpful to define a model or framework in which to examine production. This section introduces and discusses such a framework—the *production possibilities frontier.*

PRODUCING GOOD GRADES IN COLLEGE

When we think of producing goods, we usually think of goods such as cars, computers, furniture, and so on. That is, we think of goods that are produced by business firms. But individuals produce things every day. For example, college students sometimes work at producing "good grades" in their courses. They use both labor and time to produce good grades.

To illustrate, suppose you are taking two courses this semester, sociology and economics. Because you have a part-time job and many other responsibilities, you decide you can spend only 6 hours a week studying these two subjects. If you study economics for 4 hours, you have 2 hours to study sociology; if you study economics for 5 hours, you have 1 hour to study sociology.

Now let's suppose that the more time you spend studying economics, the higher the grade you will earn in economics; the less time you spend studying economics, the lower the grade you will earn. The same holds for sociology.

Exhibit 1a shows the combination of grades you can earn with 6 hours of study. For example, if you study sociology for 6 hours and economics for 0 hours, you will get a 90 in sociology and a 60 in economics. In Exhibit 1b, this combination of grades is identified by point *A*.

(1) Hours Spent Studying Sociology	(2) Grade in Sociology	(3) Hours Spent Studying Economics	(4) Grade in Economics	(5) Point in Part (b)
6	90	0	60	A
5	85	1	65	B
4	80	2	70	C
3	75	3	75	D
2	70	4	80	E
1	65	5	85	F
0	60	6	90	G

(a)

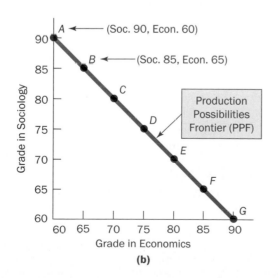

(b)

exhibit 1

Production Possibilities Frontier for Grades

Part (a) shows the different combinations of grades that can be earned in sociology and economics by studying 6 hours per week. The data in columns (2) and (4) of part (a) are plotted as points *A–G* in part (b). Connecting points *A–G* in (b) gives us a production possibilities frontier for grades.

Now look again at the table in part (a). If you study sociology for 5 hours and economics for 1 hour, you will get an 85 in sociology and a 65 in economics. This combination of grades is identified by point *B* in the graph in part (b).

In part (a), we have continued listing the possible combinations of grades based on the number of hours spent studying each subject. In part (b), we have continued to plot and identify the combinations. After all the combinations were plotted and identified, we drew a line connecting the points. This line is called a **production possibilities frontier (PPF).**[1] It gives us the combination of grades in economics and sociology that you will earn if you study a given period of time.

After a production possibilities frontier has been identified, you must identify where on that frontier you will be. Will you choose to be at point *A, B, C, D, E, F,* or *G?* Of course, no matter which point you choose, you will incur a **trade-off.** The nature of a tradeoff is that you get more of one thing but less of something else. If you choose point *A* over point *B,* you will get a higher sociology grade (90 instead of 85) but a lower economics grade (60 instead of 65).

THINKING LIKE AN ECONOMIST

According to the economist, the world is full of tradeoffs. We are regularly faced with the fact that more of one thing means less of something else. More time at work means less time at home. More reading means less time watching television. A higher grade in economics may mean a slightly lower grade in sociology. Recognizing that the world is full of tradeoffs is really no more than recognizing that we incur opportunity costs when we make choices. And why do we make choices? Scarcity.

THE ECONOMY'S PPF

Just as there is a production possibilities frontier for an individual, there is a PPF for an economy. This section discusses the straight-line PPF and the bowed-outward PPF, two possibilities for an economy's PPF.

The Straight-Line PPF: Constant Opportunity Costs

Assume three things: (1) Only two goods can be produced in an economy, computers and television sets. (2) The opportunity cost of 1 television set is 1 computer. (3) As more of one good is produced, the opportunity cost between television sets and computers is constant.

In Exhibit 2a, we have identified six combinations of computers and television sets that can be produced in an economy. For example, combination *A* is 50,000 computers and 0 television sets, combination *B* is 40,000 computers and 10,000 television sets, and so on. We plotted these six combinations of computers and television sets in Exhibit 2b. Each combination represents a different point. For example, the combination of 50,000 computers and 0 television sets is represented by point *A.* As discussed earlier, the line that connects points *A–F* is the production possibilities frontier.

The production possibilities frontier is a straight line because the opportunity cost of producing computers and television sets is constant. For example, if the economy were to move from point *A* to *B,* or from *B* to *C,* and so on, the opportunity cost of each good would remain constant at 1 for 1. To illustrate, at point *A,* 50,000 computers and 0 television sets are produced. At *B,* 40,000 computers and 10,000 television sets are produced.

Point *A:* 50,000 computers, 0 television sets
Point *B:* 40,000 computers, 10,000 television sets

Production Possibilities Frontier (PPF)
Represents the possible combinations of two goods that can be produced in a certain period of time, under the conditions of a given state of technology and fully employed resources.

Tradeoff
More of one good means less of another good.

---

1. If we were talking about the production of two goods—such as computers and television sets—instead of the "production" of sociology and economics grades, we would define a production possibilities frontier a little more completely, such as: represents the possible combinations of two goods that can be produced in a certain period of time, under the conditions of a given state of technology and fully employed resources.

Combination	Computers	and	Television Sets	Point in
	(number of units per year)			Part (b)
A	50,000	and	0	A
B	40,000	and	10,000	B
C	30,000	and	20,000	C
D	20,000	and	30,000	D
E	10,000	and	40,000	E
F	0	and	50,000	F

(a)

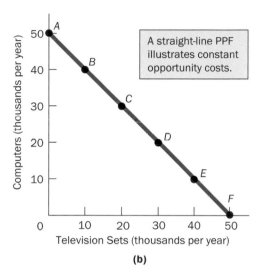

A straight-line PPF illustrates constant opportunity costs.

(b)

exhibit 2

Production Possibilities Frontier (Constant Opportunity Costs)
The economy can produce any of the six combinations of computers and television sets in part (a). We have plotted these combinations in part (b). The production possibilities frontier in part (b) is a straight line because the opportunity cost of producing either good is constant: for *every* 1 computer not produced, 1 television set is produced.

We conclude that for every 10,000 computers not produced, 10,000 television sets are produced—a ratio of 1 to 1. The opportunity cost—1 computer for 1 television set—that exists between points *A* and *B* also exists between points *B* and *C*, *C* and *D*, *D* and *E*, and *E* and *F*. In other words, opportunity cost is constant at 1 computer for 1 television set.

The Bowed-Outward (Concave-Downward) PPF: Increasing Opportunity Costs

Assume two things: (1) Only two goods can be produced in an economy, computers and television sets. (2) As more of one good is produced, the opportunity cost between computers and television sets changes.

In Exhibit 3a, we have identified four combinations of computers and television sets that can be produced in an economy. For example, combination *A* is 50,000 computers and 0 television sets, combination *B* is 40,000 computers and 20,000 television sets, and so on. We plotted these four combinations of computers and television sets in Exhibit 3b. Each combination represents a different point. The curved line that connects points *A–D* is the production possibilities frontier.

In this case, the production possibilities frontier is bowed outward (concave downward) because the opportunity cost of television sets increases as more sets are produced. To illustrate, let's start at point *A*, where the economy is producing 50,000 computers and 0 television sets, and move to point *B*, where the economy is producing 40,000 computers and 20,000 television sets.

Point *A:* 50,000 computers, 0 television sets
Point *B:* 40,000 computers, 20,000 television sets

What is the opportunity cost of a television set over this range? We see that 20,000 more television sets are produced by moving from point *A* to *B but at the cost of only 10,000 computers.* This means for every 1 television set produced, ½ computer is forfeited. Thus, the opportunity cost of 1 television set is ½ computer.

Now let's move from point *B*, where the economy is producing 40,000 computers and 20,000 television sets, to point *C*, where the economy is producing 25,000 computers and 40,000 television sets.

Point *B*: 40,000 computers, 20,000 television sets
Point *C*: 25,000 computers, 40,000 television sets

What is the opportunity cost of a television set over this range? In this case, 20,000 more television sets are produced by moving from point *B* to *C but at the cost of 15,000 computers.* This means for every 1 television set produced, ¾ computer is forfeited. Thus, the opportunity cost of 1 television set is ¾ computer.

What statement can we make about the opportunity costs of producing television sets? Obviously, as the economy produces more television sets, the opportunity cost of producing television sets increases. This gives us the bowed-outward production possibilities frontier in Exhibit 3b.

---

exhibit 3

Production Possibilities Frontier (Changing Opportunity Costs)
The economy can produce any of the four combinations of computers and television sets in part (a). We have plotted these combinations in part (b). The production possibilities frontier in part (b) is bowed outward because the opportunity cost of producing television sets increases as more television sets are produced.

Combination	Computers	and	Television Sets	Point in Part (b)
		(number of units per year)		
A	50,000	and	0	A
B	40,000	and	20,000	B
C	25,000	and	40,000	C
D	0	and	60,000	D

(a)

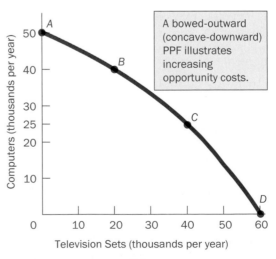

A bowed-outward (concave-downward) PPF illustrates increasing opportunity costs.

(b)

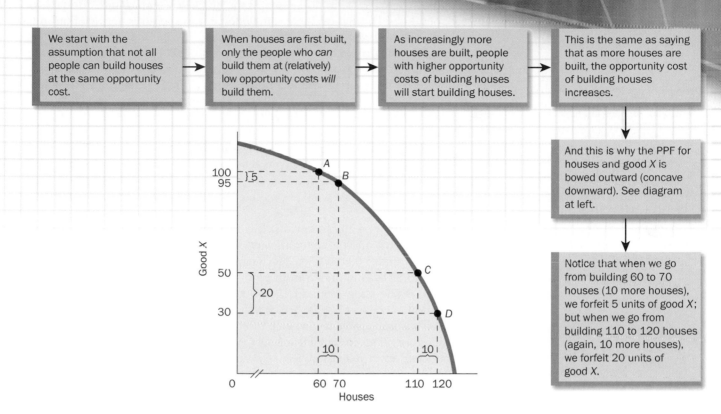

We start with the assumption that not all people can build houses at the same opportunity cost. → When houses are first built, only the people who *can* build them at (relatively) low opportunity costs *will* build them. → As increasingly more houses are built, people with higher opportunity costs of building houses will start building houses. → This is the same as saying that as more houses are built, the opportunity cost of building houses increases.

And this is why the PPF for houses and good *X* is bowed outward (concave downward). See diagram at left.

Notice that when we go from building 60 to 70 houses (10 more houses), we forfeit 5 units of good *X*; but when we go from building 110 to 120 houses (again, 10 more houses), we forfeit 20 units of good *X*.

LAW OF INCREASING OPPORTUNITY COSTS

We know that the shape of the production possibilities frontier depends on whether opportunity costs (1) are constant or (2) increase as more of a good is produced. In Exhibit 2b, the production possibilities frontier is a straight line; in Exhibit 3b, it is bowed outward. In the real world, most production possibilities frontiers are bowed outward. This means that for most goods, the opportunity costs increase as more of the good is produced. This is referred to as the **law of increasing opportunity costs.**

But why (for most goods) do the opportunity costs increase as more of the good is produced? The answer is because people have varying abilities. For example, some people are better suited to building houses than other people are. When a construction company first starts building houses, it employs the people who are most skilled at house building. The most skilled persons can build houses at lower opportunity costs than others can. But as the construction company builds more houses, it finds that it has already employed the most skilled builders, so it must employ those who are less skilled at house building. These people build houses at higher opportunity costs. Where three skilled house builders could build a house in a month, as many as seven unskilled builders may be required to build it in the same length of time. Exhibit 4 summarizes the points in this section.

THREE ECONOMIC CONCEPTS WITHIN A PPF FRAMEWORK

The PPF framework is useful for illustrating and working with economic concepts. This section looks at the economic concepts of efficiency, unemployed resources, economic growth, and an advance in technology.

exhibit 4

A Summary Statement about Increasing Opportunity Costs and a Production Possibilities Frontier That Is Bowed Outward (Concave Downward)
Many of the points about increasing opportunity costs and a production possibilities frontier that is bowed outward are summarized here.

Law of Increasing Opportunity Costs
As more of a good is produced, the opportunity costs of producing that good increase.

Efficiency

Chapter 1 discusses efficiency in terms of the right amount of something. For example, you may recall the discussion of the efficient length of time to study for an economics test. In that example, efficiency is considered in terms of an individual's actions and choices.

Economists also consider **efficiency** in terms of an economy. For example, economists often say that an economy is *efficient* if it is producing the maximum output with given resources and technology. In Exhibit 5, points *A, B, C, D,* and *E* are all efficient points. Notice that all these points lie *on* the production possibilities frontier. In other words, we are getting the most (in terms of output) from what we have (in terms of available resources and technology).

It follows that an economy is exhibiting **inefficiency** if it is producing less than the maximum output with given resources and technology. In Exhibit 5, point *F* is an inefficient point. It lies *below* the production possibilities frontier; it is below the outer limit of what is possible. In other words, we could do better with what we have.

Consider another way of viewing efficiency and inefficiency. Start at efficient point *A* in Exhibit 5 and move to efficient point *B*. We go from producing 55,000 television sets and 5,000 cars to producing fewer television sets (50,000) and more cars (15,000). Now move from point *B* back to point *A*. We go from producing 50,000 television sets and 15,000 cars to producing more television sets (55,000) and fewer cars (5,000). Notice that if we start at an efficient point—such as *A* or *B*—it is impossible to produce more of one good without producing less of another good. We can move from *A* to *B* and produce more cars but not without producing fewer television sets. *Efficiency implies that gains are impossible in one area without losses in another.* Another way to state this is that efficiency implies a *tradeoff*—before more of one good can be obtained, some of another good has to be given up. A movement between any two points on the PPF in Exhibit 5 implies a tradeoff. For example, if we move from *D* to *C,* we get 7,000 more television sets but must give up 10,000 cars.

Efficiency
In terms of production, the condition where the maximum output is produced with given resources and technology. Efficiency implies the impossibility of gains in one area without losses in another.

Inefficiency
In terms of production, the condition where less than the maximum output is produced with given resources and technology. Inefficiency implies the possibility of gains in one area without losses in another.

---

exhibit 5

Efficiency, Inefficiency, and Unemployed Resources within a PPF Framework

Points *A, B, C, D,* and *E* are efficient points. They lie on the production possibilities frontier. It is *impossible* to move away from these points and get more of one good without getting less of another good. Point *F* is an inefficient point. It lies below the production possibilities frontier. It is *possible* to move away from this point and get more of (at least) one good and no less of another. At efficient points, all resources are being used in the production of goods. At inefficient points, some resources are not being used to produce goods; that is, there are some unemployed resources.

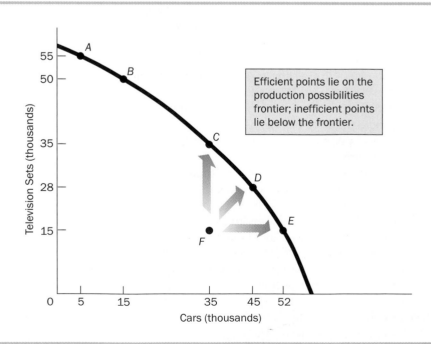

Efficient points lie on the production possibilities frontier; inefficient points lie below the frontier.

This is common sense. If efficiency exists, we already are getting the most we can out of what we have. Therefore, we cannot do better in one area (getting more of one good) without necessarily doing worse in another (getting less of another good).

Now consider inefficient point *F*, a point at which the economy is not producing the maximum output with given resources and technology. Move from point *F* to point *C*. We produce more television sets and no fewer cars. What if we move from *F* to *D*? We produce more television sets and more cars. Finally, if we move from *F* to *E*, we produce more cars and no fewer television sets. Thus, moving from *F* can give us more of at least one good and no less of another good. (Moving from *F* to *D*, we produced more of both goods.) *Inefficiency implies that gains are possible in one area without losses in another.* This is also common sense. If inefficiency exists, we are not getting the most out of what we have. Therefore, we can do better in one area without necessarily doing worse in another.

Q & A

Q: Suppose we move from point *F* to point *B* in Exhibit 5. More television sets are produced but fewer cars—in other words, more of one good but less of another. Doesn't this mean *F* is an efficient point although it was labeled an inefficient point?

A: Efficiency implies that gains are *impossible* in one area without losses in another. Point *F* does not fit this definition. We could move from *F* to *C*, *D*, or *E*—all these moves are *possible*— and get gains in one area without getting losses in another. It follows that *F* is an inefficient point. Simply because a move from *F* to *B* brings gains in one area and losses in another, it does not necessarily follow that a move from *F* to some other point would always bring the same results. As long as it is possible to move from *F* to some point and get gains in one area without getting losses in another, then *F* is an inefficient point.

Unemployed Resources

When the economy exhibits inefficiency, it is not producing the maximum output with the available resources and technology. One reason may be that the economy is not using all its resources—that is, some of its resources are unemployed, as at point *F* in Exhibit 5.

When the economy exhibits efficiency, it is producing the maximum output with the available resources and technology. This means it is using all its resources to produce goods—all its resources are employed, none are unemployed. At the efficient points *A–E* in Exhibit 5, there are no unemployed resources.

Economic Growth

Economic growth refers to the increased productive capabilities of an economy. It is illustrated by a shift outward in the production possibilities frontier. Two major factors that affect economic growth are an increase in the quantity of resources and an advance in technology.

With an increase in the quantity of resources (say, through a new discovery of resources), it is possible to produce a greater quantity of output. In Exhibit 6, an increase in the quantity of resources makes it possible to produce both more military goods and more civilian goods. Thus, the PPF shifts outward from PPF$_1$ to PPF$_2$.

Technology refers to the body of skills and knowledge concerning the use of resources in production. An advance in technology commonly refers to the ability to produce more output with a fixed quantity of resources or the ability to produce the same output with a smaller quantity of resources.

Suppose there is an advance in technology such that more military goods and more civilian goods can be produced with the same quantity of resources. As a result, the PPF in Exhibit 6 shifts outward from PPF$_1$ to PPF$_2$. The outcome is the same as when the quantity of resources is increased.

Technology
The body of skills and knowledge concerning the use of resources in production. An advance in technology commonly refers to the ability to produce more output with a fixed amount of resources or the ability to produce the same output with fewer resources.

exhibit 6

Economic Growth within a PPF Framework
An increase in resources or an advance in technology can increase the production capabilities of an economy, leading to economic growth and a shift outward in the production possibilities frontier.

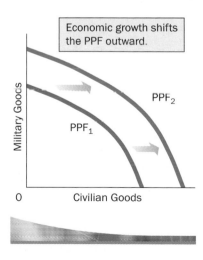

ECONOMICS IN...

Technology · Popular Culture · Everyday Life · The World

Can Technology on the Farm Affect the Number of Lawyers in the City?

There is no doubt that an advance in technology affects the industry in which it is developed and used. For example, a technological advance in the car industry will increase the output of cars; a technological advance in the house-building industry will increase the output of houses.

But can a technological advance in one industry have ripple effects beyond the industry in which it is developed and used? With this question in mind, let's start with a fact. The United States had 32.1 million farmers in 1910, 30.5 million farmers in 1940, 9.7 million farmers in 1970, and about 4.8 million farmers in 2000. Farmers accounted for 34.9 percent of the U.S. population in 1910, 23.2 percent in 1940, 4.8 percent in 1970, and only 1.9 percent in 2000. Where did all the farmers go and why did they leave farming?

Many farmers left farming because farming has experienced major technological advances during this century. Where farmers once farmed with minimal capital equipment, today they use computers, tractors, pesticides, cellular phones, and much more. As a result, more food can be produced with fewer farmers.

Because fewer farmers were needed to produce food, many farmers left the farms and entered the manufacturing and service industries. In other words, people who were once farmers (or whose parents and grandparents were farmers) began to produce cars, airplanes, television sets, and computers. They became attorneys, accountants, and police officers.

What should we learn from this? First, a technological advance in one sector of the economy may make it possible to produce goods in another sector of the economy. Technological advances in agriculture made it possible for fewer farmers to produce more food, thus releasing some farmers to produce other things. In other words, there may be more services in the world in part because of agriculture's technological advances.

Second, technological advances may affect the composition of employment. The technological advances in agriculture resulted in (1) a smaller percentage of people working in rural areas on farms and (2) a larger percentage of people working in manufacturing and services in the cities and suburbs. (Is the growth of the suburbs in the last 50 years due in part to technological advances on farms?)

Self-Test *(Answers to Self-Test questions are in the Self-Test Appendix.)*

1. What does a straight-line production possibilities frontier (PPF) represent? What does a bowed-outward PPF represent?

2. Would you expect to see more intense political battles in a growing economy or in a stagnant economy, *ceteris paribus*? Why? (Hint: Think in terms of the PPF.)

3. A politician says, "If you elect me, we can get more of everything we want." Under what condition(s) is the politician telling the truth?

4. In an economy there is only one combination of goods that is efficient. True or false? Explain your answer.

TRADE OR EXCHANGE

Trade (Exchange)
The process of giving up one thing for something else.

Trade or **exchange** is the process of giving up one thing for something else. Usually, money is traded for goods and services. Trade is all around us; we are involved with it every day. Few of us, however, have considered the full extent of trade.

THE PURPOSE OF TRADE

Why do people trade? Why do they exchange things? They do so in order to make themselves better off. When a person voluntarily trades $100 for a jacket, she is saying "I prefer to have the jacket instead of the $100." And, of course, when the seller of the jacket voluntarily sells the jacket for $100, he is saying, "I prefer to have the $100 instead of the jacket." In short, through trade or exchange, each person gives up something he or she values less for something he or she values more.

PERIODS RELEVANT TO TRADE

Three time periods are relevant to the trading process.

Before the Trade

Before a trade is made, a person is said to be in the **ex ante** position. For example, suppose Ramona has the opportunity to trade what she has, $2,000, for something she does not have, a big screen television set. In the ex ante position, she will think that she will be better off with either (1) the television set or (2) $2,000 worth of other goods. If she believes she will be better off with the television set than with $2,000 worth of other goods, she will make the trade. Individuals will make a trade only if they believe ex ante (before) the trade that the trade will make them better off.

Ex Ante
Phrase that means "before," as in before a trade.

At the Point of Trade

Suppose Ramona now gives $2,000 to the person in possession of the television set. Does Ramona still believe she will be better off with the television set than with the $2,000? Of course she does. Her action testifies to this fact.

After the Trade

After a trade is made, a person is said to be in the **ex post** position. Suppose two days have passed. Does Ramona still feel the same way about the trade as she did before the trade and at the point of trade? Maybe, maybe not. She may look back on the trade and regret it. She may say that if she had it to do over again, she would not trade the $2,000 for the big screen television set. In general, though, people expect a trade to make them better off, and usually the trade meets their expectations. But there are no guarantees that a trade will meet expectations because no one in the real world can see the future.

Ex Post
Phrase that means "after," as in after a trade.

MEASURING THE BENEFITS OF TRADES

Economists determine the benefits of a trade by examining the trade in terms of both the consumer's or buyer's point of view and the producer's or seller's point of view. They then use these two points of view to analyze various trading situations.

Thinking of Trade from the Consumer's or Buyer's Point of View

Suppose you would be willing to pay a maximum of $10 to see a new movie release. But at the movie theater, you are charged only $7. The difference between the maximum price you are willing and able to pay to see the movie and the price you actually pay is **consumers' surplus.** In this case, consumers' surplus is $3.

Consumers' Surplus (CS)
The difference between the maximum price a buyer is willing and able to pay for a good or service and the price actually paid. CS = Maximum buying price − Price paid.

$$\text{Consumers' surplus} = \text{Maximum buying price} - \text{Price paid}$$

Obviously, a buyer prefers a large consumers' surplus to a small consumers' surplus. You would have preferred to pay only $6 for the movie and obtain $4 worth of consumers' surplus.

Thinking of Trade from the Producer's or Seller's Point of View

Now consider the seller. Suppose the minimum price the owner of the theater would have accepted for admission is $5. But she doesn't sell tickets for $5; she

ECONOMICS IN...

What Do Blue Jeans and Rock 'n' Roll Have to Do with the Fall of the Berlin Wall?

The Berlin Wall once stood as the symbol of communism and the Cold War. Today, the Berlin Wall is gone and the Cold War is over. What happened? Was the military strength of the United States too much for the former Soviet Union to cope with continually? Some people think this is exactly what happened. Other people think that blue jeans and rock music had more to do with the decline of the Soviet Union and the demise of communism in Eastern Europe than did the military might of the United States.

Tension may develop between political parties in the United States because each party wants to be at a different point on the production possibilities frontier. Only through economic growth will that tension subside and then only for a while. Some economists and political scientists believe that one reason for the downfall of communism in the Soviet Union and Eastern Europe was the political tension that developed between government leaders and the majority of the people.

Consider the PPF framework shown in Exhibit 7a. Suppose the majority of the people in the Soviet Union wanted to be at point 1, producing C_1 consumer goods (blue jeans and rock music) and M_1 military goods. The government leaders, however, wanted to be at point 2, producing C_2 consumer goods and M_2 military goods. The majority of the people wanted more consumer goods than the government wanted to produce, and the government wanted more military goods than the people wanted to produce.

Is there any evidence that this scenario actually took place in the Soviet Union? Many Soviet scholars think it did. Even Soviet leaders admitted this. In May 1990, Eduard Shevardnadze, the Soviet foreign minister at the time, said that the Kremlin's emphasis on military goods and a large army was contrary to what the majority of the people wanted.[2]

Furthermore, numerous accounts of life in the former Soviet Union suggest that the majority of the people were not satisfied with the quality or quantity of consumer goods they were able to purchase. People complained of continual food shortages, shoddy products, telephone service that often broke down, and much much more.

To get an idea of Soviet economic priorities, consider that in 1980, 12.9 percent of all expenditures were for the military.

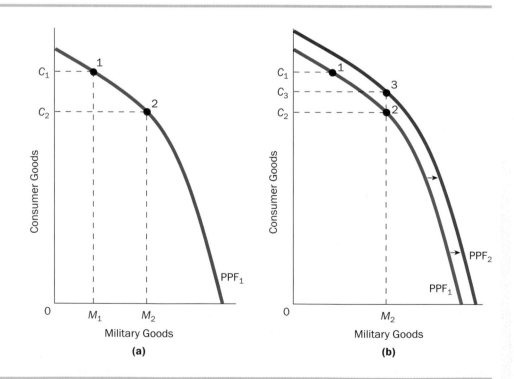

exhibit 7

The Collapse of the Former Soviet Union within a PPF Framework
In (a) we have hypothesized that the majority of the people in the former Soviet Union wanted to be at point 1 on the production possibilities frontier and that government leaders wanted to be at point 2. Given the difference between the points, we would expect some tension between the people and the government leaders. It is possible for the people to get more of what they want (consumer goods) through economic growth, as shown in (b). Through economic growth, it is possible to move from point 2 on PPF_1 to point 3 on PPF_2, bringing the people closer to their preferred amount of consumer goods (C_1). Without economic growth, the tension between the two groups may build and become "explosive."

2. See Walter Friedenberg, "Shevardnadze Warns of Explosion," *Washington Times*, sec. A, 7 May 1990. p. 1.

In contrast, the percentage of total military expenditures in most other countries was between 2 and 6 percent. It was 5.3 percent in the United States, for example. As for consumer goods, in the Soviet Union at the end of the 1980s, there were approximately 330 television sets for every 1,000 persons and 12 telephones for every 100 persons. In the United States, there were 815 television sets for every 1,000 persons and 51 telephones for every 100 persons.

As long as the Soviet Union experienced some economic growth and all the growth didn't go to the military, it was possible to alleviate some of the tension between the people and the government leaders. For example, suppose economic growth shifted the production possibilities frontier outward from PPF_1 to PPF_2 as shown in Exhibit 7b. In this case, the Soviet Union could maintain military goods production at M_2, while increasing consumer goods production to C_3, which is closer to the amount of consumer goods, C_1, that the majority of the people wanted.

But there is reason to believe that the Soviet Union didn't experience much economic growth. On February 17, 1988, Soviet leader Mikhail Gorbachev told the Central Committee of the Communist Party that the Soviet economy had not grown in 20 years.[3] In other words, it is possible that for 20 years there was constant tension between the people and the government leaders. Couldn't this lead to an "explosion" of sorts?

Some political scientists and economists believe that the popular revolt against communism that took place in the late 1980s and early 1990s was just this explosion. The Berlin Wall, once the symbol of communism for many, began to crack, metaphorically speaking. Then it came crumbling down, literally.

The bigger lesson to learn can be expressed in terms of the production possibilities frontier. A country that locates itself at a point on the production possibilities frontier where the majority of people do not want it to be is likely to experience greater political instability than a country that does not.

---

charges \$7. The difference between the price paid for the ticket and the minimum price the seller would be willing and able to sell the ticket for is **producers' (or sellers') surplus.** For this trade, the producers' surplus is \$2.

$$\text{Producers' (or sellers') surplus} = \text{Price received} - \text{Minimum selling price}$$

A seller prefers a large producers' surplus. The seller would have preferred to sell the movie ticket for \$8 and receive \$3 worth of producers' surplus.

Will a Policy Make You Better Off or Worse Off?

Many different policies and laws are put into effect by governments and organizations each year. For example, the federal government may change its tariff policy and place a tariff (tax) on certain imported goods. Or it could subsidize the production of wheat, corn, or sugar. HMOs (health maintenance organizations) may institute a policy in which they will pay for only some of the medicines you may need. The state legislators in your state may increase or decrease the tuition at a state-supported college or university. The federal government may block a merger between two major companies that produce and sell office supplies. When you hear about a new policy or law, you may naturally wonder "How does this affect me? Will I be better off or worse off?"

To answer these questions, you need to remember that you do many things. You buy goods, you sell goods, you may work for a company, you may own your own business. In other words, you wear many hats. One day you wear the hat of a buyer, the next day, that of a seller. On any given day, you may wear both the hat of an employee and the hat of a buyer. As a buyer, there is an easy way to figure out how a policy will affect you. Simply ask, "As a result of the policy, will my consumers' surplus rise, fall, or stay the same?" If it will rise, then as a buyer, the policy will make you better off. If it will fall, then you will be worse off. If it will stay the same, then your situation will be unchanged. Later

---

3. Communique on the Plenary Session of the Central Committee of the Communist Party of the Soviet Union, *Pravda* and *Izvestiya*, 18 February 1988. Some economists think that Gorbachev's statement was slightly exaggerated. It is likely that the former Soviet economy experienced some growth, but not much. Even with economic growth, if the population grew faster than the economy, per capita consumer goods would decline.

Terms of Trade
How much of one thing is given up for how much of something else.

Transaction Costs
The costs associated with the time and effort needed to search out, negotiate, and consummate an exchange.

chapters show how the concept of consumers' surplus can be used to determine how a given policy or change in policy will affect an individual.

Trade and the Terms of Trade

Suppose Emilio walks into a bookstore and browses through a few of the best-sellers. Minutes later he walks to the counter with a book, takes $30 out of his wallet (the price of the book), gives it to the cashier, and walks out. Away from the store, he thinks, "They charged too much for the book; I've been taken."

Given Emilio's thoughts and accepting that he is currently in the ex post position, is it correct to assume that he now regrets the trade that he made only moments earlier? The answer may be yes. But probably, Emilio is simply expressing his discontent over paying as much for the book as he did. He would rather have paid less for the book and received more consumers' surplus, as would any buyer.

This example illustrates the difference between trade and the terms of trade. *Trade* refers to the process whereby "things" (money, goods, services, and so on) are given up in order to obtain something else. The **terms of trade** refer to *how much* of one thing is given up for *how much* of something else. For example, if $30 is traded for a best-selling book, the terms of trade are 1 bestseller for $30. If the price of a loaf of bread is $2.50, the terms of trade are 1 loaf of bread for $2.50. Buyers and sellers can always think of more advantageous terms of exchange. Buyers prefer lower prices, sellers prefer higher prices.

Knowing the difference between trade and the terms of trade prevents us from believing that someone has been harmed by an exchange when the person claims to have been "taken" or "ripped off." Many times, the person is expressing his or her desire to have paid less (if a buyer) or to be paid more (if a seller) for the good or service that was exchanged.

COSTS OF TRADES

As always, economists consider both benefits and costs. They want to determine what costs are involved in a trade and whether the costs may prevent a trade from taking place.

Unexploited Trades

Suppose Smith wants to buy a red 1965 Ford Mustang in excellent condition. The maximum price she is willing and able to pay for the Mustang is $30,000. Also suppose that Jones owns a red 1965 Ford Mustang in excellent condition. The minimum price he is willing and able to sell the Mustang for is $23,000. Obviously, Smith's maximum buying price ($30,000) is greater than Jones's minimum selling price ($23,000), so a potential trade or exchange exists.

Will the potential trade between Smith and Jones become an actual exchange? The answer to this question may depend on the transaction costs. **Transaction costs** are the costs associated with the time and effort needed to search out, negotiate, and consummate a trade. To illustrate, neither Smith nor Jones may know that the other exists. Suppose Smith lives in Roanoke, Virginia, and Jones lives 40 miles away in Blacksburg, Virginia. Each needs to find the other, which may take time and money. Perhaps Smith can put an ad in the local Blacksburg newspaper stating that she is searching for a 1965 Ford Mustang in mint condition. Alternatively, Jones can put an ad in the local Roanoke newspaper stating that he has a 1965 Ford Mustang to sell. The ad may or may not be seen by the relevant party and then acted upon. Our point is a simple one: Transaction costs sometimes keep potential trades from turning into actual trades.

Consider another example. Suppose Kurt hates to shop for clothes because shopping takes too much time. He has to get in his car, drive to the mall, park the car, walk into the mall, look in different stores, try on different clothes, pay for the items, get back in his car, and drive home. Suppose Kurt spends an average of 2 hours when he shops and he estimates that an hour of his time is worth $30. It follows, then, that Kurt incurs $60 worth of transaction costs when he buys clothes. Usually, he is not willing to incur the transaction costs necessary to buy a pair of trousers or a shirt.

Now, suppose we ask Kurt if he would be more willing to buy clothes if shopping were easier. Suppose, we say, the transaction costs associated with buying clothes could be lowered from $60 to less than $10. At lower transaction costs, Kurt says that he would be willing to shop more often.

How can transaction costs be lowered? Both people and computers can help lower the transaction costs of trades. For example, real estate brokers lower the transaction costs of selling and buying a house. Jim has a house to sell but doesn't know how to find a buyer. Karen wants to buy a house but doesn't know how to find a seller. Enter the real estate broker, who brings buyers and sellers together. In so doing, she lowers the transaction costs of buying and selling a house.

As another example, consider e-commerce on the Internet. Ursula can buy a book by getting in her car, driving to a bookstore, getting out of her car, walking into the bookstore, looking at the books on the shelves, taking a book to the cashier, paying for it, leaving the store, getting back in her car, and returning home. Or, Ursula can buy a book over the Internet. She can click on one of the online booksellers, search for the book by title, read a short description of the book, and then click on 1-Click Buying. Buying on the Internet has lower transaction costs than shopping at a store because online buying requires less time and effort. Before online book buying and selling, were there potential book purchases and sales that weren't being turned into actual book purchases and sales? There is some evidence that there were.

Turning Potential Trades into Actual Trades

Some people are always looking for ways to earn a profit. Can what you have learned about exchange and transaction costs help you earn money? It would seem that one way to earn a profit is to turn potential trades into actual trades by lowering transaction costs. Consider the following example. Buyer Smith is willing to pay a maximum price of $400 for good X; Seller Jones is willing to accept a minimum price of $200 for good X. Currently, the transaction costs of the exchange are $500, evenly split between Buyer Smith and Seller Jones.

Buyer Smith thinks, "Even if I pay the lowest possible price for good X, $200, I will still have to pay $250 in transaction costs, bringing my total to $450. The maximum price I am willing to pay for good X is $400, so I will not make this purchase."

Seller Jones thinks, "Even if I receive the highest possible price for good X, $400, I will still have to pay $250 in transaction costs, leaving me with only $150. The minimum price I am willing to accept for good X is $200, so I will not make this sale."

This potential trade will not become an actual trade, unless someone can lower the transaction costs. One role of an entrepreneur is to try *to turn potential trades into actual trades by lowering transaction costs.* Suppose Entrepreneur Brown can lower the transaction costs for Buyer Smith and Seller Jones to $10 each, asking $60 from each person for services rendered. Also, Entrepreneur Brown negotiates the price of good X at $300. Will the potential exchange become an actual exchange?

Buyer Smith thinks, "I am willing to pay a maximum of $400 for good X. If I purchase good X through Entrepreneur Brown, I will pay $300 to Seller Jones, $10 in transaction costs, and $60 to Brown. This is a total of $370, leaving me with a consumers' surplus of $30. It is worthwhile for me to purchase good X."

Seller Jones thinks, "I am willing to sell good X for a minimum of $200. If I sell good X through Entrepreneur Brown, I will receive $300 from Buyer Smith and will have to pay $10 in transaction costs and $60 to Brown. That will leave me with $230, or $30 worth of sellers' surplus. It is worthwhile for me to sell good X."

Thus, an entrepreneur can earn a profit by finding a way to lower transaction costs. As a result, a potential exchange turns into an actual exchange.

TRADES AND THIRD-PARTY EFFECTS

Consider two trades. In the first, Harriet pays 80 cents to Taylor for a pack of chewing gum. In this trade, both Harriet and Taylor are made better off (they wouldn't have traded otherwise) and no one is made worse off.

In the second trade, Bob pays $4 to George for a pack of cigarettes. Bob takes a cigarette, lights it, and smokes it. It happens that he is near Caroline when he smokes the cigarette, and she begins to cough because she is sensitive to cigarette smoke. In this trade, both Bob, who buys the cigarettes, and George, who sells the cigarettes, are made better off. But Caroline, who had nothing to do with the trade, is made worse off. In this exchange, a third party, Caroline, is adversely affected by the exchange between George and Bob.

These examples show that some trades affect only the parties involved in the exchange, and some trades have *third-party effects* (someone other than the parties involved in the exchange is affected). In the cigarette example, the third-party effect was negative; there was an adverse effect on Caroline, the third party. Sometimes economists call adverse third party effects *negative externalities*. A later chapter discusses this topic in detail.

Self-Test

1. The maximum price a buyer is willing and able to pay for a good is $100,000. The minimum price a seller is willing to accept for the good is $89,000. The price paid for the good is $92,000. What is the producers' surplus? What is the consumers' surplus?

2. What are transaction costs? Are the transaction costs of buying a house likely to be greater or less than those of buying a car? Explain your answer.

3. "I bought a computer and I feel ripped off," Cynthia says. Does it follow that in the ex post position Cynthia regrets having purchased the computer? Explain your answer.

4. Give an example of a trade without third-party effects. Next, give an example of a trade with third-party effects.

PRODUCTION, TRADE, AND SPECIALIZATION

The first section of this chapter discusses production; the second section discusses trade. From these two sections, you might conclude that production and trade are unrelated activities. However, they are not: Before you can trade, you need to produce something. This section ties production and trade together and also shows how the benefits one receives from trade can be affected by how one produces.

PRODUCING AND TRADING

To show how a change in production can benefit traders, we eliminate anything and everything extraneous to the process. Thus, we eliminate money and consider a barter, or moneyless, economy.

In this economy, there are two individuals, Elizabeth and Brian. They live near each other and each engages in two activities: baking bread and growing apples. Let's suppose that within a certain period of time, Elizabeth can produce 20 loaves of bread and no apples, or 10 loaves of bread and 10 apples, or no bread and 20 apples. In other words, three points on Elizabeth's production possibilities frontier correspond to 20 loaves of bread and no apples, 10 loaves of bread and 10 apples, and no bread and 20 apples.

As a consumer, Elizabeth likes to eat both bread and apples, so she decides to produce (and consume) 10 loaves of bread and 10 apples.

Within the same time period, Brian can produce 10 loaves of bread and no apples, or 5 loaves of bread and 15 apples, or no bread and 30 apples. In other words, these three combinations correspond to three points on Brian's production possibilities frontier. Brian, like Elizabeth, likes to eat both bread and apples, so he decides to produce and consume 5 loaves of bread and 15 apples. Exhibit 8 shows the combinations of bread and apples that Elizabeth and Brian can produce.

Elizabeth thinks that both she and Brian may be better off if each specializes in producing only one of the two goods and trading it for the other. In other words, Elizabeth should produce either bread or apples but not both. Brian thinks this may be a good idea but is not sure what good each person should specialize in producing.

An economist would advise each to produce the good that he or she can produce at a lower cost. In economics, a person who can produce a good at a lower cost than another person can is said to have a **comparative advantage** in the production of that good.

Comparative Advantage
The situation where someone can produce a good at lower opportunity cost than someone else can.

Exhibit 8 shows that for every 10 units of bread Elizabeth does not produce, she can produce 10 apples. In other words, the opportunity cost of producing one loaf of bread (B) is one apple (A):

$$\text{Opportunity costs for Elizabeth: } 1B = 1A$$
$$1A = 1B$$

As for Brian, for every 5 loaves of bread he does not produce, he can produce 15 apples. So, for every 1 loaf of bread he does not produce, he can produce 3 apples. It follows, then, that for every one apple he chooses to produce, he forfeits ⅓ loaf of bread.

$$\text{Opportunity costs for Brian: } 1B = 3A$$
$$1A = \tfrac{1}{3}B$$

Comparing opportunity costs, we see that Elizabeth can produce bread at a lower opportunity cost than Brian can. (Elizabeth forfeits 1 apple when she produces 1 loaf of bread, whereas Brian forfeits 3 apples when he produces 1 loaf of bread.) On the other hand, Brian can produce apples at a lower opportunity cost than Elizabeth can. We conclude that Elizabeth has a comparative advantage in the production of bread and Brian has a comparative advantage in the production of apples.

Suppose each person specializes in the production of the good in which he or she has a comparative advantage. This means Elizabeth produces only bread and produces 20 loaves. Brian produces only apples and produces 30 apples.

Elizabeth		Brian	
Bread	Apples	Bread	Apples
20	0	10	0
10	10	5	15
0	20	0	30

exhibit 8

Production by Elizabeth and Brian
The exhibit shows the combinations of goods each can produce individually in a given time period.

		No Specialization and No Trade	Specialization and Trade	Gains from Specialization and Trade
Elizabeth	Consumption of Loaves of Bread	10	12	+2
	Consumption of Apples	10	12	+2
Brian	Consumption of Loaves of Bread	5	8	+3
	Consumption of Apples	15	18	+3

Now suppose that Elizabeth and Brian decide to trade 8 loaves of bread for 12 apples. In other words, Elizabeth produces 20 loaves of bread and then trades 8 of the loaves for 12 apples. After the trade, Elizabeth consumes 12 loaves of bread and 12 apples. Compare this situation with what she consumed when she didn't specialize and didn't trade. In that situation, she consumed 10 loaves of bread and 10 apples. Clearly, Elizabeth is better off when she specializes and trades than when she does not. But what about Brian?

Brian produces 30 apples and trades 12 of them to Elizabeth for 8 loaves of bread. In other words, he consumes 8 loaves of bread and 18 apples. Compare this situation with what he consumed when he didn't specialize and didn't trade. In that situation, he consumed 5 loaves of bread and 15 apples. Thus, Brian is also better off when he specializes and trades than when he does not.

Exhibit 9 summarizes consumption for Elizabeth and Brian. It shows that both Elizabeth and Brian make themselves better off by specializing in the production of one good and trading for the other.

Self-Test

1. If George can produce either (a) 10X and 20Y or (b) 5X and 25Y, what is the opportunity cost to George of producing one more X?

2. Harriet can produce either (a) 30X and 70Y or (b) 40X and 55Y; Bill can produce either (c) 10X and 40Y or (d) 20X and 20Y. Who has a comparative advantage in the production of X? in Y? Explain your answers.

PRODUCING, TRADING, AND ECONOMIC SYSTEMS

Producing and trading are major economic activities in every country of the world, not just the United States. But the laws, regulations, traditions, and social institutions that affect producing and trading are not the same in all countries. This leads us to a discussion of economic systems.

ECONOMIC SYSTEMS

Economic System
The way in which society decides to answer key economic questions—in particular those questions that relate to production and trade.

An **economic system** refers to the way in which a society decides to answer key economic questions—in particular those questions that relate to production and trade. Four questions that relate to production are:

- What goods will be produced?
- How will the goods be produced?
- For whom will the goods be produced?
- Where on the PPF will the economy operate?

Two questions that relate to trade are:

- What is the nature of trade?
- What function do prices serve?

There are hundreds of countries in the world but only two major economic systems: the *capitalist* (or market) economic system and the *socialist* economic system. One might think that every country's economy would fall neatly into one of these two categories, but things are not so simple. Most countries have chosen "ingredients" from both economic systems. These countries have economies that are neither purely capitalist nor purely socialist; instead, they are some mixture of both and are therefore called *mixed economies*. For example, the economic system that, to different degrees, exists in the United States, Canada, Australia, and Japan, among other countries, is generally known as **mixed capitalism.**

Think of capitalism and socialism as occupying opposite ends of an economic spectrum. Countries' economies lie along the spectrum. Some are closer to the capitalist end and some are closer to the socialist end.

In the following discussion, we identify how the capitalist and socialist economic systems deal with issues that relate to production and trade.

Mixed Capitalism
An economic system characterized by largely private ownership of the factors of production, market allocation of resources, and decentralized decision making. Most economic activities take place in the private sector in this system, but government plays a substantial economic and regulatory role.

BUT FIRST A WARNING

In our discussion of the two major economic systems—capitalism and socialism—we *deliberately* present each system as the polar opposite of the other: If capitalism says no, then socialism says yes; if capitalism chooses black, then socialism chooses white; if capitalism is up, then socialism is down.

Unless you keep our premise in mind, you are likely to think, "But capitalist countries don't always do things the opposite way of socialist countries. Sometimes they do things similarly."

Remember we said that most countries of the world are neither purely capitalist nor purely socialist and that most countries fall somewhere between the two polar extremes. Thus, it naturally follows that there are elements of capitalism and socialism in most countries.

However, our purpose here is not to figure out the precise breakdown between capitalism and socialism for any given country. We are not interested in saying that the United States is X percent capitalist and Y percent socialist. Our purpose is to outline the two opposite ways of dealing with questions and issues that relate to production and trade. One of these ways is called capitalism; the other, socialism.

ECONOMIC SYSTEMS AND THE PPF

Look back at Exhibit 1 (page 41), the PPF for producing good grades that relates "grade in sociology" to "grade in economics." In this case, the student chooses where on the PPF he or she will locate. In Exhibit 1, for example, the student decides whether to locate at point A, or at point B, and so on.

A different situation exists for an economy's PPF. Look back at Exhibit 5 (page 46), which shows an economy's PPF with respect to television sets and cars. Who decides where the economy will locate on this PPF?

The answer to this question has much to do in defining the difference between capitalism and socialism. To illustrate, suppose that an economy is currently located at point B in Exhibit 5. At point B, 50,000 television sets and 15,000 cars are produced. Who or what made the decision that 50,000 television sets and 15,000 cars would be produced instead of, say, 35,000 television sets and 35,000 cars (point C)?

In a capitalist economic system, the market (consisting of buyers and sellers) decides. For example, suppose the economy was initially at point A, producing 55,000 television sets and only 5,000 cars. Then people began to increase their buying of cars and decrease their buying of television sets. Would business firms respond to this change in buying behavior? In a capitalist economic system, the answer is yes. Through their buying behavior, buyers send signals to producers/sellers, and producers/sellers respond accordingly. They respond accordingly because no producer/seller wants to produce goods that buyers do not want to buy. To do otherwise is to invite economic failure.

In a socialist economic system, the market would not dictate where on the PPF the economy operates. Instead, government would play a large role in making this decision. For example, in the days of the Soviet Union, the government had much to say concerning what goods were produced and how many units of each good were produced.

THREE ECONOMIC QUESTIONS THAT DEAL WITH PRODUCTION

Every society must answer these three economic questions:

1. What goods will be produced?
2. How will the goods be produced?
3. For whom will the goods be produced?

Let's examine how these questions about production are answered in a capitalist economic system and in a socialist economic system.

What Goods Will Be Produced?

This question is really another way of asking, Where on its PPF will an economy operate? As stated earlier, in a capitalist economic system, those goods will be produced that the market (buyers and sellers) want to be produced. If there are enough buyers who want to buy a particular good or service, then it is likely that the good or service will be produced and offered for sale. This is both a strength and weakness of capitalism, some people say.

People want to buy food, cars, houses, a night out at the opera, books, and so on, and under capitalism, these goods and services are produced. Furthermore, when preferences change and people want to buy more of one good and less of another, sellers usually respond accordingly.

But there are a few goods produced under capitalism that some people do not think should be produced. Pornography is produced under capitalism, although some people would prefer that it not be produced.

In a socialist economic system, government plays a large role in determining what is produced. The degree to which ordinary citizens, working through their government, will have their buying preferences met largely depends on how responsive and open the government is.

How Will the Goods Be Produced?

Under capitalism, how the goods will be produced depends on the decisions of private producers. If private producers want to produce television sets with 10 units of capital and 100 units of labor, then so be it. If they want to produce television sets with robotics, then again it will be done. Private producers make the decisions as to how they will produce goods.

Under socialism, government plays a large role in determining how goods will be produced. For example, government might decide to have food produced on large collective farms instead of small private farms.

For Whom Will the Goods Be Produced?

Under capitalism, the goods will be produced for those persons who are able and willing to pay the prices for the goods. Government doesn't decide who will or will not have a television set, car, or house. If you want a television set and are able and willing to pay the price of the television set, then the television set is yours.

Under socialism, there is more government control over who gets what goods. For example, within a socialist economic system there may be a redistribution of funds from Smith to Jones. Or perhaps goods are given to Jones even though he is unable to pay the prices of these goods.

The layperson looks at countries and sees differences. For example, people speak French in France and English in the United States; the crime rate is higher in the United States than Belgium; and so on. The economist knows that there are some things that are the same for all countries. The United States has to decide what goods to produce, and China has to decide what goods to produce. The United States has to decide how goods will be produced, and Brazil has to decide how goods will be produced. The United States has to deal with scarcity and its effects, and so do South Korea, Pakistan, India, and Canada.

TRADE AND PRICES

Capitalism and socialism have different views of trade and prices. We outline these differences in the following paragraphs.

Trade

Consider an ordinary, everyday exchange of $100 for some clothes. Under capitalism, it is generally assumed that both the buyer and seller of the clothes benefit from the trade or else they would not have entered into it. Under socialism, the view often expressed is that one person in a trade is being made better off at the expense of the other person. In this example, perhaps the clothes seller took advantage of the buyer by charging too much money for the clothes.

Prices

When we buy something in a market—whether it is a car, a house, or a loaf of bread—we pay a price. Prices are a common market phenomenon. Under capitalism, price (1) rations goods and services, (2) conveys information, and (3) serves as an incentive to respond to information.

As discussed in Chapter 1, price is a rationing device. Those people who are willing and able to pay the price of a good, obtain the good; those persons who are either unwilling or unable to pay, do not obtain the good. In a world of scarcity, where people's wants outstrip the resources available to satisfy those wants, some type of rationing device is necessary. It may be price, first-come-first-served, brute force, or something else. For capitalist thinkers, there needs to be some way of determining who gets what of the available resources, goods, and services. Price serves this purpose.

Now consider an example to see how price can convey information and serve as an incentive to respond to information. Suppose Tom buys a dozen oranges each week for 40 cents an orange. One day, a devastating freeze hits the Florida orange groves and destroys half the orange crop. As a result, there are fewer oranges in the world and price rises to 60 cents an orange. Tom notices the higher price of oranges and wonders what caused the price to rise. He does not know about the freeze, and even if he did, he might not connect the freeze with a reduced supply of oranges and higher orange prices. Nevertheless, Tom responds to the higher price of oranges by reducing his weekly purchase from 12 oranges to 8 oranges.

Let's consider the role price has played in this example. First, through an increase in price, the "information" of the freeze was conveyed to buyers. Specifically, price has transmitted information on the relative scarcity of a good. The higher price of oranges is saying "There has been a cold spell in Florida resulting in fewer oranges. The gap between people's wants for oranges and the amount of oranges available to satisfy those wants has widened."

Second, by rising, price has provided Tom with an incentive to reduce the quantity of oranges he consumes. Tom responds to the information of the increased relative scarcity of oranges, even without knowing about Florida weather conditions.

Under socialism, price is viewed as being set by greedy businesses with vast economic power. Perhaps because of this, socialists usually stand ready to "control" price. For example, under socialism it is not uncommon to pass a law making it illegal to charge more than a certain price for, say, gasoline or rental homes. It is also not uncommon to pass a law that makes it illegal to pay less than a certain dollar wage to a worker.

By passing laws that make it illegal to charge more than a certain price for certain goods and services, socialists seek to reduce some of the economic power that they believe sellers have over consumers. By passing laws that make it illegal to pay less than a certain wage to workers, socialists seek to reduce some of the economic power that they believe the owners of businesses have over workers.

Self-Test

1. What are the three economic questions that deal with production that every society must answer?

2. How is trade viewed in a capitalist economic system?

3. What does an economic system have to do with where on its PPF the economy operates?

A Reader Asks...

How Will Economics Help Me If I Am a History Major?

I'm a history major taking my first course in economics. But quite frankly, I don't see how economics will be of much use in my study of history. Any thoughts on the subject?

Economics often plays a major role in historical events. For example, the feature "What Do Blue Jeans and Rock 'n' Roll Have to Do With the Fall of the Berlin Wall?" discusses the collapse of the Soviet Union—certainly a historical event. But was that historical event based in part on economics? Did the low economic growth of the Soviet Union contribute to its collapse? Did the ratio of civilian goods to military goods play a role in the collapse?

There are many other places where understanding economics may help you understand a historical event or period. If, as a historian, you study the Great Depression, you will need to know something about the stock market, tariffs, and more. If you study the California Gold Rush, you will need to know about supply, demand, and prices. If you study the history of prisoner-of-war camps, you will need to know about how and why people trade

and about money. If you study the Boston Tea Party, you will need to know about government grants of monopoly and about taxes.

Economics can also be useful in another way. Suppose you learn in your economics course what can and cannot cause inflation. We'll say you learn that X can cause inflation and that Y cannot. Then one day you read an article in which a historian says that Y caused the high inflation in a certain country and that the high inflation led to a public outcry, which was then met with stiff government reprisals. Without an understanding of economics, you might be willing to accept what the historian has written. But with your understanding of economics, you know that events could not have happened as the historian reports because Y, which the historian claims caused the high inflation, could not have caused the high inflation.

In conclusion, a good understanding of economics will not only help you understand key historical events but also help you discern inaccuracies in recorded history.

An Economy's Production Possibilities Frontier

- An economy's production possibilities frontier (PPF) represents the possible combinations of two goods that the economy can produce in a certain period of time, under the conditions of a given state of technology and fully employed resources.

Increasing and Constant Opportunity Costs

- A straight-line PPF represents constant opportunity costs: increased production of one good comes at constant opportunity costs.
- A bowed-outward (concave-downward) PPF represents the law of increasing opportunity costs: increased production of one good comes at increased opportunity costs.

Efficiency and Inefficiency

- All points on the PPF are efficient points; all points below the PPF are inefficient.
- Efficiency implies that gains are impossible in one area without losses in another. Inefficiency implies that gains are possible in one area without losses in another.
- When the economy is efficient, it is employing all its resources. When the economy is inefficient, some resources are unemployed.

Economic Growth and the PPF

- Economic growth is illustrated by a shift outward in the PPF. Two major factors that affect economic growth are an increase in the quantity of resources and an advance in technology.

Trade or Exchange

- People trade in order to make themselves better off. Exchange is a utility-increasing activity.
- The three time periods relevant to the trading process are (1) the ex ante period, which is the time before the trade is made; (2) the point of trade; and (3) the ex post period, which is the time after the trade has been made.
- There is a difference between trade and the terms of trade. Trade refers to the act of giving up one thing for something else. For example, a person may trade money for a car. The terms of trade refer to *how much* of one thing is traded for *how much* of something else. For example, how much money ($25,000? $30,000?) is traded for one car.

Consumers' Surplus and Producers' Surplus

- Consumers' surplus is the difference between the maximum price buyers are willing and able to pay for a good and the price actually paid for the good.

- Producers' surplus is the difference between the price sellers receive for a good and the minimum price for which they would have sold the good.
- The more consumers' surplus that buyers receive, the better off they are. The more producers' surplus that sellers receive, the better off they are.

Transaction Costs

- Transaction costs are the costs associated with the time and effort needed to search out, negotiate, and consummate a trade. Some potential exchanges are not realized because of high transaction costs. Lowering transaction costs can turn a potential exchange into an actual exchange.
- One role of an entrepreneur is to try to lower transaction costs.

Comparative Advantage and Specialization

- Individuals can make themselves better off by specializing in the production of the good in which they have a comparative advantage and then trading some of that good for other goods. A person has a comparative advantage in the production of a good if he or she can produce the good at a lower opportunity cost than another person can.

Economic Systems

- An economic system refers to the way in which a society decides to answer key economic questions—in particular those questions that relate to production and trade.
- There are two major economic systems: the capitalist (or market) economic system and the socialist economic system.
- One of the key differences between capitalism and socialism is how decisions are made with respect to where on the PPF the economy will operate. Under capitalism, the market (buyers and sellers) largely determines at which point on the PPF the economy will operate. Under socialism, government plays a large role in determining at which point on the PPF the economy will operate.
- Three economic questions that relate to production that every society must answer are: (1) What goods will be produced? (2) How will the goods be produced? (3) For whom will the goods be produced?
- Under capitalism, price (1) rations goods and services, (2) conveys information, and (3) serves as an incentive to respond to information. Under socialism, price is viewed as being set by greedy businesses with vast economic power.

Production Possibilities Frontier
   (PPF)
Tradeoff
Law of Increasing Opportunity
   Costs
Efficiency

Inefficiency
Technology
Trade (Exchange)
Ex Ante
Ex Post
Consumers' Surplus (CS)

Producers' (Sellers') Surplus (PS)
Terms of Trade
Transaction Costs
Comparative Advantage
Economic System
Mixed Capitalism

Economic Connections to You

Economic facts, actions, and changes create ripples that move away from their point of origin. Eventually, these ripples can intersect your life and have an effect on you. Consider the following example.

A country "decides" where on its PPF to locate. If a country decides to produce relatively many consumer goods and relatively few other types of goods (say, military goods), its citizens will be affected in two ways. First, a majority of the population will probably work in the sector of the economy that produces consumer goods. Second, people will likely have a wide variety of consumer goods and services from which to choose. If

a country decides to produce more military goods than consumer goods, the majority of the population will probably work in the military goods sector of the economy and its people will likely have little choice of consumer goods and services. Thus, there is a connection between where your country locates on its PPF and your desires as a consumer and worker—an economic connection to you.

Based on the material in this chapter, identify other ways in which economic facts, actions, and changes create ripples that eventually affect you.

Questions and Problems

1. Describe how each of the following would affect the U.S. production possibilities frontier: (a) an increase in the number of illegal aliens entering the country; (b) a war; (c) the discovery of a new oil field; (d) a decrease in the unemployment rate; (e) a law that requires individuals to enter lines of work for which they are not suited.

2. Explain how the following can be represented in a PPF framework: the finiteness of resources implicit in the scarcity condition; choice; and opportunity cost.

3. What condition must hold for the production possibilities frontier to be bowed outward (concave downward)? to be a straight line?

4. Give an example to illustrate each of the following: (a) constant opportunity costs; (b) increasing opportunity costs.

5. Why are most production possibilities frontiers for goods bowed outward, or concave downward?

6. Within a PPF framework, explain each of the following: (a) a disagreement between a person who favors more domestic welfare spending and one who favors more national defense spending; (b) an increase in the population; (c) a technological change that makes resources less specialized.

7. Some people have said that during the Cold War the Central Intelligence Agency (CIA) regularly estimated (a) the total quantity of output produced in the Soviet Union and (b) the total quantity of civilian goods produced in the Soviet Union. Of what interest would these data, or the information that might be deduced from them, be to the CIA? (Hint: Think in terms of the PPF.)

8. Suppose a nation's PPF shifts inward as its population grows. What happens, on average, to the material standard of living of the people? Explain your answer.

9. "A nation may be able to live beyond its means, but the world cannot." Do you agree or disagree? Explain your answer.

10. Use the PPF framework to explain something in your everyday life that was not mentioned in the chapter.

11. Describe the three time periods relevant to the trading process.

12. Are all exchanges or trades beneficial to both parties in the ex post position? Explain your answer.

13. If Donovan agrees to trade $50 for a painting, what can we say about the utility he gets from the $50 compared with the utility he expects to get from the painting?

14. A person who benefits from a trade can be disgruntled over the terms of trade. Do you agree or disagree? Explain your answer.

15. Explain how an economist might use the concepts of consumers' surplus and producers' surplus.

16. Buyers would rather pay lower prices for the goods they buy and sellers would rather receive higher prices for the goods they sell. Why?

17. Give an example of a negative third-party effect (negative externality).

18. A capitalist would be much less likely to support controls on prices and wages than would a socialist. Why?

19. Some people argue that capitalism and socialism are usually evaluated only on economic grounds, where capitalism has a clear advantage. But in order to evaluate the two economic systems evenhandedly, other factors should be considered as well—justice, fairness, the happiness of people living under both systems, the crime rate, the standard of living of those at the bottom of the economic ladder, and much more. Do you think this is the proper way to proceed? Why or why not?

20. The *convergence hypothesis,* first proposed by a Soviet economist, suggests that over time the capitalist economies will become increasingly socialistic and the socialist economies will become increasingly capitalistic. Do you believe the convergence hypothesis has merit? What real-world evidence can you cite to prove or disprove the hypothesis?

Working with Numbers and Graphs

1. Xavier is willing and able to pay up to $40 for a good that he buys for $22. Keri is willing and able to sell the good to Xavier for no less than $21. What does consumers' surplus equal? What does producers' (sellers') surplus equal?

2. Tina can produce any of the following combinations of goods X and Y: (a) 100X and 0Y, (b) 50X and 25Y, and (c) 0X and 50Y. David can produce any of the following combinations of goods X and Y: (a) 50X and 0Y, (b) 25X and 40Y, and (c) 0X and 80Y. Who has a comparative advantage in the production of good X? of good Y? Explain your answer.

3. Using the data in Problem 2, prove that both Tina and David can be made better off through specialization and trade.

4. Exhibit 6 represents an advance in technology that made it possible to produce more of both military and civilian goods. Represent an advance in technology that makes it possible to produce more of only civilian goods. Does this indirectly make it possible to produce more military goods? Explain your answer.

5. In the following figure, which graph depicts a technological breakthrough in the production of good X only?

6. In the preceding figure, which graph depicts a change in the PPF that is a likely consequence of war?

7. If PPF$_2$ in the following graph is the relevant production possibilities frontier, then which points are unattainable? Explain your answer.

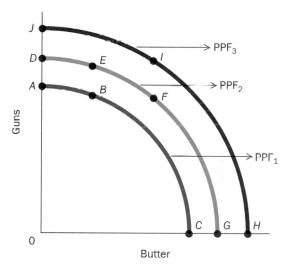

8. If PPF$_1$ in the figure above is the relevant production possibilities frontier, then which point(s) represent efficiency? Explain your answer.

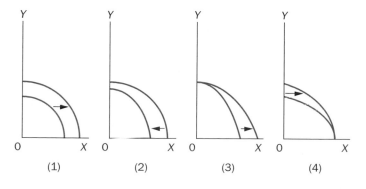

(1)   (2)   (3)   (4)

1. Go to *http://stats.bls.gov*. Select "Economy at a Glance." What is the current unemployment rate?

2. Go to *http://www.stls.frb.org/fred*. FRED is the economic database of the Federal Reserve. Under Data Categories, click on "Business/Fiscal" and then on "Capacity Utilization: Manufacturing—Percent of Capacity—1948.1." This number represents the percentage of our total manufacturing capacity being used. What is that percentage today?

3. Click "Back" and select "Total Industrial Production Index." What is the value for 1940.01 (January 1940)? What is the value for today? If this value represents production in the economy, where is the PPF for 1940 in relation to the PPF today?

Log on to the Arnold Xtra! Web site now (*http://arnoldxtra.swcollege.com*) for additional learning resources such as practice quizzes, help with graphing, video clips, and current event applications.

ch.3

SUPPLY AND DEMAND: THEORY

Thomas Carlyle, the historian and philosopher, said: "It is easy to train economists. Just teach a parrot to say Supply and Demand." In a way, Carlyle was right—economists do mention "supply and demand" often. But they do it for a reason. Supply and demand are powerful forces, forces that together explain much of what goes on in the world. Economists use supply and demand to explain why there are shortages, why prices rise and fall, and even why an auctioneer calls out certain prices.

Chapter Road Map

This chapter is about markets. A market exists anytime people come together to trade. Every market has two sides—a buying (demand) side and a selling (supply) side. We discuss both sides of a market in this chapter. We look first at demand—define what it is, identify the law of demand, and discuss those factors that can change demand. Then we discuss supply in a similar way. Finally, we put supply and demand together and discuss how the prices and quantities of goods in a market are determined.

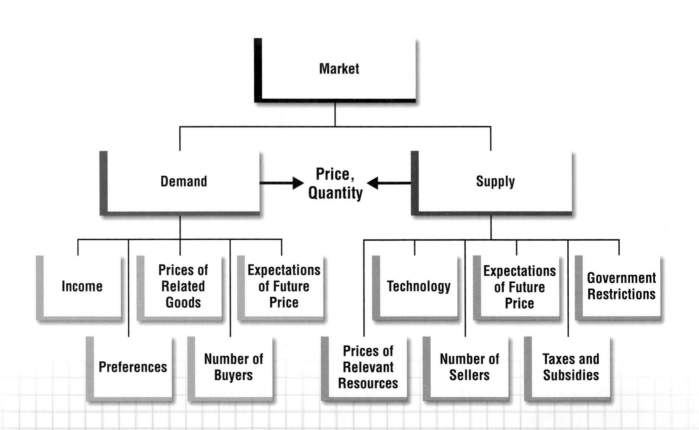

DEMAND

The word **demand** has a precise meaning in economics. It refers to (1) the willingness and ability of buyers to purchase different quantities of a good (2) at different prices (3) during a specific time period (per day, week, and so on).[1] For example, we can express part of John's demand for magazines by saying that he is willing and able to buy 10 magazines a month at $4 per magazine and that he is willing and able to buy 15 magazines a month at $3 per magazine.

Remember this important point about demand: Unless *both* willingness and ability to buy are present, a person is not a buyer and *there is no demand*. For example, Josie may be willing to buy a computer but be unable to pay the price; Tanya may be able to buy but be unwilling. Neither Josie nor Tanya demands a computer.

Q & A

Q: If a person is willing and able to buy a particular car at $40,000, will she actually make this purchase?

A: Not necessarily. Willingness and ability to buy refer to the buyer, but both a buyer and a seller are required for a trade to be made. A person may be willing and able to buy a particular car for $40,000, but that car may not currently exist, or it may exist but the seller may not be willing to sell it for $40,000.

THE LAW OF DEMAND

Will people buy more units of a good at lower prices than at higher prices? For example, will people buy more personal computers at $1,000 per computer than at $4,000 per computer? If your answer is yes, you instinctively understand the law of demand. The **law of demand** states that as the price of a good rises, the quantity demanded of the good falls, and as the price of a good falls, the quantity demanded of the good rises, *ceteris paribus*. Simply put, the law of demand states that the price of a good and the quantity demanded of the good are inversely related, *ceteris paribus*:

$$P\uparrow Q_d\downarrow$$
$$P\downarrow Q_d\uparrow \text{ ceteris paribus}$$

where P = price and Q_d = quantity demanded.

Quantity demanded is the *number of units* of a good that individuals are willing and able to buy at a particular price during some time period. For example, suppose individuals are willing and able to buy 100 TV dinners per week at the price of $4 per unit. Therefore, 100 units is the quantity demanded of TV dinners at $4.

THINKING LIKE AN ECONOMIST

When Bill says, "The more income a person has, the more expensive cars (Porsches, Corvettes) he will buy," he is not thinking like an economist. An economist knows that the ability to buy something does not necessarily imply the willingness to buy it. After all, Bill Gates, the billionaire cofounder of Microsoft, Inc., has the ability to buy many things that he chooses not to buy.

ABSOLUTE PRICE AND RELATIVE PRICE

In economics, there are absolute (or money) prices and relative prices. The **absolute price** of a good is the price of the good in money terms. For example, the absolute price of a car may be $30,000. The **relative price** of a good is the

---

Demand
The willingness and ability of buyers to purchase different quantities of a good at different prices during a specific time period.

Law of Demand
As the price of a good rises, the quantity demanded of the good falls, and as the price of a good falls, the quantity demanded of the good rises, *ceteris paribus*.

Absolute (Money) Price
The price of a good in money terms.

Relative Price
The price of a good in terms of another good.

---

1. Demand takes into account *services* as well as goods. Goods are tangible and include such things as shirts, books, and television sets. Services are intangible and include such things as dental care, medical care, and an economics lecture. To simplify the discussion, we refer only to *goods*.

price of the good *in terms of another good.* For example, suppose the absolute price of a car is $30,000 and the absolute price of a computer is $2,000. The relative price of a car—that is, the price of a car in terms of computers—is 15 computers. A person gives up the opportunity to buy 15 computers when he or she buys a car.

For this example, the relative price of a car is computed as follows:

$$\text{Relative price of a car (in terms of computers)} = \frac{\text{Absolute price of a car}}{\text{Absolute price of a computer}}$$

$$= \frac{\$30,000}{\$2,000}$$

$$= 15$$

Thus, the relative price of a car in this example is 15 computers.

Now let's compute the relative price of a computer, that is, the price of a computer in terms of a car:

$$\text{Relative price of a computer (in terms of cars)} = \frac{\text{Absolute price of a computer}}{\text{Absolute price of a car}}$$

$$= \frac{\$2,000}{\$30,000}$$

$$= 1/15$$

Thus, the relative price of a computer in this example is $\frac{1}{15}$ of a car. A person gives up the opportunity to buy $\frac{1}{15}$ of a car when he or she buys a computer.

Now consider this question: What happens to the relative price of a good if its absolute price rises and nothing else changes? For example, if the absolute price of a car rises from $30,000 to $40,000 what happens to the relative price of a car? Obviously, it rises from 15 computers to 20 computers. In short, if the absolute price of a good rises and nothing else changes, then the relative price of the good rises too.

Knowing the difference between absolute price and relative price can help you understand some important economic concepts. In the next section, relative price is used in the explanation of why price and quantity demanded are inversely related.

WHY QUANTITY DEMANDED GOES DOWN AS PRICE GOES UP

The law of demand states that price and quantity demanded are inversely related, but it does not say why they are inversely related. We identify two reasons. The first reason is that *people substitute lower-priced goods for higher-priced goods.*

Often many goods serve the same purpose. Many different goods will satisfy hunger, and many different drinks will satisfy thirst. For example, both orange juice and grapefruit juice will satisfy thirst. Suppose that on Monday, the price of orange juice equals the price of grapefruit juice. Then on Tuesday, the price of orange juice rises. As a result, some people will choose to buy less of the relatively higher-priced orange juice and more of the relatively lower-priced grapefruit juice. In other words, a rise in the price of orange juice will lead to a decrease in the quantity demanded of orange juice.

The second reason for the inverse relationship between price and quantity demanded has to do with the **law of diminishing marginal utility,** which states that for a given time period, the marginal (additional) utility or satisfaction gained by consuming equal successive units of a good will decline as the amount consumed increases. For example, you may receive more utility or satisfaction from eating your first hamburger at lunch than from eating your second

Law of Diminishing Marginal Utility
For a given time period, the marginal (additional) utility or satisfaction gained by consuming equal successive units of a good will decline as the amount consumed increases.

and, if you continue on, more utility from your second hamburger than from your third.

What does this have to do with the law of demand? Economists state that the more utility you receive from a unit of a good, the higher price you are willing to pay for it; the less utility you receive from a unit of a good, the lower price you are willing to pay for it. According to the law of diminishing marginal utility, individuals obtain less utility from additional units of a good. It follows that they will only buy larger quantities of a good at lower prices. And this is the law of demand.

FOUR WAYS TO REPRESENT THE LAW OF DEMAND: WORDS, SYMBOLS, NUMBERS, CURVE

The law of demand can be expressed in four ways:

1. In words: "As price rises, quantity demanded falls . . ."
2. In symbols: $P\uparrow Q_d\downarrow$ . . .
3. In terms of a demand schedule
4. In terms of a demand curve

A **demand schedule** is the numerical representation of the law of demand. A demand schedule for good X is illustrated in Exhibit 1a.

In Exhibit 1b, the four price-quantity combinations in part (a) are plotted and the points connected, giving us a (downward-sloping) demand curve. A (downward-sloping) **demand curve** is the graphical representation of the inverse relationship between price and quantity demanded specified by the law of demand. In short, the demand curve is a picture of the law of demand.

Demand Schedule
The numerical tabulation of the quantity demanded of a good at different prices.

(Downward-sloping) Demand Curve
The graphical representation of the law of demand.

INDIVIDUAL DEMAND CURVE AND MARKET DEMAND CURVE

An individual demand curve represents the price-quantity combinations of a particular good for a *single buyer*. For example, a demand curve could show Jones's demand for CDs. A market demand curve represents the price-quantity combinations of a particular good for *all buyers*. In this case, the demand curve would show all buyers' demand for CDs.

Exhibit 2 shows how a market demand curve can be derived by "adding" individual demand curves. The demand schedules for Jones, Smith, and other buyers are shown in part (a). The market demand schedule is obtained by adding the quantities demanded at each price. For example, at $12, the quantities demanded are 4 units for Jones, 5 units for Smith, and 100 units for other buyers. Thus, a total of 109 units are demanded at $12. In (b) the data points for the demand schedules are plotted and "added" to produce a market demand

Demand Schedule for Good X		
Price (dollars)	Quantity Demanded	Point in Part (b)
4	10	A
3	20	B
2	30	C
1	40	D

(a)

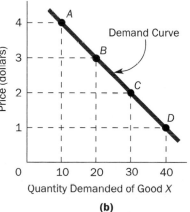

Quantity Demanded of Good X

(b)

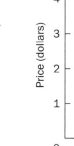

exhibit 1

Demand Schedule and Demand Curve
Part (a) shows a demand schedule for good X. Part (b) shows a demand curve, obtained by plotting the different price-quantity combinations in part (a) and connecting the points. On a demand curve, the price (in dollars) represents price per unit of the good. The quantity demanded, on the horizontal axis, is always relevant for a specific time period (a week, a month, and so on).

Price	Quantity Demanded			
	Jones	Smith	Other Buyers	All Buyers
$15	1	2	20	23
14	2	3	45	50
13	3	4	70	77
12	4 +	5 +	100 =	109
11	5 +	6 +	130 =	141
10	6	7	160	173

(a)

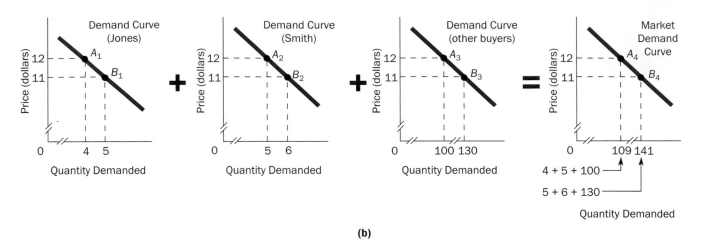

(b)

exhibit 2

Deriving a Market Demand Schedule and a Market Demand Curve
Part (a) shows four demand schedules combined into one table. The market demand schedule is derived by adding the quantities demanded at each price. In (b), the data points from the demand schedules are plotted to show how a market demand curve is derived. Only two points on the market demand curve are noted.

curve. The market demand curve could also be drawn directly from the market demand schedule.

CHANGES IN DEMAND MEAN SHIFTS IN DEMAND CURVES

Suppose that currently a specific demand exists for oranges, computers, houses, and cars. Will the demand for each of these goods be the same next year as it is today? If your answer is "Maybe not," then you instinctively understand that the demand for any good can change. Saying the demand for a good can change is the same as saying the demand for a good can increase or decrease.

What does it mean if the demand for a good *increases?* It means that buyers are willing and able to buy *more* of the good at all prices. For example, suppose that in January individuals are willing and able to buy 600 pairs of blue jeans at $60 each and that in February they are willing to buy 900 pairs of blue jeans at $60 each. An increase in demand shifts the entire demand curve to the right, as shown in Exhibit 3a.

The demand for a good *decreases* if people are willing and able to buy *less* of the good at all prices. For example, suppose that in January individuals are willing and able to buy 600 pairs of blue jeans at $60 each and that in February they are willing to buy 300 pairs of blue jeans at $60 each. A decrease in demand shifts the entire demand curve to the left, as shown in Exhibit 3b.

WHAT FACTORS CAUSE THE DEMAND CURVE TO SHIFT?

We know the demand for any good can change. But *why* would the demand change? For example, if the demand for blue jeans is higher in February than in January, what happened to cause the demand for blue jeans to rise? What caused

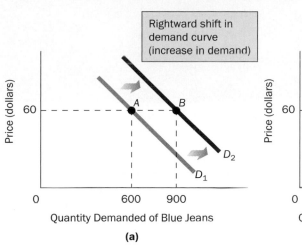

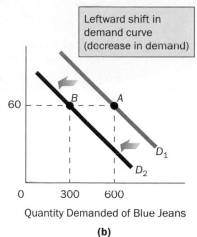

exhibit 3

Shifts in the Demand Curve
(a) The demand curve shifts rightward from D_1 to D_2. This represents an increase in demand for blue jeans: At each price the quantity demanded is greater than before. For example, the quantity demanded at $60 increases from 600 units to 900 units.
(b) The demand curve shifts leftward from D_1 to D_2. This represents a decrease in demand for blue jeans: At each price the quantity demanded is less. For example, the quantity demanded at $60 declines from 600 units to 300 units.

people to want to buy more blue jeans at each and every price? The factors that can change demand include (1) income, (2) preferences, (3) prices of related goods, (4) number of buyers, and (5) expectations of future price.

Income

As a person's income changes (increases or decreases), his or her demand for a particular good may rise, fall, or remain constant.

For example, suppose that Jack's income rises. As a consequence, his demand for CDs rises. For Jack, CDs are a *normal good*. A **normal good** is one in which as income rises, demand for the good rises; and as income falls, demand for the good falls.

Income↑ + Demand↑ = Normal good
Income↓ + Demand↓ = Normal good

Now suppose Marie's income rises. As a consequence, her demand for canned baked beans falls. For Marie, canned banked beans are an *inferior good*. An **inferior good** is one in which as income rises, demand for the good falls, and as income falls, demand for the good rises.

Income↑ + Demand↓ = Inferior good
Income↓ + Demand↑ = Inferior good

Finally, suppose George's income rises, and his demand for toothpaste neither rises nor falls. For George, toothpaste is neither a normal good nor an inferior good. Instead, it is a *neutral good*. A **neutral good** is one in which as income rises or falls, the demand for the good does not change.

Preferences

People's preferences affect the amount of a good they are willing to buy at a particular price. A change in preferences in favor of a good shifts the demand curve rightward. A change in preferences away from the good shifts the demand curve leftward. For example, if people begin to favor Tom Clancy novels to a greater degree than previously, the demand for Clancy novels increases and the demand curve shifts rightward.

Normal Good
A good the demand for which rises (falls) as income rises (falls).

Inferior Good
A good the demand for which falls (rises) as income rises (falls).

Neutral Good
A good the demand for which does not change as income rises or falls.

Popular Culture | Technology | Everyday Life | The World

Why Does Mickey Mouse Charge Such Goofy Prices?

The Walt Disney Company operates two major theme parks in the United States, Disneyland in California and Disney World in Florida. Every year millions of people visit each site. The ticket price for visiting Disneyland or Disney World differs depending on how many days a person visits the theme park. For example, in the past, Disneyland sold one-, two-, and three-day passports (tickets). On the day we checked, the price of a one-day passport was $38, the price of a two-day passport was $68, and the price of a three-day passport was $95.

How are the prices for one-, two-, and three-day passports related? If we take the price of a one-day passport ($38) and double it, we get $76. But Disneyland doesn't charge visitors $76 for visiting two days; it charges $68. Why does Disneyland charge less than double the price of a one-day passport for a two-day passport? Similarly, triple the price of a one-day passport is $114. But Disneyland doesn't charge $114 for a three-day passport; it charges $95. Why does Disneyland charge less than triple the price of a one-day passport for a three-day passport?

Disneyland is effectively telling a visitor that if she wants to visit the theme park for one day, she has to pay $38. But if she wants to visit the theme park for two days, the second day will only cost her $30 more, not $38 more. And if she wants to visit the theme park for three days, the third day will only cost her $27 more, not $38 more. In short, for a three-day passport, Disneyland charges $38 for the first day, $30 for the second day, and $27 for the third day, for a grand total of $95.

Why does Disneyland charge less for the second day than the first day? Why does it charge less for the third day than the second day?

An economic concept, the *law of diminishing marginal utility,* is the reason behind Disneyland's pricing scheme. The law of diminishing marginal utility states that as a person consumes additional units of a good, eventually the utility from each additional unit of the good decreases. Assuming the law of diminishing marginal utility holds for Disneyland, individuals will get more utility from the first day at Disneyland than the second day and more utility from the second day than the third day. The less utility or satisfaction a person gets from something, the lower the dollar amount he is willing to pay for it. Thus, a person would not be willing to pay as much for the second day at Disneyland as the first, and he would not be willing to pay as much for the third day as the second. Disneyland knows this and therefore prices its one-, two-, and three-day passports accordingly.

Prices of Related Goods

There are two types of related goods: substitutes and complements. Two goods are **substitutes** if they satisfy similar needs or desires. For many people Coca-Cola and Pepsi-Cola are substitutes. If two goods are substitutes, as the price of one rises (falls), the demand for the other rises (falls). For instance, higher Coca-Cola prices will increase the demand for Pepsi-Cola as people substitute Pepsi for the higher-priced Coke (Exhibit 4a). Other examples of substitutes are coffee and tea, corn chips and potato chips, two brands of margarine, and foreign and domestic cars.

Substitutes
Two goods that satisfy similar needs or desires. If two goods are substitutes, the demand for one rises as the price of the other rises (or the demand for one falls as the price of the other falls).

If $P_X\uparrow$ and $D_Y\uparrow$ then X and Y are substitutes.
If $P_X\downarrow$ and $D_Y\downarrow$ then X and Y are substitutes.

Two goods are **complements** if they are consumed jointly. For example, tennis rackets and tennis balls are used together to play tennis. If two goods are complements, as the price of one rises (falls), the demand for the other falls (rises).

Complements
Two goods that are used jointly in consumption. If two goods are complements, the demand for one rises as the price of the other falls (or the demand for one falls as the price of the other rises).

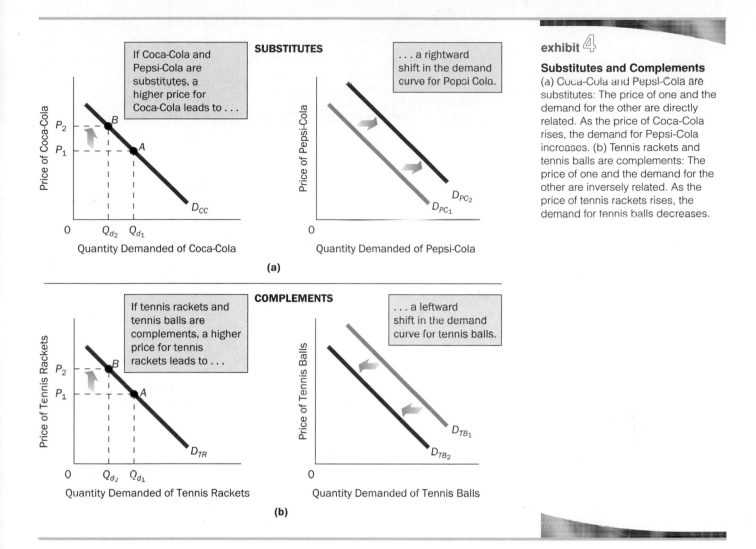

exhibit 4

SUBSTITUTES

If Coca-Cola and Pepsi-Cola are substitutes, a higher price for Coca-Cola leads to . . .

. . . a rightward shift in the demand curve for Pepsi-Cola.

(a)

COMPLEMENTS

If tennis rackets and tennis balls are complements, a higher price for tennis rackets leads to . . .

. . . a leftward shift in the demand curve for tennis balls.

(b)

Substitutes and Complements
(a) Coca-Cola and Pepsi-Cola are substitutes: The price of one and the demand for the other are directly related. As the price of Coca-Cola rises, the demand for Pepsi-Cola increases. (b) Tennis rackets and tennis balls are complements: The price of one and the demand for the other are inversely related. As the price of tennis rackets rises, the demand for tennis balls decreases.

For example, higher tennis racket prices will decrease the demand for tennis balls, as Exhibit 4b shows. Other examples of complements are cars and tires, light bulbs and lamps, and golf clubs and golf balls.

If $P_A \uparrow$ and $D_B \downarrow$ then A and B are complements.
If $P_A \downarrow$ and $D_B \uparrow$ then A and B are complements.

Number of Buyers

The demand for a good in a particular market area is related to the number of buyers in the area: More buyers, higher demand; fewer buyers, lower demand. The number of buyers may increase owing to a higher birthrate, increased immigration, the migration of people from one region of the country to another, and so on. The number of buyers may decrease owing to a higher death rate, war, the migration of people from one region of the country to another, and so on.

Expectations of Future Price

Buyers who expect the price of a good to be higher next month may buy the good now—thus increasing the current demand for the good. Buyers who expect the price of a good to be lower next month may wait until next month to buy the good—thus decreasing the current demand for the good.

For example, suppose that you are planning to buy a house. One day you hear that house prices are expected to go down in a few months. Consequently, you decide to hold off your purchase of a house for a few months. Alternatively, if you hear that prices are expected to rise in a few months, you might go ahead and purchase a house now.

A CHANGE IN DEMAND VERSUS A CHANGE IN QUANTITY DEMANDED

A *change (increase or decrease) in demand* refers to a *shift* in the demand curve, as illustrated in Exhibit 5a.

Change in demand = Shift in demand curve

For example, saying that the demand for apples has increased is the same as saying that the demand curve for apples has shifted rightward. The factors that can change demand (shift the demand curve) include income, preferences, prices of related goods, number of buyers, and expectations of future price.

A *change in quantity demanded* refers to a *movement* along a demand curve, as shown in Exhibit 5b.

Change in quantity demanded = A movement from one point to another point on the same demand curve

Own Price
The price of a good. For example, if the price of oranges is $1, this is (its) own price.

The *only* factor that can *directly* cause a change in the quantity demanded of a good is a change in the price of the good—that is, its **own price.** For example, a change in the price of computers brings about a change in the quantity demanded of computers. A change in the price of lamps brings about a change in the quantity demanded of lamps.

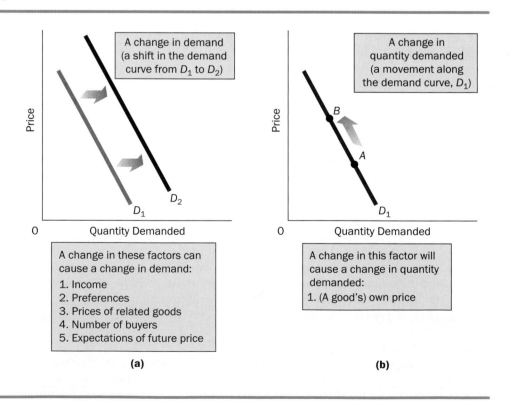

exhibit 5

A Change in Demand versus a Change in Quantity Demanded
(a) A change in demand refers to a shift in the demand curve. A change in demand can be brought about by a number of factors (see the exhibit and text). (b) A change in quantity demanded refers to a movement along a given demand curve. A change in quantity demanded is brought about only by a change in (a good's) own price.

A change in demand (a shift in the demand curve from D_1 to D_2)

A change in quantity demanded (a movement along the demand curve, D_1)

A change in these factors can cause a change in demand:
1. Income
2. Preferences
3. Prices of related goods
4. Number of buyers
5. Expectations of future price

A change in this factor will cause a change in quantity demanded:
1. (A good's) own price

(a)

(b)

ECONOMICS IN...

Does the Law of Demand Explain Obesity?

An accepted definition of obesity is that a person is considered obese if his weight in pounds exceeds 4.25 percent of the square of his height in inches. For example, suppose a person weighs 200 pounds and is 5 feet tall. The person's height in inches is 60; the square of 60 is 3,600. Because 200 (weight in pounds) is 5.5 percent of 3,600 (square of height in inches), the person is obese.

Steven Landsburg, an economist and a contributing columnist to the magazine *Slate*, reports that 21.1 percent of the people in Georgia are obese according to this definition. Ten years earlier, only 9.5 percent of Georgians were obese (using the same definition of obesity). Landsburg asks the question: Why are we getting so fat?[2]

The rise of obesity in Georgia is mirrored across the country, says Landsburg. He reports that obesity has been rising in every age group, in every race, in both males and females, and in every state. In 1991, a little over 12 percent of the people in the country were obese; in 1999, almost 20 percent were.

How does Landsburg explain the rise in obesity? He partly explains it using the law of demand. The law of demand states that as the price of something falls, the quantity demanded of it rises, *ceteris paribus*. So, if the quantity demanded of obesity has risen in recent years, has the price of obesity fallen to bring this about? Landsburg argues that in the 1990s, drugs were developed that reduce cholesterol and increase life expectancy. In other words, these drugs decrease two of the many undesirable consequences of obesity—high cholesterol and shorter life expectancy. Thus, these drugs have reduced the price of obesity. As a result, the quantity demanded of obesity has risen.

It is important to distinguish between a change in demand (shift in the demand curve) and a change in quantity demanded (movement along a demand curve), as the next section illustrates.

MEALS AT RESTAURANTS AND THE LAW OF DEMAND

Your friend says, "I've noticed that the price of dining out at restaurants has gone up. I've also noticed that more people are eating at restaurants. But the law of demand predicts the opposite. It states that if the price of a good rises, less of that good will be consumed. Obviously, the law of demand must be wrong."

Suppose we accept as truth that the price of dining out at restaurants has gone up and that more people are eating at restaurants. Does it follow that the law of demand does not hold? Not at all. The inverse relationship between price and quantity demanded holds, *ceteris paribus*. What your friend has observed is a case where all other things were not constant.

To illustrate, consider Exhibit 6a. Your friend may initially have observed two points, *A* and *B*, where *B* represents a higher price and a greater consumption of meals than *A*. From this he concluded that people buy more restaurant meals at higher prices than at lower prices. Your friend sees the demand curve as sloping upward, as in Exhibit 6b.

However, the 14 million meals consumed at point *B* are not the result of a higher price but of a higher demand curve, as in Exhibit 6c. The consumption of meals has increased from 10 million to 14 million because the demand curve has shifted rightward from D_1 to D_2 (owing perhaps to a rise in incomes or a change in preferences), not because price has increased from $10 to $15 (as your friend mistakenly thought was the case).

---

2. Steven Landsburg, "Why Are We Getting So Fat?" *Slate*, 1 May 2001.

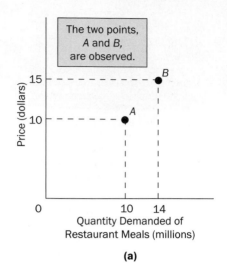

The two points, A and B, are observed.

(a)

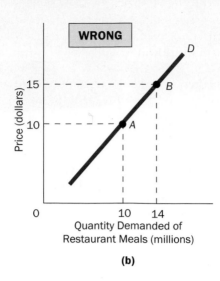

WRONG

(b)

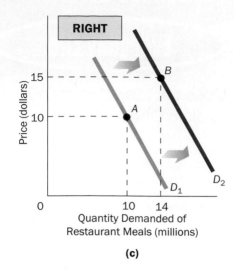

RIGHT

(c)

exhibit 6

The Law of Demand Holds
Your friend initially observes the equivalent of points A and B in (a). He believes that higher restaurant prices cause people to buy more restaurant meals. That is, he thinks (b) is the accurate representation of buying behavior. He is mistaken, however, People buy more restaurant meals because the demand curve for restaurant meals has shifted rightward, as in (c).

Supply
The willingness and ability of sellers to produce and offer to sell different quantities of a good at different prices during a specific time period.

Law of Supply
As the price of a good rises, the quantity supplied of the good rises, and as the price of a good falls, the quantity supplied of the good falls, ceteris paribus.

(Upward-sloping) Supply Curve
The graphical representation of the law of supply.

Self-Test *(Answers to Self-Test questions are in the Self-Test Appendix.)*

1. As Sandi's income rises, her demand for popcorn rises. As Mark's income falls, his demand for prepaid telephone cards rises. What kinds of goods are popcorn and telephone cards for the people who demand each?

2. Why are demand curves downward-sloping?

3. Give an example that illustrates how to derive a market demand curve.

4. What factors can change demand? What factors can change quantity demanded?

SUPPLY

Just as the word *demand* has a specific meaning in economics, so does the word *supply*. **Supply** refers to (1) the willingness and ability of sellers to produce and offer to sell different quantities of a good (2) at different prices (3) during a specific time period (per day, week, and so on).

THE LAW OF SUPPLY

The **law of supply** states that as the price of a good rises, the quantity supplied of the good rises, and as the price of a good falls, the quantity supplied of the good falls, *ceteris paribus*. Simply put, the price of a good and the quantity supplied of the good are directly related, *ceteris paribus*. (Quantity supplied is the number of units of a good sellers are willing and able to produce and offer to sell at a particular price.) The (upward-sloping) **supply curve** is the graphical representation of the law of supply (see Exhibit 7).

The law of supply can be summarized as follows:

$$P\uparrow Q_s\uparrow$$
$$P\downarrow Q_s\downarrow \text{ ceteris paribus}$$

where P = price and Q_s = quantity supplied.

The law of supply holds for the production of most goods. It does not hold when there is no time to produce more units of a good. For example, suppose a theater in Atlanta is sold out for tonight's play. Even if ticket prices increased from $30 to $40, there would be no additional seats in the theater. There is no time to produce more seats. The supply curve for theater seats is illustrated in Exhibit 8a. It is fixed at the number of seats in the theater, 500.[3]

The law of supply also does not hold for goods that cannot be produced over any period of time. For example, the violinmaker Antonio Stradivari died in 1737. A rise in the price of Stradivarius violins does not affect the number of Stradivarius violins supplied, as Exhibit 8b illustrates.

Q & A

Q: According to the law of supply, price and quantity supplied are directly related. The upward-sloping supply curve is the graphical representation of this law. But then, what do the vertical supply curves in Exhibit 8 represent? It can't be the law of supply.

A: They represent an independent relationship between price and quantity supplied.

WHY MOST SUPPLY CURVES ARE UPWARD-SLOPING

The reason why most supply curves are upward-sloping involves the law of diminishing marginal returns, which is discussed in a later chapter. For now, we say that an upward-sloping supply curve reflects the fact that under certain conditions, a higher price is an incentive to producers to produce more of a good. The incentive is in the form of higher profits. For example, if the price of books rises, book companies will earn higher profits per book, assuming all other things (for example, per-unit costs) are held constant. The expectation of higher profits encourages the companies to increase the quantity of books they supply to the market.

Generally though, costs do not remain constant as more of a good is provided because of the law of increasing opportunity costs. As discussed in Chapter 2, the law states that increased production of a good comes at increased opportunity costs. Thus, an upward-sloping supply curve reflects the fact that costs rise when more units of a good are produced, so a higher price is necessary to elicit more output.

exhibit

A Supply Curve
The upward-sloping supply curve is the graphical representation of the law of supply, which states that price and quantity supplied are directly related, *ceteris paribus*. On a supply curve, the price (in dollars) represents price per unit of the good. The quantity supplied, on the horizontal axis, is always relevant for a specific time period (a week, a month, and so on).

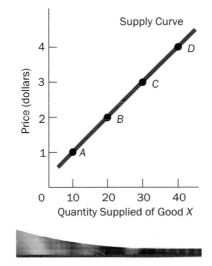

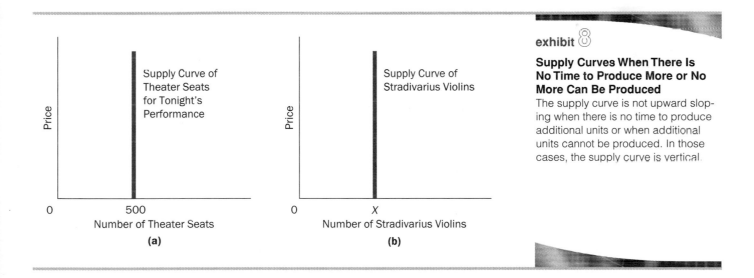

(a)

(b)

exhibit 8

Supply Curves When There Is No Time to Produce More or No More Can Be Produced
The supply curve is not upward sloping when there is no time to produce additional units or when additional units cannot be produced. In those cases, the supply curve is vertical.

---

3. The vertical supply curve is said to be *perfectly inelastic*.

THE MARKET SUPPLY CURVE

An individual supply curve represents the price-quantity combinations for a single seller. The market supply curve represents the price-quantity combinations for all sellers of a particular good. Exhibit 9 shows how a market supply curve can be derived by "adding" individual supply curves. In (a), a **supply schedule,** the numerical tabulation of the quantity supplied of a good at different prices, is given for Brown, Alberts, and other suppliers. The market supply schedule is obtained by adding the quantities supplied at each price, *ceteris paribus*. For example, at $11, the quantities supplied are 2 units for Brown, 3 units for Alberts, and 98 units for other suppliers. Thus, a total of 103 units are supplied at $11. In (b), the data points for the supply schedules are plotted and "added" to produce a market supply curve. The market supply curve could also be drawn directly from the market supply schedule.

CHANGES IN SUPPLY MEAN SHIFTS IN SUPPLY CURVES

Just as demand can change, so can supply. The supply of a good can rise or fall. What does it mean if the supply of a good *increases*? It means that suppliers are willing and able to produce and offer to sell *more* of the good at all prices. For example, suppose that in January sellers are willing and able to produce and offer for sale 600 shirts at $25 each and that in February they are willing and able to produce and sell 900 shirts at $25 each. An increase in supply shifts the entire supply curve to the right, as shown in Exhibit 10a.

The supply of a good *decreases* if sellers are willing and able to produce and offer to sell *less* of the good at all prices. For example, suppose that in January sellers are willing and able to produce and offer for sale 600 shirts at $25 each

Supply Schedule
The numerical tabulation of the quantity supplied of a good at different prices.

exhibit 9

Deriving a Market Supply Schedule and a Market Supply Curve
Part (a) shows four supply schedules combined into one table. The market supply schedule is derived by adding the quantities supplied at each price. In (b), the data points from the supply schedules are plotted to show how a market supply curve is derived. Only two points on the market supply curve are noted.

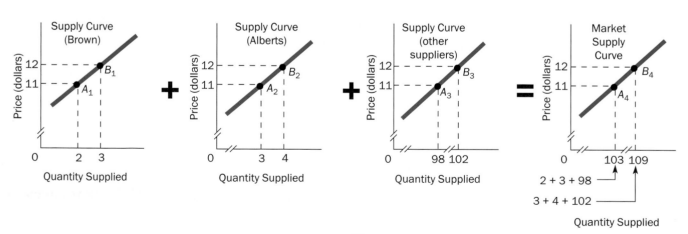

	Quantity Supplied			
Price	Brown	Alberts	Other Suppliers	All Suppliers
$10	1	2	96	99
11	2 +	3 +	98 =	103
12	3 +	4 +	102 =	109
13	4	5	106	115
14	5	6	108	119
15	6	7	110	123

(a)

(b)

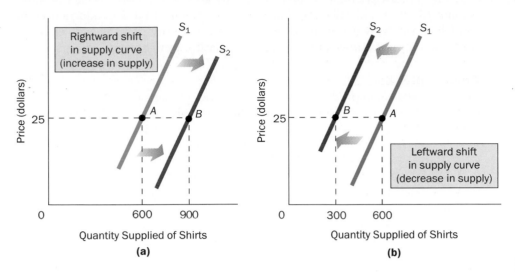

exhibit 10

Shifts in the Supply Curve
(a) The supply curve shifts rightward from S_1 to S_2. This represents an increase in the supply of shirts: At each price the quantity supplied of shirts is greater. For example, the quantity supplied at $25 increases from 600 shirts to 900 shirts. (b) The supply curve shifts leftward from S_1 to S_2. This represents a decrease in the supply of shirts: At each price the quantity supplied of shirts is less. For example, the quantity supplied at $25 decreases from 600 shirts to 300 shirts.

and that in February they are willing and able to produce and sell only 300 shirts at $25 each. A decrease in supply shifts the entire supply curve to the left, as shown in Exhibit 10b.

WHAT FACTORS CAUSE THE SUPPLY CURVE TO SHIFT?

We know the supply of any good can change. But what causes supply to change? What causes supply curves to shift? The factors that can change supply include (1) prices of relevant resources, (2) technology, (3) number of sellers, (4) expectations of future price, (5) taxes and subsidies, and (6) government restrictions.

Prices of Relevant Resources

Resources are needed to produce goods. For example, wood is needed to produce doors. If the price of wood falls, it becomes less costly to produce doors. How will door producers respond? Will they produce more doors, the same number of doors, or fewer doors? With lower costs and prices unchanged, the profit from producing and selling doors has increased; as a result, there is an increased incentive to produce doors. Door producers will produce and offer to sell more doors at each and every price. Thus, the supply of doors will increase and the supply curve of doors will shift rightward. If the price of wood rises, it becomes more costly to produce doors. Consequently, the supply of doors will decrease and the supply curve of doors will shift leftward.

Technology

In Chapter 2, technology is defined as the body of skills and knowledge concerning the use of resources in production. Also, an advance in technology refers to the ability to produce more output with a fixed amount of resources, thus reducing per-unit production costs. To illustrate, suppose it currently takes $100 to produce 40 units of a good. The per-unit cost is therefore $2.50. If an advance in technology makes it possible to produce 50 units at a cost of $100, then the per-unit cost falls to $2.00.

If per-unit production costs decline, we expect the quantity supplied of a good to increase. Why? The reason is that lower per-unit costs increase profitability and therefore provide producers with an incentive to produce more. For

http://

Go to *http://stats.bls.gov/ppi/home.htm*. Under "Economic News Releases," select "PPI News Release (TXT)," and then choose Table 2. The PPI measures prices of the resources (inputs) used in production. Try to find resources whose prices have risen more than 10 percent in the past year. What consumer products will be affected by this resource price increase? What will happen to the supply of these products? Answer the same questions for a resource whose price has fallen more than 10 percent.

example, if corn growers develop a way to grow more corn using the same amount of water and other resources, it follows that per-unit production costs will fall, profitability will increase, and growers will want to grow and sell more corn at each price. The supply curve of corn will shift rightward.

Number of Sellers
If more sellers begin producing a particular good, perhaps because of high profits, the supply curve will shift rightward. If some sellers stop producing a particular good, perhaps because of losses, the supply curve will shift leftward.

Expectations of Future Price
If the price of a good is expected to be higher in the future, producers may hold back some of the product today (if possible; for example, perishables cannot be held back). Then, they will have more to sell at the higher future price. Therefore, the current supply curve will shift leftward. For example, if oil producers expect the price of oil to be higher next year, some may hold oil off the market this year to be able to sell it next year. Similarly, if they expect the price of oil to be lower next year, they might pump more oil this year than previously planned.

Taxes and Subsidies
Some taxes increase per-unit costs. Suppose a shoe manufacturer must pay a $2 tax per pair of shoes produced. This tax leads to a leftward shift in the supply curve, indicating that the manufacturer wants to produce and offer to sell fewer pairs of shoes at each price. If the tax is eliminated, the supply curve shifts rightward.

(Production) Subsidy
A monetary payment by government to a producer of a good or service.

Subsidies have the opposite effect. Suppose the government subsidizes the production of corn by paying corn farmers $2 for every bushel of corn they produce. Because of the subsidy, the quantity supplied of corn is greater at each price and the supply curve of corn shifts rightward. Removal of the subsidy shifts the supply curve of corn leftward. A rough rule of thumb is that we get more of what we subsidize and less of what we tax.

Government Restrictions
Sometimes government acts to reduce supply. Consider a U.S. import quota on Japanese television sets. An import quota, or quantitative restriction on foreign goods, reduces the supply of Japanese television sets. It shifts the supply curve leftward. The elimination of the import quota allows the supply of Japanese television sets in the United States to shift rightward.

Licensure has a similar effect. With licensure, individuals must meet certain requirements before they can legally carry out a task. For example, owner-operators of day-care centers must meet certain requirements before they are allowed to sell their services. No doubt this reduces the number of day-care centers and shifts the supply curve of day-care centers leftward.

A CHANGE IN SUPPLY VERSUS A CHANGE IN QUANTITY SUPPLIED
A *change in supply* refers to a *shift* in the supply curve, as illustrated in Exhibit 11a. For example, saying that the supply of oranges has increased is the same as saying that the supply curve for oranges has shifted rightward. The factors that can change supply (shift the supply curve) include prices of relevant resources, technology, number of sellers, expectations of future price, taxes and subsidies, and government restrictions.

A *change in quantity supplied* refers to a *movement* along a supply curve as in Exhibit 11b. The *only* factor that can *directly* cause a change in the quantity supplied of a good is a change in the price of the good, or own price.

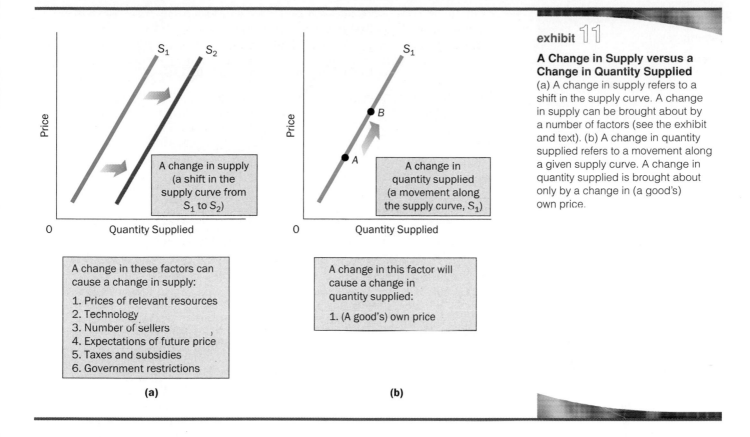

exhibit 11

A Change in Supply versus a Change in Quantity Supplied
(a) A change in supply refers to a shift in the supply curve. A change in supply can be brought about by a number of factors (see the exhibit and text). (b) A change in quantity supplied refers to a movement along a given supply curve. A change in quantity supplied is brought about only by a change in (a good's) own price.

In left panel (a): S_1, S_2; Price (vertical axis); Quantity Supplied (horizontal axis); 0 at origin.

A change in supply (a shift in the supply curve from S_1 to S_2)

A change in these factors can cause a change in supply:
1. Prices of relevant resources
2. Technology
3. Number of sellers
4. Expectations of future price
5. Taxes and subsidies
6. Government restrictions

(a)

In right panel (b): S_1; Price (vertical axis); Quantity Supplied (horizontal axis); 0 at origin; points A and B.

A change in quantity supplied (a movement along the supply curve, S_1)

A change in this factor will cause a change in quantity supplied:
1. (A good's) own price

(b)

Self-Test

1. What would the supply curve for houses (in a given city) look like for a time period of (a) the next 10 hours and (b) the next 3 months?

2. What happens to the supply curve if each of the following occurs?
   a. There is a decrease in the number of sellers.
   b. A per-unit tax is placed on the production of a good.
   c. The price of a relevant resource falls.

3. Why do most supply curves slope upward?

THE MARKET: PUTTING SUPPLY AND DEMAND TOGETHER

In this section, we put supply and demand together and discuss the market. The purpose of the discussion is to gain some understanding about how prices are determined. Have you ever wondered why the price, say, of a car is $25,000? Why isn't the price $20,000 or $40,000?

SUPPLY AND DEMAND AT WORK AT AN AUCTION

Imagine you are at an auction where bushels of corn are bought and sold. At this auction, the auctioneer will adjust the corn price to sell all the corn offered for sale. The supply curve of corn is vertical, as in Exhibit 12. It intersects the horizontal axis at 40,000 bushels; that is, quantity supplied is 40,000 bushels. The demand curve for corn is downward-sloping. Furthermore, suppose each potential buyer of corn is sitting in front of a computer that immediately registers the

exhibit 12

Supply and Demand at Work at an Auction

Q_d = quantity demanded; Q_s = quantity supplied. The auctioneer calls out different prices, and buyers record how much they are willing and able to buy. At prices of $6.00, $5.00, and $4.00, quantity supplied is greater than quantity demanded. At prices of $1.25 and $2.25, quantity demanded is greater than quantity supplied. At a price of $3.10, quantity demanded equals quantity supplied.

Quantity Supplied and Demanded
(thousands of bushels of corn)

Surplus (Excess Supply)
A condition in which quantity supplied is greater than quantity demanded. Surpluses occur only at prices above equilibrium price.

Shortage (Excess Demand)
A condition in which quantity demanded is greater than quantity supplied. Shortages occur only at prices below equilibrium price.

Equilibrium Price (Market-Clearing Price)
The price at which quantity demanded of the good equals quantity supplied.

Equilibrium Quantity
The quantity that corresponds to equilibrium price. The quantity at which the amount of the good that buyers are willing and able to buy equals the amount that sellers are willing and able to sell, and both equal the amount actually bought and sold.

Disequilibrium Price
A price other than equilibrium price. A price at which quantity demanded does not equal quantity supplied.

number of bushels he or she wants to buy. For example, if Nancy Bernstein wants to buy 5,000 bushels of corn, she simply keys "5,000" into her computer. The auction begins. (Follow along in Exhibit 12 as we relay what is happening at the auction.) The auctioneer calls out the price:

- **$6.00.** The potential buyers think for a second, and then each registers the number of bushels he or she is willing and able to buy at that price. The total is 10,000 bushels, which is the quantity demanded of corn at $6.00. The auctioneer, realizing that 30,000 bushels of corn (40,000 − 10,000 = 30,000) will go unsold at this price, decides to lower the price per bushel to:
- **$5.00.** The quantity demanded increases to 20,000 bushels, but still the quantity supplied of corn at this price is greater than the quantity demanded. The auctioneer calls out:
- **$4.00.** The quantity demanded increases to 30,000 bushels, but the quantity supplied at $4.00 is still greater than the quantity demanded. The auctioneer drops the price down to:
- **$1.25.** At this price, the quantity demanded jumps to 60,000 bushels, but that is 20,000 bushels more than the quantity supplied. The auctioneer calls out a higher price:
- **$2.25.** The quantity demanded drops to 50,000 bushels, but buyers still want to buy more corn at this price than there is corn to be sold. The auctioneer calls out:
- **$3.10.** At this price, the quantity demanded of corn is 40,000 bushels and the quantity supplied of corn is 40,000 bushels. The auction stops. The 40,000 bushels of corn are bought and sold at $3.10 per bushel.

THE LANGUAGE OF SUPPLY AND DEMAND: A FEW IMPORTANT TERMS

If quantity supplied is greater than quantity demanded, a **surplus** or **excess supply** exists. If quantity demanded is greater than quantity supplied, a **shortage** or **excess demand** exists. In Exhibit 12, a surplus exists at $6.00, $5.00, and $4.00. A shortage exists at $1.25 and $2.25. The price at which quantity demanded equals quantity supplied is the **equilibrium price** or **market-clearing price.** In our example, $3.10 is the equilibrium price. The quantity that corresponds to the equilibrium price is the **equilibrium quantity.** In our example, it is 40,000 bushels of corn. Any price at which quantity demanded is not equal to quantity supplied is a **disequilibrium price.**

The Stock Market and the Housing Market

On August 29, 2002, at 10:00 A.M., the price of a share of IBM stock was $76.81. A few seconds later, the price had risen to $77.05. Obviously, the stock market is a market that equilibrates quickly. If demand rises at the current equilibrium price, initially there is a shortage of the stock. The price is bid up and there is no longer a shortage. All this happens in seconds.

Now consider a house offered for sale in any city in the country. It is not uncommon for the sale price of a house to remain the same even though the house does not sell for months. For example, a person offers to sell her house for $400,000. One month passes, no sale; two months pass, no sale; three months pass, no sale; and so on. Ten months later, the house has still not sold and the price is still $400,000.

Is $400,000 the equilibrium price of the house? Obviously not. At equilibrium price, quantity supplied equals quantity demanded. In this case at equilibrium price, there would be a buyer for the house and a seller of the house.

However, at a price of $400,000, there is a seller of the house but no buyer. There is no doubt that the price of $400,000 is above equilibrium price. At $400,000, there is a surplus in the market; equilibrium has not been achieved.

Some people may be tempted to argue that supply and demand are at work in the stock market but not in the housing market. A better explanation, though, is that not all markets equilibrate at the same speed. While it may take only seconds for the stock market to go from surplus or shortage to equilibrium, it may take months for the housing market to do so.

A market that exhibits either a surplus ($Q_s > Q_d$) or a shortage ($Q_d > Q_s$) is said to be in **disequilibrium.** A market in which quantity demanded equals quantity supplied ($Q_d - Q_s$) is said to be in **equilibrium.** Equilibrium is identified by the letter E in Exhibit 12.

![Q & A]

Q: Some people use the words *shortage* and *scarcity* as synonyms. Do they refer to the same thing?

A: No. Scarcity is the condition where wants are greater than the resources available to satisfy them. Shortage is the condition where quantity demanded is greater than quantity supplied. A shortage occurs at any disequilibrium price that is below equilibrium price (for example, $2.25 in Exhibit 12). Scarcity occurs at all prices. Even at equilibrium price ($3.10 in Exhibit 12), where quantity demanded equals quantity supplied, scarcity exists.

Disequilibrium
A state of either surplus or shortage in a market.

Equilibrium
Equilibrium means "at rest." Equilibrium in a market is the price-quantity combination from which there is no tendency for buyers or sellers to move away. Graphically, equilibrium is the intersection point of the supply and demand curves.

MOVING TO EQUILIBRIUM: WHAT HAPPENS TO PRICE WHEN THERE IS A SURPLUS OR A SHORTAGE?

What did the auctioneer do when the price was $6.00 and there was a surplus of corn? He lowered the price. What did the auctioneer do when the price was $2.25 and there was a shortage of corn? He raised the price. The behavior of the auctioneer can be summarized this way: If a surplus exists, lower price; if a shortage exists, raise price. This is how the auctioneer moved the corn market into equilibrium.

Not all markets have auctioneers. (When was the last time you saw an auctioneer in the grocery store?) But many markets act *as if* an auctioneer were calling out higher and lower prices until equilibrium price is reached. In many real-world auctioneerless markets, prices fall when there is a surplus and rise when there is a shortage. Why?

Why Does Price Fall When There Is a Surplus?

In Exhibit 13, there is a surplus at a price of $15: quantity supplied (150 units) is greater than quantity demanded (50 units). Suppliers will not be able to sell all they had hoped to sell at $15. As a result, their inventories will grow beyond the level they hold in preparation for demand changes. Sellers will want to reduce their inventories. Some will lower prices to do so, some will cut back on production, others will do a little of both. As shown in the exhibit, there is a tendency for price and output to fall until equilibrium is achieved.

Why Does Price Rise When There Is a Shortage?

In Exhibit 13, there is a shortage at a price of $5: quantity demanded (150 units) is greater than quantity supplied (50 units). Buyers will not be able to buy all they had hoped to buy at $5. Some buyers will bid up the price to get sellers to sell to them instead of to other buyers. Some sellers, seeing buyers clamor for the goods, will realize that they can raise the price on the goods they have for sale. Higher prices will also call forth added output. Thus, there is a tendency for price and output to rise until equilibrium is achieved.

Q & A   **Q:** In Exhibit 13, the horizontal axis is labeled "Quantity." In earlier exhibits in this chapter, either "Quantity Demanded" or "Quantity Supplied" was on the horizontal axis, depending on whether we were discussing demand or supply. Why are we switching to "Quantity"?

---

exhibit 13

Moving to Equilibrium
If there is a surplus, sellers' inventories rise above the level they hold in preparation for demand changes. Sellers will want to reduce their inventories. As a result, price and output fall until equilibrium is achieved. If there is a shortage, some buyers will bid up price to get sellers to sell to them instead of to other buyers. Some sellers will realize they can raise the price on the goods they have for sale. Higher prices will call forth added output. Price and output rise until equilibrium is achieved. (Note: Recall that price, on the vertical axis, is price per unit of the good, and quantity, on the horizontal axis, is for a specific time period. In this text, we do not specify this on the axes themselves, but consider it to be understood.

Price	Q_s	Q_d	Condition
$15	150	50	Surplus
10	100	100	Equilibrium
5	50	150	Shortage

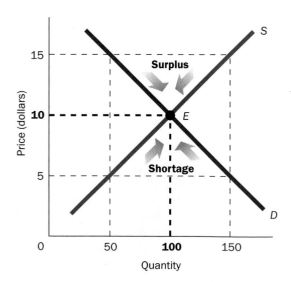

A: If we are discussing only demand, as in Exhibit 1, we put "Quantity Demanded" on the axis. If we are discussing only supply, as in Exhibit 7, we put "Quantity Supplied" on the axis. But when we discuss both demand and supply, as in Exhibit 13, we put "Quantity" on the axis, which is understood as the shortened version of "Quantity Demanded and Supplied."

MOVING TO EQUILIBRIUM: MAXIMUM AND MINIMUM PRICES

The discussion of surpluses illustrates how a market moves to equilibrium, but there is another way to show this. Exhibit 14 shows the market for good *X*. Look at the first unit of good *X*. What is the *maximum price buyers would be willing to pay* for it? The answer is $70. This can be seen by following the dotted line up from the first unit of the good to the demand curve. What is the *minimum price sellers need to receive before they would be willing to sell* this unit of good *X*? It is $10. This can be seen by following the dotted line up from the first unit to the supply curve. Because the maximum buying price is greater than the minimum selling price, the first unit of good *X* will be exchanged.

What about the second unit? Here the maximum price buyers are willing to pay is $60, and the minimum price sellers need to receive is $20. The second unit of good *X* will be exchanged. In fact, exchange will occur as long as the maximum buying price is greater than the minimum selling price. The exhibit shows that a total of four units of good *X* will be exchanged. The fifth unit will not be exchanged because the maximum buying price ($30) is less than the minimum selling price ($50).

In the process just described, buyers and sellers trade money for goods as long as both benefit from the trade. The market converges on a quantity of 4 units of good *X* and a price of $40 per unit. This is equilibrium. In other words, *mutually beneficial trade drives the market to equilibrium.*

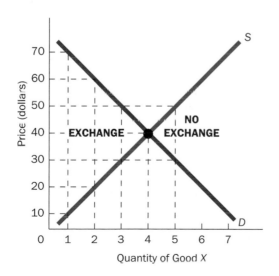

Units of Good *X*	Maximum Buying Price	Minimum Selling Price	Result
1st	$70	$10	Exchange
2nd	60	20	Exchange
3rd	50	30	Exchange
4th	40	40	Exchange
5th	30	50	No Exchange

exhibit 14

Moving to Equilibrium in Terms of Maximum and Minimum Prices
As long as the maximum buying price is greater than the minimum selling price, an exchange will occur. This condition is met for units 1–4. The market converges on equilibrium through a process of mutually beneficial exchanges.

Q: It appears that in equilibrium the maximum buying price and the minimum selling price are the same. Is this correct?

A: Yes. In Exhibit 14, at the equilibrium quantity (4 units), the maximum buying price and the minimum selling price are the same—$40.

VIEWING EQUILIBRIUM IN TERMS OF CONSUMERS' AND PRODUCERS' SURPLUS

Chapter 2 discusses the key economic concepts of consumers' surplus and producers' surplus. This section looks at how these concepts are related to equilibrium.

In Exhibit 15a, consumers' surplus is represented by the shaded triangle. This triangle includes the area under the demand curve and above the equilibrium price. Recall that the definition of consumers' surplus is the highest price buyers are willing to pay minus the price they pay. For example, the window in (a) shows that buyers are willing to pay as high as $7 for the 50th unit, but only pay $5. Thus, the consumers' surplus on the 50th unit of the good is $2. If we add the consumers' surplus on each unit of the good between and including the first and the 100th (100 units being the equilibrium quantity), we obtain the shaded consumers' surplus triangle.

In Exhibit 15b, producers' surplus is represented by the shaded triangle. This triangle includes the area above the supply curve and under the equilibrium price. Keep in mind the definition of producers' surplus—the price received by the seller minus the lowest price the seller would accept for the good. For example, the window in (b) shows that sellers would have sold the 50th unit for as low as $3 but actually sold it for $5. Thus, the producers' surplus on the 50th unit of the good is $2. If we add the producers' surplus on each unit of the good between and including the first and the 100th, we obtain the shaded producers' surplus triangle.

Now consider consumers' surplus and producers' surplus at the equilibrium quantity. Exhibit 16 shows that consumers' surplus at equilibrium is equal to areas $A + B + C + D$, and producers' surplus at equilibrium is equal to areas $E + F + G + H$. At any other exchangeable quantity, such as at 25, 50, or 75 units, both consumers' surplus and producers' surplus are less. For example, at 25 units, consumers' surplus is equal to area A and producers' surplus is equal to

exhibit 15

Consumers' and Producers' Surplus

(a) Consumers' surplus. As the shaded area indicates, the difference between the maximum or highest amount buyers would be willing to pay and the price they actually pay is consumers' surplus. (b) Producers' surplus. As the shaded area indicates, the difference between the price sellers receive for the good and the minimum or lowest price they would be willing to sell the good for is producers' surplus.

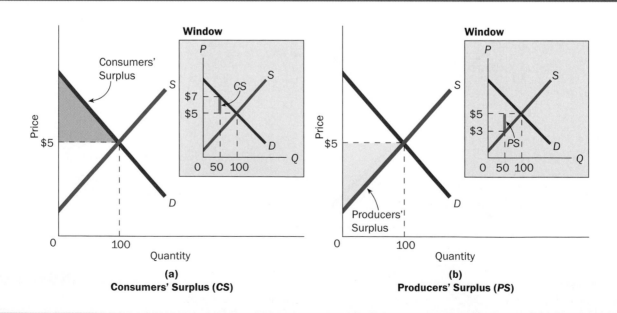

(a)
Consumers' Surplus (CS)

(b)
Producers' Surplus (PS)

Quantity (units)	Consumers' Surplus	Producers' Surplus
25	A	E
50	A + B	E + F
75	A + B + C	E + F + G
100 (Equilibrium)	A + B + C + D	E + F + G + H

(a)

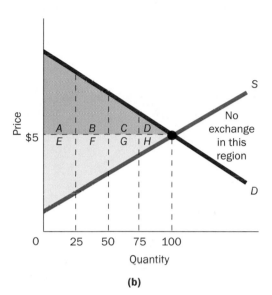

(b)

area E. At 50 units, consumers' surplus is equal to areas A + B and producers' surplus is equal to areas E + F.

Is there a special property to equilibrium? At equilibrium, both consumers' surplus and producers' surplus are maximized. In short, the sum of consumers' and producers' surplus is maximized.

WHAT CAN CHANGE EQUILIBRIUM PRICE AND QUANTITY?

Equilibrium price and quantity are determined by supply and demand. Whenever demand changes or supply changes or both change, equilibrium price and quantity change. Exhibit 17 illustrates eight different cases where this occurs. Cases (a)–(d) illustrate the four basic changes in supply and demand, where either supply or demand changes. Cases (e)–(h) illustrate changes in both supply and demand.

- (a) Demand rises (the demand curve shifts rightward), and supply is constant (the supply curve does not move). Equilibrium price rises, equilibrium quantity rises.
- (b) Demand falls, supply is constant. Equilibrium price falls, equilibrium quantity falls.
- (c) Supply rises, demand is constant. Equilibrium price falls, equilibrium quantity rises.
- (d) Supply falls, demand is constant. Equilibrium price rises, equilibrium quantity falls.
- (e) Demand rises and supply falls by an equal amount. Equilibrium price rises, equilibrium quantity is constant.
- (f) Demand falls and supply rises by an equal amount. Equilibrium price falls, equilibrium quantity is constant.

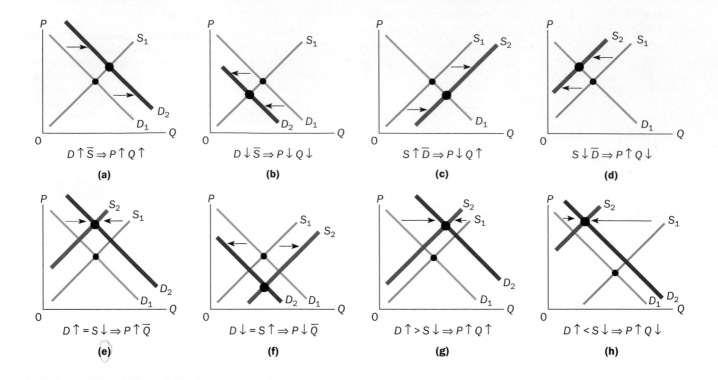

$D \uparrow \overline{S} \Rightarrow P \uparrow Q \uparrow$

(a)

$D \downarrow \overline{S} \Rightarrow P \downarrow Q \downarrow$

(b)

$S \uparrow \overline{D} \Rightarrow P \downarrow Q \uparrow$

(c)

$S \downarrow \overline{D} \Rightarrow P \uparrow Q \downarrow$

(d)

$D \uparrow = S \downarrow \Rightarrow P \uparrow \overline{Q}$

(e)

$D \downarrow = S \uparrow \Rightarrow P \downarrow \overline{Q}$

(f)

$D \uparrow > S \downarrow \Rightarrow P \uparrow Q \uparrow$

(g)

$D \uparrow < S \downarrow \Rightarrow P \uparrow Q \downarrow$

(h)

exhibit 17

Equilibrium Price and Quantity Effects of Supply Curve Shifts and Demand Curve Shifts

The exhibit illustrates the effects on equilibrium price and quantity of a change in demand, a change in supply, or a change in both. Below each diagram the condition leading to the effects is noted, using the following symbols: (1) a bar over a letter means *constant* (thus, $\overline{S}$ means that supply is constant); (2) a downward-pointing arrow ($\downarrow$) indicates a fall; (3) an upward-pointing arrow ($\uparrow$) indicates a rise. A rise (fall) in demand is the same as a rightward (leftward) shift in the demand curve. A rise (fall) in supply is the same as a rightward (leftward) shift in the supply curve.

- (g) Demand rises by a greater amount than supply falls. Equilibrium price and quantity rise.
- (h) Demand rises by a lesser amount than supply falls. Equilibrium price rises, equilibrium quantity falls.

Self-Test

1. When a person goes to the grocery store to buy food, there is no auctioneer calling out prices for bread, milk, and other items. Therefore, supply and demand cannot be operative. Do you agree or disagree? Explain your answer.

2. The price of a given-quality personal computer is lower today than it was five years ago. Is this necessarily the result of a lower demand for computers? Explain your answer.

3. What is the effect on equilibrium price and quantity of the following?
   a. A decrease in demand that is greater than the increase in supply
   b. An increase in supply
   c. A decrease in supply that is greater than the increase in demand
   d. A decrease in demand

PRICE CONTROLS

Because scarcity exists, there is a need for a rationing device—such as dollar price. But price is not always permitted to be a rationing device. Sometimes price is controlled. There are two types of price controls: price ceilings and price floors. In the discussion of price controls, the word *price* is used in the generic sense. It refers to the price of an apple, for example, the price of labor (wage), the price of credit (interest rate), and so on.

PRICE CEILING: DEFINITION AND EFFECTS

A **price ceiling** is a government-mandated maximum price above which legal trades cannot be made. For example, suppose the government mandates that the maximum price at which good X can be bought and sold is $8. It follows that $8 is a price ceiling. If $8 is below the equilibrium price of good X, as in Exhibit 18, any or all of the following effects may arise.[4]

Shortages

At the $12 equilibrium price in Exhibit 18, the quantity demanded of good X (150) is equal to the quantity supplied (150). At the $8 price ceiling, a shortage exists. The quantity demanded (190) is greater than the quantity supplied (100). When a shortage exists, there is a tendency for price and output to rise to equilibrium. But when a price ceiling exists, this tendency cannot be realized because it is unlawful to trade at the equilibrium price.

Price Ceiling
A government-mandated maximum price above which legal trades cannot be made.

Fewer Exchanges

At the equilibrium price, 150 units of good X are bought and sold. At the price ceiling in Exhibit 18, 100 units of good X are bought and sold. (Buyers would prefer to buy 190 units, but only 100 are supplied.) We conclude that price ceilings cause fewer exchanges to be made.

Nonprice Rationing Devices

If the equilibrium price of $12 fully rationed good X before the price ceiling was imposed, it follows that a (lower) price of $8 can only partly ration this good. In short, price ceilings prevent price from rising to the level sufficient to ration goods fully. But if price is responsible for only part of the rationing, what accounts for the rest? The answer is some other (nonprice) rationing device, such as first-come-first-served (FCFS).

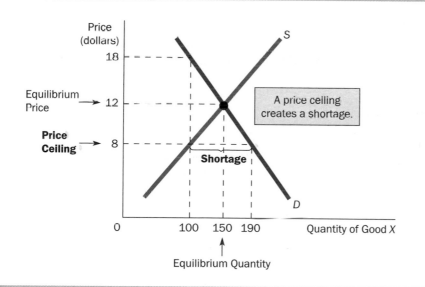

exhibit 18

A Price Ceiling
The price ceiling is $8 and the equilibrium price $12. At $12, quantity demanded − quantity supplied. At $8, quantity demanded > quantity supplied. (Recall that price, on the vertical axis, always represents price per unit. Quantity, on the horizontal axis, always holds for a specific time period.)

---

4. If a price ceiling is above the equilibrium price (say, $8 is the price ceiling and $4 is the equilibrium price), it has no effects. Usually, however, a price ceiling is below the equilibrium price. The price ceilings discussed here hold for a particular market structure and not necessarily for all market structures. The relevant market structure is usually referred to as a perfectly competitive market, a price-taker market, or a perfect market. In this market, there are enough buyers and sellers so that no single buyer can influence price.

In Exhibit 18, 100 units of good X will be sold at $8 although buyers are willing to buy 190 units at this price. What happens? Possibly, good X will be sold on an FCFS basis for $8 per unit. In other words, to buy good X, a person must not only pay $8 per unit but also be one of the first people in line.

Buying and Selling at a Prohibited Price

Buyers and sellers may regularly circumvent a price ceiling by making their exchanges "under the table." For example, some buyers may offer some sellers more than $8 per unit for good X. No doubt some sellers will accept the offers. But why would some buyers offer more than $8 per unit when they can buy good X for $8? The answer is because not all buyers can buy the amount of good X they want at $8. As Exhibit 18 shows, there is a shortage. Buyers are willing to buy 190 units at $8, but sellers are willing to sell only 100 units. In short, 90 fewer units will be sold than buyers would like to buy. Some buyers will go unsatisfied. How, then, does any one buyer make it more likely that sellers will sell to him or her instead of to someone else? The answer is by offering to pay a higher price. Because it is illegal to pay a higher price, the transaction must be made "under the table."

Tie-in Sales

Tie-in Sale
A sale whereby one good can be purchased only if another good is also purchased.

In Exhibit 18, the maximum price buyers would be willing and able to pay per unit for 100 units of good X is $18. (This is the price on the demand curve at a quantity of 100 units.) The maximum legal price, however, is $8. This difference between two prices often prompts a **tie-in sale,** a sale whereby one good can be purchased only if another good is also purchased. For example, if Ralph's Gas Station sells gasoline to customers only if they buy a car wash, the two goods are linked together in a tie-in sale.

Suppose that the sellers of good X in Exhibit 18 also sell good Y. They might offer to sell buyers good X at $8 only if the buyers agree to buy good Y at, say, $10. We choose $10 as the price for good Y because that is the difference between the maximum per-unit price buyers are willing and able to pay for 100 units of good X (specifically, $18) and the maximum legal price ($8).

In New York City and other communities with rent-control laws, tie-in sales sometimes result from rent ceilings on apartments. Occasionally, in order to rent an apartment, an individual must agree to buy the furniture in the apartment.

THINKING LIKE AN ECONOMIST *Economists think in terms of unintended effects. For example, a price ceiling policy intended to lower prices for the poor may cause shortages, the use of nonprice rationing devices, illegal market transactions, and tie-in sales. When we consider both the price ceiling and its effects, it is not clear that the poor have been helped. The economist knows that wanting to do good (for others) is not sufficient. It is important to know how to do good too.*

DO BUYERS PREFER LOWER PRICES TO HIGHER PRICES?

"Of course," someone might say, "buyers prefer lower prices to higher prices. What buyer would want to pay a higher price for anything?" But wait a minute. Price ceilings are often lower than equilibrium prices. Does it follow that buyers prefer price ceilings to equilibrium prices? Not necessarily. Price ceilings have effects that equilibrium prices do not: shortages, use of first-come-first-served as a rationing device, tie-in sales, and so on. A buyer could prefer to pay a higher price (an equilibrium price) than to pay a lower price and have to deal with the effects of a price ceiling. All we can say for certain is that buyers prefer lower prices to higher prices, *ceteris paribus.* As in many cases, the *ceteris paribus* condition makes all the difference.

PRICE FLOOR: DEFINITION AND EFFECTS

A **price floor** is a government-mandated minimum price below which legal trades cannot be made. For example, suppose the government mandates that the minimum price at which good X can be sold is $20. It follows that $20 is a price floor (see Exhibit 19). If the price floor is above the equilibrium price, the following two effects arise.[5]

Price Floor
A government-mandated minimum price below which legal trades cannot be made.

Surpluses

At the $15 equilibrium price in Exhibit 19, the quantity demanded of good X (130) is equal to the quantity supplied (130). At the $20 price floor, a surplus exists. The quantity supplied (180) is greater than the quantity demanded (90). A surplus is usually a temporary state of affairs. When a surplus exists, there is a tendency for price and output to fall to equilibrium. But when a price floor exists, this tendency cannot be realized because it is unlawful to trade at the equilibrium price.

Fewer Exchanges

At the equilibrium price in Exhibit 19, 130 units of good X are bought and sold. At the price floor, 90 units are bought and sold. (Sellers want to sell 180 units, but buyers buy only 90.) We conclude that price floors cause fewer exchanges to be made.

Self-Test

1. Do buyers prefer lower prices to higher prices?

2. "When there are long-lasting shortages, there are long lines of people waiting to buy goods. It follows that the shortages cause the long lines." Do you agree or disagree? Explain your answer.

3. Who might argue for a price ceiling? a price floor?

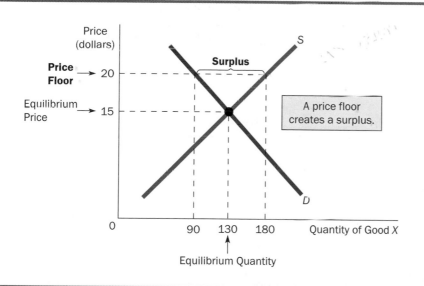

exhibit 19

A Price Floor
The price floor is $20 and the equilibrium price is $15. At $15, quantity demanded = quantity supplied. At $20, quantity supplied > quantity demanded.

---

5. If a price floor is below the equilibrium price (say, $20 is the price floor and $25 is the equilibrium price), it has no effects. Usually, however, a price floor is above the equilibrium price. As with price ceilings, the price floor effects discussed here hold for a perfectly competitive market. See footnote 4.

How Does Knowing about Supply and Demand Help Me?

Some things are interesting but not useful. Other things are useful but not interesting. For example, supply and demand are interesting, but not useful. Learning how to fix a car is useful, but not particularly interesting. Am I wrong? Have I missed something? Is knowledge of supply and demand useful? If it is, what can you do with it?

A knowledge of supply and demand can be used both to explain and to predict. Let's look at prediction first. Suppose you learn that the federal government is going to impose a quota on imported television sets. What will happen when the quota is imposed? With your knowledge of supply and demand, you can predict that the price of television sets will rise. In other words, you can use your knowledge of supply and demand to predict what will happen. Stated differently, you can use your knowledge of supply and demand to see into the future. Isn't the ability to see into the future useful?

Supply and demand also allows you to develop richer and fuller explanations of events. To illustrate, suppose there is a shortage of apples in country *X*. The cause of the shortage, someone says, is that apple growers in the country are simply growing too few apples. Well, of course, it is true that apple growers are growing "too few" apples as compared to the number of apples consumers want to buy. But does this explanation completely account for the shortage of apples? Your knowledge of supply and demand will prompt you to ask *why* apple growers are growing too few apples. When you understand that quantity supplied is related to price, you understand that apple growers will grow more apples if the price of apples is higher. What is keeping the price of apples down? Could it be a price ceiling? Without a price ceiling, the price of apples would rise, and apple growers would grow (and offer to sell) more apples. The shortage of apples will vanish.

In other words, without a knowledge of supply and demand you may have been content to explain the shortage of apples by saying that apple growers are growing too few apples. With your knowledge of supply and demand, you delve deeper into why apple growers are growing too few apples.

Chapter Summary

Demand

- The law of demand states that as the price of a good rises, the quantity demanded of the good falls, and as the price of a good falls, the quantity demanded of the good rises, *ceteris paribus*. The law of demand holds that price and quantity demanded are inversely related.
- Quantity demanded is the total number of units of a good that buyers are willing and able to buy at a particular price.
- A (downward-sloping) demand curve is the graphical representation of the law of demand.
- Factors that can change demand and cause the demand curve to shift include income, preferences, prices of related goods (substitutes and complements), number of buyers, and expectations of future price.
- The only factor that can directly cause a change in the quantity demanded of a good is a change in the good's own price.

Absolute Price and Relative Price

- The absolute price of a good is the price of the good in money terms.
- The relative price of a good is the price of the good in terms of another good.

Supply

- The law of supply states that as the price of a good rises, the quantity supplied of the good rises, and as the price of a good falls, the quantity supplied of the good falls, *ceteris paribus*. The law of supply asserts that price and quantity supplied are directly related.
- The law of supply does not hold when there is no time to produce more units of a good or when goods cannot be produced at all (over any period of time).
- The upward-sloping supply curve is the graphical representation of the law of supply. More generally, a supply curve (no matter how it slopes) represents the relationship between price and quantity supplied.

- Factors that can change supply and cause the supply curve to shift include prices of relevant resources, technology, number of sellers, expectations of future price, taxes and subsidies, and government restrictions.
- The only factor that can directly cause a change in the quantity supplied of a good is a change in the good's own price.

The Market

- Demand and supply together establish equilibrium price and quantity.
- A surplus exists in a market if, at some price, quantity supplied is greater than quantity demanded. A shortage exists if, at some price, quantity demanded is greater than quantity supplied.
- Mutually beneficial trade between buyers and sellers drives the market to equilibrium.
- The sum of consumers' surplus and producers' surplus is maximized at equilibrium.

Price Ceilings

- A price ceiling is a government-mandated maximum price. If a price ceiling is below the equilibrium price, some or all of the following effects arise: shortages, fewer exchanges, nonprice rationing devices, buying and selling at prohibited prices, and tie-in sales.
- Consumers do not necessarily prefer (lower) price ceilings to (higher) equilibrium prices. They may prefer higher prices and none of the effects of price ceilings to lower prices and some of the effects of price ceilings. All we can say for sure is that consumers prefer lower prices to higher prices, *ceteris paribus*.

Price Floors

- A price floor is a government-mandated minimum price. If a price floor is above the equilibrium price, the following effects arise: surpluses and fewer exchanges.

Key Terms and Concepts

Demand	Neutral Good	Shortage (Excess Demand)
Law of Demand	Substitutes	Equilibrium Price (Market-Clearing
Absolute (Money) Price	Complements	Price)
Relative Price	Own Price	Equilibrium Quantity
Law of Diminishing Marginal Utility	Supply	Disequilibrium Price
Demand Schedule	Law of Supply	Disequilibrium
Demand Curve	Supply Curve	Equilibrium
Normal Good	Supply Schedule	Price Ceiling
Inferior Good	Subsidy	Tie-in Sale
	Surplus (Excess Supply)	Price Floor

Economic Connections to You

Economic facts, actions, and changes create ripples that move away from their point of origin. Eventually, these ripples can intersect your life and have an effect on you. Consider the following example.

An economic change, such as a change in supply due to the price of a relevant resource, can raise or lower the price of a good. The price of one meg of RAM, a key component of a computer, fell from $2,867 in 1982 to $36 in 1996. Thus, it became cheaper for firms to produce computers. This increased the sup-

ply of computers and, in turn, lowered the price of computers. As a result, more universities, high schools, and individuals could afford to buy computers. Thus, there is a connection between the price change of a relevant resource and your access to a computer—an economic connection to you.

Based on the material in this chapter, identify other ways in which economic facts, actions, and changes create ripples that eventually affect you.

Questions and Problems

1. True or false? As the price of oranges rises, the demand for oranges falls, *ceteris paribus*. Explain your answer.
2. "The price of a bushel of wheat, which was $3.00 last month, is $3.70 today. The demand curve for wheat must have shifted rightward between last month and today." Discuss.
3. "Some goods are bought largely because they have 'snob appeal.' For example, the residents of Beverly Hills gain prestige by buying expensive items. In fact, they won't buy some items unless they are expensive. The law of demand, which holds that people buy more at lower prices than higher prices, obviously doesn't hold for the residents of Beverly Hills. The following rules apply in Beverly Hills: high prices, buy; low prices, don't buy." Discuss.
4. "The price of T-shirts keeps rising and rising, and people keep buying more and more. T-shirts must have an upward-sloping demand curve." Identify the error.
5. Predict what would happen to the equilibrium price of marijuana if it were legalized.
6. Compare the ratings for television shows with prices for goods. How are ratings like prices? How are ratings different from prices? (Hint: How does rising demand for a particular television show manifest itself?)
7. Do you think the law of demand holds for criminal activity? Do potential criminals "buy" less (more) crime, the higher (lower) the "price" of crime, *ceteris paribus*? Explain your answer.
8. Many movie theaters charge a lower admission price for the first show on weekday afternoons than for a weeknight or weekend show. Explain why.
9. A Dell computer is a substitute for a Compaq computer. What happens to the demand for Compaqs and the quantity demanded of Dells as the price of a Dell falls?
10. Describe how each of the following will affect the demand for personal computers: (a) a rise in incomes (assuming computers are a normal good); (b) a lower expected price for computers; (c) cheaper software; (d) computers become simpler to operate.
11. Describe how each of the following will affect the supply of personal computers: (a) a rise in wage rates; (b) an increase in the number of sellers of computers; (c) a tax placed on the production of computers; (d) a subsidy placed on the production of computers.
12. The law of demand specifies an inverse relationship between price and quantity demanded, *ceteris paribus*. Is the "price" in the law of demand absolute price or relative price? Explain your answer.
13. Use the law of diminishing marginal utility to explain why demand curves slope downward.
14. Explain how the market moves to equilibrium in terms of shortages and surpluses and in terms of maximum buying prices and minimum selling prices.
15. Identify what happens to equilibrium price and quantity in each of the following cases:
    a. Demand rises and supply is constant
    b. Demand falls and supply is constant
    c. Supply rises and demand is constant
    d. Supply falls and demand is constant
    e. Demand rises by the same amount that supply falls
    f. Demand falls by the same amount that supply rises
    g. Demand falls by less than supply rises
    h. Demand rises by more than supply rises
    i. Demand rises by less than supply rises
    j. Demand falls by more than supply falls
    k. Demand falls by less than supply falls
16. Many of the proponents of price ceilings argue that government-mandated maximum prices simply reduce producers' profits and do not affect the quantity supplied of a good on the market. What must the supply curve look like before a price ceiling does not affect quantity supplied?

Working with Numbers and Graphs

1. If the absolute price of good X is $10 and the absolute price of good Y is $14, then what is (a) the relative price of good X in terms of good Y and (b) the relative price of good Y in terms of good X?
2. Price is $10, quantity supplied is 50 units, and quantity demanded is 100 units. For every $1 rise in price, quantity supplied rises by 5 units and quantity demanded falls by 5 units. What is the equilibrium price and quantity?
3. Draw a diagram that shows a larger increase in demand than the decrease in supply.
4. Draw a diagram that shows a smaller increase in supply than the increase in demand.

5. At equilibrium in the following figure, what area(s) does consumers' surplus equal? producers' surplus?

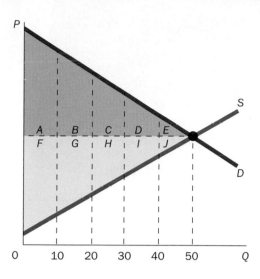

6. At what quantity in the preceding figure is the maximum buying price equal to the minimum selling price?

7. Diagrammatically explain why there are no exchanges in the area where the supply curve is above the demand curve.

8. In the following figure, can the movement from point 1 to point 2 be explained by a combination of an increase in the price of a substitute and a decrease in the price of nonlabor resources? Explain your answer.

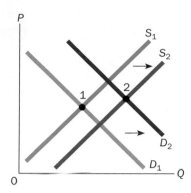

9. The demand curve is downward-sloping, the supply curve is upward-sloping, and the equilibrium quantity is 50 units. Show on a graph that the difference between the maximum buying price and minimum selling price is greater at 25 units than at 33 units.

10. Diagrammatically show and explain why a price ceiling that is above the equilibrium price will not prompt a tie-in sale.

Internet Activities

Go to *http://w3.access.gpo.gov/eop/* and make sure that the button next to the 2002 Economic Report is clicked. In the Search box, key "B-60" and then click "SUBMIT." From the results, find Table B-60, "Consumer Price Indexes for Major Expenditure Classes," and click the "TXT" icon. Assume the numbers listed are the generic prices for the goods. Also, a food number of 100 last year and of 120 this year means that food prices have risen by 20 percent.

1. Did the price of housing rise in 2001? Draw two different supply and demand diagrams that could account for the change in the price of housing. If the number of houses sold increased, which of your diagrams more likely represents the market?

2. Assume the number of houses sold increased and we know the costs of production rose as well. Draw a supply and demand diagram that shows the changes in both supply and demand that are necessary to explain the data.

3. Which is rising faster, the price of housing or the price of transportation? Are housing and transportation substitutes? (If I work where houses are expensive, can I lower my housing costs by driving from somewhere else? Can I cut my driving costs by living closer to work?) If they are substitutes, what do you think will happen in the housing and transportation markets in the future?

4. What is happening to the price of medical care relative to other goods and services? Are there substitutes for medical care? What is the likely impact on other markets (specify which markets) of the rising costs of medical care?

Log on to the Arnold Xtra! Web site now (*http://arnoldxtra.swcollege.com*) for additional learning resources such as practice quizzes, help with graphing, video clips, and current event applications.

ch.4

SUPPLY AND DEMAND: PRACTICE

The last chapter presented the theory of supply and demand. You learned about demand, supply, the law of demand, the law of supply, the factors that can change demand, the factors that can change supply, and so on. The theory of supply and demand is of little use if you cannot apply it. This chapter applies that theory to explain such things as gold prices, gas prices, health care, getting a seat at a Las Vegas show, being admitted to college, traffic congestion on a freeway, and much more.

Chapter Road Map

Most of what economists do is explain and predict.

For example, they might explain why interest rates went up,

why house prices went down, or why economic growth wasn't as rapid in

one decade as in another. They might predict what will happen to the federal budget

in the next few years, at what rate the price level will rise over the next year, or if the unemploy-

ment rate will rise or fall.

To assist them in their explanations and predictions, economists use theories. One theory widely used

by economists to explain and predict is the theory of supply and demand.

Each of the 21 applications in this chapter asks a specific question and each uses the theory of supply and demand to

either explain something or predict something. As you read the applications, ask yourself two questions: (1) What question is

being asked and answered? (2) Is the theory of supply and demand being used to explain something or to predict something?

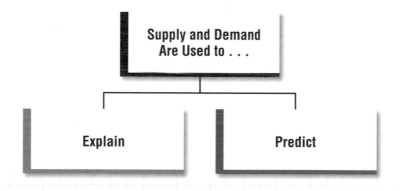

The first thought many economists have about any question is to ask themselves how it fits into the notion of supply and demand. . . . I am a supply-and-demand economist. When I come across something, I ask myself what is being transferred here and where does the supply come from and where does the demand come from.[1]

—Robert Solow
Winner of the 1987 Nobel Prize in Economics

APPLICATION 1: WHY DO COLLEGES USE GPAs, ACTs, AND SATs FOR PURPOSES OF ADMISSION?

At many colleges and universities, a student pays part of the price of his or her education (by way of tuition payments) and taxpayers and private donors pay part (by way of tax payments and charitable donations, respectively). Thus, the tuition that students pay to attend colleges and universities is usually less than the equilibrium tuition. To illustrate, suppose a student pays tuition T_1 at a given college or university. As shown in Exhibit 1, T_1 is below the equilibrium tuition, T_E. At T_1, the number of students who want to attend the university (N_1) is greater than the number of openings at the university (N_2); that is, quantity demanded is greater than quantity supplied. The university receives more applications for admission than there are places available. Something has to be done. But what?

The college or university is likely to ration its available space by a combination of money price and some other nonprice rationing devices. The student must pay the tuition, T_1, *and* meet the standards of the nonprice rationing devices. Colleges and universities usually use such things as GPAs (grade point averages), ACT scores, and SAT scores as rationing devices.

THINKING LIKE AN ECONOMIST

The layperson sees a university that requires a GPA of 3.8 and an SAT score of 1100 or better for admission. An economist sees a rationing device. The economist then

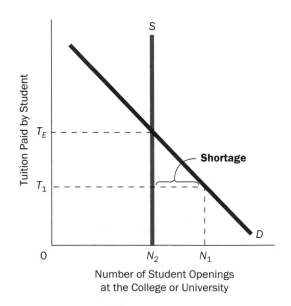

exhibit 1

College and University Admissions
If the college or university charges T_1 in tuition (when T_E is the equilibrium tuition), a shortage will be generated. The college or university will then use some nonprice rationing device, such as GPAs, ACTs, and SATs, as admission criteria.

---

1. Interview with Robert Solow. The entire interview is in *Economics* by Roger A. Arnold (St. Paul, Minnesota: West Publishing Company, 1992).

goes on to ask why this particular nonprice rationing device is being used. He reasons that there would be no need for a nonprice rationing device if (dollar) price were fully rationing the good or service.

Self-Test *(Answers to Self-Test questions are in the Self-Test Appendix.)*

1. Suppose the demand rises for admission to a university but both the tuition and the number of openings in the entering class remain the same. Will this affect the admission standards of the university? Explain your answer.

2. Administrators and faculty at state colleges and universities often say that their standards of admission are independent of whether there is a shortage or surplus of openings at the university. Do you think this is true? Do you think that faculty and administrators ignore surpluses and shortages of openings when setting admission standards? Explain your answer.

APPLICATION 2: CAN PREJUDICE AFFECT WAGES?

Suppose there are three groups of people, *A*, *B*, and *C*. The members of group *A* are always employers and the members of groups *B* and *C* are always employees. The employers in group *A* have no hiring preference for either group of employees. Let's assume that there are 100 members of group *B* and 100 members of group *C* and that the members of groups *B* and *C* are equally productive workers. Because the workers in groups *B* and *C* are equally productive and because employers show no preference for hiring one group of workers over the other, the demand for group B workers is the same as the demand for group *C* workers. As Exhibit 2a and b show, when the demand for and supply of *B* and *C* workers is the same, each *B* and *C* worker receives a wage rate of W_1.

Now suppose some (but not all) employers in group *A* become prejudiced against the members of group *B*. Let's call this subset of employers the *discriminator employers.*

The discriminator employers do not want to hire group *B* workers. As a result, the demand for *B* workers falls, and as shown in Exhibit 2c, the demand curve for *B* workers shifts leftward from D_{B_1} to D_{B_2}. For a given supply curve (S_{B_1}), the wage rate for *B* workers falls. Thus, apparently, employer prejudice results in lower wages for the group at which the prejudice is directed.

However, some economists point out that the story may not end here. They argue that in competitive product markets, the discriminator employers might be forced out of business by the nondiscriminator employers. Why might this happen?

exhibit 2

Employer Prejudice and Wages
Group *A* consists of employers, and groups *B* and *C* consist of equally productive workers. Part (a) shows the market for *B* workers. Part (b) shows the market for *C* workers. In each market the equilibrium wage rate is W_1. Later, some employers become prejudiced against *B* workers and no longer hire *B* workers. As a result, the demand curve for *B* workers shifts leftward from D_{B_1} to D_{B_2}, as shown in (c). The wage rate in the market for *B* workers falls from W_1 to W_2. Now, nondiscriminator employers may hire more *B* workers because *B* workers are as productive as *C* workers but work at a lower wage rate. As a result, the labor costs of the nondiscriminator employers fall. Nondiscriminator employers are able to lower their prices and, thus, force their discriminator competitors out of business. The prejudice that discriminator employers expressed toward *B* workers may eventually adversely affect these employers.

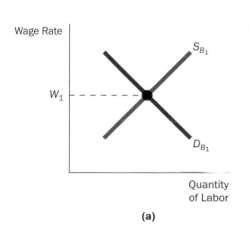

(a)

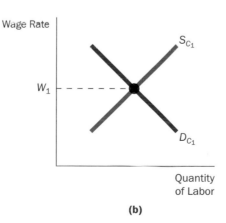

(b)

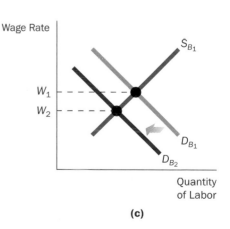

(c)

Let's look at how the prejudice of some employers might affect the nondiscriminator employers. The nondiscriminator employers realize that *B* and *C* workers are equally productive, but that it costs less to hire *B* workers than it does to hire *C* workers. So, nondiscriminator employers start to hire more *B* workers, and as a result, their labor costs decline. The nondiscriminator employers can now lower the price of their product and, thus, force their prejudiced competitors out of business. In other words, the prejudice that discriminator employers earlier expressed in the labor market might eventually adversely affect them.

Self-Test

1. If B workers are more productive than C workers, will the demand for B workers be greater than, less than, or the same as the demand for C workers?

2. How can a discriminator employer be hurt by his discriminatory actions?

APPLICATION 3: WHAT WILL HAPPEN TO THE PRICE OF MARIJUANA IF THE PURCHASE AND SALE OF MARIJUANA ARE LEGALIZED?

In the United States, the purchase or sale of marijuana is unlawful. However, there is still a demand for and supply of marijuana. There is also an equilibrium price of marijuana. Let's say that price is P_1.

Suppose that beginning tomorrow, the purchase and sale of marijuana become legal. Would P_1 rise, fall, or remain the same?

The answer, of course, depends on what we think will happen to the demand for and supply of marijuana. If the purchase and sale of marijuana are legal, then some people currently producing corn and wheat might choose instead to produce and sell marijuana. So, the supply of marijuana would rise. If nothing else changes, the price of marijuana would fall.

But something else is likely to change. If marijuana consumption is no longer illegal, then the number of people who want to buy and consume marijuana will likely rise. In other words, there will be more buyers of marijuana. This will increase the demand for marijuana.

Thus, decriminalizing the purchase and sale of marijuana is likely to shift both the marijuana demand and supply curves to the right. If the demand curve shifts to the right by the same amount as the supply curve shifts to the right, the price of marijuana will not change. If the demand curve shifts to the right by more than the supply curve shifts to the right, the price of marijuana will rise. If the supply curve shifts to the right by more than the demand curve shifts to the right, the price of marijuana will fall.

Q & A **Q:** So the price of marijuana may stay the same, rise, or fall, depending on how much the demand for marijuana rises relative to how much the supply of marijuana rises. But what will happen to the equilibrium quantity of marijuana? Will it rise, fall, or stay the same?

A: It will rise. If demand and supply rise, the new equilibrium quantity will be greater than the old equilibrium quantity. Draw it and see.

Self-Test

1. What will happen to the price of marijuana if the supply of increases by more than the demand for it?

2. What will happen to the quantity of marijuana (purchased and sold) if the demand for marijuana rises by more than the supply of marijuana falls?

APPLICATION 4: THE MINIMUM WAGE LAW

Recall that a price floor is a legislated minimum price below which trades cannot legally be made. The *minimum wage* is a price floor—a government-mandated minimum price for labor. It affects the market for unskilled labor. In Exhibit 3, the minimum wage is W_M and the equilibrium wage is W_E. At the equilibrium wage, N_1 workers are employed. At the higher minimum wage, N_3 workers want to work but only N_2 actually do work. There is a surplus of workers equal to $N_3 - N_2$ in this unskilled labor market. In addition, fewer workers are working at the minimum wage (N_2) than at the equilibrium wage (N_1). Overall, the effects of the minimum wage are (1) a surplus of unskilled workers and (2) fewer workers employed.

Suppose two economists decide to test the theory that as the minimum wage rises some unskilled workers will lose their jobs. They look at the number of unskilled workers before and after the minimum wage is raised, and, surprisingly, they find that the number of unskilled workers is the same. Do you think this is sufficient evidence to say that an increase in the minimum wage does not cause some workers to lose their jobs?

We'll leave that question hanging while we consider whether or not the economists have adequately tested their theory. Suppose instead of focusing on the number of people who lose their jobs, they look at the people who keep their jobs but have their hours reduced as a result of the higher minimum wage.

Let's look at an example. Suppose a local hardware store currently employs David and Francesca to work after school cleaning up and stocking the store. The owner of the store pays each of them the minimum wage of, say, $5.15 an hour. Then, the minimum wage is raised to $6.75 an hour. Will either David or

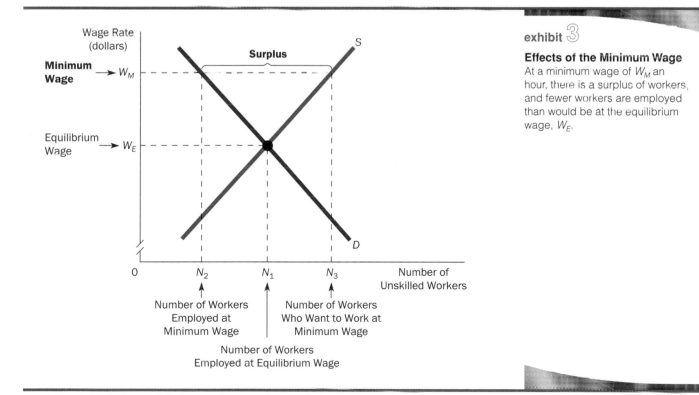

exhibit 3

Effects of the Minimum Wage
At a minimum wage of W_M an hour, there is a surplus of workers, and fewer workers are employed than would be at the equilibrium wage, W_E.

Francesca lose their jobs as a result? Not necessarily. Instead, the owner of the store could reduce the number of hours he employs the two workers. For example, instead of having each of them work 20 hours a week, he might ask each to work only 14 hours a week.[2]

Now, let's reconsider our original question: Has the higher minimum wage eliminated jobs? In a way, no. It has, however, reduced the number of hours a person works in a job. (Of course, if we define a job as including both a particular task and a certain number of hours completing that task, then the minimum wage increase has eliminated "part" of the job.) This discussion argues for changing the label on the horizontal axis in Exhibit 3 from "Number of Unskilled Workers" to "Number of Unskilled Labor Hours."

Q & A

Q: Isn't the minimum wage necessary to guarantee everybody a decent wage? If the minimum wage didn't exist, wouldn't employers hire workers for next to nothing?

A: Employers may want to hire workers for "next to nothing," but the wages workers receive depend on the demand for and supply of labor. In other words, employers do not set wages at whatever level they like. In a competitive market setting, the forces of supply and demand determine equilibrium wages.

As to the minimum wage guaranteeing a decent wage, suppose Johnny Bates, a 17-year-old in Chicago, finds that his labor is worth $5.00 an hour to employers. If the government mandates that Johnny must be paid $6.00 an hour ($1.00 more an hour than he's currently worth to employers), no employer will hire him. So the minimum wage does not guarantee Johnny a decent wage; in fact, it may guarantee him no wage.

THINKING LIKE AN ECONOMIST

In economics, some questions relate to "direction" and some to "magnitude." For example, suppose someone asks, "If the demand for labor is downward-sloping and the labor market is competitive, how will a minimum wage (above the equilibrium wage) affect employment?" This person is asking a question that relates to the direction of the change in employment. Usually, these types of questions can be answered by applying a theory. Applying the theory of demand, an economist might say, "At higher wages, the quantity demanded of labor, or the employment level, will be lower than at lower wages." The word "lower" speaks to the directional change in employment.

Now suppose someone asks, "How much will employment decline?" This person is asking a question that relates to magnitude. Usually, questions that deal with magnitude can be answered only through some kind of empirical (data-collecting and analyzing) work. In other words, we would have to collect employment figures at the equilibrium wage and at the minimum wage and then find the difference.

Self-Test

1. When the labor supply curve is upward-sloping, a minimum wage law that sets the wage rate above its equilibrium level creates a surplus of labor. If the labor supply curve is vertical, does a surplus of labor still occur? Explain your answer.

2. Someone says that an increase in the minimum wage will not cause firms to hire fewer workers. What is this person assuming?

---

2. Our two economists need to find data that relate not only to how many, if any, people lose their jobs as a result of the higher minimum wage, but also how many people who keep their jobs end up working fewer hours.

APPLICATION 5: PRICE CEILING
IN THE KIDNEY MARKET

Just as there are people who want to buy houses, computers, and books, there are people who want to buy kidneys. These people have kidney failure and either will die without a new kidney or will have to endure years of costly and painful dialysis. This demand for kidneys is shown as D_K in Exhibit 4.

The supply of kidneys is shown as S_K in Exhibit 4. Notice that at $0 price, the quantity supplied of kidneys is 350. These kidneys are from people who donate their kidneys to others, asking nothing in return. They may donate their kidneys upon their death or may donate one of their two kidneys while living. We have drawn the supply curve as upward-sloping because we assume that some people who today are unwilling to donate a kidney for $0 might be willing to do so for some positive dollar amount. Specifically, we assume that as the price of a kidney rises, the quantity supplied of kidneys will rise.

If there were a free market in kidneys, the price of a kidney would be P_1 in Exhibit 4. At this price, 1,000 kidneys would be purchased and sold—1,000 kidney transplants would occur.

Today, there is no free market in kidneys. Buying or selling kidneys is illegal at any dollar amount. In essence, then, there is a price ceiling in the kidney market and the ceiling is set at $0. What is the effect of this price ceiling?

If the demand curve for kidneys and the supply curve of kidneys intersected at $0, there would be neither a surplus nor a shortage of kidneys. But there is evidence that the demand and supply curves do not intersect at $0; they look more like those shown in Exhibit 4. In other words, there is a shortage of kidneys at $0: the quantity supplied of kidneys is 350 and the quantity demanded is 1,500. (Although these are not the actual numbers of kidneys demanded and supplied at $0, they are representative of the current situation in the kidney market.)

The last chapter describes the possible effects of a price ceiling set below equilibrium price: shortages, nonprice rationing devices, fewer exchanges, tie-in sales, and buying and selling at prohibited prices (in other words, illegal trades). Are any of these effects occurring in the kidney market?

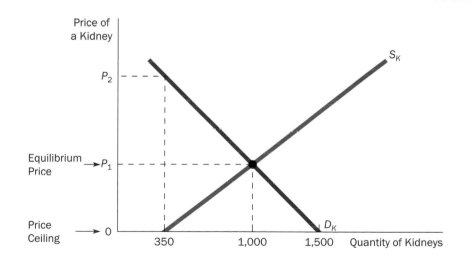

exhibit 4

The Market for Kidneys
We have identified the demand for kidneys as D_K and the supply of kidneys as S_K. Given the demand for and supply of kidneys, the equilibrium price of a kidney is P_1. It does not follow, though, that simply because there is an equilibrium price, people will be allowed to trade at this price. Today, it is unlawful to buy and sell kidneys at any positive price. In short, there is a price ceiling in the kidney market and the ceiling is $0. At the price ceiling, there is a shortage of kidneys, a nonprice rationing device for kidneys (first-come-first-served), fewer kidney transplants (than there would be at P_1), and illegal purchases and sales of kidneys.

First, there is evidence of a shortage. In almost every country in the world, there are more people on national lists who want a kidney than there are kidneys available. Some of these people die waiting for a kidney.

Second, as just indicated, the nonprice rationing device used in the kidney market is (largely) first-come-first-served. A person who wants a kidney registers on a national waiting list. How long one waits is a function of how far down the list one's name appears.

Third, there are fewer exchanges; not everyone who needs a kidney gets a kidney. With a price ceiling of $0, only 350 kidneys are supplied. All these kidneys are from people who freely donate their kidneys. If P_1 were permitted, some people who are unwilling to supply a kidney (at $0) would be willing to do so. In short, monetary payment would provide the incentive for some people to supply a kidney. At P_1, 1,000 kidneys are demanded and supplied, so more people would get kidney transplants when the price of a kidney is P_1 (1,000 in total) than when the price of a kidney is $0 (350 in total). More transplants, of course, means fewer people die waiting for a kidney.

Fourth, kidneys are bought and sold at prohibited prices. People buy and sell kidneys today; they just do so illegally. There are stories of people who need kidneys paying between $25,000 and $200,000 for a kidney.

Some people argue that a free market in kidneys would be wrong. Such a system would place the poor at a disadvantage. Think of it: A rich person who needed a kidney could buy the kidney he needed, but a poor person could not. The rich person would get a second chance at life, the poor person would not. No one particularly enjoys contemplating this stark reality.

But consider another stark reality. If it is unlawful to pay someone for a kidney, fewer kidneys will be forthcoming. In other words, the quantity supplied of kidneys is less at $0 than at, say, $20,000. Fewer kidneys supplied means, in turn, fewer kidney transplants. And fewer kidney transplants means more people will die from kidney failure.

Q & A

Q: Do economists have to analyze the price of *everything?* A price for a house is all right, but a price for a kidney is unsettling.

A: Economists simply (1) determine whether an equilibrium price exists and then (2) identify the effects of the equilibrium price (a) being the legal price and (b) not being the legal price. In the kidney market, whether we like it or not, there exists an equilibrium price for kidneys. But just because it exists, it doesn't follow that people will be allowed to legally trade at this price. The economist identifies the pricing effects in two different settings. In one setting, the legal price is not the equilibrium price; in the other setting, the legal price is the equilibrium price. That's the extent of the economist's work.

Self-Test

1. A shortage of kidneys for transplants is a consequence of the price of a kidney being below equilibrium price. Do you agree or disagree? Explain your answer.

2. Suppose the price ceiling in the kidney market is $0. Will there be a shortage of kidneys? Explain your answer.

APPLICATION 6: CRISIS IN THE ELECTRICITY MARKET

In 2001, some California residents and businesses endured electricity blackouts; they had to do without electricity for one or two hours a day. During these hours, they couldn't run air conditioners, turn on lights, watch television, and so on.

In economic terms, a blackout is simply a shortage—the quantity demanded of a good or service is greater than the quantity supplied of the good or service.

During the blackouts in California, Californians wanted to buy more electricity than there was electricity available.

But why was there a shortage of electricity? Why were there blackouts? The answer has to do with supply, demand, and price.

In California, as in other states, some companies are power distributors and other companies are power generators. A power generator generates electricity. It then sells the electricity it has generated to a power distributor, which in turn sells the electricity to consumers.

Essentially, there are two electricity markets in California. The first market, shown in Exhibit 5a, is the retail electricity market. The demand for retail electricity comes from individuals and businesses. The supply of this electricity comes from the power distributors.

The second market, shown in Exhibit 5b, is the wholesale electricity market. The demand for wholesale electricity comes from the power distributors, and the supply of this electricity comes from the power generators.

Let's suppose that both markets are currently at point 1 in parts (a) and (b). In this case, power distributors buy electricity in the wholesale electricity market for P_1 and then turn around and sell it in the retail electricity market for P_1. For example, they might buy electricity for 10 cents a kilowatt hour and sell it for 10 cents a kilowatt hour. (If you want the power distributors to sell electricity for a price a few cents more than the price they pay for the electricity, it does not change the analysis.)

Now suppose a state law is passed that places a price ceiling on retail electricity but not on wholesale electricity. For example, let's say the price ceiling on retail electricity is set at P_1 (in Exhibit 5a) and the price of wholesale electricity is

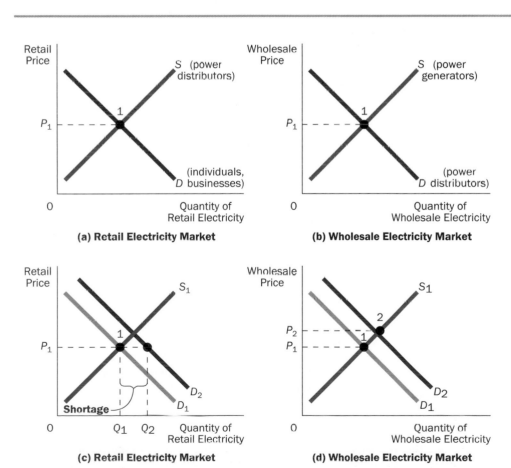

(a) Retail Electricity Market

(b) Wholesale Electricity Market

(c) Retail Electricity Market

(d) Wholesale Electricity Market

exhibit 5

Supply, Demand, and the Electricity Market
Part (a) shows the retail electricity market; part (b) shows the wholesale electricity market. The demand for electricity in the retail market comes from individuals and businesses; the supply comes from power distributors. The demand for electricity in the wholesale market comes from power distributors; the supply comes from power generators.

In 1996, the California legislature passed a law that set a ceiling on the retail price of electricity but allowed the wholesale price of electricity to be determined by supply and demand. What happens if demand for electricity rises in the retail market, as shown in (c)? Increased demand in the retail market causes increased demand in the wholesale market, as shown in (d). The wholesale price of electricity rises to P_2, but the retail price is prevented by law from rising. As a result, there is a shortage of electricity in the retail market. Shortages show up as blackouts.

determined by the forces of supply and demand. In essence, the retail electricity market is a controlled market, and the wholesale electricity market is a free market. To a large degree, this is exactly the situation in California because of a state law passed in 1996.

No problems ensue, of course, as long as the demand and supply curves remain as they are in parts (a) and (b). But suppose they change, as they did in California.

Suppose the demand for retail electricity rises from D_1 to D_2, as shown in part (c). A higher demand for retail electricity (coming from individuals and businesses) will cause power distributors to demand more generated electricity in the wholesale electricity market. So demand in that market rises from D_1 to D_2, as shown in part (d). As a result, the wholesale price of electricity rises to P_2.

Now power distributors must pay P_2 for the electricity they buy—but they must continue to sell electricity in the retail market at the price ceiling, P_1. At P_1 in the retail market, quantity demanded of electricity (Q_2) is greater than quantity supplied (Q_1); in other words, there is a shortage of electricity. Shortages of electricity are manifested as blackouts.

In reality, rising demand in the retail and wholesale electricity markets wasn't the only change in California. Supply changed, too. Supply changed because natural gas prices increased fourfold in 2000. Many of the power plants that generate electricity are fueled by natural gas. The increase in natural gas prices made generating electricity more expensive and shifted the supply curve of electricity (in the wholesale electricity market) to the left. As a result, the wholesale price of electricity was driven up even further.

Daniel McFadden, who won the Nobel Prize in Economics in 2000, summed up the electricity crisis in California: "The source of the [electricity] crisis was rigid regulation of retail prices in the face of rapid increases in wholesale prices driven by increased fuel prices and increased demand in the national electricity market."[3]

Self-Test

1. Retail and wholesale electricity markets are in equilibrium, as shown in Exhibit 5a and b. In addition, there is a price ceiling in the retail market, set at P_1, but no price ceiling in the wholesale market. Finally, fuel costs rise, causing the supply of electricity in the wholesale market to shift left. What happens to the wholesale price of electricity? What happens to the supply of electricity in the retail market? Is there a shortage, surplus, or equilibrium in the retail market? Explain your answer.

2. In our discussion, there was a price ceiling in the retail electricity market but not in the wholesale market. Suppose there had been. Specifically, suppose the price ceiling had been set at P_1 in both markets (shown in Exhibit 5a and b). Would this have averted the blackouts?

APPLICATION 7: IF GOLD PRICES ARE THE SAME EVERYWHERE, THEN WHY AREN'T HOUSE PRICES?

The price of an ounce of gold is the same everywhere in the world. For example, the price of an ounce of gold is the same in London as it is in New York City. House prices are not the same everywhere, though. For example, the median price of a house in Los Angeles, California, is higher than the median price of a house in Dubuque, Iowa. Why are gold prices the same everywhere while house prices are different?

To answer the question, let's look at what would happen if gold prices were not the same everywhere in the world. Let's assume the price of an ounce of

---

3. Daniel McFadden, "California Needs Deregulation Done Right," *Wall Street Journal,* 13 February 2001.

gold is $250 in London and $300 in New York City. What happens? Obviously this difference in prices for the same good presents a profit opportunity. People will buy gold in London for $250 an ounce, ship it to New York City, and sell it for $300 an ounce. If we ignore the costs of transporting the gold, a $50 profit per ounce is earned. When an opportunity exists for profit—by buying low and selling high—individuals are quick to try to capture the profit.

As gold is moved from London to New York in search of profit, the supply of gold in London will fall and the supply of gold in New York will rise. A falling gold supply in London will push up the price of gold (from $250), and a rising gold supply in New York will push down the price of gold (from $300). As the London gold price rises and the New York gold price falls, a point will eventually be reached where the two prices are the same. When the London price and New York price for gold are the same, profit cannot be earned by moving gold from London to New York. In short, any difference in the price of gold in various locations will quickly be eliminated by changes in the supply of gold in the various locations.

Can the same hold for houses? If the price of a house in Los Angeles is higher than the price of a house in Dubuque, is it possible to move houses and land from Dubuque to Los Angeles? Of course not. We can't pick up a house and its lot in Dubuque and move them to Los Angeles, in the process reducing the supply of houses and land in Dubuque and increasing the supply of houses and land in Los Angeles. Because the supply of houses and land cannot be reshuffled the way the supply of gold can be, we expect differences in house prices in various locations but not differences in gold prices.

Self-Test

1. What causes the price of gold to be the same in New York and London?
2. The price of a Toyota Camry is nearly the same in Miami as it is in Dallas. Why?

APPLICATION 8: GAS PRICES AFTER THE ATTACK ON THE WORLD TRADE CENTER AND THE PENTAGON

On September 11, 2001, terrorists hijacked commercial jets and flew them into the twin towers of the World Trade Center in New York City and into the Pentagon in Washington, D.C. Another hijacked jet crashed in rural Pennsylvania.

Hours after the attack, gas prices at some gas stations across the country began to rise. For example, one station in Oklahoma City raised the price of a gallon of unleaded gas from $1.68 to $5.00. A station in North Dakota raised its price of unleaded gas from $1.76 a gallon to $3.29 a gallon. A station in Illinois increased gas prices from an average of $1.88 a gallon to $4.00 a gallon.

Many people claimed that these gas stations were trying to cheat the public. Customers called Consumer Hot Lines and reported the higher prices. State officials, including the governors of many states, were fast to respond. Gas station owners were threatened with fines or lawsuits if they didn't bring gas prices back down. Prices were down in two days.

Let's consider two economic questions relevant to this incident: Why did gas prices at some stations rise? Why did prices soon return to "normal" (pre-terrorist attack) levels?

Prices might have risen because some gas station owners mistakenly thought that as a result of the terrorist attack, the demand for gas had increased and the supply of gas would soon decrease. Recall that expectation of future price is one factor that can change the current demand for a good. A gas station owner may have reasoned this way: Because of the terrorist attack, some Americans may expect a higher price for gas in the future. If they expect a higher future price, they will increase the current demand for gas. If the current demand for gas rises, price will rise.

Expectation of future price can also change the supply of a good. Again, a gas station owner could have reasoned this way: The terrorist attack may cause (my) gas suppliers to expect a higher price for gas in the future. If they expect a higher future price, they will prefer to sell gas later instead of now. The current supply of gas will fall. If the current supply of gas falls, price will rise.

Thus, expecting higher demand and lower supply, some gas station owners posted higher gas prices.

But were their expectations correct? We think not. Keep in mind that when some gas station owners were raising gas prices, many others were not. It was not uncommon for one station to be selling gas at $4.00 a gallon while a station across the street was selling gas at $1.88 a gallon. What would you think if you were the gas station owner who had posted the $4.00-a-gallon price? Would you think that people were going to see your higher price and come to your station? Or would you think that maybe your price was too high? Would you realize that the demand for gas hadn't increased and that the supply of gas wasn't likely to decrease?

If you're greedy—and no one accused the gas station owners in question of being anything but greedy—you wouldn't want to lose business by posting a price that was too high.

Some people argue that prices returned to "normal" levels because gas station owners were threatened with fines and lawsuits. But even without consumer complaints and the threat of fines and lawsuits, these gas station owners would have lowered prices to previous levels. Not lowering prices would have invited economic loss. If you think supply and demand have changed and most of the world (in the form of your competitors) is telling you that it hasn't, then your misperception of reality may be costly to you.

In the end, real supply and demand determined the price of gas, not the demand and supply some gas station owners imagined.

Q & A

Q: Can you give another example of a seller who thinks the equilibrium price of a good is higher than it actually is?

A: Consider a person who decides to sell her house. Suppose the equilibrium price for houses similar to hers is $200,000. If the house seller does not know this, she may post a price of $250,000, thinking it is the equilibrium price. With time, though, she will learn that her price of $250,000 is too high. At her price, there is a surplus of her house: there is one seller and no buyers. Eventually, she will drop the price until the house sells.

This example is really the same as the gas station example. In that example, gas station owners thought equilibrium prices were higher than they were. In time, the gas station owners learned. In the house example, the house seller thinks the equilibrium price is higher than it is. In time, she will learn.

The lesson here is a simple one: Prices are not always at their equilibrium levels, but they are always *moving toward* their equilibrium levels.

Self-Test

1. Carl argues that higher prices are caused by greed, not supply and demand (demand rises or supply falls). What might be wrong with the greed explanation of higher prices?

2. Recall from the last chapter that demand changes if income, preferences, prices of related goods, number of buyers, or expectations of future price change. Which factor is particularly relevant during a disaster? Explain your answer.

APPLICATION 9: HEALTH CARE AND THE RIGHT TO SUE YOUR HMO

A discussion of renters, landlords, and eviction notices is relevant to the right to sue an HMO. So, we begin with an analysis of two laws related to eviction of a renter. Under law 1, a renter has 30 days to vacate an apartment after being served with an eviction notice. Under law 2, the renter has 90 days to evacuate.

Landlords will find it less expensive to rent apartments under law 1 than under law 2. Under law 1, the most money a landlord can lose after serving an eviction notice is 30 days' rent. Under law 2, a landlord can lose 90 days' rent. Obviously, losing 90 days' rent is more costly than losing 30 days' rent.

A different supply curve of apartments exists under each law. The supply curve under law 1 (S_1 in Exhibit 6) will lie to the right of the supply curve under law 2 (S_2 in the exhibit). Again, that's because it is less expensive to supply apartments under law 1 than under law 2.

If the supply curve is different under the two laws, the equilibrium rent will be different too. As shown in Exhibit 6, the supply curve under law 1 lies to the right of the supply curve under law 2, so the equilibrium rent will be lower under law 1 (R_1) than under law 2 (R_2).

In conclusion, under law 1, a renter pays lower rent (good) and has fewer days to vacate the apartment (bad). Under law 2, a renter pays a higher rent (bad) and has more days to vacate the apartment (good). Who pays for the additional days to vacate the apartment under law 2? The renter pays for these additional days by paying higher rent.

Now let's turn from apartments to health care. You may frequently hear people complain about their health maintenance organizations (HMOs). The complaints are diverse and wide-ranging. One common complaint is that patients cannot sue their HMOs in state and federal courts for denial of benefits and poor-quality care.

Some people argue that patients should have the right to sue their HMOs. Let's consider two settings: one in which patients cannot sue their HMOs and one in which patients can sue.

An HMO's liability cost is lower if patients cannot sue than if they can sue. A difference in liability costs will be reflected in different supply curves. To illustrate,

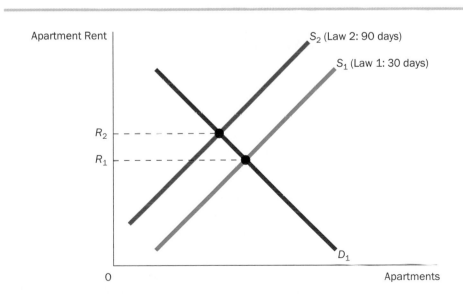

Apartment Rent / Apartments

S_2 (Law 2: 90 days)

S_1 (Law 1: 30 days)

R_2

R_1

D_1

0

exhibit 6

Apartment Rent and the Law
Under law 1, a renter has 30 days to leave an apartment after receiving an eviction notice from his or her landlord. Under law 2, a renter has 90 days to leave an apartment after receiving an eviction notice from his or her landlord. The cost to the landlord of renting an apartment is higher under law 2 than law 1, and so the supply curve of apartments under law 1 lies to the right of the supply curve of apartments under law 2. Different supply curves mean different rents. Apartment rent is higher under law 2 (R_2) than under law 1 (R_1).

recall that any single point on a supply curve is the minimum price sellers need to receive before they would be willing and able to sell that particular unit of a good.

Suppose when patients cannot sue, an HMO is willing and able to provide health care to John for $300 a month. If patients can sue, is the HMO still willing and able to provide health care to John for $300 a month? Not likely. Because of the higher liability cost due to the patient's ability to sue, the HMO is no longer willing and able to provide health care to John for $300 month. It will, however, be willing and able to provide health care to John for, say, $350 a month.

Saying a seller's minimum price for providing a good or service rises is the same as saying the seller's supply curve has shifted upward and to the left. In other words, the supply curve of HMO-provided health care will shift upward and to the left if patients have the right to sue. This is the same way the supply curve of apartments moved in Exhibit 6.

Will a difference in supply curves affect the price patients pay for their HMO-provided health care coverage? Yes. One effect of moving from a setting where patients do not have the right to sue to one where patients do have the right to sue is that patients will have to pay more for their HMO-provided health care coverage.

Economists don't determine whether patients having the right to sue is good or bad or right or wrong. Economists use their tools (in this instance, supply and demand) to point out that things people want, such as the right to sue their HMOs, often come with price tags. Individuals must decide whether the price they pay is worth what they receive in return.

Self-Test

1. Economists often say, "There is no such thing as a free lunch." How is this saying related to patients moving from a system where they cannot sue their HMOs to one where they can?

2. A professor tells her students that they can have an extra week to complete their research papers. Under what condition are the students made better off with the extra week? Can you think of a case where the students would actually be made worse off by the extra week?

APPLICATION 10: DO YOU PAY FOR THINGS EVEN WHEN THERE IS NO EXPLICIT PRICE? OR, DO YOU PAY FOR GOOD WEATHER?

Some places in the country are considered to have better weather than other places have. For example, most people would say the weather in San Diego, California, is better than the weather in Fargo, North Dakota. Often, a person in San Diego will say, "You can't beat the weather today. And the good thing about it is that you don't have to pay a thing for it. It's free."

In one sense, the San Diegan is correct: There is no weather market. Specifically, no one comes around and asks San Diegans to pay a certain dollar amount for the weather on a given day.

But in another sense, the San Diegan is incorrect. Fact is, San Diegans indirectly pay for their good weather. How do they pay? To enjoy the weather in San Diego on a regular basis, you have to live in San Diego—you have to have housing. There is a demand for housing in San Diego, just as there is a demand for housing in other places. Is the demand for housing in San Diego higher than it would be if the weather were not so good? Without the good weather, living in San Diego would not be as pleasurable and, therefore, the demand to live there would be lower. In short, the demand for housing in San Diego is higher because San Diego enjoys good weather. It follows that the price of housing is higher too. Thus, San Diegans indirectly pay for their good weather because they pay higher housing prices than they would if San Diego had bad weather.

Was our representative San Diegan right when he said the good weather was free?

Self-Test

1. Give an example to illustrate that someone may "pay" for clean air in much the same way that she "pays" for good weather.

2. If people pay for good weather, who ultimately receives the "good-weather payment"?

APPLICATION 11: PAYING ALL PROFESSORS THE SAME SALARY

In college, you take various courses. You may take courses in accounting, economics, English, and history. From your perspective, the professors in the courses may do much the same work. Each professor regularly comes to class, lectures and leads discussions, holds office hours, gives tests and exams, grades those tests and exams, and so on. Does it follow, then, that all professors of equal experience ought to be paid the same salary? In other words, if a professor in computer science with 10 years of experience earns $100,000 a year, should a professor in history with 10 years of experience earn $100,000 a year too? If your answer is yes, then what might the effects of such a policy be?

Let's again turn to supply and demand for an answer. Exhibit 7a shows the market for accounting professors; Exhibit 7b, the market for history professors. In each market there is a demand for and supply of professors. However, the equilibrium wage in the accounting market (W_A) is higher than the equilibrium wage in the history market (W_H).

exhibit 7

Paying Professors the Same Salary
Suppose the market supply and demand conditions are as shown in (a) for accounting professors and as shown in (b) for history professors. Consequently, the equilibrium wage in the two markets would be different. As shown, the equilibrium wage for accounting professors (W_A) is higher than the equilibrium wage for history professors (W_H). What happens if both accounting and history professors are paid W_A? A surplus of history professors appears. What happens if both accounting and history professors are paid W_H? A shortage of accounting professors appears. Paying all college professors the same salary when there are differences in demand and supply creates shortages and surpluses.

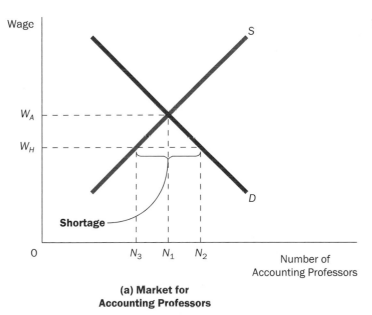

(a) Market for Accounting Professors

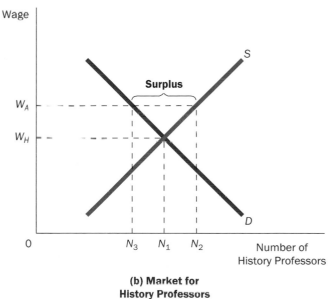

(b) Market for History Professors

Go to *http://www.colorado.edu/pba/fcq*, and click "By college, subject, and course number." Next, select "College of Arts and Sciences," and then "Economics." Look at the course evaluations for Econ 1000, which show actual student evaluations received by professors. Do some professors get higher grades from their students than other professors do? Do some professors expect less work? Are some more accessible than others? What impact do you think publishing this information will have on the quality of teaching? How might it affect the amount of work professors require of their students?

If accounting and history professors are each paid their respective equilibrium wage, neither market will be in shortage or surplus. But pay both professors the same wage when their equilibrium wages are different, and shortages or surpluses will appear.

For example, suppose both accounting and history professors are paid the higher wage, W_A. The accounting market remains in equilibrium, but a surplus appears in the history market. There will be more historians who want to work at colleges (N_2) than colleges will hire (N_3).

Or suppose both accounting and history professors are paid the lower wage, W_H. The history market remains in equilibrium, but a shortage appears in the accounting market. Colleges will want to hire more accountants (N_2) than will be willing to work at the colleges (N_3).

Sitting in class, you may think that while the supply-and-demand analysis of the accounting and history markets is interesting, it does not affect you. What does it matter if your professors are paid the same or not?

But look at the number of professors hired in each market at the equilibrium wage and at the disequilibrium wage. In the accounting market, when the wage is W_A, N_1 accounting professors are hired. At W_H, only N_3 are hired because N_3 is the number of accounting professors who are willing and able to work at W_H. N_3 is less than N_1.

In the history market, when the wage is W_H, N_1 history professors are hired. At W_A, N_3 are hired because N_3 is the number of history professors colleges are willing and able to hire at W_A. N_3 is less than N_1.

In short, more professors are working at colleges teaching students when professors are paid equilibrium wages than when they are paid disequilibrium wages. So, how professors are paid affects the student-to-faculty ratio. Instead of 40 students per faculty member at disequilibrium wages, we might have 30 students per faculty member at equilibrium wages.

Self-Test

1. Suppose the supply of biology and computer science professors is the same but the demand for computer scientists is greater than the demand for biologists. Furthermore, suppose both biologists and computer scientists are paid the same wage. If a shortage exists in both fields, in which field is the shortage greater? Explain your answer.

2. Under what condition might an economist propose that all college professors (irrespective of their field) be paid the same?

APPLICATION 12: ARE NEW CAR COMPANIES HURT BY THE USED CAR MARKET?

New car dealers sometimes complain that the used car market hurts them. They argue that the demand for new cars would be higher if the used car market did not exist. How so? Consider Shelly, who just bought a new car. She plans to keep the car for six years, after which time she will sell it on the used car market. The person who buys Shelly's used car might have bought a new car instead had the used car market not existed. In other words, without the used car market, there would be more buyers for new cars, and therefore the demand for new cars would be higher.

But new car dealers may overlook an important fact. People may have stronger preferences for a new car if a used car market exists than if it does not exist. To illustrate, suppose we ask Shelly two questions. First, "What is the maximum price you would pay for a new Honda Accord if you *could not sell* the car at a later date (in other words, if there is no used car market)?" Let's assume she answers $20,000. Second, "What is the maximum price you would pay for a new Honda Accord if you *could sell* the car at a later date (in other words, if the used car market exists)?" If her answer is more than $20,000—say, $23,000—then her demand for a new car is higher when the used car market exists than when it does not exist.

Is Shelly's maximum price for a Honda Accord likely to be higher with the used car market than without it? We think so. The ability to sell something purchased earlier is valuable to people, and they are willing to pay for this option.

In conclusion, the existence of the used car market implies (1) fewer buyers for new cars and (2) a stronger preference for new cars. Fewer buyers for new cars means a *lower demand* for new cars, but a stronger preference for new cars means a *higher demand* for new cars. Which variable affects demand more? We do not know. But certainly it is possible for the two variables to cancel each other out so that on net, the demand for new cars is the same with the used car market as without it.

Self-Test

1. Suppose a company is building new houses in an undeveloped area of a community. The local government imposes a special tax on the buyers of these new homes, the revenues of which will be used for road construction in and around the new development. The people who buy the new houses complain that no one else has to pay a special tax for road construction, so why should they? There is little doubt that they believe they pay the full tax, but do they? Explain your answer.

2. Some companies offer rebates on the goods they sell. For example, they may advertise a good for, say, $40, but then offer a $10 rebate for buying the good. They argue that this effectively reduces the price to $30 (after the rebate). Are there similarities between rebates and being able to sell your old car on the used car market?

APPLICATION 13: SUPPLY AND DEMAND ON A FREEWAY

What does a traffic jam on a busy freeway in any large city have to do with supply and demand? Actually, it has quite a bit to do with supply and demand. Look at it this way: There is a demand for driving on the freeway and a supply of freeway space. The supply of freeway space is fixed (freeways do not expand and contract over a day, week, or month). The demand, however, fluctuates. It is higher at some times than at other times. For example, we would expect the demand for driving on the freeway to be higher at 8 A.M. (rush hour) than at 11 P.M. But even though the demand may vary, the money price for driving on the freeway is always the same—zero. A zero money price means that motorists do not pay tolls to drive on the freeway.

Exhibit 8 shows two demand curves for driving on the freeway: $D_{8A.M.}$ and $D_{11P.M.}$ We have assumed the demand at 8 A.M. is greater than at 11 P.M. We have also assumed that at $D_{11P.M.}$ and zero money price the freeway market clears: Quantity demanded of freeway space equals quantity supplied of freeway space. At the higher demand, $D_{8A.M.}$, however, this is not the case. At zero money price, a shortage of freeway space exists: Quantity demanded of freeway space is greater than quantity supplied of freeway space. The shortage appears in the form of freeway congestion, bumper-to-bumper traffic. One way to eliminate the shortage is through an increase in the money price of driving on the freeway at 8 A.M. For example, as Exhibit 8 shows, a toll of 70 cents would clear the freeway market at 8 A.M.

exhibit 8

Freeway Congestion and Supply and Demand

The demand for driving on the freeway is higher at 8 A.M. than at 11 P.M. At zero money price and $D_{11P.M.}$, the freeway market clears. At zero money price and $D_{8A.M.}$, there is a shortage of freeway space, which shows up as freeway congestion. At a price (toll) of 70 cents, the shortage is eliminated and freeway congestion disappears.

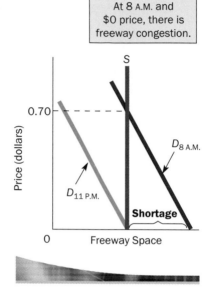

At 8 A.M. and $0 price, there is freeway congestion.

If charging different prices (tolls) at different times of the day on freeways sounds like an unusual idea, consider how Miami Beach hotels price their rooms. They charge different prices for their rooms at different times of the year. During the winter months when the demand for vacationing in Miami Beach is high, the hotels charge higher prices than when the demand is (relatively) low. If different prices were charged for freeway space at different times of the day, freeway space would be rationed the same way Miami Beach hotel rooms are rationed.

Before we leave this topic, let's consider the three alternatives usually proposed for freeway congestion. Some people propose tolls, some propose building more freeways, and others propose encouraging carpooling. Tolls deal with the congestion problem by adjusting price to its equilibrium level, as shown in Exhibit 8. Building more freeways deals with the problem by increasing supply. In Exhibit 8, it would be necessary to shift the supply curve of freeway space to the right so there is no longer any shortage of space at 8 A.M. More carpooling deals with the problem by decreasing demand. Two people in one car takes up less space on a freeway than two people in two cars. In Exhibit 8, if through carpooling the demand at 8 A.M. begins to look like the demand at 11 P.M., then there is no longer a shortage of freeway space at 8 A.M.

THINKING LIKE AN ECONOMIST

The economist knows that when there are buyers and sellers of anything (bread, cars, or freeway space), only three conditions are possible—equilibrium, shortage, or surplus. When the economist sees traffic congestion, the first thing that comes to mind is that there is a shortage of road space. Buy why is there a shortage? The economist knows that shortages occur at prices below equilibrium price. In other words, price is too low.

Self-Test

1. In Exhibit 8, at what price is there a surplus of freeway space at 8 A.M.?

2. If the driving population increases in an area and the supply of freeway space remains constant, what will happen to freeway congestion? Explain your answer.

APPLICATION 14: WHAT DOES PRICE HAVE TO DO WITH GETTING TO CLASS ON TIME?

Class starts at 10 o'clock in the morning. At 10:09, Pam Ferrario walks in late. She apologizes to the instructor, saying, "I've been on campus for 20 minutes, but I couldn't find a parking space." Her classmates nod, knowing full well what she is talking about. Here at the university, especially between the hours of 8 A.M. and 2 P.M., parking spaces are hard to find.

This scene is replayed every day at many universities and colleges across the country. Students are late for class because on many days there isn't a parking space to be found. Why can't students find parking spaces? The immediate answer is because there is a shortage of parking spaces. But why is there a shortage of parking spaces? There is a shortage of parking spaces for the same reason there is any shortage: the equilibrium price is not being charged.

Who pays for the shortage of parking spaces? The students pay—not in money, but in time. Because students know parking spaces on campus are hard to find, they often leave home or work sooner than they would if there were no shortages. Or like Pam Ferrario, they pay by being late to class.

Are there alternatives to the *pay-in-time* and *pay-in-being-late-to-class* schemes for rationing campus parking spots? Some economists have suggested a *pay-in-price* scheme. For example, the university could install meters in the parking lot and raise the fee high enough so that between the hours of 8 A.M. and 2 P.M., the quantity demanded for parking spaces equals the quantity supplied.

Such suggestions are sometimes criticized on the basis that students must pay the fee, no matter how high, in order to attend classes. But that's not exactly true. Parking off campus and using public transportation are sometimes alternatives. But this is not really the main point. The issue isn't paying or not paying, but choosing *how* to pay—in dollar price, time, or being late for class.

Some economists have taken the pay-in-price scheme further and have argued that parking spots should be auctioned on a yearly basis. In other words, a student would rent a parking spot for a year. This way the student would always know that a parking spot would be open when he or she arrived at the campus. People who parked in someone else's spot would be ticketed by campus police.

Additionally, under this scheme, a student who rented a parking spot and chose not to use it between certain hours of the day could rent it to someone else during this period. So we would expect to see notices like this on campus billboards:

PARKING SPOT FOR RENT
Near Arts Building and Student Union. Ideal for liberal arts students. Available on a 2–12 hour basis between 12 noon and 12 midnight. Rate: 50 cents per hour. Call 555-3564.

THINKING LIKE AN
ECONOMIST

The economist knows that just because someone doesn't pay a price in money terms, it doesn't mean there is no price to pay. People can pay for something in time. In fact, when money prices are below equilibrium levels, individuals usually pay in terms of something else (such as time).

Self-Test

1. If a person pays for something in terms of time, he or she is really paying in terms of money. Do you agree or disagree? Explain your answer.

2. Suppose at the price of $1 a day for parking, quantity supplied is equal to quantity demanded. What happens if the demand for parking rises more than the supply of parking and the price of parking is kept constant at $1 a day?

APPLICATION 15: AISLE SEATS ON COMMERCIAL AIRPLANES

You may have noticed that there are the same number of aisle seats as there are middle seats on commercial airplanes. For example, if there are 50 aisle seats, there are 50 middle seats too. Thus, the supply curve for aisle seats and middle seats is the same (a vertical line at 50 seats). But demand is not the same for the two types of seats because most people prefer aisle seats. So, the demand curve for aisle seats is to the right of the demand curve for middle seats.

What effect will this preference have on price? Well, if the demand for aisle seats is higher than the demand for middle seats but the supply of both types of seats is the same, then the equilibrium price will be higher for aisle seats than for middle seats. For example, suppose the equilibrium price for a middle seat is $100. Then, the equilibrium price for an aisle seat will be, perhaps, $145.

But airlines charge the same price for aisle and middle seats. In other words, if they are charging the equilibrium price for the middle seat, then they must be charging a below-equilibrium price for the aisle seat. At a below-equilibrium price, there will be a shortage of aisle seats. More people will want aisle seats (say, 80) than there are aisle seats available (say, 50). Suppose you are one of the 80 people who wants an aisle seat. How can you be one of the 50 people to get one? One way is to be one of the first 50 people to ask for an aisle seat. In other words, aisle seats are likely to be rationed by first-come-first-served. The people who are first to check in at the airport get the aisle seats (no flyer ever asks for a middle seat); the latecomers get the middle seats.

This analysis raises some additional questions for you to think about: If the equilibrium price for an aisle seat is higher than the equilibrium price for a middle seat, then why don't the airlines charge higher prices for aisle seats than for middle seats? Why not fully ration all seats by dollar price instead of rationing aisle seats partly by dollar price and partly by first-come-first-served?

THINKING LIKE AN ECONOMIST

The economist knows that it is often possible to break one market into submarkets. For example, the market for seats on an airplane can be broken into three submarkets: one for window seats, one for aisle seats, and one for middle seats. If the demand and supply conditions in these submarkets are not identical, then neither will be the equilibrium price. When airlines sell all seats for the same price, one or more submarkets will be out of equilibrium. Economists look for the consequences of disequilibria in markets.

Self-Test

1. Southwest Airlines is one of the few airlines that will not reserve seats for customers. In other words, buying a ticket on Southwest permits one to enter the airplane, but once on the airplane, it is up to the customer to locate a seat. Will the lines of people waiting to board a Southwest Airlines flight be longer than, shorter than, or the same length as the lines of people waiting to board airline flights where reserved seats are permitted?

2. There are two flights, A and B. The demand for aisle seats on flight A is greater than the demand for aisle seats on flight B, but the demand for middle seats on both flights is the same. If the same price is charged for an aisle seat and a middle seat and that price equals the equilibrium price for middle seats, then on which flight will the rationing device first-come-first-served be more extensively employed?

3. How is the discussion about seats on a commercial airline similar to the discussion of paying all professors the same wage?

APPLICATION 16: 10 O'CLOCK CLASSES IN COLLEGE

A situation similar to aisle seats on an airplane occurs for some university and college classes. Suppose an economics class is offered in the same classroom at 10 o'clock in the morning and at 8 o'clock at night. Most students would prefer the 10 A.M. class to the 8 P.M. class. Notice in Exhibit 9 that the supply of seats in the class is the same at each time but the demand to occupy those seats is not. Because the demand is greater for the 10 A.M. class than for the 8 P.M. class, the equilibrium price for the 10 A.M. class is higher than the equilibrium price for the 8 P.M. class.

But the university or college charges the same tuition no matter what time students choose to take the class. The university doesn't charge students a higher tuition if they enroll in 10 A.M. classes than if they enroll in 8 P.M. classes.

Suppose a tuition of T_1 is charged for all classes and T_1 is the equilibrium tuition for 8 P.M. classes (see Exhibit 9). It follows that T_1 is below the equilibrium tuition for 10 A.M. classes. At T_1, the quantity demanded of seats for 10 o'clock classes will be greater than the quantity supplied; more students will want the 10 o'clock class than there is space available.

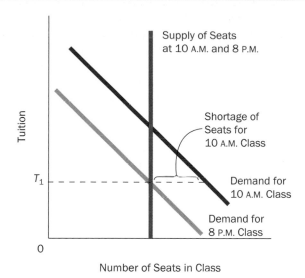

exhibit 9

The Supply and Demand for College Classes at Different Times
A given class is offered at two times, 10 A.M. and 8 P.M. The supply of seats in the classroom is the same at both times; however, the student demand for the 10 o'clock class is higher than the demand for the 8 o'clock class. The university charges the same tuition, T_1, regardless of which class a student takes. At this tuition, there is a shortage of seats for the 10 o'clock class. Seats are likely to be rationed on a first-come-first-served (first to register) basis or on seniority (seniors take precedence over juniors, etc.).

How will the university allocate the available seats? It may do it the same way that airlines ration aisle seats, that is, on a first-come-first-served basis. Those students who are first to register get the 10 A.M. class; the latecomers have to take the 8 P.M. class. Or the university could ration these "high demand classes" by giving their upperclass students (seniors) first priority.

THINKING LIKE AN ECONOMIST

The layperson sees students clamoring to get 10 A.M. classes and concludes that the demand is high for classes at this time. He then wonders why the university doesn't schedule more 10 A.M. classes. The economist knows that what the layperson sees is as much an effect of price as of demand. The demand for 10 A.M. classes may be high, but the quantity demanded may not be if the price is high enough. In fact, even though the demand for various classes at various times may be different, there is some set of prices that will make the quantity demanded of each class the same.

Self-Test

1. Suppose college students are given two options. With option A, the price a student pays for a class is always the equilibrium price. For example, if the equilibrium price to take Economics 101 is $600 at 10 A.M. and is $400 at 4 P.M., then students pay more for the 10 A.M. class than they do for the 4 P.M. class. With option B, the price a student pays for a class is the same regardless of the time the class is taken. When given the choice between options A and B, many students would say they prefer option B to A. Is this the case for you? If so, why would this be your choice?

2. How is the analysis of the 10 o'clock class similar to the analysis of aisle seats on commercial airplanes?

APPLICATION 17: TIPPING AT A LAS VEGAS SHOW

Most of the big hotel-casinos in Las Vegas have elaborate entertainment shows. To get a good seat at many (but not all) Las Vegas shows, you have to tip (in advance) the person who seats you. Tourists in Las Vegas usually complain, "I don't know why I have to pay that guy $20 to walk me to my seat. It's ridiculous." But is it?

In Las Vegas, all tickets for the same show sell for the same price (unlike tickets for a Broadway play, baseball game, or symphony concert). Buying a ticket to a Las Vegas show guarantees a seat, but it could be *any* seat in the house. It could be a good seat up front or a bad seat way in the back.

The show, therefore, has two markets: a market for good seats and a market for bad seats.[4] In each market there is a demand for and a supply of seats. The bad seats market is shown in Exhibit 10a, the good seats market in Exhibit 10b.

Normally, different market conditions (different demand and supply curves) would bring about different equilibrium prices. The hotel-casino, however, sells all tickets for the same price, say $50. This is the equilibrium price in the bad seats market, but as the exhibit shows, it is a below-equilibrium price in the good seats market. The result is a shortage of good seats.

How are the "too few" good seats rationed? They are rationed by price, but in an unusual way. As the exhibit shows, the equilibrium price for a good seat is $70: $50 is paid to the hotel-casino that sells you the ticket and $20 is paid as a tip to the person who seats you at the show. In other words, the tip is equal to the difference between the equilibrium price for a good seat and the admission price for the show (which is equal to the equilibrium price of a bad seat).

Tip for a good seat = Equibrium price of a good seat
                     − Admission price to the show

An interesting question to ask is: Why don't the hotel-casinos sell tickets to their shows the same way a ticket to a baseball game or a Broadway play is sold? Broadway plays and baseball games have reserved seating, and you pay a higher price for a better seat. Why not do the same in Las Vegas? Don't the owner-operators of the hotel-casinos in Las Vegas realize they are losing $20 on each good seat? Why don't they capture this $20 instead of letting their employees get it?

exhibit 10

Good and Bad Seats at a Las Vegas Show

If demand and supply conditions are different in the good seats and bad seats markets but the same price is charged in both markets, then at least one market is in disequilibrium. We have assumed the bad seats market is in equilibrium at $50, but at this price, there is a shortage in the good seats market. To get a good seat a customer must pay a tip equal to the difference between the equilibrium price for a good seat and the $50 admission price to the show.

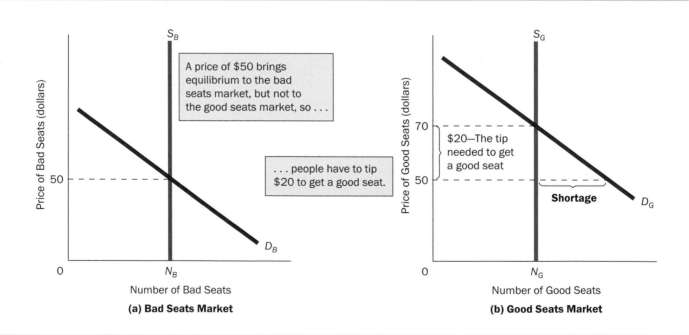

A price of $50 brings equilibrium to the bad seats market, but not to the good seats market, so . . .

. . . people have to tip $20 to get a good seat.

$20—The tip needed to get a good seat

Shortage

(a) Bad Seats Market

(b) Good Seats Market

---

4. A person can see the show from a "bad" or "not-so-good" seat; but it is not so easy or comfortable to see the show from a bad seat as from a good seat.

As odd as it may sound, Las Vegas hotel-casino owner-operators may want the price of a good seat to be too low (below equilibrium). If it is, it will generate a shortage of good seats, which will result in people trying to get the good seats in numerous ways. Many people visiting Las Vegas, who are unfamiliar with how things work, may think that the way to get a good seat for a show is to arrive at the show door early. The showroom is usually just off the casino. If enough people think they can get a good seat by being one of the first in line, long lines of people will be waiting in the casino for the showroom doors to open. Interestingly enough, people waiting in line near blackjack tables, roulette wheels, and hundreds of slot machines can do only one thing: gamble. It is very common to see people playing slot machines while standing in line for a show. The hotel-casinos, in other words, may deliberately price good show seats too low, knowing that this will lead to long lines of people with time to gamble. What the hotel-casino loses on the show may be more than made up for at the slot machines.

THINKING LIKE AN ECONOMIST

At first glance, it looks as if the hotel-casino loses revenue when it chooses not to set equilibrium prices for the various submarkets of seats at a show. For example, when the equilibrium price of a good seat is $70 and the equilibrium price of a bad seat is $50, then the hotel-casino loses $20 on each good seat if it charges $50 for all seats. The first reaction may be to ask, "Why would the hotel-casino forfeit $20 per good seat?" The layperson might answer this question by saying that the hotel-casino simply made a mistake, or that it doesn't know what the equilibrium price is for various seats, or something along these lines. The economist wonders: Is there a good, solid economic reason for the hotel-casinos to forfeit income? The answer is yes if by forfeiting income in one area the hotel-casinos more than compensate for it in another. The reaction of the economist is not to say the hotel-casino has made a mistake, but to ask what the hotel-casino knows that she doesn't.

Self-Test

1. At a Broadway show, good seats fetch higher prices than not-so-good seats. A seat up front may cost $150, while a seat in the back of the playhouse might sell for less than half this amount. Why doesn't Broadway price its tickets the same way that Las Vegas prices its tickets?

2. What does the tip for a good seat depend upon?

APPLICATION 18: WHAT IS THE PRICE OF AN "A"?

The law of demand doesn't operate just on goods with explicit prices. Unpopular teachers sometimes try to increase class enrollment by raising the average grade of the students in their courses, thereby reducing the price of the course to the student.
—Richard Posner, *Economic Analysis of the Law*

At many universities and colleges, students can take a given course from any one of several professors. For example, Francine may be able to take English 101 from Professor Brown or Professor Lawson. Now suppose that both Professor Brown and Professor Lawson are considered good instructors, but students consider

Professor Lawson slightly better than Professor Brown. For example, on a scale of 1 to 10, Professor Brown gets an 8 and Professor Lawson gets a 10. Will Francine necessarily take the course from Professor Lawson instead of Professor Brown? No. Professor Brown may "compensate" for a relatively lesser reputation by lowering the price of the course to the student. For example, Professor Brown may lower the time it takes a student in his class to get a good grade. To illustrate, suppose that the average student has to work seven hours a week to get an "A" in Professor Lawson's class, but only six hours a week to get an "A" in Professor Brown's class. The demand (of students) to get into Lawson's class may be higher than the demand to get into Brown's class (because Lawson is considered a better instructor, she is, in some sense, a "higher-quality" good). However, the price of an "A" in Brown's class is certainly lower than in Lawson's class. (See Exhibit 11.)

Is it possible for the same number of students to want to be in each of the two professors' classes? It certainly is, as Exhibit 11 shows. Quantity demanded of seats in class (1 seat = 1 student) is 30 in both Brown's class and Lawson's class.

THINKING LIKE AN ECONOMIST

The economist knows that low demand and low price can generate the same quantity demanded as high demand and high price. In fact, low demand and low price can generate an even greater quantity demanded than that generated by high demand and high price. For example, suppose students choose professor A over professor B for a given course. Does it follow that the demand is greater for professor A than for professor B? Not necessarily, says the economist. Professor A may simply charge a much lower price for a good grade than professor B charges. In fact, the demand for professor B may be higher than the demand for professor A, but professor B charges such a high price for a good grade relative to professor A that more students want to take professor A's class.

Self-Test

1. If more people want to read romance novels than classic novels, it holds that the demand for romance novels is greater than the demand for classic novels. Do you agree or disagree? Explain your answer.

2. Popularity is a function of demand, not price. Do you agree or disagree? Explain your answer.

exhibit 11

The Price of an "A"
Both Brown and Lawson are good professors, but students perceive Lawson as slightly better than Brown. The demand (by students) to be in Lawson's class is greater than the demand to be in Brown's class. However, Brown charges a lower price for an "A" than does Lawson. At the prices that each charges, the same number of students want to be in Brown's class (30) as want to be in Lawson's class (30).

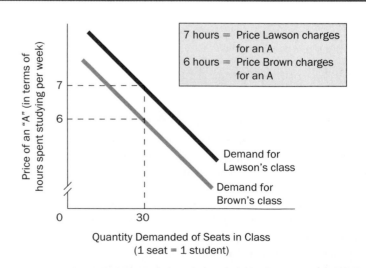

7 hours = Price Lawson charges for an A
6 hours = Price Brown charges for an A

Price of an "A" (in terms of hours spent studying per week)

Demand for Lawson's class
Demand for Brown's class

Quantity Demanded of Seats in Class (1 seat = 1 student)

APPLICATION 19: WHY ARE SPEEDING TICKETS SO EXPENSIVE? OR, TWO WAYS TO GET THE SAME PRICE

Drivers usually speed more often than they get caught for speeding. For example, Jenny may drive over the speed limit 40 times a year, but only get caught once every two years. The price for speeding is equal to the price of a speeding ticket times the probability of getting caught. For example, if there is a 1 in 20 chance of being caught for speeding and the price of a speeding ticket is $200, then the price for speeding is not $200, but $\frac{1}{20}$ of $200, or $10.

Price of speeding = Speeding ticket price × Probability of getting caught for speeding

Suppose a police force has six police officers whose job is to apprehend speeders. With six officers working each day, the probability of a speeder being caught for speeding is, say, 5 percent (1 in 20 chance). We would expect that the lower the price of speeding, the more people will speed. Suppose the data look like this:

Speeding Ticket	Probability of Getting Caught for Speeding	Price of Speeding (Speeding Ticket × Probability of Getting Caught)	Number of People Who Will Speed
$200	5 percent (0.05)	$10.00	100
$100	5 percent	$ 5.00	200
$ 50	5 percent	$ 2.50	400

According to these data, if a speeding ticket is set at $100, the price of speeding is $5 and 200 people will speed. What is the cost to taxpayers of apprehending speeders?[5] It is the sum of the cost per day of hiring the six police officers. If each police officer is paid $200 a day, then the daily cost is $1,200.

Now suppose the taxpayers decide they want to cut costs in half by reducing the number of police officers from six to three. However, they don't want any more people to speed than have been speeding. They think more people are likely to speed if there are fewer officers patrolling. Let's say that with only three officers patrolling, the probability of being caught for speeding falls from 5 percent to 2.5 percent. If this is the case, then at the current price for a speeding ticket ($100), the price of speeding falls to $2.50. We know from the data that if the price of speeding is $2.50, 400 people will speed.

How can the taxpayers cut the police force, reduce costs, and make sure that no more people speed each day? They can increase the price of a speeding ticket. For example, if the price of a speeding ticket is raised to $200, and the probability of getting caught for speeding is 2.5 percent, the price of speeding is $5. This is the same price of speeding as when the ticket price was $100 and the probability of getting caught was 5 percent.

$200 speeding ticket and 2.5 percent chance of being caught = $5
$100 speeding ticket and 5 percent chance of being caught = $5

It follows that the same number of people will speed (200) at the $200 ticket price and a 2.5 percent probability of getting caught as were speeding at the $100 ticket price and 5 percent probability of getting caught. But police costs will be lower ($600 instead of $1,200) with three officers and a $200 ticket price than with six officers and a $100 ticket price.

So, why are speeding tickets so expensive? By charging a high price to speeders who get caught, taxpayers can reduce police costs without increasing the number of speeders.

---

5. Of the 200 speeders, 5 percent (10 of them) will be caught for speeding.

THINKING LIKE AN ECONOMIST

The economist knows that there is often more than one way to achieve a particular outcome. For example, there are at least two ways to reduce the number of speeders. One way is to increase the number of police officers, which increases the number of speeders apprehended. As the probability of being apprehended for speeding rises, there will be fewer speeders. Another way is to increase the price of a speeding ticket. As the price of a speeding ticket rises, the quantity consumed of "speeding" by speeders will decline.

Self-Test

1. A friend calls you on the telephone and tells you to be careful driving to work today because there is a "speed trap" near 12th Street and Georges Avenue. If you drive slower near the "speed trap" than you usually do, what does this tell you about your behavior and the price of speeding tickets?

2. If police officers receive an increase in their income, do you think the price of a speeding ticket is likely to fall, rise, or stay the same? Explain your answer.

APPLICATION 20: WILL A SELF-INTERESTED, PROFIT-SEEKING OIL PRODUCER CONSERVE OIL FOR THE FUTURE?

Tex Baldwin is an oil producer; he pumps crude oil from under his property and sells it to refineries. It costs him $10 to extract one barrel of oil and he sells each barrel for $15. At this $15 price, he pumps and sells 1 million barrels of crude oil each year. In other words, at $15 per barrel, quantity supplied is 1 million barrels.

One day Tex reads a report indicating that in five years oil will be relatively more scarce than it is today; as a result, the price of oil will rise to $30 a barrel. Tex can continue to pump and sell oil today or he can leave the oil in the ground and pump and sell it in five years. Tex Baldwin is interested in maximizing his profits. Do you predict he will pump and sell now or pump and sell in five years?

Let's analyze Tex's situation. If he pumps and sells oil today, he earns a profit of $5 per barrel; if he pumps and sells oil five years from now, he will earn a profit of $20 per barrel.[6] Of course, if he leaves the oil in the ground, he cannot earn interest on the $5 profit per barrel. Suppose he can earn 5 percent interest on every $1 he saves. Thus, a profit of $5 a barrel today will return approximately $6.40 in five years. Comparing $6.40 a barrel with $20 a barrel, Tex realizes that he will maximize his profits by leaving the oil in the ground.

Instead of reducing the quantity of oil he supplies to the market from 1 million barrels to nothing, Tex decides to cut back to supplying 100,000 barrels. He needs some income to meet his annual financial obligations.

Before Tex expected the price of oil to rise, he supplied 1 million barrels of oil to the market; afterward, he supplied 100,000 barrels. This is how we define a decrease in the supply of oil: less oil supplied at a given price. In other words, as the expected price of oil increased, the current supply of oil decreased.

From a societal perspective, it is interesting that Tex, who only wants to maximize his profits, ends up conserving a resource (oil) that is expected to become relatively more scarce in the future. In fact, because of his desire for profit, oil in the future will likely be relatively less scarce than initially expected (after all, Tex is saving oil for the future). The individual's desire for profit does not necessarily conflict with society's need to conserve resources.

---

6. We are assuming that the cost of extracting oil is not higher in five years than it is today.

The layperson often thinks that greed, self-interest, or the desire for profit could never be a motivation behind conservation. The economist knows this is not true. When the expected price of a resource is higher than the current price, the resource owner may simply conserve (hold on to) the resource today and wait to sell it in the future. In short, the economist knows that greedy, self-interested, profit-seekers care not only about current prices but also about future prices.

Self-Test

1. Suppose there is oil under a 100 square mile area in Texas that no one owns. Since the area belongs to no one, anyone who wants to drill for the oil can do so freely. The difference between this case and the case discussed in the application is that Tex owned the land in the application but no one owns this land. Is oil (under the ground) that is owned by someone more or less likely to be conserved than oil (under the ground) that is owned by no one? Explain your answer.

2. Suppose Tex Baldwin expects to die in a year. Is he more or less likely to conserve oil for the future? Does it matter to your answer whether Tex has children or not?

APPLICATION 21: WHERE WILL PEOPLE BUY RELATIVELY MORE APPLES?

Apples grow in the state of Washington and do not grow in New York City. In which place, Washington or New York City, would you predict that relatively more high-quality apples are consumed, *ceteris paribus?* The layperson's prediction is usually, "Washington—because people in Washington have greater access to high-quality apples."

Is this the same prediction and explanation an economist would offer? To see, let's consider the matter carefully. Suppose that both high-quality and medium-quality apples are grown in the state of Washington. Their absolute or money prices are 10 cents and 5 cents, respectively. It follows that the relative price of a high-quality apple is 2 medium-quality apples.

Now suppose the cost of transporting apples to New York City is 5 cents per apple, irrespective of quality. In New York City, therefore, the price of a high-quality apple is 15 cents and the price of a medium-quality apple is 10 cents. It follows that the relative price of a high-quality apple is 1.5 medium-quality apples. In short, although the absolute prices of both types of apples is higher in New York City than in Washington, the relative price of high-quality apples is lower in New York City than in Washington.

An economist would predict that relatively more high-quality apples will be eaten where high-quality apples are relatively cheaper. This is in New York City.

Q & A

Q: Is there a difference between New Yorkers buying *relatively more* high-quality apples and New Yorkers buying *more* high-quality apples?

A: Yes. *More* indicates a larger absolute number; *relatively more* indicates a greater percentage. For example, New Yorkers may be buying relatively more high-quality apples than Washingtonians, but they are still buying fewer high-quality apples.

Let's say that Washingtonians buy 10,000 high-quality apples and 30,000 medium-quality apples, and New Yorkers buy 5,000 high-quality apples and 7,500 medium-quality apples. Washingtonians buy *more* high-quality apples, but New Yorkers buy *relatively more* high-quality apples. Of the 12,500 apples that New Yorkers buy, 40 percent are high-quality apples; of the 40,000 apples that Washingtonians buy, 25 percent are high-quality apples.

When is a change not a change? To answer this question, consider two goods, X and Y. The price of X is $40 and the price of Y is $80. At these absolute prices, if a person purchases one unit of Y, she gives up the opportunity to buy two units of X. Now suppose the prices of X and Y double: X is now $80 and Y is $160. Are these changes in absolute prices really a change? Some people would say yes; after all, X went from $40 to $80 and Y went from $80 to $160. But other people would say no because at the higher absolute prices a person still gives up two units of X to purchase one unit of Y.

According to economists, equal percentage changes in absolute prices do not constitute a meaningful change. A meaningful change is one that causes peoples' behavior to change. According to economists, only relative changes (such as a change in the relative price of a good) can do this.

A Reader Asks...

How Do I Find My Own Supply-and-Demand Applications?

I can understand an economist's applications of supply and demand, but I don't know how to apply supply and demand myself. How do I find my own supply-and-demand applications?

You can proceed in several ways, two of which we discuss here. First, you can heed the words of Robert Solow, "I am a supply-and-demand economist. When I come across something, I ask myself what is being transferred here and where does the supply come from and where does the demand come from."

We can reformulate what Solow has said into a single question: Is trade involved? This is the relevant supply-and-demand question because supply and demand are about trade. In other words, when you observe something, simply ask: Is this about trade? If you are driving on a freeway, ask: Is driving on a freeway about trade? Specifically, is something being "bought" and "sold"? If so, what? If you are applying to college, ask: Is this about trade? What is being bought and sold?

A second way to proceed is to look for surpluses and shortages around you. Surpluses and shortages are manifestations of market disequilibrium. If you find them, you can be fairly sure that supply and demand are rele-

vant. If you are sitting in a classroom with empty seats, ask: Is there a surplus or shortage here? In this case, of course, there is a surplus, which should lead you to think about price. Surpluses exist when prices are too high. Why is the price too high? If you observe more people applying to a particular college than the college will admit, ask: Is there a surplus or shortage here? In this case there is a shortage, which again should lead you to think about price. Shortages exist when prices are too low. Why is price too low?

The key to finding your own supply-and-demand applications is to (1) observe things around you and then (2) ask questions about the things you observe. If you are sitting in a restaurant eating a meal, ask questions about what you observe. Is trade involved here? Yes. Is the restaurant filled to capacity and is there a line of people waiting to get in? Yes. Are there more people who want to eat at this restaurant than there are spaces to accommodate them? Yes. Is there a shortage here? Yes. Why do shortages exist? Prices are too low. Why doesn't the restaurant raise its prices and eliminate the shortage?

The process isn't that hard, is it?

Chapter Summary

Why Do Colleges Use GPAs, ACTs, and SATs for Purposes of Admission?

- Colleges and universities charging students less than the equilibrium tuition for admission create a shortage of spaces at the colleges or universities. Consequently, colleges and universities have to impose

some nonprice rationing device, such as GPAs or ACT or SAT scores.

Can Prejudice Affect Wages?

- Prejudice directed by employers toward a group of employees can lower the demand for and the wages of these employees. If these lower-wage employees are as productive as the higher-wage employees who have not felt the effects of prejudice, then nondiscriminator employers can lower their costs by hiring the lower-wage employees. Nondiscriminator employers are then able to underprice discriminator employers.

Legalization of Marijuana
- If the purchase and sale of marijuana are legalized, the price of marijuana may rise, fall, or remain the same. The price will depend on whether the demand for marijuana rises by more than, less than, or equal to the rise in the supply of marijuana.

The Minimum Wage
- A minimum wage (above equilibrium wage) reduces the number of unskilled workers working or reduces the number of unskilled labor hours purchased by employers.

Price Ceiling in the Kidney Market
- Currently, there is a price ceiling in the kidney market, and the price is set at $0. Many of the effects of a price ceiling (shortages, fewer exchanges, and so on) are seen in the kidney market.

Crisis in the Electricity Market
- A shortage of electricity is likely to result in a setting where (1) prices in the wholesale electricity market rise due to increased demand and higher generating costs and (2) prices in the retail electricity market are controlled.

Gold Prices and House Prices
- Gold prices are the same everywhere in the world, but house prices are not. When the price of a good is higher in one location than in another location and that good can be moved from the lower-priced location to the higher-priced location, then the price of the good will end up being the same in both locations. Obviously, if the good cannot be moved from the lower-priced location to the higher-priced location, then the price of the good will not end up being the same in both locations.

Gas Prices
- After the September 11 attack on the World Trade Center and the Pentagon, gas prices at some gas stations increased. A few days later, prices were back down to pre-attack levels. Did the prices fall to normal levels because gas station owners were threatened with fines and lawsuits or because supply and demand hadn't changed in a way to justify the higher prices? We think it the latter. Although some gas station owners raised prices, other gas station owners held prices constant. Obviously, the gas station owners who raised prices would have lost considerable business if they had kept gas prices at significantly higher levels than the levels elsewhere.

Health Care and the Right to Sue an HMO
- The supply curve of HMO-provided health care will shift upward and to the left if patients have the right to sue. As a result, patients will pay more for their HMO-provided health care coverage when they have the right to sue than when they do not have the right to sue.

Do You Pay for Good Weather?
- If good weather gives people utility, then the demand for and the price of housing will be higher in a city with good weather than in a city with bad weather. Conclusion: People who buy houses in good-weather locations indirectly pay for the good weather.

Paying All Professors the Same Salary
- Suppose the equilibrium wage rate as determined by supply and demand conditions is higher, say, for a biology professor than for a history professor. If both professors are paid the equilibrium wage in biology, then there will be a surplus of history professors. If both professors are paid the equilibrium wage in history, then there will be a shortage of biology professors.

Are New Car Companies Hurt by the Used Car Market?
- The demand for new cars is as high as it is (and prices of new cars are as high as they are) because the buyer of a new car can sell the car (later) as a used car. In other words, what a buyer of a car anticipates he can do as the seller of the car influences how high his demand will be and how high a price he will pay.

Supply and Demand on a Freeway
- The effect of a disequilibrium price for driving on a freeway is a traffic jam. If the price to drive on a freeway is $0 and at this price the quantity demanded of freeway space is greater than the quantity supplied, then there will be a shortage of freeway space that will manifest itself as freeway congestion.

What Does Price Have to Do with Getting to Class on Time?
- If price doesn't fully ration campus parking spots, something will. The rationing device may be first-come-first-served, which often prompts students to leave for campus at earlier times than they would if price rationed parking spots.

Aisle Seats on Commercial Airplanes
- If the supply for two goods is the same but the demand is different, then charging the same price for the two goods means that equilibrium is not achieved for at least one of the goods. If equilibrium is not

achieved, then there is either a shortage or a surplus. In the commercial airplanes application, there was a shortage of aisle seats. This prompted a nonprice rationing device: first-come-first-served.

10 O'Clock Classes in College

- Colleges usually charge the same tuition for a class no matter when the class is taken. The supply of seats in the class may be the same at each time, but the demand for the class may be different at different times. Thus at least for some classes, the quantity demanded of seats (in the class) will be greater than the quantity supplied. Thus, some nonprice rationing device will have to be used to achieve equilibrium.

Tipping at a Las Vegas Show

- A disequilibrium price for good seats in a Las Vegas showroom gives rise to an unusual rationing device. The price of a good seat is equal to (1) the price of admission to the showroom, which is equivalent to the price of a bad seat; plus (2) a tip equal to the difference between the equilibrium price for a good seat and the admission price. In other words, there are two components to the price of a good seat.

What Is the Price of an "A"?

- The law of demand can explain how a difference in the price of earning an "A" in two different classes could explain the difference in the quantity demanded of each class. The lower the price, the greater the quantity demanded, *ceteris paribus.*

Why Are Speeding Tickets So Expensive?

- The law of demand and an understanding of two ways to approximate the same price of speeding can explain the rationale for high-priced speeding tickets.
- Price of speeding = Speeding ticket price × Probability of getting caught for speeding. It follows that there are two ways to raise the price of speeding: (1) raise the price of a speeding ticket, or (2) raise the probability of getting caught for speeding. In addition, a higher price for a speeding ticket and a lower probability of getting caught can give us the same price for speeding as a lower price for a speeding ticket and a higher probability of getting caught.

Will a Self-Interested, Profit-Seeking Oilman Conserve Oil for the Future?

- An expected price can affect current behavior and change both current supply and future supply. Specifically, if an oil producer believes the expected price of oil will be sufficiently higher than the current price, he may decrease the amount of oil that he currently supplies to the market and increase the amount of oil that he supplies to the market in the future.

Where Will People Buy Relatively More Apples?

- Economists predict that relatively more is purchased of goods that are relatively lower priced, *ceteris paribus.* Thus, New Yorkers will buy relatively more high-quality apples than Washingtonians, even though the absolute price of high-quality apples is higher in New York City than in Washington.

Economic Connections to You

Economic facts, actions, and changes create ripples that move away from their point of origin. Eventually, these ripples can intersect your life and have an effect on you. In this chapter, we have given numerous examples of how demand, supply, and price could affect you. For example, if a below-equilibrium price is charged to park in a parking lot, you may end up wasting time looking for a place to park. Use what you have learned in this chapter to come up with your (original) application of supply, demand, and price.

1. Harvard, Stanford, and Yale all charge relatively high tuition. Still, each uses ACT and SAT scores as admission criteria. Are charging a relatively high tuition and using standardized test scores (as admission criteria) inconsistent? Explain your answer.

2. Suppose the purchase and sale of marijuana are legalized and the price of marijuana falls. What explains the lower price of marijuana?

3. The minimum wage in year 1 is $1 higher than the equilibrium wage. In year 2, the minimum wage is increased so that it is $2 above the equilibrium wage. We observe that the same number of people are working at the minimum wage in year 2 as in year 1. Does it follow that an increase in the minimum wage does not cause some workers to lose their jobs? Explain your answer.

4. Explain how prejudiced employers can be hurt by their own prejudice.

5. In our discussion of the kidney market, we represent the demand curve for kidneys as downward-sloping and the supply curve of kidneys as upward-sloping. At the end of the discussion we state, "If it is unlawful to pay someone for a kidney, fewer kidneys will be forthcoming. In other words, the quantity supplied of kidneys is less at $0 than at, say, $20,000. Fewer kidneys supplied means, in turn, fewer kidney transplants." Would there be fewer kidney transplants if the supply curve of kidneys is vertical? Explain your answer.

6. Explain how a price ceiling in the retail electricity market can lead to blackouts.

7. What do the applications about freeway congestion, campus parking, 10 o'clock classes, and Las Vegas showrooms have in common?

8. Why might Las Vegas hotel-casinos choose not to charge the equilibrium price for the good seats in their showrooms?

9. Do you think there is likely to be a bigger price difference between candy bars in different locations or between cars in different locations? Explain your answer.

10. Economics has been called the "dismal science" because it sometimes "tells us" that things are true when we would prefer they were false. For example, although there are no free lunches, might we prefer that there were? Was there anything in this chapter that you learned was true that you would have preferred to be false? If so, identify it. Then explain why you would have preferred it to be false.

11. In the discussion of health care and the right to sue your HMO, we state, "Saying a seller's minimum price for providing a good or service rises, is the same as saying the seller's supply curve has shifted upward and to the left." Does it follow that if a seller's minimum price falls, the supply curve shifts downward and to the right? Explain your answer.

12. Application 10 explains that even though no one directly and explicitly pays for good weather ("Here is $100 for the good weather"), still it is possible to pay for good weather indirectly, such as through housing prices. Identify three other things (besides good weather) that you believe people pay for indirectly.

13. If the equilibrium wage for economics professors is higher than the equilibrium wage for history professors, which professors (do you think) are more likely to argue that all professors should be paid the same? Explain your answer.

14. Application 12 suggests that the used car market may not hurt companies that build and sell new cars. Do you think that the used housing market may not hurt companies that build and sell new houses? Explain your answer.

15. Suppose there exists a costless way to charge drivers on the freeway. Under this costless system, tolls on the freeway would be adjusted according to traffic conditions. For example, when traffic is usually heavy, such as from 6:30 A.M. to 9:00 A.M. on a weekday, the toll to drive on the freeway would be higher than the toll would be when traffic is light. In other words, freeway tolls would be used to equate the demand for freeway space and the supply of freeway space. Would you be in favor of such a system to replace our current (largely, zero-price) system? Explain your answer.

16. Wilson walks into his economics class 10 minutes late because he couldn't find a place to park. Because of his tardiness, he doesn't hear the professor tell the class there will be a quiz at the next class session. At the next class session, Wilson is unprepared for the quiz and ends up failing it.
   a. Might Wilson's failing the quiz have anything to do with the price of parking? Explain your answer.
   b. Suppose Wilson says to his professor: "If this university had set equilibrium prices for parking, I wouldn't have been late to class, and therefore, I would have heard about the upcoming quiz, studied for it, and probably passed it. It's not my fault I failed the quiz. It's the university's fault for not setting the equilibrium price for parking." What would you say if you were the professor?

17. University A charges more for a class for which there is high demand than for a class for which there is low demand. University B charges the same for all classes. All other things being equal between the two universities, which university would you prefer to attend? Explain your answer.

1. The price to drive on a freeway is $0 at all times of the day. This price establishes equilibrium at 3 A.M. but is too low to establish equilibrium at 5 P.M. There is a shortage of freeway space at 5 P.M.
   a. Graphically show and explain how carpooling may eliminate the shortage.
   b. Graphically show and explain how building more freeways may eliminate the shortage.
2. Diagrammatically show and explain why there is a shortage of classroom space for some college classes and a surplus for others.
3. Smith has been trying to sell his house for six months, but so far, there are no buyers. Draw the market for Smith's house.

4. According to students, Professor Smith teaches a better economics class than Professor Jones. Everything else between the two professors is the same—how they grade, the number of assignments they give, the time they teach their classes, and so on.
   a. Draw the student demand to get into Professor Smith's class in relation to the student demand to get into Professor Jones's class.
   b. If the same dollar tuition is charged for both classes, whose class is more likely to have a shortage of seats? Explain your answer.

1. Go to *http://www.usatoday.com* and select and read any story in the newspaper. What was the story about? Put the central idea of the story into economic terms or diagrams if it is possible to do so.
2. Go to *http://www.dailynews.yahoo.com* and select and read any current news item. What was the news item about? Put the central idea of the news item into economic terms or diagrams, if it is possible to do so.
3. Go to *http://www.forbes.com* and select and read any story. What was the story about? Put the central idea of the story into economic terms or diagrams, if it is possible to do so.
4. Go to *http://www.economist.com* and select and read any story. What was the story about? Put the central idea of the story into economic terms or diagrams, if it is possible to do so.
5. Go to *http://www.businessweek.com* and select and read any story. What was the story about? Put the central idea of the story into economic terms or diagrams, if it is possible to do so.

Log on to the Arnold Xtra! Web site now (*http://arnoldxtra.swcollege.com*) for additional learning resources such as practice quizzes, help with graphing, video clips, and current event applications.

ch.5

ELASTICITY

In New York City, a Broadway play is performed in a theater that has 1,500 seats. Will the play take in more revenue if the average ticket price for a performance is $40 or if it is $65? If you said $65, then here's another question: Will the play take in more revenue if the average ticket price for a performance is $65 or if it is $80? If you said $80, then here's still another question: Will the play take in more revenue if the average ticket price for a performance is $80 or if it is $100? Are you beginning to get suspicious? Perhaps it has occurred to you that the highest ticket price won't generate the greatest amount of revenue. But then, which ticket price will? The answer may surprise you.

Chapter Road Map

In this chapter, we discuss four elasticity concepts—price elasticity of demand, cross elasticity of demand, income elasticity of demand, and price elasticity of supply. Each of four elasticity concepts deals with two variables. Price elasticity of demand deals with price and quantity demanded; cross elasticity of demand deals with the price of one good and the quantity demanded of another good; income elasticity of demand deals with income and quantity demanded; price elasticity of supply deals with price and quantity supplied.

In addition, we discuss the determinants of price elasticity of demand and the relationship between price elasticity of demand and total revenue.

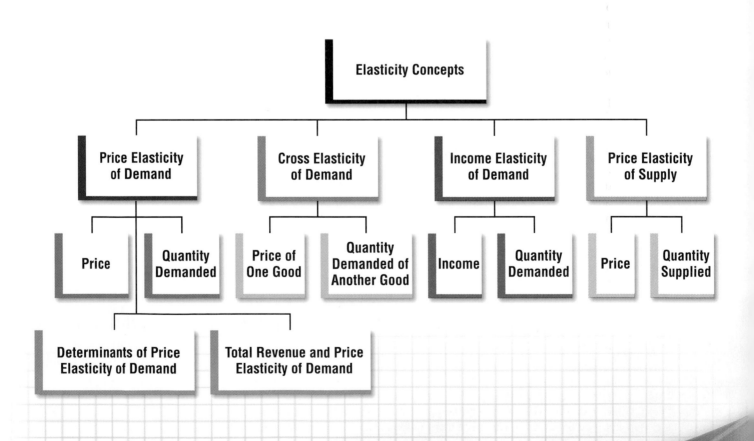

ELASTICITY: PART 1

The law of demand states that price and quantity demanded are inversely related, *ceteris paribus*. But it doesn't tell us by what percentage quantity demanded changes as price changes. Suppose price rises by 10 percent. As a result, quantity demanded falls. But by what percentage does it fall? The notion of price elasticity of demand can help answer this question. The general concept of elasticity provides a technique for estimating the response of one variable to changes in some other variable. It has numerous applications in economics.

PRICE ELASTICITY OF DEMAND

Have you ever watched any of the TV shopping networks, such as QVC or the Home Shopping Network? Every now and then, the people on these networks will offer computers for sale. For example, QVC will often advertise Dell Computers for sale. You may hear the following: "Today, we're going to be offering this Dell computer, along with a printer, digital camera, flat-panel monitor, and scanner all for the unbelievable price of $2,100."

If you watch the bottom of your television screen, you will sometimes see how many computers QVC is selling at this price. No matter how many computers are being sold, one question almost always pops into the minds of the top managers of both QVC and Dell. It is, "How many more computers could we have sold if the price had been, say, $100 lower?" A similar question is, "How many fewer computers would we have sold if the price had been, say, $100 higher?"

Specifically, QVC and Dell managers want to know the *price elasticity of demand* for the computer that is being offered for sale. **Price elasticity of demand** is a measure of the responsiveness of quantity demanded to changes in price. More specifically, it addresses the "percentage change in quantity demanded for a given percentage change in price."

Let's say that QVC raises the price of the computer by 10 percent and, as a result, quantity demanded for the computer falls by 20 percent. If we take the percentage change in quantity demanded—20 percent—and divide it by the percentage change in price—10 percent—we have what economists call the *coefficient of price elasticity of demand* (E_d).

$$E_d = \frac{\text{Percentage change in quantity demanded}}{\text{Percentage change in price}} = \frac{\% \Delta Q_d}{\% \Delta P}$$

In the formula, E_d = coefficient of price elasticity of demand or simply elasticity coefficient, % = percentage, and Δ stands for "change in."

If we carry out the calculation in our simple example—where quantity demanded changes by 20 percent and price changes by 10 percent—we get the number 2. An economist would say, "Price elasticity of demand is 2."

What Does Price Elasticity of Demand Equal to 2 Mean?

A price elasticity of demand equal to 2 means that any percentage change in quantity demanded will be 2 times the percentage change in price.[1] In other words, if price changes 1 percent, quantity demanded will change 2 percent, or if price changes 10 percent, quantity demanded will change 20 percent.

Where Is the Missing Minus Sign?

We know that price and quantity demanded move in opposite directions. When price rises, quantity demanded falls; when price falls, quantity demanded rises. In other words, if the price rises by 10 percent, then the quantity demanded might fall by 20 percent. Now, if you divide a *minus 20 percent* by a *positive 10 percent*, you don't get 2; you get −2. In other words, instead of saying that the price elasticity

Price Elasticity of Demand
A measure of the responsiveness of quantity demanded to changes in price.

---

1. This assumes we are changing price from its current level.

of demand is 2, you might think that the price elasticity of demand is −2. However, by convention, economists usually simplify things by speaking of the "absolute value" of the price elasticity of demand; thus, they drop the minus sign.

CALCULATING PRICE ELASTICITY OF DEMAND

Before you can compute a percentage change in anything, you need *two* numbers. For example, before you can compute the percentage change in your income, you need to know what your income *was* and what it *is*. For example, suppose your income last year was $50,000 and your income this year is $60,000. To find the percentage change in your income, you would find the absolute difference in income between the two years ($10,000) and divide it by your income last year ($50,000). This gives you a 20 percent rise in your income.

To compute price elasticity of demand, we obviously need (1) two prices and (2) two quantities demanded. With this in mind, look at Exhibit 1, where two points are identified on a demand curve. Let's calculate the price elasticity of demand for (1) a fall in price and (2) a rise in price.

1. **Calculating price elasticity of demand for a fall in price.** We start at $12 and lower price to $10. This is a 16.7 percent fall in price ($2/$12 = 16.7%). As shown in Exhibit 1, as we lower price from $12 to $10, quantity demanded rises from 50 units to 100 units. This is a 100 percent rise in quantity demanded (50 units/50 units = 100%). Dividing a 100 percent change in quantity demanded by a 16.7 percent change in price gives us an elasticity coefficient of 5.98. In other words, price elasticity of demand is 5.98.

2. **Calculating price elasticity of demand for a rise in price.** This time, we start at $10 and raise the price to $12. This is a 20 percent rise in price ($2/$10 = 20%). As shown in Exhibit 1, as we raise price from $10 to $12, quantity demanded falls from 100 units to 50 units. This is a 50 percent fall in quantity

exhibit 1

Calculating Price Elasticity of Demand
We identify two points on a demand curve. At one point, price is $12 and quantity demanded is 50 units. At the other point, price is $10 and quantity demanded is 100 units. When calculating price elasticity of demand, we use the *average* of the two prices and the *average* of the two quantities demanded. The formula for price elasticity of demand is

$$E_d = \frac{\dfrac{\Delta Q}{Q_{d\,Average}}}{\dfrac{\Delta P}{P_{Average}}}.$$

For the example, the calculation is

$$E_d = \frac{\dfrac{50}{75}}{\dfrac{2}{11}} = 3.67.$$

demanded (50 units/100 units = 50%). Dividing a 50 percent change in quantity demanded by a 20 percent change in price gives us an elasticity coefficient of 2.5. In other words, price elasticity of demand is 2.5.

The Problem

We have a problem here. If we start at $12 and lower price to $10, price elasticity of demand turns out to be 5.98, but if we start at $10 and raise price to $12, price elasticity of demand turns out to be 2.5. In other words, we get a different elasticity coefficient between the same two points on a given demand curve, depending on the point where we initially start. This problem results from the standard practice of using the initial value as the base value when computing percentage changes.

How Economists Have Solved the Problem

Economists have "solved" this problem by computing what they call *arc elasticity* or *average elasticity*. In practice, this means that instead of taking $12 or $10 as the original (initial, starting, or base) value, they choose the *average* of these two prices as the original value. The average of $12 and $10 is $11.

Similarly, instead of taking 50 units or 100 units as the original (initial, starting, or base) value, they choose the *average* of these two quantities demanded as the original value. The average of 50 units and 100 units is 75 units.

Formula for Calculating Price Elasticity of Demand

Here is the specific formula that economists use to calculate price elasticity of demand.[2]

$$E_d = \frac{\dfrac{\Delta Q_d}{Q_{d\,Average}}}{\dfrac{\Delta P}{P_{Average}}}$$

In the formula, ΔQ_d stands for the absolute change in Q_d. For example, if Q_d changes from 50 units to 100 units, then the change is 50 units. ΔP stands for the absolute change in price. For example, if price changes from $12 to $10, then the change in price is $2. $Q_{dAverage}$ stands for the average of the two quantities demanded and $P_{Average}$ stands for the average of the two prices.

For the price and quantity demanded data in Exhibit 1, the calculation is

$$E_d = \frac{\dfrac{50}{75}}{\dfrac{2}{11}} = 3.67$$

Q & A

Q: Is 3.67 the price elasticity of demand at the point higher up on the demand curve in Exhibit 1, the point lower down on the demand curve, or neither?

A: Neither. Because we use the "average price" and "average quantity demanded" in our price elasticity of demand equation, 3.67 may be considered the price elasticity of demand at a point *midway between the two points identified on the demand curve.*

---

2. This formula is sometimes called the midpoint formula for calculating price elasticity of demand.

FROM PERFECTLY ELASTIC TO PERFECTLY INELASTIC DEMAND

Look back at the definition of price elasticity of demand and think of it as

$$E_d = \frac{\text{Percentage change in quantity demanded}}{\text{Percentage change in price}} = \frac{\text{Numerator}}{\text{Denominator}}$$

Focusing on the numerator and denominator, we realize that (1) the numerator can be greater than the denominator, (2) the numerator can be less than the denominator, or (3) the numerator can be equal to the denominator. These three cases, along with two peripherally related cases, are discussed in the following paragraphs. Exhibits 2 and 3 provide summaries of the discussion.

Elastic Demand ($E_d > 1$)

If the numerator (percentage change in quantity demanded) is greater than the denominator (percentage change in price), the elasticity coefficient is greater than one and demand is **elastic.** This means, of course, that quantity demanded changes proportionately more than price changes. A 10 percent increase in price causes, say, a 20 percent reduction in quantity demanded ($E_d = 2$).

> Percentage change in quantity demanded > Percentage change in price →
> $E_d > 1 →$ Demand is elastic

Inelastic Demand ($E_d < 1$)

If the numerator (percentage change in quantity demanded) is less than the denominator (percentage change in price), the elasticity coefficient is less than one and demand is **inelastic.** This means that quantity demanded changes proportionately less than price changes. A 10 percent increase in price causes, say, a 4 percent reduction in quantity demanded ($E_d = 0.4$).

> Percentage change in quantity demanded < Percentage change in price →
> $E_d < 1 →$ Demand is inelastic

Unit Elastic Demand ($E_d = 1$)

If the numerator (percentage change in quantity demanded) equals the denominator (percentage change in price), the elasticity coefficient is one. This means quantity demanded changes proportionately to price changes. For example, a 10 percent increase in price causes a 10 percent decrease in quantity demanded ($E_d = 1$). In this case, demand exhibits unitary elasticity or is **unit elastic.**

Elastic Demand
The percentage change in quantity demanded is greater than the percentage change in price. Quantity demanded changes proportionately more than price changes.

Inelastic Demand
The percentage change in quantity demanded is less than the percentage change in price. Quantity demanded changes proportionately less than price changes.

Unit Elastic Demand
The percentage change in quantity demanded is equal to the percentage change in price. Quantity demanded changes proportionately to price changes.

Perfectly Elastic Demand
A small percentage change in price causes an extremely large percentage change in quantity demanded (from buying all to buying nothing).

---

exhibit 2

Price Elasticity of Demand
Demand may be elastic, inelastic, unit elastic, perfectly elastic, or perfectly inelastic.

Elasticity Coefficient	Responsiveness of Quantity Demanded to a Change in Price	Terminology
$E_d > 1$	Quantity demanded changes proportionately more than price changes: $\%\Delta Q_d > \%\Delta P$.	Elastic
$E_d < 1$	Quantity demanded changes proportionately less than price changes: $\%\Delta Q_d < \%\Delta P$.	Inelastic
$E_d = 1$	Quantity demanded changes proportionately to price change: $\%\Delta Q_d = \%\Delta P$.	Unit elastic
$E_d = \infty$	Quantity demanded is extremely responsive to even very small changes in price.	Perfectly elastic
$E_d = 0$	Quantity demanded does not change as price changes.	Perfectly inelastic

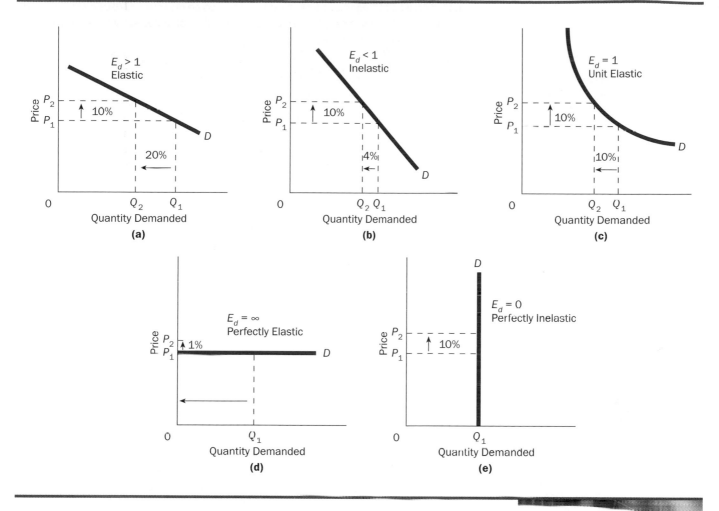

Percentage change in quantity demanded = Percentage change in price →
$E_d = 1 \rightarrow$ Demand is unit elastic

Perfectly Elastic Demand ($E_d = \infty$)

If quantity demanded is extremely responsive to changes in price, demand is **perfectly elastic.** For example, buyers are willing to buy all units of a seller's good at $5 per unit, but nothing at $5.10. A small percentage change in price causes an extremely large percentage change in quantity demanded (from buying all to buying nothing). The percentage is so large, in fact, that economists say it is "infinitely large."

Perfectly Inelastic Demand ($E_d = 0$)

If quantity demanded is completely unresponsive to changes in price, demand is **perfectly inelastic.** For example, buyers are willing to buy 100 units of good X at $10 each, and if price rises to $11, they are still willing to buy 100 units. A change in price causes no change in quantity demanded.

Q & A

Q: Suppose the price of Dogs Love It dog food rises 10 percent, and Jeremy doesn't buy any less of it per week for his dog. Does it follow that Jeremy's demand for Dogs Love It dog food is perfectly inelastic?

A: Yes, it is perfectly inelastic between the initial price and the 10 percent higher price. We qualify this answer because if price rises another 10 percent, Jeremy may cut back on his weekly purchases of Dogs Love It dog food and buy some other brand of dog food instead. The next section shows how price elasticity of demand changes as we move up some demand curves from lower to higher prices.

Q & A

Q: Aren't all demand curves downward-sloping because they express the inverse relationship between price and quantity demanded, *ceteris paribus*? In (d) and (e) in Exhibit 3, neither of the demand curves is downward-sloping. Why?

A: In the real world, no demand curves are perfectly elastic or perfectly inelastic at all prices. Thus, we ought to view the perfectly elastic and perfectly inelastic demand curves in Exhibit 3 as representations of the extreme limits between which all real-world demand curves fall.

We should add, however, that a few real-world demand curves approximate the perfectly elastic and inelastic demand curves in (d) and (e). In other words, they come very close. For example, the demand for a particular farmer's wheat approximates the perfectly elastic demand curve in (d). A later chapter discusses the perfectly elastic demand curve for firms in perfectly competitive markets.

PRICE ELASTICITY OF DEMAND AND TOTAL REVENUE (TOTAL EXPENDITURE)

Total Revenue
Price times quantity sold.

Total revenue (TR) of a seller equals the price of a good times the quantity of the good sold.[3] For example, if the hamburger stand down the street sells 100 hamburgers today at $1.50 each, its total revenue is $150.

Suppose the hamburger vendor raises the price of hamburgers to $2 each. What do you predict will happen to total revenue? Most people say it will increase; there is a widespread belief that higher prices bring higher total revenue. But total revenue may increase, decrease, or remain constant.

Suppose price rises to $2, but because of the higher price, the quantity of hamburgers sold falls to 50. Total revenue is now $100 (whereas it was $150). Whether total revenue rises, falls, or remains constant after a price change depends on whether the percentage change in quantity demanded is less than, greater than, or equal to the percentage change in price. Thus, price elasticity of demand influences total revenue.

If demand is elastic, the percentage change in quantity demanded is greater than the percentage change in price. Given a price rise of, say, 5 percent, quantity demanded falls by more than 5 percent—say, 8 percent. What happens to total revenue? Because quantity demanded falls, or sales fall off, by a greater percentage than price rises, total revenue decreases. In short, if demand is elastic, a price rise decreases total revenue.

$$\text{Demand is elastic: } P\uparrow \rightarrow TR\downarrow$$

What happens to total revenue if demand is elastic and price falls? In this case, quantity demanded rises (price and quantity demanded are inversely related) by a greater percentage than price falls, causing total revenue to increase. In short, if demand is elastic, a price fall increases total revenue.

$$\text{Demand is elastic: } P\downarrow \rightarrow TR\uparrow$$

If demand is inelastic, the percentage change in quantity demanded is less than the percentage change in price. If price rises, quantity demanded falls but by

---

3. In this discussion, "total revenue" and "total expenditure" are equivalent terms. Total revenue equals price times the quantity sold. Total expenditure equals price times the quantity purchased. If something is sold, it must be purchased, making total revenue equal to total expenditure. The term "total revenue" is used when looking at things from the point of view of the sellers in a market. The term "total expenditure" is used when looking at things from the point of view of the buyers in a market. Buyers make expenditures, sellers receive revenues.

a smaller percentage than price rises. As a result, total revenue increases. So, if demand is inelastic, a price rise increases total revenue. However, if price falls, quantity demanded rises by a smaller percentage than price falls and total revenue decreases. If demand is inelastic, a price fall decreases total revenue.

$$\text{Demand is inelastic: } P\uparrow \rightarrow TR\uparrow$$
$$\text{Demand is inelastic: } P\downarrow \rightarrow TR\downarrow$$

If demand is unit elastic, the percentage change in quantity demanded equals the percentage change in price. If price rises, quantity demanded falls by the same percentage as price rises. Total revenue does not change. If price falls, quantity demanded rises by the same percentage as price falls. Again, total revenue does not change. If demand is unit elastic, a rise or fall in price leaves total revenue unchanged.

$$\text{Demand is unit elastic: } P\uparrow \rightarrow \overline{TR}$$
$$\text{Demand is unit elastic: } P\downarrow \rightarrow \overline{TR}$$

For a review of the material in this section, see Exhibit 4.

WHEN IS A HALF-PACKED AUDITORIUM BETTER THAN A PACKED ONE?

Suppose you are the manager of a rock group that will soon go on a tour of 30 U.S. cities. In each city, the group will play in an auditorium. The auditorium in Des Moines, Iowa, seats, say, 20,000 people. Is it better to sell all 20,000 tickets for the rock group's performance or to sell less than 20,000 tickets, perhaps 10,000 tickets?

Most people will say it is better to sell 20,000 tickets than 10,000 tickets. But is it necessarily better? To sell 20,000 tickets, the price per ticket will have to be lower than the price per ticket to sell 10,000 tickets. Suppose that to sell all 20,000 tickets, the ticket price must be $10. In this case, the total revenue will be $200,000. Suppose, however, that at $25 per ticket, 10,000 tickets (and no more) can be sold. In this case, the total revenue will be $250,000. In other words, a $10 ticket price fills the auditorium to capacity and generates $200,000 total revenue. A $25 ticket price fills only half the auditorium but generates $250,000 total revenue.

Q & A   **Q:** Doesn't the analysis implicitly assume that only one ticket price, either $25 or $10, can be charged? If more than one price can be charged, then the 10,000 good seats in the auditorium might be sold for $25 each, and the remaining 10,000 not-so-good seats might be sold for $10 each. The total revenue would be $350,000 ($25 × 10,000 + $10 × 10,000 = $350,000). If only one price can be charged, a half-packed auditorium may, under certain conditions, generate more revenue than a packed auditorium. But if two prices can be charged, isn't a packed auditorium preferable to a half-packed auditorium?

A: True, the assumption is that only one price can be charged; that is, all seats must be priced at either $10 or $25, not some seats at $10 and some seats at $25. Furthermore, charging a higher price for good seats and a lower price for not-so-good seats actually happens at rock concerts, plays, basketball games, and so forth. The example has demonstrated why.

AGRICULTURE: AN APPLICATION OF PRICE ELASTICITY OF DEMAND

At the beginning of this century, one farmer produced enough food to feed 8 people. Today, one farmer produces enough food to feed 35 people. Obviously, farmers have become more productive over the years.

Increased productivity in the agricultural sector has pushed the supply curve of farm products rightward. From the perspective of consumers, this is good. Increased supply means more food at lower prices. But from the perspective of farmers, lower prices do not necessarily mean higher revenues. For example, if

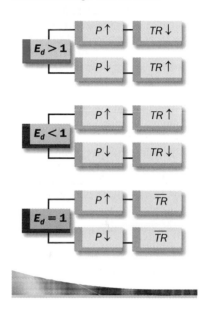

exhibit 4

Elasticities, Price Changes, and Total Revenue
If demand is elastic, a price rise leads to a decrease in total revenue (TR), and a price fall leads to an increase in total revenue. If demand is inelastic, a price rise leads to an increase in total revenue, and a price fall leads to a decrease in total revenue. If demand is unit elastic, a rise or fall in price does not change total revenue.

ECONOMICS IN...

Everyday Life   Popular Culture   Technology   The World

Can a Drug Bust Increase Drug-Related Crime?

Most people believe the sale or possession of drugs such as cocaine and heroin should be illegal. But sometimes laws may have unintended effects. Do drug laws have unintended effects? Let's analyze the enforcement of drug laws in terms of supply, demand, and price elasticity of demand.

Suppose for every $100 of illegal drug sales, 60 percent of the $100 is obtained by illegal means. That is, buyers of $100 worth of illegal drugs obtain $60 of the purchase price from criminal activities such as burglaries, muggings, and so on.

We assume the demand for and supply of cocaine in a particular city are represented by D_1 and S_1 in Exhibit 5. The equilibrium price of $50 an ounce and the equilibrium quantity of 1,000 ounces gives cocaine dealers a total revenue of $50,000. If 60 percent of this total revenue is obtained by the criminal activities of cocaine buyers, then $30,000 worth of crime has been committed to purchase the $50,000 worth of cocaine.

Now suppose there is a drug bust in the city. As a result, the drug enforcement authorities reduce the supply of cocaine. The supply curve shifts leftward from S_1 to S_2. The equilibrium price rises to $120 an ounce and the equilibrium quantity falls to 600 ounces. The demand for cocaine is inelastic between the two prices, at 0.607. When demand is inelastic, an increase in price will raise total revenue. The total revenue received by cocaine dealers is now $72,000. If, again, we assume that 60 percent of the total revenue comes from criminal activity, then $43,200 worth of crime has been committed to purchase the $72,000 worth of cocaine.

Our conclusion: If the demand for cocaine is inelastic and people commit crimes to buy drugs, then a drug bust can actually increase the amount of drug-related crime. Obviously, this is an unintended effect of drug enforcement.

exhibit 5

Drug Busts and Drug-Related Crime

In the exhibit, P = price of cocaine, Q = quantity of cocaine, and TR = total revenue from selling cocaine. At a price of $50 for an ounce of cocaine, equilibrium quantity is 1,000 ounces and total revenue is $50,000. If $60 of every $100 cocaine purchase is obtained through crime, then $30,000 worth of crime is committed to purchase $50,000 worth of cocaine. As a result of a drug bust, the supply of cocaine shifts leftward; the price rises and the quantity falls. Because we have assumed the demand for cocaine is inelastic, total revenue rises to $72,000. Sixty percent of this comes from criminal activities, or $43,200.

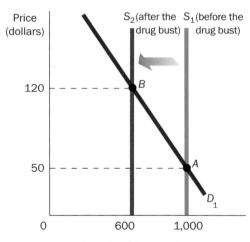

	P	Q	TR	Dollar Amount of *TR* Obtained Through Crime
Before Drug Bust	$50	1,000	$50,000	$30,000
After Drug Bust	120	600	72,000	43,200

the demand curve for a particular food is inelastic, a lower price brings lower, not higher, revenues.

Exhibit 6a illustrates a rightward shift in the supply curve for a particular food, due to an increase in productivity. As a result, equilibrium price falls and equilibrium quantity rises. Because the demand curve between the two equilibrium points, E_1 and E_2, is inelastic, total revenue is less at E_2 than at E_1.

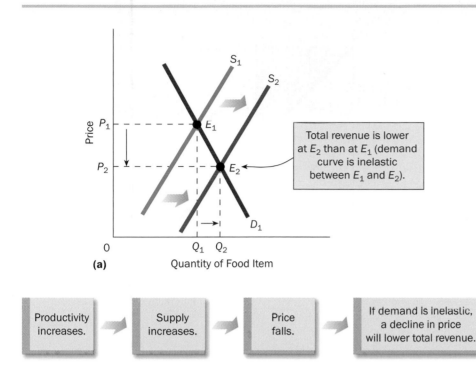

(a)

Quantity of Food Item

Total revenue is lower at E_2 than at E_1 (demand curve is inelastic between E_1 and E_2).

| Productivity increases. | → | Supply increases. | → | Price falls. | → | If demand is inelastic, a decline in price will lower total revenue. |

(b)

exhibit 6

High Productivity Doesn't Always Benefit Farmers as a Group
(a) Owing to increased agricultural productivity, the supply curve shifts rightward from S_1 to S_2. As a result, equilibrium price falls and equilibrium quantity rises. The demand curve between E_1 and E_2 is inelastic (the percentage change in quantity demanded is less than the percentage change in price), so total revenue is lower at E_2 than at E_1. In summary, increased productivity results in lower prices for consumers and lower revenues for farmers. (b) We show the links between productivity increases and a decline in total revenue. For farmers as a group, increased productivity can lead to lower incomes.

In summary, increased productivity results in lower prices for consumers and lower revenues for farmers. These results are summarized in Exhibit 6b.

Self-Test *(Answers to Self-Test questions are in the Self Test Appendix.)*

1. On Tuesday, price and quantity demanded are $7 and 120 units, respectively. Ten days later, price and quantity demanded are $6 and 150 units, respectively. What is the price elasticity of demand between the price of $7 and $6?
2. What does a price elasticity of demand of 0.39 mean?
3. Identify what happens to total revenue as a result of each of the following: (a) price rises and demand is elastic; (b) price falls and demand is inelastic; (c) price rises and demand is unit elastic; (d) price rises and demand is inelastic; (e) price falls and demand is elastic.
4. Alexi says, "When a seller raises his price, his total revenue rises." What is Alexi implicitly assuming?

ELASTICITY: PART 2

This section discusses the elasticity ranges of a straight-line downward-sloping demand curve and the determinants of price elasticity of demand.

PRICE ELASTICITY OF DEMAND ALONG A STRAIGHT-LINE DEMAND CURVE

The price elasticity of demand for a straight-line downward-sloping demand curve varies from highly elastic to highly inelastic. To illustrate, consider the price elasticity of demand at the upper range of the demand curve in Exhibit 7a. No matter whether the price falls from $9 to $8, or rises from $8 to $9, using the price elasticity of demand formula (identified earlier in the chapter), we calculate price elasticity of demand as 5.66.[4]

---

4. Keep in mind that our formula uses the average of the two prices and the average of the two quantities demanded. You may want to look back at the formula to refresh your memory.

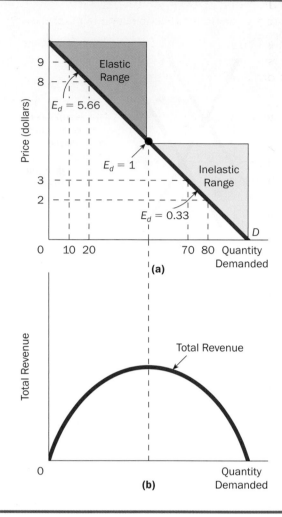

exhibit 7

Price Elasticity of Demand along a Straight-Line Demand Curve

In (a), the price elasticity of demand varies along the straight-line downward-sloping demand curve. There is an elastic range to the curve (where $E_d > 1$) and an inelastic range (where $E_d < 1$). At the midpoint of any straight-line downward-sloping demand curve, price elasticity of demand is equal to 1 ($E_d = 1$).

Part (b) shows that in the elastic range of the demand curve, total revenue rises as price is lowered. In the inelastic range of the demand curve, further price declines result in declining total revenue. Total revenue reaches its peak when price elasticity of demand equals 1.

Now consider the price elasticity of demand at the lower range of the demand curve in Exhibit 7a. No matter whether the price falls from \$3 to \$2, or rises from \$2 to \$3, we calculate the price elasticity of demand as 0.33.

In other words, along the range of the demand curve we have identified, price elasticity goes from being greater than 1 (5.66) to being less than 1 (0.33). Obviously, on its way from being greater than 1 to being less than 1, price elasticity of demand must be equal to 1. In Exhibit 7a, we have identified price elasticity of demand as equal to 1 at the *midpoint* of the demand curve.[5]

What do the elastic and inelastic ranges along the straight-line downward-sloping demand curve mean in terms of total revenue? If we start in the elastic range of the demand curve in Exhibit 7a and lower price, total revenue rises. This is shown in Exhibit 7b. In other words, as price is coming down within the elastic range of the demand curve in (a), total revenue is rising in (b).

When price has fallen enough such that we move into the inelastic range of the demand curve in (a), further price declines simply lower total revenue, as shown in (b). It holds, then, that total revenue is at its highest—its peak—when price elasticity of demand equals 1.

---

5. For any straight-line downward-sloping demand curve, price elasticity of demand equals 1 at the midpoint of the curve.

DETERMINANTS OF PRICE ELASTICITY OF DEMAND

Four factors that are relevant to the determination of price elasticity of demand are:

1. Number of substitutes
2. Necessities versus luxuries
3. Percentage of one's budget spent on the good
4. Time

Because all four factors interact, we hold all other things constant as we discuss each.

Number of Substitutes

Suppose good *A* has 2 substitutes and good *B* has 15 substitutes. Assume that each of the 2 substitutes for good *A* is as good (or close) a substitute for that good as each of the 15 substitutes is for good *B*.

Let the price of each good rise by 10 percent. The quantity demanded of each good decreases. Will the "percentage change in quantity demanded of good *A*" be greater or less than the "percentage change in quantity demanded of good *B*"? That is, will quantity demanded be more responsive to the 10 percent price rise in the good that has 2 substitutes (good *A*) or to the good that has 15 substitutes (good *B*)? The answer is the good with 15 substitutes, good *B*. This occurs because the greater the opportunities for substitution (there is more chance of substituting a good for *B* than for *A*), the greater the cutback in the quantity of the good purchased as its price rises. When the price of good *A* rises 10 percent, people can turn to 2 substitutes. Quantity demanded of good *A* falls, but not by as much as if 15 substitutes had been available, as there were for good *B*.

The relationship between the availability of substitutes and price elasticity is clear: *The more substitutes for a good, the higher the price elasticity of demand; the fewer substitutes for a good, the lower the price elasticity of demand.*

For example, the price elasticity of demand for Chevrolets is higher than the price elasticity of demand for all cars. This is because there are more substitutes for Chevrolets than there are for cars. Everything that is a substitute for a car (bus, train, walking, bicycle, and so on) is also a substitute for a specific type of car, such as a Chevrolet; but some things that are substitutes for a Chevrolet (Ford, Toyota, Chrysler, Mercedes-Benz, and so on) are not substitutes for a car. Instead, they are simply types of cars.

Thus, the relationship above can be stated as: *The more broadly defined the good, the fewer the substitutes; the more narrowly defined the good, the greater the substitutes.* There are more substitutes for this economics textbook than there are for textbooks. There are more substitutes for Coca-Cola than there are for soft drinks.

Necessities versus Luxuries

Generally, *the more that a good is considered a luxury (a good that we can do without) rather than a necessity (a good that we can't do without), the higher the price elasticity of demand.* For example, consider two goods—jewelry and a medicine for controlling high blood pressure. If the price of jewelry rises, it is easy to cut back on jewelry purchases. No one really needs jewelry in order to live. However, if the price of the medicine for controlling one's high blood pressure rises, it is not so easy to cut back on it. We expect the price elasticity of demand for jewelry to be higher than the price elasticity of demand for medicine used to control high blood pressure.

Percentage of One's Budget Spent on the Good

Claire Rossi has a monthly budget of $3,000. Of this monthly budget, she spends $3 per month on pens and $400 per month on dinners at restaurants. In percentage terms, she spends 0.1 percent of her monthly budget on pens and 13 percent of her monthly budget on dinners at restaurants. Suppose both the price of pens and

http://

Go to *http://www.travelocity.com*. In the "From:" and "To:" boxes under "Find me the best round-trip," enter LAX and SFO, respectively. Count the number of airlines that have nonstop flights. Click "New Flight Search," and change SFO to SMF. Count the number of airlines that have nonstop flights. Do you think the price elasticity of demand is greater for the LAX-SFO trip or the LAX-SMF trip? Explain your answer.

Why Did Burger King Hire Shaq?

Many companies hire celebrities to advertise their products. In the past, Shaquille O'Neal was hired to advertise Burger King, Cindy Crawford was hired to advertise Pepsi, Jerry Seinfeld to advertise American Express, and Michael Jordan to advertise products such as Gatorade and Nike.

Why do companies hire celebrities to pitch their wares? The obvious answer is to get the attention of consumers. When people see a sports star, television star, model, or movie star talking about a product, they are likely to take notice.

But there are other ways companies can get the attention of consumers, so maybe another factor is involved. Some economists have hypothesized that this other factor is related to price elasticity of demand and total revenue.

Consider the case of basketball star Shaquille O'Neal, who has advertised Burger King in the past. What message was Burger King trying to convey with its ads showing Shaq ordering a Whopper? The message may have been this: For Shaq, there is only one hamburger—no substitutes.

If the buying public accepts this message—if buyers believe there are no substitutes for a Whopper or if they want to do what Shaq does—then the price elasticity of a Whopper declines. The fewer substitutes, the lower the price elasticity of demand.

And if it is possible to get the demand for Whoppers to become inelastic (at least for a short range of the demand curve above current price), then Burger King can raise both price and total revenue. Remember, if demand is inelastic, an increase in price leads to higher total revenue.

Does Burger King want to increase its total revenue? Under the conditions stated here, it certainly does.

It's true that, at a higher price, fewer Whoppers will be sold. But profit is the objective, not number of Whoppers sold. Profit is the difference between total revenue and total cost. If the demand for a Whopper is inelastic, a price increase will raise total revenue. It will also mean fewer Whoppers sold, which will lower costs. If revenues rise and costs decline, profits rise.

Our concluding point is a simple one: The discussion of price elasticity of demand in this chapter isn't so far removed from the discussions in the offices of major companies and advertising firms as you may have thought.

---

the price of dinners at restaurants double. Would Claire be more responsive to the change in the price of pens or dinners at restaurants? The answer is the price of dinners at restaurants. The reason is that a doubling in price of a good on which Claire spends 0.1 percent of her budget is not felt as strongly as a doubling in price of a good on which she spends 13 percent. Claire is more likely to ignore the doubling in the price of pens than she is the doubling in the price of dinners at restaurants. Buyers are (and thus quantity demanded is) more responsive to price the larger the percentage of their budget that goes for the purchase of the good. *The greater the percentage of one's budget that goes to purchase a good, the higher the price elasticity of demand; the smaller the percentage of one's budget that goes to purchase a good, the lower the price elasticity of demand.*

Time

As time passes, buyers have greater opportunities to be responsive to a price change. If the price of electricity went up today, and you knew about it, you probably would not change your consumption of electricity today as much as you would three months from today. As time passes, you have more chances to change your consumption by finding substitutes (natural gas), changing your lifestyle (buying more blankets and turning down the thermostat at night), and so on. We conclude: *The more time that passes (since the price change), the higher the price elasticity of demand for the good; the less time that passes, the lower the price elasticity of demand for the good.*[6] In other words, price elasticity of demand for a good is higher in the long run than in the short run.

For example, consider gasoline consumption patterns in the period 1973–1975. Gasoline prices increased a dramatic 71 percent during this period. The consumption of gasoline didn't fall immediately and sharply. Motorists didn't immediately stop driving big gas-guzzling cars. As time passed, however, many car owners traded in their big cars for compact cars. Car buyers became more concerned with the miles a car could travel per gallon of gas. People began to form carpools. The short-run price elasticity of demand for gasoline was estimated at 0.2; the long-run price elasticity of demand for gasoline was estimated at 0.7, 3½ times larger.

Self-Test

1. If there are 7 substitutes for good X and demand is inelastic, does it follow that if there are 9 substitutes for good X demand will be elastic? Explain your answer.

2. Price elasticity of demand is predicted to be higher for which good of the following combinations of goods: (a) Compaq computers or computers; (b) Heinz ketchup or ketchup; (c) Perrier water or water? Explain your answers.

OTHER ELASTICITY CONCEPTS

This section looks at three other elasticities: cross elasticity of demand, income elasticity of demand, and price elasticity of supply. Then, the relationship between taxes and elasticity is explored.

CROSS ELASTICITY OF DEMAND

Cross elasticity of demand measures the responsiveness in the quantity demanded of one good to changes in the price of another good. It is defined as the percentage change in the quantity demanded of one good divided by the percentage change in the price of another good.

> **Cross Elasticity of Demand**
> Measures the responsiveness in quantity demanded of one good to changes in the price of another good.

$$E_c = \frac{\text{Percentage change in quantity demanded of one good}}{\text{Percentage change in price of another good}}$$

where E_c stands for coefficient of cross elasticity of demand, or elasticity coefficient.[7]

This concept is often used to determine whether two goods are substitutes or complements and the degree to which one good is a substitute for or complement to another. Consider two goods: Skippy peanut butter and Jif peanut butter. Suppose that when the price of Jif peanut butter increases by 10 percent, the quantity demanded of Skippy peanut butter increases by 45 percent. The cross elasticity of demand for Skippy with respect to the price of Jif is written

$$E_c = \frac{\text{Percentage change in quantity demanded of Skippy}}{\text{Percentage change in price of Jif}}$$

In this case, the cross elasticity of demand is a positive 4.5. When the elasticity coefficient is positive, the percentage change in the quantity demanded of one

---

6. If we say, "The more time that passes (since the price change), the higher the price elasticity of demand," wouldn't it follow that price elasticity of demand gets steadily larger? For example, might it be that on Tuesday the price of good X rises, and 5 days later, $E_d = 0.70$, 10 days later it is 0.76, and so on toward infinity? This is not exactly the case. Obviously, there comes a time when quantity demanded is no longer adjusting to a change in price (just as there comes a time when there are no longer any ripples in the lake from the passing motorboat). Our conditional statement ("the more times that passes . . .") implies this condition.

7. A question normally arises: How can E_d and E_c both be the elasticity coefficient? It is a matter of convenience. When speaking about price elasticity of demand, the coefficient of price elasticity of demand is referred to as the "elasticity coefficient." When speaking about cross elasticity of demand, the coefficient of cross elasticity of demand is referred to as the "elasticity coefficient." The practice holds for other elasticities as well.

ECONOMICS IN...

Will High Taxes on Cigarettes Reduce Smoking?

In recent years, there have been attempts to raise the taxes on cigarettes. The stated purpose of the increase in taxes is to make smoking more expensive in the hope that people will quit smoking or reduce the amount they smoke or never start smoking.

But will higher taxes on cigarettes cause millions of smokers to stop or cut back on smoking? Will it prevent many teenagers from starting to smoke and reduce the number of teenagers who are smoking? If the demand curve for cigarettes is downward-sloping, higher cigarette prices (brought about by higher taxes) will decrease the quantity demanded of cigarettes. But the question is: How much? Thus, price elasticity of demand is needed for the analysis.

To take an extreme case, suppose the demand curve for cigarettes is perfectly inelastic between the current price and the new, higher price brought about through higher taxes. In this case, the quantity demanded of cigarettes will not change. If the demand curve is inelastic (but not perfectly inelastic), the decline in the quantity demanded of cigarettes will be less than the percentage increase in the price of cigarettes.

The anti-tobacco lobby would prefer that the demand curve for cigarettes be highly elastic. In this case, the percentage change in the quantity demanded of cigarettes will be greater than the percentage change in price. Many more people will stop smoking if cigarette demand is elastic than if it is inelastic.

Another consideration is that the elasticity of demand for cigarettes may be different for adults than it is for teenagers. In fact, some studies show that teenagers are much more sensitive to cigarette price than adults are. In other words, the elasticity of demand for cigarettes is greater for teenagers than for adults.

One study found the elasticity of demand for cigarettes to be 0.35 (in the long run). This study did not separate adult smoking and teenage smoking. Another study looked at only teenage smoking and concluded that for every 10 percent rise in price, quantity demanded would decline by 12 percent. In other words, demand for cigarettes by teenagers is elastic. For those who want to use higher cigarette taxes as a means of curtailing teenage smoking, that is encouraging news.

---

good (numerator) moves in the same direction as the percentage change in the price of another good (denominator). This is representative of goods that are substitutes. As the price of Jif rises, the demand curve for Skippy shifts rightward, causing the quantity demanded of Skippy to increase at every price.[8] We conclude that if $E_c > 0$, the two goods are substitutes.

$$E_c > 0 \rightarrow \text{Goods are substitutes}$$

If the elasticity coefficient is negative, $E_c < 0$, the two goods are complements.

$$E_c < 0 \rightarrow \text{Goods are complements}$$

A negative elasticity coefficient occurs when the percentage change in the quantity demanded of one good (numerator) and the percentage change in the price of another good (denominator) move in opposite directions. Consider an example. Suppose the price of cars increases by 5 percent and the quantity demanded of car tires decreases by 10 percent. Calculating the cross elasticity of demand, we have -10 percent/5 percent $= -2$. Cars and car tires are complements.

The concept of cross elasticity of demand can be very useful. Suppose a company sells cheese. A natural question might be: What goods are substitutes for cheese? The answer would help identify the company's competitors. The company could find out which goods are substitutes for cheese by calculating the

---

8. Recall that if two goods are substitutes, a rise in the price of one good causes the demand for the other good to increase.

cross elasticity of demand between cheese and other goods. A positive cross elasticity of demand would indicate the two goods were substitutes; and the higher the cross elasticity of demand, the greater the degree of substitution.

INCOME ELASTICITY OF DEMAND

Income elasticity of demand measures the responsiveness of quantity demanded to changes in income. It is defined as the percentage change in quantity demanded of a good divided by the percentage change in income.

$$E_y = \frac{\text{Percentage change in quantity demanded}}{\text{Percentage change in income}}$$

where E_y = coefficient of income elasticity of demand, or elasticity coefficient.

Income elasticity of demand is positive, $E_y > 0$, for a *normal good*. Recall that a normal good is one whose demand, and thus quantity demanded, increases, given an increase in income. Thus, the variables in the numerator and denominator in the income elasticity of demand formula move in the same direction.

$$E_y > 0 \rightarrow \text{Normal good}$$

In contrast to a normal good, the demand for an *inferior good* decreases as income increases. Income elasticity of demand for an inferior good is negative, $E_y < 0$.

$$E_y < 0 \rightarrow \text{Inferior good}$$

To calculate the income elasticity of demand for a good, we use the same approach that we used to calculate price elasticity of demand.

$$E_y = \frac{\dfrac{\Delta Q_d}{Q_{dAverage}}}{\dfrac{\Delta Y}{Y_{Average}}}$$

where $Q_{dAverage}$ is the average quantity demanded and $Y_{Average}$ is the average income.

Suppose income increases from $500 to $600 per month and, as a result, quantity demanded of good X increases from 20 units to 30 units per month. We have

$$E_y = \frac{\dfrac{10}{25}}{\dfrac{100}{550}} = 2.2$$

E_y is a positive number, so good X is a normal good. Also, because $E_y > 1$, demand for good X is said to be **income elastic.** This means the percentage change in quantity demanded of the good is greater than the percentage change in income. If $E_y < 1$, the demand for the good is said to be **income inelastic.** If $E_y = 1$, then it is **income unit elastic.**

Q: Can a good be both normal and income inelastic?

A: Yes, it can. For a normal good, $E_y > 0$. For an income inelastic good, $E_y < 1$. Suppose that for good X, $E_y = 0.8$. This is a positive number (hence, X is a normal good) that is less than one (hence, X is income inelastic). Food, tobacco, and health-related drugs have been calculated to have elasticity coefficients greater than 0 but less than 1.

ECONOMICS IN...

Everyday Life **Popular Culture** **Technology** **The World**

Are Children Substitutes or Complements?

Not all parents are alike. Some parents spend a lot of time with their children, some do not. Some parents (of similar incomes) spend a lot of money on their children, some do not. Some parents are strict disciplinarians, some are not. Which parental behavioral differences are significant? For example, if parents A and parents B spend different amounts of time reading to their children at bedtime, is this difference a significant difference? Are children who are read to a lot different from children who are read to very little or not at all? If not, then perhaps this parental difference does not matter.

One difference in parental behavior that may be significant is whether parents treat their children as substitutes or as complements. To illustrate, suppose Bob is the father of two boys, Zack, 4 years old, and Dylan, 6 years old. Bob spends time with each of his boys and the amount of time he spends with each boy often depends on the "price" the son "charges" his father to be with him. For example, Zack is a little harder to be around than Dylan (he asks for more things from his father, he doesn't seem to be as happy doing certain things, and so on), so that the "price" Bob has to pay to be around Zack is higher than the price he has to pay to be around Dylan.

How will a change in the price each son charges his father influence the time the father spends with the other son? This question involves cross elasticity of demand, where

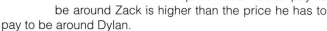

$$E_c = \frac{\text{Percentage change in quantity}}{\text{Percentage change in price Zack}}$$
$$\text{demanded of time spent with Dylan}$$
$$\text{charges his father to be with him}$$

Suppose Zack increases the price he charges his father to be with him. He demands more of his father, he seems less content when his father suggests certain activities, and so on. How will Bob react? If an increase in the price he has to pay to be with Zack increases the amount of time he wants to spend with Dylan, then as far as Bob is concerned, Dylan and Zack are substitutes ($E_c > 0$). But if an increase in the price he has to pay to be with Zack causes Bob to decrease the time he spends with Dylan, then Dylan and Zack are complements ($E_c < 0$).

In the first case, where the two boys are substitutes, the father may be saying, "I like to be with both of my boys, but if one makes it harder for me to be with him, I'll spend less time with him and I'll spend more time with the other." In the second case, where the two boys are complements, the father may be saying, "I like to be with both of my boys, but if one makes it harder for me to be with him, I'll spend less time with him and less time with the other too."

Does it matter to the two boys whether they are viewed by their father as substitutes or complements? Consider things from Dylan's perspective. Suppose he wants his father to spend more time with him. If Zack raises the price to his father of being with him (Zack) and Dylan and Zack are substitutes, then Dylan will benefit from Zack's raising the price. His father will spend less time with Zack and more with him. But if Zack and Dylan are complements, an increase in the price Zack charges his father to be with him (Zack) will cause his father to spend less time with Dylan.

Will Dylan act differently to Zack depending on whether he perceives himself as a substitute or a complement? If he perceives himself as a substitute, he may urge Zack to act up with Dad, knowing that this means Dad will spend more time with him, Dylan. But if he perceives himself as a complement, he may urge Zack to be good with Dad, knowing that if Zack charges his father a lower price to be around him (Zack) this will increase the amount of time the father will spend with Dylan.

TRAFFIC JAMS IN BANGKOK, SÃO PAULO, AND CAIRO

Bangkok is famous for its all-day traffic jams. The traffic jams and long delays in São Paulo are becoming legendary. To go from the center of the city to the airport, 19 miles away, takes 45 minutes on a good day and 2½ hours on a bad day. Cairo often has bumper-to-bumper traffic. In much of the world, traffic jams are becoming more common. What is the cause? Although there are many reasons for increased traffic jams, one reason involves income elasticity of demand. Income has been rising in many countries of the world and the income elasticity of car ownership in many countries is approximately 2. Certainly there would be fewer traffic jams, and fewer delays, if income elasticity of car ownership were lower.

PRICE ELASTICITY OF SUPPLY

Price elasticity of supply measures the responsiveness of quantity supplied to changes in price. It is defined as the percentage change in quantity supplied of a good divided by the percentage change in the price of the good.

$$E_s = \frac{\text{Percentage change in quantity supplied}}{\text{Percentage change in price}}$$

where E_s stands for coefficient of price elasticity of supply, or elasticity coefficient. We use the same approach to calculate price elasticity of supply that we used for price elasticity of demand.

In addition, supply can be classified as elastic, inelastic, unit elastic, perfectly elastic, or perfectly inelastic (Exhibit 8). Elastic supply ($E_s > 1$) refers to a percentage change in quantity supplied that is greater than the percentage change in price.

Percentage change in quantity supplied > Percentage change in price →
$E_s > 1 →$ Elastic supply

Price Elasticity of Supply
Measures the responsiveness of quantity supplied to changes in price.

exhibit 8

Price Elasticity of Supply
(a) The percentage change in quantity supplied is greater than the percentage change in price: $E_s > 1$ and supply is elastic. (b) The percentage change in quantity supplied is less than the percentage change in price: $E_s < 1$ and supply is inelastic. (c) The percentage change in quantity supplied is equal to the percentage change in price: $E_s = 1$ and supply is unit elastic. (d) A small change in price changes quantity supplied by an infinite amount: $E_s = \infty$ and supply is perfectly elastic. (e) A change in price does not change quantity supplied: $E_s = 0$ and supply is perfectly inelastic.

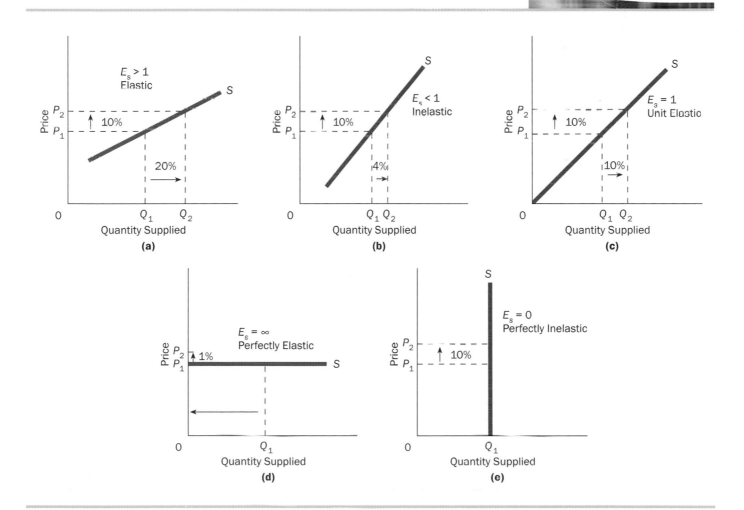

Inelastic supply ($E_s < 1$) refers to a percentage change in quantity supplied that is less than the percentage change in price.

Percentage change in quantity supplied < Percentage change in price →
$E_s < 1$ → Inelastic supply

Unit elastic supply ($E_s = 1$) refers to a percentage change in quantity supplied that is equal to the percentage change in price.

Percentage change in quantity supplied = Percentage change in price →
$E_s = 1$ → Unit elastic supply

Perfectly elastic supply ($E_s = \infty$) represents the case where a small change in price changes quantity supplied by an infinitely large amount (and thus the supply curve, or a portion of the overall supply curve, is horizontal). Perfectly inelastic supply ($E_s = 0$) represents the case where a change in price brings no change in quantity supplied (and thus the supply curve, or a portion of the overall supply curve, is vertical).

See Exhibit 9 for a review of the elasticity concepts.

PRICE ELASTICITY OF SUPPLY AND TIME

The longer the period of adjustment to a change in price, the higher the price elasticity of supply. (We are referring to goods whose quantity supplied can increase with time. This covers most goods. It does not, however, cover original Picasso paintings.) There is an obvious reason for this: Additional production takes time.

For example, suppose the demand for new housing increases in your city. Further, suppose this increase in demand occurs all at once on Tuesday. This places upward pressure on the price of housing. Will the number of houses supplied be much different on Saturday than it was on Tuesday? No, it won't. It will take time for suppliers to determine whether the increase in demand is permanent. If they decide it is a temporary state, not much will be done. If contractors decide it is permanent, they need time to move resources from the production of other things into the production of additional new housing. Simply put, the

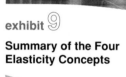

exhibit 9

Summary of the Four Elasticity Concepts

Type	Definition	Possibilities	Terminology
Price elasticity of demand	$\dfrac{\text{Percentage change in quantity demanded}}{\text{Percentage change in price}}$	$E_d > 1$ $E_d < 1$ $E_d = 1$ $E_d = \infty$ $E_d = 0$	Elastic Inelastic Unit elastic Perfectly elastic Perfectly inelastic
Cross elasticity of demand	$\dfrac{\text{Percentage change in quantity demanded of one good}}{\text{Percentage change in price of another good}}$	$E_c < 0$ $E_c > 0$	Complements Substitutes
Income elasticity of demand	$\dfrac{\text{Percentage change in quantity demanded}}{\text{Percentage change in income}}$	$E_y > 0$ $E_y < 0$ $E_y > 1$ $E_y < 1$ $E_y = 1$	Normal good Inferior good Income elastic Income inelastic Income unit elastic
Price elasticity of supply	$\dfrac{\text{Percentage change in quantity supplied}}{\text{Percentage change in price}}$	$E_s > 1$ $E_s < 1$ $E_s = 1$ $E_s = \infty$ $E_s = 0$	Elastic Inelastic Unit elastic Perfectly elastic Perfectly inelastic

change in quantity supplied of housing is likely to be different in the long run than in the short run, given a change in price. This translates into a higher price elasticity of supply in the long run than in the short run.

THINKING LIKE AN ECONOMIST

In a way, this chapter is about ratios. Ratios describe how one thing changes (the numerator) relative to a change in something else (the denominator). For example, when we discuss price elasticity of demand, we investigate how quantity demanded changes as price changes; when we discuss income elasticity of demand, we explore how quantity demanded changes as income changes. Economists often think in terms of ratios because they are often comparing the change in one variable to the change in another variable.

THE RELATIONSHIP BETWEEN TAXES AND ELASTICITY

Before discussing how elasticity affects taxes and tax revenues, we explore how supply and demand determine who pays a tax.

Who Pays the Tax?

Many people think that if government places a tax on the seller of a good, then the seller actually pays the tax. However, there is a difference between the *placement* and the *payment* of a tax. Furthermore, placement does not guarantee payment.

Suppose the government imposes a tax on sellers of VCR tapes. They are taxed $1 for every tape they sell. VCR tape sellers are told: Sell a tape, send $1 to the government. This government action changes equilibrium in the VCR tape market. To illustrate, in Exhibit 10, before the tax is imposed, the equilibrium price and quantity of tapes are $8 and Q_1, respectively. The tax per tape shifts the supply curve leftward from S_1 to S_2. The vertical distance between the two supply curves represents the $1 per tape tax.

Why does the vertical distance between the two curves represent the $1 per tape tax? This is because what matters to sellers is how much they keep for each tape sold, not how much buyers pay. For example, if sellers are keeping $8 per tape for Q_1 tapes before the tax is imposed, then they want to keep $8 per tape for Q_1 tapes after the tax is imposed. But if the tax is $1, the only way they can keep $8 per tape for Q_1 tapes is to receive $9 per tape. They receive $9 per

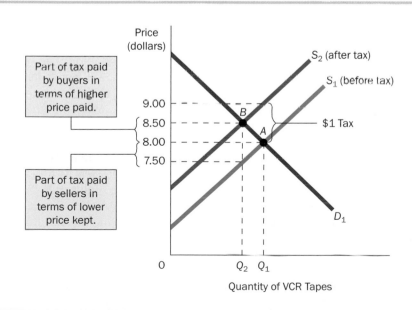

Part of tax paid by buyers in terms of higher price paid.

Part of tax paid by sellers in terms of lower price kept.

exhibit 10

Who Pays the Tax?
A tax placed on the sellers of VCR tapes shifts the supply curve from S_1 to S_2 and raises the equilibrium price from $8.00 to $8.50. Part of the tax is paid by buyers through a higher price paid ($8.50 instead of $8.00), and part of the tax is paid by sellers through a lower price kept ($7.50 instead of $8.00).

tape from buyers, turn over $1 to the government, and keep $8. In other words, each quantity on the new supply curve, S_2, corresponds to a $1 higher price than it did on the old supply curve, S_1. *It does not follow, though, that the new equilibrium price will be $1 higher than the old equilibrium price.*

The new equilibrium is at a price of $8.50 and quantity of Q_2. Buyers pay $8.50 per tape (after the tax is imposed) as opposed to $8.00 (before the tax was imposed). The difference between the new price and the old price is the amount of the $1.00 tax that buyers pay per tape. In this example, buyers pay 50 cents, or one-half of the $1.00 tax per tape.

Before the tax: Buyers pay $8.00.
After the tax: Buyers pay $8.50.

The sellers receive $8.50 per tape from buyers (after the tax is imposed) as opposed to $8.00 per tape (before the tax was imposed), but they do not get to keep $8.50 per tape. One dollar has to be turned over to the government, leaving the sellers with $7.50. Before the tax was imposed, however, sellers received and kept $8.00 per tape. As we noted, it is the price that sellers get to keep that is relevant to them. The difference between $8.00 and $7.50 is the amount of the tax per tape that sellers pay. In this example, the sellers pay 50 cents, or one-half of the $1.00 tax per tape.

Before the tax: Sellers receive $8.00 and keep $8.00.
After the tax: Sellers receive $8.50 and keep $7.50.

We conclude that the full tax was *placed* on the sellers, but they *paid* only one-half of the tax, whereas none of the tax was placed on buyers, but they paid one-half of the tax too. What is the lesson? Government can place a tax on whomever it wants, but the laws of supply and demand determine who actually ends up paying the tax.

 **THINKING LIKE AN ECONOMIST** *According to a layperson, if the government places a tax on A, then A pays the tax. The economist knows that the placement and the payment of a tax are two different things. Government may determine the placement of a tax, but supply and demand determine the payment of a tax.*

Elasticity and the Tax

In our tax example, the tax was $1 and the buyers paid half the tax and the sellers paid half the tax. This result does not occur in every situation. The buyer can pay more than half the tax. In fact, the buyer can pay the full tax if demand for the good is perfectly inelastic, as in Exhibit 11a. The tax shifts the supply curve from S_1 to S_2 and the equilibrium price rises from $8.00 to $9.00. In other words, if demand is perfectly inelastic and a tax is placed on the sellers of a good, buyers will end up paying the full tax in terms of a higher price.

Parts (b)–(d) of Exhibit 11 show other cases. In part (b), demand is perfectly elastic. The tax shifts the supply curve from S_1 to S_2, but there is no change in equilibrium price. We conclude that sellers must pay the full tax if demand is perfectly elastic.

In part (c), supply is perfectly elastic and buyers pay the full tax. In part (d), a change in price causes no change in quantity supplied. If sellers try to charge a higher price than $8 for their good (and thus try to get buyers to pay some of the tax), a surplus will result, driving the price back down to $8. In this case, sellers pay the full tax. Although it is not shown in the exhibit, sellers would receive $8, turn over $1 to the government, and keep $7 for each unit sold.

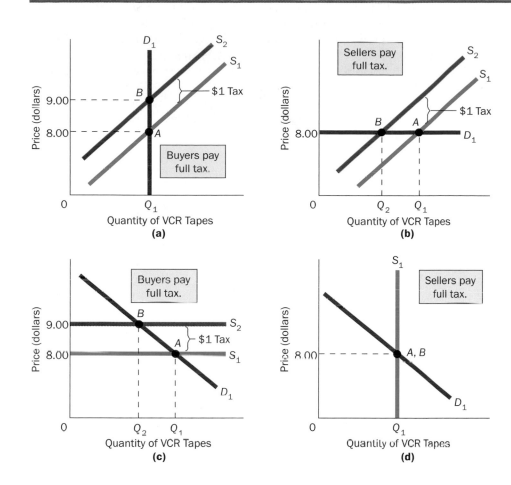

exhibit 11

Different Elasticities and Who Pays the Tax

Four extreme cases are illustrated here. If demand is perfectly inelastic (a) or if supply is perfectly elastic (c), buyers pay the full tax even though the tax may be placed entirely on sellers. If demand is perfectly elastic (b) or if supply is perfectly inelastic (d), the full tax is paid by the sellers.

Degree of Elasticity and Tax Revenue

Suppose there are two sellers: *A* and *B*. *A* faces a perfectly inelastic demand for her product and is currently selling 10,000 units a month. *B* faces an elastic demand for his product and is currently selling 10,000 units a month.

Government is thinking about placing a $1 tax per unit of product sold on one of the two sellers. If government's objective is to maximize tax revenues, which seller should it tax and why? The answer is *A,* the seller facing the inelastic demand curve.

To illustrate, in Exhibit 12, the demand curve facing seller *A* is D_1; the demand curve facing seller *B* is D_2. S_1 represents the supply curve for both firms. Currently, both firms are at equilibrium at point *A,* selling 10,000 units.

If government places a $1 tax per unit sold on seller *A,* the supply curve shifts to S_2 and equilibrium is now at point *C.* Because demand is perfectly inelastic, *A* still sells 10,000 units. Tax revenue equals the tax ($1) times 10,000 units, or $10,000.

If government places the $1 tax per unit sold on seller *B,* tax revenue will be only $8,000. When the tax shifts the supply curve to S_2, equilibrium moves to point *B,* where only 8,000 units are sold.

The lesson: Given the $1 tax per unit sold, tax revenues are maximized by placing the tax on the seller who faces the more inelastic (less elastic) demand curve.

exhibit 12

Maximizing Tax Revenues

Two sellers, A and B, are each currently selling 10,000 units of their good. A faces the demand curve D_1 and B faces D_2. If the objective is to maximize tax revenues with a $1 tax per unit of product sold and only one seller can be taxed, taxing A will maximize tax revenues and taxing B will not. Note that after the tax has been placed, the supply curve shifts from S_1 to S_2. A is in equilibrium at point C, selling 10,000 units, and B is in equilibrium at point B, selling 8,000 units. Because tax revenues equal the tax per unit times the quantity of output sold, taxing A raises $10,000 in tax revenues whereas taxing B raises $8,000.

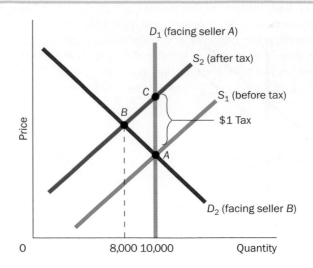

Self-Test

1. What does an income elasticity of demand of 1.33 mean?

2. If supply is perfectly inelastic, what does this signify?

3. Why will government raise more tax revenue if it applies a tax to a good with inelastic demand than if it applies the tax to a good with elastic demand?

4. Under what condition would a per-unit tax placed on the sellers of computers be fully paid by the buyers of computers?

A Reader Asks...

Is the Type of Thinking Inherent in Elasticity Useful?

The elasticity concepts in this chapter are interesting, and I'm sure they're useful to business firms. But I don't really see how thinking about elasticities helps me in any fundamental way. Any comments?

Elasticity (price, income, supply, cross) relates to a change in one thing relative to a change in something else. Thinking in terms of these types of relationships can help you gain insight into certain phenomena. For example, consider this question: If car companies increase the number of miles a car can travel on a gallon of gasoline, will cars cause more or less pollution as a result?

Now the answer most people will give is "less pollution." They reason this way: (1) If fuel economy increases, the average miles per gallon for a car will rise—say, from 27 mpg to 40 mpg. (2) Because they can travel more miles per gallon, people will have to buy fewer gallons of gasoline to get from one point to another. (3) Consequently,

people will buy and burn less gas. (4) This results in less pollution because burning gas causes carbon monoxide (pollution).

This argument sounds reasonable, and it could very well be true. But thinking "elastically" allows us to see why it might not be true. Things could unfold this way: (1) Because fuel economy increases, the cost per mile of travel declines. For example, if the price of one gallon of gas is $1.70 and a car gets 27 mpg, the cost per mile is $0.0629; but if the price is $1.70 and the car gets 40 mpg, the cost per mile is $0.0425. (2) At a lower cost per mile of travel, people will decide to travel more—after all, we assume the demand curve for traveling is downward sloping.

Thinking elastically, we now know that an increase in fuel economy can increase, decrease, or leave constant the gallon consumption of gasoline per month. It all depends on the percentage decline in gas consumption due to a higher mpg relative to the percentage increase in gas consumption due to a lower cost per mile of travel. For example, if the percentage decline in gas consumption due to a higher mpg is smaller than the percentage increase in gas consumption due to a lower cost per mile, then gas consumption will rise. Thus, car pollution will rise. We could not have easily come up with this conclusion had we not looked at the percentage change in one thing relative to the percentage change in something else. This type of thinking, of course, is inherent in the elasticity concepts discussed in this chapter.

Chapter Summary

Price Elasticity of Demand

- Price elasticity of demand is a measure of the responsiveness of quantity demanded to changes in price: E_d = percentage change in quantity demanded/percentage change in price.
- If the percentage change in quantity demanded is greater than the percentage change in price, demand is elastic. If the percentage change in quantity demanded is less than the percentage change in price, demand is inelastic. If the percentage change in quantity demanded is equal to the percentage change in price, demand is unit elastic. If a small change in price causes an infinitely large change in quantity demanded, demand is perfectly elastic. If a change in price causes no change in quantity demanded, demand is perfectly inelastic.
- The coefficient of price elasticity of demand (E_d) is negative, signifying the inverse relationship between price and quantity demanded. For convenience, however, the absolute value of the elasticity coefficient is used.

Total Revenue and Price Elasticity of Demand

- Total revenue equals price times quantity sold. Total expenditure equals price times quantity purchased. Total revenue equals total expenditure.
- If demand is elastic, price and total revenue are inversely related: As price rises (falls), total revenue falls (rises).
- If demand is inelastic, price and total revenue are directly related: As price rises (falls), total revenue rises (falls).
- If demand is unit elastic, total revenue is independent of price: As price rises (falls), total revenue remains constant.

Determinants of Price Elasticity of Demand

- The more substitutes for a good, the higher the price elasticity of demand; the fewer substitutes for a good, the lower the price elasticity of demand.
- The more that a good is considered a luxury instead of a necessity, the higher the price elasticity of demand.

- The greater the percentage of one's budget that goes to purchase a good, the higher the price elasticity of demand; the smaller the percentage of one's budget that goes to purchase a good, the lower the price elasticity of demand.
- The more time that passes (since a price change), the higher the price elasticity of demand; the less time that passes, the lower the price elasticity of demand.

Cross Elasticity of Demand

- Cross elasticity of demand measures the responsiveness in the quantity demanded of one good to changes in the price of another good: E_c = Percentage change in quantity demanded of one good/Percentage change in the price of another good.
- If $E_c > 0$, two goods are substitutes. If $E_c < 0$, two goods are complements.

Income Elasticity of Demand

- Income elasticity of demand measures the responsiveness of quantity demanded to changes in income: E_y = Percentage change in quantity demanded/Percentage change in income.
- If $E_y > 0$, the good is a normal good. If $E_y < 0$, the good is an inferior good.
- If $E_y > 1$, demand is income elastic. If $E_y < 1$, demand is income inelastic. If $E_y = 1$, demand is income unit elastic.

Price Elasticity of Supply

- Price elasticity of supply measures the responsiveness of quantity supplied to changes in price: E_s = Percentage change in quantity supplied/Percentage change in price.
- If the percentage change in quantity supplied is greater than the percentage change in price, supply is elastic. If the percentage change in quantity supplied is less than the percentage change in price, supply is inelastic. If the percentage change in quantity supplied is equal to the percentage change in price, supply is unit elastic.

- Price elasticity of supply is higher in the long run than in the short run.

Taxes and Elasticity

- There is a difference between the placement and payment of a tax. For example, a tax may be placed on the seller of a good and both the seller and buyer end up paying the tax.
- In this chapter, we discuss a per-unit tax that was placed on the seller of a specific good (VCR tapes). This tax shifted the supply curve of VCR tapes leftward. The vertical distance between the old supply curve (before the tax) and the new supply curve (after the tax) was equal to the per-unit tax.

- If a per-unit tax is placed on the seller of a good, both the buyer and the seller will pay part of the tax if the demand curve is downward-sloping and the supply curve is upward-sloping. The more inelastic the demand, the larger the percentage of the tax paid by the buyer. The more elastic the demand, the smaller the percentage of the tax paid by the buyer. When demand is perfectly inelastic, buyers pay the full tax. When demand is elastic, sellers pay the full tax. Also, when supply is perfectly elastic, buyers pay the full tax. When supply is perfectly inelastic, sellers pay the full tax.

Key Terms and Concepts

Price Elasticity of Demand
Elastic Demand
Inelastic Demand
Unit Elastic Demand
Perfectly Elastic Demand

Perfectly Inelastic Demand
Total Revenue
Cross Elasticity of Demand
Income Elasticity of Demand
Income Elastic

Income Inelastic
Income Unit Elastic
Price Elasticity of Supply

Economic Connections to You

Economic facts, actions, and changes create ripples that move away from their point of origin. Eventually, these ripples can intersect your life and have an effect on you. Consider the following example.

When a tax is placed on sellers, the amount of the tax actually paid by the sellers depends on price elasticity of supply and demand. A U.S. senator proposes that a tax of $100 for every unit sold be placed on firms in the computer industry. The senator thinks the computer industry is awash in high profits and believes the firms in the industry should shoulder their fair share of the tax burden. The senator's pro-

posal is passed into law. However, the firms in the computer industry don't pay the full tax. Part of the tax is paid by computer buyers in the form of higher computer prices. You pay part of the tax when you buy a new computer. Thus, there is a connection between the economic concept of price elasticity of demand and the price you pay for a computer—an economic connection to you.

Based on the material in this chapter, identify other ways in which economic facts, actions, and changes create ripples that eventually affect you.

Questions and Problems

1. Explain how a seller can determine whether the demand for his or her good is inelastic, elastic, or unit elastic between two prices.
2. Suppose the current price of gasoline at the pump is $1 per gallon and that one million gallons are sold per month. A politician proposes to add a 10-cent tax to the price of a gallon of gasoline. She says the tax will generate $100,000 tax revenues per month (one mil-

lion gallons × $0.10 = $100,000). What assumption is she making?
3. Suppose a straight-line downward-sloping demand curve shifts rightward. Is the price elasticity of demand higher, lower, or the same between any two prices on the new (higher) demand curve than on the old (lower) demand curve?

4. Suppose Austin, Texas, is hit by a tornado that destroys 25 percent of the housing in the area. Would you expect the total expenditure on housing after the tornado to be greater than, less than, or equal to what it was before the tornado?

5. Which good in each of the following pairs of goods has the higher price elasticity of demand? (a) airline travel in the short run or airline travel in the long run; (b) television sets or Sony television sets; (c) cars or Toyotas; (d) telephones or AT&T telephones; (e) popcorn or Orville Redenbacher's popcorn?

6. How might you determine whether toothpaste and mouthwash manufacturers are competitors?

7. Assume the demand for product A is perfectly inelastic. Further, assume that the buyers of A get the funds to pay for it by stealing. If the supply of A decreases, what happens to its price? What happens to the amount of crime committed by the buyers of A?

8. Suppose you learned that the price elasticity of demand for wheat is 0.7 between the current price for wheat and a price $2 higher per bushel. Do you think farmers collectively would try to reduce the supply of wheat and drive the price up $2 higher per bushel? Why? Assuming that they would try to reduce

supply, what problems might they have in actually doing so?

9. It has been said that if government wishes to tax certain goods, it should tax goods that have inelastic rather than elastic demand. What is the rationale for this statement?

10. In 1947, the U.S. Justice Department brought a suit against the DuPont Company (which at the time sold 75 percent of all the cellophane in the United States) for monopolizing the production and sale of cellophane. In court, the DuPont Company tried to show that cellophane was only one of several goods in the market in which it was sold. It argued that its market was not the cellophane market but the "flexible packaging materials" market, which included (besides cellophane) waxed paper, aluminum foil, and so forth. DuPont pointed out that it had only 20 percent of all sales in this more broadly defined market. Using this information, discuss how the concept of cross elasticity of demand would help establish whether DuPont should have been viewed as a firm in the cellophane market or as a firm in the "flexible packaging materials" market.

Working with Numbers and Graphs

1. A college raises its annual tuition from $2,000 to $2,500, and its student enrollment falls from 4,877 to 4,705. Compute the price elasticity of demand. Is demand elastic or inelastic?

2. As the price of good X rises from $10 to $12, the quantity demanded of good Y rises from 100 units to 114 units. Are X and Y substitutes or complements? What is the cross elasticity of demand?

3. The quantity demanded of good X rises from 130 to 145 units as income rises from $2,000 to $2,500 a month. What is the income elasticity of demand?

4. The quantity supplied of a good rises from 120 to 140 as price rises from $4 to $5.50. What is price elasticity of supply?

5. In the following figure, what is the price elasticity of demand between the two prices on D_1? on D_2?

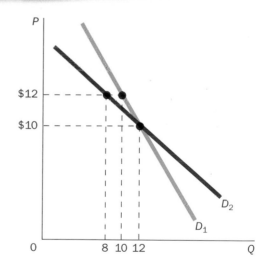

Go to *http://www.census.gov/statab/www/freq.html*. Select "Consumer Price Indexes—Selected Items." More than one table is provided, so be sure to select the correct CPI table.

1. Compare the changes in the price of ground beef over the years with the changes in the price of poultry. If we know that poultry sales fell 10 percent and that ground beef sales increased 20 percent, do you think that poultry and ground beef are substitutes? Explain your answer.
2. If the quantity of eggs purchased fell in 1998, would this be consistent with a movement along the demand curve for eggs or a shift in the demand curve for eggs? Explain your answer.
3. Check cable prices and TV prices. Is it possible to tell if cable services and TV sets are complements or substitutes? Explain your answer.
4. By what percentage did college tuition rise in the 1990s? Assuming that college administrators will raise tuition only if they expect higher revenues, what assumption must they have made about the price elasticity of demand for college?

Log on to the Arnold Xtra! Web site now (*http://arnoldxtra.swcollege.com*) for additional learning resources such as practice quizzes, help with graphing, video clips, and current event applications.

ch.6

CONSUMER CHOICE: MAXIMIZING UTILITY AND BEHAVIORAL ECONOMICS

When you purchase a computer, a book, a piece of jewelry, or something as small as a bag of potato chips, what do you think about just before you make the purchase? You may say, "I just ask myself if I want it or not." This would be the response of many people. Some economists have taken this response, put it under a microscope, and concluded that it is as if you say to yourself, "The marginal utility of this item divided by its price is greater than the marginal utility of other items divided by their prices, so I am going to make this purchase because it will increase my overall utility." You may not believe now that you or anyone else would think this, but you may believe differently after you study this chapter.

This chapter is about how consumers make choices. Most

economists hold that consumers, in choosing the way they do, try to max-

imize their utility or satisfaction. A discussion of utility maximization leads naturally

to discussions of the difference between total utility and marginal utility, the law of diminishing

marginal utility, consumer equilibrium, and the law of demand.

In recent years, some economists have questioned whether consumers make choices the way some of

the traditional economic models hypothesize they do. The issues that these economists have raised fall into what has

come to be known as behavioral economics, which we also discuss in this chapter.

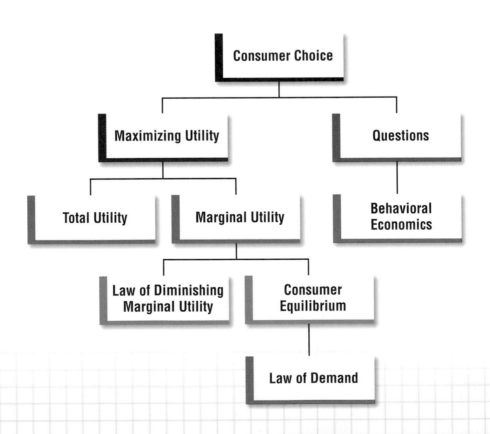

UTILITY THEORY

Water is cheap and diamonds are expensive. But water is necessary to life and diamonds are not. Isn't it odd—paradoxical?—that what is necessary to life is cheap and what is not necessary to life is expensive? The eighteenth-century economist Adam Smith wondered about this question. He observed that often things that have the greatest value in use, or are the most useful, have a relatively low price, and things that have little or no value in use have a high price. Smith's observation came to be known as the **diamond-water paradox,** or the paradox of value. The paradox challenged economists, and they sought a solution to it. This section begins to develop parts of the solution they found.

UTILITY, TOTAL AND MARGINAL

Saying that a good gives you **utility** is the same as saying that it has the power to satisfy wants, or that it gives you satisfaction. For example, suppose you buy your first unit of good X. You obtain a certain amount of utility, say, 10 **utils** from it. (Utils are an artificial construct used to "measure" utility; we realize you have never seen a util—no one has.)

You buy a second unit of good X. Once again, you get a certain amount of utility from this second unit, say, 8 utils. You purchase a third unit and receive 7 utils. The sum of the amounts of utility you obtain from each of the three units is the *total utility* you receive from purchasing good X—which is 25 utils. **Total utility** is the total satisfaction one receives from consuming a particular quantity of a good (in this example, three units of good X).

Total utility is different from marginal utility. **Marginal utility** is the additional utility gained from consuming an additional unit of good X. Marginal utility is the change in total utility divided by the change in the quantity consumed of a good:

$$MU = \Delta TU / \Delta Q$$

where the change in the quantity consumed of a good is usually equal to one unit.

To illustrate, suppose you receive 50 utils of total utility from consuming one apple and 80 utils of total utility from consuming two apples. What is the marginal utility of the second apple, or, in other words, what is the additional utility of consuming an additional apple? It is 30 utils.

LAW OF DIMINISHING MARGINAL UTILITY

Do you think the marginal utility of the second unit is greater than, less than, or equal to the marginal utility of the first unit? Before answering, consider the difference in marginal utility between the third unit and the second unit, or between the fifth unit and the fourth unit (had we extended the number of units consumed). In general, we are asking whether the marginal utility of the unit that comes next is greater than, less than, or equal to the marginal utility of the unit that comes before.

Economists have generally answered "less than." The **law of diminishing marginal utility** states that for a given time period, the marginal utility gained by consuming equal successive units of a good will decline as the amount consumed increases. In terms of our artificial units, utils, this means that the number of utils gained by the consumption of the first unit of a good is greater than the number of utils gained by the second (which is greater than the number gained by the third, which is greater than the number gained by the fourth, and so on).

The law of diminishing marginal utility is illustrated in Exhibit 1. The table in part (a) shows both the total utility of consuming a certain number of units of a good and the marginal utility of consuming additional units. The graph in part (b) shows total utility, and the graph in part (c) shows marginal utility. Notice how

Diamond-Water Paradox
The observation that those things that have the greatest value in use sometimes have little value in exchange and those things that have little value in use sometimes have the greatest value in exchange.

Utility
A measure of the satisfaction, happiness, or benefit that results from the consumption of a good.

Util
An artificial construct used to measure utility.

Total Utility
The total satisfaction a person receives from consuming a particular quantity of a good.

Marginal Utility
The additional utility a person receives from consuming an additional unit of a particular good.

Law of Diminishing Marginal Utility
The marginal utility gained by consuming equal successive units of a good will decline as the amount consumed increases.

exhibit 1

Total Utility, Marginal Utility, and the Law of Diminishing Marginal Utility

TU = total utility and MU = marginal utility. (a) Both total utility and marginal utility are expressed in utils. Marginal utility is the change in total utility divided by the change in the quantity consumed of the good, $MU = \Delta TU/\Delta Q$. (b) Total utility. (c) Marginal utility. Together, (b) and (c) demonstrate that total utility can increase (b) as marginal utility decreases (c).

(1) Units of Good X	(2) Total Utility (utils)	(3) Marginal Utility (utils)
0	0	—
1	10	10
2	19	9
3	27	8
4	34	7
5	40	6

(a)

> This is a total utility curve. It is derived by plotting the data in columns 1 and 2 in part (a) and then connecting the points.

> This is a marginal utility curve. It is derived by plotting the data in columns 1 and 3 in part (a) and then connecting the points.

(b)

(c)

the graphs in (b) and (c) show that total utility can increase as marginal utility decreases. This will be important in helping unravel the diamond-water paradox.

The law of diminishing marginal utility is based on the idea that if a good has a variety of uses but only one unit of the good is available, then the consumer will use the first unit to satisfy his or her most urgent want. If two units are available, the consumer will use the second unit to satisfy a less urgent want.

To illustrate, suppose that good X can be used to satisfy wants A through E, with A being the most urgent want and E being the least urgent want. Also, B is more urgent than C, C is more urgent than D, and D is more urgent than E. We can chart the wants as follows:

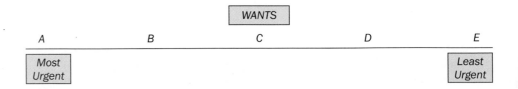

Suppose the first unit of good X can satisfy any one—but only one—of wants A through E. Which want will an individual choose to satisfy? The answer is the most urgent want—A. The individual chooses to satisfy A instead of B, C, D, or E because people will ordinarily satisfy their most urgent want before all others. If you were dying of thirst in a desert (having gone without water for three days)

and came across a quart of water, would you drink it or use it to wash your hands? You would drink it, of course. You would satisfy your most urgent want first. Washing your hands in the water would give you less utility than drinking the water.

The Law and the One-Hundredth Game of Chess

According to our definition of the law of diminishing marginal utility—the marginal utility gained by consuming equal successive units of a good will decline as the amount consumed increases—marginal utility begins to decline with the second unit of a good consumed. Occasionally, this doesn't appear to be the case. For example, someone may mention that his first chess game did not give him as much utility as his one-hundredth game. When he played his first chess game, he did not know how to play chess very well, but when he played his one-hundredth game, he did. The same can be said of other games such as golf and tennis. In short, sometimes you derive more utility from something as you get better at it.

Does this invalidate the law of diminishing marginal utility? Some economists think not. They argue that a person's first game of chess may not be the same good as his one-hundredth game. Although to an onlooker the first and the one-hundredth games may appear to be much alike (they use the same board and so forth), from the viewpoint of the chess player, there may be a large difference between the first game of chess and the one-hundredth game. In fact, the difference may be so large that we are dealing with two different goods.

This general problem has led some economists to refer to the less emphatic *principle* of diminishing marginal utility, rather than to the *law* of diminishing marginal utility. Other economists have simply noted that there are exceptions to the law of diminishing marginal utility. Still others have said that it is important to define the law (or principle) of diminishing marginal utility as follows: *The marginal utility associated with consuming equal successive units of a good will eventually decline as the amount consumed increases.* The key word is *eventually*. These economists state that a person may enjoy, say, the first piece of pizza immensely and the second even more, but *eventually* there comes a point when one piece of pizza (say, the fourth) brings less utility than the previous piece (the third). This last version of the law of diminishing marginal utility is consistent with the law as expressed by William Stanley Jevons, one of the founders of marginal utility theory. Jevons said that "the degree of utility varies with the quantity of commodity, and ultimately decreases as that quantity increases."

The Law and Boredom

Excitement is usually connected with high marginal utility, boredom with low marginal utility. The road from excitement to boredom is by way of repetition: doing the same thing repeatedly.

Doing the same thing repeatedly is similar to consistently consuming additional units of a good—to which the law of diminishing marginal utility applies. Does the law of diminishing marginal utility explain why we get bored?

Consider watching reruns on television. Few people want to watch a television show more than once in a season—hence, the declines in ratings after reruns begin. People know they will probably be bored seeing the show a second time. Not wanting to see a show more than once implicitly recognizes the validity of the law of diminishing marginal utility.

Or, consider the first few miles of a long-distance trip. Those early miles are usually the most exciting. As the day wears on and the miles roll by, boredom sets in. Are yawns the sign of boredom? Are yawns the sign of the law of diminishing marginal utility at work?

http://

Go to *http://www.yahoo.com*, and key "Chess" in the Search box. Next, select "play chess with your friends in Yahoo!" Here you can play chess online with people from around the world. How many people are currently playing chess? Suppose you will play 50 games of chess in the next two years in each of two settings. In setting *A*, you always play chess with the same person. In setting *B*, you always play the next chess game with a different person. In which setting, *A* or *B*, do you think the marginal utility of the 40th game of chess will be higher? From your answer, what do you conclude about the marginal utility of playing chess?

Cuban Cigars

The law of diminishing marginal utility explains why people trade. To illustrate, consider two people, Smith and Jones. Smith has 100 apples and Jones has 100 oranges. As Smith consumes her apples, marginal utility declines. Her tenth apple doesn't give her as much utility as her ninth, and so on. The same is true for Jones with respect to oranges. In other words, as Smith and Jones begin to consume what they have, marginal utility falls.

At some point, Smith's marginal utility of consuming another apple is likely less than her marginal utility of consuming something different—say, an orange. And at some point, Jones's marginal utility of consuming another orange is likely less than his marginal utility of consuming something different—say, an apple. When this point comes, Smith and Jones will trade. For Smith, the marginal utility of an apple will be less than the marginal utility of an orange, and she will gladly trade an apple for an orange. For Jones, the marginal utility of an orange will be less than the marginal utility of an apple, and he will gladly trade an orange for an apple.

Suppose the law of diminishing marginal utility did not exist. Smith would have the same marginal utility when she consumed her first and her one-hundredth apple and this marginal utility would always be greater than her marginal utility of an orange. The same would be true for Jones with respect to oranges. In this case, Smith and Jones would not trade with each other. It is the law of diminishing marginal utility, at work on both apples and oranges, that gets Smith and Jones to eventually trade with each other.

What holds for individuals in a country holds for individuals in different countries. Cubans may like cigars, but at some point, the marginal utility of a cigar is less than the marginal utility of some good produced in another country and Cubans are happy to trade cigars for other goods. Chileans might like grapes, but at some point, the marginal utility of a grape is less than the marginal utility of some good produced in another country and Chileans are then happy to trade grapes for other goods.

THE MILLIONAIRE AND THE PAUPER: WHAT THE LAW SAYS AND DOESN'T SAY

Who gets more utility from one more dollar, a poor man or a millionaire? Most people would say that a poor man gets more utility from one more dollar because the poor man has so many fewer dollars than the millionaire. "What's an extra dollar to a millionaire?" they ask. Then they answer, "Nothing. A millionaire has so many dollars, one more doesn't mean a thing."

Some people think the law of diminishing marginal utility substantiates the claim that a millionaire gets less utility from one more dollar than a poor man does. Unfortunately, though, this is a misreading of the law. In terms of this example, the law says that for the millionaire, an additional dollar is worth less than the dollar that preceded it; and for the poor man, an additional dollar is worth less than the dollar that preceded it. Let's say the millionaire has $2 million, and the poor man has $1,000. We now give each of them one more dollar. The law of diminishing marginal utility says (1) the additional dollar is worth less to the millionaire than her two-millionth dollar, and (2) the additional dollar is worth less to the poor man than his one-thousandth dollar. That is all the law says. We do not and cannot know whether the additional dollar is worth more or less to the millionaire than it is to the poor man. In summary, the law says something about the millionaire and about the poor man (both persons value the last dollar less than the next-to-last dollar), but it does not say anything about the millionaire's utility compared to the poor man's utility.

To compare the utility the millionaire gets from the additional dollar with the utility the poor man gets from it is to fall into the trap of making an **interpersonal utility comparison.** The utility obtained by one person cannot be scientifically or objectively compared with the utility obtained from the same thing by another person because utility is subjective. Who knows for certain how much satisfaction (utility) the millionaire gets from the additional dollar compared with that of the poor man? The poor man may care little for money; he may shun it, consider the love of it the root of all evil, and prefer to consume the things in life that do not require money. On the other hand, the millionaire may be interested only in amassing more money. We should not be so careless as to "guess" at the utility one person obtains from consuming a certain item, compare it to our "guess" of the utility another person obtains from consuming the same item, and then call these "guesses" scientific facts.

Interpersonal Utility Comparison
Comparing the utility one person receives from a good, service, or activity with the utility another person receives from the same good, service, or activity.

THE SOLUTION TO THE DIAMOND-WATER PARADOX

Goods have both total utility and marginal utility. Take water, for example. Water is extremely useful; we cannot live without it. We would expect its total utility (its total usefulness) to be high. But we would expect its marginal utility to be low because water is relatively plentiful. As the law of diminishing marginal utility states, the utility of successive units of a good diminishes as consumption of the good increases. In short, water is immensely useful, but there is so much of it that individuals place relatively little value on another unit of it.

In contrast, diamonds are not as useful as water. We would expect the total utility of diamonds to be lower than the total utility of water. However, we would expect the marginal utility of diamonds to be high. Why? There are relatively few diamonds in the world, so the consumption of diamonds (in contrast to the consumption of water) takes place at relatively high marginal utility. Diamonds, which are rare, get used only for their few valuable uses. Water, being plentiful, gets used for its many valuable uses and for its not-so-valuable uses (such as spraying the car with the hose for two more minutes even though you are 99 percent sure that the soap is fully rinsed off).

In conclusion, the total utility of water is high because water is extremely useful. The total utility of diamonds is low in comparison because diamonds are not as useful as water. The marginal utility of water is low because water is so plentiful that people end up consuming it at low marginal utility. The marginal utility of diamonds is high because diamonds are so scarce that people end up consuming them at high marginal utility.

Do prices reflect total or marginal utility? Marginal utility.

 Q: Isn't it possible for water to be more expensive than diamonds?

A: Yes, it is possible. If the supply of water is unusually limited for some reason, such as during a drought, the price of water is likely to be higher than the price of diamonds. In some arid parts of the world, water is in unusually short supply and people have been known to trade their diamonds and precious metals, or even fight, for some of it.

IS GAMBLING WORTH THE EFFORT?

Is gambling in a fair game worth the effort? The answer is no if the person derives no pleasure from gambling itself and only gambles to win.

Let's begin our analysis by defining a fair game. A fair game is one in which the value of the expected gain equals the wager made. For example, if you bet $1 to have a 10 percent chance to win $10, the game is fair: $1 (the wager) is equal to the probability of winning (10 percent) times the win ($10).

Fair Game: Wager = Probability of winning × Winnings

But now consider the diminishing marginal utility of money: The last dollar brings less utility than the next-to-last dollar, and so on. This means the money that may be lost in a wager has a higher per-unit utility than an equal amount of money that may be won. Because of diminishing marginal utility, *losing a dollar bet in a fair game causes you to lose more utility than winning a dollar causes you to gain utility*. We conclude that under the conditions stated—a fair game and no pleasure derived from gambling itself—gambling is a losing proposition.

Self-Test *(Answers to Self-Test questions are in the Self-Test Appendix.)*

1. State and solve the diamond-water paradox.

2. If total utility is falling, what does this imply for marginal utility? Give an arithmetical example to illustrate your answer.

3. When would the total utility of a good and the marginal utility of a good be the same?

CONSUMER EQUILIBRIUM AND DEMAND

This section identifies the condition necessary for consumer equilibrium and then discusses the relationship between it and the law of demand. The analysis is based on the assumption that individuals seek to maximize utility.

EQUATING MARGINAL UTILITIES PER DOLLAR

Suppose there are only two goods in the world, apples and oranges. At present, a consumer is spending his entire income consuming 10 apples and 10 oranges a week. We assume that the marginal utility and price of each are as follows:[1]

$$MU_{oranges} = 30 \text{ utils}$$
$$MU_{apples} = 20 \text{ utils}$$
$$P_{oranges} = \$1$$
$$P_{apples} = \$1$$

The marginal (last) dollar spent on apples returns 20 utils per dollar, and the marginal (last) dollar spent on oranges returns 30 utils per dollar. The ratio of MU_O/P_O (O = oranges) is greater than the ratio of MU_A/P_A (A = apples): $MU_O/P_O > MU_A/P_A$.

A consumer who found himself in this situation one week would redirect his purchases of apples and oranges the next week. He would think: If I buy an orange, I receive more utility (30 utils) than if I buy an apple (20 utils). It's better to buy one more orange with a dollar and one less apple. I gain 30 utils from buying the orange, which is 10 utils more than if I buy the apple.

But what happens as the consumer buys one more orange and one less apple? The marginal utility of oranges falls (recall what the law of diminishing marginal utility says happens as a person consumes additional units of a good), and the marginal utility of apples rises (the consumer is consuming fewer apples). Because the consumer has bought one more orange and one less apple, he now has 11 oranges and 9 apples. At this new combination of goods,

$$MU_{oranges} = 25 \text{ utils}$$
$$MU_{apples} = 25 \text{ utils}$$
$$P_{oranges} = \$1$$
$$P_{apples} = \$1$$

---

1. You may wonder where we get these marginal utility figures. They are points on hypothetical marginal utility curves, such as the one in Exhibit 1. The important point is that one number is greater than the other. We could easily have picked other numbers, such as 300 and 200, and so on.

Here the ratio MU_O/P_O equals the ratio MU_A/P_A. The consumer is getting exactly the same amount of utility (25 utils) per dollar from each of the two goods. There is no way for the consumer to redirect his purchases (buy more of one good and less of another good) and have more utility. Thus, the consumer is in equilibrium. In short, a consumer is in equilibrium when he or she derives the same marginal utility per dollar for all goods. The condition for **consumer equilibrium** is

$$MU_A/P_A = MU_B/P_B = MU_C/P_C = \ldots = MU_Z/P_Z$$

where the letters A–Z represent all the goods a person buys.[2]

Consumer Equilibrium
Occurs when the consumer has spent all income and the marginal utilities per dollar spent on each good purchased are equal: $MU_A/P_A = MU_B/P_B = MU_C/P_C = \ldots = MU_Z/P_Z$, where the letters A–Z represent all the goods a person buys.

Q & A

Q: If a person is in consumer equilibrium, does it follow that she has maximized her total utility?

A: Yes, it does. By spending her dollars on goods that give her the greatest marginal utility and in the process bringing about the consumer equilibrium condition, she is adding as much to her total utility as she can possibly add.

THINKING LIKE AN ECONOMIST

Consumers have an objective—to maximize (total) utility. They are constrained by income and prices. They make choices in a particular way—by equating the marginal utility-price ratio (MU/P) for all goods purchased, that is, by equating marginal utilities per dollar. The key word is marginal. Economists rely on the idea of marginal magnitudes because they are the significant magnitudes when economic actors seek to meet their objectives. Thinking in terms of marginal magnitudes is part of the economic way of thinking.

CONSUMER EQUILIBRIUM AND THE LAW OF DEMAND

Suppose the consumer purchases 11 oranges and 9 apples and $MU_O/P_O = MU_A/P_A$. What happens if the price of oranges falls from $1 each to $0.50 each? The situation is as follows:

$$MU_{oranges} = 25 \text{ utils}$$
$$MU_{apples} = 25 \text{ utils}$$
$$P_{oranges} = \$0.50$$
$$P_{apples} = \$1.00$$

Now, $MU_O/P_O > MU_A/P_A$. The fall in the price of oranges has moved the consumer into disequilibrium. He will attempt to restore equilibrium by buying more oranges because he derives more utility per dollar from buying oranges than from buying apples.

How is a consumer moving from disequilibrium to equilibrium in order to maximize utility related to the law of demand? This behavior illustrates the inverse relationship between (own) price and quantity demanded as expressed in the law of demand: As the price of a good rises (falls), the quantity demanded of the good falls (rises), *ceteris paribus.*

Exhibit 2 illustrates another example. There are two goods, A and B. Currently, the price of both goods is $1 each. At this price, the consumer buys 1 unit of good A and 6 units of good B. As shown in the exhibit, the marginal utility of the first unit of good A is 12 utils, and the marginal utility of the sixth unit of good B is also 12 utils. The consumer is in equilibrium where

$$MU_A/P_A = MU_B/P_B$$
$$12 \text{ utils}/\$1.00 = 12 \text{ utils}/\$1.00$$

---

2. We are assuming here that the consumer exhausts his or her income and that saving is treated as a good.

exhibit 2

Consumer Equilibrium and a Fall in Price

Initially, the price of both good *A* and good *B* is $1.00. The consumer is in equilibrium buying 1 unit of good *A* and 6 units of good *B*. Then the price of good *A* falls to $0.50. No longer is the consumer in equilibrium. To restore herself to equilibrium, she buys more of good *A* and less of good *B*. As she does this, the marginal utility of good *A* decreases and the marginal utility of good *B* increases. At the new set of prices, $0.50 for *A* and $1.00 for *B*, the consumer is back in equilibrium when she purchases 6 units of good *A* and 4 units of good *B*.

Now suppose the price of good *A* falls to $0.50. This changes the situation to the following:

$$MU_A/P_A > MU_B/P_B$$
$$12 \text{ utils}/\$0.50 > 12 \text{ utils}/\$1.00$$

In this situation, the consumer is gaining more utility per dollar by purchasing good *A* than by purchasing good *B*. To stay within the limits of her budget, she decides to buy more of good *A* and less of good *B*. We see that she buys 5 more units of good *A*, for a total of 6 units, and 2 fewer units of good *B*, for a total of 4 units. As she buys more units of good *A*, the marginal utility of good *A* decreases (law of diminishing marginal utility). The marginal utility of the sixth unit of good *A* is 8 utils. As the consumer cuts back on her purchases of good *B*, the marginal utility of good *B* increases. The marginal utility of the fourth unit of good *B* is 16 utils. At the new set of prices, $0.50 for good *A* and $1.00 for good *B*, the consumer is in equilibrium when she buys 6 units of good *A* and 4 units of good *B*. We have the following condition:

$$MU_A/P_A = MU_B/P_B$$
$$8 \text{ utils}/\$0.50 = 16 \text{ utils}/\$1.00$$

The consumer receives equal marginal utility per dollar from purchasing goods *A* and *B*.

INCOME AND SUBSTITUTION EFFECTS

Consider what happens when the absolute price of one good falls and the absolute prices of all other goods remain constant. Suppose the absolute price of computers falls, and the absolute prices of all other goods remain constant. Two things occur: First, the relative price of computers falls. Second, a consumer's real income, or purchasing power, rises.

A person's **real income,** or purchasing power, rises if with a given absolute (or dollar) income, he or she can purchase more goods and services. To illus-

Real Income
Income adjusted for price changes. A person has more (less) real income as the price of a good falls (rises), *ceteris paribus.*

ECONOMICS IN...

How You Pay for Good Weather

Suppose there are two cities that are alike in every way except one—the weather. We'll call one city Good-Weather-City (*GWC*) and the other Bad-Weather-City (*BWC*). In *GWC*, temperatures are moderate all year (75 degrees) and the sky is always blue. In *BWC*, the winter brings snow and freezing rain and the summer brings high humidity and high temperatures. *BWC* has all the forms of weather that people dislike. We assume people get more utility from living in good weather than in bad weather. We also assume the median price of a home in the two cities is the same—$200,000.

In terms of marginal utility and housing prices,

$$MU_{GWC}/P_{H,GWC} > MU_{BWC}/P_{H,BWC}$$

That is, the marginal utility of living in *GWC* (MU_{GWC}) divided by the price of a house in *GWC* ($P_{H,GWC}$) is greater than the marginal utility of living in *BWC* (MU_{BWC}) divided by the price of a house in *BWC* ($P_{H,BWC}$). In other words, there is greater utility per dollar in *GWC* than in *BWC*.

What will people do? At least some people will move from *BWC* to *GWC*. Those people in *BWC* who want to move will put their houses up for sale. This will increase the supply of houses for sale and lower the price. As these people move to *GWC*, they increase the demand for houses and the house prices in *GWC* begin to rise.

This process will continue until the price of a house in *GWC* has risen high enough, and the price of a house in *BWC* has fallen low enough, so that the *MU/P* ratios in the two cities are the same. In other words, the process continues until this condition is reached:

$$MU_{GWC}/P_{H,GWC} = MU_{BWC}/P_{H,BWC}$$

When this has occurred, one receives the same utility per dollar in the two cities. In other words, the two cities are the same.

Now let's consider a young couple that has to choose between living in the two cities. Is it clear that the young couple will choose *GWC* instead of *BWC* because *GWC* has a better climate? Not at all. *GWC* has a better climate than *BWC*, but *BWC* has lower housing prices. One member of the couple says, "Let's live in *GWC*. Think of all that great weather we'll enjoy. We can go outside every day." The other member of the couple says, "But if we live in *BWC*, we can have either a much bigger and better house for the money or more money to spend on things other than housing. Think of the better cars and clothes we'll be able to buy or the vacations we'll be able to take because we won't have to spend as much money to buy a house."

What has happened is that the initial greater satisfaction of living in *GWC* (the higher utility per dollar) has been eroded by people moving to *GWC* and raising housing prices. *GWC* doesn't look as good as it once did.

On the other hand, *BWC* doesn't look as (relatively) bad as it once did. It still doesn't have the good climate that *GWC* has, but it has lower housing prices now. The utility per dollar of living in *BWC* has risen as a consequence of housing prices falling.

In other words, as long as one city is better (in some way) than another, people will move to the relatively better city. In the process, they will change things just enough so that it is no longer relatively better. In the end, you have to pay for paradise.

---

trate, suppose Barbara's income is $100 per week and there are only two goods in the world, *A* and *B*, whose prices are $50 and $25, respectively. With her $100 income, Barbara purchases 1 unit of good *A* and 2 units of good *B* per week, for a total of 3 units of the two goods.

Now, suppose the price of good *A* falls to $25, *ceteris paribus*. The lower price allows Barbara to purchase more of the two goods. She can purchase 2 units of good *A* and 2 units of good *B*, for a total of 4 units of the two goods. Given this, we say that Barbara's real income has risen as a result of the fall in the price of good *A*. With her $100 income, Barbara is able to purchase more goods.

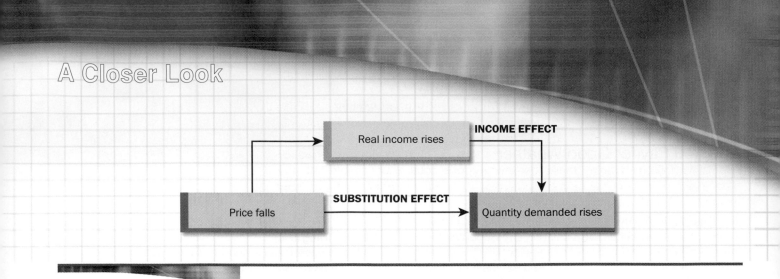

Income and Substitution Effects
A fall in price leads to an increase in quantity demanded—directly through the substitution effect and indirectly through the income effect (assuming the good is a normal good).

Substitution Effect
The portion of the change in the quantity demanded of a good that is attributable to a change in its relative price.

Income Effect
The portion of the change in the quantity demanded of a good that is attributable to a change in real income (brought about by a change in absolute price).

Go to *http://w3.access.gpo.gov/ usbudget/*, and select "search selected documents on-line." Next select "All Budget Publications," key "Health Care" in the Search Terms box, and then click "Submit." Select "Strengthening Health Care." Read the publication. Identify any statements in the publication that either explicitly or implicitly deal with (1) costs and benefits, (2) the law of diminishing marginal utility, (3) income effects, or (4) substitution effects.

A fall in the relative price of a good will, and a rise in real income can, lead to greater purchases of the good.[3] The portion of the change in the quantity demanded of a good that is attributable to a change in its relative price is referred to as the **substitution effect** (see Exhibit 3). The portion of the change in the quantity demanded of a good that is attributable to a change in real income, brought about by a change in absolute price, is referred to as the **income effect** (see Exhibit 3).

Suppose the price of normal good *A* falls from $10 to $8, *ceteris paribus*. As a result, the quantity demanded of good *A* rises from 100 units to 143 units. A portion of the 43-unit increase in the quantity demanded is due to the relative price of good *A* falling, and a portion of the 43-unit increase in the quantity demanded is due to real income rising. Suppose quantity demanded rises from 100 units to 129 units because the relative price of good *A* falls. This would be the extent of the substitution effect: People purchase 29 more units of good *A* because it has become relatively cheaper to purchase. The difference between 143 units and 129 units, or 14 units, would be the extent of the income effect: People purchase 14 more units of good *A* because their real incomes have risen.

SHOULD THE GOVERNMENT PROVIDE THE NECESSITIES OF LIFE FOR FREE?

Sometimes you will hear people say, "Food and water are necessities of life. No one can live without them. It is wrong to charge for these goods. The government should provide them free to everyone."

Or you might hear, "Medical care is a necessity to those who are sick. Without it, people will either experience an extremely low quality of life (you can't experience a high quality of life when you are feeling sick) or die. Making people pay for medical care is wrong. The government should provide it free to the people who need it."

Each of these statements labels something as a necessity of life (food and water, medical care) and then makes the policy proposal that government should provide the necessity for free.

Suppose government did give food, water, and medical care to everyone for free—in other words, at zero price (although not at zero taxes). At zero price, people would want to consume these goods up to the point of zero marginal utility for each good. They would do so because if the marginal utility of the good (expressed in dollars) is greater than its price, one could derive more utility from purchasing the good than one would lose in parting with the dollar price of the good. In other words, if the price of a good is $5, an individual will

---

3. Specifically, a rise in real income will lead to greater purchases of a good if the good is a normal good. It will not, if the good is an inferior good. See the discussion of normal and inferior goods in Chapter 3.

continue consuming it as long as the marginal utility she derives from it is greater than $5. If the price is $0, she will continue to consume the good as long as the marginal utility she derives from it is greater than $0.

Resources must be used to produce every unit of a good consumed. If the government uses scarce resources to provide goods that have low marginal utility (which food, water, and medical care would have at zero price), then fewer resources are available to produce other goods. However, if some resources are withdrawn from producing these low-utility goods, total utility would fall very little. The resources could then be redirected to producing goods with a higher marginal utility, thereby raising total utility.

The people who argue that certain goods should be provided free implicitly assume that the not-so-valuable uses of food, water, and medical care are valuable enough to warrant a system of taxes to pay for the complete provision of these goods at zero price. It is questionable, however, if the least valuable uses of food, water, and medical care are worth the sacrifices of other goods that would necessarily be forfeited if more of these goods were produced.

Think about this: Currently, water is relatively cheap, and people use it to satisfy its more valuable uses and its not-so-valuable uses too. But suppose water were cheaper than it is? Suppose it had a zero price? Would it be used to satisfy its more valuable uses, its not-so-valuable uses, and its absolutely least valuable use? If food had a zero price, would it be used to satisfy its more valuable uses, its not-so-valuable uses, and its absolutely least valuable use (food fights perhaps)?

Self-Test

1. Alesandro purchases two goods, X and Y, and the utility gained for the last unit purchased of each is 16 utils and 23 utils, respectively. The prices of X and Y are $1 and $1.75, respectively. Is Alesandro in consumer equilibrium? Explain your answer.

2. The text states that as the price of a normal good falls, quantity demanded rises from 100 units to 143 units. It then explains that a portion of the increase is due to the substitution effect and a portion of the increase is due to the income effect. Why is it important to specify a normal good? Would the result be different for an inferior good?

BEHAVIORAL ECONOMICS

Economists are interested in how people behave. This chapter has shown how economists predict people will behave when the MU/P ratio for one good is greater than it is for another good. In this situation, economic theory predicts that individuals will buy more of the good with the higher MU/P ratio and less of the good with the lower MU/P ratio. In other words, individuals, seeking to maximize their utility, buy more of one good and less of another good until the MU/P ratio for all goods is the same.

In traditional economic theories and models, individuals are assumed to be rational, self-interested, and consistent. For about the last 30 years, behavioral economists have challenged the traditional economic models. Behavioral economists argue that some human behavior does not fit neatly—at minimum, easily—into the traditional economic framework. In this section, we describe some of the findings of behavioral economists.

ARE PEOPLE WILLING TO REDUCE OTHERS' INCOMES?

Two economists, Daniel Zizzo and Andrew Oswald, set up a series of experiments with four groups, each with four people. Each person was given the same amount of money and asked to gamble with the new money. At the end of each act of gambling, two of the four persons in each group had won money and two had lost money. Then each of the four people in each group was given the opportunity to pay some amount of money to reduce the take of the others in the group. In other words, suppose that in the group consisting of Smith, Jones, Brown, and Adams, Smith and Adams had more money after gambling and Jones and Brown had less money. All four were given the opportunity to reduce the amount of money held by the others in the group. For example, Brown could pay to reduce Smith's money, Jones could pay to reduce Adams's, and so on.

At this point, some people argue that no one will spend his money to hurt someone else if it means leaving himself poorer. However, Zizzo and Oswald found that 62 percent of the participants did just that—they made themselves worse off in order to make someone else worse off.

Why might people behave this way? One explanation is that individuals are concerned with relative rank and status more than with absolute well-being. Thus, the poorer of the two individuals doesn't mind paying, say, 25 cents if it means that he can reduce the richer person's take by, say, $1. After the 25 cents is spent by the poorer person, the gap between him and the richer person is smaller.

Some economists argue that such behavior is irrational and inconsistent with utility maximization. Other economists say it is no such thing. They argue that if people get utility from relative rank, then, in effect, what is happening is that people are buying a move up the relative rank ladder by reducing the size of the gap between themselves and others.

IS $1 ALWAYS $1?

Do people treat money differently depending upon where it comes from? Traditional economics argues that they should not—after all, a dollar is a dollar is a dollar. Specifically, $1 that someone gives to you as a gift is no different than $1 you earn or $1 you find on the street. When people treat some dollars differently from other dollars, they are *compartmentalizing*. They are saying that dollars in some compartments (of their minds) are to be valued differently than dollars in other compartments.

Let's consider the following situation. Suppose you plan to see a Broadway play, the ticket for which costs $100. You buy the $100 ticket on Monday in order to see the play on Friday night. When Friday night arrives, you realize you have lost the ticket. *Do you spend another $100 to buy another ticket (assuming another ticket can be purchased)?*[4]

Now let's change the circumstances slightly. Suppose instead of buying the ticket on Monday, you plan to buy the ticket at the ticket window on Friday night. At the ticket window on Friday night, you realize you have lost $100 somewhere between home and the theater. *Assuming you still have enough money to buy a $100 ticket to the play, do you buy it?*

Now, regardless of how you answer each question, some economists argue that your answers should be consistent. In other words, if you say no to the first question, you should say no to the second question. If you say yes to the first question, you should say yes to the second question. That's because the two questions, based on two slightly two different settings, essentially present you with the same choice.

However, many people, when asked the two questions, say that they will not pay an additional $100 to buy a second ticket (having lost the first $100 ticket) but will spend an additional $100 to buy a first ticket (having lost $100 in cash between home and the theater). Why? Some people argue that spending an additional $100 on an additional ticket is the same as paying $200 to see the play—and that is just too much to pay. However, they don't see themselves as

---

4. The idea for this example comes from Gary Belsky and Thomas Gilovich, *Why Smart People Make Big Money Mistakes and How to Correct Them* (New York: Simon and Schuster, 1999).

spending $200 to see the play when they lose $100 and pay $100 for a ticket. In either case, though, $200 is gone.

Behavioral economists argue that people who answer the two questions differently (yes to one and no to the other) are compartmentalizing. They are treating two $100 amounts in two different ways—as if they come from two different compartments. For example, the person who says she will not buy a second $100 ticket (having lost the first $100 ticket) but will buy a first ticket (having lost $100 cash), is effectively saying by her behavior that $100 lost on a ticket is different than $100 lost in cash.

Let's consider another situation. Suppose you earn $1,000 by working hard at a job and also win $1,000 at the roulette table in Las Vegas. Would you feel freer to spend the $1,000 won in Las Vegas than to spend the $1,000 you worked hard to earn? If the answer is yes, then you are treating money differently depending on where it came from and what you had to do to get it. Nothing is necessarily wrong or immoral about that, but still it is interesting because $1,000 is $1,000 is $1,000— no matter where it came from and no matter what you had to do to get it.

Finally, let's look at an experiment conducted by two marketing professors. Drazen Prelec and Duncan Simester once organized a sealed-bid auction to a Boston Celtics game. Half the participants in the auction were told that if they had the winning bid, they had to pay in cash. The other half of the participants in the auction were told that if they had the winning bid, they had to pay with a credit card.

One would think that the average bid from the people who had to pay cash would be the same as the average bid from the people who had to pay with a credit card—assuming that the two groups were divided randomly and that no group showed a stronger or weaker preference for seeing the Celtics game. But this didn't happen. The average bid of the people who had to pay with a credit card was higher than the average bid of the people who had to pay with cash. In other words, using a credit card somehow caused people to bid higher dollar amounts than they would have bid had they known they were going to pay cash. Money from the credit card compartment seemed to be more quickly or easily spent than money from the cash compartment.

COFFEE MUGS AND THE ENDOWMENT EFFECT

In one economic experiment, coffee mugs were allocated randomly to half the people in a group. Each person with a mug was asked to state a price at which he would be willing to sell his mug. Each person without a mug was asked to state a price at which he would be willing to buy a mug.

It turns out that, even though the mugs were allocated randomly (dispelling the idea that somehow the people who received a mug valued it more than the people who did not receive one), the lowest price at which the owner of a mug would sell the mug was, on average, higher than the highest price at which a buyer of a mug would pay to buy a mug. In other words, it is as if sellers said they wouldn't sell mugs for less than $15 and buyers said they wouldn't buy mugs for more than $10.

This outcome—which is called the *endowment effect*—is odd. It's odd because even though there is absolutely no reason to believe that the people who received the mugs valued them more than the people who didn't receive them, it turns out that people place a higher value on something (like a mug) simply because they own it. In other words, people seem to show an inclination to hold on to what they have.

If this holds for you, think of what it means. When you go into a store to buy a sweater, you say the sweater is worth no more to you than, say, $40. In other words, you are not willing to pay more than $40 for the sweater. But if someone gave you the sweater as a gift and you were asked to sell it, you wouldn't be willing to sell it for less than, say, $50. Simply owning the sweater makes it more valuable to you.

The economist David Friedman says that such behavior is not limited to humans.[5] He points out that some species of animals exhibit territorial behavior—that is, they are more likely to fight to keep what they have than to fight to get what they don't have. As Friedman notes, "It is a familiar observation that a dog will fight harder to keep his own bone than to take another dog's bone."

Friedman argues that this type of behavior in humans makes perfect sense in a hunter-gatherer society. Here is what Friedman has to say:

"Now consider the same logic [found in the fact that a dog will fight harder to keep the bone he has than to take a bone from another dog] in a hunter-gatherer society—in which there are no external institutions to enforce property rights. Imagine that each individual considers every object in sight, decides how much each is worth to him, and then tries to appropriate it, with the outcome of the resulting Hobbesian struggle determined by some combination of how much each wants things and how strong each individual is. It does not look like a formula for a successful society, even on the scale of a hunter-gatherer band.

"There is an alternative solution, assuming that humans are at least as smart as dogs, robins, and fish. Some method, possibly as simple as physical possession, is used to define what "belongs to" whom. Each individual then commits himself to fight very hard to protect his "property"—much harder than he would be willing to fight in order to appropriate a similar object from someone else's possession—with the commitment made via some psychological mechanism presumably hardwired into humans. The result is both a considerably lower level of (risky) violence and a considerably more prosperous society.

"The fact that the result is attractive does not, of course, guarantee that it will occur—evolution selects for the reproductive interest of the individual, not the group. But in this case they are the same. To see that, imagine a population in which some individuals have adopted the commitment strategy [outlined above—that is, fighting for what you physically possess], and some have adopted different commitment strategies—for example, a strategy of fighting to the death for whatever they see as valuable. It should be fairly easy to see that individuals in the first group will, on average, do better for themselves—hence have (among other things) greater reproductive success—than those in the second group.

"How do I commit myself to fight very hard for something? One obvious way is some psychological quirk that makes that something appear very valuable to me. Hence the same behavior pattern that shows up as territorial behavior in fish and ferocious defense of bones in dogs shows up in Cornell students [who were given the coffee mugs] as an endowment effect. Just as in the earlier cases, behavior that was functional in the environment in which we evolved continues to be observed, even in an environment in which its function has largely disappeared."[6]

In other words, we value *X* more highly if we have it than if we do not have it because such behavior at one point in our evolution made possible a system of property rights in a world where the alternative was the Hobbesian jungle.

Self-Test

1. Brandon's grandmother is very cautious about spending money. Yesterday, she gave Brandon a gift of $100 for his birthday. Brandon also received a gift of $100 from his father, who isn't nearly as cautious about spending money as Brandon's grandmother

---

5. See his "Economics and Evolutionary Psychology" at his Web site, *http://www.daviddfriedman.com*.

6. See page 10 of the earlier cited work.

is. Brandon believes that it would somehow be wrong to spend his grandmother's gift on frivolous things, but that it wouldn't be wrong to spend his father's gift on such things. Is Brandon compartmentalizing? Explain your answer.

2. Summarize David Friedman's explanation of the endowment effect.

A Reader Asks...
Do People Really Equate Marginal Utility–Price Ratios?

Am I expected to believe that real people actually go around with marginal utility–price ratios in their heads and that they behave according to how these ratios change? After all, most people don't even know what marginal utility is.

We could answer that most people may not know the laws of physics, but this doesn't prevent their behavior from being consistent with the law of physics. But we present a different argument. First, let's review how a person who equates MU/P ratios behaves in accordance with the law of demand. When the MU/P ratio for good A is equal to the MU/P ratio for good B, the person is in consumer equilibrium. Suppose the price of good A falls so that the MU/P ratio for good A is now greater than the MU/P ratio for B. What does the individual do? In order to maximize utility, we predicted that the person would buy more of good A because he receives more utility per dollar buying A than he does buying B. Buying more A when the price of good declines—in order to maximize utility—is consistent with the law of demand, which states that price and quantity demanded are inversely related, *ceteris paribus*. In other words, to act in accordance with the law of demand is consistent with equating MU/P ratios.

Now our real question is "Is it possible that people can act in a manner consistent with the law of demand, even though they don't know what the law of demand says?" If the answer is yes, then they are acting *as if* they are equating MU/P ratios in their heads.

But let's not talk about people for a minute. Let's talk about rats. Certainly rats do not understand what marginal utility is. They will not be able to define it, com-

pute it, or do anything else with it. But do they act *as if* they equate MU/P ratios? Do they observe the law of demand?

With these questions in mind, consider an experiment conducted by economists at Texas A&M University, who undertook to study the "buying" behavior of two white rats. Each rat was put in a laboratory cage with two levers. By pushing one lever, they obtained root beer; by pushing the other lever, they obtained nonalcoholic collins mix. Every day, each of the rats was given a "fixed income" of 300 pushes. (When the combined total of pushes on the two levers reached 300, the levers could not be pushed down until the next day.) The prices of root beer and collins mix were both 20 pushes per milliliter of beverage. Given this income and the price of root beer and collins mix, one rat settled in to consuming 11 milliliters of root beer and 4 milliliters of collins mix. The other rat settled in to consuming almost all root beer.

Then the prices of the two beverages were changed. The price of collins mix was halved while the price of root beer was doubled.[7] Using economic theory, we would predict that with these new prices, the consumption of collins mix would increase and the consumption of root beer would decrease. This is exactly what happened. Both rats began to consume more collins mix and less root beer. In short, both rats had downward-sloping demand curves for collins mix and root beer.

The point? If the behavior of rats is consistent with the law of demand and the law of demand is consistent with equating MU/P ratios, then do you really have to know you are equating MU/P ratios before you can be doing it? Obviously not.

Chapter Summary

The Law of Diminishing Marginal Utility
- The law of diminishing marginal utility holds that as the amount of a good consumed increases, the marginal utility of the good decreases.
- The law of diminishing marginal utility should not be used to make interpersonal utility comparisons.

For example, the law does not say that a millionaire receives less (or more) utility from an additional dollar than a poor man receives. Instead, it says that for both the millionaire and the poor man, the last dollar has less value for both the millionaire and the poor man than the next-to-last dollar.

---

7. The researchers raised the price of root beer by reducing the quantity of root beer dispensed per push. This is the same as increasing the number of pushes necessary to obtain the original quantity of root beer.

The Diamond-Water Paradox

- The diamond-water paradox states that what has great value in use sometimes has little value in exchange and what has little value in use sometimes has great value in exchange. A knowledge of the difference between total utility and marginal utility is necessary to unravel the diamond-water paradox.
- A good can have high total utility and low marginal utility. For example, water's total utility is high, but because water is so plentiful, its marginal utility is low. In short, water is immensely useful, but it is so plentiful that individuals place relatively low value on another unit of it. In contrast, diamonds are not as useful as water, but because there are few diamonds in the world, the marginal utility of diamonds is high. In summary, a good can be extremely useful and have a low price if the good is in plentiful supply (high value in use, low value in exchange). On the other hand, a good can be of little use and have a high price if the good is in short supply (low value in use, high value in exchange).

Consumer Equilibrium

- Individuals seek to equate marginal utilities per dollar. For example, if a person receives more utility per dollar spent on good A than on good B, she will reorder her purchases and buy more A and less B. There is a tendency to move away from the condition $MU_A/P_A > MU_B/P_B$ to the condition $MU_A/P_A =$ MU_B/P_B. The latter condition represents consumer equilibrium (in a two-good world).

Marginal Utility Analysis and the Law of Demand

- Marginal utility analysis can be used to illustrate the law of demand. The law of demand states that price and quantity demanded are inversely related, *ceteris paribus*. Starting from consumer equilibrium in a world in which there are only two goods, A and B, a fall in the price of A will cause MU_A/P_A to be greater than MU_B/P_B. As a result, the consumer will purchase more of good A to restore herself to equilibrium.

Behavioral Economics

- Behavioral economists argue that some human behavior does not fit neatly—at minimum, easily—into the traditional economic framework.
- Behavioral economists believe they have identified human behaviors that are inconsistent with the model of men and women as rational, self-interested, and consistent. These behaviors include the following: (1) Individuals are willing to spend some money to lower the incomes of others even if it means their incomes will be lowered. (2) Individuals don't always treat $1 as $1; some dollars seem to be treated differently from other dollars. (3) Individuals sometimes value X more if it is theirs than if it isn't theirs and they are seeking to acquire it.

Key Terms and Concepts

Diamond-Water Paradox	Marginal Utility	Real Income
Utility	Law of Diminishing Marginal Utility	Substitution Effect
Util	Interpersonal Utility Comparison	Income Effect
Total Utility	Consumer Equilibrium	

Economic Connections to You

Economic facts, actions, and changes create ripples that move away from their point of origin. Eventually, these ripples can intersect your life and have an effect on you. Consider the following example.

The federal government, after intense pressure by the U.S. auto industry, imposes a quota on foreign cars imported into the United States. As a result, the average price of cars sold in the United States rises. You were in consumer equilibrium before the quota—with the marginal utility–price ratio for all goods the same. Now you are no longer in consumer equilibrium. As a result, you change the quantities of some of the goods you buy. Thus, there is a connection between an economic action by the government and the combination of goods you purchase— an economic connection to you.

Based on the material in this chapter, identify other ways in which economic facts, actions, and changes create ripples that eventually affect you.

1. "If we take $1 away from a rich person and give it to a poor person, the rich person loses less utility than the poor person gains." Comment.
2. Is it possible to get so much of a good that it turns into a bad? If so, give an example.
3. If a person consumes fewer units of a good, will marginal utility of the good increase as total utility decreases? Why or why not?
4. If the marginal utility of good A is 4 utils and its price is $2 and the marginal utility of good B is 6 utils and its price is $1, is the individual consumer maximizing (total) utility if she spends a total of $3 by buying one unit of each good? If not, how can more utility be obtained?
5. Individuals who buy second homes usually spend less for them than they do for their first homes. Why is this the case?
6. Describe five everyday examples of you or someone else making an interpersonal utility comparison.
7. Is there a logical link between the law of demand and the assumption that individuals seek to maximize util-

ity? (Hint: Think of how the condition for consumer equilibrium can be used to express the inverse relationship between price and quantity demanded.)
8. List five sets of two goods (each set is composed of two goods; for example, diamonds and water is one set) where the good with the greater value in use has lower value in exchange than does the good with the lower value in use.
9. Do you think people with high IQs are in consumer equilibrium (equate marginal utilities per dollar) more often than people with low IQs? Why or why not?
10. What is the endowment effect?
11. After each toss of the coin, one person has more money and one person has less. If the person with less money cares about relative rank and status, will he be willing to pay, say, $1 to reduce the other person's winnings by, say, 50 cents? Will he be willing to pay 25 cents to reduce the other person's winnings by $1? Explain your answers.

1. The marginal utility for the third unit of X is 60 utils and the marginal utility for the fourth unit of X is 45 utils. If the law of diminishing marginal utility holds, what is the minimum total utility?
2. Fill in blanks A–D in the following table.

Units of Good Consumed	Total Utility (utils)	Marginal Utility (utils)
1	10	10
2	19	_A_
3	_B_	8
4	33	_C_
5	35	_D_

3. The total utilities of the first five units of good X are 10, 19, 26, 33, and 40 utils, respectively. In other words, the total utility of one unit is 10 utils, the total utility of two units is 19 utils, and so on. What is the marginal utility of the third unit?

Use the following table to answer questions 4 and 5.

Units of Good X	TU of Good X (utils)	Units of Good Y	TU of Good Y (utils)
1	20	1	19
2	35	2	32
3	48	3	40
4	58	4	45
5	66	5	49

4. If George spends $5 (total) a week on good X and good Y and if the price of each good is $1 per unit, then how many units of each good does he purchase to maximize utility?
5. Given the number of units of each good George purchased in Question 4, what is his total utility?
6. Draw the marginal utility curve for a good that has constant marginal utility.
7. The marginal utility curve for units 3–5 of good X is below the horizontal axis. Draw the corresponding part of the total utility curve for good X.

1. Go to *http://www.bls.gov/cex/*. Under "Economic News Releases:" click "News Release," and then select "Consumer Expenditures in . . ."

    a. Have consumer expenditures risen by a greater percentage than consumer prices? If so, how would you explain this fact?

    b. Are there any substitutions among goods and services that you can identify? What goods or services are being substituted for other goods and services?

    c. What is the average monthly amount spent on food? Divide this dollar amount by the average number of persons per household. You now have the average monthly expenditure on food per person. Is your monthly spending on food more than, less than, or equal to this dollar amount?

2. Return to the main page. Under "Multiyear Tables," select the latest table, making sure to select (TXT). Identify the average annual amount spent on health care. Is the dollar amount in the last year more than or less than the dollar amount in the earliest year? By simply looking at the dollar amounts for each year, can you tell why they are changing from one year to the next? Does your answer to this last question cause you to reconsider your answer to Question 1b? Why or why not?

3. Return to the main page. Under "Tables Created by BLS," find "One Year Tables" and select "Composition of Consumer Unit (TXT)." Compare the data for "husbands and wives, oldest child under 6" with "husbands and wives, oldest child 6 to 17." Which category of family (oldest child under 6 or oldest child 6 to 17) spends more on vehicles? Which category of family spends more on food? If your answer to both questions is the same, do you think the family that spends more on both food and vehicles is spending less on something else (as compared to the other family)? Explain your answer.

Log on to the Arnold Xtra! Web site now (*http://arnoldxtra.swcollege.com*) for additional learning resources such as practice quizzes, help with graphing, video clips, and current event applications.

BUDGET CONSTRAINT AND INDIFFERENCE CURVE ANALYSIS

This chapter uses marginal utility theory to discuss consumer choice. Sometimes budget constraint and indifference curve analysis is used instead, especially in upper-division economics courses. We examine this important topic in this appendix.

THE BUDGET CONSTRAINT

Societies have production possibilities frontiers, and individuals have **budget constraints.** The budget constraint is built on two prices and the individual's income. To illustrate, consider O'Brien, who has a monthly income of $1,200. In a world of two goods, X and Y, O'Brien can spend his total income on X, he can spend his total income on Y, or he can spend part of his income on X and part on Y. Suppose the price of X is $100 and the price of Y is $80. Given this, if O'Brien spends his total income on X, he can purchase a maximum of 12 units; if he spends his total income on Y, he can purchase a maximum of 15 units. Locating these two points on a two-dimensional diagram and then drawing a line between them, as shown in Exhibit 1, gives us O'Brien's budget constraint. Any point on the budget constraint, as well as any point below it, represents a possible combination (bundle) of the two goods available to O'Brien.

Budget Constraint
All the combinations or bundles of two goods a person can purchase given a certain money income and prices for the two goods.

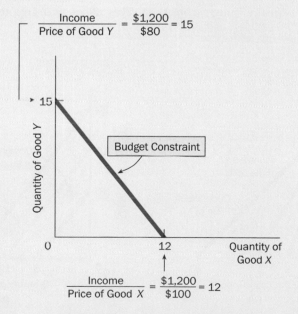

$$\frac{\text{Income}}{\text{Price of Good } Y} = \frac{\$1,200}{\$80} = 15$$

$$\frac{\text{Income}}{\text{Price of Good } X} = \frac{\$1,200}{\$100} = 12$$

exhibit 1

The Budget Constraint
An individual's budget constraint gives us a picture of the different combinations (bundles) of two goods available to the individual (this assumes a two-good world; for a many-good world, we could put one good on one axis and "all other goods" on the other). The budget constraint is derived by finding the maximum amount of each good an individual can consume (given his or her income and the prices of the two goods) and connecting these two points.

The slope of the budget constraint has special significance. The absolute value of the slope represents the relative prices of the two goods, X and Y. This slope, or P_X/P_Y, is equal to 1.25, indicating that the relative price of 1 unit of X is 1.25 units of Y.

WHAT WILL CHANGE THE BUDGET CONSTRAINT?

The budget constraint is built on two prices and the individual's income. This means that if any of the three variables changes (either of the prices or the individual's income), the budget constraint changes. Not all changes are alike, however. Consider a fall in the price of good X from $100 to $60. With this change, the maximum number of units of good X purchasable with an income of $1,200 rises from 12 to 20. The budget constraint revolves away from the origin, as shown in Exhibit 2a. Notice that the number of O'Brien's possible combinations of the two goods increases; there are more bundles of the two goods available after the price decrease than before.

Consider what happens to the budget constraint if the price of good X rises. If it goes from $100 to $150, the maximum number of units of good X falls from 12 to 8. The budget constraint revolves toward the origin. As a consequence, the number of bundles available to O'Brien decreases. We conclude that a change in the price of either good changes the slope of the budget constraint, with the result that relative prices and the number of bundles available to the individual also change.

We turn now to a change in income. If O'Brien's income rises to $1,600, the maximum number of units of X rises to 16 and the maximum number of units of Y rises to 20. The budget constraint shifts rightward (away from the origin) and is parallel to the old budget constraint. As a consequence, the number of bundles available to O'Brien increases (Exhibit 2b). If O'Brien's income falls from $1,200 to $800, the extreme end points on the budget constraint become 8 and 10 for X and Y, respectively. The budget constraint shifts leftward (toward the origin) and is parallel to the old budget constraint. As a consequence, the number of bundles available to O'Brien falls (Exhibit 2b).

INDIFFERENCE CURVES

An individual can, of course, choose any bundle of the two goods on or below the budget constraint. We assume that she spends her total income and therefore chooses a point on the budget constraint. This raises two important questions:

exhibit 2

Changes in the Budget Constraint
(a) A change in the price of good X or good Y will change the slope of the budget constraint. (b) A change in income will change the position of the budget constraint while the slope remains constant. Whenever a budget constraint changes, the number of combinations (bundles) of the two goods available to the individual changes too.

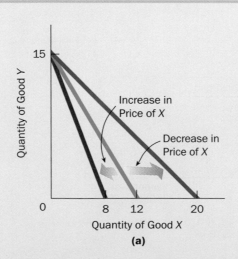

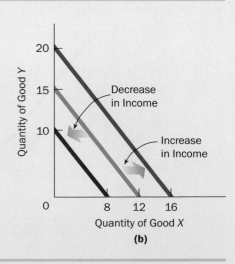

(1) Which bundle of the many bundles of the two goods does the individual choose? (2) How does the individual's chosen combination of goods change given a change in prices or income? Both questions can be answered by combining the budget constraint with the graphical expression of the individual's preferences—that is, indifference curves.

CONSTRUCTING AN INDIFFERENCE CURVE

Is it possible to be indifferent between two bundles of goods? Yes, it is. Suppose bundle *A* consists of 2 pairs of shoes and 6 shirts and bundle *B* consists of 3 pairs of shoes and 4 shirts. A person who is indifferent between these two bundles is implicitly saying that it doesn't matter which bundle he has; one is as good as the other. He is likely to say this, though, only if he receives equal total utility from the two bundles. If this were not the case, he would prefer one bundle to the other.

If we tabulate all the different bundles from which the individual receives equal utility, we have an **indifference set.** We can then plot the data in the indifference set and draw an **indifference curve.** Consider the indifference set illustrated in Exhibit 3a. There are four bundles of goods, *A–D;* each bundle gives the same total utility as every other bundle. These equal-utility bundles are plotted in Exhibit 3b. Connecting these bundles in a two-dimensional space gives us an indifference curve.

CHARACTERISTICS OF INDIFFERENCE CURVES

Indifference curves for goods have certain characteristics that are consistent with reasonable assumptions about consumer behavior.

1. **Indifference curves are downward-sloping (from left to right).** The assumption that consumers always prefer more of a good to less requires that indifference curves slope downward left to right. Consider the alternatives to downward-sloping: vertical, horizontal, and upward-sloping (left to right). A horizontal or vertical curve would combine bundles of goods some of which had more of one good and no less of another good than other bundles (Exhibit 4a–b). (If bundle *B* contained more of one good and no less of another good than bundle *A,* would an individual be *indifferent* between the two bundles? No, he or she wouldn't. Individuals prefer more to less.) An upward-sloping curve would combine bundles of goods some of which had

Indifference Set
Group of bundles of two goods that give an individual equal total utility.

Indifference Curve
Represents an indifference set. A curve that shows all the bundles of two goods that give an individual equal total utility.

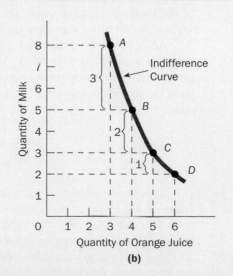

An Indifference Set		
Bundle	**Milk (units)**	**Orange Juice (units)**
A	8	3
B	5	4
C	3	5
D	2	6

(a)

(b)

exhibit 3

An Indifference Set and an Indifference Curve

An indifference set is a number of bundles of two goods in which each bundle yields the same total utility. An indifference curve represents an indifference set. In this exhibit, data from the indifference set (a) are used to derive an indifference curve (b).

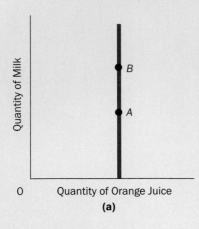

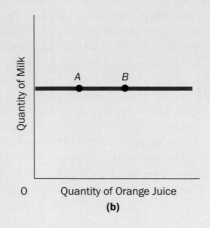

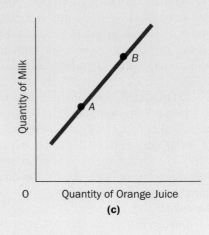

(a)   **(b)**   **(c)**

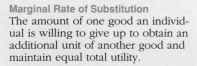

exhibit 4

Indifference Curves for Goods Do Not Look Like This

(a) Bundle *B* has more milk and no less orange juice than bundle *A*, so an individual would prefer *B* to *A* and not be indifferent between them. (b) Bundle *B* has more orange juice and no less milk than bundle *A*, so an individual would prefer *B* to *A* and not be indifferent between them. (c) Bundle *B* has more milk and more orange juice than bundle *A*, so an individual would prefer *B* to *A* and not be indifferent between them.

Marginal Rate of Substitution
The amount of one good an individual is willing to give up to obtain an additional unit of another good and maintain equal total utility.

more of *both* goods than other bundles (Exhibit 4c). A simpler way of putting it is to say that indifference curves are downward-sloping because a person has to get more of one good in order to maintain his or her level of satisfaction (utility) when giving up some of another good.

2. **Indifference curves are convex to the origin.** This implies that the slope of the indifference curve becomes flatter as we move down and to the right along the indifference curve. For example, at 8 units of milk (point *A* in Exhibit 3b), the individual is willing to give up 3 units of milk to get an additional unit of orange juice (and thus move to point *B*). At point *B*, where she has 5 units of milk, she is willing to give up only 2 units of milk to get an additional unit of orange juice (and thus move to point *C*). Finally, at point *C*, with 3 units of milk, she is now willing to give up only 1 unit of milk to get an additional unit of orange juice. We conclude that the more of one good that an individual has, the more units he or she will give up to get an additional unit of another good; the less of one good that an individual has, the fewer units he or she will give up to get an additional unit of another good. Is this reasonable? The answer is yes. Our observation is a reflection of diminishing marginal utility at work. As the quantity of a good consumed increases, the marginal utility of that good decreases; therefore we reason that the more of one good an individual has, the more units he or she can (and will) sacrifice to get an additional unit of another good and still maintain total utility. Stated differently, if the law of diminishing marginal utility did not exist then it would not make sense to say that indifference curves of goods are convex to the origin.

An important peripheral point about marginal utilities is that *the absolute value of the slope of the indifference curve*—which is called the **marginal rate of substitution**—*represents the ratio of the marginal utility of the good on the horizontal axis to the marginal utility of the good on the vertical axis:*

$$\frac{MU_{\text{good on horizontal axis}}}{MU_{\text{good on vertical axis}}}$$

Let's look carefully at the words in italics. First, we said that the absolute value of the slope of the indifference curve is the marginal rate of substitution. The marginal rate of substitution (*MRS*) is the amount of one good an individual is willing to give up to obtain an additional unit of another good and maintain equal total utility. For example, in Exhibit 3b, we see that moving from point *A* to point *B*, the individual is willing to give up 3 units of milk to get an additional unit of orange juice, with total utility remaining constant (between points A and B). The marginal rate of substitution is therefore 3 units of milk for 1 unit of orange juice in the area between points A and B. And as we said, the absolute value of the slope of the indifference curve, the marginal rate of substitution, is equal to the ratio of the MU of the good on the horizontal axis to the MU of the good on the vertical axis. How can this be? Well, if it is true that an individual giving up 3 units of milk and receiving 1 unit of orange juice maintains her total utility, it follows that (in the area under consideration) the marginal utility of orange juice is approximately three times the marginal utility of milk. In general terms

$$\text{Absolute value of the slope of the indifference curve} = \text{Marginal rate of substitution}$$

$$= \frac{MU_{\text{good on horizontal axis}}}{MU_{\text{good on vertical axis}}}$$

3. **Indifference curves that are farther from the origin are preferable because they represent larger bundles of goods.** In Exhibit 3b only one indifference curve is drawn. However, different bundles of the two goods exist and have indifference curves passing through them. These bundles have less of both goods or more of both goods than those in Exhibit 3b. Illustrating a number of indifference curves on the same diagram gives us an **indifference curve map.** Strictly speaking, an indifference curve map represents a number of indifference curves for a given individual with reference to two goods. A "mapping" is illustrated in Exhibit 5.

Notice that although only five indifference curves have been drawn, many more could have been added. For example, there are many indifference curves between I_1 and I_2.

Also notice that the farther away from the origin an indifference curve is, the higher total utility it represents. You can see this by comparing point A on I_1 and point B on I_2. At point B there is the same amount of orange juice as at point A, but more milk. Point B is therefore preferable to point A, and because B is on I_2 and A is on I_1, I_2 is preferable to I_1. The reason for this is simple: An individual receives more utility at any point on I_2 (because more goods are available) than at any point on I_1.

Indifference Curve Map
Represents a number of indifference curves for a given individual with reference to two goods.

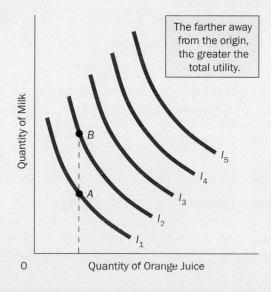

The farther away from the origin, the greater the total utility.

exhibit 5

An Indifference Map
A few of the many possible indifference curves have been drawn. Any point in the two-dimensional space is on an indifference curve. Indifference curves farther away from the origin represent greater total utility than those closer to the origin.

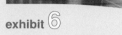

Transitivity
The principle whereby if *A* is preferred to *B*, and *B* is preferred to *C*, then *A* is preferred to *C*.

exhibit 6

Crossing Indifference Curves Are Inconsistent with Transitive Preferences

Point *A* lies on both indifference curves I_1 and I_2. This means that the individual is indifferent between *A* and *B* and between *A* and *C*, which results in her (supposedly) being indifferent between *B* and *C*. But individuals prefer "more to less" (when it comes to goods) and, thus, would prefer *C* to *B*. We cannot have transitive preferences and make sense of crossing indifference curves.

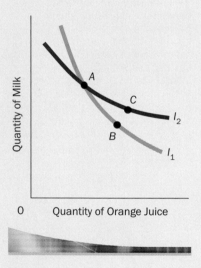

4. **Indifference curves do not cross.** Indifference curves do not cross because individuals' preferences are **transitive.** Consider the following example. If Kristin prefers Coca-Cola to Pepsi-Cola and she also prefers Pepsi-Cola to root beer, then it follows that she prefers Coca-Cola to root beer. If she preferred root beer to Coca-Cola, she would be contradicting her earlier preferences. To say that an individual has transitive preferences means that he or she maintains a logical order of preferences during a given time period. Consider what indifference curves that crossed (intersected) would represent. In Exhibit 6, indifference curves I_1 and I_2 intersect at point *A*. Notice that point *A* lies on *both* I_1 and I_2. Comparing *A* and *B*, we hold that the individual must be indifferent between them because they lie on the same indifference curve. The same holds for *A* and *C*. But if the individual is indifferent between *A* and *B* and between *A* and *C*, it follows that she must be indifferent between *B* and *C*. But *C* has more of both goods than *B*, and thus the individual will not be indifferent between *B* and *C*; she will prefer *C* to *B*. We cannot have transitive preferences and make sense of crossing indifference curves. We can, however, have transitive preferences and make sense of non-crossing indifference curves. We go with the latter.

THE INDIFFERENCE MAP AND THE BUDGET CONSTRAINT COME TOGETHER

At this point, we bring the indifference map and the budget constraint together to illustrate consumer equilibrium. We have the following facts: (1) The individual has a budget constraint. (2) The absolute value of the slope of the budget constraint is the relative prices of the two goods under consideration, say, P_X/P_Y. (3) The individual has an indifference map. (4) The absolute value of the slope of the indifference curve at any point is the marginal rate of substitution, which is equal to the marginal utility of one good divided by the marginal utility of another good; for example, MU_X/MU_Y.

With this information, what is the necessary condition for consumer equilibrium? Obviously, the individual will try to reach a point on the highest indifference curve she can reach. This point will be where the slope of the budget constraint is equal to the slope of an indifference curve (or where the budget constraint is tangent to an indifference curve). At this point, consumer equilibrium is established and the following condition holds:

Slope of budget constraint = slope of indifference curve

$$\frac{P_X}{P_Y} = \frac{MU_X}{MU_Y}$$

This condition is met in Exhibit 7 at point *E*. Note that it looks similar to the condition for consumer equilibrium earlier in this chapter. By rearranging the terms in the condition, we get[1]

$$\frac{MU_X}{P_X} = \frac{MU_Y}{P_Y}$$

FROM INDIFFERENCE CURVES TO A DEMAND CURVE

We can now derive a demand curve within a budget constraint–indifference curve framework. Exhibit 8a shows two budget constraints, one reflecting a $10 price for good *X* and the other reflecting a $5 price for good *X*. Notice that as the price

---

1. Start with $P_X/P_Y = MU_X/MU_Y$ and cross multiply. This gives $P_X MU_Y = P_Y MU_X$. Next divide both sides by P_X. This gives $MU_Y = P_Y MU_X/P_X$. Finally, divide both sides by P_Y. This gives $MU_Y/P_Y = MU_X/P_X$.

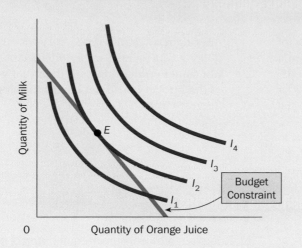

exhibit 7

Consumer Equilibrium
Consumer equilibrium exists at the point where the slope of the budget constraint is equal to the slope of an indifference curve, or where the budget constraint is tangent to an indifference curve. In the exhibit, this point is E. Here $P_X/P_Y = MU_X/MU_Y$; or rearranging, $MU_X/P_X = MU_Y/P_Y$.

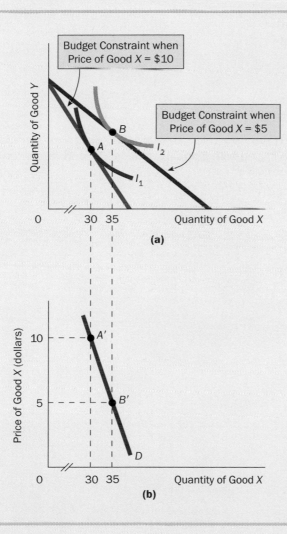

exhibit 8

From Indifference Curves to a Demand Curve
(a) At a price of $10 for good X, consumer equilibrium is at point A with the individual consuming 30 units of X. As the price falls to $5, the budget constraint moves outward (away from the origin), and the consumer moves to point B and consumes 35 units of X. Plotting the price-quantity data for X gives a demand curve for X in (b).

of X falls, the consumer moves from point A to point B. At B, 35 units of X are consumed; at A, 30 units of X were consumed. We conclude that a lower price for X results in greater consumption of X. By plotting the relevant price and quantity data, we derive a demand curve for good X in (b).

- A budget constraint represents all combinations of bundles of two goods a person can purchase given a certain money income and prices for the two goods.
- An indifference curve shows all the combinations or bundles of two goods that give an individual equal total utility.
- Indifference curves are downward-sloping, convex to the origin, and do not cross. The farther away from the origin an indifference curve is, the greater total utility it represents for the individual.
- Consumer equilibrium is at the point where the slope of the budget constraint equals the slope of the indifference curve.

Questions and Problems

1. Diagram the following budget constraints:
   a. Income = $4,000; P_X = $50; P_Y = $100
   b. Income = $3,000; P_X = $25; P_Y = $200
   c. Income = $2,000; P_X = $40; P_Y = $150
2. Explain why indifference curves (a) are downward-sloping, (b) are convex to the origin, and (c) do not cross.
3. Explain why consumer equilibrium is equivalent using marginal utility and indifference curve analysis.
4. Derive a demand curve using indifference curve analysis.

Log on to the Arnold Xtra! Web site now (*http://arnoldxtra.swcollege.com*) for additional learning resources such as practice quizzes, help with graphing, video clips, and current event applications.

ch.7

THE FIRM

Everyone deals with business firms on a daily basis. People buy goods from firms—cars, clothes, food, books, entertainment, and so on. And people work for firms as accountants, truck drivers, lawyers, secretaries, clerks, and vice presidents. Our lives are constantly intermingled with business firms—as buyers of goods or as sellers of our labor services or as both.

Even though we deal with business firms daily, most of us probably know little about them. Why do firms exist? What purpose do they serve? Why are they structured the way they are? What are their objectives?

Chapter Road Map

In the next chapter, we begin discussing many of the technical details of business firms. But before we start talking about production, costs, revenue, market structures, and more, we need to provide some basic background information about business firms. In this chapter we discuss why firms exist, the objective of the firm, and the various types of firms. This basic information is necessary for you to understand the "ins" and "outs" of business firms in the following chapters.

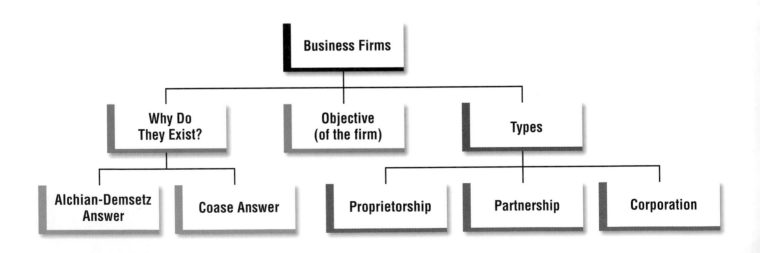

WHY FIRMS EXIST

A **business firm** is an entity that employs resources, or factors of production, to produce goods and services to be sold to consumers, other firms, or the government. This section starts with a basic question: Why do firms exist?[1]

THE MARKET AND THE FIRM: INVISIBLE HAND VERSUS VISIBLE HAND

In our discussion of supply and demand, the market guides and coordinates individuals' actions. Moreover, the market does this in an impersonal manner. No one orders buyers to reduce quantity demanded when price increases; they just do it. No one orders sellers to increase quantity supplied when price increases; they just do it. No one orders more resources to be moved into the production of personal computers when the demand and price for personal computers increase. The market guides individuals from the production of one good into the production of another good. It coordinates individuals' actions so that suppliers and demanders find mutual satisfaction at equilibrium. As the economist Adam Smith observed, individuals in a market setting are "led by an invisible hand to promote an end which was no part of their intention."

Contrast the invisible hand of the market with the visible hand of a manager in a firm. Who tells the employee on the assembly line to make more computer chips? The manager does. Who tells the employee to design a new engine, to paint the lamps green, to put steak and lobster on the menu? The manager does. Thus, both the invisible hand of the market and the visible hand of the manager of a firm guide and coordinate individuals' actions. There is, in other words, both **market** and **managerial coordination.**

If the market is capable of guiding and coordinating individuals' actions, why did firms (and managers) arise in the first place? In other words, we return to our original question: Why do firms exist?

THE ALCHIAN AND DEMSETZ ANSWER

Economists Armen Alchian and Harold Demsetz suggest that firms are formed when benefits can be obtained from individuals working as a team.[2] Sometimes the sum of what individuals can produce as a team is greater than the sum of what they can produce alone: Sum of team production > Sum of individual production.

Consider 11 individuals, all making shoe boxes. Each working alone produces 10 shoe boxes per day, for a total daily output of 110 shoe boxes. If they work as a team, however, the same 11 individuals can produce 140 shoe boxes. The added output (30 shoe boxes) may be reason enough for them to work together as a team.

THINKING LIKE AN ECONOMIST

Before answers come questions. The most important question is sometimes simply "Why?" The economist asks, "Why do firms exist?" This may seem as obvious as asking, "Why is there a sun?" or "Why does the sun set in the west?" But as we have seen, asking seemingly obvious questions, as well as less obvious ones, and then attempting to answer them, can expand our knowledge of the world. Why is the price of a car $15,000? Why do consumers buy more when price falls? Economists and other scientists are a lot like kids: They are forever asking why.

Business Firm
An entity that employs factors of production (resources) to produce goods and services to be sold to consumers, other firms, or the government.

Market Coordination
The process in which individuals perform tasks, such as producing certain quantities of goods, based on changes in market forces, such as supply, demand, and price.

Managerial Coordination
The process in which managers direct employees to perform certain tasks.

---

1. The word *firm* refers to a profit-seeking business enterprise, which is how we use it here. Occasionally, "business firm" or "business" is used as a reminder that these terms and "firm" are interchangeable. Of course, there are other types of firms besides business firms. We discuss a few at the end of this chapter.

2. Armen Alchian and Harold Demsetz, "Production, Information Costs, and Economic Organization," *American Economic Review* 62 (December 1972): 777–95.

SHIRKING IN A TEAM

Team production can have problems that do not occur in individual production. One problem of team production is **shirking,** which occurs when workers put forth less than the agreed-to effort. The amount of shirking increases in teams because the costs of shirking to individual team members are lower than when they work alone.

Consider five individuals, Alice, Bob, Carl, Denise, and Elizabeth, who form a team to produce light bulbs because they realize that the sum of their team production will be more than the sum of their individual production. They agree to team-produce light bulbs, sell the light bulbs, and split the proceeds five equal ways. On an average day, they produce 140 light bulbs and sell each one for $2. Total revenue per day is $280, with each of the five team members receiving $56. Then Carl begins to shirk. Owing to his shirking, production falls to 135 light bulbs per day, and total revenue falls to $270 per day. Each person now receives $54. Notice that while Carl did all the shirking, Carl's reduction in pay was only $2, one-fifth of the $10 drop in total revenue.

In situations (such as team production) where one person receives all the benefits from shirking and pays only a part of the costs, economists predict there will be more shirking than in the situation where the person who shirks bears the full cost of his or her shirking.

Q & A

Q: Suppose a firm is made up exclusively of extremely conscientious and hard-working people. Would shirking still be a problem?

A: Even though individuals may have different inclinations to shirk (given the chance, some people will shirk more than others), this does not mean that their behavior is independent of a change in the cost of shirking. As long as shirking is considered a good (Isn't it a form of leisure?) from which individuals obtain utility, lowering the cost of shirking will cause individuals to "consume" more shirking, *ceteris paribus*.

The Monitor (Manager): Taking Care of Shirking

The **monitor** (or manager) plays an important role in the firm. The monitor reduces the amount of shirking by firing shirkers and rewarding the productive members of the firm. In doing this, the monitor can preserve the benefits that often come with team production (increased output) and reduce, if not eliminate, the costs associated with team production (increased shirking). But this raises a question: *Who or what monitors the monitor?* In other words, *how can the monitor be kept from shirking?*

One possibility is to give the monitor an incentive not to shirk by making him or her a **residual claimant** of the firm. A residual claimant receives the excess of revenues over costs (profits) as income. If the monitor shirks, then profits are likely to be lower (or even zero or negative) and, therefore, the monitor will receive less income.

Can Above-Market Wages Cause People to Shirk Less?

Recently, some economists have argued that firms may find it in their best interest to pay wage rates above market levels. At first sight, this seems nonsensical. Why would an employer pay $10 per hour per worker for 200 workers when the market wage rate is, say, $9 per hour? Such an action would seemingly raise costs and lower profits.

But some economists maintain that employees who are paid above-market wage rates are less likely to shirk or are more likely to monitor themselves. The reason is that they have a greater incentive to hold on to their jobs. After all, if they lose the jobs that pay above-market wages, they will likely have to settle for new jobs that pay less. The strong desire to keep their above-market-wage jobs

"He Never Showed Up"

College professors sometimes assign group projects to their students. They ask students to form groups of, say, five students each, and then give each group a topic to research, write about, and present to the class. Moreover, the professors often assign the grade the group earns to each individual member of the group. In other words, if the group gets a "B" for its work, then each member of the group is assigned a "B."

Typically at the beginning of the project, the group meets, assigning different members of the group different tasks, and then arranges to meet later to put all their separate "parts" of the project together. Let's look at the group project from the perspective of one of the five members of the group. He could very well think, "My grade is largely dependent on what others do because I contribute only one-fifth of the work to the project. If I don't work very hard on the project, my grade will be a little lower. Therefore, there are certain costs to me for not doing my part, but there are certain benefits too. In other words, there are both costs and benefits to my shirking. I have a lot of other things to do right now so the benefits of shirking outweigh the costs. I won't spend much time on the project."

In a group project, the costs of shirking are spread over five people and the benefits are received by one. In an indi-

vidual project, both the full costs and the full benefits accrue to the same person. The difference in the two projects will affect behavior. We would predict that there will be more shirking in a group project than in an individual project because the costs of shirking are relatively lower in the group project. Often the professor will hear about this shirking. A member of the group, who does not shirk or shirks very little compared to others, says to the professor, "We were supposed to work on this project together, but Larry hasn't really been doing his part. In fact, we were supposed to meet at the library last night around seven, and he never showed up."

causes them to be more conscientious in their work and to shirk less. And if shirking is reduced, so are the monitoring (management) costs of the firm. In short, labor costs may be higher for the firm that pays above-market wage rates, but its monitoring costs will be lower. Overall, economists who advance the above-market wage theory, which is more commonly referred to as the *efficiency wage theory,* predict that firms will be willing to pay above-market wage rates only if their monitoring costs go down by more than their labor costs go up.

THINKING LIKE AN ECONOMIST

Marginal analysis, which is an integral part of microeconomic thinking, involves weighing "additional benefits" against "additional costs" when making a decision. (See Chapter 1.) This type of thinking is employed in efficiency wage theory. Suppose a firm is considering paying its employees wage rates $1 above the current market level. The action comes with potential benefits and costs. The firm's owners must ask themselves two questions: (1) How much are the additional benefits that arise from lower monitoring costs? (2) How much are the additional costs that arise from higher labor costs? Then the firm's owners must compare the two dollar amounts and take the appropriate action. If monitoring costs fall by more than labor costs rise, efficiency wage economists predict that the firm's owners will pay above-market wages; if not, they won't.

RONALD COASE ON WHY FIRMS EXIST

Ronald Coase, winner of the 1991 Nobel Prize in Economics, argued that "the main reason why it is profitable to establish a firm would seem to be that there is a cost of using the price mechanism."[3] Stated differently, firms exist in order to economize on buying and selling everything. In other words, they exist in order to reduce transaction costs.

Consider an example. Suppose it takes 20 different operations to produce good X. One way to produce good X, then, is to enter into a separate contract with everyone necessary to complete the 20 different operations. If we assume that one person completes one and only one operation, then we have 20 different contracts. Obviously, there are costs associated with preparing and monitoring these various contracts. A firm is a recipe for reducing these costs. It effectively replaces many contracts with one.

Here is what Coase has to say:

> The costs of negotiating and concluding a separate contract for each exchange transaction which takes place on a market must also be taken into account.... It is true that contracts are not eliminated when there is a firm, but they are greatly reduced. A factor of production (or the owner thereof) does not have to make a series of contracts as would be necessary, of course, if this co-operation were a direct result of the working of the price mechanism. For this series of contracts is substituted one. At this state, it is important to note the character of the contract into which a factor enters that is employed within a firm. The contract is one whereby the factor [the employee], for a certain remuneration (which may be fixed or fluctuating), agrees to obey the directions of an entrepreneur within certain limits.[4]

MARKETS: OUTSIDE AND INSIDE THE FIRM

What do we see when we put the firm under the microeconomic microscope? Basically, we see a market of sorts at work. Economics is largely about trades or exchanges; it is about market transactions. In supply-and-demand analysis, the exchanges are between buyers of goods and services and sellers of goods and services. In the theory of the firm, the exchanges take place at two levels: (1) at the level of individuals coming together to form a team and (2) at the level of workers "choosing" a monitor.

Let's look at the theory of the firm in the context of exchange. Individuals initially come together because they realize that the sum of what they can produce as a team is greater than the sum of what they can produce as individuals. In essence, each individual "trades" working alone for working in a team. Later, after the team has been formed, the team members learn that shirking reduces the amount of the added output they came together to capture in the first place. Now, the team members enter into another trade or market transaction. They trade some control over their daily behavior—specifically, they trade an environment in which the cost of shirking is low for an environment in which the cost of shirking is high—in order to receive a larger absolute amount of the potential benefits that drew them together. It is in this trade that the monitor appears: Some individuals "buy" the monitoring services that other individuals "sell."

As you continue your study of microeconomics, look for the "markets" that appear at different levels of analysis.

---

3. Ronald Coase, "The Nature of the Firm," *Economica* (November 1937).

4. Ibid.

THE OBJECTIVE OF THE FIRM

Most economists say that the firm's goal, or objective, is to maximize profits. Not all economists agree, however. William Baumol, for example, claims that firms seek to maximize sales. A. A. Berle and Gardner Means maintain that **separation of ownership from control (or management)** in business firms (especially large firms) has allowed managers to pursue their own goals, such as increasing the size of the firm or increasing the number of employees working for them, at the expense of the profit-maximization goal of the stockholders (owners) of the firm. Richard Cyert, James March, and Herbert Simon argue that rather than trying to maximize profits, the firm seeks only to achieve some satisfactory target profit level (referred to by Simon as **satisficing behavior**) and then pursues other goals.

Although these so-called sales and managerial theories of the firm explain some relevant aspects of the business firm, many economists believe they do not offer a significant alternative to profit maximization as the goal of business firms. It may be true that business firms do not attempt only to maximize profits, and goals other than profit do sometimes motivate the behavior of firms. Nonetheless, one must ask whether the theories built on the profit-maximization assumption satisfactorily describe, explain, and predict the firm's behavior. As we see in later chapters, they apparently do this quite well.

Q & A

Q: Firm *A* decides to maximize profits over a three-year time span, and firm *B* decides to maximize profits over a shorter time period, say, one year. An observer, who does not know the time span each firm has chosen, may believe firm *B* is attempting to maximize profits while firm *A* is not. In short, long-run profit maximization (three years in this example) may involve short-run behavior that appears contrary to profit maximization. And, of course, it may be contrary to profit maximization in the short run but not in the long run. Isn't this a problem with the profit-maximization hypothesis?

A: That depends on how the word *problem* is used. Certainly, this example does not call the profit-maximization hypothesis into question. In other words, nothing in this example suggests that firms do not attempt to maximize profits. Instead, the example correctly points out that (1) firms do not necessarily all maximize profits over the same time period and (2) failure to understand this can give the impression that a firm does not maximize profits when, in fact, it does.

Self-Test *(Answers to Self-Test questions are in the Self-Test Appendix.)*

1. What metaphor did Adam Smith use to convey the message that markets guide and coordinate individuals' actions in an impersonal manner?
2. Will individuals form teams or firms in all settings?
3. Why would a person shirk more in a (monitorless) team than when working alone?
4. Who, or what, monitors the monitor?

TYPES OF BUSINESS FIRMS

Business firms differ in many ways. They differ in what they produce, the number of people they employ, their revenues, their costs, where they are located, the type of advertising campaigns they run, their relationship with the government, the amount of taxes they pay, and in hundreds of other details. Many of the differences among business firms are minor, but some are not. One major difference is the firm's legal categorization. Business firms commonly fall into one of three legal categories: proprietorships, partnerships, and corporations.

Separation of Ownership from Control (or Management)
Refers to the division of interests between owners and managers that may occur in large business firms.

Satisficing Behavior
Behavior directed to meeting some satisfactory (not maximum) profit target.

http://

Go to *http://www.fortune.com*. On this page, you will find various lists. Read the following lists: (1) The Fortune 500, (2) America's Most Admired Companies, and (3) The 100 Best Companies to Work For. How many of the top 10 firms on the Fortune 500 list are also in the top 10 on the other lists? How many of the "100 Best Companies to Work For" do you recognize? Do you think that all the companies on the "100 Best Companies to Work For" list try to maximize profits? Why or why not?

Do Secretaries Who Work for Investment Banks Earn More Than Secretaries Who Work for Hotels?[5]

A person who lives in Des Moines, Iowa, pays the same price for a Snickers candy bar as a person who lives in Tucson, Arizona; a person who lives in Billings, Montana, pays the same price for a soft drink as a person who lives in Orlando, Florida. Many goods fetch the same price no matter where they are bought and sold.

If many of the same goods fetch the same price, do many of the people who do the same work earn the same wage? For example, will secretaries at different types of businesses earn the same wage? Probably not. There is some evidence that not all firms pay workers doing identical jobs the same wage. Industries where profits are higher tend to pay workers higher wages. For example, secretaries in investment banks tend to earn more than secretaries in hotels. Cleaners in law firms earn more than cleaners in hotels. Mexican truck drivers who deliver oil earn more than drivers who deliver corn. British clerical workers earn more in the computer industry than in the textile industry.

One explanation of this difference in wage rates is that secretaries working in high-profit industries are paid more than secretaries working in low-profit industries because they do

more or harder work. But there is not much evidence that this is true.

Another explanation of the difference is that the higher wage rate in some industries compensates for the relative unpleasantness of work in that industry. While wages do adjust for the degree of risk on the job, the amount of unpleasantness, and so on, there seems to be no evidence that this is the case in the examples mentioned. A secretary who works in an investment bank doesn't seem to have a more pleasant or less pleasant work environment than a secretary who works in a hotel.

Then, what does explain the difference in wage rates? Some efficiency wage theorists have hypothesized that above-equilibrium wages are paid by many high-profit industries because the managerial cost of monitoring employees in these industries is higher. They argue that in a high-profit industry, a manager's time is more valuable. In this setting, it is particularly costly for managers to monitor employees, that is, to make sure they do not shirk. Managers know that if they pay workers above-equilibrium wages, the workers will be less likely to shirk. Workers don't want to take the chance of losing jobs that pay them more than they can earn elsewhere. Therefore, to a large degree, the higher wage acts as an incentive for workers to monitor themselves. Managers in high-profit industries find it less costly to pay the higher wages that ensure employees will monitor themselves than to spend their valuable time monitoring employees. In short, if an investment banker doesn't want to waste her time monitoring her secretary's output, the easiest and least costly way to do this is to pay him more than he could earn in another job.

Proprietorship
A form of business that is owned by one individual who makes all the business decisions, receives the entire profits, and is legally responsible for the debts of the firm.

Unlimited Liability
A legal term that signifies that the personal assets of the owner(s) of a firm may be used to settle the debts of the firm.

PROPRIETORSHIPS

A **proprietorship** is a form of business that is owned by one individual who makes all the business decisions, receives the entire profits, and is legally responsible for the debts of the firm.

Being legally responsible for the debts of the business means that the sole proprietor has **unlimited liability;** that is, a sole proprietor is responsible for settling all debts of the firm even if this means selling his or her personal property (car, house, and so on) to do so.

As Exhibit 1 shows, proprietorships are the most numerous form of business firm in the United States; in 1998, 72.2 percent of all firms were proprietorships. However, they accounted for only 4.8 percent of total business revenues. Using

---

5. This feature is based on "When Paying More Costs Less," *The Economist* (30 May–5 June 1998) and Shailendra Raj Mehta, "The Law of One Price and a Theory of the Firm: A Ricardian Perspective on Interindustry Wages," *Rand Journal of Economics* (Spring 1998).

PERCENTAGE OF U.S. FIRMS

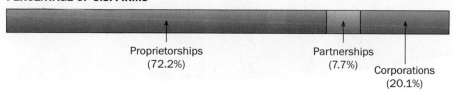

Proprietorships
(72.2%)

Partnerships
(7.7%)

Corporations
(20.1%)

PERCENTAGE OF TOTAL BUSINESS RECEIPTS

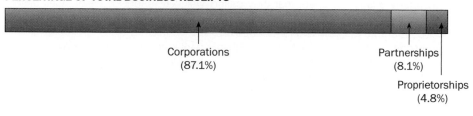

Corporations
(87.1%)

Partnerships
(8.1%)

Proprietorships
(4.8%)

exhibit 1

Forms of Business Organizations
Two criteria commonly used for classifying business firms are percentage of U.S. firms and percentage of total business revenues. Nearly three out of every four firms is a proprietorship, but they generate only 4.8 percent of total business revenues. Corporations, though relatively few in number, generate 87.1 percent of total business revenues. All data are for 1998.

this latter criterion, the much less numerous corporations are the dominant form of business firm.

Advantages of Proprietorships

There are certain advantages to proprietorships. The first advantage is that *proprietorships are easy to form and to dissolve*. To start a proprietorship, one need only meet broadly defined health and zoning regulations and register the name of the business. To dissolve the proprietorship, one need only stop doing business.

The second advantage is that *all decision-making power resides with the sole proprietor*. He or she need not consult anyone as to what product will be produced, how many units will be produced, or who will do what and when.

The third advantage is that *the profit of the proprietorship is taxed only once*. The profit of the proprietorship is the income of the sole proprietor, and as such only personal income taxes apply to it.

Disadvantages of Proprietorships

There are three major disadvantages of proprietorships. The first disadvantage is that *the sole proprietor faces unlimited liability*. The owner is responsible for all debts of the proprietorship and his or her personal property can be used to settle these debts. In short, the liability of the firm can extend beyond the confines of the business to the proprietor's home, car, boat, and savings account.

The second disadvantage is that *proprietorships have limited ability to raise funds for business expansion*. This partly explains why proprietorships are usually small business firms. Proprietorships do not find borrowing funds easy because lenders are not eager to lend funds to business firms whose success depends on only one person.

The third disadvantage is that *proprietorships usually end with the death of the proprietor*. From the point of view of the business community and the firm's employees, this is a disadvantage. Employees usually like to work for firms that offer a degree of permanency and the possibility of upward career mobility.

PARTNERSHIPS

A **partnership** is a form of business that is owned by two or more co-owners, called partners, who share any profits the business earns and who are legally responsible for any debts incurred by the firm. A partnership may be viewed as a proprietorship with more than one owner. Partners in a partnership may contribute

Partnership
A form of business that is owned by two or more co-owners (partners) who share any profits the business earns; each of the partners is legally responsible for all debts incurred by the firm.

ECONOMICS IN...

The First Killer App

Businesses must analyze a lot of data every day. Some data, such as receipts and costs, deal with day-to-day operations. Within the two broad categories of receipts and costs, there are many subcategories. Much of the data must be manipulated in order to determine the profits for the month, the amount owed in sales taxes, and so on.

But keeping records and making necessary business computations is not all that businesses do with the data they collect. Some data are used in "what if" scenarios. Will profits be higher if we purchase from supplier X instead of from supplier Y? Suppose we buy resource A instead of resource B, will we better off?

Before 1978, much of the record keeping, computations, and "what-if" scenarios were done on paper spreadsheets. Employees entered the data and made the calculations with the help of a simple calculator. Some of these calculations took hours to perform. Changing one number in one column or row of figures often meant an entire spreadsheet had to be redone by hand. Think of how much labor time could be saved if there were a quicker way to do the computational work.

A Harvard MBA student, Dan Bricklin, sitting in class doing a case study, wondered the same thing. Bricklin and a friend of his, Bob Frankston, started work on an electronic spreadsheet that they called VisiCalc (short for Visible Calculator). VisiCalc was the first electronic spreadsheet. Released in 1979, it sold for about $100.

VisiCalc was the perfect software for businesses. Employees could be more productive because VisiCalc reduced the amount of time needed to prepare spreadsheets. By making employees more productive, it lowered the costs of business. VisiCalc gave businesses the ability to keep track of their data and to make important computations in seconds instead of hours. They could create plans, forecasts, and projections easily and quickly. In fact, VisiCalc was so helpful for businesses that it gave many businesses their first real reason for buying a computer. It was the tail that wagged the dog.

VisiCalc has been called the first "killer app" (killer application)—the application that everyone has to have because it makes life so much easier, interesting, exciting, and so on. Since its introduction, many other electronic spreadsheets and more "killer apps" have been developed. But many believe it all started with VisiCalc.

different amounts of financial capital to the formation of the firm; they may agree to have different responsibilities within the firm; and they may agree to different "cuts" of the profit pie.

Advantages of Partnerships

Because partnerships are much like proprietorships, they share many of the same advantages and disadvantages. First, as for a proprietorship, *a partnership is easy to organize.*

Second, *a partnership is usually an effective form of business organization in situations where team production involves skills that are difficult to monitor.* For example, physicians and attorneys often form partnerships. Names like the Smithies and Yankelovich law firm or the Matson, Bradbury, and Chan medical clinic are not uncommon. Monitoring the job performance of such professionals would be difficult. Was our fictional Dr. Matson doing a good job or not when he talked gruffly to Mrs. Brown about her "moving aches and pains"? Was he trying to short-circuit her hypochondria, or was he simply being rude? Because Dr. Matson is a partner in the partnership, he is a residual claimant, and thus has an incentive to monitor his own work performance effectively.

Third, *in a partnership, the benefits of specialization can be realized.* If, for example, one partner in an advertising agency is better at public relations and another is better at design, then they can work at the tasks for which they are best suited.

Fourth, *the profit of the partnership is the income of the partners, and only personal income taxes apply to it.*

Disadvantages of Partnerships

First, *the partners in a partnership have unlimited liability.* In a way, this is even more of a disadvantage in a partnership than it is in a proprietorship. In a proprietorship, the proprietor incurs only his or her own debts and is solely responsible for them. In a partnership, one partner might incur the debts, but all partners are responsible for them. For example, if partner Matson incurs a debt by buying an expensive piece of medical equipment without the permission of partners Bradbury and Chan, that is too bad for partners Bradbury and Chan. They are still legally responsible for the debts incurred by Matson.

Second, *decision making in a partnership can be complicated or frustrating.* In our fictional law firm, suppose that Smithies wants to move the partnership in one direction, to specialize in corporate law, say, and Yankelovich wants to move it in another direction, to specialize in family law. Who makes the decision in this tug-of-war? Possibly no one will make the decision and things will stay as they are, which may not be a good thing for the growth of the partnership.

Third, *voluntary withdrawal by a partner from the firm or the death of a member of the firm can cause the partnership to dissolve or to be restructured.* This presents partnerships with a continuity problem, similar to the one proprietorships experience.

Q & A

Q: Isn't there such a thing as a limited partnership that avoids some of the problems of unlimited liability?

A: Yes. In a **limited partnership,** there are usually general partners and limited partners. General partners continue to have unlimited liability, but limited partners do not. The limited partner's liability is restricted to the amount he or she has invested in the firm. Usually, limited partners do not participate in the management of the firm, nor do they enter into contractual agreements on behalf of the firm.

Limited Partnership
A form of business that is organized as a partnership but that gives some of the partners the legal protection of limited liability.

CORPORATIONS

A **corporation** is a legal entity that can conduct business in its own name in the same way an individual does. Ownership of the corporation resides with stockholders who have limited liability in the debts of the corporation. As Exhibit 1 shows, corporations made up only 20.1 percent of all U.S. firms in 1998 but accounted for 87.1 percent of total business revenues. Exhibit 2 shows the top 10 firms (in terms of revenues) in the world in 2001.

Corporation
A legal entity that can conduct business in its own name the way an individual does; ownership of the corporation resides with stockholders who have limited liability in the debts of the corporation.

Rank	Company	Revenues ($ billions)
1	Wal-Mart Stores	$220
2	Exxon Mobil	191
3	General Motors	177
4	BP	174
5	Ford Motor	162
6	Enron	139
7	DaimlerChrysler	137
8	Royal Dutch/Shell Group	135
9	General Electric	126
10	Toyota Motor	121

exhibit 2

Top 10 Global Firms
The exhibit shows the top 10 global firms in terms of revenues for 2001.

Source: Fortune, April 2002

Saying One Thing and Doing Another

Have you ever proposed one thing and done another? Business leaders seem to do this all the time. Economists observe that business leaders preach the virtues of free enterprise, but at the same time seek government assistance for their businesses. For example, the owner-manager of a domestic steel company might extol the benefits of the free enterprise system when giving a speech before a civic group or answering questions for the press, but then hire lobbyists to go to Washington to argue for tariffs on foreign (imported) steel. Is this behavior hypocritical? It might be—but economists would rather try to understand this behavior than to label it.

Why do many business leaders praise free enterprise but seek government assistance that will benefit them at the expense of their competitors or at the expense of the buying public? We explain with a simple example. Suppose there are 100 businesses in the country. The owners of all the businesses advocate free enterprise. But, then, one day the owner of one business goes to Washington, D.C., to ask for government assistance, such as tax or regulation relief or a tariff imposed on foreign competitors. The owners of the other 99 businesses realize that if they don't also seek some government assistance, they may be worse off relative to the business that is receiving government assistance. In other words, if one business gets a government favor and the other businesses do not, then the relative standings of the other businesses fall. In time, all 100 businesses hire lobbyists to help them obtain government assistance.

Are all 100 businesses better off with government favors than without them? Not necessarily. The assistance one business receives may hurt another business. For example, suppose Ford Motor Company successfully lobbies for high tariffs on Japanese cars. The tariffs on Japanese imports may make Ford better off, but certainly the Americans who own or work for Toyota dealerships in the United States are made worse off. So, while each business may be helped by what government does for it, that same business may be hurt many times over by what government does for other businesses. In other words, win one time and lose ten times.

In this situation, business leaders may argue for free enterprise and an end to government favors. But unless government abolishes all business favors at once, it might be rational for a single business owner to try to keep her government favor while arguing for the abolition of all government favors. For example, company *A* might be better off if no business received government assistance, but as long as government provides assistance to any business, it is in company *A*'s best interest to keep the government favor it now receives. Company *A* sees no good reason for it to give up its government favor as long as other businesses do not give up their favors.

So, are business owners hypocritical or simply rational given their situation?

Limited Liability
A legal term that signifies that the owners (stockholders) of a corporation cannot be sued for the corporation's failure to pay its debts.

Advantages of Corporations

First, *the owners of a corporation (the stockholders) are not personally liable for the debts of the corporation.* They have **limited liability.** Limited liability assures the owners (stockholders) that if the corporation should incur debts that it cannot pay, creditors do not have recourse to the owners' personal property for payment. This means that an owner of a corporation cannot lose more than his or her investment. For example, if a person buys 100 shares of stock in corporation *XYZ* at $50 a share for a total purchase price of $5,000, he cannot lose more than $5,000.

Second, *corporations continue to exist even if one or more owners of the corporation sell their shares or die.* This is because the corporation is a legal entity in and of itself.

Third, because the corporation's life is independent of the life of any one of the owners of the corporation and there is limited liability, *corporations are usually able to raise large sums of financial capital for investment purposes.* Limited liability is a plus from the point of view of the potential investor in a corporation. She knows that she can lose only her investment and nothing more. In addition, because corporations can sell bonds and issue stock, they have means of raising financial capital that do not exist for proprietorships or partnerships. Bonds and stocks are discussed in more detail later in the chapter.

Disadvantages of Corporations

The major disadvantage of corporations is that *the profits of a corporation are taxed twice.* For example, suppose corporation *XYZ* earns a $3 million profit this year. This amount is subject to the corporate income tax. If the corporate tax is 25 percent, then $750,000 is paid in taxes and $2.25 million remains for **dividends** and other uses. Suppose half of this $2.25 million is distributed as dividends to stockholders. This is income for the stockholders and is taxed at personal income tax rates. In short, the $3 million profit is subject to both the corporate income tax and the personal income tax. Contrast this situation with the profit earned by a proprietorship. If a proprietorship had earned the $3 million profit, it would have been subject to only one tax: the personal income tax.

Dividends
A share of profits distributed to stockholders.

A second disadvantage is that *corporations are often subject to problems associated with the separation of ownership from control.* The owners of the corporation are different persons from the managers who control it on a day-to-day basis, and the owners and managers may not always agree on the corporation's objectives.

The objective of the owners might be to increase profits and raise the value of the stock they hold. The manager might want to increase the size of the corporation or hire additional personnel or contribute to the local community—all of which may work against profitability.

This possible difference in objectives between managers and owners is a subject of controversy in the economics profession. Many economists discount this problem. According to their argument, stockholders do not need to know what the managers of their corporation are doing on a daily basis. To evaluate the managers' performance, stockholders can simply watch the value of their stock. If their stock goes down in value, they can reason that present managers are not doing a good job and can organize to remove them. In short, they can monitor the managers by reading the stock market pages of their local newspaper. Also, the stockholders can make the managers "one of them" by issuing stock to the managers. Because the managers are owners, their objectives and those of stockholders should correspond. Finally, entrepreneurs are usually waiting in the wings, willing and able to make the case to stockholders that the present managers are doing a bad job and need to be replaced (by them). Their presence restrains present managers from satisfying their objectives at the expense of the objective(s) of stockholders.

Exhibit 3 summarizes the advantages and disadvantages of corporations and compares them with proprietorships and partnerships.

Self-Test

1. What type of business generates the largest percentage of total business revenues?
2. What are the advantages of a corporation?
3. What is the difference between a limited and general partner in a partnership?
4. How might the owners of a corporation solve the problems associated with separation of ownership from control?

SOME FINANCIAL ASPECTS OF FIRMS

This section provides some information about the finances of firms. In particular, we explain how a firm shows its financial status and how a corporation raises financial capital.

exhibit 3

Advantages and Disadvantages of Different Types of Business Firms

Proprietorship

Examples	Advantages	Disadvantages
1. Local barbershop 2. Many restaurants 3. Family farm 4. Carpet cleaning service	1. Easy to form and to dissolve. 2. All decision-making power resides with the sole proprietor. 3. Profit is taxed only once.	1. Proprietor faces unlimited liability. 2. Limited ability to raise funds for business expansion. 3. Usually ends with death of proprietor.

Partnership

Examples	Advantages	Disadvantages
1. Some medical offices 2. Some law offices 3. Some advertising agencies	1. Easy to organize. 2. Deals effectively with team production that involves skills difficult to monitor. 3. Benefits of specialization can be realized. 4. Profit is taxed only once.	1. Partners face unlimited liability (one partner can incur a debt and all partners are legally responsible for payment of the debt). 2. Decision making can be complex and frustrating. 3. Withdrawal or death of a partner can end partnership or cause its restructuring.

Corporation

Examples	Advantages	Disadvantages
1. Home Depot 2. AT&T 3. Wal-Mart Stores	1. Owners (stockholders) have limited liability. 2. Corporation continues if owners sell their shares of stock or die. 3. Usually able to raise large sums of financial capital.	1. Profit is taxed twice. 2. Problems may arise due to separation of ownership from control. (Some suggest "separation of ownership from control" is more illusory than real.)

THE BALANCE SHEET OF A FIRM

Balance Sheet
An accounting of the assets, liabilities, and net worth of a business firm.

Assets
Anything of value to which the firm has a legal claim.

Liabilities
Debts of the business firm.

Net Worth (Equity or Capital Stock)
Value of the business firm to its owners; it is determined by subtracting liabilities from assets.

All business firms—proprietorships, partnerships, and corporations—have a balance sheet. A **balance sheet** presents a picture of the financial status of a firm; it is an accounting of the assets and liabilities (and hence the net worth) of a firm. Exhibit 4 illustrates a balance sheet for a fictional corporation, XYZ, Inc.

On the left side of the balance sheet, **assets** are listed. An asset is anything of value to which the firm has a legal claim. On the right side of the balance sheet, **liabilities** are listed. A liability is a debt of the firm. Also listed on the right side of the balance sheet is **net worth.** Net worth, also known as **equity,** or **capital stock** (when dealing with a corporation), is the value of the business firm to its owners. It is determined by subtracting liabilities from assets.

According to XYZ's balance sheet, if the company sold its assets and paid its liabilities, it would have $90 million. This amount, or the net worth of the firm, represents the owners' claims on the assets of the firm. If liabilities exceed assets, then the firm has a negative net worth. Because a firm's net worth is equal to its assets minus its liabilities, it follows that liabilities plus net worth equal a firm's assets. In other words, the left side of the balance sheet exactly "balances" the right side.

$$\text{Net worth} = \text{Assets} - \text{Liabilities}$$

so it follows that

$$\text{Assets} = \text{Liabilities} + \text{Net worth}$$

Assets ($ millions)		Liabilities ($ millions)	
Cash	$ 5	Accounts payable	$ 10
Accounts receivable	15	Short-term debt	15
Inventory	25	Long-term debt	30
Equipment	40	Total liabilities	$ 55
Land and building	60	Net worth	90
Total assets	$145	Total liabilities and net worth	$145

exhibit 4

A Balance Sheet for XYZ, Inc.
The left side of the balance sheet lists the corporation's assets; the right side of the balance sheet lists liabilities and net worth (equity or capital stock). The net worth of a business firm is equal to assets minus liabilities. This means liabilities plus net worth equal assets, and the right side of the balance sheet exactly "balances" the left side.

FINANCING CORPORATE ACTIVITY

As mentioned earlier, corporations have options for raising financial capital that do not exist for proprietorships and partnerships. All firms can raise financial capital by borrowing from banks and other lending institutions. Corporations, however, have two other avenues: They can *sell bonds* (sometimes referred to as *issuing debt*), and they can *issue (or sell) additional shares of stock.*

A **bond** is a promise to pay for the use of someone else's money. Specifically, it is a debt obligation to repay a certain sum of money (the principal) at maturity and also to pay periodic fixed sums until that date. All bonds specify the following: (1) the maturity date, which is some date in the future, say, 2010; (2) a dollar figure, which is called the **face value (par value)** of the bond, say, $1,000; and (3) a **coupon rate** (of interest), which is stated in percentage terms, such as 10 percent.

When someone buys the bond we have just described from a corporation, the following process takes place: (1) The person who buys the bond pays some dollar amount for the bond (not necessarily the face value). So, the person has lent money to the corporation; the corporation has borrowed money from the person who bought the bond. (2) The person who buys the bond receives annual payments from the corporation equal to the coupon rate times the face value of the bond. For our bond, this payment is $100 (10% × $1,000 = $100). These $100 payments will continue each year through 2010, the maturity date. (3) When the maturity date arrives, the person who bought the bond receives the face value of the bond—$1,000.

Instead of selling bonds, a corporation may issue stock to raise financial capital. A **share of stock** is a claim on the assets of the corporation that gives the purchaser a share of the ownership of the corporation. Whereas the buyer of a corporate bond is lending funds to the corporation, the buyer of a share of stock is acquiring an ownership right in the corporation.

NONPROFIT FIRMS

There are firms other than business firms. It is important to know about them and to understand how and why they differ from business firms. This short section discusses nonprofit firms, both private and public.

A **nonprofit firm** is a firm in which there are no residual claimants; any revenues over costs must be reinvested in the firm so that "what comes in" equals "what goes out." Churches, charitable organizations, colleges, and mutual insurance companies are a few examples of nonprofit firms. All these organizations are without residual claimants. For example, a college president does not pocket any of the revenues over the costs of running the college. Any revenues that come

Bond
A debt obligation to repay a certain sum of money (the principal) at maturity and also to pay periodic fixed sums until that date.

Face Value (Par Value)
Dollar amount specified on a bond.

Coupon Rate
The percentage of the face value of a bond that is paid out regularly (usually quarterly or annually) to the holder of the bond.

Share of Stock
A claim on the assets of a corporation that gives the purchaser a share of the ownership of the corporation.

Nonprofit Firm
A firm in which there are no residual claimants; any revenues over costs must be reinvested in the firm so that "what comes in" equals "what goes out."

Go to *http://money.cnn.com/markets/ipo/.* Pickup one of the "UPCOMING IPOS." An IPO is an initial public offering, the first public sale of a company's stock. Pick one company. How many shares of stock did it sell and at what price?

into the college—through tuition fees, state appropriations, or monetary gifts—must be used for the operation of the college.

It has been argued that because no residual claimants exist in a nonprofit firm, no one within the firm has an incentive (or, at least, as strong an incentive as in a profit-maximizing business firm with residual claimants) to monitor shirking.

Also, because any funds in excess of costs cannot be taken out of the firm, it is argued that top administrators in nonprofit firms will attempt to use these "surplus" funds to make their lives more comfortable within the firm. The administrators might have large, luxurious offices and private dining rooms, pay out higher salaries than necessary in order to acquire quality personnel, or take frequent pleasurable "business" trips.

Nonprofit firms can be either private or public. A charitable organization such as the United Way is a private nonprofit firm. A police force that receives state-appropriated funds is a public nonprofit firm. One major difference between the two is who pays the costs of the firm.

In a private nonprofit firm, private citizens pay the costs. For example, the salaries of the persons who work for the local church are paid by private citizens, mostly through voluntary contributions. In a public nonprofit firm, taxpayers pay the costs. The salaries of the police in your town are paid by taxpayers.

At times the difference is not so clear-cut. Sometimes a nonprofit firm will receive some funds from taxpayers and some from private citizens who purchase the goods or services the nonprofit firm sells. State universities receive funds both from private citizens (the students who are consumers of education) and also from taxpayers. Is the state university a private nonprofit firm or a public nonprofit firm? The answer is that it is a public nonprofit firm because it is operated by persons who must answer to members of the public sector: the state governor and the regents, who are elected or publicly appointed.

A private nonprofit firm (such as a charitable organization) that doesn't satisfy the persons who contribute the funds—its customers, so to speak—is more likely to go out of business than a public nonprofit firm that doesn't satisfy its customers. The reason is that the latter receives taxpayer funds whereas the former does not. If the customers of the private nonprofit firm do not wish to continue buying what the firm is selling or wish to stop contributing, they do just that. They show their change in preferences or their dissatisfaction with the firm by stopping the flow of dollars.

The customers-as-taxpayers of the public nonprofit firm are not in the same situation. They may not like the way the public nonprofit firm is treating them or they may think the firm is doing an extremely poor job at delivering services, but unless they can convince their elected representatives to stop allocating tax funds for the public nonprofit firm, the flow of tax dollars is likely to continue.

A Reader Asks...

What's the Annual Sales Revenue at a Starbucks?

I'd like to know some of the facts and figures for business firms. For example, do most firms have many employees or only a few? What does the average small business owner get to keep from each dollar of sales? What are the safest small businesses to start, and what are the riskiest? What are the average annual sales for a Starbucks? Can you help with the answers to these questions?

Out of a total of 4.8 million firms, about 2.6 million firms have 1–4 employees and about 1 million firms have 5–9 employees. Approximately 3,400 firms have more than 2,500 employees, 4,900 firms have between 1,000 and 2,500 employees, and 8,000 firms have between 500 and 999 employees. So, while most of the firms are small firms, most people work for large firms. For example, out of a total of 108 million employees, approximately

40 million people work for the 3,400 firms that each employ more than 2,500 employees.[6]

As to the percentage of each dollar in revenue the average small business owner gets to keep, the answer is 21.5 percent. In other words, out of every dollar of revenue, the average small business owner keeps 21.5 cents. Of course, the averages vary for different types of businesses. For example, the average for legal services is 45.3 cents, while the average for hotels and motels is 4.1 cents. Here are the averages for some other types of businesses: gasoline stations—2.2 cents, heavy construction—10 cents, apparel stores—9.7 cents, furniture stores—7.2 cents, taxi and limousine service—25 cents, securities brokers—7.2 cents, automotive body shops—11.6 cents, certified public accountants—42.9 cents, dentists—36.9 cents, motion picture and sound recording studios—28.1 cents.

As to the riskiest and safest businesses, one way to measure risk is to look at the percentage of businesses in an industry that end the year with profits and the percentage that end the year with losses. For example, for the period 1998–2001, 83.5 percent of all home health care businesses ended up with profits, while only 33.8 percent of scenic and sightseeing transportation businesses did. Using this measure, some of the safer businesses are optometry services, dental services, general freight trucking, couriers, nursing services, engineering services, automotive body shops, management consulting, and food manufacturing. Some of the riskier businesses are computer and electronic products, video tape rental, oil and gas extraction, pet breeding, and commodity brokers.

Finally, what does the average Starbucks earn in revenue (not profit) in a year? The answer is $755,951. The average Gap earns $4 million; the average Home Depot, $44 million; the average Barnes & Noble, $5.7 million; the average McDonald's, $1.4 million; the average Outback Steakhouse, $3.4 million. By the way, one way to look at the relative success of a business is to compute its average annual sales revenue per square foot. For example, the average Starbucks is 1,500 square feet, while the average Home Depot is 132,000 square feet. The average Starbucks earns $504 per square foot, while the average Home Depot earns $333 per square foot. The average Nordstrom earns $342 per square foot; the average Gap, $482; the average Barnes & Noble, $243. It is interesting that while the average Barnes & Noble earns $5.7 million and the average B. Dalton Books earns $1.2 million, B. Dalton earns more per square foot ($299) than Barnes & Noble ($243).

Chapter Summary

The Firm

- Alchian and Demsetz argue that firms are formed when there are benefits from individuals working as a team; specifically, when the sum of what individuals can produce as a team is greater than the sum of what individuals can produce alone: sum of team production > sum of individual production.

- There are both advantages and disadvantages to team production. The chief advantage (in many cases) is the positive difference between the output produced by the team and the sum of the output produced by individuals working alone. The chief disadvantage is the increased shirking in teams. The role of the monitor (manager) in the firm is to preserve the increased output and reduce or eliminate the increased shirking. The monitors have a monetary incentive not to shirk their monitoring duties when they are residual claimants.

- Ronald Coase argued that firms exist in order to reduce the "costs of negotiating and concluding a separate contract for each exchange transaction which takes place on a market." In short, firms exist to reduce transaction costs.

Types of Business Firms

- A proprietorship is a form of business that is owned by one individual who makes all the business decisions, receives the entire profits, and is legally responsible for the debts of the firm. The sole proprietor has unlimited liability. The advantages of a proprietorship include the following: (1) It is easy to form and to dissolve. (2) All decision-making power resides with the sole proprietor. (3) The profits of the proprietorship are taxed only once. The disadvantages include the following: (1) The sole proprietor faces unlimited liability. (2) A proprietorship has limited ability to raise funds for business expansion. (3) It usually ends with the death of the proprietor.

- A partnership is a form of business that is owned by two or more co-owners (partners) who share any profits the business earns and who are legally responsible for any debts incurred by the firm. The advantages of a

---

6. All the data in this feature are from *http://BizStats.com*.

partnership include the following: (1) It is easy to organize. (2) It is an effective form of business organization in situations where team production involves skills that are difficult to monitor. (3) The benefits of specialization can be realized. (4) The profits of the partnership are taxed only once. The disadvantages include the following: (1) The partners have unlimited liability. (2) Decision making can be complicated and frustrating. (3) The voluntary withdrawal of a partner from the firm or the death of a partner can cause the partnership to be dissolved or restructured.

- A corporation is a legal entity that can conduct business in its own name. Corporations account for the vast majority of total business revenues. The advantages of a corporation include the following: (1) The owners (stockholders) of the corporation are not personally liable for the debts of the corporation; there is limited (not unlimited) liability. (2) The corporation continues to exist even when an owner sells his or her shares of stock or dies. (3) Corporations are usually able to raise large sums of financial capital for investment purposes. The disadvantages include the following: (1) The profits of the corporation are taxed twice. (2) There are problems associated with separation of ownership from control (although some economists maintain that no serious problems exist here that cannot be solved).

The Balance Sheet of a Firm

- A balance sheet is a picture of the financial status of a firm. Principally, a balance sheet lists a firm's assets, liabilities, and net worth. An asset is anything of value to which the firm has a legal claim. A liability is a debt of the firm. Net worth is the difference between assets and liabilities.

Financing Corporate Activity

- Corporations can either sell bonds or issue additional shares of stock to raise funds. A bond is a debt obligation that promises to pay back a certain fixed sum of money at a specific point in time and to pay a fixed sum of money periodically. A share of stock is a claim on the assets of the corporation that gives the purchaser a share of the ownership of the corporation. A bondholder of corporation X, for example, does not have an ownership right in corporation X, but a stockholder of the corporation does.

Nonprofit Firms

- Nonprofit firms are firms in which there are no residual claimants. There are both private and public nonprofit firms. One major difference between the two types is who pays the costs of the firms. In private nonprofit firms, private citizens as (voluntary) contributors or consumers do; in public nonprofit firms, taxpayers do. Because there are no residual claimants in nonprofit firms, we would expect the incentive to monitor shirking to be less. In addition, because none of the "surplus" funds can be taken out of the firm, we would expect to see top administrators in nonprofit firms using the funds in personal ways to enhance their comfort, pleasure, and status.

Key Terms and Concepts

Business Firm
Market Coordination
Managerial Coordination
Shirking
Monitor
Residual Claimants
Separation of Ownership from Control (or Management)
Satisficing Behavior

Proprietorship
Unlimited Liability
Partnership
Limited Partnership
Corporation
Limited Liability
Dividends
Balance Sheet
Assets

Liabilities
Net Worth (Equity or Capital Stock)
Bond
Face Value (Par Value)
Coupon Rate
Shares of Stock
Nonprofit Firm

1. Explain the difference between managerial coordination and market coordination.
2. Is the managerial coordination that goes on inside a business firm independent of market forces? Explain your answer.
3. Explain why even conscientious workers will shirk more when the cost of shirking falls.
4. What does the phrase "separation of ownership from control" refer to?
5. Discuss the different types of liability (limited versus unlimited) that proprietorships, partnerships, and corporations face.
6. This chapter implies that business firms might operate differently from nonprofit firms. What might account for this?
7. Profit sharing is more often found in partnerships, where the number of owners is small, than in corporations, where the number of owners tends to be relatively large. Could there be an economic reason for this? If so, what could it be?
8. Your economics class can be viewed as a team. You come together with other individuals to learn economics. There is a hierarchical scheme in the classroom. Your instructor is the monitor, and he or she tells you what to read and when the tests will be given and then grades your performance. Consider what would happen if, instead of this system, you were not graded. Would you shirk more or less? Explain your answer. In which setting would you expect to learn more economics? Why? Can you relate any of your answers to the performance of an employee in a firm? If so, explain how.
9. What differences, if any, do you think there might be between the behavior of the president of your college or university as chief administrator of a nonprofit firm and the behavior of the president of a corporation as chief administrator of a business firm?
10. Suppose an economist asks a business owner, "What is the objective of your firm?" The owner says, "To produce a quality good and sell it at a reasonable price." The economist asks, "Do you try to maximize profits?" The owner says, "No." Is it clearly the case that the owner doesn't try to maximize profits and that her goal really is what it is stated to be?
11. What does it mean to say that the profits of a corporation are taxed twice?

1. Give a numerical example that illustrates lost output due to shirking.
2. Will a person shirk more in a group of 10 persons or 100 persons, *ceteris paribus*? Why?
3. If you had to define *residual claimant* with numbers (and the minimum of words), how would you define it?

1. Go to *http://www.census.gov/prod/99pubs/99statab/sec17 .pdf*. Find Table 861.
   a. Based on number of returns, which business form—proprietorship, partnership, or corporation—grew by the largest percentage between the earliest year and the latest year identified?
   b. Each business form is divided into categories according to size of receipts. For example, there are corporations with receipts between $100,000 and $499,999, corporations with receipts between $500,000 and $999,999, and so on. In which receipts category do you find the greatest number of proprietorships? the greatest number of corporations? the greatest number of partnerships?
   c. For the latest year identified, compute average corporate receipts and average proprietorship receipts. Which is larger? Any conclusions?
   d. Look at Table 863. What percentage of total (business) profits do corporations earn?
2. Go to *http://www.sbaonline.sba.gov/*. Select "Financing Your Business," then "Loan Programs," and finally "7a Loan Guaranty." Read the page.

a. What is the 7(a) Loan Guaranty program? What is the maximum Small Business Administration (SBA) guaranty?
b. What does the SBA seek in a loan application?
c. Can an SBA loan be used to pay delinquent withholding taxes? (Select "Uses of Loan" to find the answer.) Can it be used to start a church? a casino?

3. Go to *http://www.sbaonline.sba.gov/sbdc/*. Select "SBDC Mission and Overview." What is the purpose of the Small Business Development Centers (SBDC) program? Go back and select "Your Nearest SBDC." Is there an SBDC near you?

Log on to the Arnold Xtra! Web site now (*http://arnoldxtra.swcollege.com*) for additional learning resources such as practice quizzes, help with graphing, video clips, and current event applications.

ch.8

PRODUCTION AND COSTS

If you walk into any business firm, you will see people working. If you listen to conversations, you will hear something about the kind of work they do. But behind what you see and hear in a modern business firm, there is another world—the world of production and costs. Although you don't often see this world, it is very important to the success or failure of the firm, as this chapter explains.

Chapter Road Map

Just as there are two sides to a market—a buying (demand) side and a selling (supply) side—there are two sides to a firm—a cost side and a revenue side. We examine the revenue side in the next few chapters. In this chapter, we discuss the cost side of the firm.

However, it is impossible to discuss the cost side of the firm without discussing production. We discuss production in two time periods—the short run and the long run. Production in the short run leads to the law of diminishing marginal returns and to various types of cost. Production in the long run leads to economies of scale, constant returns to scale, diseconomies of scale, and long-run average total cost.

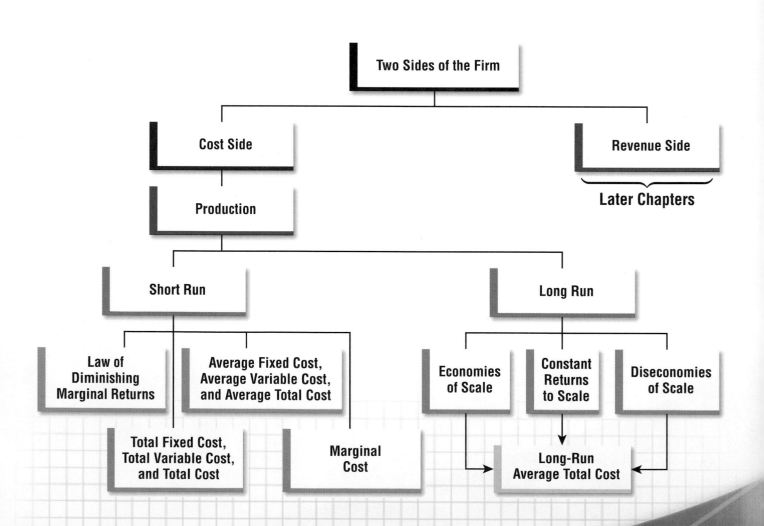

THE FIRM'S OBJECTIVE: MAXIMIZING PROFIT

Firms produce goods in order to sell the goods. Economists assume that a firm's objective in producing and selling goods is to maximize profit. **Profit** is the difference between total revenue and total cost.

Profit = Total revenue − Total cost

Recall that *total revenue* is equal to the price of a good times the quantity of the good sold. For example, if a business firm sells 100 units of X at $10 per unit, its total revenue is $1,000.

While almost everyone defines total revenue the same way, a disagreement sometimes arises as to what total cost should include. To illustrate, suppose Jill currently works as an attorney earning $80,000 a year. One day, dissatisfied with her career, Jill quits her job as an attorney and opens a pizzeria. At the end of her first year of operating the pizzeria, Jill sits down to compute her profit. She sold 20,000 pizzas at a price of $10 per pizza, so her total revenue (for the year) is $200,000. Jill computes her total costs by adding the dollar amounts she spent for everything she bought or rented to run the pizzeria. She spent $2,000 on plates, $3,000 on cheese, $4,000 on soda, $20,000 for rent in the mall where the pizzeria is located, $2,000 for electricity, and so on. The dollar payments Jill made for everything she bought or rented are called her *explicit costs*. An **explicit cost** is a cost that is incurred when an actual (monetary) payment is made. So, in other words, Jill sums her explicit costs, which turn out to be $90,000. Then Jill computes her profit by subtracting $90,000 from $200,000. This gives her a profit of $110,000.

A few days pass before Jill tells her friend Marian that she earned a $110,000 profit her first year of running the pizzeria. Marian asks: "Are you sure your profit is $110,000?" Jill assures her that it is. "Did you count the salary you earned as an attorney as a cost?" Marian asks. Jill tells Marian that she did not count the $80,000 salary as a cost of running the pizzeria because the $80,000 is not something she "paid out" to run the pizzeria. "I wrote a check to my suppliers for the pizza ingredients, soda, dishes, and so on," Jill says, "but I didn't write a check to anyone for the $80,000."

Marian tells Jill that although she (Jill) did not "pay out" $80,000 in salary to run the pizzeria, still she forfeited $80,000 to run the pizzeria. "What you could have earned but didn't is a cost to you of running the pizzeria," says Marian.

Jill's $80,000 salary is what economists call an *implicit cost*. An **implicit cost** is a cost that represents the value of resources used in production for which no actual (monetary) payment is made. It is a cost incurred as a result of a firm using resources that it owns or that the owners of the firm contribute to it.

If total cost is computed as explicit costs plus implicit costs, then Jill's total cost of running the pizzeria is $90,000 plus $80,000 or $170,000. Subtracting $170,000 from a total revenue of $200,000 leaves a profit of $30,000.

ACCOUNTING PROFIT VERSUS ECONOMIC PROFIT

Economists refer to the first profit that Jill calculated ($110,000) as *accounting profit*. **Accounting profit** is the difference between total revenue and total cost, where total cost = explicit costs. See Exhibit 1a.

Accounting profit = Total revenue − Total cost (Explicit costs)

Economists refer to the second profit calculated ($30,000) as *economic profit*. **Economic profit** is the difference between total revenue and total cost, where total cost equals the sum of explicit and implicit costs. See Exhibit 1b.

Economic profit = Total revenue − Total cost (Explicit costs + Implicit costs)

Profit
The difference between total revenue and total cost.

Explicit Cost
A cost that is incurred when an actual (monetary) payment is made.

Implicit Cost
A cost that represents the value of resources used in production for which no actual (monetary) payment is made.

Accounting Profit
The difference between total revenue and explicit costs.

Economic Profit
The difference between total revenue and total cost, including both explicit and implicit costs.

exhibit 1

Accounting and Economic Profit
Accounting profit equals total revenue minus explicit costs. Economic profit equals total revenue minus both explicit and implicit costs.

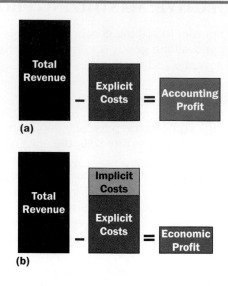

(a)

(b)

Go to *http://www.census.gov/epcd/ www/smallbus.htm*. Look at Table 1. What are the average receipts of a non-employer firm (a firm with no payroll)? Give an example of a firm that operates with only an owner and no employees. Suppose you own a nonemployer firm and earn the average receipts. If your firm has no explicit costs, are your receipts greater than the amount you can earn working for a firm with a payroll?

Q: Suppose a person has $100,000 in the bank, earning an interest rate of 5 percent a year. This amounts to $5,000 in interest a year. Now suppose this person takes the full $100,000 out of the bank in order to start a business. Is the $5,000 included in the implicit costs of owning and operating the firm?

A: Yes. To see why it would be, suppose we change the example somewhat. Instead of the person using her $100,000 to start a business, suppose she leaves her $100,000 in the bank and instead takes out a $100,000 loan at an interest rate of 5 percent. The interest she has to pay on the loan—$5,000 a year—certainly would be an explicit cost and would take away from overall profit. It just makes sense, then, to count the $5,000 interest the owner doesn't earn if she uses her own $100,000 to start the business (instead of taking out a loan) as a cost, albeit an implicit cost.

Q: When most people use the word *profit*, which profit—accounting or economic—are they referring to? Which concept of profit is it better to use?

A: When most noneconomists use the word *profit*, they usually mean accounting profit. Economic profit directs economic activity, however, as the following example illustrates.

Suppose one month after graduating from college, Marta gets a good-paying job working for a long-distance telephone company. Three years later, she thinks about leaving the company to start her own business. Will what Marta has to give up to start her company, including her well-paying job, job security, pension benefits, and so on, be important in her decision of whether or not to strike out on her own? We think she'll say yes, it is important. This, then, tells us that not only do explicit costs matter but implicit costs matter too.

We conclude that if we seek to understand and predict economic behavior, it is better to think in terms of economic profit rather than accounting profit.

ZERO ECONOMIC PROFIT IS NOT SO BAD AS IT SOUNDS

Normal Profit
Zero economic profit. A firm that earns normal profit is earning revenue equal to its total costs (explicit plus implicit costs). This is the level of profit necessary to keep resources employed in that particular firm.

Economic profit is usually lower (never higher) than accounting profit because economic profit is the difference between total revenue and total cost where total cost is the sum of explicit and implicit costs, whereas accounting profit is the difference between total revenue and only explicit costs. Thus, it is possible for a firm to earn both a positive accounting profit and a zero economic profit. In economics, a firm that makes a zero economic profit is said to be earning a **normal profit.**

Normal profit = Zero economic profit

Should the owner of a firm be worried if he has made zero economic profit for the year just ending? The answer is no. A zero economic profit—as bad as it may sound—means the owner has generated total revenue sufficient to cover total cost, that is, both explicit and implicit costs. If, for example, the owner's implicit cost is a (forfeited) $100,000 salary working for someone else, then earning a zero economic profit means he has done as well as he could have done in his next best (alternative) line of employment.

When we realize that zero economic profit (or normal profit) means "doing as well as could have been done," we understand that it isn't bad to make zero economic profit. Zero accounting profit, however, is altogether different; it implies that some part of total cost has not been covered by total revenue.

Self-Test *(Answers to Self-Test questions are in the Self-Test Appendix.)*

1. Suppose everything about two people is the same except that one person currently earns a high salary and the other person currently earns a low salary. Which is more likely to start his or her own business and why?

2. Is accounting or economic profit larger? Why?

3. When can a business owner be earning a profit but not covering his costs?

PRODUCTION

Production is a transformation of resources or inputs into goods and services. You may think of production the way you might think of making a cake. It takes certain ingredients to make a cake—sugar, flour, and so on. Similarly, it takes certain resources, or inputs, to produce a computer, a haircut, a piece of furniture, or a house.

Economists often talk about two types of inputs in the production process—fixed and variable. A **fixed input** is an input whose quantity cannot be changed as output changes. To illustrate, suppose the McMahon and McGee Bookshelf Company has rented a factory under a six-month lease: McMahon and McGee, the owners of the company, have contracted to pay the $2,300 monthly rent for six months—no matter what. Whether McMahon and McGee produce 1 bookshelf or 7,000 bookshelves, the $2,300 rent for the factory must be paid. The factory is an input in the production process of bookshelves; specifically, it is a fixed input.

A **variable input** is an input whose quantity can be changed as output changes. Examples of variable inputs for the McMahon and McGee Bookshelf Company include wood, paint, nails, and so on. These inputs can (and most likely will) change as the production of bookshelves changes. As more bookshelves are produced, more of these inputs will be purchased by McMahon and McGee; as fewer bookshelves are produced, fewer of these inputs will be purchased. Labor might also be a variable input for McMahon and McGee. As they produce more bookshelves, they might hire more employees; as they produce fewer bookshelves, they might lay off some employees.

If any of the inputs of a firm are fixed inputs, then it is said to be producing in the *short run*. In other words, the **short run** is a period in time in which some inputs are fixed.

If none of the inputs of a firm are fixed inputs—if all inputs are variable—then the firm is said to be producing in the *long run*. In other words, the **long run** is a period in time in which all inputs can be varied (no inputs are fixed).

When firms produce goods and services and then sell them, they necessarily incur costs. In this section, we discuss the production activities of the firm in the

Fixed Input
An input whose quantity cannot be changed as output changes.

Variable Input
An input whose quantity can be changed as output changes.

Short Run
A period of time in which some inputs in the production process are fixed.

Long Run
A period of time in which all inputs in the production process can be varied (no inputs are fixed).

short run, a discussion that leads to the law of diminishing marginal returns and marginal costs. In the next section, we tie the production of the firm to all the costs of production in the short run. We then turn to an analysis of production in the long run.

PRODUCTION IN THE SHORT RUN

Suppose two inputs (or resources), labor and capital, are used to produce some good. Furthermore, suppose one of those inputs—capital—is fixed. Because an input is fixed, the firm is producing in the short run.

Column 1 of Exhibit 2 shows the units of the fixed input, capital. Notice that capital is fixed at 1 unit. Column 2 shows different units of the variable input, labor. Notice that we go from zero units of labor through 10 units of labor (10 workers). Column 3 shows the quantities of output produced with one unit of capital and different amounts of labor. (The quantity of output is sometimes referred to as the *total physical product* or *TPP*.) For example, 1 unit of capital and zero units of labor produce zero output; 1 unit of capital and 1 unit of labor produce 18 units of output; 1 unit of capital and 2 units of labor produce 37 units of output; 1 unit of capital and 3 units of labor produce 57 units of output; and so on.

Column 4 shows the marginal physical product of the variable input. The **marginal physical product (MPP)** of a variable input is equal to the change in output that results from changing the variable input by one unit, *holding all other inputs fixed*. In our example, the variable input is labor, so here we are talking about the *MPP* of labor. Specifically, the *MPP* of labor is equal to the change in output, *Q*, that results from changing labor, *L*, by one unit, *holding all other inputs fixed*.

$$MPP \text{ of labor} = \Delta Q / \Delta L$$

Notice that the marginal physical product of labor first rises (18 to 19 to 20), then falls (20 to 19 to 18 to 17 to 16 to 10), and then becomes negative (-4 and -8). When the *MPP* is rising, we say there is increasing *MPP*; when it is falling, there is diminishing *MPP*; and when it is negative, there is negative *MPP*.

Focus on the point at which the *MPP* first begins to decline—with the addition of the fourth worker. The point at which the marginal physical product of labor first declines is the point at which diminishing marginal returns are said to have

Marginal Physical Product (MPP)
The change in output that results from changing the variable input by one unit, holding all other inputs fixed.

exhibit 2

Production in the Short Run and the Law of Diminishing Marginal Returns
In the short run, as additional units of a variable input are added to a fixed input, the marginal physical product of the variable input may increase at first. Eventually, the marginal physical product of the variable input decreases. The point at which marginal physical product decreases is the point at which diminishing marginal returns have set in.

(1) Fixed Input, Capital (units)	(2) Variable Input, Labor (workers)	(3) Quantity of Output, Q (units)	(4) Marginal Physical Product of Variable Input (units) $\Delta(3)/\Delta(2)$
1	0	0	
1	1	18	18
1	2	37	19
1	3	57	20
1	4	76	19
1	5	94	18
1	6	111	17
1	7	127	16
1	8	137	10
1	9	133	-4
1	10	125	-8

"set in." Diminishing marginal returns are common in production; so common, in fact, that economists refer to the **law of diminishing marginal returns** (or the law of diminishing marginal product). The law of diminishing marginal returns states that *as ever-larger amounts of a variable input are combined with fixed inputs, eventually the marginal physical product of the variable input will decline.*

Q & A

Q: Why does the *MPP* of the variable input eventually decline?

A: Think of adding agricultural workers (variable input) to 10 acres of land (fixed input). The workers must clear the land, plant the crop, and then harvest the crop. In the early stages of adding labor to the land, perhaps the *MPP* rises or remains constant. But eventually, as we continue to add more workers to the land, there comes a point where the land is over-crowded with workers. Workers are stepping around each other, stepping on the crops, and so on. Because of these problems, output growth begins to slow.

Q & A

Q: In Exhibit 2, would the firm ever hire any worker beyond the third? After all, the *MPP* of labor is at its highest (20) with the third worker. Why hire the fourth worker if the *MPP* of labor falls to 19?

A: The reason the firm may hire the fourth worker is because this worker adds output. It would be one thing if the quantity of output was 57 units with three workers and fell to 55 units with the addition of the fourth worker. But this isn't the case here. With the addition of the fourth worker, output rises from 57 units to 76 units. The firm has to ask and answer two questions: (1) What can the additional 19 units of output be sold for? (2) What does it cost to hire the fourth worker? Suppose the additional 19 units can be sold for $100 and it costs the firm $70 to hire the fourth worker. Will the firm hire the fourth worker? Yes.

MARGINAL PHYSICAL PRODUCT AND MARGINAL COST

A firm's costs are tied to its production. Specifically, the *marginal cost (MC)* of producing a good is a reflection of the marginal physical product (*MPP*) of the variable input. Our objective in this section is to prove that this last statement is true. But before we can do this, we need to define and discuss some economic cost concepts.

Some Economic Cost Concepts

Recall our earlier discussion of fixed inputs and variable inputs. Certainly a cost is incurred whenever a fixed input or variable input is employed in the production process. The costs associated with fixed inputs are called **fixed costs.** The costs associated with variable inputs are called **variable costs.**

Because the quantity of a fixed input does not change as output changes, fixed costs do not change as output changes. Payments for such things as fire insurance (the same amount every month), liability insurance, and the rental of a factory and machinery are usually considered fixed costs. Whether the business produces 1, 100, or 1,000 units of output, it is likely that the rent for its factory will not change. It will be whatever amount was agreed to with the owner of the factory for the duration of the rental agreement.

Because the quantity of a variable input changes with output, so do variable costs. For example, it takes labor, wood, and glue to produce wooden bookshelves. It is likely that the quantity of all these inputs (labor, wood, and glue) will change as the number of wooden bookshelves produced changes.

The sum of fixed costs and variable costs is **total cost (*TC*).** In other words, if total fixed costs (*TFC*) are $100 and total variable costs (*TVC*) are $300, then total cost (*TC*) is $400.

$$TC = TFC + TVC$$

Marginal Cost (*MC*)
The change in total cost that results from a change in output: $MC = \Delta TC/\Delta Q$.

Now that we know what total cost is, we can formally define marginal cost. **Marginal cost (*MC*)** is the change in total cost, *TC*, that results from a change in output, *Q*.

$$MC = \Delta TC/\Delta Q$$

The Link between *MPP* and *MC*

In Exhibit 3, we establish the link between the marginal physical product of a variable input and marginal cost. The first four columns present much of the same data that was first presented in Exhibit 2. Essentially, column 3 shows the different quantities of output produced by one unit of capital (fixed input) and various amounts of labor (variable input) and column 4 shows the *MPP* of labor. In Exhibit 3a, we have drawn the *MPP* curve, based on the data in column 4. Notice that the *MPP* curve first rises and then falls.

In column 5, we have identified the total fixed cost (*TFC*) of production as $40. (Recall that fixed costs do not change as output changes.) For column 6, we have assumed that each worker is hired for $20, so when there is only one worker, total variable cost (*TVC*) is $20; when there are two workers, total variable cost is $40; and so on. Column 7 shows total cost at various output levels; the total cost figures in this column are simply the sum of the fixed costs in column 5 and the variable costs in column 6. Finally, in column 8, we compute marginal cost. Exhibit 3b shows the *MC* curve, based on the data in column 8.

Let's focus on columns 4 and 8 in Exhibit 3, which show the *MPP* and *MC*, respectively. Notice that when the *MPP* is rising (from 18 to 19 to 20), marginal cost is decreasing (from $1.11 to $1.05 to $1.00) and when the *MPP* is falling (from 20 to 19 and so on), marginal cost is increasing (from $1.00 to $1.05 and

exhibit 3

Marginal Physical Product and Marginal Cost

(a) The marginal physical product of labor curve. The curve is derived by plotting the data from columns 2 and 4 in the exhibit. (b) The marginal cost curve. The curve is derived by plotting the data from columns 3 and 8 in the exhibit. Notice that as the *MPP* curve rises, the *MC* curve falls; and as the *MPP* curve falls, the *MC* curve rises.

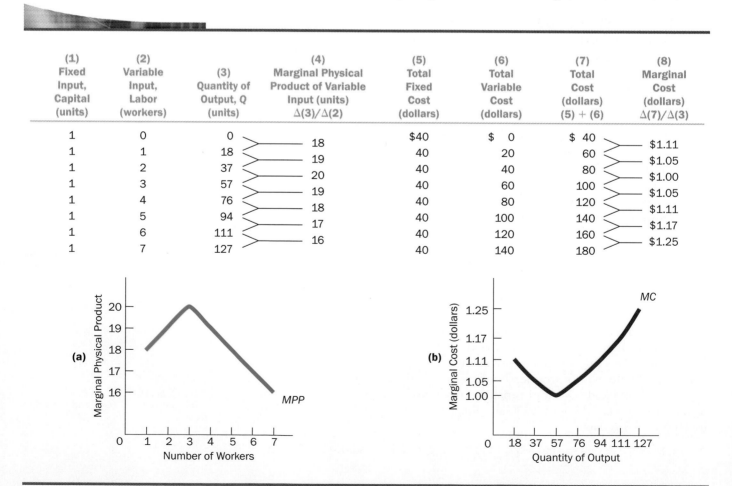

(1) Fixed Input, Capital (units)	(2) Variable Input, Labor (workers)	(3) Quantity of Output, *Q* (units)	(4) Marginal Physical Product of Variable Input (units) $\Delta(3)/\Delta(2)$	(5) Total Fixed Cost (dollars)	(6) Total Variable Cost (dollars)	(7) Total Cost (dollars) (5) + (6)	(8) Marginal Cost (dollars) $\Delta(7)/\Delta(3)$
1	0	0		$40	$ 0	$ 40	
			18				$1.11
1	1	18		40	20	60	
			19				$1.05
1	2	37		40	40	80	
			20				$1.00
1	3	57		40	60	100	
			19				$1.05
1	4	76		40	80	120	
			18				$1.11
1	5	94		40	100	140	
			17				$1.17
1	6	111		40	120	160	
			16				$1.25
1	7	127		40	140	180	

so on). In other words, the *MPP* and *MC* move in opposite directions. You can also see this by comparing the *MPP* curve with the *MC* curve. When the *MPP* curve is going up, the *MC* curve is moving down, and when the *MPP* curve is going down, the *MC* curve is going up. Of course, all this is common sense: As marginal physical product rises, or to put it differently, as the productivity of the variable input rises, we would expect costs to decline. And as the productivity of the variable input declines, we would expect costs to rise.

In conclusion, then, what the *MC* curve looks like depends on what the *MPP* curve looks like. Recall that the *MPP* curve must have a declining portion because of the law of diminishing marginal returns. So, if the *MPP* curve first rises and then (when diminishing marginal returns set in) falls, it follows that the *MC* curve must first fall and then rise.

Another Way to Look at the Relationship between *MPP* and *MC*

An easy way to see that marginal physical product and marginal cost move in opposite directions involves reexamining the definition of marginal cost. Recall that marginal cost is defined as the change in total cost divided by the change in output. The change in total cost is the additional cost of adding an additional unit of the variable input (see Exhibit 3). The change in output is the marginal physical product of the variable input. Thus, marginal cost is equal to the additional cost of adding an additional unit of the variable input divided by the input's marginal physical product. In Exhibit 3, the variable input is labor, so $MC = W/MPP$, where MC = marginal cost, W — wage, and MPP = marginal physical product of labor. The following table reproduces column 4 from Exhibit 3, notes the wage, and computes *MC* using the equation $MC = W/MPP$.

MPP	Variable Cost (W)	$\frac{W}{MPP} = MC$
18 units	$20	$20/18 = $1.11
19	20	20/19 = 1.05
20	20	20/20 = 1.00
19	20	20/19 = 1.05
18	20	20/18 = 1.11
17	20	20/17 = 1.17
16	20	20/16 = 1.25

Now, compare the marginal cost figures in the last column in the table above with the marginal cost figures in column 8 of Exhibit 3. Whether marginal cost is defined as equal to $\Delta TC/\Delta Q$ or as equal to W/MPP, the result is the same. The latter way of defining marginal cost, however, explicitly shows that as *MPP* rises, *MC* falls, and as *MPP* falls, *MC* rises.

$$\frac{W}{MPP\uparrow} = MC\downarrow$$

$$\frac{W}{MPP\downarrow} = MC\uparrow$$

AVERAGE PRODUCTIVITY

When the word *productivity* is used in the press or by the layperson, what is usually being referred to is *average physical product* instead of *marginal physical product*. To illustrate the difference, suppose one worker can produce 10 units of output a day and two workers can produce 18 units of output a day. Marginal physical product is 8 units (MPP of labor $= \Delta Q/\Delta L$). Average physical product, which is output divided by the quantity of labor, is equal to 9 units.

$$AP \text{ of labor} = Q/L$$

ECONOMICS IN...

High School Students, Staying Out Late, and More

Can marginal cost affect a person's behavior? Let's analyze two different situations in which it might.

High School Students and Staying Out Late

A 16-year-old high school student asks her parents if she can have the car tonight. She says she plans to go with some friends to a concert. Her parents ask her what time she will get home. She says that she plans to be back by midnight.

The girl's parents tell her that she can have the car and that they expect her home by midnight. If she's late, she will lose her driving privileges for a week.

Now suppose it is later that night. In fact, it is midnight and the 16-year-old is 15 minutes away from home. When she realizes she can't get home until 12:15 a.m., will she continue on home? She may not. The marginal cost of staying out later is now zero. In short, whether she arrives home at 12:15, 1:15, or 2:25, the punishment is the same: she will lose her driving privileges for a week. There is no additional cost for staying out an additional minute or an additional hour. There may, however, be additional benefits. Her "punishment" places a zero marginal cost on staying out after midnight. Once midnight has come and gone, the additional cost of staying out later is zero.

No doubt her parents would prefer her to get home at, say, 12:01 rather than at 1:01 or even later. If this is the case, then they should not have made the marginal cost of staying out after midnight zero. What they should have done is increased the marginal cost of staying out late for every minute (or 15-minute period) the 16-year-old was late. In other words, one of the parents might have said, "For the first 10 minutes you're late, you'll lose 1 hour driving privileges, for the second 10 minutes you're late, you'll lose 2 hours driv-

ing privileges, and so on." This would have presented our teen with a rising marginal cost of staying out late. With a rising marginal cost, it is more likely she will get home close to midnight.

Crime

Suppose the sentence for murder in the first degree is life imprisonment and the sentence for burglary is 10 years. In a given city, the burglary rate has skyrocketed in the past few months. Many of the residents have become alarmed. They have called on the police and other local and state officials to do something about the rising burglary rate.

Someone proposes that the way to lower the burglary rate is to increase the punishment for burglary. Instead of only 10 years in prison, make the punishment stiffer. In his zeal to reduce the burglary rate, a state legislator proposes that burglary carry the same punishment as first-degree murder: life in prison. That will certainly get the burglary rate down, he argues. After all, who will take the chance of committing a burglary if he knows that if he gets caught and convicted, he will spend the rest of his days in prison?

Unfortunately, by making the punishment for burglary and murder the same, the marginal cost of murdering someone that a person is burglarizing falls to zero. To illustrate, suppose Smith is burglarizing a home, and the residents walk in on him. Smith realizes the residents can identify him as the burglar, so he shoots and kills them. What does it matter? If he gets apprehended for burglary, the penalty will be the same as it is for murder. Raising the cost of burglary from 10 years to life imprisonment may reduce the number of burglaries, but it may have the unintended effect of raising the murder rate.

Usually, when the term *labor productivity* is used in the newspaper and in government documents, it refers to the average (physical) productivity of labor on an hourly basis. By computing the average productivity of labor for different countries and noting the annual percentage changes, we can compare labor productivity between and within countries. Government statisticians have chosen 1992 as a benchmark year (a year against which we measure other years). They have also set a productivity index, which is a measure of productivity, for 1992 equal to 100. By computing a productivity index for other years and noting whether each index is above, below, or equal to 100, they know whether productivity is rising, falling, or remaining constant, respectively. Finally, by computing the percentage change in productivity indices from one year to the next, they know the rate at which productivity is changing.

Suppose the productivity index for the United States is 120 in year 1 and 125 in year 2. The productivity index is higher in year 2 than in year 1, so labor productivity increased over the year; that is, output produced increased per hour of labor expended.

Self-Test

1. If the short run is six months, does it follow that the long run is longer than six months?

2. "As we add more capital to more labor, eventually the law of diminishing marginal returns will set in." What is wrong with this statement?

3. Suppose a marginal cost (*MC*) curve falls when output is in the range of 1 unit to 10 units, flattens out and remains constant over an output range of 10 units to 20 units, and then rises over a range of 20 units to 30 units. What does this have to say about the marginal physical product (*MPP*) of the variable input?

COSTS OF PRODUCTION: TOTAL, AVERAGE, MARGINAL

In this section, we continue our discussion of the costs of production. The easiest way to see the relationships among the various costs is with the example in Exhibit 4.

Column 1 of Exhibit 4 shows the various quantities of output, ranging from zero units to 10 units.

Column 2 shows the total fixed costs of production. We have set *TFC* at $100. Recall that fixed costs do not change as output changes. In other words, *TFC* is $100 when output is zero units, or 1 unit, or 2 units, and so on. Because *TFC* does not change as *Q* changes, the *TFC* curve in the exhibit is a horizontal line at $100.

In column 3, we have computed *average fixed cost*. **Average fixed cost (*AFC*)** is total fixed cost divided by quantity of output.

$$AFC = TFC/Q$$

Average Fixed Cost (*AFC*)
Total fixed cost divided by quantity of output: $AFC = TFC/Q$.

For example, look at the fourth entry in column 3. How did we get a dollar amount of $33.33? We simply took *TFC* at 3 units of output, which is $100, and divided by 3. Notice that the *AFC* curve in the exhibit continually declines.

In column 4, we have simply entered some hypothetical data for total variable cost (*TVC*). The *TVC* curve in the exhibit rises because it is likely that variable costs will increase as output increases.

In column 5, we have computed average variable cost. **Average variable cost (*AVC*)** is total variable cost divided by quantity of output.

$$AVC = TVC/Q$$

Average Variable Cost (*AVC*)
Total variable cost divided by quantity of output: $AVC = TVC/Q$.

For example, look at the third entry in column 5. How did we get a dollar amount of $40.00? We simply took *TVC* at 2 units of output, which is $80, and divided by 2. Notice that the *AVC* curve declines and then rises.

Column 6 shows total cost (*TC*). Total cost is the sum of total variable cost and total fixed cost. Notice that the *TC* curve does not start at zero. Why not? Because even when output is zero, there are some fixed costs. Fact is, at zero output, total fixed cost (*TFC*) is $100. It follows, then, that the total cost (*TC*) curve starts at $100 instead of at $0.

Column 7 shows average total cost. **Average total cost (*ATC*)** is total cost divided by quantity of output. Average total cost is sometimes called *unit cost*.

$$ATC = TC/Q$$

Average Total Cost (*ATC*), or Unit Cost
Total cost divided by quantity of output: $ATC = TC/Q$.

(1) Quantity of Output, Q (units)	(2) Total Fixed Cost (TFC)	(3) Average Fixed Cost (AFC) AFC = TFC/Q = (2)/(1)	(4) Total Variable Cost (TVC)	(5) Average Variable Cost (AVC) AVC = TVC/Q = (4)/(1)
0	$100	—	$ 0	—
1	100	$100.00	50	$50.00
2	100	50.00	80	40.00
3	100	33.33	100	33.33
4	100	25.00	110	27.50
5	100	20.00	130	26.00
6	100	16.67	160	26.67
7	100	14.28	200	28.57
8	100	12.50	250	31.25
9	100	11.11	310	34.44
10	100	10.00	380	38.00

exhibit 4

Total, Average, and Marginal Costs

TFC equals $100 (column 2) and TVC is as noted in column 4. From the data, we calculate AFC, AVC, TC, ATC, and MC. TFC, AFC, TVC, AVC, TC, ATC, and MC are shown in diagrams at the bottom of the corresponding columns. (Note: Scale is not the same for all diagrams.)

Alternatively, we can say that *ATC* equals the sum of *AFC* and *AVC*.

$$ATC = AFC + AVC$$

To understand why this makes sense, remember that $TC = TFC + TVC$. Thus, if we divide all total magnitudes by quantity of output (Q), we necessarily get *ATC* = *AFC* + *AVC*. Notice that the *ATC* curve falls and then rises.

Column 8 shows marginal cost (*MC*). Recall that marginal cost is the change in total cost divided by the change in output.

$$MC = \Delta TC / \Delta Q$$

The *MC* curve has a declining portion and a rising portion. What is happening to the *MPP* of the variable input when *MC* is declining? The *MPP* is rising. What is happening to the *MPP* of the variable input when *MC* is rising? *MPP* is falling. Obviously, the low point on the *MC* curve is when diminishing marginal returns set in.

THE *AVC* AND *ATC* CURVES IN RELATION TO THE *MC* CURVE

What do the average total and average variable cost curves look like in relation to the marginal cost curve? To explain, we need to discuss the **average-marginal rule,** which is best defined with an example.

Suppose there are 20 persons in a room and each person weighs 170 pounds. Your task is to calculate the average weight. This is accomplished by adding the individual weights and dividing by 20. Obviously, this average weight will be 170 pounds. Now let an additional person enter the room. We shall refer to this addi-

Average-Marginal Rule
When the marginal magnitude is above the average magnitude, the average magnitude rises; when the marginal magnitude is below the average magnitude, the average magnitude falls.

exhibit 4

Continued

(6) Total Cost (TC) $TC = TFC + TVC$ $= (2) + (4)$	(7) Average Total Cost (ATC) $ATC = TC/Q$ $= (6)/(1)$	(8) Marginal Cost (MC) $MC = \Delta TC/\Delta Q$ $= \Delta(6)/\Delta(1)$
$100.00	—	—
150.00	$150.00	$50.00
180.00	90.00	30.00
200.00	66.67	20.00
210.00	52.50	10.00
230.00	46.00	20.00
260.00	43.33	30.00
300.00	42.86	40.00
350.00	43.75	50.00
410.00	45.56	60.00
480.00	48.00	70.00

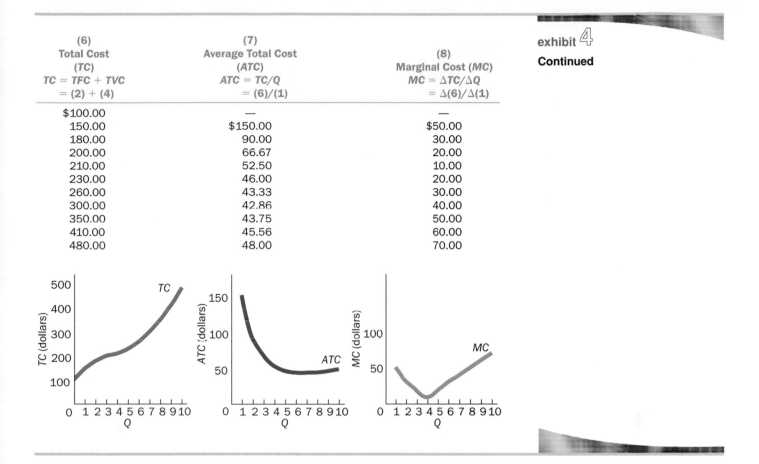

tional person as the marginal (additional) person and the additional weight he brings to the room as the marginal weight.

Let's suppose the weight of the marginal person is 275 pounds. The average weight based on the 21 persons now in the room is 175 pounds. The new average weight is greater than the old average weight. The average weight was pulled up by the weight of the additional person. In short, when the marginal magnitude is above the average magnitude, the average magnitude rises. This is one part of the average-marginal rule.

Suppose that the weight of the marginal person is less than the average weight of 170 pounds, for example, 65 pounds. Then the new average is 165 pounds. In this case, the average weight was pulled down by the weight of the additional person. Thus, when the marginal magnitude is below the average magnitude, the average magnitude falls. This is the other part of the average-marginal rule.

$$\text{Marginal} < \text{Average} \rightarrow \text{Average} \downarrow$$
$$\text{Marginal} > \text{Average} \rightarrow \text{Average} \uparrow$$

We can apply the average-marginal rule to find out what the average total and average variable cost curves look like in relation to the marginal cost curve. The following analysis holds for both the average total cost curve and the average variable cost curve.

We reason that if marginal cost is below (less than) average variable cost, average variable cost is falling; if marginal cost is above (greater than) average variable cost, average variable cost is rising. This reasoning implies that the relationship between the average variable cost curve and the marginal cost curve must look like that in Exhibit 5a. In Region 1 of (a), marginal cost is below average variable

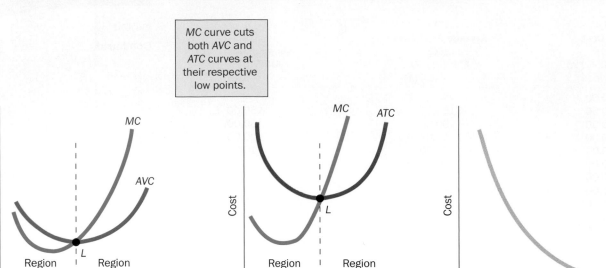

| MC curve cuts both AVC and ATC curves at their respective low points. |

(a)

(b)

(c)

exhibit 5

Average and Marginal Cost Curves
(a) The relationship between *AVC* and *MC*. (b) The relationship between *ATC* and *MC*. The *MC* curve intersects both the *AVC* and *ATC* curves at their respective low points (*L*). This is consistent with the average-marginal rule. (c) The *AFC* curve declines continuously.

cost and, consistent with the average-marginal rule, average variable cost is falling. In Region 2 of (a), marginal cost is above average variable cost, and average variable cost is rising. In summary, the relationship between the average variable cost curve and the marginal cost curve in Exhibit 5a is consistent with the average-marginal rule.

In addition, because average variable cost is pulled down when marginal cost is below it and pulled up when marginal cost is above it, it follows that the marginal cost curve must intersect the average variable cost curve at the latter's lowest point. This lowest point is point *L* in Exhibit 5a.

The same relationship that exists between the *MC* and *AVC* curves also exists between the *MC* and *ATC* curves, as shown in Exhibit 5b. In Region 1 of (b), marginal cost is below average total cost and, consistent with the average-marginal rule, average total cost is falling. In Region 2 of (b), marginal cost is above average total cost, and average total cost is rising. It follows that the marginal cost curve must intersect the average total cost curve at the latter's lowest point.

What about the average fixed cost curve? Is there any relationship between it and the marginal cost curve? The answer is no. We can indirectly see why by recalling that average fixed cost is simply total fixed cost (which is constant over output) divided by output ($AFC = TFC/Q$). As output (Q) increases and total fixed cost (TFC) remains constant, it follows that average fixed cost (TFC/Q) must decrease continuously (see Exhibit 5c).

TYING SHORT-RUN PRODUCTION TO COSTS

As we have said before, costs are tied to production. To see this explicitly, let's summarize some of our earlier discussions. See Exhibit 6.

We assume production takes place in the short run, so there is at least one fixed input. Suppose we initially add units of a variable input to the fixed input and the marginal physical product of the variable input (e.g., labor) rises. As a result of *MPP* rising, marginal cost (*MC*) falls. When *MC* has fallen enough to be below average variable cost (*AVC*), we know from the average-marginal rule that *AVC* will begin to decline. Also, when *MC* has fallen enough to be below average total cost (*ATC*), *ATC* will begin to decline.

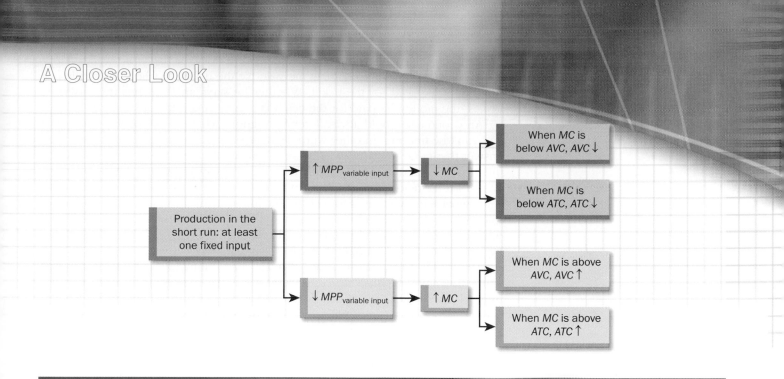

exhibit 6

Tying Production to Costs
What happens in terms of production (*MPP* rising or falling) affects *MC*, which in turn eventually affects *AVC* and *ATC*.

Eventually, though, the law of diminishing marginal returns will set in. When this happens, the *MPP* of the variable input declines. As a result, *MC* rises. When *MC* has risen enough to be above *AVC*, *AVC* will rise. Also, when *MC* has risen enough to be above *ATC*, *ATC* will rise.

We conclude: What happens in terms of production (Is *MPP* rising or falling?) affects *MC*, which in turn eventually affects *AVC* and *ATC*. In short, the cost of a good is tied to the production of that good.

ONE MORE COST CONCEPT: SUNK COST

Sunk cost is a cost incurred in the past that cannot be changed by current decisions and therefore cannot be recovered. For example, suppose a firm must purchase a $10,000 government license before it can legally produce and sell lamp poles. Furthermore, suppose the government will not buy back the license or allow it to be resold. The $10,000 the firm spends to purchase the license is a sunk cost. It is a cost that, after it has been incurred (the $10,000 was spent), cannot be changed by a current decision (the firm cannot go back into the past and undo what was done) and cannot be recovered (the government will neither buy back the license nor allow it to be resold).

Let's consider another example of a sunk cost. Suppose Jeremy buys a movie ticket, walks into the theater, and settles down to watch the movie. Thirty minutes into the movie, he realizes that he hates it. The money he paid for the ticket is a sunk cost. The cost was incurred in the past, it cannot be changed, and it cannot be recovered. (We are assuming that movie theaters do not give your money back if you dislike the movie.)

Economists' Advice: Ignore Sunk Costs

Economists advise individuals to ignore sunk costs. To illustrate, consider the case of Jeremy who bought the movie ticket but dislikes the movie. Given the constraints in this case, the movie ticket is a sunk cost. Now suppose Jeremy says the following to himself as he is watching the movie:

I paid to watch this movie, but I really hate it. Should I get up and walk out or should I stay and watch the movie? I think I'll stay and watch the movie because if I leave, I'll lose the money I paid for the ticket.

Sunk Cost
A cost incurred in the past that cannot be changed by current decisions and therefore cannot be recovered.

Can you see the error Jeremy is making? He believes that if he walks out of the theater he will lose the money he paid for the ticket. But he has already lost the money he paid for the ticket. Whether he stays and watches the movie or leaves, the money he paid for the ticket is gone forever. It is a sunk cost.

An economist would advise Jeremy to ignore what has happened in the past and can't be undone. In other words, ignore sunk costs. Instead, simply ask and answer these questions: What do I gain (what are my benefits) if I stay and watch the movie? What do I lose (what are my costs) if I stay and watch the movie? (Not: What have I already lost? Nothing can be done about what has already been lost.)

If what Jeremy expects to gain by staying and watching the movie is greater than what he expects to lose, he ought to stay and watch the movie. However, if what he expects to lose by staying and watching the movie is greater than what he expects to gain, he ought to leave.

To see this more clearly, suppose again that Jeremy has decided to stay and watch the movie *because he doesn't want to lose the price of the movie ticket.* Two minutes after he has made this decision, you walk up to Jeremy and offer him $200 to leave the theater. What do you think Jeremy will do now? Do you think he will say, "I can't leave the movie theater because if I do, I will lose the price of the movie ticket"? Or do you think he is more likely to say, "Sure, I'll take the $200 and leave the movie theater"?

Most people will say that Jeremy will take the $200 and leave the movie theater. Why? The simple reason is because if he doesn't leave, he loses the opportunity to receive $200.

Well, wouldn't he have forfeited something—albeit not $200—if he stayed at the movie theater before the $200 was offered? (Might he have given up at least $1 in benefits doing something else?) In short, didn't he have some opportunity cost of staying at the movie theater before the $200 was offered? Surely he did. The problem is that somehow, by letting sunk cost influence his decision, Jeremy was willing to ignore this opportunity cost of staying at the theater. All the $200 did was to make this opportunity cost of staying at the movie theater obvious.

Q & A

Q: Suppose Alicia purchases a pair of shoes, wears them for a few days, and then realizes they are uncomfortable. Furthermore, suppose she can't return the shoes for a refund. Are the shoes considered a sunk cost? Would an economist recommend that Alicia simply not wear the shoes? If so, this seems wasteful.

A: The purchase of the shoes represents a cost (1) incurred in the past that (2) cannot be changed by a current decision and (3) cannot be recovered; therefore, it is a sunk cost. An economist would recommend that Alicia not base her current decision to wear or not wear the shoes on what has happened and cannot be changed. If a person lets what she has done, and can't undo, influence her present decision, she runs the risk of compounding mistakes.

To illustrate, if Alicia decides to wear the uncomfortable shoes because she thinks it is a waste of money not to, then she may end up with an even bigger loss: certainly less comfort and possibly a trip to the podiatrist later. The relevant question she must ask herself is, "What will I give up by wearing the uncomfortable shoes?" and not, "What did I give up by buying the shoes?" The message here is that only the future can be affected by a present decision, never the past. Bygones are bygones, sunk costs are sunk costs.

Behavioral Economics and Sunk Cost

In one real-life experiment, two researchers randomly distributed discounts to buyers of subscriptions to Ohio University's 1982–1983 theater season.[1] One group of ticket buyers paid the normal ticket price of $15 per ticket, a second

---

1. Hal Arkes and Catherine Blumer, "The Psychology of Sunk Cost," *Organizational Behavior and Human Decision Processes* 124 (1985).

What Matters to Global Competitiveness?

What does a country need to do to be competitive in the global marketplace? The usual answer is that it needs to produce goods that people in other countries want to buy at prices they want to pay. For example, for the United States to be competitive in the global car and computer markets, U.S. firms must produce cars and computers at prices that people all over the world are willing and able to pay.

Price is a major factor in the race to be competitive in the global market. If U.S. car firms charge higher prices for their cars than German and Japanese firms charge for their similar-quality cars, then it is unlikely that U.S. firms will be competitive in the global car market. We conclude: If U.S. firms are to be competitive in the global market, they must keep their prices down, all other things being equal.

But how do firms keep their prices down? One way is to keep their unit cost, or average total cost, down. Look at it this way:

Profit per unit = Price per unit − Unit cost (or *ATC*)

The lower unit cost is, the lower price can go and still earn the producer/seller an acceptable profit per unit. In other words, to be competitive on price, firms must be competitive on unit costs; they need to find ways to lower unit cost. This chapter shows how unit cost will decline when marginal cost (*MC*) is below unit cost (*ATC*). In other words, to lower *ATC*, marginal cost must fall and go below (current) average total cost. But how do firms get *MC* to fall and eventually go below current *ATC*? This chapter also explains that before *MC* can decline, marginal physical product (*MPP*) must rise.

Let's summarize our analysis so far: To be competitive in the global marketplace, U.S. firms must be competitive on price. To be competitive on price, firms must be competitive on unit cost (*ATC*). This requires that firms get their *MC* to decline and, ultimately, go below their current *ATC*. And the way to get *MC* to decline and go below current *ATC* is to raise the marginal productivity (*MPP*) of the inputs the firms use. To a large degree, the key to becoming or staying globally competitive is to find and implement ways to increase factor productivity.

How do you fit into the picture? Your education may affect the marginal physical product (*MPP*) of labor. As you learn more things and become more skilled (more productive)—and as many others do too—the *MPP* of labor in the United States rises. This, in turn, lowers firms' marginal cost, which, one hopes, will decline enough to pull both average variable and average total costs down. As this happens, U.S. firms can become more competitive on price and still earn a profit.

group received $2 off per ticket, and a third group received $7 off per ticket. In short, some buyers paid lower ticket prices than other buyers did.

The two researchers found that people who paid more for their tickets attended the theater performances more often than those who paid less for their tickets. Now some people argue that this is because the people who paid more for their tickets somehow wanted to attend the theater more than those who paid less. But this isn't likely because the discounts to buyers were distributed randomly.

Instead, what seems to be the case here is that the more someone paid for the ticket (and everyone paid for his or her ticket before the night of the theater performance), the greater the sunk cost. And the greater the sunk cost, the more likely individuals were to attend the theater performance. In other words, (at least some) people were not ignoring sunk cost.

THINKING LIKE AN ECONOMIST *Microeconomics emphasizes that all economic actors deal with objectives, constraints, and choices. Let's focus briefly on constraints. All economic actors would prefer to have fewer rather than more constraints and to have constraints that offer more latitude rather than less latitude. For example, a firm would probably prefer to be constrained in having to buy its resources from five suppliers rather than*

"I Have to Become an Accountant"

Don: I don't like accounting, but I have to become an accountant.

Mike: Why?

Don: Because I've spent four years in college studying accounting. I spent all that money and time on accounting; I have to get some benefits from it.

Mike: The money and time you spent on accounting is a sunk cost. You can't get those back.

Don: Sure I can. All I have to do is work as an accountant. I'll be earning a good income and getting my "college investment" to pay off.

Mike: It sounds to me as if you're letting your four years in college studying accounting determine what you will do for the rest of your work life. Why do that?

Don: Because accounting is all I know how to do.

Mike: If you could do it over, what would you study and do?

Don: I'd study English literature and then I'd become a high school teacher.

Mike: Can't you still do that? You're only 24 years old.

Don: Sure, but that would mean my last four years in college were completely wasted. I'm not going to waste them.

Mike: Again, you're letting your past determine what you do now and in the future.

Don: It sounds like you're telling me to get out of accounting.

Mike: I'm not advising you to stay in or to get out of accounting. I'm simply saying that the time and money you spent getting a degree in accounting is a sunk cost and that you shouldn't let a sunk cost determine what you will do with your life.

Don: It still seems as if you're advising me to get out of accounting.

Mike: But that's not true. I'm simply saying that you ought to look at the benefits and costs of being an accountant—starting at this moment in time. You shouldn't look over your shoulder and say that because you "invested" four years in accounting that you now have to become an accountant. Those four years are gone; you can never get them back. And you shouldn't try.

Don: In other words, starting from this moment in time, I should ask myself what the costs and benefits are of becoming an accountant. If the costs are greater than the benefits, I should not become one, but if the benefits are greater than the costs, I should become one.

Mike: That's right. Let me put it to you this way. Suppose tomorrow the bottom fell out of the accounting market. Accountants couldn't earn even $100 a month. Would you still want to be an accountant?

Don: No way. It wouldn't make any sense. I couldn't earn enough income.

Mike: Well, if you wouldn't become an accountant because the benefits ($100 a month) are too low relative to the costs, wouldn't it make sense not to become an accountant if the costs are too high relative to the benefits?

Don: What do you mean?

Mike: Well, suppose that the bottom does not fall out of the accounting market and that you can earn $4,000 a month working as an accountant. The question now is: How much do you have to give up, say, in terms of less utility, to get this $4,000 a month? If you would be happy as an English literature teacher, although earning less than you would earn as an accountant, and unhappy as an accountant, then the cost of becoming an accountant and not a teacher may be more than $4,000 a month.

Don: I agree that if I become an accountant I will have to give up some happiness. But if I don't become an accountant and become a high school teacher instead, I will have to give up some income because I probably would earn less as a teacher than as an accountant. And, by the way, income gives me some happiness.

Mike: I agree. But now you're at least looking at the choice you have to make without considering something in the past that you can't change, that is, studying accounting in college.

Don: How so?

Mike: You're asking yourself what the benefits will be of becoming an accountant, and your answer seems to be the happiness or utility you'll receive from $4,000 a month. You're then asking yourself what the costs will be of becoming an accountant, and you seem to be saying that you'll have to forfeit some happiness. The question, then, becomes: Will the $4,000 a month provide you with enough utility to overcome the disutility you will feel because you're unhappy working as an accountant?

Don: But by doing this how am I ignoring sunk cost? All this seems to tell me is that economics is about utility, not money.

Mike: You're ignoring the sunk cost of obtaining an accounting degree because when you consider the costs of becoming an accountant, you are considering only what you will (in the future) give up if you become one. You're not considering what you already have (in the past) given up and that cannot be changed.

Don: And are you suggesting that this is what I should do—only consider future costs and not sunk costs?

Mike: Yes, because you're better off not trying to change something that cannot be changed. It would be a little like your trying to change the weather. You can't do it, and you shouldn't waste your time and energy trying. If you do try, you're simply forfeiting other things that you could be accomplishing.

Don: In other words, I shouldn't try to get back the sunk costs I incurred getting an accounting degree because trying to do this means that I'll be forfeiting the opportunity to do other things. I'd be compounding an error. I'd be try-ing to get back something I can't get back, and in the process, losing some important time, energy, and perhaps money that I could be using in a more "utility productive" way.

Mike: That's right.

---

only one supplier. A consumer would rather have a budget constraint of $4,000 a month instead of $2,000 a month.

Think of two persons, A and B. Person A considers sunk cost when she makes a decision, and person B ignores it when she makes a decision. Does one person face fewer constraints, ceteris paribus? The answer is that the person who ignores sunk cost when making a decision, person B, faces fewer constraints. What person A does, in fact, is act as if a constraint is there—the constraint of sunk cost, the constraint of having to rectify a past decision—when it really exists only because person A thinks it does.

In this sense, the "constraint" of sunk cost is very different from the constraint of, say, scarcity. Whether a person believes scarcity exists or not, it exists. People are constrained by scarcity, as they are by the force of gravity, whether they know it or not. But people are not constrained by sunk cost if they choose not to be constrained by it. If you choose to let bygones be bygones, if you realize that sunk cost is a cost that has been incurred and cannot be changed, then you will not be constrained by it when making a current decision.

Economists look at things this way: There are already enough constraints in the world. You are not made better off by behaving as if there is one more than there actually is.

Self-Test

1. Identify two ways to compute average total cost (*ATC*).

2. Would a business ever sell its product for less than cost? Explain your answer. (Hint: Think of sunk cost.)

3. What happens to unit costs as marginal costs rise? Explain your answer.

4. Do changes in marginal physical productivity influence unit costs? Explain your answer.

PRODUCTION AND COSTS IN THE LONG RUN

This section discusses production and long-run costs. As noted previously, in the long run there are no fixed inputs and no fixed costs. Consequently, the firm has greater flexibility in the long run than in the short run.

LONG-RUN AVERAGE TOTAL COST CURVE

In the short run, there are fixed costs and variable costs; therefore, total cost is the sum of the two. But in the long run, there are no fixed costs, so variable costs are total costs. Here we focus on (1) what the long-run average total cost (*LRATC*) curve is and (2) what it looks like.

ECONOMICS IN...

Popular Culture   Technology   Everyday Life   The World

Ignoring Sunk Cost: Country Music, No; *The Godfather*, Yes

To paraphrase Johnny Cash, the country music singer, country music is about horses, railroads, hard times, whiskey, death, love, mother, and God. The economist adds one more thing that country music is about: sunk cost.

As we state in this chapter, sunk cost is a cost that cannot be changed by current decisions and therefore cannot be recovered. Often, country music songs are about things that happened in the past that can't be changed or undone. In other words, they are about sunk cost. But instead of taking the economist's advice and ignoring sunk cost—letting bygones be bygones and not crying over spilt milk—many people in country music songs hold on to it. Consequently, country music is often sad.

For example, Michelle Wright's song "If I'm Over You" is about a woman who just can't let go of the love she's lost. She's stuck on sunk cost. Reba McEntire's song "It Don't Matter," is about a person who, because she can't get over someone she's lost, says that nothing matters anymore. (Is she letting her past adversely affect her future?) Garth Brooks's song "She's Gonna Make It" is about a man and woman who have gone their separate ways. The woman, who is doing okay, has let bygones be bygones; the man hasn't. One ignores sunk cost; the other doesn't.

Perhaps no one follows the economist's advice to ignore sunk costs better than Vito Corleone (played by Marlon Brando) in the movie *The Godfather*. Let's look at the movie in economic terms.

Vito Corleone, the head of the Corleone family, has been shot and is recuperating at home. His son Sonny, the head of the family in his absence, has sought revenge for his father's shooting and has had the son of a Mafia boss killed. In retaliation, Sonny has been killed. Vito Corleone, unaware of what has transpired, hears his wife crying and cars coming to the house. The consiglieri to the Corleone family tells Vito that Sonny has been killed. Vito begins to cry and then he says that he wants no acts of vengeance and that he wants a meeting with the heads of the five Mafia families. He then says, "This war stops now."

The death of Sonny is a sunk cost. Nothing can change the fact that Sonny is dead. When Vito Corleone says "This war stops now," he tells us that he will ignore sunk cost. Later in the movie, when he meets with the heads of the five families he explains why. He asks Philip Tattaglia, whose son was also killed, if vengeance will bring his son back. He asks him if vengeance will bring Sonny back. Then he tells the heads of the five families that he wants an end to the war for selfish reasons. Another Corleone son, Michael, is in Sicily. Vito has to bring him back to the United States soon, and he doesn't want the war to continue because he doesn't want anything to happen to Michael.

In summary, Vito Corleone, upon hearing the news of the death of Sonny, can either ignore sunk costs or not. If he doesn't ignore sunk costs and seeks revenge, he will not bring back Sonny and he may jeopardize Michael's life. If he ignores sunk costs and makes the peace, he can keep Michael safe. Sonny is a sunk cost because he can't be brought back to life. It is better not to let what has happened and cannot be changed adversely affect the future. And this is exactly what Vito Corleone does.

Consider the manager of a firm that produces bedroom furniture. When all inputs are variable, the manager must decide what the situation of the firm should be in the (upcoming) short-run period. For example, suppose he needs to determine the size of the plant; that is, he must decide whether the plant will be small, medium, or large in size. After this decision is made, he is locked in to a specific plant size; he is locked in for the short run.

Associated with each of the three different plant sizes is a short-run average total cost (*SRATC*) curve. (We discuss both short-run and long-run average total cost curves here, so we distinguish between the two with prefixes: *SR* for short run and *LR* for long run.) The three short-run average total cost curves, representing the different plant sizes, are illustrated in Exhibit 7a.

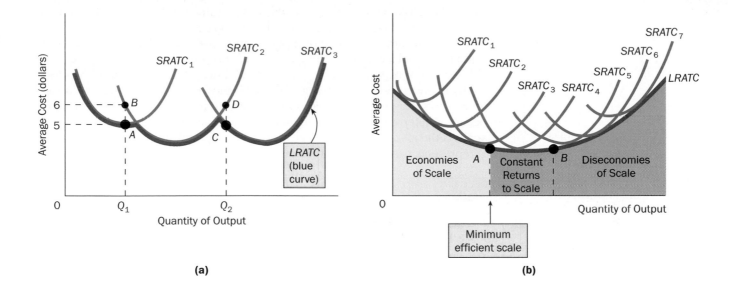

(a)

(b)

exhibit 7

Long-Run Average Total Cost Curve (LRATC)
(a) There are three short-run average total cost curves for three different plant sizes. If these are the only plant sizes, the long-run average total cost curve is the heavily shaded, blue scalloped curve. (b) The long-run average total cost curve is the heavily shaded, blue smooth curve. The *LRATC* curve in (b) is not scalloped because it is assumed that there are so many plant sizes that the *LRATC* curve touches each *SRATC* curve at only one point.

Suppose the manager of the firm wants to produce output level Q_1. Which plant size will he choose? Obviously, he will choose the plant size represented by $SRATC_1$ because this gives a lower unit cost of producing Q_1 than the plant size represented by $SRATC_2$. The latter plant size has a higher unit cost of producing Q_1 ($6 as opposed to $5).

Suppose, though, the manager chooses to produce Q_2. Which plant size will he choose now? He will choose the plant size represented by $SRATC_3$ because the unit cost of producing Q_2 is lower with the plant size represented by $SRATC_3$ than it is with that represented by $SRATC_2$.

If we were to ask the same question for every (possible) output level, we would derive the **long-run average total cost (LRATC) curve.** The *LRATC* curve shows the lowest unit cost at which the firm can produce any given level of output. In Exhibit 7a, it is those portions of the three *SRATC* curves that are tangential to the blue curve. The *LRATC* curve is the scalloped blue curve.

Exhibit 7b shows a host of *SRATC* curves and one *LRATC* curve. In this case, the *LRATC* curve is not scalloped, as it is in part (a). The *LRATC* curve is smooth in part (b) because we assume there are many plant sizes in addition to the three represented in (a). In other words, although they have not been drawn, short-run average total cost curves representing different plant sizes exist in (b) between $SRATC_1$ and $SRATC_2$ and between $SRATC_2$ and $SRATC_3$ and so on. In this case, the *LRATC* curve is smooth and touches each *SRATC* curve at one point.

ECONOMIES OF SCALE, DISECONOMIES OF SCALE, AND CONSTANT RETURNS TO SCALE

Suppose two inputs, labor and capital, are used together to produce a particular good. If inputs are increased by some percentage (say, 100 percent) and output increases by a greater percentage (more than 100 percent), then unit costs fall and **economies of scale** are said to exist.

If inputs are increased by some percentage and output increases by an equal percentage, then unit costs remain constant and **constant returns to scale** are said to exist.

If inputs are increased by some percentage and output increases by a smaller percentage, then unit costs rise and **diseconomies of scale** are said to exist.

The following arithmetical example illustrates economies of scale. Good X is made with two inputs, Y and Z, and it takes $20Y$ and $10Z$ to produce 5 units of

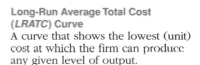

Long-Run Average Total Cost (LRATC) Curve
A curve that shows the lowest (unit) cost at which the firm can produce any given level of output.

Economies of Scale
Exist when inputs are increased by some percentage and output increases by a greater percentage, causing unit costs to fall.

Constant Returns to Scale
Exist when inputs are increased by some percentage and output increases by an equal percentage, causing unit costs to remain constant.

Diseconomies of Scale
Exist when inputs are increased by some percentage and output increases by a smaller percentage, causing unit costs to rise.

X. The cost of each unit of input *Y* is \$1 and the cost of each unit of input *Z* is \$1. Thus, a total cost of \$30 is required to produce 5 units of *X*. The unit cost (average total cost) of good *X* is \$6 ($ATC = TC/Q$).

Now consider a doubling of inputs *Y* and *Z* to 40*Y* and 20*Z* and a more than doubling in output, say, to 15 units. This means a total cost of \$60 is required to produce 15 units of *X*, and the unit cost (average total cost) of good *X* is \$4.

If, in the production of a good, economies of scale give way to constant returns to scale or diseconomies of scale, as in Exhibit 7b, the point at which this occurs is referred to as the minimum efficient scale. The **minimum efficient scale** is the lowest output level at which average total costs are minimized. Point *A* represents the minimum efficient scale in Exhibit 7b.

Q: Is there any special significance to the minimum efficient scale of output?

A: Yes, there is. Look at the long-run average total cost curve in Exhibit 7b. Between points *A* and *B* there are constant returns to scale; the average total cost is the same over the various output levels between the two points. This means that larger firms (firms producing greater output levels) within this range do not have a cost advantage over smaller firms that operate at the minimum efficient scale.

Q: Are economies of scale, diseconomies of scale, and constant returns to scale relevant to the short run, the long run, or both?

A: They are relevant only to the long run. Implicit in the definition of the terms, and explicit in the arithmetical example of economies of scale, all inputs necessary to the production of a good are changeable. Because no input is fixed, economies of scale, diseconomies of scale, and constant returns to scale must be relevant only to the long run.

In addition, the three conditions can easily be seen in the *LRATC* curve. If economies of scale are present, the *LRATC* curve is falling; if constant returns to scale are present, the curve is flat, and if diseconomies of scale are present, the curve is rising (see Exhibit 7b).

We must not confuse diminishing marginal returns with diseconomies of scale. Diminishing marginal returns are the result of using, say, a given plant size more intensively. Diseconomies of scale result from changes in the size of the plant.

WHY ECONOMIES OF SCALE?

Up to a certain point, long-run unit costs of production fall as a firm grows. There are two main reasons for this: (1) Growing firms offer greater opportunities for employees to specialize. Individual workers can become highly proficient at more narrowly defined tasks, often producing more output at lower unit costs. (2) Growing firms (especially large, growing firms) can take advantage of highly efficient mass production techniques and equipment that ordinarily require large setup costs and thus are economical only if they can be spread over a large number of units. For example, assembly line techniques are usually "cheap" when millions of units of a good are produced, and are "expensive" when only a few thousand units are produced.

WHY DISECONOMIES OF SCALE?

Diseconomies of scale usually arise at the point where a firm's size causes coordination, communication, and monitoring problems. In very large firms, managers often find it difficult to coordinate work activities, communicate their directives to the right persons in satisfactory time, and monitor personnel effectively. The business operation simply gets "too big." There is, of course, a monetary incentive not to pass the point of operation where diseconomies of scale exist. Firms will usually find ways to avoid diseconomies of scale. They will reorganize, divide operations, hire new managers, and so on.

MINIMUM EFFICIENT SCALE AND NUMBER OF FIRMS IN AN INDUSTRY

Some industries are composed of a smaller number of firms than other industries are. Or, we can say there is a different degree of concentration in different industries.

Exhibit 8 lists the minimum efficient scale (*MES*) for six industries as a percentage of U.S. consumption or total sales for that industry. Notice that firms in some industries experience economies of scale up to output levels that are a higher percentage of industry sales than firms in other industries. For example, cigarette firms reach the minimum efficient scale of plant, and thus exhaust economies of scale, at an output level of 6.6 percent of total industry sales. On the other hand, petroleum refining firms experience economies of scale only up to an output level of 1.9 percent of total industry sales. Consequently, we would expect to find fewer firms in the cigarette industry than in the petroleum refining industry. By dividing the *MES* as a percentage of U.S. consumption into 100, we can estimate the number of efficient firms it takes to satisfy U.S. consumption for a particular product. For cigarettes, it takes 15 firms (100/6.6 = 15). For petroleum refining, it takes 52 firms.

SHIFTS IN COST CURVES

In discussing the shape of short-run and long-run cost curves, we assumed that certain factors remained constant. We discuss a few of these factors here and describe how changes in them can shift cost curves.

TAXES

Consider a tax on each unit of a good produced. Suppose company *X* has to pay a tax of $3 for each unit of *X* it produces. What effects will this have on the firm's cost curves? Will the tax affect the firm's fixed costs? No, it won't. The tax is paid only when output is produced, and fixed costs are present even if output is zero. (Note that if the tax is a lump-sum tax, requiring the company to pay a lump sum no matter how many units of *X* it produces, the tax will affect fixed costs.) We conclude that the tax does not affect fixed costs and therefore cannot affect average fixed cost.

Will the tax affect variable costs? Yes, it will. As a consequence of the tax, the firm has to pay more for each unit of *X* it produces. Because variable costs rise, so does total cost. This means that average variable cost and average total cost rise, and the representative cost curves shift upward. Finally, because marginal cost is the change in total cost divided by the change in output, marginal cost rises and the marginal cost curve shifts upward.

INPUT PRICES

A rise or fall in variable input prices causes a corresponding change in the firm's average total, average variable, and marginal cost curves. For example, if the price of steel rises, the variable costs of building skyscrapers rise, and so must average variable cost, average total cost, and marginal cost. The cost curves shift upward. If the price of steel falls, the opposite effects occur.

TECHNOLOGY

Technological changes often bring either (1) the capability of using fewer inputs to produce a good (for example, the introduction of the personal computer reduced the hours necessary to key and edit a manuscript) or (2) lower input prices (technological improvements in transistors have led to price reductions in the transistor components of calculators). In either case, technological changes of this variety lower variable costs, and consequently, lower average variable cost, average total cost, and marginal cost.

exhibit 8

Minimum Efficient Scale (*MES*) for Six Industries

Source: F. M. Scherer, Alan Bechenstein, Erich Kaufer, and R. D. Murphy, *The Economics of Multiplant Operation* (Cambridge, Mass.: Harvard University Press, 1975), p. 80.

Industry	*MES* as a Percentage of U.S Consumption
Refrigerators	14.1%
Cigarettes	6.6
Beer brewing	3.4
Petroleum refining	1.9
Paints	1.4
Shoes	0.2

Self-Test

1. Give an arithmetical example to illustrate economies of scale.
2. What would the *LRATC* curve look like if there were always constant returns to scale? Explain your answer.
3. Firm *A* charged $4 per unit when it produced 100 units of good *X,* and it charged $3 per unit when it produced 200 units. Furthermore, the firm earned the same profit per unit in both cases. How can this be?

A Reader Asks...

Will a Knowledge of Sunk Cost Help Prevent Me from Making a Mistake in the Stock Market?

I have a friend who bought some stock at $40 a share. Soon after she bought the stock, it fell to $30 a share. I asked my friend if she planned to sell the stock. She said that she couldn't because if she did, she would take a $10 loss per share of stock. Is she looking at things correctly?

No, your friend is letting a past decision (the purchase of stock at $40 a share) influence a present decision (whether or not to sell the stock).

Let's go back in time, to the point when your friend was thinking about whether or not to buy the stock. Before she made the purchase, she had to have asked herself this question: "Do I think the price of the stock will rise or fall?" She must have thought the price of the stock was going to rise or else she wouldn't have purchased it.

Why, then, doesn't she ask herself the same question now that the price of the stock has fallen? Why not ask, "Do I think the price of the stock will rise or fall?" Isn't this the best question she can ask herself? If she thinks the price of the stock will rise, then she should not sell the stock. But if she thinks the price will fall, then she should sell the stock before it falls further in price.

Instead, she lets her present be influenced by her past. She cannot change the past; she cannot change the fact that the price of her stock has fallen $10 per share. But the $10 per share fall in price is a sunk cost. It is something that happened in the past and cannot be changed by a current decision. If she doesn't ignore sunk cost, she risks losing even more than she already has lost.

Chapter Summary

Explicit Cost and Implicit Cost

- An explicit cost is incurred when an actual (monetary) payment is made. An implicit cost represents the value of resources used in production for which no actual (monetary) payment is made.

Economic Profit and Accounting Profit

- Economic profit is the difference between total revenue and total cost, including both explicit and implicit costs. Accounting profit is the difference between total revenue and explicit costs. Economic profit is usually lower (never higher) than accounting profit. Economic profit (not accounting profit) motivates economic behavior.

Production and Costs in the Short Run

- The short run is a period in which some inputs are fixed. The long run is a period in which all inputs can

be varied. The costs associated with fixed and variable inputs are referred to as fixed costs and variable costs, respectively.
- Marginal cost is the change in total cost that results from a change in output.
- The law of diminishing marginal returns states that as ever-larger amounts of a variable input are combined with fixed inputs, eventually the marginal physical product of the variable input will decline. As this happens, marginal cost rises.
- The average-marginal rule states that if the marginal magnitude is above (below) the average magnitude, the average magnitude rises (falls).
- The marginal cost curve intersects the average variable cost curve at its lowest point. The marginal cost curve intersects the average total cost curve at its lowest point. There is no relationship between marginal cost and average fixed cost.

Production and Costs in the Long Run

- In the long run, there are no fixed costs, so variable costs equal total costs.
- The long-run average total cost curve is the envelope of the short-run average total cost curves. It shows the lowest unit cost at which the firm can produce any given level of output.
- If inputs are increased by some percentage and output increases by a greater percentage, then unit costs fall and economies of scale exist. If inputs are increased by some percentage and output increases by an equal percentage, then unit costs remain constant and constant returns to scale exist. If inputs are increased by some percentage and output increases by a smaller percentage, then unit costs rise and diseconomies of scale exist.
- The minimum efficient scale is the lowest output level at which average total costs are minimized.

Sunk Cost

- Sunk cost is a cost incurred in the past that cannot be changed by current decisions and therefore cannot be recovered. A person or firm that wants to minimize losses will hold sunk costs to be irrelevant to present decisions. For example, Janet buys good X for $10 on Monday with the idea of reselling it at a higher price in the near future. A week passes and the price of good X falls to $6. Some people argue that Janet should not sell good X because she will incur a loss. According to their argument, Janet should look over her shoulder, note the higher price she paid for the good, and let this fact influence her present decision. But bygones are bygones. Janet needs to ask herself, "Do I expect the price of good X to go up or down?" If the answer is down, then it is better to sell today at $6 than to sell tomorrow at an even lower price. If the answer is up, then Janet may want to sell later.

Shifts in Cost Curves

- A firm's cost curves will change owing to a change in taxes, input prices, or technology.

Key Terms and Concepts

Profit
Explicit Cost
Implicit Cost
Accounting Profit
Economic Profit
Normal Profit
Fixed Input
Variable Input
Short Run
Long Run
Marginal Physical Product (MPP)

Law of Diminishing Marginal
   Returns
Fixed Costs
Variable Costs
Total Cost (TC)
Marginal Cost (MC)
Average Fixed Cost (AFC)
Average Variable Cost (AVC)
Average Total Cost (ATC), or Unit
   Cost
Average-Marginal Rule

Sunk Cost
Long-Run Average Total Cost
   (LRATC) Curve
Economies of Scale
Constant Returns to Scale
Diseconomies of Scale
Minimum Efficient Scale

Questions and Problems

1. Illustrate the average-marginal rule in a noncost setting.
2. "People who earn big salaries are less likely to go into business for themselves than people who earn small salaries because their implicit costs are higher." Do you agree or disagree? Explain your answer.
3. The average variable cost curve and the average total cost curve get closer to each other as output increases. What explains this?
4. When would total costs equal fixed costs?
5. Is studying for an economics exam subject to the law of diminishing marginal returns? If so, what is the fixed input? What is the variable input?
6. Some individuals decry the decline of the small family farm and its replacement with the huge corporate megafarm. Discuss the possibility that this is a consequence of economies of scale.

7. We know there is a link between productivity and costs. For example, recall the link between the marginal physical product of the variable input and marginal cost. With this in mind, what link might there be between productivity and prices?

8. Some people's everyday behavior suggests that they do not hold sunk costs irrelevant to present decisions. Give some examples different from those discussed in this chapter.

9. Explain why a firm might want to produce its good even after diminishing marginal returns have set in and marginal cost is rising.

10. People often believe that large firms in an industry have cost advantages over small firms in the same industry. For example, they might think a big oil company has a cost advantage over a small oil company. For this to be true, what condition must exist? Explain your answer.

11. The government says that firm X must pay $1,000 in taxes simply because it is in the business of producing a good. What cost curves, if any, does this tax affect?

12. Based on your answer to question 11, does MC change if TC changes?

13. Under what condition would Bill Gates be the richest person in the United States and earn zero economic profit?

Working with Numbers and Graphs

1. Determine the appropriate dollar amount for each lettered space.

(1) Quantity of Output, Q (units)	(2) Total Fixed Cost (TFC)	(3) Average Fixed Cost (AFC) (AFC) = TFC/Q = (2)/(1)	(4) Total Variable Cost (TVC)	(5) Average Variable Cost (AVC) AVC = TVC/Q = (4)/(1)	(6) Total Cost (TC) TC = TFC + TVC = (2) + (4)	(7) Average Total Cost (ATC) ATC = TC/Q = (6)/(1)	(8) Marginal Cost (MC) MC = $\Delta TC/\Delta Q$ = $\Delta(6)/\Delta(1)$
0	$200	A	$ 0		V		
1	200	B	30	L	W	GG	QQ
2	200	C	50	M	X	HH	RR
3	200	D	60	N	Y	II	SS
4	200	E	65	O	Z	JJ	TT
5	200	F	75	P	AA	KK	UU
6	200	G	95	Q	BB	LL	VV
7	200	H	125	R	CC	MM	WW
8	200	I	165	S	DD	NN	XX
9	200	J	215	T	EE	OO	YY
10	200	K	275	U	FF	PP	ZZ

2. Give a numerical example to show that as marginal physical product (MPP) rises, marginal cost (MC) falls.

3. Price = $20, quantity = 400 units, unit cost = $15, implicit costs = $4,000. What does economic profit equal?

4. If economic profit equals accounting profit, what do implicit costs equal?

5. If accounting profit is $400,000 greater than economic profit, what do implicit costs equal?

6. If marginal physical product is continually declining, what does marginal cost look like? Explain your answer.

7. If the ATC curve is continually declining, what does this imply about the MC curve? Explain your answer.

1. Go to *http://www.honda.com*. Pick a model and search the site for the manufacturer's suggested retail price (MSRP). Next, go to *http://www.edmunds.com*. Click "New Cars," and then select the car you priced at Honda. Finally, select "Vehicle Prices." What is the dollar difference between the MSRP and the dealer's invoice (price)? Was the MSRP the same as stated at the Honda Web site?

2. Go the *http://www.carsdirect.com*, and select "the carsdirect.com advantage." Read the page. Click on "Back," and browse the site. Find the price of the car you selected in Question 1.

   a. How did the CarsDirect.com price compare with the MSRP and the dealer's invoice price? How much lower is it than the MSRP? Do you think you can get a lower (buying) price if you go to the car dealership in your town and negotiate a price in person? Why or why not?

   b. Do you think it affects the price you pay if CarsDirect.com gets its cars from the manufacturer instead of a dealership? Explain your answer.

   c. If CarsDirect.com obtained its cars directly from the manufacturers, would this positively or negatively affect dealers? Explain your answer.

   d. Currently, most dealers offer customers a good and a service. The *good* is a car. The *service* is the "service for the car." For example, after buying your car from the Honda dealership in town, you may return to the dealership over the years to have the car serviced. If dealers lose car-selling business to CarsDirect.com, do you think the quality of the service that dealers provide repairing cars will improve and the price of that service will fall? Why or why not?

Log on to the Arnold Xtra! Web site now (*http://arnoldxtra.swcollege.com*) for additional learning resources such as practice quizzes, help with graphing, video clips, and current event applications.

ch.9

PERFECT COMPETITION

A business firm must answer three questions. These are the same three questions that you would have to answer if you started a business. The questions are: (1) What price should we charge for the good we produce and sell? (2) How many units of the good should we produce? (3) How do we know when it would be better to shut down the business rather than to continue to operate? This chapter describes how one type of firm—the perfectly competitive firm—answers these three important questions.

Chapter Road Map

This chapter begins our discussion of market struc-

*tures. A **market structure** is a firm's particular environment, the*

characteristics of which influence the firm's pricing and output decisions. In

this and the next two chapters, we discuss four major market structure theories—the

theory of perfect competition, the theory of monopoly, the theory of monopolistic competition,

and various theories of oligopoly. This chapter focuses on the theory of perfect competition. With respect

to this theory, we discuss the perfectly competitive firm in both the short run and the long run.

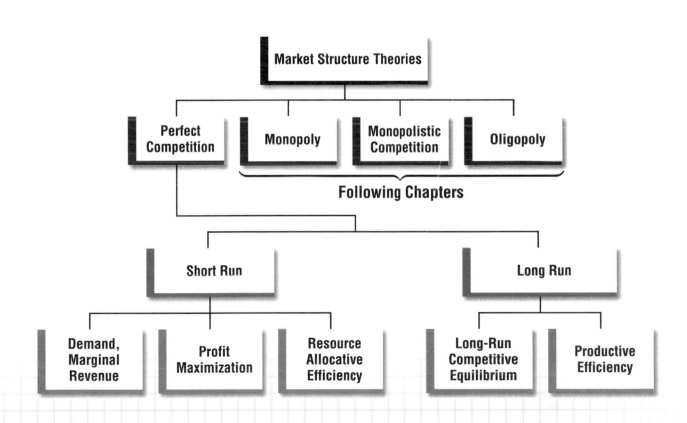

THE THEORY OF PERFECT COMPETITION

Market Structure
The particular environment of a firm, the characteristics of which influence the firm's pricing and output decisions.

Perfect Competition
A theory of market structure based on four assumptions: there are many sellers and buyers, sellers sell a homogeneous good, buyers and sellers have all relevant information, and there is easy entry into and exit from the market.

In this section, we begin our discussion of the theory of **perfect competition**, which is built on four assumptions:

1. **There are many sellers and many buyers, none of which is large in relation to total sales or purchases.** This assumption speaks to both demand (number of buyers) and supply (number of sellers). Because there are many buyers and sellers, it is reasonably assumed that each buyer and each seller acts independently of other buyers and sellers, respectively, and each is so small a part of the market that he or she has no influence on price.
2. **Each firm produces and sells a homogeneous product.** This means each firm sells a product that is indistinguishable from all other firms' products in a given industry. (For example, a buyer of wheat cannot distinguish between Farmer Stone's wheat and Farmer Gray's wheat.) As a consequence, buyers are indifferent to the sellers of the product.
3. **Buyers and sellers have all relevant information about prices, product quality, sources of supply, and so forth.** Buyers and sellers know who is selling what, at what prices, at what quality, and on what terms. In short, they know everything that relates to buying, producing, and selling the product.
4. **Firms have easy entry and exit.** New firms can enter the market easily, and existing firms can exit the market easily. There are no barriers to entry or exit.

Before discussing the perfectly competitive firm in the short run and in the long run, we discuss some of the characteristics of the perfectly competitive firm that result from these four assumptions.

A PERFECTLY COMPETITIVE FIRM IS A PRICE TAKER

Price Taker
A seller that does not have the ability to control the price of the product it sells; it takes the price determined in the market.

A perfectly competitive firm is a **price taker.** A price taker is a seller that does not have the ability to control the price of the product it sells; it takes the price determined in the market. For example, if Farmer Stone is a price taker, it follows that he can increase or decrease his output without significantly affecting the price of the product he sells.

Why is a perfectly competitive firm a price taker? A firm is restrained from being anything but a price taker if it finds itself one among many firms where its supply is small relative to the total market supply (assumption 1 in the theory of perfect competition), and it sells a homogeneous product (assumption 2) in an environment where buyers and sellers have all relevant information (assumption 3).

Q & A

Q: If the assumptions of the theory guarantee that the perfectly competitive firm is a price taker, then aren't economists choosing the assumptions necessary to give them what they want?

A: No, they aren't. Economists do not start out wanting the perfectly competitive firm to be a price taker and then choose the assumptions that will make this so. Instead, economists start out with certain assumptions and then logically conclude that the firm for which these assumptions hold, or that behaves as if these assumptions hold, is a price taker; that is, it has no control over price. Afterward, economists test the theory by observing whether it accurately predicts and explains the real-world behavior of some firms.

THE DEMAND CURVE FOR A PERFECTLY COMPETITIVE FIRM IS HORIZONTAL

In the perfectly competitive setting, there are many sellers and many buyers. Together, all buyers make up the market demand curve; together, all sellers make up the market supply curve. An equilibrium price is established at the intersection of the market demand and market supply curves (Exhibit 1a).

When the equilibrium price has been established, a single perfectly competitive firm faces a horizontal (flat, perfectly elastic) demand curve at the equilib-

http://

Go to *http://www.schwab.com/*, and select "Quotes & Research." Key "IBM" in the Free Quotes & Charts box, and click "Go." What is the current price for a share of IBM stock? Check the price of the stock in about an hour. Has the price changed? Do you think the market for IBM moves from one equilibrium to another quickly or slowly? Do you think the market for IBM stock is a perfectly competitive market? Next, click "Accounts and Services," then "Accounts and Commissions," and finally "Commissions." Read the page. Can anyone sell stocks on the Internet or does a person have to be a licensed broker? Is there easy entry into the brokerage industry? Explain your answer.

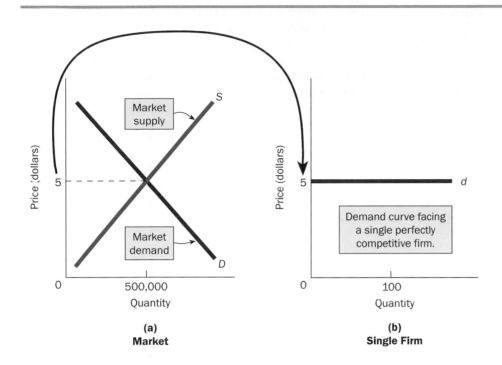

exhibit 1

Market Demand Curve and Firm Demand Curve in Perfect Competition
(a) The market, composed of all buyers and sellers, establishes the equilibrium price. (b) A single perfectly competitive firm then faces a horizontal (flat, perfectly elastic) demand curve. We conclude that the firm is a price taker; it "takes" the equilibrium price established by the market and sells any and all quantities of output at this price. (The capital *D* represents the market demand curve; the lowercase *d* represents the single firm's demand curve.)

rium price. In short, the firm "takes" the equilibrium price as given—hence, the firm is a price taker—and sells all quantities of output at this price.[1] (As an aside, an earlier chapter explains that the more substitutes for a good, the higher the price elasticity of demand. In the perfectly competitive market setting, there are many substitutes for the firm's product—so many, in fact, that the firm's demand curve is perfectly elastic.)

If a perfectly competitive firm tries to charge a price higher than the market-established equilibrium price, it won't sell any of its product. This is because the firm sells a homogeneous product, its supply is small relative to the total market supply, and all buyers are informed about where they can obtain the product at the lower price.

Also, if the firm wants to maximize profits, it will not offer to sell its good at a lower price than the equilibrium price. Why should it? It can sell all it wants at the market-established equilibrium price. Therefore, this is the only relevant price for the perfectly competitive firm.

Q & A **Q:** An earlier chapter notes that demand curves are downward-sloping. Now it appears that the demand curve for a perfectly competitive firm is not downward-sloping, but horizontal. How can this be?

A: The *market demand curve* in Exhibit 1a is downward-sloping, positing an inverse relationship between price and quantity demanded, *ceteris paribus*. The demand curve faced by a single perfectly competitive firm does not contradict this relationship; it simply represents the pricing situation in which the single perfectly competitive firm finds itself. This curve shows that a single perfectly competitive firm's supply is *such a small percentage of the total market supply* that the firm cannot perceptibly influence price by changing its quantity of output. To put it differently, the firm's supply is so small compared with the total market supply that the inverse relationship between price and quantity demanded, although present, cannot be observed on the firm's level, although it is observable on the market level.

---

1. The horizontal demand curve does not mean that the firm can sell an infinite amount at the equilibrium price; rather, it means that price will be virtually unaffected by the variations in output that the firm may find it practicable to make.

THE MARGINAL REVENUE CURVE OF A PERFECTLY COMPETITIVE FIRM IS THE SAME AS ITS DEMAND CURVE

Recall that total revenue is the price of a good times the quantity sold. If the equilibrium price is $5, as in Exhibit 2, and the perfectly competitive firm sells 100 units of its good, its total revenue is $500. Now suppose the firm sells an additional unit, bringing the total number of units sold to 101. Its total revenue is now $505.

Marginal Revenue (MR)
The change in total revenue that results from selling one additional unit of output.

The firm's **marginal revenue (MR)**—the change in total revenue (TR) that results from selling one additional unit of output (Q)—is $5.

$$MR = \Delta TR/\Delta Q$$

Notice that marginal revenue ($5) at any output level is always equal to the equilibrium price ($5). We conclude that for a perfectly competitive firm, price is equal to marginal revenue (P = MR).

For a Perfectly Competitive Firm: P = MR

If price is equal to marginal revenue, it follows that *the marginal revenue curve for the perfectly competitive firm is the same as its demand curve.*

A demand curve plots price against quantity, whereas a marginal revenue curve plots marginal revenue against quantity. If price equals marginal revenue, then the demand curve and marginal revenue curve are the same (Exhibit 2).

THEORY AND REAL-WORLD MARKETS

The theory of perfect competition describes how firms act in a market structure where (1) there are many buyers and sellers, none of which is large in relation to total sales or purchases; (2) sellers sell a homogeneous product; (3) buyers and sellers have all relevant information; and (4) there is easy entry and exit. These assumptions are closely met in some real-world markets. Examples include some agricultural markets and a small subset of the retail trade. The stock market, where there are hundreds of thousands of buyers and sellers of stock, is also sometimes cited as an example of perfect competition.

The four assumptions of the theory of perfect competition are also *approximated* in some real-world markets. In such markets, the number of sellers may not be large enough for every firm to be a price taker, but the firm's control over price may be negligible. The amount of control may be so negligible, in fact, that the firm acts as if it were a perfectly competitive firm.

---

exhibit 2

The Demand Curve and the Marginal Revenue Curve for a Perfectly Competitive Firm
(a) By computing marginal revenue, we find that it is equal to price. (b) By plotting columns 1 and 2, we obtain the firm's demand curve; by plotting columns 2 and 4, we obtain the firm's marginal revenue curve. The two curves are the same.

(1) Price	(2) Quantity	(3) Total Revenue = (1) × (2)	(4) Marginal Revenue = ΔTR/ΔQ = Δ(3)/Δ(2)
$5	1	$ 5	$5
5	2	10	5
5	3	15	5
5	4	20	5

(a)

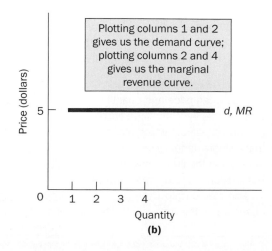

Plotting columns 1 and 2 gives us the demand curve; plotting columns 2 and 4 gives us the marginal revenue curve.

(b)

Similarly, buyers may not have all relevant information concerning price and quality, but they may still have a great deal of information, and the information they do not have may not matter. The products that the firms in the industry sell may not be homogeneous, but the differences may be inconsequential.

In short, a market that does not meet the assumptions of perfect competition may nonetheless approximate those assumptions to such a degree that it behaves *as if* it were a perfectly competitive market. If so, the theory of perfect competition can be used to predict the market's behavior.

Go to *http://www.nmpf.org/*, and select "market data & economic analysis." Explore the site for relevant information concerning the milk market. Estimate the current number of U.S. dairy farms. How is the price of milk determined? Does a single dairy farm have any influence on the price of milk?

Self-Test *(Answers to Self-Test questions are in the Self-Test Appendix.)*

1. A price taker does not have the ability to control the price of the product it sells. What does this mean?

2. Why is a perfectly competitive firm a price taker?

3. The horizontal demand curve for the perfectly competitive firm signifies that it cannot sell any of its product for a price higher than the market equilibrium price. Why can't it?

4. Suppose the firms in a real-world market do not sell a homogeneous product. Does it necessarily follow that the market is not perfectly competitive?

PERFECT COMPETITION IN THE SHORT RUN

The perfectly competitive firm is a price taker. So, for a perfectly competitive firm, price is equal to marginal revenue, $P = MR$, and therefore its demand curve is the same as its marginal revenue curve. This section discusses the amount of output the firm will produce in the short run.

WHAT LEVEL OF OUTPUT DOES THE PROFIT-MAXIMIZING FIRM PRODUCE?

Consider the situation in Exhibit 3. The perfectly competitive firm's demand curve and marginal revenue curve (which are the same) are drawn at the equilibrium price of $5. The firm's marginal cost curve is also shown. On the basis of these curves, what quantity of output will the firm produce?

The firm will continue to increase its quantity of output as long as marginal revenue is greater than marginal cost. It will not produce units of output for which marginal revenue is less than marginal cost. We conclude that the firm will

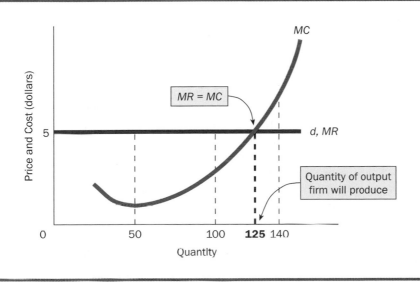

exhibit 3

The Quantity of Output the Perfectly Competitive Firm Will Produce
The firm's demand curve is horizontal at the equilibrium price. Its demand curve is its marginal revenue curve. The firm produces that quantity of output at which $MR = MC$.

Profit-Maximization Rule
Profit is maximized by producing
the quantity of output at which
$MR = MC$.

stop increasing its quantity of output when marginal revenue and marginal cost are equal. The **profit-maximization rule** for the firm says: *Produce the quantity of output at which $MR = MC$.*[2] In Exhibit 3, this is at 125 units of output. For the perfectly competitive firm, the profit-maximization rule can be written as $P = MC$ because for the perfectly competitive firm $P = MR$. In perfect competition, profit is maximized when

$$P = MR = MC$$

Q & A

Q: Why doesn't the firm in Exhibit 3 stop producing at 50 units of output? This is where the largest difference between marginal revenue and marginal cost occurs. Why does the firm continue to produce until marginal revenue equals marginal cost?

A: Suppose the firm did stop producing with unit 50. Then it wouldn't have produced unit 51, which comes with a greater marginal revenue than marginal cost. Nor would it have produced unit 52, for which marginal revenue is also greater than marginal cost. In short, the firm would not have produced some units of output for which a marginal (additional) profit could have been earned; thus, it would not have been maximizing profit. What matters is whether MR is greater than MC, not how much greater MR is than MC.

THE PERFECTLY COMPETITIVE FIRM EXHIBITS RESOURCE ALLOCATIVE EFFICIENCY

Resources (or inputs) are used to produce goods and services; for example, wood may be used to produce a chair. The resources used in the production of goods have a certain exchange value to the buyers of the goods. This exchange value is approximated by the price that people pay for the good. In other words, when Smith buys a chair for $100, one thing we know is that Smith values the resources used to produce the chair by at least $100.

Wood that is used to produce chairs can't be used to produce desks. In other words, there is an opportunity cost of producing chairs that is best measured by its marginal cost.

Now suppose 100 chairs are produced, and at this quantity, price is greater than marginal cost; for example, price is $100 and marginal cost is $75. What does this mean? Obviously, it means that buyers place a higher value on wood when it is used to produce chairs than when it is used to produce some alternative good.

Resource Allocative Efficiency
The situation that exists when firms produce the quantity of output at which price equals marginal cost: $P = MC$.

Producing a good—any good—until price equals marginal cost ensures that all units of the good are produced that are of greater value to buyers than the alternative goods that might have been produced. Stated differently, a firm that produces the quantity of output at which price equals marginal cost ($P = MC$) is said to exhibit **resource allocative efficiency.**

Does the perfectly competitive firm exhibit resource allocative efficiency? We know two things about this firm so far. First, it produces the quantity of output at which $MR = MC$. Second, for the perfectly competitive firm, $P = MR$. Well, if the perfectly competitive firm produces the output at which $MR = MC$ and for this firm, $P = MR$, then it naturally follows that it produces the output at which $P = MC$. In short, the perfectly competitive firm is resource allocative efficient.

An important point to note is that for a perfectly competitive firm, profit maximization and resource allocative efficiency are not at odds. (Might they be for other market structures? See the next two chapters.) The perfectly competitive firm seeks to maximize profit by producing the quantity of output at which $MR = MC$, and because for the firm $P = MR$, it automatically accomplishes resource allocative efficiency ($P = MC$) when it maximizes profit ($MR = MC$).

---

2. The profit-maximization rule is the same as the loss-minimization rule because it is impossible to maximize profits without minimizing losses. The profit-maximization rule holds for all firms, whether or not they are perfectly competitive.

TO PRODUCE OR NOT TO PRODUCE: THAT IS THE QUESTION

The following cases illustrate three applications of the profit-maximization (loss-minimization) rule by a perfectly competitive firm.

Case 1: Price Is above Average Total Cost

Exhibit 4a illustrates the perfectly competitive firm's demand and marginal revenue curves. If the firm follows the profit-maximization rule and produces the quantity of output at which marginal revenue equals marginal cost, it will produce 100 units of output. This will be the profit-maximizing quantity of output. Notice that at this quantity of output, price is above average total cost. Using the information in the exhibit, we can make the following calculations:

exhibit 4

Profit Maximization and Loss Minimization for the Perfectly Competitive Firm: Three Cases
(a) In Case 1, $TR > TC$ and the firm earns profits. It continues to produce in the short run. (b) In Case 2, $TR < TC$ and the firm takes a loss. It shuts down in the short run because it minimizes its losses by doing so; it is better to lose $400 in fixed costs than to take a loss of $450. (c) In Case 3, $TR < TC$ and the firm takes a loss. It continues to produce in the short run because it minimizes its losses by doing so; it is better to lose $80 by producing than to lose $400 in fixed costs.

Case 1

Equilibrium price (P)	= $15
Quantity of output produced (Q)	= 100 units
Total revenue ($P \times Q = \$15 \times 100$)	= $1,500
Total cost ($ATC \times Q = \$11 \times 100$)	= $1,100
Total variable cost ($AVC \times Q = \$7 \times 100$)	= $700
Total fixed cost ($TC - TVC = \$1,100 - \$700$)	= $400
Profits ($TR - TC = \$1,500 - \$1,100$)	= $400

We conclude that if price is above average total cost for the perfectly competitive firm, the firm maximizes profits by producing the quantity of output at which $MR = MC$.

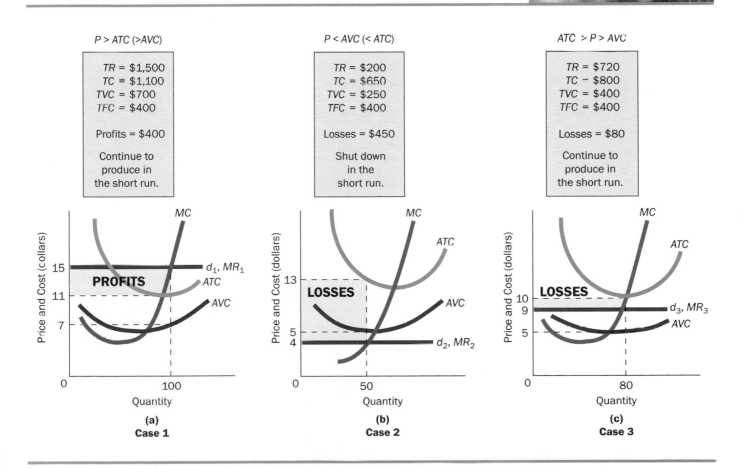

$P > ATC \ (>AVC)$	$P < AVC \ (< ATC)$	$ATC > P > AVC$
$TR = \$1,500$	$TR = \$200$	$TR = \$720$
$TC = \$1,100$	$TC = \$650$	$TC = \$800$
$TVC = \$700$	$TVC = \$250$	$TVC = \$400$
$TFC = \$400$	$TFC = \$400$	$TFC = \$400$
Profits = $400	Losses = $450	Losses = $80
Continue to produce in the short run.	Shut down in the short run.	Continue to produce in the short run.

(a) Case 1 — (b) Case 2 — (c) Case 3

Case 2: Price Is below Average Variable Cost

Exhibit 4b illustrates the case in which price is below average variable cost. The equilibrium price at which the perfectly competitive firm sells its good is $4. At this price, total revenue is less than both total cost and total variable cost, as the following calculations indicate. To minimize its loss, the firm should shut down.

Case 2	
Equilibrium price (P)	= $4
Quantity of output produced (Q)	= 50 units
Total revenue ($P \times Q = \$4 \times 50$)	= $200
Total cost ($ATC \times Q = \$13 \times 50$)	= $650
Total variable cost ($AVC \times Q = \$5 \times 50$)	= $250
Total fixed cost ($TC - TVC = \$650 - \$250$)	= $400
Profits ($TR - TC = \$200 - \$650$)	= −$450

If the firm produces in the short run, it will take a loss of $450. If it shuts down, its loss will be less. It will lose its fixed costs, which amount to the difference between total cost and variable cost ($TFC + TVC = TC$, so $TC - TVC = TFC$). This is $400 ($650 − $250). So, between the two options of producing in the short run or shutting down, the firm minimizes its losses by choosing to shut down ($Q = 0$). It will lose $400 by shutting down, whereas it will lose $450 by producing in the short run.

We conclude that if price is below average variable cost, the perfectly competitive firm minimizes losses by choosing to shut down; that is, by not producing.

Case 3: Price Is below Average Total Cost but above Average Variable Cost

Exhibit 4c illustrates the case in which price is below average total cost but above average variable cost. Here the equilibrium price at which the perfectly competitive firm sells its good is $9. If the firm follows the profit-maximization rule, it will produce 80 units of output. At this price and quantity of output, total revenue is less than total cost (hence there will be a loss), but total revenue is greater than total variable cost. The calculations are as follows:

Case 3	
Equilibrium price (P)	= $9
Quantity of output produced (Q)	= 80 units
Total revenue ($P \times Q = \$9 \times 80$)	= $720
Total cost ($ATC \times Q = \$10 \times 80$)	= $800
Total variable cost ($AVC \times Q = \$5 \times 80$)	= $400
Total fixed cost ($TC - TVC = \$800 - \$400$)	= $400
Profits ($TR - TC = \$720 - \$800$)	= −$80

If the firm decides to produce in the short run, it will take a loss of $80. Should it shut down instead? If it does, it will lose its fixed costs, which, in this case, are $400 ($TC - TVC = \$800 - \$400$). It is better to continue to produce in the short run than to shut down. Losses are minimized by producing.

We conclude that if price is below average total cost but above average variable cost, the perfectly competitive firm minimizes its losses by continuing to produce in the short run instead of shutting down.

Short-Run (Firm) Supply Curve
The portion of the firm's marginal cost curve that lies above the average variable cost curve.

Short-Run Market (Industry) Supply Curve
The horizontal "addition" of all existing firms' short-run supply curves.

Summary of Cases 1–3

We conclude: *A perfectly competitive firm produces in the short run as long as price is above average variable cost (Cases 1 and 3). A perfectly competitive firm shuts down in the short run if price is less than average variable cost (Case 2).*

$$P > AVC \rightarrow \text{Firm produces}$$
$$P < AVC \rightarrow \text{Firm shuts down}$$

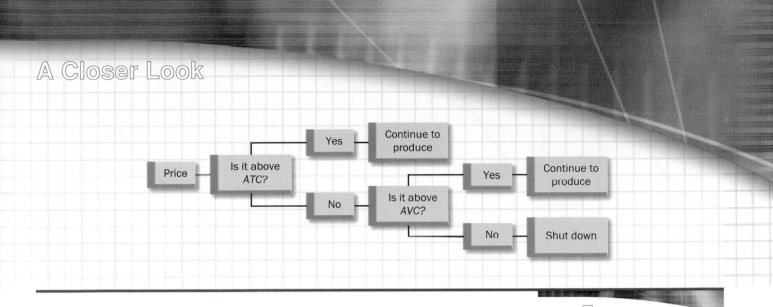

We can summarize the same information in terms of total revenue and total variable costs. *A perfectly competitive firm produces in the short run as long as total revenue is greater than total variable costs (Cases 1 and 3). A perfectly competitive firm shuts down in the short run if total revenue is less than total variable costs (Case 2).*

$$TR > TVC \rightarrow \text{Firm produces}$$
$$TR < TVC \rightarrow \text{Firm shuts down}$$

Exhibit 5 reviews some of the material discussed in this section.

THE PERFECTLY COMPETITIVE FIRM'S SHORT-RUN SUPPLY CURVE

The perfectly competitive firm produces (supplies output) in the short run if price is above average variable cost. It shuts down (does not supply output) if price is below average variable cost. It follows that the **short-run supply curve** of the firm is that portion of its marginal cost curve that lies above the average variable cost curve. In other words, only a price above average variable cost will induce the firm to supply output. The short-run supply curve of the perfectly competitive firm is illustrated in Exhibit 6.

Firm's supply curve = Portion of MC curve above AVC curve

FROM FIRM TO MARKET (INDUSTRY) SUPPLY CURVE

After we know that the firm's short-run supply curve is the part of its marginal cost curve above its average variable cost curve, it is a simple matter to derive the **short-run market (industry) supply curve.**[3] We horizontally "add" the short-run supply curves for all firms in the market or industry.

Consider, for simplicity, an industry made up of three firms, *A, B,* and *C* (see Exhibit 7a). At a price of P_1, firm *A* supplies 10 units, firm *B* supplies 8 units, and firm *C* supplies 18 units. One point on the market supply curve thus corresponds to P_1 on the price axis and 36 units (10 + 8 + 18 = 36) on the quantity axis.[4] If we follow this procedure for all prices, we have the short-run market supply curve. This market supply curve is shown in the market setting in part (b) of the exhibit.

3. In discussing market structures, the words *industry* and *market* are often used interchangeably when a single-product industry is under consideration, which is the case here.

4. We add one qualification: Each firm's supply curve is drawn on the assumption that the prices of its variable inputs are constant.

exhibit 5

What Should a Perfectly Competitive Firm Do In the Short Run?
The firm should produce in the short run as long as price (*P*) is above average variable cost (*AVC*). It should shut down in the short run if price is below average variable cost.

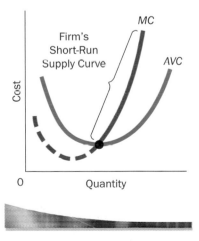

exhibit 6

The Perfectly Competitive Firm's Short-Run Supply Curve
The short-run supply curve is that portion of the firm's marginal cost curve that lies above the average variable cost curve.

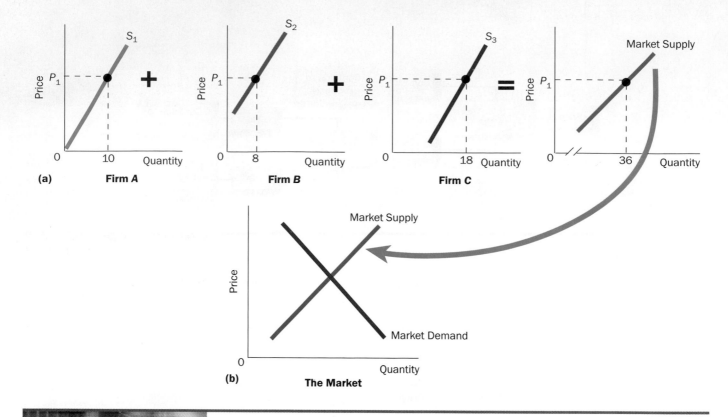

exhibit 7

Deriving the Market (Industry) Supply Curve
In (a) we "add" (horizontally) the quantity supplied by each firm to derive the market supply curve. The market supply curve and the market demand curve are shown in (b). Together, they determine equilibrium price and quantity.

This market supply curve is used along with the market demand curve (derived in Chapter 3) to determine equilibrium price and quantity.

WHY IS THE MARKET SUPPLY CURVE UPWARD-SLOPING?

Recall that in Chapter 3, when the demand and supply curves are introduced, the supply curve is drawn upward-sloping. The supply curve is upward-sloping because of the law of diminishing marginal returns. To see this, consider the following questions and answers.

 **Q:** Why do we draw market supply curves upward-sloping?

A: Because market supply curves are the horizontal "addition" of firms' supply curves and firms' supply curves are upward-sloping.

 Q: But why are firms' supply curves upward-sloping?

A: Because the supply curve for each firm is that portion of its marginal cost (*MC*) curve that is above its average variable cost (*AVC*) curve—and this portion of the *MC* curve is upward-sloping.

 Q: But why do *MC* curves have an upward-sloping portion?

A: Because of the law of diminishing marginal returns. Remember that according to the law of diminishing marginal returns, the marginal physical product (*MPP*) of a variable input eventually declines. When this happens, the *MC* curve begins to rise. We conclude that because of the law of diminishing marginal returns, *MC* curves are upward-sloping; and because *MC* curves are upward-sloping, so are market supply curves.

ECONOMICS IN...

Popular Culture   Technology   Everyday Life   The World

What Do Harry Houdini, Lucille Ball, and Bugs Bunny Have in Common?

The U.S. Postal Service has issued certain special, collector's stamps in the past. These stamps have had likenesses of Harry Houdini, James Dean, Lucille Ball, The Beatles, Niagara Falls, Alfred Hitchcock, Daffy Duck, and Bugs Bunny.

Why does the U.S. Postal Service issue these special, collector's stamps? To find out, let's analyze stamps from the point of view of the Postal Service.

Most people buy stamps to send letters or other items through the mail. When a stamp is placed on a letter, the Postal Service is required to deliver the letter to the address on the envelope. Suppose the unit variable cost (AVC) of producing a stamp is 7 cents, regardless of the likeness on the front, and the unit variable cost of delivering a letter with a stamp on it is 19 cents. The sum of the unit variable costs of producing the stamp and delivering the letter is 26 cents.

$$AVC \text{ stamp} = AVC \text{ producing the stamp} + AVC \text{ delivering the letter}$$

For purposes of simplicity, we assume that $AFC = 0$, so that $AVC = ATC$. In other words, the per-unit cost of the stamp is 26 cents. It follows, then, that if the price of a stamp is 37 cents, the U.S. Postal Service earns a per-unit profit of 11 cents per stamp issued and used.

Now suppose the U.S. Postal Service wants to increase its per-unit profit. How might it do this? One way is to issue stamps that people wouldn't put on items to be mailed. In other words, issue stamps that people want to collect.

This brings us to the special, collector's stamps the U.S. Postal Service issues and sells. Many people buy these stamps but do not use them to mail letters. They buy the stamps to collect them. But if people buy these stamps to collect them and not to use them, the U.S. Postal Service doesn't incur the unit variable cost of delivering mail for these special stamps. This means the average total cost of the collector's stamp falls by the AVC of delivering the letter, which in turn means the ATC of the stamp falls to 7 cents (the AVC of producing the stamp). Consequently, the profit per unit for issuing collector's stamps rises to 30 cents for a 37-cent stamp.

Self-Test

1. If a firm produces the quantity of output at which $MR = MC$, does it follow that it earns profits?

2. In the short run, if a firm finds that its price (P) is less than its average total cost (ATC), should it shut down its operation?

3. The layperson says that a firm maximizes profits when total revenue (TR) minus total cost (TC) is as large as possible and positive. The economist says that a firm maximizes profits when it produces the level of output at which $MR = MC$. Explain how the two ways of looking at profit maximization are consistent.

4. Why are market supply curves upward-sloping?

PERFECT COMPETITION IN THE LONG RUN

The number of firms in a perfectly competitive market may not be the same in the short run as in the long run. For example, if the typical firm is making economic profits in the short run, new firms will be attracted to the industry, and the number of firms will increase. If the typical firm is sustaining losses, some existing firms will exit the industry, and the number of firms will decrease. This process is explained in greater detail later in this section. We begin by outlining the conditions of long-run competitive equilibrium.

THE CONDITIONS OF LONG-RUN COMPETITIVE EQUILIBRIUM

Long-Run Competitive Equilibrium
The condition where $P = MC = SRATC = LRATC$. There are zero economic profits, firms are producing the quantity of output at which price is equal to marginal cost, and no firm has an incentive to change its plant size.

The following conditions characterize **long-run competitive equilibrium:**

1. **Economic profit is zero: Price (P) is equal to short-run average total cost ($SRATC$).**

$$P = SRATC$$

The logic of this condition is clear when we analyze what will happen if price is above or below short-run average total cost. If it is above, positive economic profits will attract firms to the industry in order to obtain the profits. If price is below, losses will result and some firms will want to exit the industry. Long-run competitive equilibrium cannot exist if firms have an incentive to enter or exit the industry in response to positive economic profits or losses, respectively. For long-run equilibrium to exist, there can be no incentive for firms to enter or exit the industry. This condition is brought about by zero economic profit (normal profit), which is a consequence of the equilibrium price being equal to short-run average total cost.

2. **Firms are producing the quantity of output at which price (P) is equal to marginal cost (MC).**

$$P = MC$$

As previously noted, perfectly competitive firms naturally move toward the output level at which marginal revenue, or price because $MR = P$ for a perfectly competitive firm, equals marginal cost.

3. **No firm has an incentive to change its plant size to produce its current output; that is, $SRATC = LRATC$ at the quantity of output at which $P = MC$.** To understand this condition, suppose $SRATC > LRATC$ at the quantity of output established in condition 2. If this is the case, the firm has an incentive to change plant size in the long run because it wants to produce its product with the plant size that will give it the lowest average total cost (unit cost). It will have no incentive to change plant size when it is producing the quantity of output at which price equals marginal cost and $SRATC$ equals $LRATC$.

$$SRATC = LRATC$$

The three conditions necessary for long-run competitive equilibrium can be stated as: Long-run competitive equilibrium exists when $P = MC = SRATC = LRATC$ (Exhibit 8).

Q & A

Q: It appears that long-run competitive equilibrium exists when firms have no incentive to make any changes. Is this correct?

A: Yes, it is. Specifically, long-run competitive equilibrium exists when all of the following occur:

1. **There is no incentive for firms to enter or exit the industry.** This means there are no economic profits or losses. There is, instead, zero economic profit (or normal profit), which can come about only if $P = SRATC$.
2. **There is no incentive for firms to produce more or less output.** This requires firms to produce the quantity of output at which P (or MR) = MC because any other output level does not maximize profits or minimize losses.

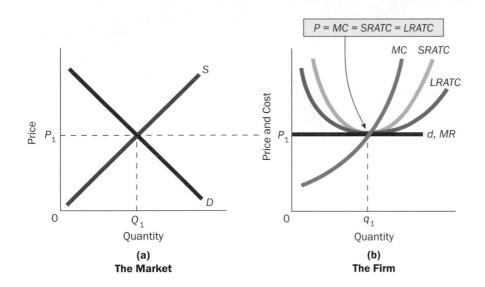

$$P = MC = SRATC = LRATC$$

(a)
The Market

(b)
The Firm

exhibit 8

Long-Run Competitive Equilibrium
(a) Equilibrium in the market. (b) Equilibrium for the firm. In (b), $P = MC$ (the firm has no incentive to move away from the quantity of output at which this occurs, q_1); $P = SRATC$ (there is no incentive for firms to enter or exit the industry); and $SRATC = LRATC$ (there is no incentive for the firm to change its plant size).

3. **There is no incentive for firms to change plant size.** Firms naturally want to produce at the lowest average total cost (unit cost) possible. If, for example, $SRATC > LRATC$ at the output level at which $MR = MC$, the firm has an incentive to change its plant size in the long run in order to produce the same output level at lower unit costs.

THE PERFECTLY COMPETITIVE FIRM AND PRODUCTIVE EFFICIENCY

A firm that produces its output at the lowest possible per unit cost (lowest ATC) is said to exhibit **productive efficiency.** The perfectly competitive firm does this in long-run equilibrium, as shown in Exhibit 8. Productive efficiency is desirable from society's standpoint because it means that perfectly competitive firms are economizing on society's scarce resources and therefore not wasting them.

To illustrate, suppose the lowest unit cost at which good X can be produced is $3—this is the minimum ATC. If a firm produces 1,000 units of good X at this unit cost, its total cost is $3,000. Now suppose the firm produces good X, not at its lowest unit cost of $3, but at a slightly higher unit cost of $3.50. Total cost is now equal to $3,500. This means resources worth $500 were employed producing good X that could have been used to produce other goods had the firm exhibited productive efficiency. Society could have been "richer" in goods and services, but now is not.

Productive Efficiency
The situation that exists when a firm produces its output at the lowest possible per unit cost (lowest ATC).

INDUSTRY ADJUSTMENT TO AN INCREASE IN DEMAND

An increase in market demand for a product can throw an industry out of long-run competitive equilibrium. Suppose we start at long-run competitive equilibrium, where $P = MC = SRATC = LRATC$. (See Exhibit 9.) Then market demand rises for the product produced by the firms in the industry. What happens? Equilibrium price rises. As a consequence, the demand curve faced by an individual firm (which is its marginal revenue curve) shifts upward.

Next, existing firms in the industry increase quantity of output because marginal revenue now intersects marginal cost at a higher quantity of output. In the long run, new firms begin to enter the industry because price is currently above average total cost and there are positive economic profits.

As new firms enter the industry, the market (industry) supply curve shifts rightward. As a consequence, equilibrium price falls. It falls until long-run competitive equilibrium is reestablished; that is, until there is, once again, zero economic profit.

Go to *http://money.cnn.com/*. Key "DIS" in the "ticket symbol" box, and click "quote." Earnings is the word sometimes used to refer to profits. Dividends are the payments (to the owners of a company) out of profits or earnings. Is there anything mentioned on this page other than profits or dividends? Is there any mention of costs, revenue, and so on? Does it follow that profit is the key variable that is used to evaluate a company? Looking at the page, what is the relevant time period used to evaluate a company's profit position? Is it 10 weeks? 20 weeks? 52 weeks?

A Closer Look

(1) The industry is in long-run competitive equilibrium. All firms earn zero economic profit.

(2) For some reason, the market demand curve rises and price rises.

(3) This raises the demand and marginal revenue curves for the firm, and it produces more output.

(4) At a higher price and demand curve, firms in the industry are now earning positive economic profits.

(5) Other firms (currently not in the industry) view the positive economic profits as an incentive to join the industry.

(6) As new firms join the industry, the market supply curve shifts to the right and price declines.

(7) This lowers the demand and marginal revenue curves for firms. Older firms, which made up the industry before market demand increased (back in Box 2), cut back output.

(8) Eventually, all firms earn zero economic profit and are in long-run competitive equilibrium.

exhibit 9

The Process of Moving from One Long-Run Competitive Equilibrium Position to Another

The exhibit describes what happens on both the market level and the firm level when demand rises and throws an industry out of long-run competitive equilibrium.

If you look at the process again, from the initial increase in market demand to the reestablishment of long-run competitive equilibrium, you will notice that price increased in the short run (owing to the increase in demand), and then decreased in the long run (owing to the increase in supply). Also, profits increased (owing to the increase in demand and consequent increase in price) and then decreased (owing to the increase in supply and consequent decrease in price). They went from zero to some positive amount and then back to zero.

The *up-and-down* movements in both price and profits in response to an increase in demand are important to note. Too often people see only the primary upward movements in both price and profits and ignore or forget the secondary downward movements. The secondary effects in price and profits are as important as the primary effects.

The process of adjustment to an increase in demand brings up an important question. If price first rises owing to an increase in market demand, and later falls owing to an increase in market supply, will the new equilibrium price be greater than, less than, or equal to the original equilibrium price? (In Exhibit 9, it is shown as equal to the original equilibrium price, but this need not be the case.)

For example, if equilibrium price is $10 before the increase in market demand, will the new equilibrium price (after market and firm adjustments have taken place) be greater than, less than, or equal to $10? The answer depends on whether increasing cost, decreasing cost, or constant cost, respectively, describes the industry in which the increase in demand has taken place.

Constant-Cost Industry

In a **constant-cost industry,** average total costs (unit costs) do not change as output increases or decreases when firms enter or exit the market or industry. If market demand increases for a good produced by firms in a constant-cost industry, price will initially rise and then will finally fall to its original level. This is illustrated in Exhibit 10a.

We start from a position of long-run competitive equilibrium where there are zero economic profits. This is at point 1. Then, demand increases and price rises from P_1 to P_2. At P_2, there are positive profits, which cause the firms currently in the industry to increase output. We move up the supply curve, S_1, from point 1 to point 2. Next, new firms, drawn by the profits, enter the industry, causing the supply curve to shift rightward.

For a constant-cost industry, output is increased without a change in the price of inputs. Because of this, the firms' cost curves do not shift. But, if costs do not rise to reduce the profits in the industry, then price must fall. (Profits can be reduced in two ways—through a rise in costs or a fall in price.) Price must fall to its original level (P_1) before profits can be zero. This implies that the supply curve shifts rightward by the same amount that the demand curve shifts rightward. In the exhibit, this is a shift from S_1 to S_2. The two long-run equilibrium points (1 and 3), where economic profits are zero, define the **long-run (industry) supply (LRS) curve.** A constant-cost industry is characterized by a horizontal long-run supply curve.

Constant-Cost Industry
An industry in which average total costs do not change as (industry) output increases or decreases when firms enter or exit the industry, respectively.

exhibit 10

Long-Run Industry Supply Curves
LRS = long-run industry supply. Each part illustrates the same scenario, but with different results depending on whether the industry has (a) constant costs, (b) increasing costs, or (c) decreasing costs. In each part, we start at long-run competitive equilibrium (point 1). Demand increases, price rises from P_1 to P_2, and there are positive economic profits. Consequently, existing firms increase output and new firms are attracted to the industry. In (a), input costs remain constant as output increases, so the firms' cost curves do not shift. Profits fall to zero through a decline in price. This implies that in a constant-cost industry, the supply curve shifts rightward by the same amount as the demand curve shifts rightward. In (b), input costs increase as output increases. Profits are squeezed by a combination of rising costs and falling prices. The new equilibrium price (P_3) for an increasing-cost industry is higher than the old equilibrium price (P_1). In (c), input costs decrease as output increases. The new equilibrium price (P_3) for a decreasing-cost industry is lower than the old equilibrium price (P_1).

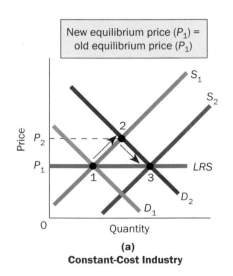

(a)
Constant-Cost Industry

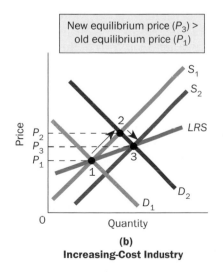

(b)
Increasing-Cost Industry

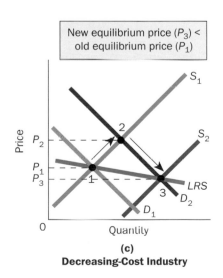

(c)
Decreasing-Cost Industry

Increasing-Cost Industry

In an **increasing-cost industry,** average total costs (unit costs) increase as output increases and decrease as output decreases when firms enter and exit the industry, respectively. If market demand increases for a good produced by firms in an increasing-cost industry, price will initially rise and then will finally fall to a level above its original level.

Consider the situation in Exhibit 10b. We start, as before, in long-run competitive equilibrium at point 1. Demand increases and price rises from P_1 to P_2. This brings about positive economic profits, which cause firms in the industry to increase output and new firms to enter the industry. So far, this is the same process as for a constant-cost industry. However, in an increasing-cost industry, as firms purchase more inputs to produce more output, some input prices rise and cost curves shift. In short, as industry output increases, profits are caught in a two-way squeeze: Price is coming down, and costs are rising. If costs are rising as price is falling, then it is not necessary for price to fall to its original level before zero economic profits rule once again. Price will not have to fall as far to restore long-run competitive equilibrium in an increasing-cost industry as in a constant-cost industry. We would expect, then, that when an increasing-cost industry experiences an increase in demand, the new equilibrium price will be higher than the old equilibrium price. This means the supply curve shifts rightward by less than the demand curve shifts rightward. An increasing-cost industry is characterized by an upward-sloping long-run supply curve.

Decreasing-Cost Industry

In a **decreasing-cost industry,** average total costs (unit costs) decrease as output increases and increase as output decreases when firms enter and exit the industry, respectively. If market demand increases for a good produced by firms in a decreasing-cost industry, price will initially rise and then will finally fall to a level below its original level. In Exhibit 10c, price moves from P_1 to P_2 and then to P_3. In such an industry, average total costs decrease as new firms enter the industry, so price must fall below its original level in order to eliminate profits. A decreasing-cost industry is characterized by a downward-sloping long-run supply curve.

WHAT HAPPENS AS FIRMS ENTER AN INDUSTRY IN SEARCH OF PROFITS?

In 1969, the first handheld calculator was introduced in the United States; it sold for $395. In 1975, Sony sold the first videocassette recorder (VCR) for a price of $1,400. In 1977, Apple Computer Corporation sold the first personal computer—it had only 4K random access memory (RAM)—for just under $1,300. In 2003, the prices of all three goods were much lower in both nominal and real (inflation-adjusted) terms, and the quality was generally much higher than when the goods were first introduced. Handheld calculators of higher quality than the one introduced in 1969 were selling for approximately $10. Videocassette recorders of higher quality than those in 1975 were selling for approximately $149. Personal home computers of much higher quality than those in 1977 were selling for approximately $600.

What brought about this sharp decrease in price and increase in quality? The entry of new firms into the calculator, VCR, and personal computer industries was partly responsible. Positive economic profits, realized by the first companies in the different industries, attracted new firms, the supply of the goods increased, and prices fell.[5] In 1970, one year after the first handheld calculator was introduced, Texas Instruments entered the industry. It was quickly followed by Canon, Hewlett-Packard, National Semi-Conductor, and Sears, to name only a few well-known companies. In the VCR industry, Sony was soon followed by RCA, Gen-

---

5. Changes in technology also occurred at about this time.

ECONOMICS IN...

Technology — Popular Culture — Everyday Life — The World

Amazon.com: There May Not Be Any Cappuccino, but There Are Millions of Books

Book superstores seem to be springing up everywhere in recent years. Usually, these superstores are about 25,000 square feet and have comfortable chairs and a coffee area. You can relax with a hot cup of cappuccino as you browse through a book you pulled off the seemingly endless rows of shelves. Companies such as Borders, Crown, Books-a-Million, and Barnes & Noble have been opening book superstores all over the country.

So far, superstores have been profitable ventures for Barnes & Noble. On average, a book superstore costs about $2 million to create and generates more than $6 million in total revenues in its first year. Barnes & Noble has stated that it plans to expand in upcoming years.

When there are positive economic profits such as these, firms outside the market will enter the market to compete for a share of the positive profits earned by existing firms. In the bookselling market, the Internet has made this easier to do. Now, instead of building a $2 million physical superstore, it is possible to "build" a book superstore in cyberspace. In other words, it is possible to compete with Barnes & Noble, Crown, and Borders—firms that have physical superstores—by selling books via the Internet.

Amazon, the first cyberspace bookseller, calls itself "Earth's Biggest Bookstore" both on the Internet and in its newspaper and magazine advertisements. In April 1997, Jeff Bezos, the CEO of Amazon, said that a list of Amazon's 2.5 million titles would fill 14 New York City phone books. In other words, in the world of book superstores, Amazon is the super book superstore.

Amazon entered the book superstore market because the brick-and-mortar superstores had proved there were profits in the market. But, Amazon entered the market in a way that had never been done before—through cyberspace.

So, what have we learned? First, when there are positive economic profits in a competitive market, existing firms will expand. This is what Barnes & Noble is doing. Second, when there are positive economic profits in a competitive market, new firms will enter the market. This is what Amazon did. Third, it is possible to enter a market today—as opposed to only a few years ago—through cyberspace. In other words, the introduction of the Internet has given potential competitors another road they can travel to enter new markets.

eral Electric, Zenith, and many others. In the personal computer industry, Apple was quickly followed by Tandy (Radio Shack), Xerox, IBM, Nippon Electric, Casio, Digital Equipment, and a host of others.

These examples illustrate how easy entry into the market can affect price and profits. They also suggest the potential benefits that incumbent firms can enjoy if they can successfully limit entry into the industry. (Consider the profits Sony would have realized if it could have legally prohibited other firms from entering the videocassette recorder industry.)

INDUSTRY ADJUSTMENT TO A DECREASE IN DEMAND

Demand can decrease as well as increase. The analysis outlined for an increase in demand can be reversed to explain industry adjustment to a decrease in demand. Starting at long-run competitive equilibrium, market demand decreases. As a consequence, in the short run, the equilibrium price falls, effectively shifting the firm's demand curve (marginal revenue curve) downward. Following this, some firms in the industry will decrease production because marginal revenue intersects marginal cost at a lower level of output, and some firms will shut down.

In the long run, some firms will leave the industry because price is below average total cost and they are suffering continual losses. As firms leave the industry, the market supply curve shifts leftward. As a consequence, the equilibrium price rises. It will rise until long-run competitive equilibrium is reestablished, that is, until there are, once again, zero economic profits (instead of negative economic profits). Whether the new equilibrium price is greater than, less than, or equal to the original equilibrium price depends on whether decreasing cost, increasing cost, or constant cost, respectively, describes the industry in which demand decreased.

Q: What motivates long-run adjustment?

A: Profit seeking by firms is behind long-run adjustment. For example, suppose that in the short run, the typical firm is earning profits. In the long run, new firms will enter the industry, causing the number of firms to increase, supply to increase, and prices to fall.

DIFFERENCES IN COSTS, DIFFERENCES IN PROFITS: NOW YOU SEE IT, NOW YOU DON'T

Suppose two farmers, Hancock and Cordero, produce wheat. Farmer Cordero grows his wheat on fertile land; Farmer Hancock grows her wheat on poor soil. Both farmers sell their wheat for the same price, but because of the difference in the quality of their land, Cordero has lower average total costs than Hancock. This is represented in Exhibit 11.

If we compare the initial situations for the two farmers (see each farmer's ATC_1), we notice that Cordero is earning profits and Hancock is not. Cordero is earning profits because he pays lower average total costs than Hancock as a consequence of farming higher-quality land. But is this situation likely to continue? Is Cordero likely to continue earning profits? The answer is no.

Individuals will bid up the price of the fertile land that Cordero farms vis-à-vis the poor-quality land that Hancock farms. In other words, if Cordero is renting his farmland, the rent he pays will increase to reflect the superior quality of the land. The rent will increase by an amount equal to the profits per time period; that is, an amount equal to the shaded portion in Exhibit 11b. If Cordero owns the land, the superior quality of the land will have a higher implicit cost attached to it (Cordero can rent it for more than Hancock can rent her land, assuming Hancock owns her land). This fact will be reflected in the average total cost curve.

exhibit 11

Differences in Costs, Differences in Profits: Now You See It, Now It's Gone

At ATC_1 for both farmers, Cordero earns profits and Hancock does not. Cordero earns profits because the land he farms is of higher quality (more productive) than Hancock's land. Eventually, this fact is taken into account, by Cordero either paying higher rent for the land or incurring implicit costs for it. This moves Cordero's ATC curve upward to the same level as Hancock's, and Cordero earns zero economic profits. The profits have gone as payment (implicit or explicit) for the higher-quality, more productive land.

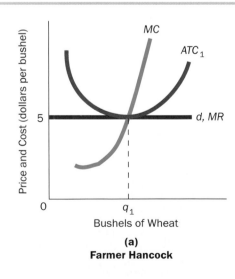

(a)
Farmer Hancock

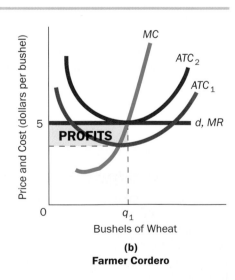

(b)
Farmer Cordero

ECONOMICS IN...

Everyday Life   Popular Culture   Technology   The World

One City, Two States

Wheat farmers are in a perfectly competitive industry. There are many buyers and sellers of wheat; wheat is a homogeneous good; buyers and sellers appear to have much (if not all) relevant information about prices, product quality, sources of supply, and so forth; and there is easy entry and exit.

Suppose the wheat industry is in long-run equilibrium, the representative wheat farmer in both Nebraska and Iowa is earning normal profits, and the market equilibrium price is $5 per bushel of wheat. Now suppose the Nebraska state government passes a law that says Nebraska wheat farmers cannot sell their wheat for more than $4 a bushel. As a result of the law, Nebraska wheat farmers will no longer be able to earn normal profits, and so they will exit the Nebraska wheat industry. Because there will initially be fewer wheat farmers, the supply of wheat will decline, and the equilibrium price of wheat will rise. As a result of the higher price of wheat, Iowa wheat farmers will earn higher-than-normal profits. If the wheat industry is a competitive industry, new farmers will enter the wheat business (in Iowa), and the price of wheat will eventually decline until wheat farmers are earning only normal profits. The outcome of the Nebraska law will be: (1) no wheat farmers in Nebraska, (2) more wheat farmers in Iowa, and (3) an equilibrium price of a bushel of wheat above $5 in the short run and, in the face of constant costs, at $5 in the long run. In short, the only thing the Nebraska law will accomplish in the long run is to rid the state of wheat farmers.

Our story about wheat farmers has relevance to a city that is located in two states—Texarkana. Half of Texarkana is in Arkansas (Texarkana, Arkansas) and half is in Texas (Texarkana,

Texas). Each half of Texarkana has a different mayor, a different sheriff, and a different city government.[6]

Each half of Texarkana also has a different number of banks. Most of the banks in the city are located in Texas. Why? To a large degree, the reason is that Arkansas has a usury law and Texas does not. Stated differently, Arkansas law limits the interest rate that can be charged on consumer loans. In Arkansas, the highest interest rate that can be charged on consumer loans is 5 percent above the discount rate charged by the Federal Reserve. (The discount rate is the interest rate that the Federal Reserve, the U.S. monetary authority, charges for loans.) At the time of this writing, 9.5 percent was the highest interest rate an Arkansas bank could charge.

If the credit industry is a competitive industry (like the wheat industry) and, at the given market equilibrium rate, lenders are earning only normal profits, then an interest-rate ceiling will have the same effect as our price ceiling on wheat. Critics of the law say that the usury law forces banks and credit businesses to leave Arkansas and go to Texas. This has largely happened in Texarkana. Most of the banks and much of the available credit businesses are in Texarkana, Texas, not Texarkana, Arkansas.

Perhaps because of the more plentiful credit in the Texas half of the city, shoppers, upper-income homeowners, and businesses tend to prefer Texarkana, Texas, to Texarkana, Arkansas. The landscape of the "two cities" has changed as a result. The upscale neighborhoods, restaurants, department stores, car dealerships, and the town's only shopping mall are all located in Texarkana, Texas.

In Exhibit 11b, ATC_2 reflects either the higher rent Cordero must pay for the superior land or the full implicit cost he incurs by farming land he owns. In either case, when the average total cost curve reflects all costs, Cordero will be in the same situation as Hancock; he, too, will be earning zero economic profits.

Where has the profit gone? It has gone as payment for the higher-quality, more productive resource responsible for the lower average total costs in the first place. Consequently, average total costs are no longer relatively lower for the person or firm that employs the higher-quality, more productive resource or input.

PROFIT AND DISCRIMINATION

A firm's discriminatory behavior can affect its profits in the context of the model of perfect competition. Let's start at the position of long-run competitive equilibrium where firms are earning zero economic profits. Consider the owner of a

---

6. This feature is based on "The bad side of town," *The Economist* (28 November 1998).

firm who chooses not to hire an excellent worker (a worker who is above average, let's say) simply because of that worker's race, religion, or gender.

If the owner of the firm discriminates in any way, what happens to his profits? If he chooses not to employ high-quality employees because of their race, religion, or gender, then his costs will rise above the costs of his competitors who hire the best employees—irrespective of race, religion, or gender. Because he is initially earning zero profit, where $TR = TC$, this act of discrimination will raise TC and push him into taking economic losses.

If the owner in the example is instead a manager, he may lose his job. Owners may decide to replace managers of firms earning subnormal profits. Thus, profit maximization by shareholders works to reduce discrimination.

Our conclusion is that if a firm is in a perfectly competitive market structure, it will pay penalties if it chooses to discriminate. This is not to say that discrimination will disappear. It only says that discrimination comes with a price tag. And according to economic theory, the more something costs, the less of it there will be, *ceteris paribus.*

Self-Test

1. If firms in a perfectly competitive market are earning positive economic profits, what will happen?

2. If firms in a perfectly competitive market want to produce more output, is the market in long-run equilibrium?

3. If a perfectly competitive market in long-run equilibrium witnesses an increase in demand, what will happen to price?

4. Suppose there are two firms, each of which produces computer software. Firm *A* employs a software genius at the same salary that firm *B* employs a mediocre software engineer. Will the firm that employs the software genius earn higher profits than the other firm, *ceteris paribus*?

TOPICS FOR ANALYSIS WITHIN THE THEORY OF PERFECT COMPETITION

This section briefly analyzes three topics within the theory of perfect competition: higher costs and higher prices, advertising, and setting prices.

DO HIGHER COSTS MEAN HIGHER PRICES?

Suppose there are 600 firms in an industry. Each firm sells the identical product at the same price. Suppose that one of these firms experiences a rise in its marginal costs of production. Someone immediately comments, "Higher costs for the firm today, higher prices for the consumer tomorrow." Her assumption is that firms that experience a rise in costs simply pass on these higher costs to consumers in the form of higher prices.

Will this occur in a perfectly competitive market structure? Remember that each firm in the industry is a price taker; furthermore, only one firm has experienced a rise in marginal cost. Because this firm supplies only a tiny percentage of the total market supply, it is unlikely that the market supply curve will undergo more than a negligible change. And if the market supply curve does not change, neither will equilibrium price. In short, a rise in costs incurred by one of many firms does not mean consumers will pay higher prices. The situation would have been different, of course, if many of the firms in the industry had experienced a rise in costs. In this case, the market supply curve would have been affected, along with price.

WILL THE PERFECTLY COMPETITIVE FIRM ADVERTISE?

Do individual farmers advertise? Have you ever seen an advertisement for, say, Farmer Johnson's milk? We think not. First, Farmer Johnson sells a homogeneous product, so advertising his milk is the same as advertising every dairy farmer's milk. Second, Farmer Johnson is in a perfectly competitive market, so he can sell all the milk he wants at the going price. Why should he advertise? From his viewpoint, advertising has costs and no benefits.

Will a perfectly competitive industry advertise? For example, if Farmer Johnson won't advertise his milk, will the milk industry advertise milk? It may. The industry as a whole may advertise milk in the hope of shifting the market demand curve for milk to the right. This is actually what the milk industry hopes to do with its commercial message, "Got milk?"

SUPPLIER-SET PRICE VERSUS MARKET-DETERMINED PRICE: COLLUSION OR COMPETITION?

Suppose the only thing you know about a particular industry is that all firms within it sell their products at the same price. To explain this, some people argue that the firms are colluding—that is, the firms come together, pick a price, and stick to it.

This, of course, is one way all firms can arrive at the same price for their products. But it is not the only way. Another way has been described in this chapter. It could be that all firms are price takers; that is, the firms are in a perfectly competitive market structure. In this case, there is no collusion.

THINKING LIKE AN ECONOMIST   *Sometimes, two or more explanations may seem equally reasonable. For example, observing that all firms within an industry sell their products for the same price, both the explanation that the firms collude on price and the explanation that the firms are price takers seem equally reasonable. But for the economist, a reasonable explanation is not sufficient; she wants the correct explanation. The economist is skeptical of any explanation that simply sounds reasonable. She has to have evidence that supports the explanation.*

Self-Test

1. In a perfectly competitive market, do higher costs mean higher prices?
2. Suppose you see a product advertised on television. Does it follow that the product cannot be produced in a perfectly competitive market?

A Reader Asks...

Does Job Security Have Anything to Do with Fixed and Variable Costs?

What is the relationship among fixed, variable, and total costs; the firm's shut-down decision; and employee job security?

Consider the total fixed cost–total cost ratio (*TFC/TC*) for firms. The greater the ratio—that is, the larger *TFC* is relative to *TC*—the more likely the firm will operate in the short run; the smaller the ratio, the less likely the firm will operate in the short run. It follows that the more likely the firm will operate in the short run, the greater the job security for the employees of the firm; the less likely the firm will operate in the short run, the lesser the job security for the employees of the firm.

To illustrate, suppose two firms, *X* and *Y*, have the following:

Firm X	Firm Y
TC = $600	TC = $600
TVC = $400	TVC = $500
TFC = $200	TFC = $100
TVC/TC = $400/$600 = 0.66	TVC/TC = $500/$600 = 0.83
TFC/TC = $200/$600 = 0.33	TFC/TC = $100/$600 = 0.17

Notice that two firms have the same total cost ($600) but that fixed and variable costs are different percentages of total cost for the two firms. Firm *X* has a lower *TVC/TC* ratio and a higher *TFC/TC* ratio than firm *Y* has. If total revenue falls to, say, $499, firm *Y* will shut down because its total revenue will be less than its total variable cost (*TVC*). However, firm *X* will continue to operate. For firm *X*, total revenue will have to fall below $400 before it will shut down. In other words, the firm with the

higher *TFC/TC* ratio (firm *X*) stays operational longer than the firm with the lower *TFC/TC* ratio (firm *Y*). It follows, then, that everything else equal between the two firms, an employee working for firm *X* is less likely to be laid off due to declining total revenue than an employee working for firm *Y*.

Chapter Summary

The Theory of Perfect Competition

- The theory of perfect competition is built on four assumptions: (1) There are many sellers and many buyers, none of which is large in relation to total sales or purchases. (2) Each firm produces and sells a homogeneous product. (3) Buyers and sellers have all relevant information with respect to prices, product quality, sources of supply, and so on. (4) There is easy entry into and exit from the industry.

- The theory of perfect competition predicts the following: (1) Economic profits will be squeezed out of the industry in the long run by the entry of new firms—that is, zero economic profit exists in the long run. (2) In equilibrium, firms produce the quantity of output at which price equals marginal cost. (3) In the short run, firms will stay in business as long as price covers average variable costs. (4) In the long run, firms will stay in business as long as price covers average total costs. (5) In the short run, an increase in demand will lead to a rise in price; whether the price in the long run will be higher than, lower than, or equal to its original level depends on whether the firm is in an increasing-, decreasing-, or constant-cost industry.

The Perfectly Competitive Firm

- A perfectly competitive firm is a price taker. It sells its product only at the market-established equilibrium price.
- The perfectly competitive firm faces a horizontal (flat, perfectly elastic) demand curve. Its demand curve and marginal revenue curve are the same. $D = MR$
- The perfectly competitive firm (as well as all other firms) maximizes profits (or minimizes losses) by producing the quantity of output at which $MR = MC$.
- For the perfectly competitive firm, price equals marginal revenue.
- A perfectly competitive firm is resource allocative efficient because it produces the quantity of output at which $P = MC$.

Production in the Short Run

- If $P > ATC\ (> AVC)$, the firm earns economic profits and will continue to operate in the short run.

- If $P < AVC\ (< ATC)$, the firm takes losses. It will shut down because the alternative (continuing to produce) increases the losses.
- If $ATC > P > AVC$, the firm takes losses. Nevertheless, it will continue to operate in the short run because the alternative (shutting down) increases the losses.
- The firm produces in the short run only when price is greater than average variable cost. Therefore, the portion of its marginal cost curve that lies above the average variable cost curve is the firm's short-run supply curve.

Conditions of Long-Run Competitive Equilibrium

- Long-run competitive equilibrium exists when (1) there is no incentive for firms to enter or exit the industry, (2) there is no incentive for firms to produce more or less output, and (3) there is no incentive for firms to change plant size. We formalize these conditions as follows: (1) Economic profits are zero. (This is the same as saying there is no incentive for firms to enter or exit the industry). (2) Firms are producing the quantity of output at which price is equal to marginal cost. (This is the same as saying there is no incentive for firms to produce more or less output. After all, when $P = MC$, it follows that $MR = MC$ for the perfectly competitive firm, and thus the firm is maximizing profits.) (3) $SRATC = LRATC$ at the quantity of output at which $P = MC$. (This is the same as saying firms do not have an incentive to change plant size.)
- A perfectly competitive firm exhibits productive efficiency because it produces its output in the long run at the lowest possible per unit cost (lowest *ATC*).

Industry Adjustment to a Change in Demand

- In a constant-cost industry, an increase in demand will result in a new equilibrium price equal to the original equilibrium price (before demand increased). In an increasing-cost industry, an increase in demand will result in a new equilibrium price that is higher than the original equilibrium price. In a decreasing-cost industry, an increase in demand will result in a new equilibrium price that is lower than the original equilibrium price.

- The long-run supply curve for <u>a constant-cost</u> industry is horizontal (flat, perfectly elastic). The long-run supply curve for an increasing-cost industry is upward-sloping. The long-run supply curve for a decreasing-cost industry is downward-sloping.

Key Terms and Concepts

Market Structure
Perfect Competition
Price Taker
Marginal Revenue (*MR*)
Profit-Maximization Rule
Resource Allocative Efficiency

Short-Run (Firm) Supply Curve
Short-Run Market (Industry)
    Supply Curve
Long Run Competitive Equilibrium
Productive Efficiency
Constant-Cost Industry

Long-Run (Industry) Supply
    (*LRS*) Curve
Increasing-Cost Industry
Decreasing-Cost Industry

Economic Connections to You

Economic facts, actions, and changes create ripples that move away from their point of origin. Eventually, these ripples can intersect your life and have an effect on you. Consider the following example:

A new industry emerges on the scene. Currently, the firms in the industry are earning extremely high (positive) economic profits. These high profits are widely reported in newspapers and magazines. Some firms outside the industry are thinking about entering this profitable market. Before they do, however, government decides to impose a heavy and permanent tax on the profits of the firms in the industry. As a result of the tax, not as many new firms enter the

market. Consequently, market supply doesn't rise so much and price doesn't fall so much as otherwise would have been the case. You must pay a higher price for products produced in this industry than you would have if the government had not imposed such a heavy tax on the profits of the firms in the industry. Thus, there is a connection between a government tax on the profits of firms in an industry and the prices you must pay for products—an economic connection to you.

Based on the material in this chapter, identify other ways in which economic facts, actions, and changes create ripples that eventually affect you.

Questions and Problems

1. True or false: The firm's entire marginal cost curve is its short-run supply curve. Explain your answer.
2. True or false: In a perfectly competitive market, firms always operate at the lowest per-unit cost. Explain your answer.
3. "Firm A, one firm in a competitive industry, faces higher costs of production. As a result, consumers end up paying higher prices." Discuss.
4. Suppose all firms in a perfectly competitive market structure are in long-run equilibrium. Then demand for the firms' product increases. Initially, price and economic profits rise. Soon afterward, the government decides to tax most (but not all) of the economic profits, arguing that the firms in the industry

did not earn them—the profits were simply the result of an increase in demand. What effect, if any, will the tax have on market adjustment?
5. Explain why one firm sometimes appears to be earning higher profits than another, but in reality is not.
6. For a perfectly competitive firm, profit maximization does not conflict with resource allocative efficiency. Do you agree? Explain your answer.
7. The perfectly competitive firm does not increase its quantity of output without limit even though it can sell all it wants at the going price. Why not?
8. Suppose you read in a business magazine that computer firms are reaping high profits. With the theory of perfect competition in mind, what do you expect to

happen over time to the following: computer prices, the profits of computer firms, the number of computers on the market, the number of computer firms?

9. In your own words, explain resource allocative efficiency.

10. The term *price taker* can apply to buyers as well as sellers. A price-taking buyer is one who cannot influence price by changing the amount she buys. What goods do you buy for which you are a price taker? What goods do you buy for which you are not a price taker?

11. Why study the theory of perfect competition if no real-world market completely satisfies each of the theory's assumptions?

12. Explain why a perfectly competitive firm will shut down in the short run if price is lower than average variable cost, but it will continue to produce if price is below average total cost but above average variable cost.

13. In long-run competitive equilibrium, $P = MC = SRATC = LRATC$. Because $P = MR$, we can write the condition as $P = MR = MC = SRATC = LRATC$. Now let's look at the condition as consisting of four parts: (a) $P = MR$, (b) $MR = MC$, (c) $P = SRATC$, and (d) $SRATC = LRATC$. To explain why $MR = MC$, (b), we say that this condition exists because the perfectly competitive firm attempts to maximize profits and this is how it does it. What is the explanation for (a), (c), and (d)?

14. Suppose the government imposes a production tax on one perfectly competitive firm in an industry. For each unit the firm produces, it must pay $1 to the government. Will consumers in this market end up paying higher prices because of the tax? Why or why not?

15. Why is the marginal revenue curve for a perfectly competitive firm the same as its demand curve?

16. Many plumbers charge the same price for coming to your house to fix a kitchen sink. Is this because plumbers are colluding together on price?

17. Do firms in a perfectly competitive market exhibit productive efficiency? Why or why not?

Working with Numbers and Graphs

1. Given the following information, state whether the firm should shut down or continue to operate in the short run.
   a. $Q = 100$; $P = \$10$; $AFC = \$3$; $AVC = \$4$
   b. $Q = 70$; $P = \$5$; $AFC = \$2$; $AVC = \$7$
   c. $Q = 150$; $P = \$7$; $AFC = \$5$; $AVC = \$6$

2. If total revenue increases at a constant rate, what does this imply about marginal revenue?

3. Using the following table, what quantity of output should the firm produce? Explain your answer.

Q	TR	TC
0	$ 0	$ 0
1	100	50
2	200	110
3	300	180
4	400	260
5	500	360
6	600	480

4. Is the firm in Question 4 a perfectly competitive firm? Explain your answer.

5. Explain how a market supply curve is derived.

6. Draw the following:
   a. A firm that earns profits
   b. A firm that incurs losses but will continue operating in the short run

c. A firm that incurs losses and will shut down in the short run

7. Why is the firm's supply curve that portion of its marginal cost curve that is above its average variable cost curve?

8. In the following figure, what area(s) represent(s) the following at Q_1?
   a. Total cost
   b. Total variable cost
   c. Total revenue
   d. Loss (negative profit)

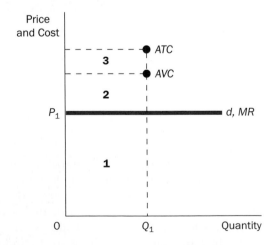

9. Why does the *MC* curve cut the *ATC* curve at the latter's lowest point?

10. Suppose all firms in a perfectly competitive market are in long-run equilibrium. Illustrate what a perfectly competitive firm will do if market demand rises.

Internet Activities

Go to *http://www.yahoo.com*. Select "Computers & Internet" (in the Directory), then "Product Information and Reviews," and finally "Desktop Computers@."

1. One of the assumptions in the theory of perfect competition is "many sellers." Do you think there are enough computer manufacturers to make the computer market a perfectly competitive market? Are you more likely to buy a computer from some of the manufacturers than from others? If your answer is yes, do you still think the computer market is a perfectly competitive market? Why or why not?

2. Click on "Dell," "Gateway," and two other computer manufacturers. Do the manufacturers produce homogeneous goods? Explain your answer. Does each manufacturer try to convince potential buyers that its computers are superior to the computers produced by other manufacturers?

3. Do you think computer buyers and sellers have "all relevant information"? Explain your answer. As a buyer, would your answer be different if you did not have Internet access and you lived in a small town with only two computer stores?

4. Do computer manufacturers have relatively easy entry into and exit out of the market? (Hint: Do all the links on the page still work?)

5. Are the computer manufacturers price takers? Explain your answer.

6. If more buyers turn to the Internet to buy computers, do you think computer prices will fall? Why or why not?

Log on to the Arnold Xtra! Web site now (*http://arnoldxtra.swcollege.com*) for additional learning resources such as practice quizzes, help with graphing, video clips, and current event applications.

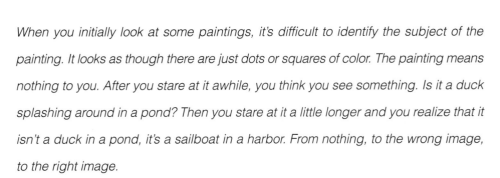

ch.10

MONOPOLY

When you initially look at some paintings, it's difficult to identify the subject of the painting. It looks as though there are just dots or squares of color. The painting means nothing to you. After you stare at it awhile, you think you see something. Is it a duck splashing around in a pond? Then you stare at it a little longer and you realize that it isn't a duck in a pond, it's a sailboat in a harbor. From nothing, to the wrong image, to the right image.

Studying monopoly progresses much the same way. At first, you may not see what it is about at all. Then you may think it is about exorbitant profits and giant corporations. Then, if you study a little more, things begin to come into sharper focus and you see what monopoly is really about.

The last chapter discusses the perfectly competitive firm. The perfectly competitive firm sells its product at the price determined in the market. This chapter discusses the monopoly firm. The monopoly firm has some control over the price at which it sells its product.

We discuss various issues related to the monopoly firm—the monopolist's demand and marginal revenue curves, the profit-maximization condition for the monopolist, the deadweight loss of monopoly, and rent seeking and monopoly. We also examine the differences between the monopoly firm that sells all units of its good at the same price (the single-price monopolist) and the monopoly firm that sells different units of its good at different prices (the price-discriminating monopolist).

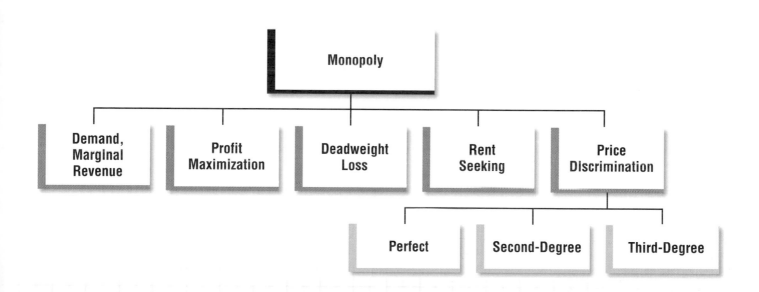

THE THEORY OF MONOPOLY

The last chapter discusses one theory of market structure—the theory of perfect competition. At the opposite end of the market structure spectrum is the theory of **monopoly.** The theory of monopoly is built on three assumptions:

Monopoly
A theory of market structure based on three assumptions: There is one seller, it sells a product for which no close substitutes exist, and there are extremely high barriers to entry.

1. **There is one seller.** This means that the firm is the industry. Contrast this situation with perfect competition, where many firms make up the industry.
2. **The single seller sells a product for which there are no close substitutes.** Because there are no close substitutes for its product, the single seller—the monopolist or monopoly firm—faces little, if any, competition.
3. **There are extremely high barriers to entry.** In the theory of perfect competition, we assume it is easy for a firm to enter the industry. In the theory of monopoly, we assume it is very hard (if not impossible) for a firm to enter the industry. Extremely high barriers keep out new firms.

Examples of monopoly include many public utilities (local public utilities such as electricity, water, and gas companies) and the U.S. Postal Service (in the delivery of first-class mail).

Q & A

Q: One of the assumptions in the theory of monopoly is that the single seller sells a product for which there are no close substitutes. Isn't deciding what constitutes a close substitute for a product a subjective matter for an individual?

A: Yes, it is. For example, someone might argue that writing a letter is a close substitute for making a telephone call, and someone else might maintain that it is not. Recall, however, that we are not trying to determine whether close substitutes exist or not, we are simply assuming that there are no close substitutes. This is part of our theory, which we hope will explain and predict the behavior of firms in some real-world markets. If the theory accurately predicts behavior in market *X*, even though some people argue that market *X* does not perfectly meet the assumption that there are no close substitutes, some economists would say, "No matter, the market behaves as if the assumption is met."

Even if the critics are right and a range of substitutes exists, it is impossible to know beforehand how close a substitute must be before the theory (that assumes no close substitutes) is not useful. In other words, even if there is a "slightly close" substitute for a seller's product, "slightly close" may not be close enough to matter.

BARRIERS TO ENTRY: A KEY TO UNDERSTANDING MONOPOLY

If a firm is a single seller of a product, why don't other firms enter the market and produce the same product? Legal barriers, economies of scale, or one firm's exclusive ownership of a scarce resource may make it difficult or impossible for new firms to enter the market.

Legal Barriers

Public Franchise
A right granted to a firm by government that permits the firm to provide a particular good or service and excludes all others from doing the same.

Legal barriers include public franchises, patents, and government licenses. A **public franchise** is a right granted to a firm by government that permits the firm to provide a particular good or service and excludes all others from doing the same (thus eliminating potential competition by law). For example, the U.S. Postal Service has been granted the exclusive franchise to deliver first-class mail. Many public utilities operate under state and local franchises, as do food and gas suppliers along many state turnpikes.

In the United States, patents are granted to inventors of a product or process for a period of 20 years. During this time, the patent holder is shielded from competitors; no one else can legally produce and sell the patented product or process. The rationale behind patents is that they encourage innovation in an economy. It is argued that few people will waste their time and money trying to invent a new product if their competitors can immediately copy the product and sell it.

ECONOMICS IN...

Monopoly and the Boston Tea Party

The original meaning of the word *monopoly* was an exclusive right to sell something. At one time, kings and queens granted monopolies to people in their favor. The monopoly entitled the person to be the sole producer or seller of a particular good. If anyone dared to compete with him, then the king or queen could have that person fined or imprisoned.

The issue of monopoly comes up in the early history of the United States. In 1767, the British Parliament passed the Townsend Acts. These acts imposed taxes (or duties) on various products that were imported into the American colonies. The taxes were so hated in the colonies that they prompted protest and noncompliance. The taxes were repealed in 1770, except for one—the tax on tea. Some historians state that the British Parliament left the tax on tea to show the colonists that it had the right to raise tax revenue without seeking colonial approval. To get around the tax, the colonists started to buy tea from Dutch traders.

Then, in 1773, the British East India Company was in financial trouble. To help solve its financial problems, it sought a special privilege—a monopoly—from the British Parliament. In response, Parliament passed the Tea Act, which granted the British East India Company the sole right—the monopoly right—to export tea to the colonies. The combination of the tax and the monopoly right given to the East India Company angered the colonists and is said to have led to the Boston Tea Party on December 16, 1773. The colonists who took part in the Boston Tea Party threw overboard 342 chests of tea owned by the monopoly-wielding East India Company.

Entry into some industries and occupations requires a government-granted license. For example, radio and television stations cannot operate without a license from the Federal Communications Commission (FCC). In most states, a person needs to be licensed to join the ranks of physicians, dentists, architects, nurses, embalmers, barbers, veterinarians, and lawyers, among others.

Some cities also use licensing as a form of legal barrier. For example, the Taxi & Limousine Commission in New York City requires a person to have a taxi license, called a *taxi medallion,* in order to own and operate a taxi in New York City. A taxi medallion is similar to a business license; a person needs it to lawfully operate a taxicab business. The number of taxi medallions (licenses) has been fixed at about 12,000 for many years. The price of a medallion changes according to changes in the demand for medallions. In 1976, a medallion was about $45,000; in 1988, it was $125,000; and in March 2002, it was $193,000. Obviously, many people find $193,000 a barrier to entering the taxi business. Thus, many economists believe that taxi medallions in New York City are a form of legal barrier.

Economies of Scale

In some industries, low average total costs (low unit costs) are obtained only through large-scale production. Thus, if new entrants are to be competitive in the industry, they must enter it on a large scale. But having to produce on this scale is risky and costly and therefore acts as a barrier to entry. If economies of scale are so pronounced in an industry that only one firm can survive in the industry, this firm is called a **natural monopoly.** Often-cited examples of natural monopoly include public utilities that provide gas, water, and electricity. A later chapter discusses government regulation of a natural monopoly.

Exclusive Ownership of a Necessary Resource

Existing firms may be protected from the entry of new firms by the exclusive or near-exclusive ownership of a resource needed to enter the industry. The classic example is the Aluminum Company of America (Alcoa), which for a time controlled almost all sources of bauxite in the United States. Alcoa was the sole producer of aluminum in the country from the late nineteenth century until the 1940s. Many people today view the DeBeers Company of South Africa as a monopoly because it controls a large percentage of diamond production and sales. Strictly speaking, DeBeers is more of a marketing cartel than a monopolist, although, as we see in the next chapter, a successful cartel acts much like a monopolist.

WHAT IS THE DIFFERENCE BETWEEN A GOVERNMENT MONOPOLY AND A MARKET MONOPOLY?

Sometimes high barriers to entry exist because competition is legally prohibited; sometimes they exist independently. When high barriers take the form of public franchises, patents, or government licenses, competition is legally prohibited. When high barriers take the form of economies of scale or exclusive ownership of a resource, competition is not legally prohibited. In these cases, nothing legally prohibits rival firms from entering the market and competing, even though they may choose not to do so. The high barrier to entry does not have a sign attached to it that reads "No competition allowed."

Some economists use the term *government monopoly* to refer to monopolies that are legally protected from competition and the term *market monopoly* to refer to monopolies that are not legally protected from competition. But these terms do not imply that one type is better or worse than the other.

Self-Test *(Answers to Self-Test questions are in the Self-Test Appendix.)*

1. John states that there are always some close substitutes for the product any firm sells, therefore the theory of monopoly (which assumes no close substitutes) cannot be useful. Comment.

2. How do economies of scale act as a barrier to entry?

3. How is a movie superstar like a monopolist?

MONOPOLY PRICING AND OUTPUT DECISIONS

A monopolist is a **price searcher;** that is, it is a seller that has the ability to control to some degree the price of the product it sells. In contrast to a price taker, a price searcher can raise its price and still sell its product—although not as many units as it could sell at the lower price. The pricing and output decisions of the price-searching monopolist are discussed in the next sections.

THE MONOPOLIST'S DEMAND AND MARGINAL REVENUE

In the theory of monopoly, the monopoly firm is the industry and the industry is the monopoly firm—they are the same. It follows that the demand curve for the monopoly firm is the market demand curve, which is downward-sloping. A downward-sloping demand curve posits an inverse relationship between price and quantity demanded: More is sold at lower prices than at higher prices, *ceteris paribus.* Unlike the perfectly competitive firm, the monopolist can raise its price and still sell its product (though not as much).

Suppose the monopolist wants to sell an additional unit of its product. What must it do? Because it faces a downward-sloping demand curve, it must necessarily lower price. For example, if the monopoly seller is selling two units of X at $10 each and wishes to sell three units, it must lower price, say, to $9.75. It sells all three units at $9.75.[1] To sell an additional unit, it must lower price on all previous units.

The monopoly seller both gains and loses by lowering price, as Exhibit 1 shows. It gains $9.75, the price of the additional unit sold because price was lowered. It loses 50 cents—25 cents on the first unit it used to sell at $10 plus 25 cents on the second unit it used to sell at $10.

Gains are greater than losses; the monopolist's net gain from selling the additional unit of output is $9.25 ($9.75 − $0.50 = $9.25). This is the monopolist's *marginal revenue:* the change in total revenue that results from selling one additional unit of output. (Total revenue is $20 when two units are sold at $10 each. Total revenue is $29.25 when three units are sold at $9.75 each. The change in total revenue that results from selling one additional unit of output is $9.25.)

Notice that the price of the good ($9.75) is greater than the marginal revenue ($9.25), $P > MR$. This is the case for a monopoly seller, or any price searcher. (Recall that for the firm in perfect competition, $P = MR$.)

For a monopolist: $P > MR$

Step by step, the effects of a price reduction can be summarized as follows:

1. To sell an additional unit of a good (per time period), the monopolist must lower price. In our example, the monopolist lowers price from $10 to $9.75.
2. The monopolist gains and loses by lowering price.
3. The gain equals the price of the product times one (one additional unit). Let's call this the *revenue gained*. In our example, revenue gained is $9.75 × 1 = $9.75. Notice that price equals revenue gained (P = revenue gained).

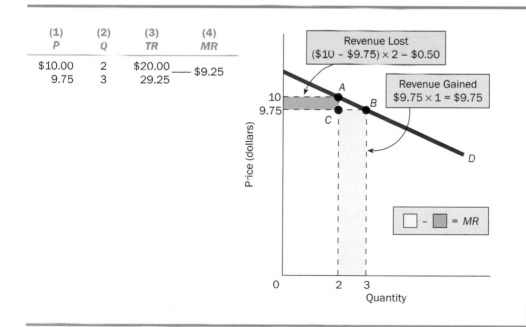

(1) P	(2) Q	(3) TR	(4) MR
$10.00	2	$20.00	$9.25
9.75	3	29.25	

Revenue Lost
($10 − $9.75) × 2 − $0.50

Revenue Gained
$9.75 × 1 = $9.75

☐ − ▨ = MR

exhibit 1

The Dual Effects of a Price Reduction on Total Revenue
To sell an additional unit of its good, a monopolist needs to lower price. This price reduction both gains revenue and loses revenue for the monopolist. In the exhibit, the revenue gained and revenue lost are shaded and labeled. Marginal revenue is equal to the larger shaded area minus the smaller.

---

1. This discussion is about how a single-price monopolist behaves. This is a monopolist that sells all units of its product for the same price. Later, we discuss a price-discriminating monopolist.

4. The loss equals the difference between the new lower price ($9.75) and the old higher price ($10) times the units of output sold *before* price was lowered. In our example, this is 25 cents × 2 = 50 cents. Let's call this the *revenue lost*.
5. Marginal revenue can be defined as revenue gained minus revenue lost.
6. P = revenue gained, MR = revenue gained − revenue lost, and revenue lost is > 0. Therefore, $P > MR$.

Q & A

Q: Earlier, it was said that to sell an additional unit, the monopolist must lower price on all previous units. This is confusing. How does the monopolist lower price on units it has already sold?

A: We shouldn't think of previous and additional as referring to an actual sequence of events. The firm doesn't sell 100 units of a good and then decide to sell one more unit. The firm is in an either-or situation. Either the firm sells 100 units over some period of time or it sells 101 units over the same period of time. If the firm wants to sell 101 units, the price per unit has to be lower than if it wants to sell 100 units.

THE MONOPOLIST'S DEMAND AND MARGINAL REVENUE CURVES ARE NOT THE SAME: WHY NOT?

In perfect competition, the firm's demand curve is the same as its marginal revenue curve. In monopoly, the firm's demand curve is not the same as its marginal revenue curve. The monopolist's demand curve lies above its marginal revenue curve.

The demand curve plots price and quantity (P and Q); the marginal revenue curve plots marginal revenue and quantity (MR and Q). Because price is greater than marginal revenue for a monopolist, its demand curve necessarily lies above its marginal revenue curve. (Note that price and marginal revenue are the same for the first unit of output, so the demand curve and the marginal revenue curve will share one point in common.) The correct relationship between a monopolist's demand and marginal revenue curves is illustrated in Exhibit 2.

IF A FIRM MAXIMIZES REVENUE, DOES IT AUTOMATICALLY MAXIMIZE PROFIT TOO?

We assume that all firms, whether price searchers or price takers, seek to maximize profit. Many of us easily fall into the trap of thinking that the price that maximizes revenue is necessarily the price that maximizes profit. But this is the case only when a firm has no variable costs, as we explain in the following paragraph.

Profit is the difference between total revenue and total cost: profit = $TR − TC$. If a firm has no variable costs, then total cost equals total fixed cost (remember that fixed cost is constant as output changes). Thus, if a firm has no variable costs, profit can be written as the difference between total revenue and total fixed cost: profit = $TR − TFC$ because $TC = TFC$. It follows that maximizing total revenue is the same as maximizing profit; every time total revenue increases, the difference between it and total cost (total fixed cost)—that is, profit—increases too.

We conclude that maximizing revenue is the same as maximizing profit only when a firm has no variable costs. It is unlikely, though, that a firm will be without variable costs. In the numerous cases in which variable costs exist, the price that maximizes revenue is not the same as the price that maximizes profit.

PRICE AND OUTPUT FOR A PROFIT-MAXIMIZING MONOPOLIST

The monopolist that seeks to maximize profit produces the quantity of output at which $MR = MC$ (as did the profit-maximizing perfectly competitive firm) and *charges the highest price per unit at which this quantity of output can be sold.*

exhibit 2

Demand and Marginal Revenue Curves

The demand curve plots price and quantity. The marginal revenue curve plots marginal revenue and quantity. For a monopolist $P > MR$, so the marginal revenue curve must lie below the demand curve. (Note that when a demand curve is a straight line, the marginal revenue curve bisects the horizontal axis halfway between the origin and the point where the demand curve intersects the horizontal axis.)

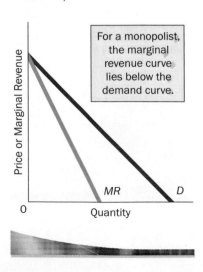

For a monopolist, the marginal revenue curve lies below the demand curve.

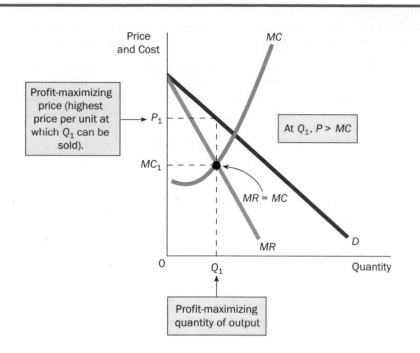

exhibit 3

The Monopolist's Profit-Maximizing Price and Quantity of Output
The monopolist produces the quantity of output (Q_1) at which $MR = MC$, and charges the highest price per unit at which this quantity of output can be sold (P_1). Notice that at the profit-maximizing quantity of output, price is greater than marginal cost, $P > MC$.

In Exhibit 3, the highest price at which Q_1, the quantity at which $MR = MC$, can be sold is P_1. Notice that at Q_1, the monopolist charges a price that is greater than marginal cost, $P > MC$. In other words, the monopolist is *not* resource allocative efficient.

Whether profits are earned depends on whether P_1 is greater or less than average total cost at Q_1. In short, the profit-maximizing price may be the loss-minimizing price. Both monopoly profits and monopoly losses are illustrated in Exhibit 4.

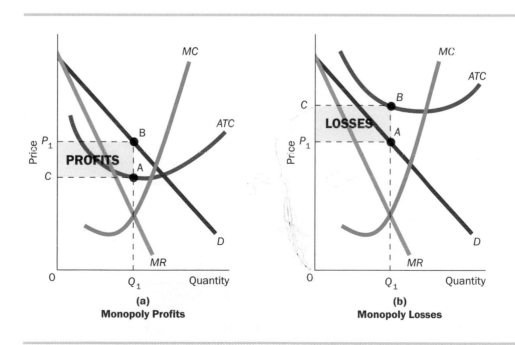

(a)
Monopoly Profits

(b)
Monopoly Losses

exhibit 4

Monopoly Profits and Losses
A monopoly seller is not guaranteed any profits. In (a), price is above average total cost at Q_1, the quantity of output at which $MR = MC$. Therefore, TR (the area $0P_1BQ_1$) is greater than TC (the area $0CAQ_1$), and profits equal the area CP_1BA. In (b), price is below average total cost at Q_1. Therefore, TR (the area $0P_1AQ_1$) is less than TC (the area $0CBQ_1$), and losses equal the area P_1CBA.

Q: Isn't it unrealistic to suggest that the monopolist can take a loss? After all, if the monopolist is the only seller in the industry, how can it take a loss?

A: Just because a firm is the only seller of a particular product does not guarantee it will earn profits. Remember, a monopolist cannot charge any price it wants for its good; it charges the highest price that the demand curve allows it to charge. In some instances, the highest price may be lower than its average total costs (unit costs). If so, there is a loss.

DIFFERENCES BETWEEN PERFECT COMPETITION AND MONOPOLY

There are some important differences between perfect competition and monopoly. Two of these differences are:

1. For the perfectly competitive firm, $P = MR$; for the monopolist, $P > MR$. The perfectly competitive firm's demand curve is its marginal revenue curve; the monopolist's demand curve lies above its marginal revenue curve.
2. The perfectly competitive firm charges a price equal to marginal cost; the monopolist charges a price greater than marginal cost.

Perfect competition: $P = MR$ and $P = MC$

Monopoly: $P > MR$ and $P > MC$

MONOPOLY, PERFECT COMPETITION, AND CONSUMERS' SURPLUS

A monopoly firm differs from a perfectly competitive firm in terms of how much consumers' surplus buyers receive. To illustrate, consider Exhibit 5, which shows a downward-sloping market demand curve, a downward-sloping marginal revenue curve, and a horizontal marginal cost (MC) curve. Although you are used to seeing upward-sloping marginal cost curves, there is nothing to prevent marginal cost from being constant over some range of output. A horizontal MC curve simply means that marginal cost is constant. If the market in Exhibit 5 is perfectly competitive, the demand curve *is* the marginal revenue curve. Therefore, the

---

exhibit 5

Monopoly, Perfect Competition, and Consumers' Surplus

If the market in the exhibit is perfectly competitive, the demand curve is the marginal revenue curve. The profit-maximizing output is Q_{PC} and price is P_{PC}. Consumers' surplus is the area $P_{PC}AB$. If the market is a monopoly market, the profit-maximizing output is Q_M and price is P_M. In this case, consumers' surplus is the area $P_M AC$. Consumers' surplus is greater in perfect competition than in monopoly; it is greater by the area $P_{PC}P_M CB$.

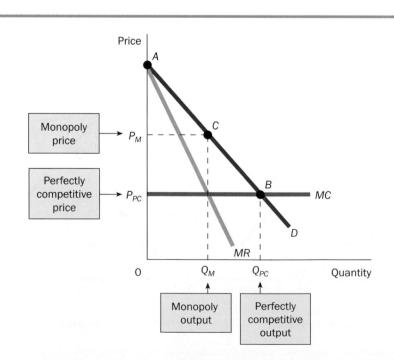

profit-maximizing output is Q_{PC}.[2] The buyer will pay P_{PC} per unit of the good. Consumers' surplus is the area under the demand curve and above the price. For the perfectly competitive firm, consumers' surplus is the area $P_{PC}AB$.

Now suppose the market is a monopoly market. In this case, the demand curve and the marginal revenue curve are different. The profit-maximizing output is where the MR curve intersects the MC curve; thus, the profit-maximizing output is Q_M. The price the buyer pays is P_M. Consumers' surplus in the monopoly case is P_MAC.

Obviously, consumers' surplus is greater in the perfectly competitive case than in the monopoly case. How much greater? It is greater by the area $P_{PC}P_MCB$. Stated differently, this is the loss in consumers' surplus due to monopolization.

Self-Test

1. Why does the monopolist's demand curve lie above its marginal revenue curve?
2. Is a monopolist guaranteed to earn profits?
3. Is a monopolist resource allocative efficient?
4. A monopolist is a price searcher. Why do you think it is called a price searcher? What is it searching for?

THE CASE AGAINST MONOPOLY

Monopoly is often said to be inefficient in comparison with perfect competition. This section examines some of the shortcomings associated with monopoly.

THE DEADWEIGHT LOSS OF MONOPOLY

Exhibit 6 shows demand, marginal revenue, marginal cost, and average total cost curves. We have made the simplifying assumption that the product is produced under constant-cost conditions; as a consequence, marginal cost equals long-run average total cost.

If the product is produced under perfect competition, output Q_{PC} is produced and is sold at a price of P_{PC}. At the competitive equilibrium output level, $P = MC$.

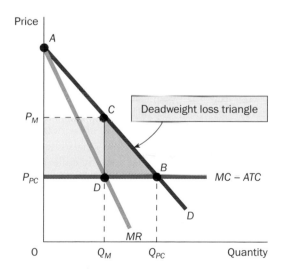

exhibit 6

Deadweight Loss and Rent Seeking as Costs of Monopoly
The monopolist produces Q_M, and the perfectly competitive firm produces the higher output level Q_{PC}. The deadweight loss of monopoly is the triangle (DCB) between these two levels of output. Rent-seeking activity is directed to obtaining the monopoly profits, represented by the area $P_{PC}P_MCD$. Rent seeking is a socially wasteful activity because resources are expended to transfer income rather than to produce goods and services.

---

2. Keep in mind that we are looking at the market demand curve, not the firm's demand curve. That is why the demand curve is downward-sloping. All market demand curves are downward-sloping.

If the product is produced under monopoly, output Q_M is produced and is sold at a price of P_M. At the monopoly equilibrium, $P > MC$.

Greater output is produced under perfect competition than under monopoly. The net value of the difference in these two output levels is said to be the **deadweight loss of monopoly.** In Exhibit 6, the value to buyers of increasing output from Q_M to Q_{PC} is equal to the maximum amount they would pay for this increase in output. This amount is designated by the area $Q_M CBQ_{PC}$. The costs that would have to be incurred to produce this additional output are designated by the area $Q_M DBQ_{PC}$. The difference between the two is the triangle DCB. *This is the amount buyers value the additional output over and above the costs of producing the additional output.* It is the loss attached to not producing the competitive quantity of output. The triangle DCB is referred to as the *deadweight loss triangle.*

We conclude that monopoly produces a quantity of output that is "too small" in comparison to the quantity of output produced in perfect competition. This difference in output results in a welfare loss to society.

Arnold Harberger was the first economist who tried to determine the actual size of the deadweight loss cost of monopoly in the manufacturing sector of the U.S. economy. He estimated the deadweight loss to be a small percentage of the economy's total output. Additional empirical work by other economists puts the figure at approximately 1 percent of total output.

RENT SEEKING

Sometimes individuals and groups try to influence public policy in the hope of redistributing (transferring) income from others to themselves. To illustrate, look again at the perfectly competitive outcome in Exhibit 6. The market produces Q_{PC} output and charges a price of P_{PC}.

Suppose one of the many firms that is currently producing some of Q_{PC} asks the government to grant it a monopoly. In other words, of the, say, 100 firms currently producing Q_{PC}, one firm, firm A, asks the government to prevent the 99 remaining firms from competing with it. Let's consider the benefits for firm A of becoming a monopolist. Currently, it is earning zero economic profit because it is selling at a price that equals ATC. If it becomes a monopolist, though, it will earn profits equal to the area $P_{PC}P_M CD$ in Exhibit 6. These profits are the result of a *transfer* from buyers to the monopolist.

To see this, let's go back to our discussion of consumers' surplus. If the market in Exhibit 6 is perfectly competitive, consumers' surplus is equal to the area $P_{PC}AB$; if the market is monopolized, consumers' surplus is equal to the area $P_M AC$. The difference is the area $P_{PC}P_M CB$. In other words, this area represents the loss in consumers' surplus if the market is monopolized. Part of this area—$P_{PC}P_M CD$—is transferred to the monopolist in terms of profits. In other words, if the market is monopolized, part of the consumers' surplus that is lost to buyers becomes profits for the monopolist. (The other part is the deadweight loss of monopoly, identified by the deadweight loss triangle.)

If firm A tries to get the government to transfer "income" or consumers' surplus from buyers to itself it is undertaking a *transfer-seeking activity.* In economics, these transfer-seeking activities are usually called **rent seeking.** In other words, firm A is rent seeking.[3]

Economist Gordon Tullock has made the point that rent-seeking behavior is individually rational but socially wasteful. To see why, let's say the profits in

---

3. The word "rent" usually confuses people. In everyday life, *rent* refers to the payment for an apartment, etc. In economics, rent, or more formally, economic rent, is a payment in excess of opportunity cost. The term *rent seeking* was introduced into economics by economist Anne Krueger in her article "The Political Economy of the Rent-Seeking Society," *American Economic Review* 64 (June 1974): 291–303.

Exhibit 6 are equal to $10 million. In other words, the area $P_{PC}P_MCD$ is equal to $10 million. Firm A wants the $10 million in profits, so it asks the government for a monopoly favor. In other words, it wants the government to prevent 99 firms from competing with it.

Firm A will not get its monopoly privilege simply by asking for it. It will have to spend money and time to convince government officials that it should be given this monopoly privilege. It will have to hire lobbyists, take politicians and other government officials to dinner, perhaps give donations to certain politicians. In other words, firm A will have to spend resources to get what it wants. All the resources firm A uses to try to bring about a transfer from buyers to itself are wasted, says Tullock. How so? Well, resources used to bring about a transfer can't be used to produce shoes, computers, television sets, and many other things that people would like to buy. The resources simply go to try to transfer income from one party to another. They don't go to produce goods and services.

Ask yourself what society would look like if no one produced anything, but only invested time and money in rent seeking. Jones would try to get what is Smith's, Smith would try to get what is Brown's, and Brown would try to get what is Thompson's. No one would produce anything; everyone would simply spend time and money trying to get what currently belongs to someone else. In this world, who would produce the food, the computers, and the cars? The answer is no one.

Tullock makes the point that the resource cost of rent seeking should be added to the deadweight loss of monopoly. In other words, according to Tullock, the overall cost of monopoly to society is higher than anyone initially thought.

THINKING LIKE AN ECONOMIST

Here is an economics joke: Two economists are walking down the street. One sees a $10 bill lying on the sidewalk and asks, "Isn't that a $10 bill?" "Obviously not," says the other. "If it were, someone would have already picked it up."

This joke tells us something about how economists think. Specifically, economists believe that if the opportunity for gain exists, it won't last long because someone will grab it—quickly. By the time you come along, it's gone.

Think of this in terms of what Gordon Tullock has said about monopoly. As a seller, being a monopolist is better than being a competitive firm. In other words, a monopoly position is "worth something." It is like a $10 bill lying on the sidewalk. Just as people will pick up a $10 bill on the sidewalk, they'll try to become monopolists.

This brings up the whole topic of rent seeking, to which Tullock first called our attention. Just as people will bend down to pick up the $10 bill, so will they invest resources in an attempt to capture the monopoly rents. In other words, no opportunity for gain is likely to be ignored.

X-INEFFICIENCY

Economist Harvey Leibenstein maintains that the monopolist is not under pressure to produce its product at the lowest possible cost. The monopolist can produce its product above the lowest possible unit cost and still survive. Certainly, the monopolist benefits if it can and does lower its costs, but the point is that it doesn't have to in order to survive (with the proviso that average total costs cannot rise so high as to be higher than price). Leibenstein refers to a monopolist operating at higher than the lowest possible cost, and to the organizational slack that is directly tied to this, as **X-inefficiency.**

It is hard to obtain accurate estimates of X-inefficiency, but whatever its magnitude, there are forces working to mitigate it. For example, if a market monopoly is being run inefficiently, other people realizing this may attempt to buy the monopoly and, if successful, lower costs to make higher profits.

X-Inefficiency
The increase in costs and organizational slack in a monopoly resulting from the lack of competitive pressure to push costs down to their lowest possible level.

PRICE DISCRIMINATION

In our discussions about monopoly, we have assumed that the monopoly seller sells all units of its product for the same price (it is a single-price monopolist). However, this is not always the case. Under certain conditions, a monopolist could practice **price discrimination.** This occurs when the seller charges different prices for the product it sells, and the price differences do not reflect cost differences.

TYPES OF PRICE DISCRIMINATION

There are three types of price discrimination: perfect price discrimination, second-degree price discrimination, and third-degree price discrimination.

Suppose a monopolist produces and sells 1,000 units of good X. If it sells each unit separately and charges the highest price each consumer would be willing to pay for the product rather than go without it, the monopolist is said to practice **perfect price discrimination.** This is sometimes called *discrimination among units.*

If it charges a uniform price per unit for one specific quantity, a lower price for an additional quantity, and so on, the monopolist practices **second-degree price discrimination.** This is sometimes called *discrimination among quantities.* For example, the monopolist might sell the first 10 units for $10 each, the next 20 units at $9 each, and so on.

If it charges a different price in different markets or charges a different price to different segments of the buying population, the monopolist practices **third-degree price discrimination.** This is sometimes called *discrimination among buyers.* For example, if your local pharmacy charges senior citizens lower prices for medicine than it charges nonsenior citizens, it practices third-degree price discrimination.

WHY A MONOPOLIST WANTS TO PRICE DISCRIMINATE

Suppose these are the maximum prices at which the following units of a product can be sold: first unit, $10; second unit, $9; third unit, $8; fourth unit, $7. If the monopolist wants to sell four units, and it charges the same price for each unit (it is a single-price monopolist), its total revenue is $28 ($7 × 4).

Now suppose the monopolist can and does practice perfect price discrimination. It charges $10 for the first unit, $9 for the second unit, $8 for the third unit, and $7 for the fourth unit. Its total revenue is $34 ($10 + $9 + $8 + $7). A comparison of total revenue when the monopolist does and does not price discriminate explains why the monopolist would want to price discriminate. A perfectly price-discriminating monopolist receives the maximum price for each unit of the good it sells; a single-price monopolist does not.

For the monopolist who practices perfect price discrimination, price equals marginal revenue, $P = MR$. To illustrate, when the monopolist sells its second unit for $9 (having sold the first unit for $10), its total revenue is $19—or its marginal revenue is $9, which is equal to price.

CONDITIONS OF PRICE DISCRIMINATION

It is obvious why the monopolist would want to price discriminate. But what conditions must exist before it can? To price discriminate, the following conditions must hold:

1. The seller must exercise some control over price; it must be a price searcher.
2. The seller must be able to distinguish among buyers who would be willing to pay different prices.
3. It must be impossible or too costly for one buyer to resell the good to other buyers. The possibility of **arbitrage,** or "buying low and selling high," must not exist.

Price Discrimination
Occurs when the seller charges different prices for the product it sells, and the price differences do not reflect cost differences.

Perfect Price Discrimination
Occurs when the seller charges the highest price each consumer would be willing to pay for the product rather than go without it.

Second-Degree Price Discrimination
Occurs when the seller charges a uniform price per unit for one specific quantity, a lower price for an additional quantity, and so on.

Third-Degree Price Discrimination
Occurs when the seller charges different prices in different markets or charges a different price to different segments of the buying population.

Arbitrage
Buying a good in a market where its price is low and selling the good in another market where its price is higher.

Why Do District Attorneys Plea Bargain?

On the television series "Law & Order," the assistant district attorney often offers the accused a chance to plead to a lesser charge in return for providing information about a crime or for agreeing to testify against someone. In short, the assistant district attorneys on "Law & Order" are willing to plea bargain.

To some people, a district attorney who plea bargains is similar to a seller who price discriminates. Let's analyze plea bargaining to see whether or not this is true. Suppose two people, Smith and Jones, have committed the same crime. The district attorney has the same type and amount of evidence against each person, and the chance of a successful prosecution is approximately the same for each case. A successful prosecution will end in each person going to prison for 25 years.

Now suppose the district attorney offers Smith a plea bargain. In exchange for Smith's testimony against someone the DA's office has been after for a long time, Smith will be charged with a lesser crime and will have to serve only 5 years in prison. Thus, Smith can pay a smaller price for his crime than Jones must pay. In other words, each person commits the same crime and each has an equal chance of being successfully prosecuted for that crime, but Smith (if he accepts the plea bargain) will serve 5 years in prison and Jones will serve 25 years in prison.

Do district attorneys want to plea bargain for a reason analogous to why sellers want to price discriminate?[4] A seller wants to price discriminate because it raises her total revenue without affecting her costs. Recall the example in the text: $10 is the highest price at which the first unit of a good can be sold, $9 is the highest price for the second unit, $8 is the highest price for the third unit, and $7 is the highest for the fourth unit. A single-price monopolist that wants to sell 4 units of the good charges a price of $7 per unit and earns total revenue of $28. But a perfectly price-discriminating monopolist charges the highest price per unit and gains total revenue of $34. In other words, price discrimination leads to higher total revenue.

District attorneys do not want to maximize total revenue, but they may want to maximize the number of successfully prosecuted crimes given certain budget constraints. Just as price discrimination leads to higher total revenue, plea bargaining may lead to more successfully prosecuted crimes. Let's consider Smith and Jones again. Each has committed the same crime. Without a plea bargain, each person goes to prison for 25 years. But if the DA offers Smith 5 years and, in return, Smith helps the DA send Brown to prison, then because of the plea bargain three crimes are successfully prosecuted—the crimes committed by Smith, Jones, and Brown.

Finally, just as certain conditions have to be met before a seller can price discriminate, certain conditions have to be satisfied before district attorneys can plea bargain successfully.

To price discriminate, a seller must exercise some control over the price of the product she sells. To plea bargain, a district attorney has to exercise some control over the sentence for the accused. In reality, district attorneys do exercise some control over sentences because they largely control the charges against the accused. If they reduce the charges (say from murder to manslaughter), they automatically affect the sentence.

A seller who price discriminates has to be able to distinguish between customers who would be willing to pay different prices for the good she sells. Similarly, a district attorney has to be able to distinguish between accused persons who do and do not have something to "sell" to the authorities. District attorneys seem to be able to do this. In many cases, the accused person who has something to "sell" will say so.

Finally, for price discrimination to exist, arbitrage has to be impossible or too costly. Obviously, it is impossible to resell a plea bargain.

---

4. Be careful here. We are not saying that a plea bargain is an act of price discrimination, broadly defined. We are saying that there are similarities between why sellers want to price discriminate and why district attorneys want to plea bargain. Later in the feature, we explain that, just as there are certain conditions that need to be met in order to price discriminate, there are certain conditions that need to be met in order for district attorneys to offer plea bargains—and there seems to be rough similarity between the two sets of conditions.

If the seller is not a price searcher, it has no control over price and therefore cannot sell a good at different prices to different buyers. Also, unless the seller can distinguish among buyers who would pay different prices, it cannot price discriminate. After all, how would it know to whom to charge the higher (lower) prices? Finally, if a buyer can resell the good, there can be no price discrimination because buyers who buy the good at a lower price will simply turn around and sell the good to other buyers for a price lower than the seller's higher price. In time, no one will pay the higher price.

MOVING TO $P = MC$ THROUGH PRICE DISCRIMINATION

The perfectly competitive firm exhibits resource allocative efficiency; it produces the quantity of output at which $P = MC$. The single-price monopolist produces the quantity of output at which $P > MC$. The single-price monopolist produces an inefficient level of output. But what about the monopolist that can and does practice perfect price discrimination? Does it, too, produce an inefficient level of output?

The answer is no. A perfectly price-discriminating monopolist does not lower price on all previous units in order to sell an additional unit of its product. For it, $P = MR$ (as is the case for the perfectly competitive firm). Naturally, when the perfectly price-discriminating monopolist produces the quantity of output at which $MR = MC$, it automatically produces the quantity where $P = MC$. In short, the perfectly price-discriminating monopolist and the perfectly competitive firm both exhibit resource allocative efficiency.

Some important points are reviewed in Exhibit 7. In part (a), the perfectly competitive firm produces where $P = MC$. In part (b), the single-price monopolist produces where $P > MC$. In part (c), the perfectly price-discriminating monopolist produces where $P = MC$. Notice one important difference between the perfectly competitive firm and the perfectly price-discriminating monopolist. Although both produce where $P = MC$, the perfectly competitive firm charges the same price for each unit of the good it sells and the perfectly price-discriminating monopolist charges a different price for each unit of the good it sells.

exhibit 7

Comparison of a Perfectly Competitive Firm, Single-Price Monopolist, and Perfectly Price-Discriminating Monopolist

For both the perfectly competitive firm and the perfectly price-discriminating monopolist, $P = MR$ and the demand curve is the marginal revenue curve. Both produce where $P = MC$. The single-price monopolist, however, produces where $P > MC$ because for it $P > MR$ and its demand curve lies above its marginal revenue curve. One difference between the perfectly competitive firm and the perfectly price-discriminating monopolist is that the former charges the same price for each unit of the good it sells and the latter charges a different price for each unit of the good it sells.

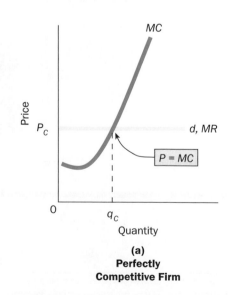

(a)
Perfectly Competitive Firm

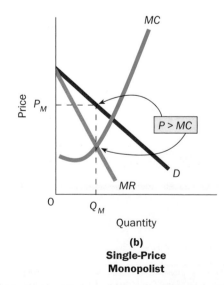

(b)
Single-Price Monopolist

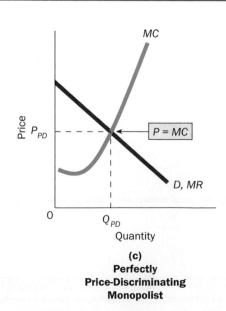

(c)
Perfectly Price-Discriminating Monopolist

Q: Suppose a firm charges one person $40 for its product and charges another person only $33. Isn't the first person paying a higher price so that the second person can pay a lower price?

A: No, this is not the case. Suppose there are two persons, O'Neill and Stevens. The maximum price O'Neill will pay for good X is $40; the maximum price Stevens will pay for good X is $33. If a monopolist can and does perfectly price discriminate, it charges O'Neill $40 and Stevens $33.

Is O'Neill somehow paying the higher price so that Stevens can pay the lower price? It is easy to see that O'Neill is not by considering whether the monopolist would have charged O'Neill a price under $40 if Stevens's maximum price had been $39 instead of $33. Probably it wouldn't—why should it when it could have received O'Neill's maximum price of $40?

Our point is that the perfectly price-discriminating monopolist tries to get the highest price from each customer, irrespective of what other customers pay. In short, the price O'Neill is charged is independent of the price Stevens is charged.

YOU CAN HAVE THE COMICS, JUST GIVE ME THE COUPONS

Third-degree price discrimination, or discrimination among buyers, is sometimes employed through the use of cents-off coupons. (Remember that third-degree price discrimination exists if a seller sells the same product at different prices to different segments of the population.)

One of the conditions of price discrimination is that the seller has to be able to distinguish among customers who would be willing to pay different prices. Would people who value their time highly be willing to pay a higher price for a product than people who do not? Some sellers think so. They argue that people who place a high value on their time want to economize on the shopping time connected with the purchase of the product. If sellers want to price discriminate between these two types of customers—charging more to customers who value time more and charging less to customers who value time less—they must determine the category into which each of their customers falls.

How would you go about this if you were a seller? What many real-world sellers do is place cents-off coupons in newspapers and magazines. They hypothesize that people who value their time relatively low are willing to spend it clipping and sorting coupons. People who place a relatively high value on their time are not.

In effect, things work much like this in, say, a grocery store:

1. The posted price for all products is the same for all customers.
2. Both Linda and Josh put product X in their shopping carts.
3. When Linda gets to the checkout counter, the clerk asks, "Do you have any coupons today?" Linda says no. She is therefore charged the posted price for all products, including X.
4. When Josh gets to the checkout counter, the clerk asks, "Do you have any coupons today?" Josh says yes and gives the clerk a coupon for product X. Josh pays a lower price for product X than Linda pays.

In conclusion, one of the uses of the cents-off coupon is to make it possible for the seller to charge a higher price to one group of customers than to another group. (We say one of the uses because cents-off coupons are also used to induce customers to try a product and so forth.)

Self-Test

1. What are some of the "costs" or shortcomings of monopoly?
2. What is the deadweight loss of monopoly?
3. Why must a seller be a price searcher (among other things) before he can price discriminate?

Do Colleges and Universities Price Discriminate?

At the university I attend, scholarships are given to students with low incomes, excellent grades, or athletic ability. Are these scholarships a form of price discrimination?

Let's ask this question: Do scholarships to these types of students (low income, high academic ability, high athletic ability) satisfy the definition of price discrimination? The low-income student might not come to the university unless he or she receives a lower tuition price (than other students pay). In other words, the university price discriminates because the scholarship, in effect, reduces the tuition the low-income student has to pay. The excellent student and the athlete have numerous universities competing for them. In other words, both have a high elasticity of demand for education at a given university because they have so many substitutes (other universities) from which to choose. Consequently, a university will have to offer them a lower tuition price to secure them as students. The university price discriminates through an academic scholarship for the excellent student and an athletic scholarship for the athlete.

Now, let's consider whether or not the university meets the conditions of a price discriminator. First, it is a price searcher. Not all universities are alike, nor do they sell a homogeneous good as they would in the case of perfect competition (price taker).

Second, the university can distinguish between students (customers) who would be willing to pay different prices. For example, the student with few universities seeking him would probably be willing to pay more than the student with many options.

Third, the service being purchased cannot be resold to someone else. For example, it is difficult to resell an economics lecture. You could, of course, tell someone what was covered in the lecture, perhaps for a small payment or a promise to do the same for you at a later time, but this would be similar to telling someone about a movie instead of the person seeing the movie herself. It is often difficult or impossible to resell something that is consumed on the premises.

Chapter Summary

The Theory of Monopoly

- The theory of monopoly is built on three assumptions: (1) There is one seller. (2) The single seller sells a product for which there are no close substitutes. (3) There are extremely high barriers to entry into the industry.
- High barriers to entry may take the form of legal barriers (public franchise, patent, government license), economies of scale, or exclusive ownership of a scarce resource.

Monopoly Pricing and Output

- The profit-maximizing monopolist produces the quantity of output at which $MR = MC$ and charges the highest price per unit at which this quantity of output can be sold.
- For the single-price monopolist, $P > MR$; therefore, its demand curve lies above its marginal revenue curve.
- The single-price monopolist sells its output at a price higher than its marginal cost, $P > MC$, and therefore is *not* resource allocative efficient.

- Consider a perfectly competitive market and a monopoly market, each with the same demand and marginal cost curves. Consumers' surplus is greater in the perfectly competitive market.

Rent Seeking

- Activity directed at competing for and obtaining transfers is referred to as rent seeking. From society's perspective, rent seeking is a socially wasteful activity. People use resources to bring about a transfer of income from others to themselves instead of producing goods and services.

Price Discrimination

- Price discrimination occurs when a seller charges different prices for its product and the price differences are not due to cost differences.
- Before a seller can price discriminate, certain conditions must hold: (1) The seller must be a price searcher. (2) The seller must be able to distinguish among customers who would be willing to pay dif-

ferent prices. (3) It must be impossible or too costly for a buyer to resell the good to others.

- A seller that practices perfect price discrimination (charges the maximum price for each unit of product sold) sells the quantity of output at which $P = MC$. It exhibits resource allocative efficiency.

- The single-price monopolist is said to produce too little output because it produces less than would be produced under perfect competition. This is not the case for a perfectly price-discriminating monopolist.

Key Terms and Concepts

Monopoly
Public Franchise
Natural Monopoly
Price Searcher

Deadweight Loss of Monopoly
Rent Seeking
X-Inefficiency
Price Discrimination

Perfect Price Discrimination
Second-Degree Price Discrimination
Third-Degree Price Discrimination
Arbitrage

Questions and Problems

1. The perfectly competitive firm exhibits resource allocative efficiency ($P = MC$), but the single-price monopolist does not. What is the reason for this difference?

2. Because the monopolist is a single seller of a product with no close substitutes, is it able to obtain any price for its good that it wants?

3. When a single-price monopolist maximizes profits, price is greater than marginal cost. This means that buyers would be willing to pay more for additional units of output than the units cost to produce. Given this, why doesn't the monopolist produce more?

4. Is there a deadweight loss if the firm produces the quantity of output at which price equals marginal cost? Explain.

5. It has been noted that rent seeking is individually rational, but socially wasteful. Explain.

6. Occasionally, students accuse their instructors, rightly or wrongly, of practicing grade discrimination. These students claim that the instructor "charges" some students a higher price for a given grade than he or she "charges" other students (by requiring some students to do more or better work). Unlike price discrimination, grade discrimination involves no money. Discuss the similarities and differences between the two types of discrimination. Which do you prefer less or perhaps dislike more? Why?

7. Make a list of real-world price discrimination practices. Do they meet the conditions posited for price discrimination?

8. For many years in California, car washes would advertise "Ladies Day." On one day during the week, a woman could have her car washed for a price lower than a man could have his car washed. Some people argued that this was a form of sexual discrimination. A California court accepted the argument and ruled that car washes could no longer have a "Ladies Day." Do you think this was a case of sexual discrimination or price discrimination? Explain your answer.

9. Make a list of market monopolies and a list of government monopolies. Which list is longer? Why do you think this is so?

10. Fast-food stores often charge higher prices for their products in high-crime areas than they charge in low-crime areas. Is this an act of price discrimination? Why or why not?

11. In general, coupons are more common on small-ticket items than they are on big-ticket items. Explain why.

12. A firm maximizes its total revenue. Does it follow that it has automatically maximized its profit too?

13. If the benefits to consumers of producing more output are greater than the costs to the monopoly firm of producing the additional output, then why doesn't the monopoly firm produce the greater output and eliminate the deadweight loss of monopoly?

1. Draw a graph that shows a monopoly firm incurring losses.

2. A monopoly firm is currently earning positive economic profit. The owner of the firm decides to sell it. He asks for a price that takes into account the economic profit. Explain and diagrammatically show what this does to the average total cost (*ATC*) curve of the firm.

3. Suppose a single-price monopolist sells its output (Q_1) at P_1. Then it raises its price to P_2 and its output falls to Q_2. In terms of *P*'s and *Q*'s, what does marginal revenue equal?

Use the following figure to answer questions 4–6.

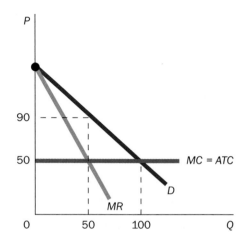

4. If the market is perfectly competitive, what does profit equal?

5. If the market is a monopoly market, what does profit equal?

6. Redraw the figure and label consumers' surplus when the market is perfectly competitive and when it is monopolized.

1. Go to *http://www.aims.ca/commentary/conversation.htm* and read the interview with James M. Buchanan. How does he define rent seeking? How does he suggest we eliminate or reduce rent seeking?

2. Go to *http://www.virtualschool.edu/cox/HuberForbes.html* and read the article "Two Cheers for Price Discrimi-

nation." How does the author define "efficient price"? How did the Supreme Court rule in the IBM case?

3. Go to *http://www4.law.cornell.edu/uscode/35/pI.html* and click on "Patent Fees." What is the filing fee for an original patent?

Log on to the Arnold Xtra! Web site now (*http://arnoldxtra.swcollege.com*) for additional learning resources such as practice quizzes, help with graphing, video clips, and current event applications.

ch.11

MONOPOLISTIC COMPETITION, OLIGOPOLY, AND GAME THEORY

How do firms in a market act toward each other? Are they fiercely competitive, much as runners are in a race? Do they act as if it's a race to the finish line and only one can be the winner? Or do firms act like people strolling in a park on a warm spring day? Do they behave as if they haven't a care in the world? Competition? Forget it. There are just too many casualties in competitive races. As you read this chapter, keep these two images in your mind. And keep two words in mind as well: competition and collusion. This chapter is about both.

Chapter Road Map

A monopoly firm is a price searcher—a seller that has the ability to control to some degree the price of the product it sells. The monopolistic competitive firm and the oligopoly firm are also price searchers.

We begin this chapter by outlining the theory of monopolistic competition, identifying both the demand curve and marginal revenue curve for the monopolistic competitive firm, discussing how the firm maximizes profit, and so on. Then, we discuss oligopoly. Instead of presenting one theory of oligopoly, we present three: the cartel theory, the kinked demand curve theory, and the price leadership theory. We also discuss strategic behavior in the context of oligopoly, which brings us to a discussion of game theory. We examine one particular game in game theory—the prisoner's dilemma. The last section of the chapter presents a few applications of the prisoner's dilemma.

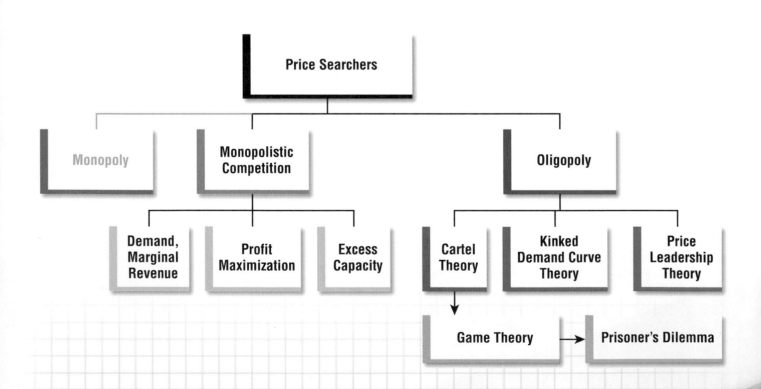

THE THEORY OF MONOPOLISTIC COMPETITION

The theory of **monopolistic competition** is built on three assumptions:

Monopolistic Competition
A theory of market structure based on three assumptions: many sellers and buyers, firms producing and selling slightly differentiated products, and easy entry and exit.

1. **There are many sellers and buyers.** This assumption holds for perfect competition too. For this reason, you might think the monopolistic competitor should be a price taker, but this is not the case. It is a price searcher, basically because of the next assumption.

2. **Each firm (in the industry) produces and sells a slightly differentiated product.** Differences among the products may be due to brand names, packaging, location, credit terms connected with the sale of the product, friendliness of the salespeople, and so forth. Product differentiation may be real or imagined. For example, aspirin may be aspirin, but if some people view a name-brand aspirin (such as Bayer) as better than a generic brand, product differentiation exists.

3. **There is easy entry and exit.** Monopolistic competition resembles perfect competition in this respect. There are no barriers to entry and exit, legal or otherwise.

Examples of monopolistic competition include retail clothing, computer software, restaurants, and service stations.

THE MONOPOLISTIC COMPETITOR'S DEMAND CURVE

The perfectly competitive firm has many rivals, all producing the same good, and so there are an endless number of substitutes for the good it produces. The elasticity of demand for its product is extremely high; so high, in fact, that the demand curve it faces is horizontal (for all practical purposes).

The monopoly firm has practically no rivals, and it produces a good for which there are no substitutes. The elasticity of demand for its product is low, and its downward-sloping demand curve reflects this fact.

What is the situation for the monopolistic competitor? Like the perfectly competitive firm, it has many rivals. But unlike the perfectly competitive firm, its rivals don't sell exactly the same product it sells. In other words, there are substitutes for its product, but not perfect substitutes. Because of this, the elasticity of demand for its product is not so great as that of the perfectly competitive firm. Nor does its demand curve look like the demand curve faced by the perfectly competitive firm. The monopolistic competitor's demand curve is not horizontal; instead, it is downward-sloping.

THE RELATIONSHIP BETWEEN PRICE AND MARGINAL REVENUE FOR A MONOPOLISTIC COMPETITOR

Because a monopolistic competitor faces a downward-sloping demand curve, it has to lower price to sell an additional unit of the good it produces. For example, let's say that it can sell 3 units at $10 each but that it has to lower its price to $9 to sell 4 units. It follows that its marginal revenue is $6 (total revenue at 3 units is $30 and total revenue at 4 units is $36), which is below its price of $9. In other words, for the monopolistic competitor $P > MR$.

HOW MUCH OUTPUT WILL THE MONOPOLISTIC COMPETITOR PRODUCE? WHAT PRICE WILL IT CHARGE?

The monopolistic competitive firm is the same as both the perfectly competitive firm and the monopoly firm in one regard. It produces the quantity of output at which $MR = MC$. We see this in Exhibit 1, where the firm produces q_1. What price does the monopolistic competitor charge for this quantity? Answer: The highest price it can charge. This is P_1 in the exhibit.

exhibit 1

The Monopolistic Competitive Output and Price

The monopolistic competitor produces that quantity of output for which $MR = MC$. This is q_1 in the exhibit. It charges the highest price consistent with this quantity, which is P_1.

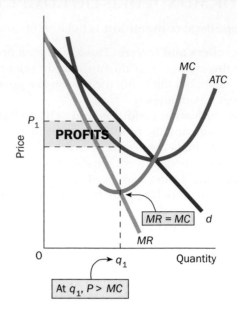

At q_1, $P > MC$

THE RELATIONSHIP BETWEEN PRICE AND MARGINAL COST FOR THE MONOPOLISTIC COMPETITOR

For the monopolistic competitor, $P > MR$. Also, the monopolistic competitor produces the quantity of output at which $MR = MC$. It follows that it must produce a level of output at which price is greater than marginal cost, $P > MC$. (This is obvious in Exhibit 1.) When a firm does not produce where $P = MC$, it does not produce the resource allocative efficient output. So, the monopolistic competitor does not exhibit resource allocative efficiency.

WILL THERE BE PROFITS IN THE LONG RUN?

Suppose the firms in a monopolistic competitive market are currently earning profits, such as the firm in Exhibit 1. Will they continue to earn profits in the long run? Most likely, they won't. The assumption of easy entry and exit precludes this. If firms in the industry are earning profits, new firms will enter the industry and reduce the demand that each firm faces. In other words, the demand curve for each firm may shift to the left. Eventually, competition will reduce economic profits to zero in the long run, as shown for the monopolistic competitive firm in Exhibit 2.

Q & A

Q: To the question of whether firms will continue to earn profits in the long run, the answer was "Most likely, they won't." Why was the answer qualified by "most likely"? Why not simply "no"?

A: The answer was qualified by "most likely" because monopolistic competition differs from perfect competition, where short-run profits attract new firms that produce the *identical* product produced by existing firms in the industry. In monopolistic competition, new firms usually produce a close substitute for the product produced by existing firms. Is this enough of a difference to upset the zero economic profit condition in the long run? In some instances, it may be. An existing firm may differentiate its product sufficiently in the minds of the buyers that, although new firms enter the industry and compete with it, it still continues to earn profits.

Firms that try to differentiate their products from those of other sellers in ways other than price are said to be engaged in *nonprice competition*. This may take the form of advertising or of trying to establish a brand name that is well respected, among other things. For exam-

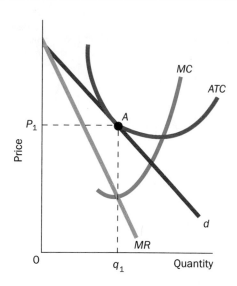

exhibit 2

Monopolistic Competition in the Long Run
Because of easy entry into the industry, there are likely to be zero economic profits in the long run for a monopolistic competitor. In other words, $P = ATC$.

ple, soft drink companies' advertising often tries to stress the uniqueness of their product. Dr. Pepper has been advertised as "the unusual one," 7-Up as "the uncola." Dell has a well-respected name in personal computers, Bayer in aspirin, Hilton in hotels. Such well-respected names sometimes sufficiently differentiate products in the minds of the buyers so that short-run profits are not easily, or completely, eliminated by the entry of new firms into the industry.

EXCESS CAPACITY: WHAT IS IT, AND IS IT "GOOD" OR "BAD"?

The theory of monopolistic competition makes one major prediction, which is generally referred to as the **excess capacity theorem.** It states that in equilibrium, a monopolistic competitor will produce an output smaller than the one that would minimize its unit costs of production.

To illustrate, look at point A in Exhibit 3a. At this point, the monopolistic competitor is in long-run equilibrium because profits are zero ($P = ATC$). Notice that point A *is not* the lowest point on the ATC curve. The lowest point on the average total cost curve is point L. We conclude that in long-run equilibrium, when the monopolistic competitor earns zero economic profits, it is not producing the quantity of output at which average total costs (unit costs) are minimized for the given scale of plant. Exhibit 3 contrasts the perfectly competitive firm and the monopolistic competitor in long-run equilibrium. In part (b), the perfectly competitive firm is earning zero economic profits, and price (P_{C_1}) equals average total cost (ATC). Furthermore, the point at which price equals average total cost (point L) is the lowest point on the ATC curve. In long-run equilibrium, the perfectly competitive firm produces the quantity of output at which unit costs are minimized.

Now look back at part (a). The monopolistic competitor is earning zero economic profits, and price (P_{MC_1}) equals average total cost. As previously noted, the monopolistic competitor does not produce the quantity of output at which unit costs are minimized. If it did, it would produce q_{MC_2}. For this reason, it has been argued that the monopolistic competitor produces "too little" output (q_{MC_1} instead of q_{MC_2}) and charges "too high" a price (P_{MC_1} instead of P_{MC_2}). With respect to the former, "too little" output translates into the monopolistic competitor underutilizing its present plant size. It is said to have *excess capacity.* In part (a), the excess capacity is equal to the difference between q_{MC_2} and q_{MC_1}.

It is sometimes argued that the monopolistic competitor operates at excess capacity because it faces a downward-sloping demand curve. Look once again at Exhibit 3a. The only way the firm would not operate at excess capacity is if its

Go to *http://www.vegas.com*. Search for "All" restaurants located on the "Strip" that have a price range of "$15 or less." How many restaurants did your search find? If you had included all price ranges, how many restaurants would your search have found? Do restaurants sell "slightly differentiated products"? Is the restaurant market a monopolistic competitive market?

Excess Capacity Theorem
States that a monopolistic competitor in equilibrium produces an output smaller than the one that would minimize its costs of production.

exhibit 3

A Comparison of Perfect Competition and Monopolistic Competition: The Issue of Excess Capacity

The perfectly competitive firm produces a quantity of output consistent with lowest unit costs. The monopolistic competitor does not. If it did, it would produce q_{MC_2} instead of q_{MC_1}. The monopolistic competitor is said to underutilize its plant size or to have excess capacity.

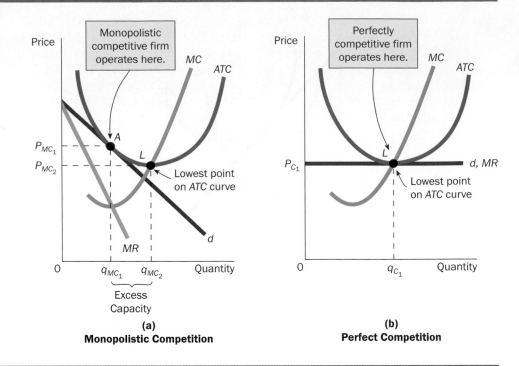

(a)
Monopolistic Competition

(b)
Perfect Competition

demand curve were tangent to the *ATC* curve at point *L*—the lowest point on the *ATC* curve. But for this to occur, the demand curve would have to be horizontal, which would require homogeneous products. It is impossible for a downward-sloping demand curve to be tangent to the *ATC* curve at point *L*.

In short, *the monopolistic competitor operates at excess capacity as a consequence of its downward-sloping demand curve,* and its downward-sloping demand curve is a consequence of differentiated products. We leave you with a question many economists ask, but do not always answer the same way: If excess capacity is the price we pay for differentiated products (more choice), is it too high a price?

Q & A

Q: The monopolistic competitor does not produce where $P = MC$, and it does not produce where $P =$ lowest *ATC*. In other words, the monopolistic competitor is neither resource allocative efficient nor productive efficient. Is this correct?

A: Yes, the monopolistic competitor exhibits neither resource allocative efficiency nor productive efficiency.

ADVERTISING AND DESIGNER LABELS

Suppose you own a business that is considered a monopolistic competitive firm. Your business is one of many sellers, you sell a product slightly differentiated from the products of your competitors, and there is easy entry into and exit from the industry. Would you rather your business were a monopoly firm instead? Wouldn't it be better for you to be the only seller of a product than to be one of many sellers? Most business owners would say yes, it is better to be a monopoly firm than a monopolistic competitive firm. This being the case, we consider how monopolistic competitors may try to become monopolists.

One possibility is through advertising. If a monopolistic competitor can, through advertising, persuade the buying public that her product is *more than just slightly differentiated* from those of her competitors, she stands a better chance of becoming a monopolist. (Remember, a monopolist produces a good for which there are no close substitutes.)

Consider an example. Many firms produce men's and women's jeans. To many people, the jeans produced by these firms look very much alike. How, then, does any one firm differentiate its product from the pack? It could add a "designer label" to the jeans to suggest that the jeans are unique—that they are the only Levi's jeans, for example. Or through advertising, it could try to persuade the buying public that its jeans are "the" jeans worn by the most famous, best-looking people living and vacationing in the most exciting places in the world.

We are not concerned here with whether the advertising is successful in meeting its objective. Our point is that firms sometimes use advertising to try to differentiate their products from their competitors' products.

Self-Test *(Answers to Self-Test questions are in the Self-Test Appendix.)*

1. How is a monopolistic competitor like a monopolist? How is it like a perfect competitor?
2. Why do monopolistic competitors operate at excess capacity?

OLIGOPOLY: ASSUMPTIONS AND REAL-WORLD BEHAVIOR

Unlike perfect competition, monopoly, and monopolistic competition, there is no one theory of **oligopoly.** However, the different theories of oligopoly do have the following common assumptions:

1. **There are few sellers and many buyers.** It is usually assumed that the few firms of an oligopoly are interdependent; each one is aware that its actions influence the other firms and that the actions of the other firms affect it. This interdependence among firms is a key characteristic of oligopoly.
2. **Firms produce and sell either homogeneous or differentiated products.** Aluminum is a homogeneous product produced in an oligopolistic market; cars are a differentiated product produced in an oligopolistic market. The oligopolist is a price searcher. Like all other firms, it produces the quantity of output at which $MR = MC$.
3. **There are significant barriers to entry.** Economies of scale are perhaps the most significant barrier to entry in oligopoly theory, but patent rights, exclusive control of an essential resource, and legal barriers also act as barriers to entry.

Which industries today are dominated by a small number of firms? Economists have developed the **concentration ratio** to help answer this question. The concentration ratio is the percentage of industry sales (or assets, output, labor force, or some other factor) accounted for by x number of firms in the industry. The "x number" in the definition is usually four or eight, but it can be any number (although it is usually small).

Oligopoly
A theory of market structure based on three assumptions: few sellers and many buyers, firms producing either homogeneous or differentiated products, and significant barriers to entry.

Concentration Ratio
The percentage of industry sales (or assets, output, labor force, or some other factor) accounted for by x number of firms in the industry.

Four-Firm Concentration Ratio: CR_4 = Percentage of industry sales accounted for by four largest firms

Eight-Firm Concentration Ratio: CR_8 = Percentage of industry sales accounted for by eight largest firms

A high concentration ratio implies that few sellers make up the industry; a low concentration ratio implies that more than a few sellers make up the industry.

Suppose we calculate a four-firm concentration ratio for industry Z. Total industry sales for a given year are $5 million, and the four largest firms in the industry account for $4.5 million in sales. The four-firm concentration ratio would be 0.90 or 90 percent ($4.5 million is 0.90 of $5 million). Industries with high four- and eight-firm concentration ratios in recent years include cigarettes, cars, tires, cereal breakfast foods, farm machinery, and soap and other detergents, to name a few.

Although concentration ratios are often used to determine the extent (or degree) of oligopoly, they are not perfect guides to industry concentration. Most important, they do not take into account foreign competition and competition from substitute domestic goods. For example, the U.S. automobile industry is highly concentrated, but it still faces stiff competition from abroad. A more relevant concentration ratio for this particular industry might be one computed on a worldwide basis.

PRICE AND OUTPUT UNDER OLIGOPOLY

There is not just one theory of oligopoly, there are many. We present three in this section: the cartel theory, the kinked demand curve theory, and the price leadership theory.

THE CARTEL THEORY

Cartel Theory
In this theory of oligopoly, oligopolistic firms act as if there were only one firm in the industry.

Cartel
An organization of firms that reduces output and increases price in an effort to increase joint profits.

The key behavioral assumption of the **cartel theory** is that oligopolists in an industry act as if there were only one firm in the industry. In short, they form a cartel in order to capture the benefits that would exist for a monopolist. A **cartel** is an organization of firms that reduces output and increases price in an effort to increase joint profits.

Let's consider the benefits that may arise from forming and maintaining a cartel. Exhibit 4 shows an industry in long-run competitive equilibrium. Price is P_1 and quantity of output is Q_1. The industry is producing the output at which price equals marginal cost and there are zero economic profits. Now suppose the firms that make up the industry form a cartel and reduce output to Q_C. The new price is P_C (cartel price), and there are profits equal to the area CP_CAB, which can be shared among the members of the cartel. With no cartel, there were no profits; with a cartel, profits are earned. Thus, the firms have an incentive to form a cartel and behave cooperatively rather than competitively.

However, firms may not be able to form a cartel, even though they have a profit incentive to do so. Also, even if they are able to form the cartel, the firms may not be able to maintain it successfully. Firms that wish to form and maintain a cartel will encounter several problems, in addition to the fact that legislation prohibits certain types of cartels in the United States. Organizing and forming a cartel involves costs as well as benefits.

exhibit 4

The Benefits of a Cartel (to Cartel Members)
We assume the industry is in long-run competitive equilibrium, producing Q_1 and charging P_1. There are no profits. A reduction in output to Q_C through the formation of a cartel raises price to P_C and brings profits of CP_CAB. (Note: In an earlier chapter, a horizontal demand curve faces the *firm*. Here a downward-sloping demand curve faces the *industry*. Don't be misled by this difference. No matter what type of demand curve we use, long-run competitive equilibrium is where $P = MC = SRATC = LRATC$.)

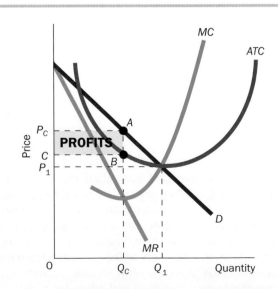

How Is a New Year's Resolution Like a Cartel Agreement?

In a cartel, one firm makes an agreement with another firm or firms. In a New Year's resolution, you essentially make an agreement with yourself. So both cases—the cartel and the resolution—involve an agreement.

Both cases also raise the possibility of cheating on the agreement. Suppose your New Year's resolution is to exercise more, take better notes in class, and read one "good" book a month. You might set such objectives for yourself because you know you will be better off in the long run if you do these things. But then the short run interjects itself into the picture. You have to decide between exercising today and plopping down in your favorite chair and watching some television. You have to decide between starting to read *Moby Dick* and catching up on the latest entertainment news in *People* magazine. The part of you that wants to hold to the resolution is at odds with the part of you that wants to watch television or read *People*. Often, the television-watching, *People*-reading part wins out. It is just too easy to break a New Year's resolution—as you probably already know.

Similarly, it is easy to break a cartel agreement. For the firm that has entered into the agreement, the lure of higher profits is often too strong to resist. In addition, the firm is concerned that if it doesn't break the agreement (and cheat), some other firm might, and then it will have lost out completely.

In short, both resolutions and cartel agreements take a lot of willpower to hold them together. And willpower, it seems, is in particularly short supply.

What, if anything, can take the place of willpower? What do both a resolution and a cartel agreement need in order to sustain long life? The answer is something or someone who will exact some penalty from the party that breaks the resolution or cartel agreement. Government sometimes plays this role for firms. Family members and friends occasionally play this role for individuals by reminding or reprimanding them if they fail to live up to their resolutions. (Usually, though, family members and friends are not successful.)

We conclude the following: First, an agreement is at the heart of both a New Year's resolution and a cartel. Second, both the resolution and the cartel are subject to cheating behavior. Third, if the resolution and the cartel are to sustain long life, they often need someone or something to prevent each party from breaking the agreement.

The Problem of Forming the Cartel

Even if it were legal, getting the sellers of an industry together to form a cartel can be costly, especially when the number of sellers is large. Each potential cartel member may resist incurring the costs of forming the cartel because it stands to benefit more if another firm does the work. In other words, each potential member has an incentive to be a free rider, that is, to stand by and take a free ride on the actions of others.

The Problem of Formulating Cartel Policy

Suppose the first problem is solved, and potential cartel members form a cartel. Now comes the problem of formulating policy. For example, firm *A* might propose that each cartel member reduce output by 10 percent, while firm *B* advocates that all bigger cartel members reduce output by 15 percent and all smaller members reduce output by 6 percent. There may be as many policy proposals as there are cartel members. Reaching agreement may be difficult. Such disagreements are harder to resolve the greater the differences among cartel members in costs, size, and so forth.

The Problem of Entry into the Industry

Even if the cartel members manage to agree on a policy that generates high profits, those high profits will provide an incentive for firms outside the industry to join the industry. If current cartel members cannot keep new suppliers from entering, the cartel is likely to break up.

The Problem of Cheating

As paradoxical as it first appears, after the cartel agreement is made, cartel members have an incentive to cheat on the agreement. Consider Exhibit 5, which shows a *representative firm* of the cartel. We compare three situations for this firm: first, the situation before the cartel is formed; second, the situation after the cartel is formed when all members adhere to the cartel price; third, the situation if the firm cheats on the cartel agreement, but the other cartel members do not.

Before the cartel is formed, the firm is in long-run competitive equilibrium; it produces output q_1 and charges price P_1. It earns zero economic profits. Next, it reduces its output to q_C as directed by the cartel (the cartel has set a quota for each member), and it charges the cartel price of P_C. Now the firm earns profits equal to the area CP_CAB.

What happens if the firm cheats on the cartel agreement and produces q_{CC} instead of the stipulated q_C? As long as other firms do not cheat, this firm views its demand curve as horizontal at the cartel price (P_C). The reason is simple: It is one of a number of firms, so it cannot affect price by changing output. Therefore, it can produce and sell additional units of output without lowering price. We conclude that if the firm cheats on the cartel agreement and other firms do not, then the cheating firm can increase its profits from the smaller amount CP_CAB to the larger amount FP_CDE. Of course, if all firms cheat, the cartel members are back where they started—with no cartel agreement and at price P_1.

This analysis illustrates a major theme of cartels: Firms have an incentive to form a cartel, but once it is formed, they have an incentive to cheat. As a result,

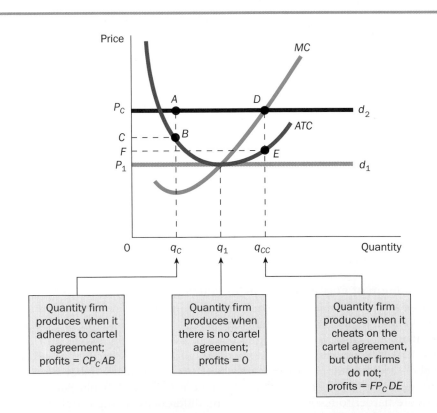

exhibit 5

The Benefits of Cheating on the Cartel Agreement

The situation for a representative firm of the cartel: in long-run competitive equilibrium, it produces q_1 and charges P_1, earning zero economic profits. As a consequence of the cartel agreement, it reduces output to q_C and charges P_C. Its profits are the area CP_CAB. If it cheats on the cartel agreement and others do not, the firm will increase output to q_{CC} and reap profits of FP_CDE. Note, however, that if this firm can cheat on the cartel agreement, so can others. Given the monetary benefits gained by cheating, it is likely that the cartel will exist for only a short time.

Quantity firm produces when it adheres to cartel agreement; profits = CP_CAB

Quantity firm produces when there is no cartel agreement; profits = 0

Quantity firm produces when it cheats on the cartel agreement, but other firms do not; profits = FP_CDE

some economists have concluded that even if cartels are formed successfully, it is unlikely that they will be effective for long.

THINKING LIKE AN ECONOMIST

In economics, there are moving targets. Consider the target of higher profits for the firms in an oligopolistic industry. After the firms form a cartel to capture the higher profits, the target of higher profits moves—to where a cartel member must cheat on the cartel to "hit" it. But if all cartel members take aim at the target's new position, the target moves back to its original position—to where cartel members must agree to stop cheating.

The layperson may think that an economic objective, or economic target, is stationary. All that an economic actor has to do to hit it is take careful aim. But the economist knows that sometimes the target moves and that careful aim is not always enough.

THE KINKED DEMAND CURVE THEORY

The behavioral assumption in the **kinked demand curve theory** is that if a single firm lowers price, other firms will do likewise, but if a single firm raises price, other firms will not follow suit. Suppose there are five firms in an industry, A, B, C, D, and E. If firm A raises its price, the other firms maintain their prices. If firm A cuts its price, the other firms match the price cut.

The kinked demand curve theory, developed in the 1930s by Paul Sweezy, is shown in Exhibit 6. The current price being charged by the firm is $25. If the firm raises its price to $27, other firms will not match it, and therefore the firm's sales will drop (from 20 to 10). In short, the demand curve for the firm above $25 is highly elastic. However, if the firm lowers its price to, say, $23, other firms will match the price cut, and therefore the firm's sales will not increase by much (only from 20 to 22). Demand is much less elastic below $25 than above it. We conclude that there is a kink in the firm's demand curve at the current price (point K in Exhibit 6). The kink signifies that other firms respond radically differently to a single firm's price hikes than to its price cuts.

Actually, there are two demand curves and two marginal revenue curves, as shown in the window in Exhibit 6. Only the thicker portions of the curves in the window are relevant, however, and thus appear in the main diagram. To illustrate,

Kinked Demand Curve Theory
A theory of oligopoly that assumes that if a single firm in the industry cuts price, other firms will do likewise, but if it raises price, other firms will not follow suit. The theory predicts price stickiness or rigidity.

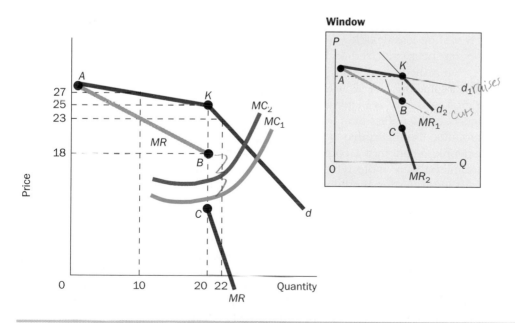

Window

exhibit 6

Kinked Demand Curve Theory
The key behavioral assumption of the theory is that rival firms will not match a price hike but will match a price cut. The theory predicts that changes in marginal costs between B and C will not cause changes in price or output. The window in the exhibit shows two demand curves and two marginal revenue curves. The firm believes it faces d_2, the more inelastic demand curve, if it cuts price; the firm believes it faces d_1, the more elastic demand curve, when it raises price. The relevant portions of each demand curve are indicated by heavy lines. Only the relevant parts of the demand and marginal revenue curves are shown in the main diagram.

starting at a price of $25, the firm believes price cuts will be matched but price hikes will not. So, when considering a price cut, the firm believes it faces the more inelastic of the two demand curves, d_2, and the corresponding marginal revenue curve, MR_2. But when considering a price hike, the firm believes it faces the more elastic of the two demand curves, d_1, and the corresponding marginal revenue curve, MR_1. It follows that the firm's demand curve includes part of d_1 and part of d_2; the firm's marginal revenue curve includes part of MR_1 and part of MR_2. This occurs because the market reacts one way to a price cut and a different way to a price hike.

Q: Why do firms match price cuts but not price hikes?

A: It has been argued that firms match price cuts because if they do not, they will lose a large share of the market. They do not match price hikes because they hope to gain market share.

Price Rigidity

Look at the marginal revenue curve for the oligopolist in the main diagram of Exhibit 6. Directly below the kink, it drops sharply. In fact, the marginal revenue curve can be viewed as three segments: a line from point A to point B, which corresponds to the upper part of the demand curve; a gap between points B and C directly below the kink in the demand curve; and a line from point C onward, which corresponds to the lower part of the demand curve (from point K onward).

The gap between points B and C represents the sharp change in marginal revenue that occurs when price is lowered below the kink on the demand curve. The gap helps explain why prices might be less flexible (more rigid) in oligopoly than in other market structures.

Recall that the oligopolistic firm produces the output at which $MR = MC$. For the firm in Exhibit 6, though, marginal cost (MC) can change between points B and C, and the firm will continue to produce the same quantity of output and charge the same price. For example, an increase in marginal cost from MC_1 to MC_2 will not lead to a change in production levels or price.

To put it differently, prices are "sticky" if oligopolistic firms face kinked demand curves. Costs can change within certain limits, and such firms will not change their prices because they expect that none of their competitors will follow their price hikes, but that all will match their price cuts.

Criticisms of the Kinked Demand Curve Theory

The kinked demand curve (and resulting MR curve) posits that prices in oligopoly will be less flexible (or more rigid) than in other market structures. The theory has been criticized on both theoretical and empirical grounds.

On a theoretical level, looking at Exhibit 6, the theory fails to explain how the original price of $25 came about. In other words, why does the kink come at $25? The theory is better at explaining things after the kink (the current price) has been identified than in explaining the placement of the kink. On empirical grounds, the theory has been challenged as a general theory of oligopoly. For example, economist George Stigler found no evidence that the oligopolists he examined were more reluctant to match price increases than price cuts, which calls into question the behavioral assumption behind the kinked demand curve theory.

THE PRICE LEADERSHIP THEORY

Price Leadership Theory
In this theory of oligopoly, the dominant firm in the industry determines price and all other firms take their price as given.

The key behavioral assumption in the **price leadership theory** is that one firm in the industry—called the dominant firm—determines price, and all other firms take this price as given. Suppose there are 10 firms in an industry, A–J, and that firm A is the dominant firm; also suppose that firm A is much larger than its rival firms. (The dominant firm need not be the largest firm in the industry; it could be the low-cost firm.) The dominant firm sets the price that maximizes its profits, and all other firms take this price as given. All other firms, then, are seen as price takers; thus, they will equate price with their respective marginal costs.

This explanation suggests that the dominant firm acts without regard to the other firms in the industry and simply forces the other firms to adapt. This is not quite correct. The dominant firm sets the price based on information it has about the other firms in the industry, as shown in Exhibit 7.

In part (a), the market demand curve and the horizontal sum of the marginal cost curves of the fringe firms (all firms other than the dominant firm) are shown. Because these fringe firms are price takers, the marginal cost curve in (a) is their supply curve. The dominant firm observes that at a price of P_1, the fringe firms alone can supply the entire market. They will supply Q_1. In short, P_1 and Q_1 define the situation in the industry or market that excludes the dominant firm.

Now add the dominant firm. It derives its demand curve, D_{DN}, by noting how much is left for it to supply at each given price. For example, at a price of P_1, the fringe firms would supply the entire market and nothing would be left for the dominant firm to supply. So a price of P_1 and an output of zero is one point on the dominant firm's demand curve, as shown in part (b). (Sometimes the dominant firm's demand curve is referred to as the *residual demand curve* for obvious reasons.) The dominant firm continues to locate other points on its demand curve by noting the difference between the market demand curve (D) and MC_F at each price below P_1.

After the dominant firm calculates its residual demand curve, it produces the quantity of output at which its marginal revenue equals its marginal cost. This level is q_{DN} in Exhibit 7b. It charges the highest price for this quantity of output, which is P_{DN}. This is the price that the dominant firm sets and the fringe firms take. Because they act as price takers, the fringe firms equate P_{DN} with marginal cost and produce q_F, as shown in part (a). The remainder of the total output produced by the industry—the difference between Q_2 and q_F—is produced by the dominant firm. This means that the distance from the origin to q_{DN} in (b) is equal to the difference between Q_2 and q_F in (a).

At one time or another, the following firms have been price leaders in their industries: R. J. Reynolds (cigarettes), General Motors (autos), Kellogg's (breakfast cereals), and Goodyear Tire and Rubber (tires).

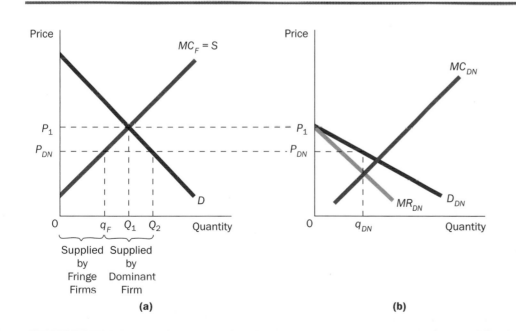

exhibit 7

Price Leadership Theory
There is one dominant firm and a number of fringe firms. (a) The horizontal sum of the marginal cost curves of the fringe firms is their supply curve. At P_1, the fringe firms supply the entire market. (b) The dominant firm derives its demand curve by computing the difference between market demand, D, and MC_F at each price below P_1. It then produces q_{DN} (where $MR_{DN} = MC_{DN}$) and charges P_{DN}. P_{DN} becomes the price that the fringe firms take. They equate price and marginal cost and produce q_F in (a). The remainder of the output—the difference between Q_2 and q_F—is produced by the dominant firm.

Self-Test

1. The text states, "Firms have an incentive to form a cartel, but once it is formed, they have an incentive to cheat." What, specifically, is the incentive to form the cartel and what is the incentive to cheat on the cartel?

2. What explains the kink in the kinked demand curve theory of oligopoly?

3. According to the price leadership theory of oligopoly, how does the dominant firm determine what price to charge?

http://

Go to *http://www.economics.harvard .edu/~aroth/barg.html*. This is a very short paper by Alvin E. Roth regarding "Bargaining" (including "Game Theory"). Read this article. What is John Nash's main contribution to game theory?

Game Theory
A mathematical technique used to analyze the behavior of decision makers who try to reach an optimal position for themselves through game playing or the use of strategic behavior, are fully aware of the interactive nature of the process at hand, and anticipate the moves of other decision makers.

GAME THEORY, OLIGOPOLY, AND CONTESTABLE MARKETS

Of the four market structures (perfect competition, monopoly, monopolistic competition, and oligopoly), oligopoly is often described as the most difficult to analyze. Analysis is difficult because of the interdependence among firms in an oligopolistic market. Economists often use game theory to get a workable understanding of this interdependence of oligopoly firms. **Game theory** is a mathematical technique used to analyze the behavior of decision makers who (1) try to reach an optimal position through game playing or the use of strategic behavior, (2) are fully aware of the interactive nature of the process at hand, and (3) anticipate the moves of other decision makers.

In this section, we describe a famous game in game theory and then use it to discuss oligopoly behavior. We also discuss the issue of contestable markets.

PRISONER'S DILEMMA

A well-known game in game theory, called *prisoner's dilemma,* illustrates a case where individually rational behavior leads to a jointly inefficient outcome. It has been described this way: "You do what is best for you, I'll do what is best for me, and somehow we end up in a situation that is not best for either of us." Here are the mechanics of the prisoner's dilemma game.

The Facts

Two men, Bob and Nathan, are arrested and charged with jointly committing a crime. They are put in separate cells so that they cannot communicate with each other. The district attorney goes to each man separately and says the following:

- If you confess to the crime and agree to turn state's evidence and your accomplice does not confess, I will let you off with a $500 fine.
- If your accomplice confesses to the crime and agrees to turn state's evidence and you do not confess, I will fine you $5,000.
- If both you and your accomplice remain silent and refuse to confess to the crime, I will charge you with a lesser crime, which I can prove you committed, and both you and your accomplice will pay fines of $2,000.
- If both you and your accomplice confess, I will fine each of you $3,000.

The Options and Consequences

Each man has two choices: confess or not confess. These choices are shown in the grid in Exhibit 8. According to the possibilities laid out by the district attorney, if both men do not confess, each pays a fine of $2,000. This is shown in box 1 in the exhibit.

If Nathan confesses and Bob does not, then Nathan gets off with the light fine of $500 and Bob pays the stiff penalty of $5,000. This is shown in box 2.

If Nathan does not confess and Bob confesses, then Nathan pays the stiff penalty of $5,000 and Bob pays the light fine of $500. This is shown in box 3.

Finally, if both men confess, each pays $3,000. This is shown in box 4.

Nathan's Choices

	Not Confess	Confess
Not Confess	**1** Nathan pays $2,000. Bob pays $2,000.	**2** Nathan pays $500. Bob pays $5,000.
Confess	**3** Nathan pays $5,000. Bob pays $500.	**4** Nathan pays $3,000. Bob pays $3,000.

Bob's Choices

exhibit 8

Prisoner's Dilemma
Nathan and Bob each have two choices: confess or not confess. No matter what Bob does, it is always better for Nathan to confess. No matter what Nathan does, it is always better for Bob to confess. Both Nathan and Bob confess and end up in box 4 where each pays a $3,000 fine. Both men would have been better off had they not confessed. That way they would have ended up in box 1 paying a $2,000 fine.

What Nathan Thinks

Nathan considers his choices and their possible outcomes. He reasons to himself, "I have two options, confess or not confess, and Bob has the same two options. Let me ask myself two questions:

- *"If Bob chooses not to confess, what is the best thing for me to do?* The answer is confess because if I do not confess, I will end up in box 1 paying $2,000, but if I confess I will end up in box 2 paying only $500. No doubt about it, if Bob chooses not to confess, I ought to confess.
- *"If Bob chooses to confess, what is the best thing for me to do?* The answer is confess because if I do not confess, I will end up in box 3 paying $5,000, but if I confess I will pay $3,000. No doubt about it, if Bob chooses to confess, I ought to confess."

Nathan's Conclusion

Nathan concludes that no matter what Bob chooses to do, not confess or confess, he is always better off if he confesses. Nathan decides to confess to the crime.

The Situation Is the Same for Bob

Bob goes through the same mental process that Nathan does. Asking himself the same two questions Nathan asked himself, Bob gets the same answers and draws the same conclusion. Bob decides to confess to the crime.

The Outcome

The DA goes to each man and asks what he has decided. Nathan says, "I confess." Bob says, "I confess." The outcome is shown in box 4 with each man paying a fine of $3,000.

Look Where They Could Be

Is there an outcome, represented by one of the four boxes, that is better for both Nathan and Bob than the outcome where each pays $3,000? Yes, there is; it is box 1. In box 1, both Nathan and Bob pay $2,000. To get to box 1, all the two men had to do was keep silent and not confess.

Changing the Game

What would happen if the DA gave Nathan and Bob another chance? Suppose she tells them that she will not accept their confessions. Instead, she wants them to talk it over together for 10 minutes, after which time she will come back, place each man in a separate room, and ask for his decision. The second time she will accept each man's decision, no matter what.

Will this change the outcome? Most people will say yes, arguing that Nathan and Bob will now see that their better choice is to remain silent, so that each ends up with a $2,000 fine instead of a $3,000 fine. Let's assume this happens, that Nathan and Bob enter into an agreement to remain silent.

Nathan's Thoughts on the Way to His Room

The DA returns and takes Nathan to a separate room. On the way, Nathan thinks to himself, "I'm not sure I can trust Bob. Suppose he goes back on our agreement and confesses. If I hold to the agreement and he doesn't, he'll end up with a $500 fine and I'll end up paying $5,000. Of course, if I break the agreement and confess and he holds to the agreement, then I'll reduce my fine to $500. Maybe the best thing for me to do is break the agreement and confess, hoping that he doesn't and I'll pay only $500. If I'm not so lucky, at least I'll protect myself from paying $5,000."

Once in the room, the DA asks Nathan what his decision is. He says, "I confess."

The Situation Is the Same for Bob

Bob sees the situation the same way Nathan does and again chooses to confess.

The Outcome Again

Both men end up confessing a second time. Each pays $3,000, realizing that if they had been silent and kept to their agreement, their fine would be only $2,000 each.

ARE OLIGOPOLY FIRMS THAT FORM A CARTEL (AND TRY TO FIX PRICES) IN A PRISONER'S DILEMMA?

Think back to our discussion of the cartel theory of oligopoly. Were the oligopoly firms that entered into a cartel agreement in a prisoner's dilemma? Most economists answer yes. To illustrate, suppose there are two firms, *A* and *B,* that produce and sell the same product and are in stiff competition with each other. Currently, the competition between them is so stiff that each earns only $10,000 profits. Soon the two firms decide to enter into a cartel agreement in which each agrees to raise prices and, after prices are raised, not to undercut the other. If they hold to the agreement, each firm will earn profits of $50,000. But if one firm holds to the cartel agreement and the other does not, the one that does not will earn profits of $100,000 and the one that does will earn $5,000 profits. Of course, if neither holds to the agreement, then both will be back where they started—earning $10,000 profits. The choices for the two firms and the possible outcomes are outlined in Exhibit 9.

Each firm is likely to behave the way our two prisoners did in our prisoner's dilemma. Each firm will see the chance to earn $100,000 by breaking the agreement (instead of $50,000 by holding to it); each will also realize that if it does not break the agreement and the other firm does, it will be in a worse situation than when it was in stiff competition with the other firm. Most economists predict that the two firms will end up in box 4 in Exhibit 9, earning the profits they did before they entered into the agreement. In summary, they will cheat on the cartel agreement and again be in competition—the very situation they wanted to escape.

An Enforcer of the Cartel Agreement

Is there any way out of the prisoner's dilemma for the two firms? The only way out is to have some entity actually enforce the cartel agreement so that the two firms do not cheat on the agreement. As odd as it may sound, sometimes government has played this role. We say this "sounds odd," because normally we think of government as trying to break up cartel agreements. After all, cartel agreements are

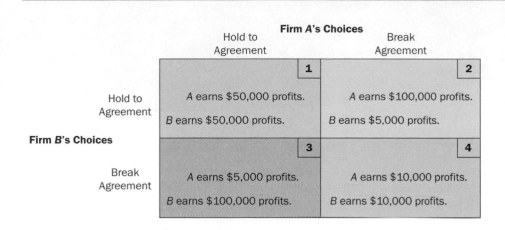

Firm A's Choices

	Hold to Agreement	Break Agreement
Hold to Agreement	**1** A earns $50,000 profits. B earns $50,000 profits.	**2** A earns $100,000 profits. B earns $5,000 profits.
Break Agreement	**3** A earns $5,000 profits. B earns $100,000 profits.	**4** A earns $10,000 profits. B earns $10,000 profits.

Firm B's Choices

illegal. Nevertheless, sometimes government acts as the enforcer, and not the eliminator, of the cartel agreement.

Consider the Civil Aeronautics Board (CAB) in the days of airline regulation. The CAB was created to protect the airlines from "cutthroat competition." It had the power to set airfares, allocate air routes, and prevent the entry of new carriers into the airline industry. In the days before deregulation, the federal government's General Accounting Office estimated that airline fares would have been, on average, as much as 52 percent lower if the CAB had not been regulating them. Clearly, the CAB was doing for the airlines—preventing price competition among airlines, allocating routes, and preventing competition—what an airline cartel would have done.

In a similar vein, Judge Richard Posner has observed that "the railroads supported the enactment of the first Interstate Commerce Act, which was designed to prevent railroads from price discrimination, because discrimination was undermining the railroad's cartels."[1]

ARE MARKETS CONTESTABLE?

The discussion of market structures, from perfect competition to oligopoly, has focused on the *number of sellers* in each market structure. In perfect competition, there are many sellers; in monopoly there is only one; in monopolistic competition, there are many; in oligopoly, there are few. The message is that the number of sellers in a market influences the behavior of the sellers within the market. For example, the monopoly seller is more likely to restrict output and charge higher prices than is the perfect competitor.

In recent years, economists have shifted the emphasis from the number of sellers in a market to the issue of *entry into and exit from an industry*. This new focus is a result of the work of William Baumol and other economists who have put forth the idea of contestable markets.

A **contestable market** is one in which the following conditions are met:

1. **There is easy entry into the market and costless exit from the market.**
2. **New firms entering the market can produce the product at the same cost as current firms.**
3. **Firms exiting the market can easily dispose of their fixed assets by selling them elsewhere** (less depreciation; thus, fixed costs are not sunk but recoverable)

Contestable Market
A market in which entry is easy and exit is costless, new firms can produce the product at the same cost as current firms, and exiting firms can easily dispose of their fixed assets by selling them.

1. Richard A. Posner, "Theories of Regulation," *Bell Journal of Economics and Management Science* 5 (Autumn): 337.

ECONOMICS IN...

Everyday Life | Popular Culture | Technology | The World

An Economic Theory of the Mafia

The U.S. government prohibits its residents from engaging in certain activities. With only a few exceptions, it forbids residents from being either buyers or sellers of illegal drugs, prostitution services, or gambling services. Because government is willing to punish anyone who goes against its prohibitions, there is a high barrier to entering the illegal drug, prostitution, and gambling markets.

Of course not everyone has abided by the government's prohibitions; there are both buyers and sellers of illegal goods and services. Consider one of the historically biggest sellers in these markets—the Mafia. The term *Mafia* has been adopted internationally to refer to an organized crime unit that sells illegal goods and services and is willing to use extreme force (violence) to protect what it perceives as its business interests.

In reality, numerous Mafia firms (often referred to as Mafia families) benefit from the high barrier to entry established by the government. Each Mafia firm faces a higher demand curve than it would if there were no legal barriers to entry. Consequently, prices and profits are higher for the few Mafia firms that supply the market.[2]

The question each Mafia firm has to ask itself is: Could its profits be even higher without the other Mafia firms? In economic terms, the question becomes: Are there benefits from moving from being one of a few oligopoly firms to being the sole monopoly firm? Or, stated differently, are there benefits from facing the entire market demand curve instead of only some fraction of it?

There are benefits, of course, but there are also costs in trying to obtain the benefits. How can a Mafia firm obtain the benefits of a monopoly? It can try to put other Mafia firms out of business by offering higher quality goods and services, lower prices, better credit terms, better delivery, and so on. Or, it can try to eliminate (literally kill) the members of the other Mafia firms. What will be the costs of using these methods?

If any one Mafia firm tries to kill its competitors, then the other Mafia firms will likely band together against it. To understand why, consider five Mafia firms, *A–E*. Firm *A* tries to elim-

inate firm *B* by killing the members of the firm. Firms *C–E* know that if firm *A* is successful, it will probably try to eliminate them next. They will then band together with firm *B* to try to eliminate firm *A*. In short, each firm will soon realize that trying to kill its competition is not likely to be a successful strategy.

This leaves the option of trying to outcompete rivals by offering lower prices, higher quality, and so on. Will the Mafia firms proceed this way? Perhaps not. They may recognize that stiff competition among them may simply reduce their profits. Instead, they may form a cartel agreement. Often in the past, Mafia cartel agreements have taken the form of dividing up the market. Each Mafia firm gets a certain geographic area in which it can exclusively supply all illegal goods and services.

But economists know that cartel agreements are notoriously unstable because there are often huge benefits from breaking the cartel agreement when others do not. Once the Mafia firms form a cartel agreement, each firm is in a prisoner's dilemma. In the end, the firms soon learn that cheating behavior puts everyone in a worse position. How then do Mafia firms make sure that each cooperates and holds to the cartel agreement? Who or what will enforce the Mafia cartel agreements?

Economist Robert Axelrod reports that the only strategy that seemingly solves the (repeated) prisoner's dilemma game and gets participants to cooperate with each other instead of cheating on each other is tit-for-tat. The tit-for-tat strategy is simple: You give to others what you get from them. When individuals know that they will get what they give, they will want to give (to others) what they want to receive from them. And what they want is cooperation, holding to the cartel agreement. They want to make sure they are in box 1 of the prisoner's dilemma payoff matrix, not box 4. (See Exhibit 8.)

Applied to Mafia firms, tit-for-tat works this way: If one Mafia family kills a member of another family, then the second family must kill someone in the first family. The message has to be that you get whatever you give. There is evidence that Mafia firms are rather efficient practitioners of tit-for-tat.

To illustrate, suppose there are currently eight firms in an industry, all of which are earning profits. Firms outside the industry notice this and decide to enter the industry (nothing prevents entry). They acquire the necessary equipment and produce the product at the same cost as current producers. Time passes, and the firms that entered the industry decide to exit it. They can either

---

2. We assume throughout our discussion that each Mafia firm faces constant marginal cost and therefore constant unit cost.

switch their machinery into another line of production or sell their equipment for what they paid for it, less depreciation.

Perhaps the most important element of a contestable market is "hit-and-run" entry and exit. New entrants can enter—hit—produce the product and take profits from current firms and then exit costlessly—run.

The theory of contestable markets has been criticized because of its assumptions—in particular, the assumption that there is extremely free entry into and costless exit from the industry. However, although this theory, like most theories, does not perfectly describe the real world, this does not of itself destroy the theory's usefulness.

At minimum, contestable markets theory has rattled orthodox market structure theory. Here are a few of its conclusions:

1. Even if an industry is composed of a small number of firms, or simply one firm, this is not evidence that the firms perform in a noncompetitive way. They might be extremely competitive if the market they are in is contestable.
2. Profits can be zero in an industry even if the number of sellers in the industry is small.
3. If a market is contestable, inefficient producers cannot survive. Cost inefficiencies invite lower-cost producers into the market, driving price down to minimum *ATC* and forcing inefficient firms to change their ways or exit the industry.
4. If, as conclusion 3 suggests, a contestable market encourages firms to produce at their lowest possible average total cost and charge $P = ATC$, it follows that they will also sell at a price equal to marginal cost. (Recall that the marginal cost curve intersects the average total cost curve at its minimum point.)

The theory of contestable markets has also led to a shift in policy perspectives. To some (but certainly not all) economists, the theory suggests a new way to encourage firms to act as perfect competitors. Rather than direct interference in the behavioral patterns of firms, efforts should perhaps be directed at lowering entry and exit costs.

APPLICATIONS OF GAME THEORY

Game theory, especially prisoner's dilemma, is applicable in a number of real-world situations. In this section, we discuss a few of these applications.

GRADES AND PARTYING

Your economics professor announces in class one day that on the next test, she will give the top 10 percent of the students in the class A's, the next 15 percent B's, and so on. You realize it takes less time studying to get, say, a 60 than a 90 on the test, so you hope everyone studies only a little. That way, you can study only a little and earn a high letter grade. But, of course, everyone in the class is thinking the same thing.

Envision yourself entering into an agreement with your fellow students. You say the following to them one day:

There are 30 students in our class. Each of us can choose to study either 2 hours or 4 hours for the test. Our relative standing in the class will be the same whether we all study for 2 hours or all study for 4 hours. So, why don't we all agree to study for only 2 hours, so we have 2 extra hours to do other things. I'd rather receive my B by studying only 2 hours instead of by having to study 4 hours.

Suppose everyone agrees with the logic of the argument and agrees to study only 2 hours. Of course, once everyone has agreed to this, there is an incentive to cheat on the agreement and study more. If everyone else in your class agrees to study 2 hours and you study 4 hours, you increase your relative standing in the class. You go from, say, a B to an A.

ECONOMICS IN...

The Industry Standard Path to Monopoly

Some economists suggest that knowledge-based industries are not the same as traditional industries, such as steel, wheat, and clothing. They argue that knowledge industries often produce network goods. A *network good* is a good whose value increases as the expected number of units sold increases. A telephone is a network good. If only 5 percent of the population owns a telephone, a telephone is not so useful to you as it would be if 50, 75, or 100 percent of the population owned a telephone. As a telephone purchaser, the more people you expect to own a telephone, the more valuable a telephone is to you.

Consider a similar example from the knowledge-based software industry. The more widely an operating system is used, the more likely it will become the standard for the industry. People will want to use the system most people are using to ensure they can "network" with others.

Another argument by economists is that knowledge industries are often characterized by the lock-in effect. The lock-in effect describes the situation where a particular product or technology becomes settled upon as the standard and is difficult to dislodge as the standard. A product in a knowledge-based industry is often difficult to use at first, and so after a customer has learned how to use the product, she doesn't want to switch to learning another. For example, after a person has learned a certain word processing program

or spreadsheet, has worked with a certain Internet browser, or has used a particular operating system, she may not want to switch to another. In other words, there may be high switching costs.

What do network goods, lock-in effects, and high switching costs have to do with monopolistic competition and oligopoly? Promoting the lock-in effect (connected with a network good) may be one way a monopolistic competitor or oligopolist can become a monopolist. For example, suppose a software company has developed a new software program. To establish its software as the industry standard, it has to get a lot of people to use the software. Initially, it may either give away its software or sell it at a very low price. As more people use the software, people not currently using it will find the software more useful. The software may snowball into the industry standard. Furthermore, if there are high switching costs, the industry standard may be immovable.

Do companies in the real world behave this way? Some economists believe that Microsoft, Inc., acted just this way with respect to its operating system and its Internet browser. Does this mean, then, that Microsoft was trying to become a monopoly? If it was, it certainly wasn't alone. Many companies have tried in the past, and try today, to become monopolies. The real question is whether or not Microsoft is now, or can become, a monopoly. Not all economists address this issue the same way. Some see Microsoft as a near-monopoly firm in the software industry. As evidence, they point to the large percentage of the market it supplies. Others argue that many of Microsoft's markets are contestable and so Microsoft cannot act like a monopolist.[3] They also argue that the lock-in effect is exaggerated today. The lock-in effect is greatly tempered, they argue, by the rapid pace of innovation, which favors the emergence of new products.

You and the other students in your class are in a prisoner's dilemma. Look at Exhibit 10, which shows the payoffs for you and for Jill, a representative other student. If both you and Jill study 4 hours, each receives an 85, which is a B (box 4). With your professor's new relative grading plan, if you study 2 hours and Jill studies 2 hours, the grade for each of you falls to 65, but now 65 is a B (box 1). In other words, comparing box 4 with box 1, box 1 is better because you receive the same letter grade (B) in both cases but spend less time studying.

---

3. For these economists, the real issue is not whether a firm is a monopolist or not, but whether it acts like one. If it doesn't act like one, then for all practical purposes, it isn't one.

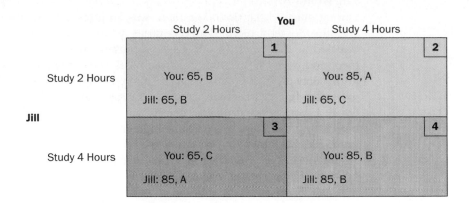

exhibit 10

Studying and Grades

Suppose your letter grade in class depends on how well you do relative to others. In this setting, you and the other students are in a prisoner's dilemma, which is shown here. If both you and Jill (a representative other student) each study 4 hours, each of you earn a point grade of 85, which is a B (box 4). If each of you study 2 hours, each of you earn a point grade of 65, which is a B (box 1). Box 1 is preferred over box 4 because you get the same letter grade in each box, but you study less in box 1 than in box 4.

If you study 4 hours while Jill studies 2 hours, your point grade rises to 85 and Jill's point grade remains at 65. In this case, 85 is an A and 65 is a C (box 2). You are better off and Jill is worse off.

If you study 2 hours while Jill studies 4 hours, Jill's point grade rises to 85 and your point grade remains at 65. Jill earns a letter grade of A, and you earn a letter grade of C.

No matter what Jill decides to do—study 2 or 4 hours—it is always better for you to study 4 hours (assuming the costs of studying additional hours are less than the benefits of studying additional hours). The same holds for Jill. Our outcome, then, is box 4, where both you and Jill study 4 hours.

Of course, once you and Jill agree to lower your study time from 4 hours to 2 hours, each of you has an incentive to cheat on the agreement. If you study 4 hours and Jill studies 2 hours, then you raise your grade to an 85, which is now an A, while Jill's grade is 65, which now becomes a C (box 2). Of course, if Jill studies 4 hours and you study 2 hours, then Jill raises her grade to an 85, which is now an A, while your grade is 65, which is now a C (box 3).

No matter what you think Jill is going to do, the best thing for you to do is study 4 hours.[4] The same holds for Jill with respect to whatever you choose to do. The outcome then is box 4, where both of you study 4 hours.

Ideally, what you need (and Jill needs too) is a way to enforce your agreement not to study more than 2 hours. How might students do this? One way is to party. That's right—party. If you can get all the students in your class together and party, you can be fairly sure that no one is studying too much.

Think about this: Students in the same class understand that (1) some professors set aside some percentage of A's for the top students in the class (no matter how low the top is) and (2) they are in a prisoner's dilemma. They realize it would be better for them to cooperate and study less than to compete and study more. Instead of actually entering into an agreement to study less (sign on the dotted line), they "think up" ways to keep the studying time down. One way to keep the studying time down—one way to enforce the implicit and unspoken agreement not to study too much—is to do things with others that do not entail studying. One "institution" that satisfies all requirements is partying—everyone is together not studying.

---

4. We are assuming here that the cost of studying two additional hours is lower than the benefits you receive by raising your grade one letter.

THE ARMS RACE

During much of the Cold War, there was an arms race between the United States and the Soviet Union. Both countries were producing armaments that were directed at the other. Occasionally, representatives of the two countries would meet and try to slow down the arms race. The United States would agree to cut armaments production if the Soviet Union did and vice versa. Many arms analysts generally agreed that the arms agreements between the United States and the Soviet Union were unsuccessful. In other words, representatives of the two countries would meet and enter into an agreement not to compete so heavily in arms production. But then, the countries would end up competing on arms production.

Were the two countries in a prisoner's dilemma? Look at Exhibit 11. When both the United States and the Soviet Union were competing on arms production, they were in box 4, each receiving a utility level of 7. Their collective objective was to move from box 4 to box 1, where each cooperated with the other and reduced its armaments production. In box 1, each country received a utility level of 10. The arms agreements that the United States and the Soviet Union entered into were an attempt to get to box 1.

Of course, after the agreement was signed, each country had an incentive to cheat on the agreement. Certainly the United States would be better off if it increased its armaments production while the Soviet Union cut back its production. Then, the United States could establish clear military superiority over the Soviet Union. The same held for the Soviet Union with respect to the United States.

Looking at the payoff matrix in Exhibit 11, it is easy to see that the best strategy for the United States is to compete; the same holds for the Soviet Union. And so the two countries ended up in box 4, racing to outproduce the other in arms.

SPEED LIMIT LAWS

Envision a world with no law against speeding. In this world, you and everyone else speeds. With everyone speeding, a good number of accidents occur each day,

exhibit 11

An Arms Race
In the days of the Cold War, the United States and the Soviet Union were said to be in an arms race. Actually, the arms race was a result of the two countries being in a prisoner's dilemma. Start with each country racing to produce more military goods than the other country; that is, each country is in box 4. In their attempt to move to box 1, they enter into an arms agreement (to reduce the rate at which they produce arms). But no matter what the Soviet Union does (hold to the arms agreement or break it), it is always better for the United States to break the agreement. The same holds for the Soviet Union with respect to the United States. The two countries end up in box 4. (Note: In the exhibit, the higher the number, the better the position for the country.)

	United States Hold to Arms Agreement	United States Break Arms Agreement
Soviet Union Hold to Arms Agreement	**1** United States, 10 Soviet Union, 10	**2** United States, 15 Soviet Union, 5
Soviet Union Break Arms Agreement	**3** United States, 5 Soviet Union, 15	**4** United States, 7 Soviet Union, 7

some of which may involve you. In time, everyone decides that something has to be done about the speeding. It is just too dangerous, everyone admits, to let the speeding continue.

Someone offers a proposal: "Let's agree that we will post signs on the road that state the maximum speed. Furthermore, let's agree here and now that we will all obey the speed limits." The proposal sounds like a good one, and so everyone agrees to follow it.

Of course, as we know by now, once the agreement not to speed is made, we have a prisoner's dilemma. Each person will be better off if he (and he alone) speeds while everyone else obeys the speed limit. In the beginning, everyone agrees to the speed limit; in the end, everyone breaks the speed limit.

What is missing, of course, is an effective enforcement mechanism. To move the speeders out of the classic prisoner's dilemma box (Box 4 in our earlier examples) to box 1, someone or something has to punish people who do not cooperate with others. A law against speeding—backed up by the police and court system—solves the prisoner's dilemma. The law, the police, and the court system change the payoff for cheating on the agreement.

THE FEAR OF GUILT AS AN ENFORCEMENT MECHANISM

Might there be a social purpose for guilt? Might there be a good reason for feeling guilty? With these two questions in mind, consider the following. John and Mary decide to get married. As part of their wedding vows, they promise to remain faithful to each other. In other words, each promises the other that he or she will not cheat.

As we have seen so many times, once an agreement is made between two parties, it is sometimes the case that each party will be better off if it "cheats" and the other party does not. In the case of John and Mary, John may think, "I can gain utility by cheating on Mary." Of course, Mary can think the same thing with respect to John. Their utility payoffs are shown in Exhibit 12.

Notice in part (a) that both Mary and John receive a utility level of 15 when one cheats but the other does not. Possibly, if each person felt some guilt over cheating on his or her partner, the utility level would be something lower than 15. In some sense, both Mary and John might prefer to feel guilty when cheating. After all, both would prefer to be in box 1, where neither is cheating, than in box 4, where both are cheating. In short, given that box 1 is better than box 4 for both Mary and John, we would expect that both would opt for some enforcement mechanism that prevented them from moving away from box 1. Think back to the speeding example. Don't the speeders actually want a law against speeding that is enforced by the police and courts?

Of course, there is no outside enforcement mechanism for John and Mary. But an internal sense of guilt over cheating, might be a good substitute for an external enforcement mechanism. Instead of the police and the court system putting John and Mary in prison for cheating, each one's sense of guilt will put him or her in a personal jail. (Isn't this what someone is implying by saying, "There is no way I can do that, I would feel too guilty." In other words, many people want to prevent themselves from suffering the pangs of guilt in much the same way they don't want to suffer the pain of prison. Both guilt pangs and prison are *bads*. Both come with disutility.)

Suppose, as shown in Exhibit 12b, a sense of guilt would change Mary's utility level in box 2 from 15 to 4 and would change John's utility level in box 3 from 15 to 4. Then, neither Mary nor John would find it advantageous to cheat on the other if his or her spouse did not cheat.[5]

---

5. Of course, the way we have structured the payoff matrix, each finds it advantageous to cheat on the other if the other cheats. In other words, if Mary does not cheat on John, then John is better off not cheating than cheating, but if Mary cheats on John, and John knows that Mary is cheating on him, than he is better off cheating than not cheating.

exhibit 12

Cheating and Guilt

Does guilt sometimes serve a useful social purpose? John and Mary are married and may be in a prisoner's dilemma. If Mary cheats on John, but John doesn't cheat on Mary, Mary may be better off and therefore moves from box 1 to box 2 in part (a). If John cheats on Mary, but Mary doesn't cheat on John, John may be better off and therefore moves from box 1 to box 3 in (a). Of course, if both cheat, they both end up in box 4, which is inferior for both to box 1. A sense of guilt for each person may change the payoffs in part (a). If each person feels guilty about cheating, then the payoff from cheating is lowered. Look at the new payoffs for each person in part (b). The payoff for cheating goes from 15 to 4 for both Mary and John. With the new, lower payoffs (resulting from a sense of guilt over cheating), both Mary and John remove themselves from a prisoner's dilemma and therefore are more likely to end up in box 1, a box that is better for both.

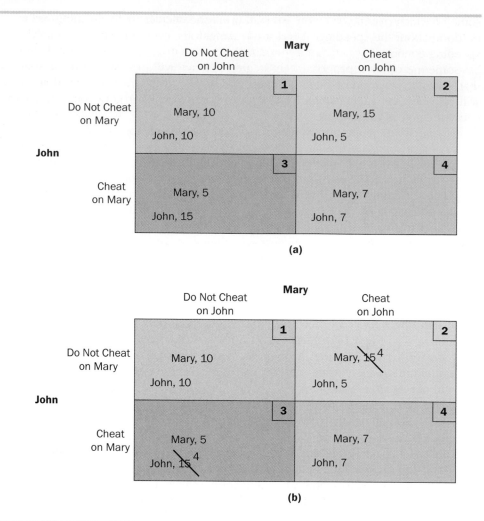

(a)

(b)

We end with a question: When is guilt good? One answer is that when the fear of guilt allows two people to remove themselves from a setting they would prefer not to be in to a better setting. In other words, if the fear of guilt moves Mary and John from box 4 to box 1 (which is what they want), then the fear of guilt is good.

A Reader Asks...

Are Some Prisoner's Dilemmas Good and Others Bad?

Are there times when we're glad that people are in a prisoner's dilemma and times when we're not glad? In other words, are there some settings in which we actually want people to end up in box 4 instead of box 1, and other settings in which we want people to end up in box 1 instead of box 4?

Let's look again at two of the prisoner's dilemma settings in the chapter. In one of our settings, two competing sellers enter into a cartel agreement to reduce or eliminate the competition between them. If the cartel agreement is successful, sellers are better off and consumers are worse off. If the cartel agreement is unsuccessful (if the cartel agreement is broken by one or both of the sellers), then sellers are worse off and consumers are better off.

The sellers, as you know, are in a prisoner's dilemma. Each seller agrees to cooperate with the other (to reduce or eliminate cooperation), but also has an incentive to cheat on the agreement. The incentive to cheat (and make oneself better off at the other's expense) is what gets each seller to break the cartel agreement. Outcome: Competition between sellers means benefits for consumers.

Consumers ought to be glad that sellers are in a prisoner's dilemma, and therefore end up in box 4 competing with each other for the consumer's business. In other words, if the sellers weren't in a prisoner's dilemma, consumers would want to put them in one.

Now consider our discussion about the arms race between the United States and the Soviet Union. Just like our two sellers, the two countries are in a prisoner's dilemma. Each country agrees to cooperate with the other (to reduce the arms race between them), but also has an incentive to cheat on any arms agreement. The incentive to cheat (and clearly establish military superiority over the other country) is what gets each country to break the arms agreement. Outcome: Arms race.

It is not clear in this case that there are any obvious beneficiaries (other than perhaps armament producers) to the two countries being stuck in a prisoner's dilemma and ending up in box 4, engaged in an arms race. So, here might be an example of a prisoner's dilemma that almost everyone would have preferred did not exist.

Chapter Summary

Monopolistic Competition

- The theory of monopolistic competition is built on three assumptions: (1) There are many sellers and buyers. (2) Each firm in the industry produces and sells a slightly differentiated product. (3) There is easy entry and exit.
- The monopolistic competitor is a price searcher.
- For the monopolistic competitor, $P > MR$, and the marginal revenue curve lies below the demand curve.
- The monopolistic competitor produces the quantity of output at which $MR = MC$. It charges the highest price per unit for this output.
- Unlike the perfectly competitive firm, the monopolistic competitor does not exhibit resource allocative efficiency.
- The monopolistic competitive firm does not earn profits in the long run (because of easy entry into the industry) unless it can successfully differentiate its product (for example, by brand name) in the minds of buyers.

Excess Capacity Theorem

- The excess capacity theorem states that a monopolistic competitor will, in equilibrium, produce an output smaller than the one at which average total costs (unit costs) are minimized. Thus, the monopolistic competitor is not productive efficient.

Oligopoly Assumptions

- There are many different oligopoly theories. All are built on the following assumptions: (1) There are few sellers and many buyers. (2) Firms produce and sell either homogeneous or differentiated products. (3) There are significant barriers to entry.
- One of the key characteristics of oligopolistic firms is their interdependence.

Oligopoly Theories

- The cartel theory assumes that firms in an oligopolistic industry act in a manner consistent with there being only one firm in the industry.
- Four problems are associated with cartels: (1) the problem of forming the cartel, (2) the problem of formulating policy, (3) the problem of entry into the industry, and (4) the problem of cheating.
- Firms that enter into a cartel agreement are in a prisoner's dilemma situation where individually rational behavior leads to a jointly inefficient outcome.
- The kinked demand curve theory assumes that if a single firm lowers price, other firms will do likewise, but if a single firm raises price, other firms will not follow suit.
- The kinked demand curve theory predicts that an oligopolistic firm will experience price stickiness or rigidity. This is because there is a gap in its marginal revenue curve in which the firm's marginal cost can rise or fall and the firm will still produce the same quantity of output and charge the same price. The evidence in some empirical tests rejects the theory.
- The price leadership theory assumes that the dominant firm in the industry determines price and all other firms take this price as given.

The Theory of Contestable Markets

- A contestable market is one in which the following conditions are met: (1) There is easy entry into the market and costless exit from it. (2) New firms entering the market can produce the product at the same costs as current firms. (3) Firms exiting the market can easily dispose of their fixed assets by selling them elsewhere (less depreciation).
- Compared to orthodox market structure theories, the theory of contestable markets places more emphasis on the issue of entry into and exit from an industry and less emphasis on the number of sellers in an industry.

Game Theory

- Game theory is a mathematical technique used to analyze the behavior of decision makers who (1) try to reach an optimal position through game playing or the use of strategic behavior, (2) are fully aware of the interactive nature of the process at hand, and (3) anticipate the moves of other decision makers.
- The prisoner's dilemma game illustrates a case where individually rational behavior leads to a jointly inefficient outcome.

Key Terms and Concepts

Monopolistic Competition
Excess Capacity Theorem
Oligopoly
Concentration Ratio

Cartel Theory
Cartel
Kinked Demand Curve Theory
Price Leadership Theory

Game Theory
Contestable Market

Questions and Problems

1. What, if anything, do all firms in all four market structures have in common?
2. What causes the unusual appearance of the marginal revenue curve in the kinked demand curve theory?
3. Would you expect cartel formation to be more likely in industries that comprise a few firms or in those that include many firms? Explain your answer.
4. Does the theory of contestable markets shed any light on oligopoly pricing theories? Explain your answer.
5. There are 60 types or varieties of product X on the market. Is product X made in a monopolistic competitive market? Explain your answer.
6. Why does interdependence of firms play a major role in oligopoly but not in perfect competition or monopolistic competition?
7. Airline companies sometimes fly airplanes that are one-quarter full between cities. Some people point to this as evidence of economic waste. What do you think? Would it be better to have fewer airline companies and more full planes?
8. Concentration ratios have often been used to note the tightness of an oligopoly market. A high concentration ratio indicates a tight oligopoly market, and a low concentration ratio indicates a loose oligopoly market. Would you expect firms in tight markets to reap higher profits, on average, than firms in loose markets? Would it matter if the markets were contestable? Explain your answers.
9. Market theories are said to have the happy consequence of getting individuals to think in more focused and analytical ways. Has this happened to you? Give examples to illustrate.
10. Give an example of a prisoner's dilemma situation other than the ones mentioned in this chapter.
11. How are oligopoly and monopolistic competition alike? How are they different?

1. Diagrammatically identify the quantity of output a monopolistic competitor produces and the price it charges.
2. Diagrammatically identify a monopolistic competitor that is incurring losses.
3. In Exhibit 6, what is the highest dollar amount to which marginal cost can rise without changing price?
4. Total industry sales are $105 million. The top four firms account for sales of $10 million, $9 million, $8 million, and $5 million, respectively. What is the four-firm concentration ratio?
5. According to the kinked demand curve theory, if the firm is considering a price hike, which demand curve in the following figure does it believe it faces and why?

6. Refer to the following figure. Because of a cartel agreement, the firm has been assigned a production quota of q_2 units. The cartel price is P_2. What are its profits equal to if it adheres to the cartel agreement? What are its profits if it breaks the cartel agreement and produces q_3?

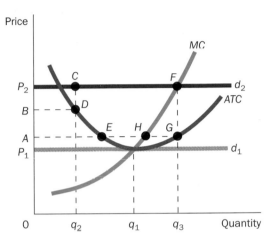

1. Go to *http://www.uscar.org/uscar/history.htm*. Read the Web page, and answer the following questions.
   a. Which U.S. automobile companies have formed "USCAR" organization?
   b. Is the U.S. car industry an oligopoly? Why or why not?
   c. The companies in this organization are cooperating with each other. Is their cooperation a subtle effort to form a cartel? Why or why not?
2. Go to *http://www.ual.com*. Select "In-flight Services" in the Travel Support category.
   a. What fast-food restaurant offers special meals for children who travel? Can you use a laptop on the airplane? Are movies provided on some airplanes?
   b. When United offers movies and fast food for kids, is it engaging in price or nonprice competition?
   c. Click on the "Back" button, and select "Red Carpet Club." Are the services of the Red Carpet Club consistent with nonprice competition? price discrimination? something else?
   d. Click on the "Back" button, and select "Special Offers" in the Planning Travel category. What are e-fares? Suppose it is 24 hours before flight departure and the airline has 30 seats available. Would it want to notify potential customers of this fact and might it sell seats at discounted prices? If there is an empty seat on an airplane about to depart, what is the marginal cost of adding an additional passenger?

3. Go to *http://www.iflyswa.com*.
   a. From viewing the Web sites for Southwest and United (earlier), which airline seems more heavily engaged in price competition?

b. Do you think Southwest's low-fare strategy will be successful? How might United compete with Southwest—by lowering prices or by offering more frills on a flight?

Log on to the Arnold Xtra! Web site now (*http://arnoldxtra.swcollege.com*) for additional learning resources such as practice quizzes, help with graphing, video clips, and current event applications.

ch.12

GOVERNMENT AND PRODUCT MARKETS: ANTITRUST AND REGULATION

If you visit Washington, D.C., you may see the building that houses the Department of Justice. One of the many duties of the Justice Department is the enforcement of the country's antitrust laws. The stated purpose of these laws is to control monopoly and to preserve and promote competition. Does it matter to your life whether the Department of Justice does a good, bad, or mediocre job of controlling monopoly and preserving and promoting competition? Does it matter how the Department of Justice goes about doing its job? It matters in more ways than you can imagine.

Chapter Road Map

In this chapter, we discuss the two major ways the federal government can influence and impact markets—through its antitrust laws and through various regulations. We describe various antitrust laws and cases and examine some of the unsettled points in antitrust law. Then, we discuss government regulation of a natural monopoly, the effects of some regulations, and various theories of regulation.

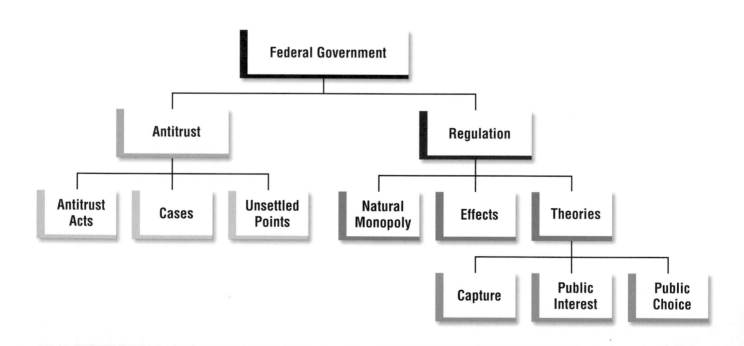

ANTITRUST

A monopoly (1) produces a smaller output than is produced by a perfectly competitive firm with the same revenue and cost considerations, (2) charges a higher price, and (3) causes a deadweight loss. Some economists argue that based on these facts, government should place certain restrictions on monopolies. Also, government should restrict the activities of cartels because the objective of a cartel is to behave as if it were a monopoly.

Other economists argue that monopolies do not have as much market power as some people think—witness the competition some monopolies face from broadly defined substitutes and imports. As for cartels, they usually contain the seeds of their own destruction. Therefore, it is only a matter of time (usually short) before they crumble naturally.

We are not concerned here with the debate about whether or not to restrict monopoly power. Instead, we examine the ways government deals with it. Two of the ways include the antitrust laws and regulation. We examine antitrust law in this section, regulation in the next.

Antitrust law is legislation passed for the stated purpose of controlling monopoly power and preserving and promoting competition. Let's look at how a few of the major antitrust acts have been used and the effects they have had.

Antitrust Law
Legislation passed for the stated purpose of controlling monopoly power and preserving and promoting competition.

ANTITRUST ACTS

A few key acts that constitute U.S. antitrust policy are the Sherman Act (1890), the Clayton Act (1914), the Federal Trade Commission Act (1914), the Robinson-Patman Act (1936), the Wheeler-Lea Act (1938), and the Celler-Kefauver Antimerger Act (1950).

The Sherman Act (1890)

The Sherman Act was passed during a period when mergers of companies were common. (A merger occurs when two companies combine under single ownership of control.) At that time, the organization that companies formed by combining together was called a **trust**; this in turn gave us the word *antitrust*.

The Sherman Act contains two major provisions:

Trust
A combination of firms that come together to act as a monopolist.

1. "Every contract, combination in the form of trust or otherwise, or conspiracy, in restraint of trade or commerce among the several states, or with foreign nations, is hereby declared to be illegal."
2. "Every person who shall monopolize, or attempt to monopolize, or combine or conspire with any other person or persons to monopolize any part of the trade or commerce . . . shall be guilty of a misdemeanor."

Some people have argued that the provisions of the Sherman Act are vague. For example, the act never explains which specific acts constitute "restraint of trade," although it declares such acts illegal.

The Clayton Act (1914)

The Clayton Act makes the following business practices illegal when their effects "may be to substantially lessen competition or tend to create a monopoly":

1. Price discrimination—charging different customers different prices for the same product where the price differences are not related to cost differences.
2. Exclusive dealing—selling to a retailer on the condition that the retailer not carry any rival products.
3. Tying contracts—arrangements whereby the sale of one product is dependent on the purchase of some other product(s).
4. The acquisition of competing companies' stock if the acquisition reduces competition. (Some say a major loophole of the act is that it does not ban the

acquisition of competing companies' physical assets, and therefore does not prevent anticompetitive mergers as it was designed to do.)

5. Interlocking directorates—an arrangement whereby the directors of one company sit on the board of directors of another company in the same industry. These were made illegal, irrespective of their effects (that is, interlocking directorates are illegal at all times, not just when their effects "may be to substantially lessen competition . . .").

The Federal Trade Commission Act (1914)

The Federal Trade Commission Act contains the broadest and most general language of any antitrust act. It declares illegal "unfair methods of competition in commerce." In essence, this amounts to declaring illegal those acts that are judged to be "too aggressive" in competition. The problem is how to decide what is fair and what is unfair, and what is aggressive but not too aggressive. This act also set up the Federal Trade Commission (FTC) to deal with "unfair methods of competition."

The Robinson-Patman Act (1936)

The Robinson-Patman Act was passed in an attempt to decrease the failure rate of small businesses by protecting them from the competition of large and growing chain stores. The large chain stores were receiving price discounts from suppliers and, in turn, were passing the discounts on to their customers. As a result, small businesses had a difficult time competing, and many of them failed. The Robinson-Patman Act prohibits suppliers from offering special discounts to large chain stores unless they also offer the discounts to everyone else. Many economists believe that, rather than preserving and strengthening competition, the Robinson-Patman Act limits it. The act seems to be more concerned about a certain group of competitors than about the process of competition and the buying public as a whole.

The Wheeler-Lea Act (1938)

The Wheeler-Lea Act empowers the Federal Trade Commission to deal with false and deceptive acts or practices. Major moves in this area have been against advertising that the FTC has deemed false and deceptive.

The Celler-Kefauver Antimerger Act (1950)

The Celler-Kefauver Act was designed to close the merger loophole in the Clayton Act (see point 4 of the Clayton Act). It bans anticompetitive mergers that occur as a result of one company acquiring the physical assets of another company.

UNSETTLED POINTS IN ANTITRUST POLICY

It is not always clear where lines should be drawn in implementing antitrust policy. Which firms should be allowed to enter into a merger, and which firms should be prohibited? What constitutes restraint of trade? Which firms should be termed "monopolists" and broken into smaller firms, and which firms should be left alone?

As you might guess, not everyone answers these questions the same way. In short, some points of antitrust policy are still unsettled. A few of the more important unsettled points are noted here.

Does the Definition of the Market Matter?

Should a market be defined broadly or narrowly? The way the market is defined helps determine whether or not a particular firm is considered a monopoly. For example, in an important antitrust suit in 1945, a court ruled that Alcoa (Aluminum Company of America) was a monopoly because it had 90 percent of the virgin aluminum ingot market. If Alcoa's market had been broadened to include stainless steel, copper, tin, nickel, and zinc (some of the goods competing with aluminum), it is unlikely that Alcoa would have been ruled a monopoly.

Hurray for Hollywood!!!

Thomas Alva Edison was born in 1847 and died in 1931. In his 84 years of life, Edison was granted 1,093 patents. Almost everyone knows the role Edison played in the development of electric light and power, but not everyone knows the role Edison played in indirectly and unwittingly making Hollywood the film capital of the world.

Our story begins with an Edison invention—a machine called the kinetophonograph. The kinetophonograph showed a moving picture that was synchronized with a phonograph record. Later, Edison invented the kinetoscope, which was a device that allowed users to deposit a coin and watch a short motion picture through a small hole.

After inventing the kinetophonograph and kinetoscope, Edison went on to construct the first building that was used solely to make movies. A hole in the ceiling of the building allowed the sun to shine through and illuminate the stage. The entire building was on a set of tracks so that it could be moved around to follow the sun. The first film that Edison produced was a 15-minute movie called *The Great Train Robbery*. Over the years, he produced more than 2,000 short films.

There is some evidence that Edison and a few other people tried to gain complete control over the movie industry in its early days. Edison played a critical role in putting together the Movie Trust, sometimes called the Edison Trust, a group of 10 film producers and distributors. It is reported that the Movie Trust tried to eliminate its competition. First, the Movie Trust entered into a contract with Eastman Kodak Company, which manufactured film, to sell film only to it. Second, the

Movie Trust refused to lease or sell equipment to certain filmmakers and theater owners.[1]

One of the independent movie producers that the Movie Trust tried to run out of the industry was Carl Laemmie. Laemmie and some other movie producers decided to leave the East Coast where the Movie Trust had the greatest control over the industry. They went to the West Coast, specifically to southern California, to get away from the stranglehold the Movie Trust had over the industry on the East Coast. Others soon followed. The rush of independent filmmakers to southern California set the stage for the development of Hollywood as the film capital of the world. In 1917, the Movie Trust was dissolved by court order, but by then, the movie industry had a new home. Laemmie, for example, founded Universal Studios in Hollywood in 1912.

Would Hollywood be the film capital of the world had it not been for the Movie Trust? It is doubtful. Without the exclusionary and anticompetitive tactics of the Movie Trust, the film capital of the world would probably be on the East Coast of the United States, probably in or near New York City.

Later court rulings have tended to define markets broadly rather than narrowly. For instance, in the DuPont case in 1956, the market relevant to DuPont was ruled to be the flexible wrapping materials market rather than the narrower cellophane market.

Concentration Ratios

Concentration ratios have often been used to gauge the amount of competition in an industry, but as pointed out in the last chapter, their use presents two major problems. First, concentration ratios do not address the issue of foreign competition. For example, the four-firm concentration ratio may be very high, but the four firms that make up the concentration ratio may still face stiff competition from abroad. Second, a four-firm concentration ratio can remain stable over time even though there is competition among the four major firms in the industry.

---

1. As an aside, the Movie Trust forbade the identification of actors in their movies because it thought that if actors became well-known, they would demand higher salaries.

Herfindahl Index
Measures the degree of concentration in an industry. It is equal to the sum of the squares of the market shares of each firm in the industry.

In 1982, the Justice Department replaced the four- and eight-firm concentration ratios with the Herfindahl index, although it too is subject to some of the same criticisms as the concentration ratios. The **Herfindahl Index** measures the degree of concentration in an industry. It is equal to the sum of the squares of the market shares of each firm in the industry:

$$\text{Herfindahl index} = (S_1)^2 + (S_2)^2 + \ldots (S_n)^2$$

where S_1 through S_n are the market shares of firms 1 through n. For example, if there are 10 firms in an industry, and each firm has a 10 percent market share, the Herfindahl index is 1,000 ($10^2 + 10^2 + 10^2 + 10^2 + 10^2 + 10^2 + 10^2 + 10^2 + 10^2 + 10^2 = 1,000$).

Exhibit 1 compares the Herfindahl index and the four-firm concentration ratio. When the four-firm concentration ratio is used, the top four firms, A–D, have a 48 percent market share, which generally is thought to describe a concentrated industry. A merger between any of the top four firms and any other firm (say, between firm B and firm G in Exhibit 1) would give the newly merged firm a greater market share than any existing firm and usually would incur frowns from the Justice Department.

The Herfindahl index for the industry is 932, however, and the Justice Department generally considers any number less than 1,000 to be representative of an unconcentrated (or competitive) industry. An index between 1,000 and 1,800 is considered to be representative of a moderately concentrated industry, and an index greater than 1,800 is representative of a concentrated industry.

Antitrust actions are usually brought by the Justice Department if (1) the index rises by 100 points or more and the (premerger) index is initially in the 1,000 to 1,800 category or (2) the index rises by 50 points or more and the (premerger) index is initially in the greater than 1,800 category.

To illustrate, suppose two firms, A and B, want to merge. The market share of firm A is 20 percent and the market share of firm B is 10 percent. In other words, together these firms account for 30 percent of the market. We assume there are 7 other firms in the industry and each has a 10 percent market share. The Herfindahl index in this industry is 1,200 ($20^2 + 10^2 + 10^2 + 10^2 + 10^2 + 10^2 + 10^2 + 10^2 + 10^2 = 1,200$).

If the merger is approved, there will be 8, not 9, firms. Moreover, the market share of the merged firm (A and B now form one firm) will be 30 percent. The

---

exhibit 1

A Comparison of the Four-Firm Concentration Ratio and the Herfindahl Index

Using the old method (in this case, the four-firm concentration ratio), the top four firms in the industry have a 48 percent market share. The Justice Department would likely frown on a proposed merger between any of the top four firms and any other firm. However, the Herfindahl index of 932 is representative of an unconcentrated industry.

Firms	Market Share
A	15%
B	12
C	11
D	10
E	8
F	7
G	7
H	6
I	6
J	6
K	6
L	6

OLD METHOD: FOUR-FIRM CONCENTRATION RATIO

15% + 12% + 11% + 10% = **48%**

NEW METHOD: HERFINDAHL INDEX

Square the market share of each firm and then add:

$(15)^2 + (12)^2 + (11)^2 + (10)^2 + (8)^2 + (7)^2 + (7)^2 + (6)^2 + (6)^2 + (6)^2 + (6)^2 + (6)^2 = $ **932**

Herfindahl index after the merger will be 1,600. In other words, there will be an increase of 400 points if the firms merge. With this substantial increase in the index, it is likely the proposed merger would be blocked.

The advantage of the Herfindahl index over the four- and eight-firm concentration ratios is that it provides information about the dispersion of firm size in an industry. For example, the Herfindahl index will distinguish between these two situations: (1) 4 firms together have a 50 percent market share and there are only 4 other firms in the industry and (2) 4 firms together have a 50 percent market share and there are 150 other firms in the industry.

The Herfindahl index and the four- and eight-firm concentration ratios have been criticized for implicitly arguing from firm size to market power. Both assume that firms that have large market shares have market power that they are likely to be abusing. But, of course, size could be a function of efficiency, and a firm with a large market share could be serving the buying public well.

Innovation and Concentration Ratios

According to the 1999 *Economic Report of the President,* more than half of all productivity gains in the U.S. economy in the last 50 years, as measured by output per labor hour, have come from innovation and technical change. Because innovation and technical change are so important to our economic well-being, some economists argue that concentration ratios should not play as large a role in determining a merger's approval. The merger's effect on innovation should also be taken into account. There is some evidence that antitrust authorities are beginning to accept this line of thinking (see the discussion of antitrust cases later in the chapter).

It used to be thought that small firms in highly competitive markets with many rivals had a stronger incentive to innovate than firms in markets where only a few firms existed and each firm had sizable market power. Increasingly, though, it is thought that these small competitive firms often face a greater risk of innovation than those firms with substantial market power. And, therefore, they innovate less.

To illustrate, consider a market with 100 firms, each of which supplies 1/100 of the market. Suppose one of these firms invests heavily in research and develops a new product or process. It has to worry about any of its 99 rivals soon developing a similar innovation and therefore reducing the value of its innovation. On the other hand, if a firm is 1 of 4 firms and has substantial market power, it doesn't face as much "innovative risk." It has only 3, not 99, rivals to worry about. All other things equal, the risk that a competing firm's successful innovations will make one's own innovations less valuable may be inversely related to the number of competitors a firm faces. And, of course, the less likely that competitors can make one's own innovations less valuable, the higher the expected return from innovating.

Today, antitrust authorities say that they consider the benefits of both competition and innovation when ruling on proposed mergers. On the one hand, increased competition lowers prices for consumers. On the other hand, monopoly power may yield more innovation. If it does, then the lower prices brought about through increased competition have to be weighed against the increased innovation that may come about through greater market concentration and monopoly power.

ANTITRUST AND MERGERS

There are three basic types of mergers.

1. A **horizontal merger** is a merger between firms that are selling similar products in the same market. For example, suppose both companies *A* and *B* produce cars. If the two companies combined under single ownership of control, it would be a horizontal merger.

Horizontal Merger
A merger between firms that are selling similar products in the same market.

Vertical Merger
A merger between companies in the same industry but at different stages of the production process.

Conglomerate Merger
A merger between companies in different industries.

2. A **vertical merger** is a merger between companies in the same industry but at different stages of the production process. Stated differently, a vertical merger occurs between companies where one buys (or sells) something from (to) the other. For example, suppose company *C*, which produces cars, buys tires from company *D*. If the two companies combined under single ownership of control, it would be a vertical merger.

3. A **conglomerate merger** is a merger between companies in different industries. For example, if company *E*, in the car industry, and company *F*, in the pharmaceutical drug industry, combined under single ownership of control, we would have a conglomerate merger.

Of the three types of mergers—vertical, horizontal, and conglomerate—the federal government looks most carefully at proposed horizontal mergers. The reason is that horizontal mergers are more likely (than vertical or conglomerate mergers) to change the degree of concentration, or competition, in an industry. For example, if General Motors (cars) and Ford Motor Company (cars) horizontally merge, competition in the car industry is likely to decrease by more than if General Motors (cars) and BF Goodrich (tires) vertically merge. In the latter case, it is even possible that the competition among car companies, and among tire companies, will be the same after the merger as it was before. This is not necessarily the case, however, and the government does not always approve vertical mergers—in some notable examples, it has not.

NINE ANTITRUST CASES AND ACTIONS

Most people agree that the stated purpose of the antitrust laws—promoting and strengthening competition—is a worthwhile goal. Often, however, the stated purpose or objective of a policy and its effects turn out to be quite different. Some economists have argued that the antitrust laws have not, in all instances, accomplished their stated objective. The following cases and actions illustrate some of the ways that courts and government policymakers have approached antitrust cases over the years.

Case 1: Von's Grocery

In 1966, the U.S. Supreme Court ruled on the legality of a merger between Von's Grocery Co. and Shopping Bag Food Stores, both of Los Angeles. Together, the two grocery chains had a little more than 7 percent of the grocery market in the Los Angeles area. However, the Supreme Court ruled that a merger between the two companies violated the Clayton Act. The Court based its ruling largely on the fact that between 1950 and the early 1960s, the number of small grocery stores in Los Angeles had declined sharply. The Court took this as an indication of increased concentration in the industry.

Economists are quick to point out that the number of firms in an industry might be falling due to technological changes, and when this happens, the average size of an existing firm rises. Justice Potter Stewart, in a dissenting opinion to the 1966 decision, argued that the Court had erroneously assumed that the "degree of competition is invariably proportional to the number of competitors."

Case 2: Utah Pie

In 1967, the Utah Pie Company, which was based in Salt Lake City, charged that three of its competitors in Los Angeles were practicing price discrimination. Utah Pie charged that these companies were selling pies in Salt Lake City for lower prices than they were selling pies near their plants of operation. The Supreme Court ruled in favor of Utah Pie.

Some economists note, though, that Utah Pie charged lower prices for its pies than did its competitors and that it continued to increase its sales volume and make a profit during the time its competitors were supposedly exhibiting anti-competitive behavior. They suggest that Utah Pie was using the antitrust laws to hinder its competition.

Case 3: Continental Airlines

In 1978, Continental Airlines set out to acquire National Airlines. The Justice Department opposed the merger of the two companies on the grounds that the merged company would dominate the New Orleans air-traffic market. The Civil Aeronautics Board (CAB) did not oppose the merger because it believed the market under consideration was contestable. Recall that firms in a contestable market that operate inefficiently or that consistently earn positive economic profits will be joined by competing firms. By refusing to oppose the merger, the CAB implied that it believed that statistical measures, such as concentration ratios, mean less than whether the market is contestable.

Case 4: IBM

In 1969, the Justice Department filed antitrust charges against IBM, saying that it had monopolized the "general-purpose computer and peripheral-equipment" industry. IBM argued that the antitrust authorities had interpreted its market too narrowly. After 13 years of litigation against IBM, the government decided to drop the suit. During the years of litigation, the computer market had changed. New competitors had entered the broadly defined computer market. Although IBM might have once dominated the mainframe computer industry, there was little evidence that it dominated the minicomputer, word processor, or computer-services market.

Case 5: Universities

For many years, the upper-level administrators of some of the country's top universities—Brown, Columbia, Cornell, Dartmouth, Harvard, MIT, Princeton, the University of Pennsylvania, and Yale—met to discuss such things as tuition, faculty salaries, and financial aid. There seemed to be evidence that these meetings occurred because the universities were trying to align tuition, faculty raises, and financial need. For example, one of the universities once wanted to raise faculty salaries by more than the others wanted and was persuaded not to do so. Also, at these meetings, the administrators compared lists of applicants to find the names of students who had applied to more than one of their schools (for example, someone might have applied to Harvard, Yale, and MIT). Then, the administrators adjusted their financial aid packages for that student so that no university was offering more than another.

The Justice Department charged the universities with a conspiracy to fix prices. Eight of the universities settled the case by agreeing to sign a consent decree to cease colluding on tuition, salaries, and financial aid. MIT did not agree to sign the consent decree and pursued the case to the Supreme Court. In 1992, the Supreme Court ruled against MIT, saying that it had violated antitrust laws.

Case 6: Microsoft and Intuit

In 1995, antitrust authorities claimed that the personal finance/checkbook software market was concentrated. Intuit's software, Quicken, was the top seller in the market with a market share of 69 percent. Microsoft's software, Money, was second with 22 percent of the market. Together, the Intuit and Microsoft market share was 91 percent.

In 1995, Microsoft agreed to acquire all Intuit stock from Intuit's shareholders and to exchange 1.336 shares of Microsoft for each share of Intuit stock. If the sale had closed, the acquisition would have cost $2 billion.

The Justice Department sought to block the Microsoft acquisition of Intuit, arguing that it would lessen competition and innovation in the personal finance/checkbook software market. They also cited a statement by Microsoft to Intuit in which Microsoft declared it would substantially increase its competitive efforts if Intuit did not agree to be acquired. Furthermore, the Justice Department argued that if Microsoft did acquire Intuit (and Quicken), this would eliminate

http://

Go to *http://www.usdoj.gov/atr/pubdocs.html*, and select "Criminal Enforcement." Under the "Other Policy Documents" menu, click on "Criminal Fines." How much money in criminal fines has the Antitrust Division of the U.S. Department of Justice ("Division") obtained since the beginning of FY 1997? What type of activities have resulted in more than 90 percent of these fines? Which is the largest fine ever imposed by the "Division"?

the chance of any new competitors in the personal finance/checkbook software market in the future. Quicken in the hands of Intuit was a strong competitor, but Quicken in the hands of powerful Microsoft would be daunting.

Case 7: Lockheed Martin and Northrop Grumman

In 1997, Lockheed Martin Corporation proposed to acquire Northrop Grumman Corporation. Both Lockheed and Northrop were leading suppliers of aircraft and electronics systems to the U.S. military. The Justice Department challenged the acquisition; it said that it would give Lockheed a monopoly in fiberoptic towed decoys and in systems for airborne early warning radar. In this case, the issue of innovation played a major role. The Justice Department noted that both Lockheed and Northrop had invested heavily in the research and development of advanced airborne early warning radar systems. If the two companies merged, research and development activities would decline and innovation would be hampered. The Justice Department blocked the acquisition of Northrop by Lockheed.

Case 8: Boeing and McDonnell Douglas

In 1997, the Federal Trade Commission approved the merger of Boeing Co. and McDonnell Douglas Corp., the two largest commercial aircraft manufacturers in the United States. Innovation was an issue in the Boeing–McDonnell Douglas case, just as it was in the Lockheed Martin–Northrop Grumman Case. However, innovation played a different role in this case. The FTC approved the merger in order to *increase* innovation. The FTC's analysis showed that McDonnell Douglas had fallen behind technologically and was no longer applying competitive innovative pressure on Boeing. The FTC felt that because McDonnell Douglas was not stimulating innovation in the aircraft manufacturing market, nothing would be lost from the standpoint of innovation in allowing the two firms to merge. In fact, something might be gained. McDonnell Douglas's assets might be put to better use by a technologically advanced company like Boeing.

Case 9: Genetech and Roche

In 1990, the FTC challenged the acquisition of Genetech, Inc., by Roche Holdings., Ltd. The FTC argued that Genetech and Roche were currently both trying to find a treatment for AIDS and HIV infection. The Commission argued that if the two companies were allowed to merge, the competition between the two firms to be the first to develop a treatment for AIDS and HIV would no longer exist. This would make the development of a successful treatment less likely.

ANTITRUST AND NETWORK MONOPOLIES

A network connects things. For example, a telephone network connects telephones, the Internet (which is a network of networks) connects computers, a bank network may connect ATMs (automatic teller machines). A **network good** is a good whose value increases as the expected number of units sold increases. A telephone is a network good. You buy a telephone in order to network with other people. It has little value to you if you expect only a hundred people to buy telephones. Its value increases if you expect thousands of people to buy telephones.

Software is also a network good in the sense that if Smith buys software X and Jones also buys software X, then they can easily exchange documents with each other. As new buyers buy a network good, present owners of the good receive greater benefits. This is because the network connects them to more people. For example, if Brown and Thompson also buy software X, Smith and Jones will receive greater benefits because they can exchange documents with two more people.

Let's see how the production and sales of a network good can lead to monopoly. Suppose that three companies, A, B, and C, make some version of network good X. Company A makes the most popular version of good X, or has the greatest "network-worthiness" linked to its good. Consequently, people who are thinking of buying good X buy it from company A. As more people purchase good X from company A, the "network-worthiness" increases even more. This prompts even more people to buy good X from company A rather than to buy it from the other two companies. Eventually, the customers of companies B and C may switch to company A, and at some point, almost everyone buys good X from company A. Company A is a network monopoly.

Currently, the antitrust authorities move against a network monopoly based on how it behaves, not because of what it is. For example, the authorities would not issue a complaint against company A in our example unless it undertook predatory or exclusionary practices to *maintain* its monopoly position.

Q & A

Q: Earlier it was stated that economists are still undecided as to whether market share assists or detracts from innovation. For example, it was argued that 1 firm among 4 firms may have less "innovative risk" than 1 firm among 100 firms. Therefore, the firm with a larger market share would innovate more, *ceteris paribus*. It seems that a network monopoly will have a large market share. Does it follow that it will be a major innovator?

A: Actually, the situation may be somewhat different for network monopolies. There are sometimes high switching costs that accompany a network monopoly. To illustrate, suppose firm A produces network good A. Network good A begins to sell quite well. Because it is a network good, its robust sales increase the value of the good to potential customers. Potential customers turn into actual customers, and before long, good A has set the market, or industry, standard.

Because network good A is now the industry standard and because network goods (especially those related to the high-tech industries) are sometimes difficult to learn, it may have a "lock" on the market. Specifically, there is a **lock-in effect** that increases the costs of switching from good A to another good. Because of the (relatively) high switching costs, good A has some staying power in the market. Firm A, the producer of good A, thus has staying power too. This may cause firm A to rest on its laurels, so to speak. Instead of innovating, instead of trying to outcompete its existing and future rivals with better production processes or better products, it may do very little. Firm A will realize that the high switching costs keep customers from changing to a different network good. Some economists suggest that in this environment, the network monopoly may have little reason to innovate.

> **Lock-In Effect**
> Descriptive of the situation where a particular product or technology becomes settled upon as the standard and is difficult or impossible to dislodge as the standard.

THE UNITED STATES OF AMERICA VERSUS MICROSOFT: CIVIL ACTION NO. 98-1232

On May 18, 1998, the U.S. Department of Justice joined with 20 states and issued a civil action complaint against Microsoft, Inc. The action claimed basis in Sections 1 and 2 of the Sherman Act. The complaint claimed that Microsoft possesses monopoly power in the market for personal computer operating systems. It stated that (1) Microsoft Windows is used on more than 80 percent of Intel-based PCs and (2) there are high barriers to entry in the market for PC operating systems essentially because Microsoft Windows is a network good that is the industry standard.

The Justice Department claimed that Microsoft was using its dominance in the personal computer operating systems market not only to maintain monopoly power but also to gain dominance in the Internet browser market. The Justice Department claimed that Microsoft, which packages its Internet browser with Windows, required computer manufacturers to agree, as a condition for receiving licenses to install Windows on their products, not to remove Microsoft's browser and not to allow a more prominent display of a rival browser. The Justice Department also claimed that Microsoft refused to display the icons of Internet Service Providers (ISPs) on the main Windows screen unless the ISPs would first agree to withhold information from their customers about non-Microsoft browsers.

In the antitrust case, Microsoft argued that it did not have a monopoly in the operating systems market. It stated that it was part of a cutthroat software industry where today's industry leaders could go out of business tomorrow. It essentially argued that none of its business practices hurt any consumers and that all were necessary to its survival. Microsoft claimed that if it was guilty of anything, it was guilty of charging prices that were too low. It charged nothing, for example, for its Internet browser. Furthermore, Microsoft said that the addition of its browser to Windows was not an attempt to monopolize anything; it was an attempt to provide the buying public with a better product. In short, the browser was simply a new feature of Windows and not an illegal tie-in that violated a consent degree that Microsoft had signed in 1995.

Some economists contended that Microsoft's low pricing strategy made sense. They argued that it approximated marginal cost pricing. After all, software, once written, costs very little for each additional copy. Also, low prices are simply a way to sell a lot of copies—and what is wrong with that?

Critics contended that the low prices to gain customers worked to Microsoft's advantage because its operating system was a network good. Low prices mean more customers, and more customers mean Microsoft would eventually become the industry standard. Once there, it would wield its market power to maintain its current position and would try to establish itself as a monopolist in other markets (such as the browser market).

On Friday, November 4, 1999, Judge Thomas Penfield Jackson, the judge who heard the case against Microsoft, issued his findings of fact. Findings of fact simply present the facts of the case as the judge sees them; it does not constitute a ruling in the case. (The ruling was to come later.) In his findings of fact, Judge Jackson essentially agreed with the case the Justice Department made against Microsoft. He said that Microsoft is not only a monopolist in the operating systems market but also that it used its monopoly power to thwart competition. Specifically, it tied its operating system (Windows) together with its browser (Internet Explorer) not for purposes of efficiency and not to satisfy consumers, but in order to establish a monopoly position in the browser market and to preserve its monopoly position in the operating systems market.

Before issuing his final judgment in the case, Judge Jackson appointed Judge Richard Posner, chief of the 7th U.S. Circuit of Appeals, to try to mediate a settlement between the government and Microsoft. After a few months, mediation talks broke down. There was to be no settlement between the two parties.

On Monday, April 3, 2000, Judge Jackson issued a ruling in the case. He ruled that Microsoft had violated the Sherman Act. The judge wrote that Microsoft was guilty of "unlawfully tying its Web browser" to Windows. He continued by saying that "Microsoft's anticompetitive actions trammeled the competitive process through which the computer software industry generally stimulates innovation."

On July 7, 2000, Judge Jackson issued his final ruling in the case. He ordered that Microsoft be split into two companies—one for operating systems and one for applications. Bill Gates said that Microsoft would appeal the ruling to a higher court.

The U.S. Court of Appeals heard the case months later. On June 28, 2001, the U.S. Court of Appeals reversed Judge Jackson's order to break up Microsoft, but it agreed with some of the judge's findings—specifically, that Microsoft had broken federal antitrust law. The appeals court sent the Microsoft case back to a lower court, but this time to a different judge.

The new judge, U.S. District Judge Colleen Kollar-Kotelly, ordered both Microsoft and the Justice Department to set out the key issues in the case and determine how it might proceed. Before Judge Kollar-Kotelly issued a decision in the case, Microsoft and the Justice Department announced on November 2, 2001, that they had reached a settlement that would end the case. Under the settlement, Microsoft would make portions of its Windows software code available

The Bill Gates Deposition

Before the Microsoft case went to trial, Bill Gates was deposed by the attorneys for the Justice Department. Here are some excerpts from the deposition that took place on Friday, August 28, 1998, at One Microsoft Way, Redmond, Washington. The "Q" stands for questioner and the "A" stands for answerer, who is Bill Gates.

Excerpt 1

Q: In January 1996, you [Mr. Gates] were aware that there were non-Microsoft browsers that were being marketed; is that correct?

A: I can't really confine it to that month, but I'm sure in that time period I was aware of other browsers being out.

Q: And were those non-Microsoft browsers, or at least some of them, being marketed in competition with Microsoft's browsers?

A: Users were making choices about which browser to select.

Q: Is the term "competition" a term that you're familiar with, Mr. Gates?

A: Yes.

Q: And does it have a meaning in the English language that you're familiar with?

A: Any lack of understanding of the question doesn't stem from the use of that word.

Q: And you understand what is meant by non-Microsoft browsers, do you not, sir?

A: No.

Q: You don't? Is that what you're telling me? You don't understand what that means?

A: You'll have to be more specific. What—

Q: Do you understand what is meant by non-Microsoft browsers?

A: In the right context, I'd understand that.

Excerpt 2

Q: Okay. Let me ask you to look at Trial Exhibit 560. This is a message from you to Mr. Ballmer and Mr. Chase with a copy to Mr. Maritz and some other people also given copies dated August 15, 1997, at 4:07 P.M. on the subject of IBM and Netscape, correct?

A: Uh-huh.

Q: And you type in here "Importance: High."

A: No.

Q: No?

A: No, I didn't type that.

Q: Who typed in "High"?

A: A computer.

Q: A computer. Why did the computer type in "High"?

A: It's an attribute of the e-mail.

Q: And who set the attribute of the e-mail?

A: Usually the sender sends that attribute.

Q: Who is the sender here, Mr. Gates?

A: In this case it appears I'm the sender.

Q: Yes. And so you're the one who set the high designation of importance, right, sir?

A: It appears I did that. I don't remember doing that specifically.

Excerpt 3

Q: When you refer to an Internet browser share here, sir, what is the share of?

A: Browser usage.

Q: Of course, you don't say "browser usage" here, do you, sir?

A: No, it says "share."

Q: Now, let's say that you meant browser usage because that's what your testimony is. What browser usage were you talking about in terms of what your share of browser usage was? What browsers?

A: I'm not getting your question. Are you trying to ask what I was thinking when I wrote this sentence?

Q: Let me begin with that. What were you thinking when you—

A: I don't remember specifically writing this sentence.

Q: Does that mean you can't answer what you were thinking when you wrote the sentence?

A: That's correct.

Q: So since you don't have an answer to that question, let me put a different question.

A: I have an answer. The answer is I don't remember.

Q: You don't remember what you meant. Let me try to ask you—

A: I don't remember what I was thinking.

Q: Is there a difference between remembering what you were thinking and remembering what you meant?

A: If the question is what I meant when I wrote it, no.

Q: So you don't remember what you were thinking when you wrote it and you don't remember what you meant when you wrote it; is that fair?

A: As well as not remembering writing it.

to competitors and Microsoft would allow computer manufacturers to choose the products they would load onto their machines without the threat of any retaliation from Microsoft.

Some of the states that had joined the Justice Department in its initial action against Microsoft accepted the settlement and some did not. As of this writing, nine states had not accepted the settlement and Microsoft continues to fight off the sanctions that the nine states are requesting.

Self-Test (Answers to Self-Test questions are in the Self-Test Appendix.)

1. Why does it matter whether a market is defined broadly or narrowly for purposes of antitrust policy?

2. There are 20 firms in an industry and each firm has a 5 percent market share. What is the four-firm concentration ratio and the Herfindahl index for this industry?

3. What is the advantage of the Herfindahl index over the four- and eight-firm concentration ratios? Explain your answer.

REGULATION

This section examines the types of regulation, theories of regulation, the stated objectives of regulatory agencies, and the effects of regulation on natural and other monopolies.

THE CASE OF NATURAL MONOPOLY

Recall that if economies of scale are so pronounced or large in an industry that only one firm can survive, that firm is a *natural monopoly*. Firms that supply local electricity, gas, and water service are usually considered natural monopolies.

Consider the natural monopoly situation in Exhibit 2. There is one firm in the market and it produces Q_1 units of output at an average total cost of ATC_1. (Q_1 is the output at which $MR = MC$; to simplify the diagram, the MR curve is not shown.)

At Q_1, there is an inefficient allocation of resources. Resource allocative efficiency exists when the marginal benefit to demanders of the resources used in

exhibit 2

The Natural Monopoly Situation
The only existing firm produces Q_1 at an average total cost of ATC_1 (Q_1 is the output at which $MR = MC$, although to simplify the diagram the MR curve is not shown.) Resource allocative efficiency exists at Q_2. There are two ways to obtain this output level: (1) The only existing firm can increase its production to Q_2, or (2) a new firm can enter the market and produce Q_3, which is the difference between Q_2 and Q_1. The first way minimizes total cost, the second way does not. This, then, is a natural monopoly situation: One firm can supply the entire output demanded at a lower cost than two or more firms can.

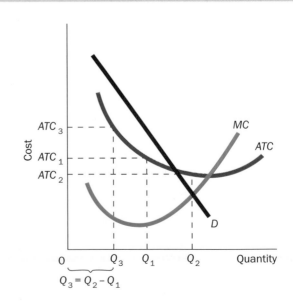

the goods they buy equals the marginal cost to suppliers of the resources they use in the production of the goods they sell. In Exhibit 2, resource allocative efficiency exists at Q_2, corresponding to the point where the demand curve intersects the MC curve.

There are two ways to reach the higher, efficient quantity of output, Q_2: (1) The firm currently producing Q_1 could increase its output to Q_2. (2) Another firm could enter the market and produce Q_3—the difference between Q_2 and Q_1.

Different costs are associated with each way. If a new firm enters the market and produces Q_3, it incurs an average total cost of ATC_3. Thus, both firms together produce Q_2, but the new firm incurs average total costs of ATC_3, while the existing firm incurs average total costs of ATC_1.

If, instead, the firm currently in the market increases its production to Q_2, it incurs average total costs of ATC_2. As long as the objective is to increase output to the level of resource allocative efficiency, it is cheaper (lower total costs) to have the firm currently in the market increase its output to Q_2 rather than to have two firms together produce Q_2.

Natural monopoly exists where one firm can supply the entire output demanded at lower cost than two or more firms can. It is a natural monopoly because a monopoly situation will naturally evolve over time as the low-cost producer undercuts its competitors.

Will the natural monopolist charge the monopoly price? Some economists say yes. See Exhibit 3, where the natural monopoly firm produces Q_1, at which marginal revenue equals marginal cost, and charges price P_1, which is the highest price per unit consistent with the output it produces.

Because it charges the monopoly price, some people argue that the natural monopoly firm should be regulated. What form should the regulation take? This question is addressed next.

REGULATING THE NATURAL MONOPOLY

The natural monopoly may be regulated through price, profit, or output regulation.

1. **Price regulation.** Marginal cost pricing is one form of price regulation. The objective is to set a price for the natural monopoly firm that equals marginal cost at the quantity of output at which demand intersects marginal cost. In Exhibit 4, this price is P_1. At this price, the natural monopoly takes a loss. At Q_1, average total cost is greater than price, and thus total cost is greater than

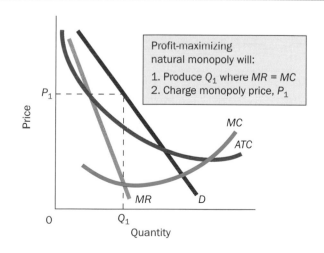

Profit-maximizing natural monopoly will:

1. Produce Q_1 where $MR = MC$
2. Charge monopoly price, P_1

exhibit 3

The Profit-Maximizing Natural Monopoly
The natural monopoly that seeks to maximize profits will produce the quantity of output at which $MR = MC$ and charge the (monopoly) price, P_1.

total revenue.[2] Obviously, the natural monopoly would rather go out of business than be subject to this type of regulation unless it receives a subsidy for its operation.

2. **Profit regulation.** Government may want the natural monopoly to earn only zero economic profits. If so, government will require the natural monopoly to charge a price of P_2 (because $P_2 = ATC$) and to supply the quantity demanded at that price (Q_2). This form of regulation is often called *average-cost pricing*. Theoretically, this may seem like a good way to proceed, but in practice it often turns out differently. The problem is that if the natural monopoly is always held to zero economic profits—and is not allowed to fall below or rise above this level—then it has an incentive to let costs rise. Higher costs—in the form of higher salaries or more luxurious offices—simply mean higher prices to cover the higher costs. In this case, it is unlikely that average cost pricing is an efficient way to proceed.

3. **Output regulation.** Government can mandate a quantity of output it wants the natural monopoly to produce. Suppose this is Q_3 in Exhibit 4. Here, there are positive economic profits because price is above average total cost at Q_3. It is possible, however, that the natural monopoly would want even higher profits. At a fixed quantity of output, this can be obtained by lowering costs. The natural monopolist might lower costs by reducing the quality of the good or service it sells, knowing that it faces no direct competition and that it is protected (by government) from competitors.

Regulation of a natural monopoly does not always turn out the way it was intended. Government regulation of a natural monopoly—whether it takes the form of price, profit, or output regulation—can distort the incentives of those who operate the natural monopoly. For example, if profit is regulated to the extent that zero economic profits are guaranteed, then the natural monopoly has

exhibit 4

Regulating a Natural Monopoly
The government can regulate a natural monopoly through (1) price regulation, (2) profit regulation, or (3) output regulation. Price regulation usually means marginal cost pricing, and profit regulation usually means average cost pricing.

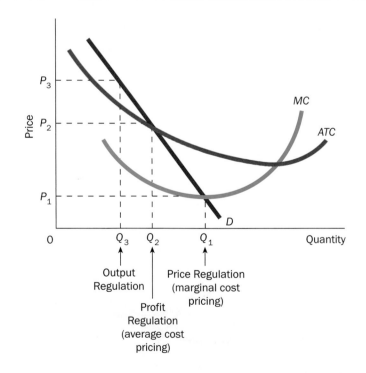

---

2. Remember that $TC = ATC \times Q$ and $TR = P \times Q$. Here $ATC > P$, so it follows that $TC > TR$.

little incentive to hold costs down. Furthermore, the owners of the natural monopoly have an incentive to try to influence the government officials or other persons who are regulating the natural monopoly.

In addition, each of the three types of regulation requires information. For example, if the government wishes to set price equal to marginal cost or average total cost for the natural monopoly, it must know the cost conditions of the firm.

Three problems arise in gathering information: (1) The cost information is not easy to determine, even for the natural monopoly itself. (2) The cost information can be rigged (to a degree) by the natural monopoly, and therefore the regulators will not get a true picture of the firm. (3) The regulators have little incentive to obtain accurate information because they are likely to keep their jobs and prestige even if they work with less-than-accurate information. (This raises a question: Who will ensure that the regulators do a good job?)

Finally, there is the issue of **regulatory lag,** which is indirectly related to information. Regulatory lag refers to the time period between when a natural monopoly's costs change and when the regulatory agency adjusts prices for the natural monopoly. For example, suppose the rates your local gas company charges customers are regulated. The gas company's costs rise, and it seeks a rate hike through the local regulatory body. The rate hike is not likely to be approved quickly. The gas company will probably have to submit an application for a rate hike, document its case, have a date set for a hearing, argue its case at the hearing, and then wait for the regulatory agency to decide on the merits of the application. Many months may pass between the beginning of the process and the end. During that time, the regulated firm is operating in ways and under conditions that both the firm and the regulatory body might not have desired.

Regulatory Lag
The time period between when a natural monopoly's costs change and when the regulatory agency adjusts prices for the natural monopoly.

THINKING LIKE AN ECONOMIST

The public is perhaps naturally inclined to think that a solution (such as regulation) to a problem (such as monopoly) is better than no solution at all—that something is better than nothing. The economist has learned, though, that a "solution" can do one of three things: (1) solve a problem, (2) not solve a problem but do no damage, (3) make the problem worse. Thinking in terms of the entire range of possibilities is natural for an economist, who, after all, understands that solutions come with both costs and benefits.

REGULATING INDUSTRIES THAT ARE NOT NATURAL MONOPOLIES

Some firms are regulated even though they are not natural monopolies. For instance, in the past, government has regulated both the airline and trucking industries. In the trucking industry, the Interstate Commerce Commission (ICC) fixed routes, set minimum freight rates, and erected barriers to entry. In the airline industry, the Civil Aeronautics Board (CAB) did much the same thing. Some economists view the regulation of competitive industries as unnecessary. They see it as evidence that the firms that are being regulated are controlling the regulation to reduce their competition. We discuss this in greater detail next.

THEORIES OF REGULATION

The **capture theory of regulation** holds that no matter what the motive is for the initial regulation and the establishment of the regulatory agency, eventually the agency will be "captured" (controlled) by the special interests of the industry that is being regulated. The following are a few of the interrelated points that have been put forth to support this hypothesis:

Capture Theory of Regulation
Holds that no matter what the motive is for the initial regulation and the establishment of the regulatory agency, eventually the agency will be "captured" (controlled) by the special interests of the industry that is being regulated.

1. In many cases, persons who have been in the industry are asked to regulate the industry because they know the most about it. Such regulators are likely to feel a bond with people in the industry, see their side of the story more often than not, and thus be inclined to cater to them.

Getting a Taxi in London

There are two types of taxis in London: large, black cabs and small minicabs. Size is not the only difference between the two types of taxis.[3] Black cabs are licensed and regulated, minicabs are not. Black cabs usually charge twice the rate that minicabs charge, black cabs can pick up patrons on the street and minicabs cannot (you have to call for a minicab), and drivers of black cabs have to learn "the Knowledge," whereas drivers of minicabs do not. "The Knowledge" requires prospective drivers to memorize more than 16,000 streets in a 113-square-mile area, along with every church, restaurant, and theater on those streets. Most applicants take two to three years to master "the Knowledge," and only 3 of every 10 pass.

In recent years, minicab drivers have been taking away business from the drivers of black cabs. As a result, the drivers of black cabs have started to fight back. First, they want the government to require minicab drivers to learn "the Knowledge." This will definitely thin the ranks of cab drivers. Second, they want government to continue to forbid minicab drivers from picking up passengers on the streets. Minicab drivers have argued for that right. The drivers of the black cabs maintain that their goal is to protect the public from the discomfort of riding in a small cab whose driver likely does not know every byway in London. That the measures, if passed, would raise the income of the drivers of the black cabs is, of course, a happy coincidence.

Our purpose here is not to side with the drivers of either the black cabs or the minicabs, but to point out what economists have known for a long time: regulation, of almost any variety, comes with both benefits and costs. It might be interesting, though, to ask taxicab customers whether they think the benefits of riding in a large, well-kept black cab with a knowledgeable driver at the wheel are worth double the fare. Some people might even suggest another possibility: allowing minicabs and black cabs to compete openly so customers—not government—could decide which cabs best serve their needs.

---

2. At regulatory hearings, members of the industry attend in greater force than do taxpayers and consumers. The industry turns out in force because the regulatory hearing can affect it substantially and directly. In contrast, the effect on individual taxpayers and consumers is usually small and indirect (the effect is spread over millions of people). Thus, regulators are much more likely to hear and respond to the industry's side of the story.

3. Members of the regulated industry make a point of getting to know the members of the regulatory agency. They may talk frequently about business matters; perhaps they socialize. The bond between the two groups grows stronger over time. This may have an impact on regulatory measures.

4. After they either retire or quit their jobs, regulators often go to work for the industries they once regulated.

Public Interest Theory of Regulation
Holds that regulators are seeking to do, and will do through regulation, what is in the best interest of the public or society at large.

Public Choice Theory of Regulation
Holds that regulators are seeking to do, and will do through regulation, what is in their best interest (specifically to enhance their power and the size and budget of their regulatory agencies).

The capture theory is markedly different from what has come to be called the **public interest theory of regulation.** This theory holds that regulators are seeking to do, and will do through regulation, what is in the best interest of the public or society at large.

An alternative to both theories is the **public choice theory of regulation.** This theory suggests that to understand the decisions of regulatory bodies, we must first understand how the decisions affect the regulators themselves. For

---

3. Adapted from Dana Milbank, "The London Taxi May Go the Way of London Bridge," *Wall Street Journal,* 7 April 1995, p. 1.

example, a regulation that increases the power of the regulators and the size and budget of the regulatory agency should not be viewed the same way as a regulation that decreases the agency's power and size. The theory predicts that the outcomes of the regulatory process will tend to favor the regulators instead of either business interests or the public.

Here, then, are three interesting, different, and at first sight, believable theories of regulation. Economists have directed much effort to testing the three theories. There is no clear consensus yet, but in the area of business regulation, the adherents of the capture and public choice theories have been increasing.

SOCIAL REGULATION

When the word *regulation* is used, different people often think of different things. Some people may think of the price and profit regulation that is part of regulating a natural monopoly. Others may think of what has been referred to as *social regulation*. Social regulation is concerned with the conditions under which goods and services are produced and the safety of these items for the consumer. For example, the Occupational Safety and Health Administration (OSHA) is a regulatory government agency concerned with protecting workers against occupational injuries and illnesses. The Consumer Product Safety Commission (CPSC) specifies minimum standards for potentially unsafe products. One of its responsibilities is to make sure toy manufacturers meet certain standards so their toys won't harm the children who use them. The Environmental Protection Agency (EPA) regulates the amount of pollution business firms can emit into the air or waterways.

As with almost any type of government regulation, not everyone agrees on the worth of social regulation. Some people argue that the bulk of social regulation is too costly to taxpayers and reflects an intrusive, meddlesome government. The proponents of social regulation believe that while the costs are high, the benefits are even higher. They say, for example, that highway fatalities would be 40 percent higher in the absence of auto safety features mandated through regulation, that mandated childproof lids have resulted in 90 percent fewer child deaths caused by accidental swallowing of poisonous substances, and that government regulations on the use of asbestos save between 630 and 2,553 persons from dying of cancer each year.

The proponents of social regulation also argue that government regulation of and vigilance over business is important because atrocious things can happen without it. For example, they cite the case of Beech-Nut Nutrition Corporation, a baby food manufacturer, which, in 1987, pleaded guilty to 215 felony counts. The company had sold millions of containers of sugared water and flavoring that it had labeled "100 percent apple juice." The case of Cordis Corporation is also often cited. Cordis Corporation produced and sold thousands of pacemakers that it knew were defective. Many of the pacemakers failed. The company ended up pleading guilty to 25 criminal violations.

THE COSTS AND BENEFITS OF REGULATION

Suppose a business firm is polluting the air with smoke from its factories. The government passes an environmental regulation requiring such firms to purchase antipollution devices that reduce the smoke emitted into the air.

What are the benefits of this kind of regulation? The obvious benefit is cleaner air. But cleaner air can lead to other benefits. For example, people may have fewer medical problems in the future. In some parts of the country, pollution from cars and factories causes people to cough, feel tired, and experience eye discomfort. More importantly, some people have chronic medical problems from constantly breathing dirty air. Government regulation that reduces the amount of pollution in the air clearly helps these people.

But regulation usually doesn't come with benefits only. It comes with costs too. For example, when a business firm incurs the cost of antipollution devices,

ECONOMICS IN...

"Why Am I Always Flying to Dallas?"

The shortest distance between two points is a straight line. Some say that the airline industry doesn't care much about straight lines (or, obviously, about short distances). It cares about hubs and spokes.

Suppose you want to go from Phoenix to New York City. The shortest route is the direct route: Phoenix directly to New York. Very likely, however, you won't be able to get a direct flight. Often (but not always) you will be routed through Dallas or Chicago. In other words, you will get on the plane in Phoenix, get off the plane in Dallas, get on another plane in Dallas, fly to New York, and finally get off the plane in New York. This is referred to as the hub-and-spoke delivery system. The hub represents the center of an airline network; the spokes (much like the spokes on a bicycle wheel) represent origin and destination cities and are always linked through the hub.

The hub-and-spoke system has been used more often since airline deregulation. In several instances, airline departures from major hubs (such as Dallas and Chicago) have doubled. Most economists believe the increased use of the hub-and-spoke system, which makes average travel time longer, is the result of increased price competition brought on by deregulation.

After deregulation, airlines were under greater pressure to compete on price; thus, it became more important to cut costs. One way to cut costs is to use bigger planes because bigger planes cost less to operate per seat mile. But the bigger planes have to be filled. To accomplish both objectives—flying bigger planes that are more fully occupied—the airlines began to gather passengers at one spot. Then at the hub, they could put more passengers on one plane and fly them to the same destination. For example, instead of flying people in Phoenix and people in Albuquerque directly but separately to New York, both groups of people are flown first to Dallas, and then the combined group is flown to New York.

This system may have benefits that offset the costs of inconvenience and longer travel time. Some people think it is better to pay lower airline ticket prices and reach one's destination a little later than to pay higher prices and get there sooner. They also maintain that increased use of the hub-and-spoke system has given passengers more options to travel on different airlines (in Dallas, numerous airlines can fly you to New York) at more convenient times (numerous flights leave Dallas every hour).

---

its overall costs of production rise. Simply put, it is costlier for the business firm to produce its product after the regulation is imposed. As a result, the business firm may produce fewer units of its product, raising its product price and causing some workers to lose their jobs.

If you are the worker who loses your job, you may view the government's insistence that businesses install antipollution devices differently than if, say, you are the person suffering from chronic lung disease. If you have asthma, less pollution may be the difference between your feeling well and your feeling sick. If you are a worker for the business firm, less pollution may end up costing you your job. Ideally, you prefer to have a little less pollution in your neighborhood, but perhaps not at the cost of losing your job.

Are economists for or against government regulation of the type described? The answer is neither. The job of the economist is to make the point that regulation involves both benefits and costs. To the person who only sees the costs, the economist asks: But what about the benefits? And to the person who only sees the benefits, the economist asks: But what about the costs? Then, the economist goes on to outline the benefits and the costs as best she can.

SOME EFFECTS OF REGULATION ARE UNINTENDED

Besides outlining the benefits and costs of regulation, the economist tries to point out the unintended effects that can occur with regulation. To illustrate, consider the example concerning fuel standards that is discussed in an earlier chapter. Suppose the government requires new cars to get an average of 40 miles per gallon of gasoline instead of, say, 30 miles per gallon. Many people will say that this is a good thing. They will reason that if car companies are made to produce cars that get better mileage, people will not need to buy and burn as much gasoline. When less gasoline is burned, less air pollution will be produced.

There is no guarantee the regulation will have this effect, though. The effects could be quite different. If cars are more fuel-efficient, people will buy less gasoline to drive from one place to another—say, from home to college. This means that the (dollar) cost per mile of traveling will fall. As a result of cheaper traveling costs, people might begin to travel more. Leisure driving on the weekend might become more common. People might begin to drive farther on vacations, and so on. If people begin to travel more, then the gasoline saving that resulted from the higher fuel economy standards might be offset or even outweighed. And more gasoline consumption due to more travel will mean more gasoline will be burned and more pollutants will end up in the air.

In other words, a regulation requiring car companies to produce cars that get better fuel mileage may have an unintended effect. The net result might be that people purchase and burn more gasoline and thus produce more air pollution, not less as the government intended.

DEREGULATION

In the early 1970s, many economists, basing their arguments on the capture and public choice theories of regulation, argued that regulation was actually promoting and protecting market power instead of reducing it. They argued for deregulation. And since the late 1970s, many industries have been deregulated, including airlines, trucking, long-distance telephone service, and more.

Consider a few details that relate to the deregulation of the airline industry. The Civil Aeronautics Act, which was passed in 1938, gave the Civil Aeronautics Authority (CAA) the authority to regulate airfares, the number of carriers on interstate routes, and the pattern of routes. The CAA's successor, the Civil Aeronautics Board (CAB), regulated fares in such a way that major air carriers could meet their average costs. An effect of this policy was that fares were raised so high-cost, inefficient air carriers could survive. In addition, the CAB did not allow price competition between air carriers. As a result, air carriers usually competed in a nonprice dimension: They offered more scheduled flights, better meals, more popular in-flight movies, and so forth.

In 1978, under CAB chairman Alfred Kahn, an economist, the airline industry was deregulated. With deregulation, airlines can compete on fares, initiate service along a new route, or discontinue a route. Empirical research after deregulation showed that passenger miles increased and fares decreased. For example, in 1978, fares fell 20 percent, and between 1979 and 1984, fares fell approximately 14 percent.

Deregulation has also led to a decline in costs in various industries. For example, a recent study by Clifford Winston of the Brookings Institution shows that since deregulation, costs in the airline industry have fallen 24 percent (per unit of output); in trucking, operating costs have fallen 30–35 percent per mile; in railroads, there has been a 50 percent decline in costs per ton-mile and a 141 percent increase in productivity; and in natural gas, there has been a 35 percent decline in operating and maintenance expenses.[4]

---

4. See The Economic Report of the President, 1997, p. 190.

Corporate Scandals, Corporate Oaths

Before people buy or sell stocks, they usually acquire some information. For example, if you were thinking about buying a company's stock, you would want to know what the company's profits were last year, what the company's plans were for the future, how much the company was spending on research and new equipment, and so on.

Now suppose the information you acquired about a company was false. Instead of earning, say, $100 million in profits in the last quarter, the company actually took a loss—but you didn't know this. With false information, you are likely to make a mistake; perhaps you would buy the stock when you otherwise wouldn't have.

In recent years, many people have made decisions based on inaccurate information provided to them by companies. Enron, at one time the sixth-largest company in the United States, announced in November 2001 that it had camouflaged a huge debt in a web of "off balance sheet" partnerships and, thus, had overstated its profits by $600 million.

Another company, Adelphia Communications, did much the same thing when it excluded billions of dollars in liabilities from its financial statements and inflated its profits.

WorldCom erroneously reported billions of dollars in normal operating expenses as investments, thus making its profits appear larger than they were. Think of the investors who had bought stock in WorldCom for $60 a share and after WorldCom's misdeeds became public, sold their stock for 20 cents a share.

A natural question is, "Where were the auditors—the accounting firms that are supposed to make sure companies provide accurate reports?" One well-known accounting firm, Arthur Andersen, was shredding documents. On June 15, 2002, a Texas jury found Arthur Andersen guilty of obstructing justice in its role of shredding documents related to its former client, Enron.

Enron, Adelphia, and WorldCom weren't the only companies facing corporate scandals in 2001 and 2002. In what seemed like a-scandal-a-week environment, the Securities and Exchange Commission (SEC) issued Order 4-460. (The SEC states that its primary mission "is to protect investors and maintain the integrity of the securities markets.")

Order 4-460 required the chief executive officers (CEOs) of 942 multibillion-dollar companies to sign a "statement under oath" that the financial reports their companies submitted were true and omitted no essential facts. These "statements under oath" were to be delivered to the Secretary of the SEC on or before August 14, 2002.

Most of the CEOs complied with the order. Some of the CEOs only signed the oath *after* restating their company's profits downward. For example, Household International restated its profits downward by $386 million (over the period of 1994 through the second quarter of 2002).

To see the statements of oath submitted by the CEOs of various companies, you may want to visit the SEC Web site at *http://www.sec.gov/*.

Self-Test

1. What is a criticism of average cost pricing?
2. State the essence of the capture theory of regulation.
3. What is the difference between the capture theory and the public choice theory of regulation?
4. Are economists for or against social regulation?

Were Sotheby's and Christie's Engaged in Price Fixing?

Not too long ago, I read that the two major auction houses, Sotheby's and Christie's, were engaged in price fixing. What were the details?

Sotheby's (founded in 1744) and Christie's (founded in 1766) are the two biggest auction houses in the world. In 1983, A. Alfred Taubman, a Michigan shopping-mall magnate, bought Sotheby's (some say for his wife as a wedding present). In 1994, Taubman appointed Diana Brooks president and CEO of Sotheby's. In 1997, the U.S. Justice Department began investigating possible collusion between Sotheby's and Christie's to fix the prices people paid to have their items auctioned.

Under American law, accused conspirators are encouraged to confess and to name others involved in the conspiracy. In fact, the first party to do this is given leniency. Christopher Davidge, the president and CEO of Christie's,

came forth and turned over papers describing the price-fixing arrangement with Sotheby's.

According to Diana Brooks, who pleaded guilty to the charge, she had been ordered by Taubman to enter into the illegal collusive agreement with Christie's. Taubman claimed that Brooks was lying. Taubman's spokesman declared, "We believe that Mrs. Brooks is lying to save her skin and that she has a clear motivation for doing so."

On April 23, 2002, A. Alfred Taubman was sentenced to a year and a day in prison and fined $7.5 million for leading a six-year price-fixing scheme with its chief competitor Christie's that is said to have swindled more than $100 million from their customers. In handing down the sentence, the judge said, "Price fixing is a crime whether it's committed in the grocery store or the halls of a great auction house."

Chapter Summary

Dealing with Monopoly Power

- A monopoly produces less than a perfectly competitive firm produces (assuming the same revenue and cost conditions), charges a higher price, and causes a deadweight loss. This is the monopoly power problem, and solving it is usually put forth as a reason for antitrust laws and/or government regulatory actions. Some economists note, though, that government antitrust and regulatory actions do not always have the intended effect. Also, sometimes they are implemented where there is no monopoly power problem to solve.

Antitrust Laws

- Two major criticisms have been directed at the antitrust acts. First, some argue that the language in the laws is vague; for example, even though the words "restraint of trade" are used in the Sherman Act, the act does not clearly explain what actions constitute a restraint of trade. Second, it has been argued that some antitrust acts appear to hinder, rather than promote, competition; an example is the Robinson-Patman Act.
- There are a few unsettled points in antitrust policy. One centers on the proper definition of a market. Should a market be defined narrowly or broadly? How this question is answered will have an impact on which firms are considered monopolies. In addition,

the use of concentration ratios for identifying monopolies or deciding whether to allow two firms to enter into a merger has been called into question. Recently, concentration ratios have been largely replaced (for purposes of implementing antitrust policy) with the Herfindahl index. This index is subject to some of the same criticisms as the concentration ratios. Antitrust authorities are also beginning to consider the benefits of innovation in ruling on proposed mergers.

Regulation

- Even if we assume that the intent of regulation is to serve the public interest, it does not follow that this will be accomplished. To work as desired, regulation must be based on complete information (the regulatory body must know the cost conditions of the regulated firm, for example), and it must not distort incentives (to keep costs down, for example). Many economists are quick to point out that neither condition is likely to be fully met. In itself, this does not mean that regulation should not be implemented, but only that regulation may not have the expected effects.
- Government uses three basic types of regulation to regulate natural monopolies: price, profit, or output regulation. Price regulation usually means marginal cost price regulation, that is, setting $P = MC$. Profit

regulation usually means zero economic profits. Output regulation specifies a particular quantity of output that the natural monopoly must produce.

- The capture theory of regulation holds that no matter what the motive is for the initial regulation and the establishment of the regulatory agency, eventually the agency will be "captured" (controlled) by the special interests of the industry that is being regulated. The public interest theory holds that regulators are seeking to do, and will do through regulation, what is in the best interest of the public or society at large. The public choice theory holds that regulators are seeking to do, and will do through regulation, what is in their best interest (specifically, to enhance their power and the size and budget of their regulatory agencies).

Key Terms and Concepts

Antitrust Law
Trust
Herfindahl Index
Horizontal Merger
Vertical Merger

Conglomerate Merger
Network Good
Lock-In Effect
Regulatory Lag
Capture Theory of Regulation

Public Interest Theory of
Regulation
Public Choice Theory of
Regulation

Economic Connections to You

Economic facts, actions, and changes create ripples that move away from their point of origin. Eventually, these ripples can intersect your life and have an effect on you. Consider the following example.

An economic researcher, working alone for years, develops a new measure for gauging the amount of competition in a market. He publishes a paper on the new measure that is widely accepted in the economics profession. Eventually, officials in the Antitrust Division of the Department of Justice begin to use the new measure to decide whether or not mergers should be permitted. The measure is not really effective at gauging the amount of competition in a market, but this is not known at the time. So, antitrust officials continue to make decisions based on the

measure. Years later, an economist points out a fundamental error in the measure. Convinced of the error, antitrust officials stop using the measure to gauge competition. In the interim, however, mergers were blocked that could have led to cost efficiencies and lower prices and mergers were permitted that resulted in substantially less competition in the market. You end up buying lower-quality, higher-priced goods because the measure was flawed. Thus, there is a connection between an economic measure and the quality and price of goods you purchase—an economic connection to you.

Based on the material in this chapter, identify other ways in which economic facts, actions, and changes create ripples that eventually affect you.

Questions and Problems

1. Why was the Robinson-Patman Act passed? the Wheeler-Lea Act? the Celler-Kefauver Antimerger Act?
2. Explain why defining a market narrowly or broadly can make a difference in how antitrust policy is implemented.
3. What is one difference between the four-firm concentration ratio and the Herfindahl index?
4. How does a vertical merger differ from a horizontal merger? Why would the government look more carefully at one than at the other?

5. What is the implication of saying that regulation is likely to affect incentives?
6. Explain price regulation, profit regulation, and output regulation.
7. Why might profit regulation lead to rising costs for the regulated firm?
8. What is the major difference between the capture theory of regulation and the public interest theory of regulation?

9. George Stigler and Claire Friedland studied both unregulated and regulated electric utilities and found no difference in the rates charged by them. One could draw the conclusion that regulation is ineffective when it comes to utility rates. What ideas or hypotheses presented in this chapter might have predicted this result?

10. The courts have ruled that it is a reasonable restraint of trade (and therefore permissible) for the owner of a business to sell his business and sign a contract with the new owner saying he will not compete with her within a vicinity of, say, 100 miles, for a period of, say, 5 years. If this is a reasonable restraint of trade, can you give an example of what you would consider an unreasonable restraint of trade? Explain how you decide what is a reasonable restraint of trade and what isn't.

11. In your opinion, what is the best way to deal with the monopoly power problem? Do you advocate antitrust laws or regulation, or something else we didn't discuss? Give reasons for your answer.

12. It is usually asserted that public utilities such as electric companies and gas companies are natural monopolies. But an assertion is not proof. How would you go about trying to prove (disprove) that electric companies and the like are (are not) natural monopolies? (Hint: You might consider comparing the average total cost of a public utility that serves many customers with the average total cost of a public utility that serves relatively few customers.)

13. Discuss the advantages and disadvantages of regulation (as you see it).

Working with Numbers and Graphs

1. Calculate the Herfindahl index and the four-firm concentration ratio for the following industry:

Firms	Market Share
A	17%
B	15
C	14
D	14
E	12
F	10
G	9
H	9

Use the following figure to answer Questions 2–4.

2. Is the firm in the figure a natural monopoly? Explain your answer.

3. Will the firm in the figure earn profits if it produces Q_3 and charges P_3? Explain your answer.

4. Which quantity in the figure is consistent with profit regulation? With price regulation? Explain your answers.

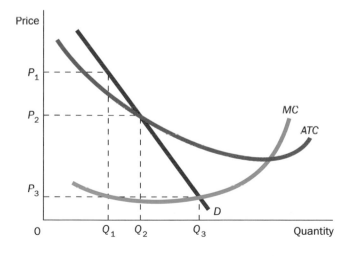

1. Go to *http://www.usdoj.gov/atr/overview.html*.
   a. What is the stated mission of the Antitrust Division of the U.S. Department of Justice?
   b. Click on "Antitrust Enforcement and the Consumer." What penalties might be imposed on someone found in violation of antitrust law?
   c. Can a private citizen sue a company she believes has violated one or more antitrust laws?
2. Go to *http://www.ftc.gov/ftc/mission.htm*. What is the mission of the Federal Trade Commission? What is the difference between what the FTC does and what the Antitrust Division of the Department of Justice does?
3. Go to *http://www.ftc.gov/ftc/consumer.htm*. Click on "Advertising," and select the "TEXT" icon next to "FTC Guide Concerning the Use of the Word Free." What is the definition of "free"? Suppose a seller usually sells good X for $10 and good Y for $4. If he makes the following offer, "Buy good X for $14 and get good Y for free," has he done anything wrong? Explain your answer.

Log on to the Arnold Xtra! Web site now (*http://arnoldxtra.swcollege.com*) for additional learning resources such as practice quizzes, help with graphing, video clips, and current event applications.

FACTOR MARKETS:
WITH EMPHASIS ON THE LABOR MARKET

Employees want to know why their salaries can't be higher; they would like to have more income for spending and saving. As an employee, you might wonder, "Why am I not getting paid $10,000 more? Why not $20,000 more?" Of course, employers look at salaries in another way; they would like to pay lower salaries. Your employer may look at your salary and wonder, "Why couldn't I have paid $10,000 less? Why not $20,000 less?"

Salaries are determined by economic forces. This chapter identifies the factors and the process that will be at work determining your pay. Is this chapter relevant to you? Without a doubt.

For most of this book, we have discussed firms as sellers

in product markets. But firms are buyers too. Firms buy factors of pro-

duction (resources, inputs). In other words, while firms are sellers in product, or

goods, markets, they are buyers in factor, or resource, markets. Buyer one day, seller the next.

In this chapter, we discuss firms as buyers—buyers of factors, or resources. We start by dis-

cussing factors in general. Then we turn to a discussion of a factor that most people are very interested in—

labor. Stated differently, we turn to a discussion of the labor market, where the demand for and supply of labor

occupy center stage. We study the demand for and supply of labor in order to gain a fuller understanding of the forces

that determine wages.

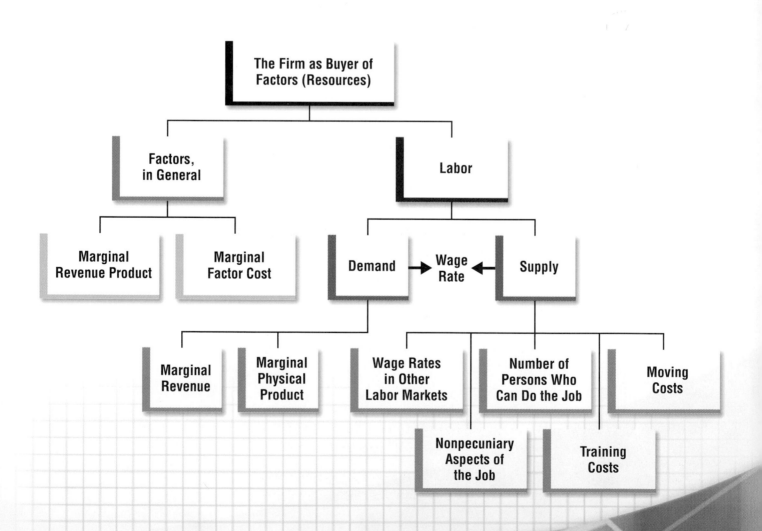

FACTOR MARKETS

Just as there is a demand for and supply of a product, there is a demand for and a supply of a factor or resource (such as the demand for and supply of labor).

THE DEMAND FOR A FACTOR

Why do firms purchase factors? The answer is obvious—to produce products to sell. This is true for all firms, whether they are perfectly competitive firms or oligopolistic firms or whatever. For example, farmers buy tractors and fertilizer in order to produce crops to sell. General Motors buys steel in order to build cars to sell.

The demand for factors is a **derived demand.** It is derived from and directly related to the demand for the product that the resources go to produce. If the demand for the product rises, the demand for the factors used to produce the product rises. If the demand for the product falls, the demand for the factors used to produce the product falls. For example, if the demand for a university education falls, so does the demand for university professors. If the demand for computers rises, so does the demand for skilled computer workers.

When the demand for a seller's product rises, the seller needs to decide how much more of a factor it should buy. The concepts of marginal revenue product and marginal factor cost are relevant to this decision.

> **Derived Demand**
> Demand that is the result of some other demand. For example, factor demand is the result of the demand for the products that the factors go to produce.

MARGINAL REVENUE PRODUCT: TWO WAYS TO CALCULATE IT

Marginal revenue product (MRP) is the additional revenue generated by employing an additional factor unit. For example, if a firm employs one more unit of a factor and its total revenue rises by $20, the *MRP* of the factor equals $20. Marginal revenue product can be calculated in two ways:

> **Marginal Revenue Product (MRP)**
> The additional revenue generated by employing an additional factor unit.

$$MRP = \Delta TR/\Delta \text{Quantity of the factor}$$

or

$$MRP = MR \times MPP$$

where TR = total revenue, MR = marginal revenue, and MPP = marginal physical product.

Method 1: $MRP = \Delta TR/\Delta$Quantity of the Factor

Look at Exhibit 1a. Column 1 shows the different quantities of factor X. Column 2 shows the quantity of output produced at the different quantities of factor X.

Column 3 lists the price and the marginal revenue of the product that the factor goes to produce. Notice that this is $5. Also, notice that we have assumed the seller is a perfectly competitive firm. How do you know this? The reason is that we have assumed the price of the product (P) equals the product's marginal revenue (MR). For a perfectly competitive firm, $P = MR$.

In column 4, we calculate the total revenue, or price times quantity. In column 5, we calculate the marginal revenue product (*MRP*) by dividing the change in total revenue (from column 4) by the change in the quantity of the factor.

Method 2: $MRP = MR \times MPP$

Now look at Exhibit 1b. Columns 1 and 2 are the same as in Exhibit 1a.

In column 3, we calculate the marginal physical product (*MPP*) of factor X. Recall that *MPP* is the change in the quantity of output divided by the change in the quantity of the factor.

Column 4 lists the price and marginal revenue of the product. Again, notice that price equals marginal revenue, so the firm is perfectly competitive. Column 4 is the same as column 3 in part (a).

exhibit 1

Calculating Marginal Revenue Product (*MRP*)

There are two methods of calculating *MRP*. Part (a) shows one method (*MRP* = Δ*TR*/ΔQuantity of the factor), and (b) shows the other (*MRP* = *MR* × *MPP*).

(1) Quantity of Factor X	(2) Quantity of Output, Q	(3) Product Price, Marginal Revenue (P = MR)	(4) Total Revenue TR = P × Q = (3) × (2)	(5) Marginal Revenue Product of Factor X MRP = ΔTR/ΔQuantity of factor X = Δ(4)/Δ(1)
0	10*	$5	$ 50	—
1	19	5	95	$45
2	27	5	135	40
3	34	5	170	35
4	40	5	200	30
5	45	5	225	25

(a)

(1) Quantity of Factor X	(2) Quantity of Output, Q	(3) Marginal Physical Product MPP = Δ(2)/Δ(1)	(4) Product Price, Marginal Revenue (P = MR)	(5) Marginal Revenue Product of Factor X MRP = MR × MPP = (4) × (3)
0	10*	—	$5	—
1	19	9	5	$45
2	27	8	5	40
3	34	7	5	35
4	40	6	5	30
5	45	5	5	25

(b)

*Because the quantity of output is 10 at 0 units of factor X, other factors (not shown in the exhibit) must also be used to produce the good.

exhibit 2

The *MRP* Curve Is the Firm's Factor Demand Curve

The data in columns (1) and (5) in Exhibit 1b are plotted to derive the *MRP* curve. The *MRP* curve shows the various quantities of the factor the firm is willing to buy at different prices, which is what a demand curve shows. The *MRP* curve is the firm's factor demand curve.

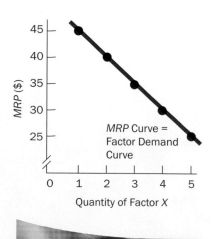

In column 5, we calculate the *MRP* by multiplying the marginal revenue (in column 4) times *MPP* (in column 3). The *MRP* figures in column 5 of (b) are the same as the *MRP* figures in column 5 of (a), showing that *MRP* can be calculated in two ways.

THE *MRP* CURVE IS THE FIRM'S FACTOR DEMAND CURVE

Look again at column 5 in Exhibit 1b, which shows the *MRP* for factor *X*. By plotting the data in column 5 against the quantity of the factor (shown in column 1), we derive the *MRP* curve for factor *X*. This curve is the same as the firm's demand curve for factor *X* (or, simply, the firm's factor demand curve). See Exhibit 2.

MRP curve = Factor demand curve

Q: Why is the *MRP* curve, or factor demand curve, in Exhibit 2 downward-sloping?

A: Remember that *MRP* can be calculated in two ways. In one of those ways, *MRP* = *MR* × *MPP*. What do we know about *MPP*, the marginal physical product of a factor? According to the law of diminishing marginal returns, eventually the *MPP* of a factor will diminish. Because *MRP* is equal to *MR* × *MPP* and *MPP* will eventually decline, it follows that *MRP* will eventually decline too.

VALUE MARGINAL PRODUCT

Value marginal product (*VMP*) is equal to the price of the product times the marginal physical product of the factor:

$$VMP = P \times MPP$$

For example, if $P = \$10$ and $MPP = 9$ units, then $VMP = \$90$. Think of VMP as a measure of the value that each factor unit adds to the firm's product. Or you can think of it simply as "MPP measured in dollars."

Value Marginal Product (*VMP*)
The price of the good multiplied by the marginal physical product of the factor: $VMP = P \times MPP$.

Q: Why might a firm want to know the *VMP* of a factor?

A: Put yourself in the shoes of an owner of a firm that produces computers. Suppose one of the factors you need to produce computers is labor. Currently, you are thinking of hiring an additional worker. Whether or not you actually hire the additional worker will depend on (1) how much better off you are—in dollars and cents—with the additional worker than without him or her and (2) what you have to pay to hire the worker. Simply put, you want to know what the worker will do for you and what you will have to pay for the worker. The *VMP* of a factor is a dollar measure of how much an additional unit of the factor will do for you.

AN IMPORTANT QUESTION: IS *MRP* = *VMP*?

In the earlier computations of *MRP* (shown in Exhibit 1), price (P) was equal to marginal revenue (MR) because we assumed the firm was perfectly competitive. Because $P = MR$ for a perfectly competitive firm, does it follow that for a perfectly competitive firm $MRP = VMP$? The answer is yes.

Given that

$$MRP = MR \times MPP$$

and

$$VMP = P \times MPP$$

then because $P = MR$ for a perfectly competitive firm, it follows that

$$MRP = VMP \text{ for a perfectly competitive firm}$$

See Exhibit 3a.

exhibit 3

MRP and VMP Curves
$MRP = MR \times MPP$ and $VMP = P \times MPP$. (a) The *MRP* (factor demand) curve and *VMP* curve. These are the same for a price taker, or perfectly competitive firm, because $P = MR$. (b) The *MRP* (factor demand) curve and *VMP* curve for a firm that is a price searcher (monopolist, monopolistic competitor, oligopolist). The *MRP* curve lies below the *VMP* curve because for these firms, $P >$ MR.

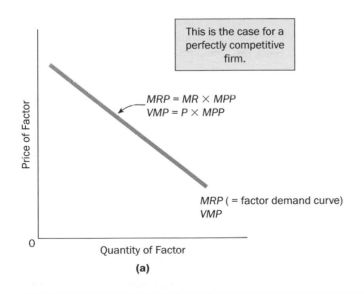

This is the case for a perfectly competitive firm.

$MRP = MR \times MPP$
$VMP = P \times MPP$

MRP (= factor demand curve)
VMP

Price of Factor

Quantity of Factor

(a)

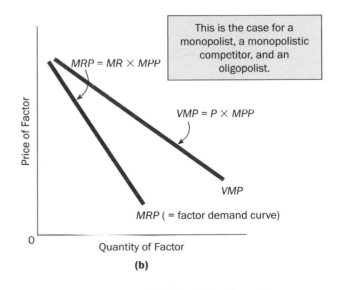

This is the case for a monopolist, a monopolistic competitor, and an oligopolist.

$MRP = MR \times MPP$

$VMP = P \times MPP$

VMP

MRP (= factor demand curve)

Price of Factor

Quantity of Factor

(b)

Q: The conclusion is that "*MRP = VMP* for a perfectly competitive firm." Nothing is said about other types of firms—such as monopolists, monopolistic competitors, and oligopolists. These firms all face downward-sloping demand curves for their products. Does *MRP = VMP* for them?

A: No. For any firm that is a price searcher, or faces a downward-sloping demand curve, price is greater than marginal revenue: *P > MR*. If *P > MR* for these firms, then it follows that *VMP > MRP*.

Given that

$$MRP = MR \times MPP$$

and

$$VMP = P \times MPP$$

then because *P > MR* for monopolists, monopolistic competitors, and oligopolists, it follows that

$$VMP > MRP \text{ for monopolists, monopolistic competitors, and oligopolists}$$

See Exhibit 3b.

MARGINAL FACTOR COST

Marginal factor cost (*MFC*) is the additional cost incurred by employing an additional factor unit. It is calculated as

$$MFC = \Delta TC / \Delta \text{Quantity of the factor}$$

where *TC* = total costs.

Let's suppose a firm is a **factor price taker.** This means it can buy all it wants of a factor at the equilibrium price. For example, suppose the equilibrium price for factor *X* is $5. If a firm is a factor price taker, it can buy any quantity of factor *X* at $5 per factor unit (see Exhibit 4a).

What would the marginal factor cost (*MFC*) curve (the firm's factor supply curve) look like for this kind of firm? It would be horizontal (flat, or perfectly elastic), as shown in Exhibit 4b.[1]

HOW MANY UNITS OF A FACTOR SHOULD A FIRM BUY?

Suppose you graduate with a B.A. in economics and go to work for a business firm. The first day on the job, you are involved in a discussion about factor *X*. Your employer asks you, "How many units of this factor should we buy?" What would you say?

Recall that economists often make use of marginal analysis. An economist is likely to answer this question by saying, "Continue buying additional units of the factor until the additional revenue generated by employing an additional factor unit is equal to the additional cost incurred by employing an additional factor unit." Simply stated, keep buying additional units of the factor, until *MRP = MFC*. In Exhibit 5, *MRP* equals *MFC* at a factor quantity of Q_1.

---

1. Although the *MFC*, or factor supply curve, for the single factor price taker is horizontal, the market supply curve is upward-sloping. This is similar to the situation for the perfectly competitive firm where the firm's demand curve is horizontal but the market (or industry) demand curve is downward-sloping. In factor markets, we are simply talking about the supply side of the market instead of the demand side. The firm's supply curve is flat because it can buy additional factor units without driving up the price of the factor; it buys a relatively small portion of the factor. For the industry, however, higher factor prices must be offered to entice factors (such as workers) from other industries. The difference in the two supply curves—the firm's and the industry's—is basically a reflection of the different sizes of the firm and the industry.

(1) Quantity of Factor X	(2) Price of Factor X	(3) Total Cost $TC = (2) \times (1)$	(4) $MFC = \Delta TC / \Delta \text{quantity}$ of the factor $= \Delta(3)/\Delta(1)$
0	$5	$ 0	—
1	5	5	$5
2	5	10	5
3	5	15	5
4	5	20	5
5	5	25	5
6	5	30	5

(a)

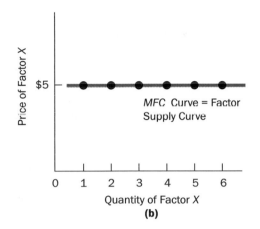

(b)

exhibit 4

Calculating *MFC* and Deriving the *MFC* Curve (the Firm's Factor Supply Curve)
In (a), *MFC* is calculated in column 4. Notice that the firm is a factor price taker because it can buy any quantity of factor *X* at a given price ($5, as shown in column 2). In (b), the data from columns (1) and (4) are plotted to derive the *MFC* curve, which is the firm's factor supply curve.

THINKING LIKE AN ECONOMIST

In the product market, a firm produces that quantity of output at which marginal revenue equals marginal cost, MR = MC. *In the factor market, a firm buys the factor quantity at which marginal revenue product equals marginal factor cost,* MRP = MFC. *The economic principle of equating additional benefits with additional costs holds in both markets.*

WHEN THERE IS MORE THAN ONE FACTOR, HOW MUCH OF EACH FACTOR SHOULD THE FIRM BUY?

Up until now, we have only discussed the purchase of one factor. Suppose we have two factors. For example, suppose a firm requires two factors, labor and capital, to produce its product. How does it combine these two factors to minimize costs? Does it combine, say, 20 units of labor with 5 units of capital, or perhaps 15 units of labor with 8 units of capital?

The firm purchases the two factors until the ratio of *MPP* to price for one factor equals the ratio of *MPP* to price for the other factor. In other words,

$$\frac{MPP_L}{P_L} = \frac{MPP_K}{P_K}$$

This is the **least-cost rule.** To understand the logic behind it, consider an example. Suppose (1) the price of labor is $5, (2) the price of capital is $10, (3) an extra unit of labor results in an increase in output of 25 units, and (4) an extra unit of capital results in an increase in output of 25 units. Finally, assume the firm currently spends an extra $5 on labor and an extra $10 on capital.

Least-Cost Rule
Specifies the combination of factors that minimizes costs. This requires that the following condition be met: $MPP_1/P_1 = MPP_2/P_2 = \ldots = MPP_n/P_n$, where the numbers stand for the different factors.

exhibit 5

Equating *MRP* and *MFC*
The firm continues to purchase a factor as long as the factor's *MRP* exceeds its *MFC*. In the exhibit, the firm purchases Q_1.

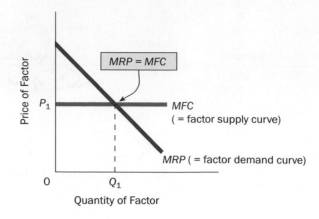

Go to *http://stats.bls.gov/mfp/home.htm*, and click on "Economic News Releases." Select "Multifactor Productivity Trends," and click on "Table 1. Private. . . " Since 1996, has labor productivity been rising faster or slower than capital productivity? If labor productivity (*MPP* of labor) rises faster than capital productivity (*MPP* of capital), do you think this will affect how much labor and capital firms buy? Explain your answer in terms of the least-cost rule.

Notice that MPP_L/P_L is greater than MPP_K/P_K: 25/\$5 > 25/\$10. Thus, in this example, a dollar spent on labor is more effective at raising output than a dollar spent on capital. In fact, it is twice as effective.

The firm is not minimizing costs. It now spends an additional \$15 (\$5 on labor and \$10 on capital) and produces 50 additional units of output. If it spends an extra \$10 on labor and \$0 on capital, it can still produce the 50 additional units of output, but will save \$5. To minimize costs, the firm will rearrange its purchases of factors until the least-cost rule is met.

Q: If $MPP_L/P_L > MPP_K/P_K$, how does the firm equalize the two ratios?

A: It buys more labor and less capital. As this happens, the *MPP* of labor falls and the *MPP* of capital rises, bringing the two ratios closer in line. The firm continues to buy more of the factor whose *MPP*-to-price ratio is larger. It stops when the two ratios are equal.

THINKING LIKE AN ECONOMIST

We can compare a firm's least-cost rule with the way buyers allocate their consumption dollars. A buyer of goods in the product market chooses combinations of goods so that the marginal utility of good A divided by the price of good A is equal to the marginal utility of good B divided by the price of good B; that is, $MU_A/P_A = MU_B/P_B$.

A firm buying factors in the factor market chooses combinations of factors so that the marginal physical product of, say, labor divided by the price of labor (the wage rate) is equal to the marginal physical product of capital divided by the price of capital; that is, $MPP_L/P_L = MPP_K/P_K$.

Consumers buy goods the same way firms buy factors. This points out something that you may have already sensed. Economic principles are few, but they sometimes seem numerous because we find them in so many different settings.

The same economic principle lies behind equating the MU/P *ratio for different goods in the product market and equating the* MPP/P *ratio for different resources in the resource market.[2] In short, there are not two different economic principles at work—one in the product market and another in the factor market—but only one economic principle at work in two markets. That principle simply says that economic actors will, in their attempt to meet their objectives, arrange their purchases in such a way that they receive equal additional benefits per dollar of expenditure.*

Seeing how a few economic principles operate in many different settings is part of the economic way of thinking.

---

2. The "*P*" in *MU/P* stands for product price; the "*P*" in *MPP/P* stands for factor price.

Why Jobs Don't Always Move to the Low-Wage Country

Are tariffs needed to protect U.S. workers? Some people think so. They argue that without tariffs, U.S. companies will relocate to countries where wages are lower. They will produce their products there, and then transport them into the United States to sell. Tariffs will make this scenario less likely because the gains the companies receive in lower wages will be offset by the tariffs imposed on their goods.

What this argument overlooks is that U.S. companies are not only interested in what they pay workers; they are also interested in the marginal productivity of the workers.

For example, suppose a U.S. worker earns $10 an hour and a Mexican worker earns $4 an hour. Also, suppose the marginal physical product (MPP) of the U.S. worker is 10 units of good X and the MPP of the Mexican worker is 2 units of good X. Thus, we have lower wages in Mexico and higher productivity in the United States. Where will the company produce?

The answer is in the United States, because more output is produced per $1 of cost in the United States than in Mexico:

$$\text{Output produced per \$1 of cost} = \frac{\text{MPP of the factor}}{\text{Cost of the factor}}$$

To illustrate, at an MPP of 10 units of good X and a wage rate of $10, U.S. workers produce 1 unit of good X for every $1 they are paid:

$$\frac{\text{MPP of U.S. labor}}{\text{Wage rate of U.S. labor}} = \frac{10 \text{ units of good } X}{\$10}$$
$$= 1 \text{ unit of good } X \text{ per } \$1$$

In Mexico, at an MPP of 2 units and a wage rate of $4, workers produce 1/2 unit of good X for every $1 they are paid:

$$\frac{\text{MPP of Mexican labor}}{\text{Wage rate of Mexican labor}} = \frac{2 \text{ units of good } X}{\$4}$$
$$= 1/2 \text{ unit of good } X \text{ per } \$1$$

Thus, the company gets more output per $1 of cost by using U.S. labor. It is cheaper to produce the good in the United states than it is in Mexico—even though wages are lower in Mexico.

In other words, businesses look at the following ratios:

(1)	(2)
MPP of labor in U.S.	MPP of labor in Mexico
Wage rate in U.S.	Wage rate in Mexico

If ratio (1) is greater than ratio (2), U.S. companies will hire labor in the United States. As they do this, the MPP of labor in the United States will decline. (Remember the law of diminishing marginal returns?) Companies will continue to hire labor in the United States until ratio (1) is equal to ratio (2).

Self-Test *(Answers to Self-Test questions are in the Self-Test Appendix.)*

1. When a perfectly competitive firm employs one worker, it produces 20 units of output, and when it employs two workers, it produces 39 units of output. The firm sells its product for $10 per unit. What is the marginal revenue product connected with hiring the second worker?

2. What is the difference between marginal revenue product (MRP) and value marginal product (VMP)?

3. What is the distinguishing characteristic of a factor price taker?

4. How much labor should a firm purchase?

THE LABOR MARKET

Labor is a factor of special interest because at one time or another, most people find themselves in the labor market. This section first discusses the demand for labor, then the supply of labor, and finally the two together. The discussion focuses on the firm that is a price taker in the product market (in other words, a perfectly competitive firm) and also is a price taker in the factor market.[3]

SHIFTS IN A FIRM'S *MRP*, OR FACTOR DEMAND, CURVE

As mentioned earlier, a firm's *MRP* curve is its factor demand curve, and marginal revenue product equals marginal revenue times marginal physical product:

$$MRP = MR \times MPP \tag{1}$$

For a perfectly competitive firm, where $P = MR$, we can write equation (1) as

$$MRP = P \times MPP \tag{2}$$

Now consider the demand for a specific factor input, labor. As the price of the product that labor produces changes, the factor demand curve for labor shifts. In Exhibit 6, we start with a product price of $10 and curve MRP_1. At the wage rate of W_1, the firm hires Q_1 labor.

Suppose product price rises to $12. As we can see from equation (2), *MRP* rises. At each wage rate, the firm wants to hire more labor. For example, at W_1, it wants to hire Q_2 labor instead of Q_1. In short, a rise in product price shifts the firm's *MRP*, or factor demand, curve rightward.

If product price falls from $10 to $8, *MRP* falls. At each wage rate, the firm wants to hire less labor. For example, at W_1, it wants to hire Q_3 labor instead of Q_1. In short, a fall in product price shifts the firm's *MRP*, or factor demand, curve leftward.

Changes in the *MPP* of the factor—reflected in a shift in the *MPP* curve—also change the firm's *MRP* curve. As we can see from equation (2), an increase in, say, the *MPP* of labor will increase *MRP* and shift the *MRP*, or factor demand,

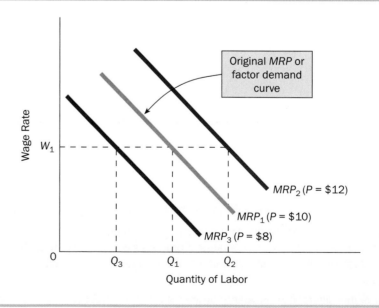

exhibit 6

Shifts in the Firm's *MRP*, or Factor Demand, Curve

It is always the case that $MRP = MR \times MPP$. For a perfectly competitive firm, where $P = MR$, it follows that $MRP = P \times MPP$. If P changes, *MRP* will change. For example, if product price rises, *MRP* rises, and the firm's *MRP* curve (factor demand curve) shifts rightward. If product price falls, *MRP* falls, and the firm's *MRP* curve (factor demand curve) shifts leftward. If *MPP* rises (reflected in a shift in the *MPP* curve), *MRP* rises and the firm's *MRP* curve shifts rightward. If *MPP* falls, *MRP* falls and the firm's *MRP* curve shifts leftward.

Original *MRP* or factor demand curve

MRP_2 ($P = 12)

MRP_1 ($P = 10)

MRP_3 ($P = 8)

Wage Rate — Quantity of Labor

3. It is important to keep in mind that the labor market we discuss here is a labor market in which neither buyers nor sellers have any control over wage rates. Because of this, supply and demand are our analytical tools. In the next chapter, we modify this analysis.

ECONOMICS IN...

How May Crime, Outsourcing, and Multitasking Be Related?

Consider three seemingly unrelated images of life in the United States in recent years:

- A lower crime rate. For example, violent crime, property crime, and homicides were all down in the late 1990s.
- More people choosing to multitask—that is, to work on more than one task at a time. For example, if you drive a car at the same time you talk to your office on your cell phone, you are multitasking.
- Increasingly more professional people outsourcing their routine tasks. They are hiring people to run errands, buy groceries, plan parties, drop off dry cleaning, take pets to the vet, and so on.

Could all three images be the result of the same thing—higher real wages?[4] How might higher real wages affect crime, multitasking, and outsourcing? Let's consider crime first. There are both costs and benefits to committing a crime. As long as the benefits are greater than the costs, crimes will be committed; increase the costs of crime relative to the benefits, and the crime rate will decline. Suppose part of the cost of crime is equal to the probability of being sentenced to jail times the real wage that would be earned if the person were not in jail.

Part of the cost of crime = Probability of jail sentence
× Real Wage

If this is the case, then as the real wage rises, the overall cost of crime rises and fewer crimes will be committed.

How does the real wage relate to individuals outsourcing their routine tasks? To illustrate, suppose John and Mary are married and have two daughters. Currently, Mary works as a physician and John works part-time as an accountant. Because John has chosen to work part-time, he takes care of many of the routine household tasks. He buys the groceries, runs the errands, and so on. If the real wage rises for accountants, John may rethink his part-time work. An increase in the real wage is the same as an increase in the reward from working, and so John may choose to work more. In fact, it may be cheaper for him to work full-time and pay someone else to run the errands, buy the groceries, and so on.

Finally, what about multitasking? As the real wage rises, one's time becomes more valuable. And, as time becomes more valuable, people will want to economize on it. One way to economize on time is to do several things at the same time. Instead of spending 20 minutes driving to work and another 10 minutes talking on the phone, why not "kill two birds with one stone" and talk on the phone while driving to work? Ten minutes are saved this way.

If higher real wages can affect the crime rate, the amount of outsourcing, and the degree to which people multitask, it is important to know what can cause real wages to rise. One way real wages can rise is through a technological advance that increases the quality of the capital goods used by labor. To illustrate, consider a technological advance that makes it possible for computers to complete more tasks in less time. As a result, the productivity of labor rises and the demand curve for labor shifts to the right. Higher demand for labor increases the nominal wage rate and, as long as the price level doesn't rise by more than the nominal wage rate, the real wage rises too.

Can a technological advance indirectly lead to a lower crime rate, more outsourcing, and greater multitasking? We think so.

---

curve rightward. A decrease in *MPP* will decrease *MRP* and shift the *MRP*, or factor demand, curve leftward.[5]

Q & A

Q: Considering the factor labor, if there is either a change in the price of the product labor produces or a change in the *MPP* of labor (reflected in a shift in the *MPP* curve), the (factor) demand curve for labor shifts. Is this correct?

A: Yes, that is correct.

---

4. Nominal wages are dollar wages—such as $30 an hour. Real wages are nominal wages adjusted for price changes. Stated differently, real wages measure what nominal wages can actually buy in terms of goods and services. So when real wages rise, people can buy more goods and services.

5. Notice here that we are talking about a change in *MPP* that is reflected in a shift in the *MPP* curve; we are not talking about a movement along a given *MPP* curve.

MARKET DEMAND FOR LABOR

We would expect the market demand curve for labor to be the horizontal "addition" of the firms' demand curves (*MRP* curves) for labor. However, this is not the case, as Exhibit 7 illustrates.

Assume two firms, *A* and *B,* make up the buying side of the factor market. Also assume that the product price for both firms is P_1. Parts (a) and (b) in the exhibit show the *MRP* curves for the two firms based on this product price.

At a wage rate of W_1, firm *A* purchases 100 units of labor. This is the amount of labor at which its marginal revenue product equals marginal factor cost (or the wage). At this same wage rate, firm *B* purchases 150 units of labor. If we horizontally "add" the *MRP* curves of firms *A* and *B,* we get the *MRP* curve in (c) where the two firms together purchase 250 units of labor at W_1.

Now assume the wage rate increases to W_2. In (c), firms *A* and *B* move up the given MRP_{A+B} curve and purchase 180 units of labor. This may seem to be the end of the process, but, of course, it is not. A higher wage rate increases each firm's costs and thus shifts its supply curve leftward. This leads to an increase in product price to P_2.

Recall that the firm's marginal revenue product is equal to marginal revenue (or price, when the firm is perfectly competitive) times marginal physical product: $MRP = MR \times MPP = P \times MPP$. If price rises, so does *MRP;* thus, each firm faces a new *MRP* curve at the wage rate W_2. Parts (a) and (b) in Exhibit 7 illustrate these new *MRP* curves for firms *A* and *B,* and (c) shows the horizontal "addition" of the new *MRP* curves. The firms together now purchase 210 units of labor at W_2.

After all adjustments have been made, connecting the units of labor purchased by both firms at W_1 and W_2 gives the market demand curve in (c).

THE ELASTICITY OF DEMAND FOR LABOR

The **elasticity of demand for labor** is the percentage change in the quantity demanded of labor divided by the percentage change in the price of labor (the wage rate).

$$E_L = \frac{\text{Percentage change in quantity demanded of labor}}{\text{Percentage change in wage rate}}$$

Elasticity of Demand for Labor
The percentage change in the quantity demanded of labor divided by the percentage change in the wage rate.

exhibit 7

The Derivation of the Market Demand Curve for Labor Units
Two firms, *A* and *B,* make up the buying side of the market for labor. At a wage rate of W_1, firm *A* purchases 100 units of labor and firm *B* purchases 150 units. Together, they purchase 250 units, as illustrated in (c). The wage rate rises to W_2, and the amount of labor purchased by both firms initially falls to 180 units, as shown in (c). Higher wage rates translate into higher costs, a fall in product supply, and a rise in product price from P_1 to P_2. Finally, an increased price raises *MRP* and each firm has a new *MRP* curve. The horizontal "addition" of the new *MRP* curves shows they purchase 210 units of labor. Connecting the units of labor purchased by both firms at W_1 and W_2 gives the market demand curve.

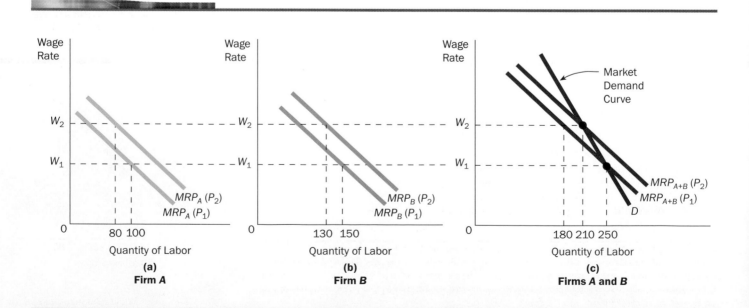

where E_L = coefficient of elasticity of demand for labor, or simply elasticity coefficient.

For example, suppose when the wage rate changes by 20 percent, the quantity demanded of a particular type of labor changes by 40 percent. Then, the elasticity of demand for this type of labor is 2 (40 percent/20 percent), and the demand between the old wage rate and the new wage rate is elastic. There are three main determinants of elasticity of demand for labor.

Elasticity of Demand for the Product That Labor Produces

If the demand for the product that labor produces is highly elastic, a small percentage increase in price (say, owing to a wage increase that shifts the supply curve for the product leftward) will decrease quantity demanded of the product by a relatively large percentage. In turn, this will greatly reduce the quantity of labor needed to produce the product, implying the demand for labor is highly elastic too.

The relationship between the elasticity of demand for the product and the elasticity of demand for labor is as follows: *The higher the elasticity of demand for the product, the higher the elasticity of demand for the labor that produces the product; the lower the elasticity of demand for the product, the lower the elasticity of demand for the labor that produces the product.*

Ratio of Labor Costs to Total Costs

Labor costs are a part of total costs. Consider two situations. In one, labor costs are 90 percent of total costs, and in the other, labor costs are only 5 percent of total costs. Now suppose wages increase by $2 per hour. Total costs are affected more when labor costs are 90 percent of total costs (the $2 per hour wage increase is being applied to 90 percent of all costs) than when labor costs are only 5 percent of total costs. Thus, price rises by more when labor costs are a larger percentage of total costs. And, of course, the more price rises, the more quantity demanded of the product falls. It follows that labor, being a derived demand, is affected more. In short, the decline in the quantity demanded of labor is greater for a $2-per-hour wage increase when labor costs are 90 percent of total costs than when labor costs are 5 percent of total costs.

The relationship between the labor cost–total cost ratio and the elasticity of demand for labor is as follows: *The higher the labor cost–total cost ratio, the higher the elasticity of demand for labor (the greater the cutback in labor for any given wage increase); the lower the labor cost–total cost ratio, the lower the elasticity of demand for labor (the less the cutback in labor for any given wage increase).*

Number of Substitute Factors

The more substitutes there are for labor, the more sensitive buyers of labor will be to a change in the price of labor. This principle was established in the discussion of price elasticity of demand. The more possibilities for substituting other factors for labor, the more likely firms will cut back on their use of labor if the price of labor rises. *The more substitutes for labor, the higher the elasticity of demand for labor; the fewer substitutes for labor, the lower the elasticity of demand for labor.*

THE SUPPLY OF LABOR

As the wage rate rises, the quantity supplied of labor rises, *ceteris paribus*. The upward-sloping labor supply curve in Exhibit 8 illustrates this.

At a wage rate of W_1, individuals are willing to supply 100 labor units. At the higher wage rate of W_2, individuals are willing to supply 200 labor units. Some individuals who were not willing to work at a wage rate of W_1 are willing to work at a wage rate of W_2, and some individuals who were working at W_1 will be willing to supply more labor units at W_2. At the even higher wage rate of W_3, individuals are willing to supply 280 labor units.

exhibit 8

The Market Supply of Labor
A direct relationship exists between the wage rate and the quantity of labor supplied.

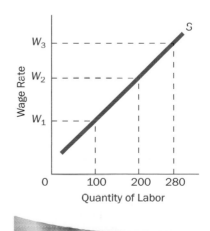

ECONOMICS IN...

What Is the Wage Rate for a Street-Level Pusher in a Drug Gang?

Gangs that deal drugs exist in almost every large city in the United States. It is not uncommon to see a 16- or 17-year-old gang member selling or delivering drugs in Los Angeles, New York, Chicago, Houston, or elsewhere. Often, in a public debate about drugs in one of these cities, someone will say, "No wonder these kids sell drugs; it's the best job they can get. When your alternatives are working at McDonald's earning the minimum wage or selling drugs for big money, you sell drugs. If we want to get kids off the streets and out of gangs, and if we want to stop them from selling drugs, we have to have something better for them than the minimum wage."

But we wonder? Do the young gang members who sell and deliver drugs really earn "big money"? Economics would predict that they wouldn't. After all, one would think that the supply of people who can sell or deliver drugs is rather large. In fact, a recent study found that low-level foot soldiers in a drug gang actually earned very low wages.

Steven Levitt, an economist, and Sudhir Venkatesh, a sociologist, analyzed the data set of a drug-selling street gang.[6] They estimated that the average hourly wage rate in the gang was $6 at the time they started the study and $11 at the time they finished.[7] They also noted that the distribution of wages was extremely skewed. Actual street-level dealers (foot soldiers) appeared to earn less than the minimum wage. According to Levitt and Vankatesh, "While these wages are almost too low to be believable, there are both theoretical arguments and corroborating empirical evidence in support of these numbers. From a theoretical perspective, it is hardly surprising that foot-soldier wages would be low given the minimal skill requirements for the job and the presence of a 'reserve army' of potential replacements among the rank and file."[8]

Substitution and Income Effects

Exhibit 8 shows an upward-sloping *market* supply curve of labor. But let's consider an individual's supply curve of labor—say, John's supply curve of labor. Is it upward-sloping? It is if the substitution effect (of a change in the wage rate) outweighs the income effect. To illustrate, suppose John currently earns $10 an hour and works 40 hours a week. If John's wage rate rises to, say, $15 an hour, he will feel two effects, each pulling him in opposite directions.

One effect is the *substitution effect*. Here is how it works: As the wage rate rises, John recognizes that the monetary reward from working has increased. As a result, John will want to work more—say, 45 hours a week instead of 40 hours (+5 hours).

The other effect is the *income effect*. Here is how it works: As the wage rate rises, John knows that he can earn $600 a week (40 hours at $15 an hour) instead of $400 a week (40 hours at $10 an hour). If leisure is a normal good (the demand for which increases as income increases), then John will want to consume more leisure as his income rises. But the only way to consume more leisure is to work fewer hours. Let's say John wants to decrease his work hours per week from 40 to 37 hours (−3 hours).

The substitution effect pulls John in one direction (toward working 5 more hours) and the income effect pulls John in the opposite direction (toward working 3 fewer hours). Which effect is stronger? In our numerical example, the sub-

---

6. *An Economic Analysis of a Drug-Selling Gang's Finances,* NBER Working Paper No. W6592, June 1998, National Bureau of Economic Research, Cambridge, Massachusetts.

7. Wage rates are in 1995 dollars.

8. Ibid., p. 17.

stitution effect is stronger, so on net, John wants to work two more hours a week as his wage rate rises. This means John's supply curve of labor is upward-sloping between a wage rate of $10 and $15.

CHANGES IN THE SUPPLY OF LABOR
Changes in the wage rate change the quantity supplied of labor units. But what changes the entire labor supply curve? Two factors of major importance are wage rates in other labor markets and the nonmoney, or nonpecuniary, aspects of a job.

Wage Rates in Other Labor Markets
Deborah currently works as a technician in a television manufacturing plant. She has skills suitable for a number of jobs. One day, she learns that the computer manufacturing plant on the other side of town is offering 33 percent more pay per hour. Deborah is also trained to work as a computer operator, so she decides to leave her current job and apply for work at the computer manufacturing plant. In short, the wage rate offered in other labor markets can bring about a change in the supply of labor in a particular labor market.

Nonmoney, or Nonpecuniary, Aspects of a Job
Other things held constant, people prefer to avoid dirty, heavy, dangerous work in cold climates. An increase in the overall "unpleasantness" of a job (for example, an increased probability of contracting lung cancer working in an asbestos factory) will cause a decrease in the supply of labor to that firm or industry. An increase in the overall "pleasantness" of a job (for example, employees are now entitled to a longer lunch break and use of the company gym) will cause an increase in the supply of labor to that firm or industry.

PUTTING SUPPLY AND DEMAND TOGETHER
Exhibit 9 illustrates a particular labor market. The equilibrium wage rate and quantity of labor are established by the forces of supply and demand. At a wage rate of W_2, there is a surplus of labor. Some people who want to work at this wage rate will not be able to find jobs. A subset of this group will begin to offer their services for a lower wage rate. The wage rate will move down until it reaches W_1.

At a wage rate of W_3, there is a shortage of labor. Some demanders of labor will begin to bid up the wage rate until it reaches W_1. At the equilibrium wage rate, W_1, the quantity supplied of labor equals the quantity demanded of labor.

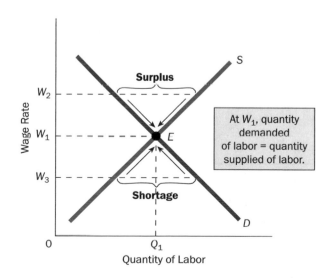

exhibit 9

Equilibrium in a Particular Labor Market
The forces of supply and demand bring about the equilibrium wage rate and quantity of labor. At the equilibrium wage rate, the quantity demanded of labor equals the quantity supplied. At any other wage rate, there is either a surplus or a shortage of labor.

WHY DO WAGE RATES DIFFER?

To discover why wage rates differ, we must determine what conditions would be necessary for everyone to receive the same pay. Assume the following conditions hold:

1. The demand for every type of labor is the same. (Throughout our analysis, any wage differentials caused by demand are short-run differentials.)
2. There are no special nonpecuniary aspects to any job.
3. All labor is ultimately homogeneous and can costlessly be trained for different types of employment.
4. All labor is mobile at zero cost.

Given these conditions, there would be no difference in wage rates in the long run. To illustrate, consider Exhibit 10, where two labor markets, A and B, are shown. Initially, the supply conditions are different, with a greater supply of workers in labor market B (represented by S_B) than in labor market A (represented by S_A). Because of the different supply conditions, more labor is employed in labor market B (Q_B) than in labor market A (Q_A), and the equilibrium wage rate in labor market B ($10) is lower than the equilibrium wage rate in labor market A ($30).

The differences in the wage rates between the two labor markets will not last. We have assumed (1) labor can move costlessly from one labor market to another (so why not move from the lower-paying job to the higher-paying job?), (2) there are no special nonpecuniary aspects to any job (there is no nonpecuniary reason for not moving), (3) labor is ultimately homogeneous (workers who work in labor market B can work in labor market A), and (4) if workers need training to make a move from one labor market to another, they not only are capable of being trained but also can acquire the training costlessly.

As a result, some workers in labor market B will relocate to labor market A, decreasing the supply of workers to S'_B in labor market B and increasing the supply of workers to S'_A in labor market A. The relocation of workers ends when the equilibrium wage rate in both markets is the same—$20. We conclude that wage rates will not differ in the long run if our four conditions hold.

Because we know the conditions under which wage rates will not differ, we now know why wage rates do differ. Obviously, they differ because demand conditions are not the same in all labor markets (important to explain short-run wage differentials only) and because supply conditions are not the same in all

exhibit 10

Wage Rate Equalization across Labor Markets

Given the four necessary conditions (noted in the text), there will be no wage rate differences across labor markets. We start with a wage rate of $30 in labor market A and a wage rate of $10 in labor market B. Soon some individuals in B relocate to A. This increases the supply in one market (A), driving down the wage rate, and decreases the supply in the other market (B), driving up the wage rate. Equilibrium comes when the same wage rate is paid in both labor markets. This outcome critically depends on the necessary conditions holding.

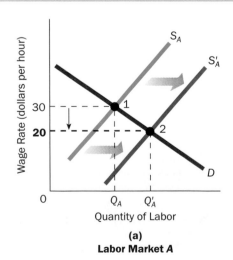

(a)
Labor Market A

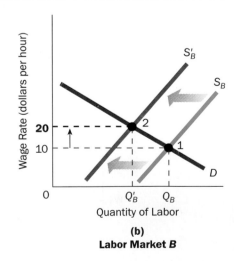

(b)
Labor Market B

markets: there are nonpecuniary aspects to different jobs, labor is not homogeneous, labor cannot be retrained without cost, and labor is not costlessly mobile.

WHY DEMAND AND SUPPLY DIFFER IN DIFFERENT LABOR MARKETS

Saying that wage rates differ because demand and supply conditions in different labor markets differ raises the question of why this is the case. Let's consider what factors affect the demand for and supply of labor.

Demand for Labor

We know that the firm's *MRP* curve is its factor demand curve, so we need to look at what affects the components of *MRP*, namely, *MR* and *MPP*.

Marginal revenue is indirectly affected by product supply and demand conditions because these conditions determine price. ($MR = \Delta TR / \Delta Q$ and $TR = P \times Q$). Thus, product demand and supply conditions affect factor demand. In short, because the supply and demand conditions in different product markets are different, it follows that the demand for labor in different labor markets will be different too.

The second factor, the marginal physical product of labor, is affected by individual workers' *own abilities and skills* (both innate and learned), the *degree of effort* they put forth on the job, and the *other factors of production* available to them. With respect to the latter, American workers are more productive than workers in many other countries because they work with many more capital goods and much more technical know-how. If all individuals had the same innate and learned skills and abilities, applied the same degree of effort on the job, and worked with the same amount and quality of other factors of production, wages would differ less than they currently do.

Supply of Labor

Why are the supply conditions in different labor markets different? First, as noted earlier, jobs have *different nonpecuniary qualities*. Working as a coal miner in West Virginia is not so attractive a job as working as a gardener at a lush resort in Hawaii. We would expect this fact to be reflected in the supply of coal miners and gardeners.

Second, supply is also a reflection of the *number of persons who can actually do a job*. Williamson may want to be a nuclear physicist, but may not have the ability in science and mathematics to be one. Johnson may want to be a basketball player, but may not have the ability to be one.

Third, even if individuals have the ability to work at a certain job, they may perceive the *training costs as too high* (relative to the perceived benefits) to train for it. Mendoza may have the ability to be a brain surgeon, but views the years of schooling required to become one too high a price to pay.

Fourth, sometimes supply in different labor markets reflects a difference in the *cost of moving* across markets. Wage rates might be higher in Alaska than in Alabama for comparable labor because the workers in Alabama find the cost of relocating to Alaska too high relative to the benefits of receiving a higher wage.

Q & A

Q: Do the same factors that affect the demand for and supply of labor also affect the wage rate labor is paid?

A: Yes, they do. Because the wage rate is determined by supply and demand forces, the factors that affect these forces indirectly affect wage rates. Exhibit 11 summarizes these factors.

WHY DID YOU CHOOSE THE MAJOR THAT YOU CHOSE?

Our lives are sometimes influenced by what happens in labor markets. Consider a college student who is trying to decide whether to major in accounting or English. The student believes that English is more fun and interesting but that accounting,

What factors affect the wage rate in a single competitive labor market?
The supply of and demand for labor.

But what factors affect labor supply and demand?
Many factors. We categorize them accordingly.

Demand for Labor

- Because the *MRP* curve is the factor demand curve, we need to look at what affects the components of *MRP*, namely, *MR* (or *P*, if the firm is a product price taker) and *MPP* of labor.

Supply of Labor

- Wage rates in other labor markets
- Nonpecuniary aspects of the job
- Number of persons who can do the job
- Training costs
- Moving costs

MR

- Product supply and demand conditions determine price and therefore indirectly affect marginal revenue ($MR = \Delta TR/\Delta Q$ and $TR = P \times Q$, so we can see the link between *P* and *MR*)

MPP of Labor

- Own abilities and skills
- Degree of effort on the job
- Other factors of production labor has available

exhibit 11

The Wage Rate
A step-by-step framework that describes the factors that affect the wage rate.

on average, will earn her enough additional income to compensate for the lack of fun in accounting. Specifically, at a $40,000 annual salary for accounting and a $30,000 annual salary for English, the student is indifferent between accounting and English. But at a $41,000 annual salary for accounting and a $30,000 annual salary for English, accounting moves ahead.

Of course, what accounting "pays" is determined by the demand for and supply of accountants. When we realize this, we realize that other people influenced the person's decision to go into accounting. To illustrate, suppose Congress passes more intricate tax laws that require more accountants to figure them out. This increases the demand for accountants which, in turn, raises the wage rate for accountants. And an increase in the wage rate that accountants receive increases the probability that more people—perhaps you—will major in accounting and not in English, philosophy, or history.

As you can see, economics—in which markets play a major role—helps explain why part of your life is the way it is.

MARGINAL PRODUCTIVITY THEORY

Let's analyze some of the things we know from this chapter:

1. If a firm is a factor price taker, marginal factor cost is constant and equal to factor price, $MFC = P$. Suppose the factor price taker hires labor. For the firm, $MFC = W$, where *W* is the wage rate.
2. Firms hire the factor quantity at which $MRP = MFC$.
3. Taking points 1 and 2 together, a factor price taker pays labor a wage equal to its marginal revenue product: $W = MRP$. That is, because $MFC = W$ (point 1) and $MRP = MFC$ (point 2), it follows that $W = MRP$.

4. If a firm is a perfectly competitive firm, $MRP = VMP$.
5. If a firm is both perfectly competitive (a product price taker) and a factor price taker, it pays labor a wage equal to its value marginal product: $W = VMP$. That is, because $W = MRP$ (point 3) and $MRP = VMP$ (point 4), it follows that $W = VMP$.

This is the **marginal productivity theory,** which states that if a firm sells its product and purchases its factors in competitive or perfect markets (that is, it is a perfectly competitive firm and a factor price taker), it pays its factors their MRP or VMP (the two are equal for a product price taker).

In other words, the theory holds that under the competitive conditions specified, if a factor unit is withdrawn from the productive process and the amount of all other factors remains the same, then the decrease in the value of the product produced equals the factor payment received by the factor unit. To illustrate, suppose Wilson works for a perfectly competitive firm (firm X) producing good X. One day he quits his job (but nothing else relevant to the firm changes). As a result, the total revenue of the firm falls by $100. If Wilson was paid $100, then he received his MRP. He was paid a wage equal to his contribution to the productive process.[9]

Marginal Productivity Theory
States that firms in competitive or perfect product and factor markets pay factors their marginal revenue products.

Q & A

Q: Aren't some workers paid less than their MRPs (less than their contributions to the productive process)? If so, isn't this evidence sufficient to reject the marginal productivity theory?

A: The theory specifies that the firm sells its product and purchases its factors in competitive, or perfect (price-taker), markets. Not all firms fit into this category; thus, certainly some workers are not paid their MRPs. (Marginal productivity theory and market imperfections are discussed in the next chapter.)

Q & A

Q: Are workers who work for firms that "sell their products and purchase their factors in competitive markets" paid their MRPs?

A: The proponents of marginal productivity theory argue that employees in this setting are paid wages that over time closely approximate their MRPs. In other words, not all employees are paid their exact MRPs, but most employees in this setting are paid close to their MRPs. The critics of the theory point out that it is very difficult for firms to measure the value of their employees' marginal products accurately. The proponents argue that the firms have a monetary incentive to make a reasonable estimate. They add that firms interview and screen potential employees, as well as regularly evaluate current employees, to acquire information on workers' MRPs.

Self-Test

1. The demand for labor is a derived demand. What could cause the firm's demand curve for labor to shift rightward?
2. Suppose the coefficient of elasticity of demand for labor is 3. What does this mean?
3. Why are wage rates higher in one competitive labor market than in another? In short, why do wage rates differ?
4. Workers in labor market X do the same work as workers in labor market Y, but they earn $10 less per hour. Why?

---

9. Recall that there are two ways to calculate MRP: $MRP = \Delta TR/\Delta$ quantity of the factor, and $MRP = MR \times MPP$. In this example, we use the first method. When Wilson quits his job, the change in the denominator is 1 factor unit. If, as a result, TR falls by $100, then the change in the numerator must be $100.

Is Kobe Bryant Worth Millions of Dollars a Year?

Many players of professional sports earn millions of dollars each year. For example, in baseball, Barry Bonds earned about $18 million in 2002; in basketball, Kobe Bryant earned about $13 million.

Watching the multimillionaires playing baseball and basketball, no doubt many spectators will say, sarcastically, "Can you imagine getting paid that much money to play a game?" Or, "Do you think anyone is really worth that much money?"

What do you think? Is Kobe Bryant worth $13 million a year? Before you can accurately answer the question, you need to determine what it means to say a person is worth a certain salary—whether the salary is $13 million or $13,000.

Consider this example. Suppose if a firm hires a person, she will generate $90,000 a year in additional revenue for the firm but that the firm will have to pay her only $75,000 a year. Is she worth $75,000? The obvious answer is yes. The additional benefits of hiring her ($90,000) are greater than the additional costs of hiring her ($75,000). Another way of saying this is that her marginal revenue product (*MRP*) is greater than her marginal factor cost (*MFC*). In this setting, a person is worth hiring at a particular salary as long as the person's (annual) *MRP* is greater than her (annual) salary.

So, is Kobe Bryant worth $13 million a year? There is no way to know for sure without knowing his *MRP*. If his *MRP* is greater than $13 million a year, then he is worth $13 million. He might be worth even more. If his *MRP* is less than $13 million, then he isn't worth $13 million. We can say one thing, though: Certainly, the owners of the L.A. Lakers expected Kobe's *MRP* to be greater than $13 million a year or they wouldn't have paid him that amount.

LABOR MARKETS AND INFORMATION

This section looks at job hiring, employment practices, and employment discrimination and how information, or the lack of it, affects these processes.

SCREENING POTENTIAL EMPLOYEES

Employers typically do not know exactly how productive a potential employee will be. What the employer wants, but lacks, is complete information about the potential employee's future job performance.

This raises two questions: Why would an employer want complete information about a potential employee's future job performance? What does the employer do because he or she lacks complete information?

The answer to the first question is obvious. Employers have a strong monetary incentive to hire good, stable, quick-learning, responsible, hardworking, punctual employees. One study found that corporate spending on training employees reached $40 billion annually. Obviously, corporations want to see the highest return possible for their training expenditures, so they try to hire employees who will make the training worthwhile. This is where screening comes in.

Screening is the process used by employers to increase the probability of choosing "good" employees based on certain criteria. For example, an employer

Screening
The process used by employers to increase the probability of choosing "good" employees based on certain criteria.

might ask a young college graduate searching for a job what his or her GPA was in college. This is a screening mechanism. The employer might know from past experience that persons with high GPAs turn out to be better employees, on average, than persons with low GPAs. Screening is one thing an employer does because he or she lacks complete information.

PROMOTING FROM WITHIN

Sometimes employers promote from within the company because they have more information about company employees than about potential employees.

Suppose the executive vice president in charge of sales is retiring from Trideck, Inc. The president of the company could hire an outsider to replace the vice president, but often she will select an insider about whom she has some knowledge. What may look like discrimination to outsiders—"That company discriminates against persons not working for it"—may simply be a reflection of the difference in costs to the employer of acquiring relevant information about employees inside and outside the company.

IS IT DISCRIMINATION OR IS IT AN INFORMATION PROBLEM?

Suppose the world is made up of just two kinds of people: those with characteristic X and those with characteristic Y. We call them X people and Y people, respectively. Over time, we observe that most employers are X people and that they tend to hire and promote proportionally more X than Y people. Are the Y people being discriminated against?

They could be. Nothing we have said so far rules this out. But, then, it may be that X people rarely hire or promote Y people because over time X employers have learned that Y people, on average, do not perform as well as X people.

So, in this example, we simply state that X people are not discriminating against Y people. Instead, Y people are not being hired and promoted as often as X people because, for whatever reason, Y people, on average, are not as productive as X people.

Suppose in this environment an extremely productive Y person applies for a job with an X employer. The problem is that the X employer does not know—she lacks complete information—about the full abilities of the Y person. Furthermore, acquiring complete information is costly. She bases her decision to reject the Y person's job application on what she knows about Y people, which is that, on average, they are not as productive as X people. She doesn't do this because she has something against Y people, but because it is simply too costly for her to acquire complete information on every potential employee—X or Y.

We do not mean to imply that everything that looks like discrimination is really a problem of the high cost of information. Nonetheless, sometimes what looks like discrimination ("he doesn't like me, I'm a Y person") is a consequence of living in a world where acquiring complete information is "too costly."

Legislation mandating equal employment opportunities requires employers to absorb some information costs in order to open up labor markets to all. All but the smallest of firms are required to search for qualified Y persons who can perform the job even if the employer believes that the average Y person cannot. Requiring employers to forgo the use of a screening mechanism will likely increase firm costs and raise prices to consumers, but the premise of the legislation is that those costs are more than outweighed by the social benefits of having more Y persons in the mainstream of society.

Does Education Matter to Income?

The greater the demand for my labor and the smaller the supply, the higher the wage I'll be paid. One of the things that can shift the factor demand curve for my labor to the right (and thus bring me a higher wage) is a rise in "my MPP." Is this where education plays a role? Does more education lead to a higher MPP and higher wages?

Certainly, there are people with little education who earn high salaries, but generally speaking, more education does seem to raise one's productivity. And as a result, it tends to raise one's pay. For example, in 1999, a person with only a high school diploma had average annual earnings of $24,572; a person with a bachelor's degree, $45,678; and a person with a master's degree, $55,641.

Let's also consider Charles, who is 22 years old and has just completed his associate's degree. He is trying to decide whether or not to continue his education. In 1999, a person with an associate's degree (as the highest degree) had average annual earnings of $32,152. Let's look at Charles's lifetime earnings in two cases.

If Charles stops his education with an associate's degree and works until he is 65 years old, he will earn $32,152 each year for 43 years.[10] That is a total of $1,382,536. If,

however, Charles goes on to get a master's degree and we assume it takes him 6 more years of schooling to do so, then he will earn $55,641 each year for the next 37 years. That is a total of $2,058,717. The difference in lifetime earnings for a person with an associate's degree and a person with a master's degree is $676,181. Stated differently, Charles's lifetime earnings will be almost 50 percent higher with a master's degree than with an associate's degree (as the highest degree).

The difference in lifetime earnings is even greater for a person with a doctorate. (In 1999, a person with a doctorate had average annual earnings of $86,833). If we assume a doctorate requires 2 years of additional schooling beyond a master's degree, then the total lifetime earnings with a doctorate will be $3,039,155. It follows, then, that the difference in lifetime earnings (between an associate's degree and a doctorate) is $1,656,619. This is 119 percent more lifetime earnings.

Or we can think of it this way. If going from an associate's degree to a doctorate more than doubles Charles's lifetime earnings, it is as if he produces a clone of his associate-degree self during his 8 more years of schooling. (What do you produce in school? Nothing. Wrong, you produce clones of yourself.)

Chapter Summary

Derived Demand

- The demand for a factor is derived—hence, it is called a *derived demand*. Specifically, it is derived from and directly related to the demand for the product that the factor goes to produce; for example, the demand for auto workers is derived from the demand for autos.

MRP, MFC, VMP

- Marginal revenue product (*MRP*) is the additional revenue generated by employing an additional factor unit. Marginal factor cost (*MFC*) is the additional cost incurred by employing an additional factor unit. The profit-maximizing firm buys the factor quantity at which $MRP = MFC$.
- The *MRP* curve is the firm's factor demand curve; it shows how much of a factor the firm buys at different prices.
- Value marginal product (*VMP*) is a measure of the value that each factor unit adds to the firm's product. Whereas $MRP = MR \times MPP$, $VMP = P \times MPP$. For a perfectly competitive firm, $P = MR$, so $MRP = VMP$.

For a monopolist, a monopolistic competitor, or an oligopolist, $P > MR$, so $VMP > MRP$.

The Least-Cost Rule

- A firm minimizes costs by buying factors in the combination at which the *MPP*-to-price ratio for each factor is the same. For example, if there are two factors, labor and capital, the least-cost rule reads $MPP_L/P_L = MPP_K/P_K$.

Labor and Wages

- A change in the price of the product labor produces or a change in the marginal physical product of labor (reflected in a shift in the *MPP* curve) will shift the demand curve for labor.
- The higher (lower) the elasticity of demand for the product labor produces, the higher (lower) the elasticity of demand for labor. The higher (lower) the labor cost–total cost ratio, the higher (lower) the elasticity of demand for labor. The more (fewer) substitutes for labor, the higher (lower) the elasticity of demand for labor.

---

10. We are not adjusting in our example for annual percentage increases in earnings.

- As the wage rate rises, the quantity supplied of labor rises, *ceteris paribus*.
- At the equilibrium wage rate, the quantity supplied of labor equals the quantity demanded of labor.

Demand for and Supply of Labor

- The demand for labor is affected by (1) marginal revenue and (2) marginal physical product. The supply of labor is affected by (1) wage rates in other labor markets, (2) nonpecuniary aspects of the job, (3) number of persons who can do the job, (4) training costs, and (5) moving costs.

Marginal Productivity Theory

- Marginal productivity theory states that firms in competitive or perfect product and factor markets pay factors their marginal revenue products.

Key Terms and Concepts

Derived Demand
Marginal Revenue Product (*MRP*)
Value Marginal Product (*VMP*)

Marginal Factor Cost (*MFC*)
Factor Price Taker
Least-Cost Rule

Elasticity of Demand for Labor
Marginal Productivity Theory
Screening

Economic Connections to You

Economic facts, actions, and changes create ripples that move away from their point of origin. Eventually, these ripples can intersect your life and have an effect on you. Consider the following example.

People begin to save a larger percentage of their incomes. As a result, the supply of funds available for loans expands. In turn, this lowers the price of a loan, or the interest rate. At lower interest rates, businesses begin to borrow more funds and buy more capital equipment. As a result of their buying more capital equipment, the marginal productivity of (your) labor rises. This raises the demand for your labor. If nothing else changes, your wages will rise. Thus, there is a connection between an increase in savings and the amount of income you earn—an economic connection to you.

Based on the material in this chapter, identify other ways in which economic facts, actions, and changes create ripples that eventually affect you.

Questions and Problems

1. The supply curve is horizontal for a factor price taker; however, the industry supply curve is upward-sloping. Explain why this occurs.
2. What forces and factors determine the wage rate for a particular type of labor?
3. What is the relationship between labor productivity and wage rates?
4. What might be one effect of government legislating wage rates?
5. Using the theory developed in this chapter, explain the following: (a) why a worker in Ethiopia is likely to earn much less than a worker in Japan; (b) why the army expects recruitment to rise during economic recessions; (c) why basketball stars earn relatively large incomes; (d) why jobs that carry a health risk offer higher pay than jobs that do not, *ceteris paribus*.
6. Discuss the factors that might prevent the equalization of wage rates for identical or comparable jobs across labor markets.
7. Prepare a list of questions that an interviewer is likely to ask an interviewee in a job interview. Try to identify which of the questions are part of the interviewer's screening process.
8. Explain why the market demand curve for labor is not simply the horizontal "addition" of the firms' demand curves for labor.
9. Discuss the firm's objective, its constraints, and how it makes its choices in its role as a buyer of resources.
10. Explain the relationship between each of the following pairs of concepts: (a) the elasticity of demand for a product and the elasticity of demand for the labor that produces the product; (b) the labor cost–total cost ratio and the elasticity of demand for labor; (c) the number of substitutes for labor and the elasticity of demand for labor.

1. Determine the appropriate numbers for the lettered spaces.

(1) Units of Factor X	(2) Quantity of Output	(3) Marginal Physical Product of X (MPP_X)	(4) Product Price, Marginal Revenue (P = MR)	(5) Total Revenue	(6) Marginal Revenue Product of X (MRP_X)
0	15	0	$8	F	L
1	24	A	8	G	M
2	32	B	8	H	N
3	39	C	8	I	O
4	45	D	8	J	P
5	50	E	8	K	Q

2. If the price of a factor is constant at $48, how many units of the factor will the firm buy?

3. On the same diagram, draw the *VMP* curve and the *MRP* curve for an oligopolist. Explain why the curves look the way you draw them.

4. Explain why the factor supply curve is horizontal for a factor price taker.

5. Look at the two factor demand curves in the following figure. Is the price of the product that labor goes to produce higher for MRP_2 than for MRP_1? Explain your answer.

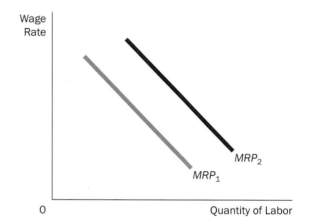

1. Go to *http://stats.bls.gov/eag/eag.us.htm*, and click the graph icon next to "Unemployment rate." The striped or shaded areas represent recessions. Did the unemployment rate continue to rise after the 1990–1991 recession ended? Why might this occur?

2. Click on the "Back" button, and then on the graph icon next to "Average Hourly Earnings." Did the recessions cause a dip in average hourly earnings? Are you surprised by the answer to this question? Why or why not?

3. Click on the "Back" button, and then on the graph icon next to "Employment Cost Index." Did the reces-

sions affect the rate of change in (1) wages and salaries and (2) benefits? If so, explain how the recessions changed the rate of change in each.

4. Click on the "Back" button, and then on the graph icon next to "Productivity." What is the relationship between (labor) productivity and output since 1995:3? What is the relationship between output and hours of all persons in the nonfarm business sector since 1995:3? Is the growth in the rate of output greater than or less than the growth rate in productivity since 1995:3?

Log on to the Arnold Xtra! Web site now (*http://arnoldxtra.swcollege.com*) for additional learning resources such as practice quizzes, help with graphing, video clips, and current event applications.

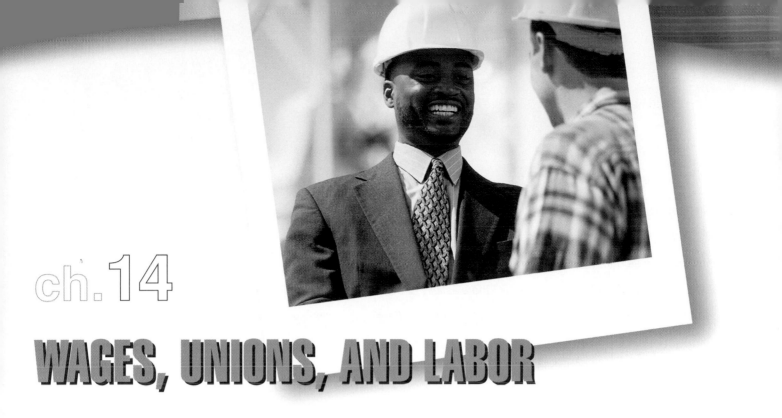

WAGES, UNIONS, AND LABOR

Certain organizations seem to engender controversy. Labor unions are one such organization. Some people are definitely pro-union; others are definitely anti-union. And, there are many millions of people in between who know what unions are, but don't really know how unions can affect their lives. In this chapter, we hope to discuss labor unions in an objective, unbiased way. The topics include the objectives, practices, and effects of unions, among other things.

This chapter mainly focuses on labor unions. Specifically,

we discuss the objectives, practices, and effects of unions. The labor

union is often said to have one of three objectives, as shown below. To obtain its

objective, the union will attempt to affect the elasticity of demand for union labor and/or the

demand for or supply of union labor or it will attempt to affect wages directly. Finally, we discuss the

effect labor unions may have on wages, prices, and productivity and efficiency.

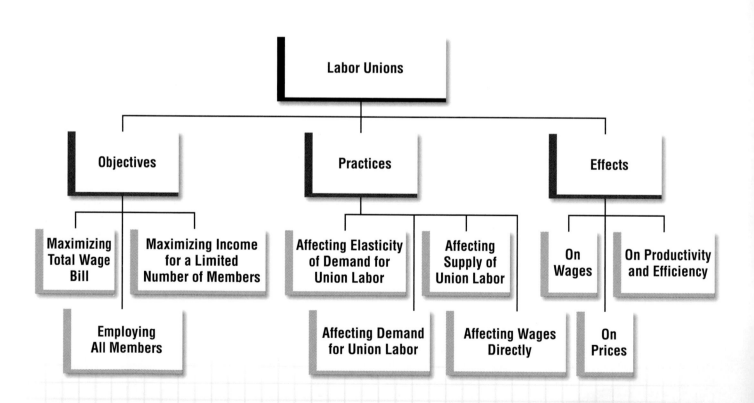

THE FACTS AND FIGURES OF LABOR UNIONS

This section discusses the different types of labor unions and gives some statistics that place unions within the overall labor force.

TYPES OF UNIONS

Economists often speak of three different types of labor unions: craft (trade) unions, industrial unions, and public employee unions. A **craft** or **trade union** is a union whose membership is made up of individuals who practice the same craft or trade. Examples include the plumbers', electricians', and musicians' unions.

An **industrial union** is a union whose membership is made up of workers who work in the same firm or industry but do not all practice the same craft or trade. Examples include the autoworkers' and the steelworkers' unions. For an industrial union to be successful, it must unionize all firms in an industry. If it does not, union firms will face competition from (possibly lower-cost) nonunion firms, which may lead to a decrease in the number of union firms and workers.

A **public employee union** is a union whose membership is made up of workers who work for the local, state, or federal government. Examples include teachers', police, and firefighters' unions. During the past two decades, this has been one of the fastest-growing subsets of the union movement.

Besides these three types of unions, some economists hold that employee associations, such as the American Medical Association (AMA), the American Association of University Professors (AAUP), and the American Bar Association (ABA), are a type of union. An **employee association** is an organization whose members belong to a particular profession. Many people would probably not place professional employee associations into the union category. Some economists argue, however, that employee associations often have the same objectives and implement the same practices to meet those objectives as craft, industrial, and public employee unions; consequently, these associations should be considered unions.

A FEW FACTS AND FIGURES

Union membership as a percentage of the labor force (total number of union members divided by total workforce) was 5.6 percent in 1910, rising to about 12 percent in 1920. By 1930, it was down to about 7.4 percent, and in 1934 it fell to approximately 5 percent. From the late 1930s until the mid-1950s, union membership as a percentage of the labor force grew. It reached its peak of 25 percent in the mid-1950s. In recent years, it has declined. In 1983 it was 20.1 percent, in 1997 it was 14.1 percent, and in 2001 it was 13.5 percent.

OBJECTIVES OF LABOR UNIONS

Labor unions usually seek one of three objectives: to employ all their members, to maximize the total wage bill, or to maximize income for a limited number of union members.

EMPLOYMENT FOR ALL MEMBERS

One possible objective of a labor union is employment for all its members. To illustrate, suppose the demand curve in Exhibit 1 represents the demand for labor in a given union. Also assume the total membership of the union is Q_1. If the objective of the union is to have its total membership employed, then the wage rate that must exist in the market is W_1. At W_1, firms want to hire the total union membership.

MAXIMIZING THE TOTAL WAGE BILL

The total wage bill received by the membership of a union is equal to the wage rate times the number of labor hours worked. One possible objective of a labor union is to maximize this dollar amount; that is, to maximize the number of dollars coming *from* the employer *to* union members.

Craft (Trade) Union
A union whose membership is made up of individuals who practice the same craft or trade.

Industrial Union
A union whose membership is made up of individuals who work in the same firm or industry but do not all practice the same craft or trade.

Public Employee Union
A union whose membership is made up of individuals who work for the local, state, or federal government.

Employee Association
An organization whose members belong to a particular profession.

http://

Go to *http://www.teamster.org/*, and read the page. Next, select and read "Divisions." Is the International Brotherhood of Teamsters a craft (trade) union, an industrial union, or a public employee union? Click the "Back" button, and choose "Organizing" from the Select Department box. Then select "Recent Organizing Victories." Does the union try to organize employees in different industries or in only one industry?

exhibit 1

Labor Union Objectives

If total membership in the union is Q_1, and the union's objective is employment for all its members, it chooses W_1. If the objective is to maximize the total wage bill, it chooses W_2, where the elasticity of demand for labor equals 1. If the union's objective is to maximize the income of a limited number of union workers (represented by Q_3), it chooses W_3.

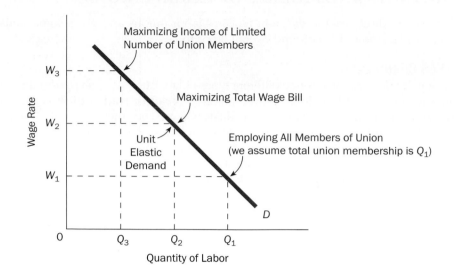

In Exhibit 1, the wage rate that maximizes the total wage bill is W_2. At W_2, the quantity of labor is Q_2 and the elasticity of demand for labor is equal to 1. Recall that total revenue (or total expenditure) is maximized when price elasticity of demand is equal to 1, or demand has unit elasticity. It follows that the total wage bill is maximized at that point where the demand for labor is unit elastic. Note, however, that less union labor is working at W_2 than at W_1, indicating that there is a tradeoff between higher wages and the employment of union members.

MAXIMIZING INCOME FOR A LIMITED NUMBER OF UNION MEMBERS

Some economists have suggested that a labor union might want neither total employment of its membership nor maximization of the total wage bill. Instead, it might prefer to maximize income for a limited number of union members, perhaps those with the most influence or seniority in the union. Suppose this group is represented by Q_3 in Exhibit 1. The highest wage at which this group can be employed is W_3; thus, the union might seek this wage rate instead of any lower wage.

Q & A

Q: Exhibit 1 suggests that the union must make a wage-employment tradeoff. It can get higher wage rates, but some of the union members will lose their jobs in the process. Is this correct?

A: Yes, a higher wage rate means fewer union members employed, *ceteris paribus*. The union is likely to be aware that this wage-employment tradeoff exists. Notice also that this wage-employment tradeoff depends on the elasticity of demand for labor.

Consider the demand for labor in two unions, *A* and *B*, in Exhibit 2. Suppose both unions bargain for a wage increase from W_1 to W_2. The quantity of labor drops much more in union *B*, where demand for labor is elastic between the two wage rates, than in union *A*, where the demand for labor is inelastic between the two wage rates. We would expect union *B* to be less likely than union *A* to push for higher wages, *ceteris paribus*. The reason is that the wage-employment tradeoff is more pronounced for union *B* than for union *A*. It is simply costlier (in terms of union members' jobs) for union *B* to push for higher wages than it is for union *A* to do so.

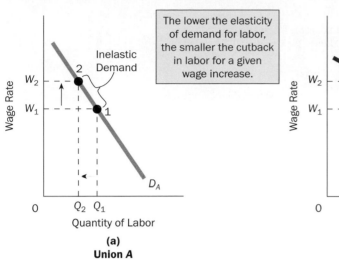

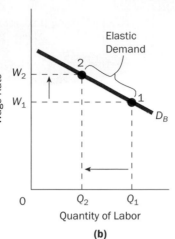

The lower the elasticity of demand for labor, the smaller the cutback in labor for a given wage increase.

(a)
Union A

(b)
Union B

exhibit 2

The Wage-Employment Tradeoff: Two Cases
For union A, which has an inelastic demand for its labor between W_1 and W_2, a higher wage rate brings about a smaller cutback in the quantity of labor than for union B, which has an elastic demand for its labor between W_1 and W_2. We predict that union B will be less likely to push for higher wages than union A because its wage-employment tradeoff is more pronounced.

PRACTICES OF LABOR UNIONS

This section explains how labor unions try to meet their objectives by influencing one or more of the following factors: the elasticity of demand for labor, the demand for labor, and the supply of labor. We also discuss how unions can directly affect wages.

AFFECTING ELASTICITY OF DEMAND FOR UNION LABOR

Exhibit 2 shows that the lower the elasticity of demand for labor, the smaller the cutback in labor for any given wage increase. Obviously, the smaller the cutback in labor for a given wage increase, the better it is from the viewpoint of the labor union. Given a choice between losing either 200 jobs or 50 jobs because of a wage rate increase of $2, the labor union prefers to lose the smaller number of jobs. Thus, a labor union looks for ways to lower the elasticity of demand for its labor. It does this mainly by attempting to reduce the availability of substitutes.

Availability of Substitute Products

Consider the autoworkers' union, whose members produce American automobiles. We know that the lower the elasticity of demand for American automobiles, the lower the elasticity of demand for the labor that produces automobiles. We would expect, then, that unions would attempt to reduce the availability of substitutes for the products they produce through such means as import restrictions. The autoworkers' union, for example, has in past years proposed restrictions on Japanese car imports.

Availability of Substitute Factors

The fewer the substitute factors for union labor, the lower the elasticity of demand for union labor. There are two general substitutes for union labor: nonunion labor and certain types of machines. For example, a musical synthesizer (which can sound like many different instruments) is a substitute for a group of musicians playing different instruments. Labor unions have often attempted to reduce the availability of substitute factors—both the nonunion labor variety and the nonhuman variety. Thus, labor unions commonly oppose the relaxation of immigration

ECONOMICS IN...

Technology, the Price of Competing Factors, and Displaced Workers[1]

For most of the eighteenth century in England, spinners and weavers worked on hand-operated spinning wheels and looms. Then in the 1770s, a mechanical spinner was invented. This new machine required steam or water power and so yarn-spinning factories were set up near water mills. The factory workers, working with mechanical spinners, could produce 100 times more yarn in a day than they could produce using hand-operated spinners.

Because of the increased supply of yarn, the price fell and the quantity demanded of yarn increased substantially. In turn, this increased the demand for weavers, who continued to use hand-operated looms. As a result of the increased demand for weavers, their wages increased. In reaction to the higher wages for weavers, entrepreneurs and inventors began to experiment with different kinds of weaving machines. Their experiments began to pay off; in 1787, the power loom was invented, although it was not perfected until the 1820s. By the

1830s, two workers using a power loom could produce in one day 20 times what a weaver could produce on a hand-operated loom.

Soon, the weavers who used hand-operated looms found themselves without jobs. They had been displaced by the introduction of the power loom. Some of the displaced workers showed their frustration and anger at their predicament by burning power looms and factories.

The story of spinners and weavers in eighteenth-century England helps us to realize two important points about technology. First, as long as there are advancements in technology, some workers will be temporarily displaced. Second, an advancement in technology often has an identifiable cause; it doesn't simply fall out of the sky. If it had not been for the higher weavers' wages, it is not clear that the power loom would have been invented.

laws, they usually favor the repatriation of illegal aliens, they generally are in favor of a high minimum wage (which increases the relative price of nonunion labor vis-à-vis union labor), and they usually oppose machines that can be substituted for their labor. Also, in the area of construction, unions usually specify that certain jobs can be done by, say, electricians only (thus prohibiting substitute factors from being employed on certain jobs).

AFFECTING THE DEMAND FOR UNION LABOR

Labor unions can try to meet their objectives by increasing the demand for union labor. All other things held constant, this leads to higher wage rates and more union labor employed. How can labor unions increase the demand for their labor? Consider the following possibilities.

Increasing Product Demand

Unions occasionally urge the buying public to buy the products produced by union labor. Unions advertise, urging people to "look for the union label" or to look for the label that reads "Made in the U.S.A." As mentioned earlier, they sometimes also support legislation that either keeps out imports altogether or makes them more expensive.

---

1. This feature is based on Elizabeth Hoffman, "How Can Displaced Workers Find Better Jobs?" in *Second Thoughts: Myths and Morals of U.S. Economic History,* ed. by Donald McCloskey (Oxford: Oxford University Press, 1993).

Increasing Substitute Factor Prices

If union action leads to a rise in the relative price of factors that are substitutes for union labor, the demand for union labor rises. (Recall that if X and Y are substitutes and the price of X rises, so does the demand for Y.) For this reason, unions have often lobbied for an increase in the minimum wage—the wage received mostly by unskilled labor, which is a substitute for skilled union labor. The first minimum wage legislation was passed at a time when many companies were moving from the unionized North to the nonunionized South. The minimum wage made the nonunionized, relatively unskilled labor in the South more expensive and is said to have slowed the movement of companies to the South.

Increasing Marginal Physical Product

If unions can increase the productivity of their members, the demand for their labor will rise. With this in mind, unions prefer to add skilled labor to their ranks, and they sometimes undertake training programs for new entrants.

AFFECTING THE SUPPLY OF UNION LABOR

A third way labor unions try to meet their objectives is by decreasing the supply of labor. A decreased supply translates into higher wage rates. How might the labor union decrease the supply of labor from what it might be if the labor union did not exist? One possibility is to control the supply of labor in a market.

Craft unions, in particular, have been moderately successful in getting employers to hire only union labor. In the past, they were successful at turning some businesses into closed shops. A **closed shop** is an organization in which an employee must belong to the union before he or she can work. (In contrast, in an *open shop,* an employer may hire union or nonunion workers.) When unions can determine, or at least control in some way, the supply of labor in a given market, they can decrease it from what it would ordinarily have been. They can do this by restricting membership, by requiring long apprenticeships, or by rigid certification requirements. The closed shop was prohibited in 1947 by the Taft-Hartley Act.

The union shop, however, is legal in many states today. A **union shop** is an organization that does not require individuals to be union members in order to be hired, but does require them to join the union within a certain period of time after becoming employed.

Today, unions typically argue for union shops, against open shops, and against the prohibition of closed shops. They also typically argue against state right-to-work laws (which some, but not all, states have), which make it illegal to require union membership for purposes of employment. (The Taft-Hartley Act allowed states to pass right-to-work laws and thus to override federal legislation that legalized union shops.) In short, the union shop is illegal in right-to-work states.

AFFECTING WAGES DIRECTLY: COLLECTIVE BARGAINING

Besides increasing wage rates indirectly by influencing the demand for and supply of their labor, unions can directly affect wage rates through collective bargaining. **Collective bargaining** is the process whereby wage rates are determined by the union bargaining with management on behalf of all its members. In collective bargaining, union members act together as a single unit in order to increase their bargaining power with management. On the other side of the market, the employers of labor may also band together and act as one unit. Their objective is the same as the union's: to increase their bargaining power.

Closed Shop
An organization in which an employee must belong to the union before he or she can be hired.

Union Shop
An organization in which a worker is not required to be a member of the union to be hired, but must become a member within a certain period of time after being employed.

Collective Bargaining
The process whereby wage rates and other issues are determined by a union bargaining with management on behalf of all union members.

What Are College Professors' Objectives?

Labor unions try to meet their objectives by influencing the elasticity of demand for labor and the demand for labor. To influence these factors, they try to (1) reduce the availability of substitute products, (2) reduce the availability of substitute factors, (3) increase demand for the product they produce, (4) increase substitute factor prices, and (5) increase the *MPP* of their members. Labor unions try to do (1) and (2) because they want the elasticity of demand for their labor to be low (so that any wage increase only slightly reduces the quantity demanded of union labor). They try to do (3), (4), and (5) because they want the demand for their labor to be high (so that they will receive high wages). Thus, labor unions have as overall objectives to reduce the wage-employment tradeoff and to raise their wages. Unionized workers are not the only group of people with these overall objectives.

Consider (classroom) college professors. Do college professors do some of the same things that labor unions do? Do they try to reduce their wage-employment tradeoff and raise their wages? There is some (anecdotal) evidence that they do. This evidence is often found by listening to the way college professors discuss college education. Let's examine the behavior of college professors in terms of three of the five factors mentioned with respect to labor unions: (1) reduce the availability of substitute services, (2) reduce the availability of substitute factors, and (3) increase demand for what they sell.

Reduce the Availability of Substitute Services

Classroom college professors often argue that the college classroom is the best setting in which to learn. In a classroom, lectures can be given, discussions carried out, questions asked and answered, and so on.[2] In other words, courses on the Internet, correspondence courses, and other such educational settings cannot take the place of the college classroom experience. This would imply that the classroom experience is unique. But if it is unique, there are no substitutes for it.

Recall that the fewer substitutes there are for a good or service, the lower the price elasticity of demand for that good or service, *ceteris paribus*. And, of course, as the elasticity of demand for the service college professors provide decreases, the wage-employment tradeoff diminishes for the professors.

Are college professors simply acting selfishly when they argue this way? Or are they stating the truth? The answer to both questions could be yes. It may be true that the college classroom is the best setting in which to learn, and it may also be true that it is in the best interest of college professors to make sure that students (customers) understand this.

Reduce the Availability of Substitute Factors

College professors often argue against large classes (90 students or more). They say that students can get a better education when classes are smaller—ideally about 30 students. In a smaller class, the professor can give students greater individualized attention, can discuss things with them that are impossible to discuss in large lecture halls, can give them more writing assignments, which are important to their education, and so on.

All this sounds reasonable, and it may be true. But arguing against large classes is also a way of trying to reduce the availability of substitute factors. To illustrate, suppose there are 10 economics professors at one college, each professor teaches 3 classes a semester, and classes are limited to 30 students each. Thus, there are 30 economics classes offered each semester. Furthermore, suppose students may enroll in any of the 30 economics classes available. In this setting, Professor Jones, say, teaches 3 classes and there are 9 professors who are substitutes for him (who teach a total of 27 substitute courses for his courses).

Then one day, 1 of the 10 economics professors retires from the college. The college mandates that the new professor who replaces her must teach 3 classes each semester and each class must have 90 students. Thus, the new professor teaches three times as many students each semester as every other professor.

By raising class size for the new professor, is the university adding only 1 professor or the equivalent of 3 professors?

Look at it from Professor Jones's point of view. He still teaches 3 classes a semester, and there are still only 9 professors who are substitutes for him. But under the 1 class = 30 students rule, the new professor is doing her job and the job of 2 other professors. It is as if the new professor brought 2 other (shadow) professors with her; she walked into the college as 3 people, not as a single person. So, instead of Professor Jones having 9 other professors who are substitutes for him (together teaching 27 substitute classes), he effectively has 11 other professors who are substitutes for him (together teaching 33 substitute classes). In conclusion, when Professor Jones argues against big classes, he effectively argues against substitutes for himself.

---

2. The author of this text is a college professor and often finds he argues this way. He is not saying anything about college professors in this feature that may not hold for him too.

Increasing Demand for What Professors Sell

Most college professors argue in favor of subsidies for higher education.[3] Occasionally, a university professor may say that all higher education should be privatized and that government shouldn't use tax dollars to subsidize a person's college education, but this is a rare event. Most college professors are in favor of subsidies for college education and many of them would like to see these subsidies increased. We do not mean to imply that professors' arguments for subsidizing higher education are fallacious; we only state that they make these arguments. But certainly, subsidies for higher education cause the demand for a college education to be higher than it would be otherwise. And, if the demand for a college education is higher, so is the demand for college professors because the demand for college professors is a derived demand.

Conclusion

Many college professors argue that the college classroom is the best setting in which to learn. They also argue against large classes and in favor of subsidies for higher education. They may be honest in the arguments they put forth to support their positions and, moreover, their arguments may be solid and true. Still, these positions, if realized, have the effect of reducing the college professor wage-employment tradeoff and increasing college professors' salaries.

From the viewpoint of the labor union, collective bargaining is unlikely to be successful unless the union can strike. A **strike** occurs when unionized employees refuse to work at a certain wage or under certain conditions. Exhibit 3 illustrates the effects of successful union collective bargaining.

Suppose the initial wage rate that exists in the labor market is the competitive wage rate W_1. This is the wage rate that would exist if each employee were to bargain separately with management. The equilibrium quantity of labor is Q_1.

Management and the union (which represents all labor in this market) now sit down at a collective bargaining session. The union specifies that it wants a wage rate of W_2 and says that *none of its members will work at a lower wage rate*. This means the union holds that the new supply curve is $S'S$—or the heavy supply curve. In effect, the union is telling management that it cannot hire anyone for a wage rate lower than W_2 and if it wants to hire more workers than want to work at this wage rate—represented by Q_3—it will have to increase the wage rate.

Whether the union can bring about this higher wage rate (W_2) depends on whether it can prevent labor from working at less than this wage. That is, if management does not initially agree to W_2, the union will have to call a strike and show management that it cannot hire any labor for a wage rate lower than W_2. It has to convince management that the new supply curve looks the way the union says it looks. We assume in Exhibit 3 that the strike threat, or actual strike, is successful for the union and management agrees to the higher wage rate of W_2. As a result, the quantity of labor employed, Q_2, is less than it would have been at W_1. The new equilibrium is at point B instead of point A.

STRIKES

The purpose of a strike is to convince management that the supply curve is what the union says it is. Often, this depends on the ability of striking union employees to prevent nonstriking and nonunion employees from working for management at a lower wage rate than the union is seeking through collective bargaining. For example, if management can easily hire individuals at a wage rate lower than W_2 in Exhibit 3, it will not be convinced that the heavy supply curve is the relevant supply curve.

Strike
The situation in which union employees refuse to work at a certain wage or under certain conditions.

---

3. For purposes here, think of the subsidy as a dollar rebate for each unit of education purchased. This has the effect of shifting the demand curve upward a vertical distance equal to the subsidy.

exhibit 3

Successful Collective Bargaining by the Union

We start at a wage rate of W_1. The union's objective is to increase the wage rate to W_2. This means the union holds that the new supply curve of labor is $S'S$—the heavy supply curve. To convince management that the new supply curve looks as the union says it does, the union will have to either threaten a strike or call one. We assume that the union is successful at raising the wage rate to W_2. As a consequence, the quantity of labor employed is less than it would have been at W_1.

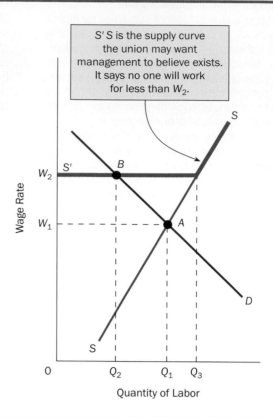

> $S'S$ is the supply curve the union may want management to believe exists. It says no one will work for less than W_2.

Self-Test *(Answers to Self-Test questions are in the Self-Test Appendix.)*

1. What will lower the demand for union labor?
2. What is the difference between a closed shop and a union shop?
3. What is the objective of a strike?

EFFECTS OF LABOR UNIONS

What are the effects of labor unions on wage rates? Are the effects the same in all labor markets? These two questions are addressed in this section.

THE CASE OF MONOPSONY

Monopsony
A single buyer in a factor market.

A single buyer in a factor market is known as a **monopsony.** Some economists refer to a monopsony as a "buyer's monopoly." A monopoly is a single seller of a product; a monopsony is a single buyer of a factor.

Suppose a firm in a small town is the only buyer of labor because there are no other firms for miles around. This firm would be considered a monopsony. Because it is a monopsony, it cannot buy additional units of a factor without increasing the price it pays for the factor (in much the same way that a monopolist in the product market cannot sell an additional unit of its good without lowering price). The reason is that the supply of labor it faces is the market supply of labor.

For the monopsonist, marginal factor cost increases as it buys additional units of a factor, and the supply curve of the factor is different from the monopsonist's marginal factor cost curve.

As shown in Exhibit 4, marginal factor cost increases as additional units of the factor are purchased. Notice in part (a) that as workers are added, the wage rate rises. For example, for the monopsonist to employ two workers, the wage rate

(1) Workers	(2) Wage Rate	(3) Total Labor Cost (1) × (2)	(4) Marginal Factor Cost $\frac{\Delta(3)}{\Delta(1)}$
0	—	—	—
1	$6.00	$ 6.00	$6.00
2	6.05	12.10	6.10
3	6.10	18.30	6.20
4	6.15	24.60	6.30
5	6.20	31.00	6.40

(a)

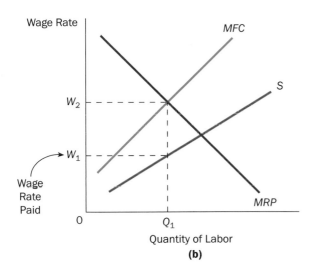

(b)

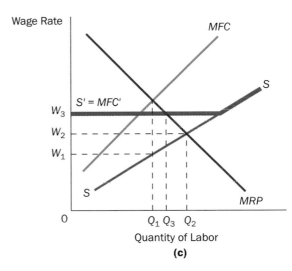

(c)

exhibit 4

The Labor Union and the Monopsonist
(a) For the monopsonist, MFC > wage rate. This implies that the supply curve the monopsonist faces lies below its MFC curve. (b) The monopsonist purchases Q_1 quantity of labor and pays a wage rate of W_1, which is less than MRP (labor is being paid less than its MRP). (c) If the labor union succeeds in increasing the wage rate from W_1 to W_3 through collective bargaining, then the firm will also hire more labor (Q_3 instead of Q_1). We conclude that in the case of monopsony, higher wage rates (over a range) do not imply fewer persons working.

must rise from $6.00 per hour to $6.05. To employ three workers, the monopsonist must offer to pay $6.10. Comparing column 2 with column 4, we notice that the marginal factor cost for a monopsonist is greater than the wage rate (in the same way that for a monopolist, price is greater than marginal revenue). Plotting columns 1 and 2 gives the supply curve for the monopsonist (see Exhibit 4b); plotting columns 1 and 4 gives the monopsonist's MFC curve. Because MFC > wage rate, it follows that the supply curve lies below the MFC curve.

Exhibit 4b shows that the monopsonist chooses to purchase Q_1 units of labor (where MRP = MFC) and that it pays a wage rate of W_1. (W_1 is the wage rate necessary to get Q_1 workers to offer their services.)

If the monopsonist were to pay workers what their services were worth to it (as represented by the MRP curve), it would pay a higher wage. Some persons contend that labor unions and collective bargaining are necessary in situations such as this, where labor is being paid less than its marginal revenue product. Furthermore, they argue that successful collective bargaining on the part of the labor union in this setting will not be subject to the wage-employment tradeoff it encounters in other settings. This is illustrated in Exhibit 4c.

Successful collective bargaining by the labor union moves the wage rate from W_1 to W_3 in part (c). The labor union is essentially saying to the monopsonist that it cannot hire any labor below W_3. This changes the monopsonist's marginal factor cost curve from MFC to MFC', which corresponds to the new supply curve the monopsonist faces, $S' S$. The monopsonist once again purchases that quantity of labor at which marginal revenue product equals marginal factor cost. But now, because the marginal factor cost curve is MFC', equality is at Q_3 workers and a

ECONOMICS IN...

"Are You Ready for Some Football?"

Sometimes firms that sell a similar good try to form a cartel so they can act as a monopoly. Can this behavior occur when firms buy a factor? Do firms that buy a specific factor sometimes try to form a cartel so they can act as a monopsony? No doubt you know such a "firm." Many universities and colleges have banded together to buy the services of college-bound athletes. In other words, they have entered into a cartel agreement to reduce the monetary competition among themselves for college-bound athletes. The National Collegiate Athletic Association (NCAA) is the cartel or monopsony enforcer. How does all this work?

The NCAA sets certain rules and regulations by which its member universities and colleges must abide or else face punishment and fines. For example, universities and colleges are prohibited from offering salaries to athletes to play on their teams. They are prohibited from "making work" for them at the university or paying them relatively high wage rates for a job that usually pays much less—for example, paying athletes $30 an hour to reshelve books in the university library. Universities and colleges are also prohibited from offering inducements such as cars, clothes, and trips to attract athletes.

The stated objectives of these NCAA regulations are to maintain the amateur standing of college athletes, to prevent the rich schools from getting all the good players, and to enhance the competitiveness of college sports. Some economists suggest that some schools may have other objectives. They note that college athletics can be a revenue-raising activity for schools and that these institutions would rather pay college athletes less than their marginal revenue products (the way a monopsony does) to play sports.

Currently, universities and colleges openly compete for athletes by offering scholarships, free room and board, and school jobs. They also compete in terms of their academic reputations and the reputations of their sports programs (obviously, some find it easier to do this than others). Although it is prohibited, some universities and colleges compete for athletes in ways not sanctioned by the NCAA; that is, they compete "under the table." This is evidence, some economists maintain, that some schools are cheating on the cartel agreement. Such cheating usually benefits the college athletes, who receive a "payment" for their athletic abilities that is closer to their marginal revenue products. For example, it has occasionally been noted that some college athletes, many of whom come from families of modest means, drive flashy, expensive cars in college. Where do they get these cars? Often they come from community friends of the university or boosters of its sports program. Such payments to college athletes may be prohibited by the NCAA, but as we saw earlier, members of cartels (of the monopoly or monopsony variety) usually find ways of evading the rules.

Not all economists agree that the NCAA is a cartel. Some economists argue that paying college athletes would diminish the reputation of college athletics, which would decrease the public demand for college sports programs. They conclude that the NCAA imposes its rules and regulations—one of which is that college athletes should not be paid to play sports—in order to keep college sports nonprofessional and in relatively high demand, and not to suppress players' wages.

---

wage rate of W_3. We conclude that over a range, there is no wage-employment tradeoff for the labor union when it faces a monopsonist. It is possible to raise both the wage rate and the number of workers employed.

Q & A   **Q:** An earlier chapter explains that the minimum wage, which is an example of a price floor, reduces the number of persons working in the labor market in which it is effective. In the monopsony setting, however, this does not seem to be the case. In fact, if W_3 in Exhibit 4c is considered a minimum wage—in that the monopsonist cannot hire anyone for a lower wage—then it seems to increase rather than decrease employment. Is this right?

A: Yes, that is right. Consider two peripheral points, though. First, W_3 is a higher wage rate than the wage rate that would maximize total employment. The wage rate that maximizes total employment occurs where supply and demand intersect. In Exhibit 4c, this is where the *MRP* curve, or the factor demand curve, intersects the supply curve (*SS*) of labor. Here Q_2 workers would be employed at a wage rate of W_2.

Second, notice that even in a monopsony setting, it is not possible to raise wage rates continually and increase employment too. For example, in part (c), if the wage rate were raised above where the original *MFC* curve intersects the *MRP* curve, then the monopsonist would purchase a quantity of labor less than Q_1, the quantity it originally purchased.

 Q: Are there many instances of monopsony in the real world?

A: The evidence seems to show that there are few instances of (pure) monopsony in the real world. Some economists argue that many firms have some degree of monopsony power—that is, their *MFC* curves are not perfectly elastic. Historically, the "company town" fits the description of monopsony. Today, it is easy for labor to move from city to city and from firm to firm, so that most workers have opportunities to work for a number of firms, not just one.

THINKING LIKE AN ECONOMIST *An economist rarely answers questions without specifying the condition under which the answer is true. For example, if asked, "Does the minimum wage increase or decrease the number of persons working in the unskilled labor market?" the economist would answer, "In the case of monopsony, the minimum wage can increase the number of persons working; in the case of perfect competition, the minimum wage decreases the number of persons working." Sometimes the layperson misunderstands this type of response, thinking the economist is giving an ambiguous answer or hedging his bets. But the economist is simply trying to be as precise as possible.*

UNIONS' EFFECTS ON WAGES

Most studies show that some unions have increased their members' wages substantially, whereas other unions have not increased their members' wages at all. Work by H. Gregg Lewis concludes that during the period 1920–1979, the average wage of union members was 10 to 15 percent higher than that of comparable nonunion labor. (Keep in mind, though, that the union-nonunion wage differential can differ quite a bit in different years and between industries.) For data on this subject, see Exhibit 5.

Exhibit 6 illustrates the theoretical basis of the observation that higher union wages lead to lower nonunion wages, or to a union-nonunion wage gap. Two sectors of the labor market are shown: the unionized sector in part (a) and the nonunionized sector in part (b). We assume that labor is homogeneous and that the wage rate is $15 in both sectors.

The labor union either collectively bargains to a higher wage rate of $18 or manages to reduce supply so that $18 comes about (the exhibit shows a decrease in supply). As a consequence, less labor is employed in the unionized sector. If we hold that the persons who now are not working in the unionized sector can work in the nonunionized sector, it follows that the supply of labor in the nonunionized sector increases from S_{NU} to S'_{NU} and the wage rate in the nonunionized sector falls to $12. We conclude that there are theoretical and empirical reasons for believing that labor unions increase the wages of union employees and decrease the wages of nonunion employees.

Do the higher wages that union employees receive through unionization outweigh the lower wages that nonunion employees receive in terms of the percentage of the national income that goes to labor? It appears not. The percentage of the national income that goes to labor (union plus nonunion labor) has been fairly constant over time. In fact, it was approximately the same when unions were

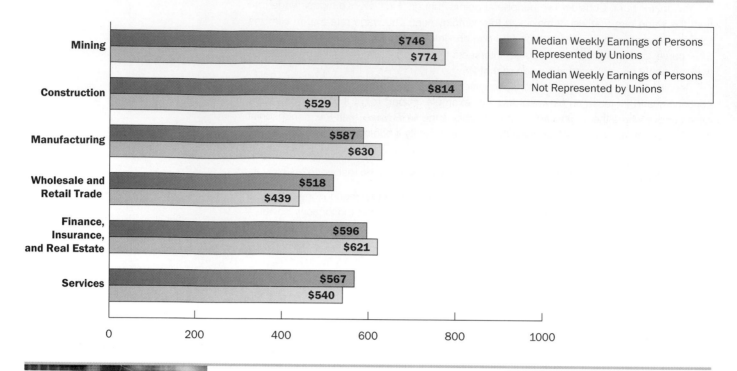

Mining	$746	$774
Construction	$814	$529
Manufacturing	$587	$630
Wholesale and Retail Trade	$518	$439
Finance, Insurance, and Real Estate	$596	$621
Services	$567	$540

Median Weekly Earnings of Persons Represented by Unions

Median Weekly Earnings of Persons Not Represented by Unions

0   200   400   600   800   1000

exhibit 5

Median Weekly Earnings in the Union and Nonunion Sectors, Selected Industries, 2000

In three of the six (selected) industries shown, union workers earned a higher weekly salary in 2000 than did nonunion workers. Overall in 2000, the median weekly salary was $696 for a union worker and $542 for a nonunion worker (not shown).

Source: Statistical Abstract of the United States, 2001.

weak and union membership was relatively low as when unions were strong and union membership was relatively high.

Q & A

Q: The layperson's view of labor unions is that they obtain higher wages for their members at the expense of the owners of the firms, not at the expense of other workers. The preceding comments suggest this may not be true. Why don't the higher wages that go to union employees come out of profits?

A: It is important to differentiate between the short run and the long run here. In the theory of perfect competition, when there were short-run profits, new firms entered the industry, the industry supply curve shifted rightward, prices fell, and profits were competed away. In the long run, there was zero economic profit.

In addition, when there were short-run losses, firms exited the industry, the industry supply curve shifted leftward, prices increased, and losses finally disappeared. In the long run, there was zero economic profit.

Within this market structure, consider a labor union that manages to obtain higher wages for its members. It is possible that in the short run these higher wages will diminish profits—the way any cost increase would diminish profits, *ceteris paribus*—but in the long run there will be adjustments as firms exit the industry, supply curves shift, and prices change. In the long run, zero economic profit will exist. We conclude that it is possible in the short run for "higher wages to come out of profits," but in the long run this isn't likely to be the case.

THINKING LIKE AN ECONOMIST *Economists make the important distinction between primary and secondary effects, or between what happens in the short run and what happens in the long run. For example, we have just seen that higher wages may initially come at the expense of profits, but as time passes, this may not continue to be the case.*

UNIONS' EFFECTS ON PRICES

One effect of labor unions is that union wages are relatively higher and nonunion wages are relatively lower. The higher union wages mean higher costs for the

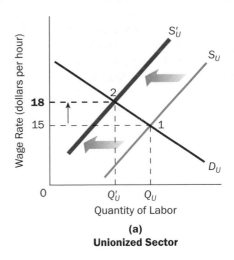

Changes in supply conditions and wage rates in the unionized sector can cause changes in supply and wage rates in the nonunionized sector.

(a)
Unionized Sector

(b)
Nonunionized Sector

firms that employ union labor, and higher costs affect supply curves, which in turn affect product prices. We conclude that higher union wages will cause higher prices for the products that the union labor produces. Conversely, lower nonunion wages mean lower costs for the firms that employ nonunion labor and thus lower prices for the products produced by nonunion labor.

UNIONS' EFFECTS ON PRODUCTIVITY AND EFFICIENCY: TWO VIEWS

There are two major views of the effects labor unions have on productivity and efficiency.

The Traditional (or Orthodox) View

The traditional view holds that labor unions have a negative impact on productivity and efficiency. Its proponents make the following arguments: (1) Labor unions often have unnecessary staffing requirements and insist that only certain persons be allowed to do certain jobs. Because of this, the economy operates below its potential—that is, inefficiently. (2) Strikes disrupt production and prevent the economy from realizing its productive potential. (3) Labor unions drive an artificial wedge between the wages of comparable labor in the union and nonunion sectors of the labor market.

This last point warrants elaboration. Look again at Exhibit 6. Remember, we are dealing with homogeneous labor and we start with the same wage rate in both sectors of the labor market. Union efforts increase the wage rate in the union sector and decrease the wage rate in the nonunion sector.

At this point, the marginal revenue product of persons who work in the union sector is higher than the marginal revenue product of individuals who work in the nonunion sector. (We are farther up the factor demand curve, or *MRP* curve, in the union than in the nonunion sector.) If labor could move from the nonunionized sector to the unionized sector, it would be moving from where it is worth less to where it is worth more. But this cannot happen owing to the supply-restraining efforts of the union. Economists call this a misallocation of labor; not all labor is employed where it is most valuable.

A New View: The Labor Union as a Collective Voice

There is evidence that in some industries, union firms have a higher rate of productivity than nonunion firms. Some economists believe that this is a result of the labor union's role as a collective voice mechanism for its members. Without a labor union, workers who are disgruntled with their jobs, who feel taken advantage of by

exhibit 6

The Effect of Labor Unions on Union and Nonunion Wages
We begin at a wage rate of $15 in both the unionized sector, (a), and the nonunionized sector, (b). Next, the union manages to increase its wage rate to $18 either through collective bargaining or by decreasing the supply of labor in the unionized sector (shown). Fewer persons now work in the unionized sector, and we assume that those persons who lose their jobs move to the nonunionized sector. The supply of labor in the nonunionized sector rises, and the wage rate falls.

Go to *http://www.uaw.org.* Under the "ABOUT UAW" menu, select "Questions & Answers," and then click on "How does union pay compare to non-union pay?" What was the average union wage rate in the most recent year reported? What was the average nonunion wage rate in the most recent year reported?

their employers, or who feel unsafe in their work will leave their jobs and seek work elsewhere. This "job exiting" comes at a cost; it raises the turnover rate, results in lengthy job searches during which individuals are not producing goods and services, and raises training costs. Such costs can be reduced, it is argued, when a labor union acts as a collective voice for its members. Instead of individual employees having to discuss ticklish employment matters with their employer, the labor union does it for them. Overall, the labor union makes the employees feel more confident, less intimidated, and more secure in their work. Such positive feelings usually mean happier, more productive employees. Some proponents of this view also hold that the employees are less likely to quit their jobs. In fact, there is evidence that unionism does indeed reduce job quits.

Critics have contended, though, that the reduced job quits are less a function of the labor union as a collective voice mechanism than of the labor union as an institution capable of increasing its members' wages. It has also been noted that the productivity-increasing aspects of the labor union, which are linked to its role as a collective voice mechanism, are independent of the productivity-decreasing aspects of the labor union in its role as "monopolizer of labor."

Self-Test

1. What is a major difference between a monopsonist and a factor price taker?
2. Under what conditions will the minimum wage increase the number of people working?
3. How could a collectively bargained higher wage rate in the unionized sector of the economy lead to a lower wage rate in the nonunionized sector of the economy?

A Reader Asks...
What Are the Facts of Labor Unions?

Earlier in the chapter, it's noted that 13.5 percent of the labor force is comprised of union workers. In what state is union membership the largest percentage of the work force? Is union membership greater in some industries than others? Is the private sector more or less unionized than the public sector?

Here is some information about labor unions, some of which will answer your questions:

- The four states with the highest union membership rates are New York, Hawaii, Alaska, and Michigan (in order)—all with membership rates over 20 percent in 2001. The two states with the lowest membership rates (below 5 percent) are North Carolina and South Carolina.
- Six states—California, New York, Illinois, Michigan, Ohio, and Pennsylvania—account for 35 percent of all workers but have 50 percent of all union members.
- In 2001, workers in the public sector had unionization rates that were four times higher than their counterparts in the private sector.
- The unionization rate of government workers is about 37.4 percent, compared with 9.0 percent among private sector employees.

- Protective service workers—a group that includes police officers and firefighters—has the highest unionization rate (38 percent) among all occupations.
- The nonagricultural industry with the lowest unionization rate (2.1 percent) is finance, insurance, and real estate.
- Union membership rates of government employees have held steady since 1983, while those of private nonagricultural employees have declined.
- Unionization membership rates are higher among men (15.1 percent) than women (11.7 percent).
- African-American men have the highest rate of union membership among all major worker groups.
- Workers ages 45 to 54 are more likely to be unionized than either their younger or older counterparts.
- Full-time workers are more than twice as likely as part-time workers to be members of a union.
- There are approximately 1.6 million workers who are not union members but who are represented by unions at their place of work.
- In 2001, about 16.3 million workers in the United States were members of a labor union.

Types of Unions

- There are three different types of labor unions: craft (or trade) unions, industrial unions, and public employee unions. Some economists hold that employee associations are also a type of union.

Objectives of a Union

- Objectives of a union include (1) employment for all its members, (2) maximization of the total wage bill, and (3) maximization of the income for a limited number of union members. A labor union faces a wage-employment tradeoff; higher wage rates mean less labor union employment. There is an exception, however. When a labor union faces a monopsonist, it is possible for the union to raise both wage rates and employment of its members (over a range). Exhibit 4c illustrates this.

Practices of a Labor Union

- To soften the wage-employment tradeoff, a labor union seeks to lower the elasticity of demand for its labor. Ways of doing this include (1) reducing the availability of substitute products and (2) reducing the availability of substitute factors for labor.
- Union wage rates can be increased indirectly by increasing the demand for union labor or by reducing the supply of union labor or can be increased directly by collective bargaining. To increase demand for its labor, a union might try to increase (1) the demand for the good it produces, (2) substitute factor prices, or (3) its marginal physical product. To decrease the supply of its labor, a union might argue for closed and union shops and against right-to-work laws.
- In a way, successful collective bargaining on the part of a labor union changes the supply curve of labor that the employer faces. The labor union is successful if, through its collective bargaining efforts, it can prevent the employer from hiring labor at a wage rate below a union-determined level. In this case, the supply curve of labor becomes horizontal at this wage rate. See Exhibit 3.

Monopsony

- For a monopsonist, marginal factor cost rises as it buys additional units of a factor and its supply curve lies below its marginal factor cost curve. The monopsonist buys the factor quantity at which $MRP = MFC$. The price of the factor is less than the monopsonist's marginal factor cost, so the monopsonist pays the factor less than its marginal revenue product.

Effects of Unions

- There is evidence that labor unions generally have the effect of increasing their members' wage rates (over what they would be without the union) and lowering the wage rates of nonunion labor.
- The traditional view of labor unions holds that unions negatively affect productivity and efficiency. They do this by (1) arguing for and often obtaining unnecessary staffing requirements, (2) calling strikes that disrupt production, and (3) driving an artificial wedge between the wages of comparable labor in the union and nonunion sectors.
- The "new" view of labor unions holds that labor unions act as a collective voice mechanism for individual union employees and cause them to feel more confident in their jobs and less intimidated by their employers. This leads to more productive employees, who are less likely to quit, and so forth.

Key Terms and Concepts

Craft (Trade) Union	Employee Association	Collective Bargaining
Industrial Union	Closed Shop	Strike
Public Employee Union	Union Shop	Monopsony

1. What is the difference between a craft (trade) union and an industrial union?
2. What view is a labor union likely to hold on each of the following issues? (a) Easing of the immigration laws; (b) a quota on imported products; (c) free trade; (d) a decrease in the minimum wage.
3. Most actions or practices of labor unions are attempts to affect one of three factors. What are these three factors?
4. Explain why the monopsonist pays labor a wage rate less than labor's marginal revenue product.
5. It has been suggested that organizing labor unions is easier in some industries than in others. What industry characteristics make unionization easier?
6. What is the effect of labor unions on nonunion wage rates?
7. Some persons argue that a monopsony firm exploits its workers if it pays them less than their marginal revenue products. Others disagree. They say that as long as the firm pays the workers their opportunity costs (which must be the case or the workers would not stay with the firm), the workers are not being exploited. This suggests that there are two definitions of exploitation: (a) paying workers below their marginal revenue products (even if wages equal the workers' opportunity costs) and (b) paying workers below their opportunity costs. Keeping in mind that this may be a subjective judgment, which definition of exploitation do you think is more descriptive of the process and why?

8. A discussion of labor unions will usually evoke strong feelings. Some people argue vigorously against labor unions; others argue with equal vigor for labor unions. Some people see labor unions as the reason why the workers in this country enjoy as high a standard of living as they do; others see labor unions as the reason the country is not so well off economically as it might be. Speculate on why the topic of labor unions generates such strong feelings and emotions and often such little analysis.
9. What forces may lead to the breakup of an employer (monopsony) cartel?

1. Determine the appropriate numbers for the lettered spaces:

(1) Workers	(2) Wage Rate	(3) Total Labor Cost	(4) Marginal Factor Cost
1	A	$12.00	$12.00
2	$12.10	24.20	E
3	12.20	C	F
4	B	D	12.60

2. Which demand curve for labor in the following figure exhibits the most pronounced wage-employment tradeoff? Explain your answer.

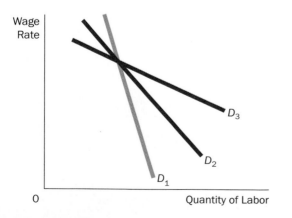

3. Consider the monopsony setting in the following figure. In the absence of collective bargaining:

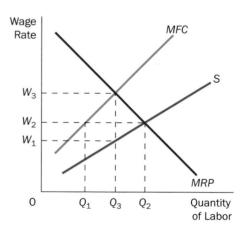

   a. What wage rate does the monopsony pay?
   b. What quantity of labor does the monopsony hire?
   c. If the monopsony were to pay labor what its services are worth, what wage rate would it pay?
4. Diagrammatically explain how changes in supply conditions and wage rates in the unionized sector can cause changes in supply and wage rates in the nonunionized sector.

1. Go to *http://www.aflcio.org*. Locate the center column of the home page, which lists various economic and social issues. Click on an issue that interests you. What is the position of the AFL-CIO on the issue? Is your position on the issue the same as the position of the AFL-CIO? If not, explain your position. If so, explain why you agree with the position of the AFL-CIO.

2. Go to *http://www.msf.org.uk/*. Which union in which country provides this Web site? Select "What is MSF?" and read this Web page.
   a. What does MSF stand for?
   b. How does it operate?
   c. Are there any differences between MSF and the AFL-CIO? If so, describe them.

Log on to the Arnold Xtra! Web site now (*http://arnoldxtra.swcollege.com*) for additional learning resources such as practice quizzes, help with graphing, video clips, and current event applications.

ch.15

THE DISTRIBUTION OF INCOME AND POVERTY

A random sample of people from the general population will have various incomes. Some people will be in the top 20 percent of income earners, some in the lowest 20 percent, and many others in between these two extremes. In other words, some people earn high incomes, and many earn middle incomes. What factors might influence the amount of income a person earns? Why are some people more likely to be poor than others? Why are some people more likely to be rich than others? You'll find the answers to these questions and many other questions about the distribution of income and poverty in this chapter.

Chapter Road Map

In this chapter, we discuss income and poverty.

First, we discuss the distribution of income and various issues

related to it, including the different percentages of total income earned by

various income groups, the measurement of income inequality, the reasons for income

inequality, and various normative standards of the income distribution. We then turn to poverty

and a discussion of what poverty is, who the poor are, and the justification for government redistribu-

tion programs to the poor.

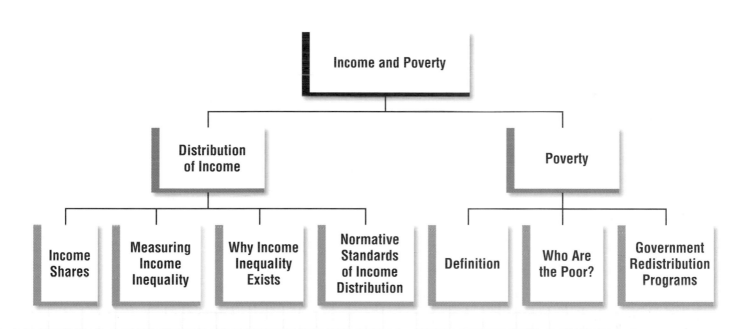

SOME FACTS ABOUT INCOME DISTRIBUTION

In discussing public policy issues, we sometimes speak of a fact when we should speak of facts. A single fact is usually not as informative as facts are, in much the same way that a single snapshot in time does not tell as much of a story as a moving picture—a succession of snapshots through time. This section presents a few facts about the distribution of income.

WHO ARE THE RICH AND HOW RICH ARE THEY?

By many interpretations, the lowest fifth (lowest quintile) of households is considered poor, the top fifth is considered rich, and the three-fifths in between are considered middle income.[1]

In 2000, the lowest fifth (the poor) received 3.6 percent of the total money income, the second fifth received 8.9 percent, the third fifth received 14.9 percent, the fourth fifth received 23.0 percent, and the top fifth received 49.6 percent (see Exhibit 1).

Now we know that the lowest 20 percent received 3.6 percent of the total money income in 2000, but what does this represent in absolute dollars for the average household in this category? In 2000, the mean annual household income of the lowest fifth was $10,190. For the second fifth, the mean annual household income was $25,334; for the third fifth, it was $42,361; for the fourth fifth, it was $65,729; and for the top fifth, it was $141,620.

Has the income distribution become more or less equal over time? Exhibit 2 shows the income shares of households in 1967 and 2000. In 1967, the highest fifth (top) of households accounted for 43.8 percent of all income; in 2000, the percentage had risen to 49.6 percent.

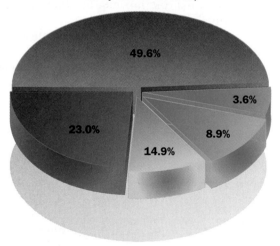

exhibit 1

Distribution of Household Income Shares, 2000

The annual income shares for different quintiles of households is shown here.

Source: U.S. Bureau of the Census

INCOME SHARE
(percentage of total
money income received)

49.6%
3.6%
23.0%
8.9%
14.9%

QUINTILE	MEAN HOUSEHOLD INCOME (dollars)	
Lowest Fifth	10,190	
Second Fifth	25,334	
Third Fifth	42,361	
Fourth Fifth	65,729	
Highest Fifth	141,620	

---

1. A household consists of all people who occupy a housing unit. It includes the related family members and all unrelated people.

INCOME SHARE (PERCENT)

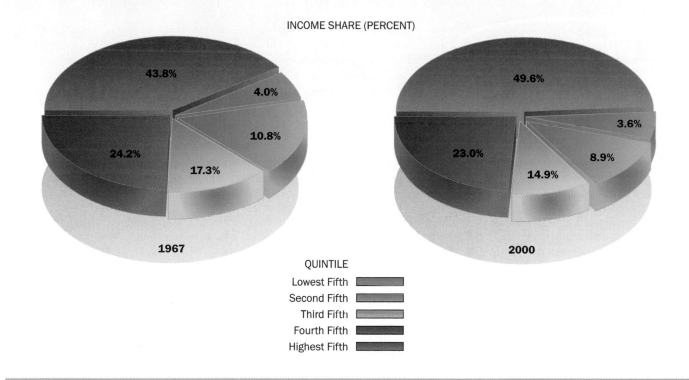

1967

43.8%

4.0%

10.8%

17.3%

24.2%

2000

49.6%

3.6%

8.9%

14.9%

23.0%

QUINTILE

Lowest Fifth

Second Fifth

Third Fifth

Fourth Fifth

Highest Fifth

exhibit 2

Income Distribution, 1967 and 2000

A comparison of income shares in 1967 with those in 2000 shows that there was less income equality (more income inequality) in 2000 than in 1967. Note that income shares have not been adjusted for direct taxes.

Source: U.S. Bureau of the Census

At the other end of the income spectrum, in 1967, the lowest fifth received 4.0 percent of all income; in 2000, the percentage had fallen to 3.6 percent. The middle groups—the three-fifths of income recipients between the lowest fifth and the highest fifth—accounted for 52.3 percent of all income in 1967 and 46.8 percent in 2000. We conclude that the income distribution in the United States was less equal (more unequal) in 2000 than in 1967.

THE INCOME DISTRIBUTION AND COMPUTERS

What has caused the increasing inequality of income in the United States during the last three decades? Some people think that computers explain the increasing income inequality. They believe computers complement the skills of the more sophisticated, knowledgeable workers, raising their productivity and thus raising their incomes. This explanation, while perhaps plausible, is suspicious. First, the increasing income inequality precedes the use of personal computers. Second, just because income inequality and the use of computers occur at about the same time, it does not follow that one causes the other. In other words, association does not mean causation. Third, some economists have found that wages and income inequality increased with the use of pencils, but no one is willing to make the case that pencils can shift the income distribution.

CAN ALL PEOPLE BECOME BETTER OFF AS THE INCOME DISTRIBUTION BECOMES MORE UNEQUAL?

People often think that if the income distribution has become more unequal, some group of income earners is worse off. For example, suppose you read in the newspaper that the bottom fifth of income earners received 6 percent of the total income last year, but received only 5 percent this year. Would you think these income earners had "lost some ground" in a year? Would you think they were worse off this year compared to last year? Many people would think so. But an increasingly unequal income distribution is not necessarily a sign of an income group being worse off.

"I'm Waiting Until the Price Comes Down"

Often, when new products are first introduced in the market, many people consider them to be "too expensive" to buy. For example, this was true for VCRs and video recorders. In time, though, the prices of these items came down, and increasingly more people purchased them. Goods initially purchased by a few ended up being goods purchased by many.

Today, many people consider HDTV sets to be "too expensive." Often, a person is heard to say, "I think I'm going to wait until the price comes down before I buy one." People increasingly expect new goods to start out at high prices and then come down in price over time. Wait long enough, and you can get it at a "good" price.

There is a reason for this expectation. Many of the new products introduced in U.S. economic history fit this profile. For example, in terms of hours of labor needed to purchase various goods, prices have come down for many goods over time. In 1908, it took the average worker 4,696 hours of labor to buy an automobile; in 1970, it took 1,397 hours; and in 1997, it took 1,365 hours. Cars have gotten cheaper over time, as measured by the number of hours of labor it takes to buy one. The same holds for refrigerators, long-distance telephone calls, air travel, microwave ovens, color television sets, cellular phones, VCRs, and computing power.[2] For example, while it took 562 labor hours of income to buy a color television when it first came out, it took only 23 hours in 1997. It took 95 labor hours of income to buy soft contact lenses when they were first introduced in the 1970s, but it only took 4 hours in 1997. Some economists have argued that the falling prices of many goods (in terms of labor hours needed to work to purchase them) makes many of the goods that once only the rich could have purchased now available to individuals at the lower end of the income distribution.

To illustrate, suppose society is made up of five individuals, *A–E*. *A* earns $20,000, *B* earns $10,000, *C* earns $5,000, *D* earns $2,500, and *E* earns $1,250. The total income in this society is $38,750, and the distribution of income is certainly unequal. *A* earns 51.61 percent of the income, *B* earns 25.81 percent, *C* earns 12.90 percent, *D* earns 6.45 percent, and *E* earns only 3.23 percent.

Now suppose each person receives additional real income. *A* receives $10,000 more real income for a total of $30,000, *B* receives $3,000 more real income for a total of $13,000, *C* earns $2,000 more real income for a total of $7,000, *D* earns $1,000 more real income for a total of $3,500, and *E* earns $200 more real income for a total of $1,450. In terms of real income, each of the five persons is better off. But the income distribution has become even more unequal. For example, *A* (at the top fifth of income earners) now receives 54.60 percent of all income instead of 51.61 percent, and *E* (at the bottom fifth of income earners) now receives 2.64 percent instead of 3.22 percent. A newspaper headline might read, "The rich get richer as the poor get poorer." People reading this headline might naturally think that the poor in society are now worse off. But we know they are not worse off in terms of the goods and services they can purchase. They now have more real income than they had when the income distribution was less unequal. In short, it is possible for everyone to be better off even though the income distribution has become more unequal.

THE INCOME DISTRIBUTION ADJUSTED FOR TAXES AND IN-KIND TRANSFER PAYMENTS

Government can change the distribution of income. One of the ways it does this is through the use of taxes and transfer payments. Economists speak of ex ante and ex post distributions of income. The **ex ante distribution** of income is the

Ex Ante Distribution (of Income)
The before-tax-and-transfer-payment distribution of income.

---

2. This feature is based on W. Michael Cox, "The Low Cost of Living," *Wall Street Journal,* 9 April 1998, p. A22.

before-tax-and-transfer-payment distribution of income. The **ex post distribution** of income is the after-tax-and-transfer-payment distribution of income. **Transfer payments** are payments to persons that are not made in return for goods and services currently supplied.

The income distributions in Exhibit 2 do not take into account taxes or **in-kind transfer payments,** that is, transfer payments, such as medical assistance and subsidized housing, that are paid in a specific good or service rather than in cash. However, the distributions do take into account cash (monetary) transfer payments, such as direct monetary welfare assistance and Social Security benefits. When the figures in Exhibit 2 are adjusted for taxes and in-kind transfers, the income distributions are more equal because the in-kind payments go largely to the lowest-income groups while the taxes are paid largely by the highest-income groups.

THE EFFECT OF AGE ON THE INCOME DISTRIBUTION

In analyzing the income distribution, it is important to distinguish between people who are poor for long periods of time (sometimes their entire lives) and people who are poor temporarily. Consider Sherri Holmer, who attends college and works part-time as a waitress at a nearby restaurant. Currently, her income is so low that she falls into the lowest fifth of income earners. But it isn't likely that this will always be the case. After she graduates from college, Sherri's income will probably rise. If she is like most people, her income will rise during her twenties, thirties, and forties. In her late forties or early fifties, her income will take a slight downturn and then level off.

It is possible, in fact highly likely, that a person in her late twenties, thirties, or forties will have a higher income than another person in her early twenties or sixties, even though their total lifetime incomes will be identical. If we view each person over time, income equality is greater than if we view each person at a particular point in time (say, when one person is 58 years old and the other is 68).

To illustrate, look at Exhibit 3, which shows the incomes of John and Stephanie in different years. In 2000, John is 18 years old and earning $10,000 per year and Stephanie is 28 years old and earning $30,000. The income distribution between John and Stephanie is unequal in 2000.

Ten years later, the income distribution is still unequal, with Stephanie earning $45,000 and John earning $35,000. In fact, the income distribution is unequal in every year shown in the exhibit. However, the total income earned by each person is $236,000, giving a perfectly equal income distribution over time.

In the United States, there seems to be quite a bit of upward income mobility over time. The University of Michigan's Panel Survey on Dynamics tracked

Year	John's Age	John's Income	Stephanie's Age	Stephanie's Income
2000	18 years	$ 10,000	28 years	$30,000
2010	28	35,000	38	45,000
2020	38	52,000	48	60,000
2030	48	64,000	58	75,000
2040	58	75,000	68	26,000
Total		$236,000		$236,000

exhibit 3

Income Distribution at One Point in Time and Over Time
In each year, the income distribution between John and Stephanie is unequal, with Stephanie earning more than John in 2000, 2010, 2020, and 2030 and John earning more than Stephanie in 2040. In the five years specified, however, both John and Stephanie earned the same total income of $236,000, giving a perfectly equal income distribution over time.

50,000 Americans for 17 years. Of the people in the lowest fifth of the income distribution in 1975, only 5.1 percent were still there in 1991—but 29 percent of them were in the highest fifth.

A SIMPLE EQUATION

Before discussing the possible sources or causes of income inequality, we need to identify the factors that determine a person's income. The following simple equation combines four of them—labor income, asset income, transfer payments, and taxes:

Individual income = Labor income + Asset income + Transfer payments − Taxes

Labor income is equal to the wage rate an individual receives times the number of hours he or she works. Asset income consists of such things as the return to saving, the return to capital investment, and the return to land. Transfer payments and taxes have already been discussed. This equation provides a quick way of focusing on the direct and indirect factors that affect an individual's income and the degree of income inequality. The next section examines the conventional ways that income inequality is measured.

Q & A

Q: One of the factors in the income equation is transfer payments, which include both cash and in-kind payments. According to the equation, if a person receives an in-kind transfer—such as free food—his income increases. But this doesn't make sense. How can a free good increase a person's income? After all, food isn't money.

A: We are interested in how much a person can consume. An individual who earns $15,000 per year and doesn't have to pay apartment rent is better off (in having more goods and services) than a person who earns $15,000 per year and does have to pay apartment rent. The first person is better off than his absolute level of money income would lead us to believe. By including in-kind transfers, among other things, in individual income, we are trying to take into account this quality of being "better off." Although most government income figures do not take into account in-kind transfers, most economists argue that simple money income is not so accurate a measure of one's command over goods and services as is a measurement of income that adjusts for in-kind transfers.

THINKING LIKE AN ECONOMIST

To many people, poor is poor. This is not the case for the economist. The economist wants to know why the person is poor. Is he poor because he is young and just starting out in life? Would he be poor if we were to consider the in-kind benefits he receives? Some people argue that when someone is poor, you don't ask questions, you simply try to help him. But the economist knows that not everyone is in the same situation for the same reason. The reason may determine whether or not you proceed with help, and if you do proceed, just how you do so. Both the disabled elderly person and the young, smart college student may earn the same low income, but you may feel it more important to help the disabled elderly person than the college student.

Self-Test *(Answers to Self-Test questions are in the Self-Test Appendix.)*

1. How can government change the distribution of income?

2. Income inequality at one point in time is sometimes consistent with income equality over time. Comment.

3. Smith and Jones have the same income this year, $40,000. Does it follow that their income came from the same sources? Explain your answer.

MEASURING INCOME EQUALITY

Two commonly used measures of income inequality are the Lorenz curve and the Gini coefficient. We explain and discuss both measures in this section.

THE LORENZ CURVE

The **Lorenz curve** represents the distribution of income; it expresses the relationship between cumulative percentage of households and *cumulative percentage of income*. Exhibit 4 shows a hypothetical Lorenz curve.

The data in part (a) are used to plot the Lorenz curve in part (b). According to (a), the lowest fifth of households has an income share of 10 percent, the second fifth has an income share of 15 percent, and so on. The Lorenz curve in (b) is derived by plotting five points. Point *A* represents the cumulative income share of the lowest fifth of households (10 percent of income goes to the lowest fifth of households). Point *B* represents the cumulative income share of the lowest fifth plus the second fifth (25 percent of income goes to two-fifths, or 40 percent, of the income recipients). Point *C* represents the cumulative income share of the lowest fifth plus the second fifth plus the third fifth (45 percent of income goes to three-fifths, or 60 percent, of the income recipients). The same procedure is used for points *D* and *E*. Connecting these points gives the Lorenz curve that represents the data in (a); the Lorenz curve is another way of depicting the income distribution in (a). Exhibit 5 illustrates the Lorenz curve for the United States based on the (money) income shares in Exhibit 1.

Lorenz Curve
A graph of the income distribution. It expresses the relationship between cumulative percentage of households and cumulative percentage of income.

exhibit 4

A Hypothetical Lorenz Curve
The data in (a) were used to derive the Lorenz curve in (b). The Lorenz curve shows the cumulative percentage of income earned by the cumulative percentage of households. If all households received the same percentage of total income, the Lorenz curve would be the line of perfect income equality. The bowed Lorenz curve shows an unequal distribution of income. The more bowed the Lorenz curve is, the more unequal the distribution of income.

Quintile	Income Share (percent)	Cumulative Income Share (percent)
Lowest fifth	10%	10%
Second fifth	15	25
Third fifth	20	45
Fourth fifth	25	70
Highest fifth	30	100

(a)

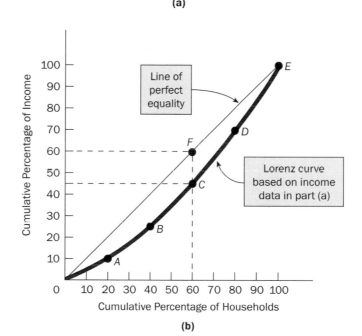

(b)

exhibit 5

Lorenz Curve for the United States, 2000
This Lorenz curve is based on the 2000 income shares for the United States.

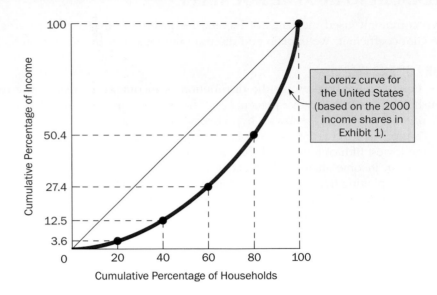

Lorenz curve for the United States (based on the 2000 income shares in Exhibit 1).

Cumulative Percentage of Income

Cumulative Percentage of Households

What would the Lorenz curve look like if there were perfect income equality among different households? In this case, every household would receive exactly the same percentage of total income, and the Lorenz curve would be the line of perfect income equality illustrated in Exhibit 4b. At any point on this 45° line, the cumulative percentage of income (on the vertical axis) equals the cumulative percentage of households (on the horizontal axis). For example, at point *F*, 60 percent of the households receive 60 percent of the total income.

THE GINI COEFFICIENT

Gini Coefficient
A measure of the degree of inequality in the income distribution.

The **Gini coefficient,** which is a measure of the degree of inequality in the income distribution, is used in conjunction with the Lorenz curve. It is equal to the area between the line of perfect income equality (or 45° line) and the actual Lorenz curve divided by the entire triangular area under the line of perfect income equality.

$$\text{Gini Coefficient} = \frac{\text{Area between the line of perfect income equality and actual Lorenz curve}}{\text{Entire triangular area under the line of perfect income equality}}$$

Exhibit 6 illustrates both the line of perfect income equality and an actual Lorenz curve. The Gini coefficient is computed by dividing the shaded area (the area between the line of perfect income equality and the actual Lorenz curve) by the area *0AB* (the entire triangular area under the line of perfect income equality).

The Gini coefficient is a number between 0 and 1. At one extreme, the Gini coefficient equals 0 if the numerator in the equation is 0. A numerator of 0 means there is no area between the line of perfect income equality and the actual Lorenz curve, implying that they are the same. It follows that a Gini coefficient of 0 means perfect income equality.

At the other extreme, the Gini coefficient equals 1 if the numerator in the equation is equal to the denominator. If this is the case, the actual Lorenz curve is as far away from the line of perfect income equality as is possible. It follows that a Gini coefficient of 1 means complete income inequality. (What would the actual Lorenz curve look like if there were complete income inequality? In this situation, one person would have all the total income, and no one else would have any

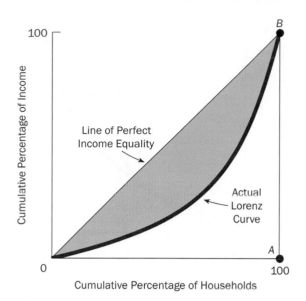

100

Cumulative Percentage of Income

B

Line of Perfect
Income Equality

Actual
Lorenz
Curve

A

0   100

Cumulative Percentage of Households

exhibit 6

The Gini Coefficient
The Gini coefficient is a measure of the degree of income inequality. It is equal to the area between the line of perfect income equality and the actual Lorenz curve divided by the entire triangular area under the line of perfect income equality. In the diagram, this is equal to the shaded portion divided by the triangular area 0AB. A Gini coefficient of 0 means perfect income equality; a Gini coefficient of 1 means complete income inequality. The larger the Gini coefficient, the greater the income inequality; the smaller the Gini coefficient, the lower the income inequality.

income. In Exhibit 6, a Lorenz curve representing complete income inequality would lie along the horizontal axis from 0 to *A* and then move from *A* to *B*.)

If a Gini coefficient of 0 represents perfect income equality and a Gini coefficient of 1 represents complete income inequality, then it follows that the larger the Gini coefficient, the higher the degree of income inequality and the smaller the Gini coefficient, the lower the degree of income inequality. In 2000, the Gini coefficient in the United States was 0.460; in 1984, the Gini coefficient in the United States was 0.415.

A LIMITATION OF THE GINI COEFFICIENT

Although we can learn the degree of inequality in the income distribution from the Gini coefficient, we have to be careful not to misinterpret it. For example, suppose the Gini coefficient is 0.33 in country 1 and 0.25 in country 2. We know the income distribution is more equal in country 2 than in country 1. But, in which country does the lowest fifth of households receive the larger percentage of income? The natural inclination is to answer in the country with the more equal income distribution—country 2. However, this may not be true.

To see this, consider Exhibit 7, which shows two Lorenz curves. Overall, Lorenz curve 2 is closer to the line of perfect income equality than Lorenz curve 1 is; thus, the Gini coefficient for Lorenz curve 2 is smaller than the Gini coefficient for Lorenz curve 1. But notice that the lowest 20 percent of households has a smaller percentage of total income with Lorenz curve 2 than with Lorenz curve 1.

Our point is that the Gini coefficient cannot tell us what is happening in different quintiles. We should not jump to the conclusion that because the Gini coefficient is lower in country 2 than in country 1, the lowest fifth of households has a greater percentage of total income in country 2 than in country 1.

http://

Go to *http://www.census.gov/hhes/www/income.html*, and select "Historical Income Tables." Click on "Income Inequality" under CPI-U-RS, and then select table "F-4." What is the Gini Ratio (Gini Coefficient)? How is the Gini Ratio related to the Lorenz Curve? Overall, would you say there is greater or less income inequality in the United States since the 1940s?

Self-Test

1. Starting with the top fifth of income earners and proceeding to the lowest fifth, suppose the income share of each group is 40 percent, 30 percent, 20 percent, 10 percent, and 5 percent. Can these percentages be right?

2. Country *A* has a Gini coefficient of 0.45. What does this mean?

exhibit 7

Limitation of the Gini Coefficient
By itself the Gini coefficient cannot tell us anything about the income share of a particular quintile. Although there is a tendency to believe that the bottom quintile receives a larger percentage of total income the lower the Gini coefficient, this need not be the case. In the diagram, the Gini coefficient for Lorenz curve 2 is lower than the Gini coefficient for Lorenz curve 1. But, the bottom 20 percent of households obtains a smaller percentage of total income in the lower Gini coefficient case.

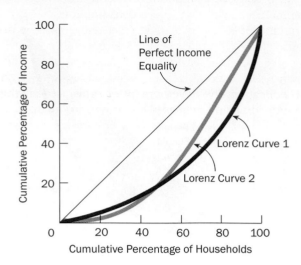

WHY INCOME INEQUALITY EXISTS

Why does income inequality exist? This question can be answered by focusing on our simple equation:

Individual income = Labor income + Asset income + Transfer payments − Taxes

Generally, income inequality exists because people do not receive the same labor income, asset income, and transfer payments, or pay the same taxes. But why don't they receive, say, the same labor income and asset income? This section discusses some of the specific reasons for income inequality by focusing on factors that often contribute to differences in labor and asset income. The next section looks at some of the proposed standards of income distribution.

FACTORS CONTRIBUTING TO INCOME INEQUALITY

Six factors that contribute to income inequality are innate abilities and attributes, work and leisure, education and other training, risk taking, luck, and wage discrimination.

Innate Abilities and Attributes

Individuals are not all born with the same innate abilities and attributes. People vary in the degree of intelligence, good looks, and creativity they possess. Some individuals have more marketable innate abilities and attributes than others have. For example, the man or woman born with exceptionally good looks, the "natural" athlete, or the person who is musically gifted or mathematically adept is more likely to earn a higher income than someone with lesser abilities or attributes.

Work and Leisure

There is a tradeoff between work and leisure: More work means less leisure, less work means more leisure. Some individuals will choose to work more hours (or take on a second job) and thus have less leisure. This choice will be reflected in their labor income. They will earn a larger income than those persons who choose not to work more, *ceteris paribus.*

Education and Other Training

Economists usually refer to schooling and other types of training as an "investment in human capital." In order to buy a capital good, or invest in one, a person has to give up present consumption. A person does so in the hope that the capital good will increase his or her future consumption.

Schooling can be looked on as capital. First, one must give up present consumption to obtain it. Second, by providing individuals with certain skills and knowledge, schooling can increase their future consumption over what it would be without the schooling. Schooling, then, is human capital. In general, **human capital** refers to education, the development of skills, and anything else that is particular to the individual and increases his or her productivity.

Contrast a person who has obtained an education with a person who has not. The educated person is likely to have certain skills, abilities, and knowledge that the uneducated person lacks. Consequently, he or she is likely to be worth more to an employer. Most college students know this; it is part of the reason they are college students.

Human Capital
Education, development of skills, and anything else that is particular to the individual and increases his or her productivity.

Risk Taking

Individuals have different attitudes toward risk. Some individuals are more willing to take on risk than others are. Some of the individuals who are willing to take on risk will do well and rise to the top of the income distribution and some will fall to the bottom. Those individuals who prefer to play it safe aren't as likely to reach the top of the income distribution or to hit the bottom.

Luck

When individuals can't explain why something has happened to them, they often say it was the result of good or bad luck. At times, the good or bad luck explanation makes sense; at other times, it is more a rationalization than an explanation.

Good and bad luck may influence incomes. For example, the college student who studies biology only to find out in her senior year that the bottom has fallen out of the biology market has experienced bad luck. The farmer who hits oil while digging a well has experienced good luck. An automobile worker who is unemployed owing to a recession he had no part in causing is experiencing bad luck. A person who trains for a profession in which there is an unexpected increase in demand experiences good luck.

Although luck can and does influence incomes, it is not likely to have (on average) a large or long-run effect. The person who experiences good luck today, and whose income reflects this fact, isn't likely to experience luck-boosting income increases time after time. In the long run, such factors as innate ability and attributes, education, and personal decisions (how much work, how much leisure?) are more likely to have a larger, more sustained effect on income than luck will have.

Wage Discrimination

Wage discrimination exists when individuals of equal ability and productivity, as measured by their marginal revenue products, are paid different wage rates by the same employer. It is a fact that in the period as a whole since World War II, the median income of African Americans has been approximately 60 percent that of whites. It is also a fact that since the late 1950s, women working full-time have earned approximately 60 percent of the male median income. Are these differences between white and black incomes and between male and female incomes due wholly to discrimination? Most empirical studies show that approximately half the differences are due to differences in education, productivity, and job training (although one may ask if discrimination has anything to do with the education, productivity, and job training differences). The remainder of the wage differential is due to other factors, one of which is hypothesized to be discrimination.

Most people agree that discrimination exists, although they differ on the degree to which they think it affects income. Also, we should note that discrimination is not always directed at employees by employers. For example, consumers

Wage Discrimination
The situation that exists when individuals of equal ability and productivity (as measured by their contribution to output) are paid different wage rates.

Winner-Take-All Markets[3]

Two economists, Robert Frank and Philip Cook, published a book in 1995 titled *The Winner-Take-All Society*. In the book, they argue that there are more winner-take-all markets today than in the past. A winner-take-all market is one in which the top producer or performer in the market earns appreciably more than others in the market earn. In fact, the top producers earn so much more than others that it is as if they "take it all."

For example, in making major movies, the producer, director, and leading actor may earn much more than anyone else involved in the movie. In the sports market, the highest-paid players on a professional baseball, football, or basketball team usually earn more than their fellow players. For example, the last year that Michael Jordan played basketball with the Chicago Bulls, he earned 121 times the salary of the lowest-paid player.

Frank and Cook state that there is nothing new about winner-take-all markets in sports and entertainment. What is new, they argue, is that winner-take-all is becoming a common feature of other markets. Winner-take-all is becoming increasingly more descriptive in such fields as law, journalism, design, investment banking, and medicine.

Do the data support what Frank and Cook are saying? Recent statistics show that "within-group" income inequality has been rising. In other words, the "winnings" have come to be concentrated on a smaller percentage of people in an industry. To illustrate, in 1974, major U.S. CEOs (chief executive officers) earned an average of 35 times the amount an average American production worker earned; by 1990, this multiple had jumped to 150. There are other examples that illustrate the same phenomenon, prompting Frank and Cook to comment that we are increasingly coming to live in a winner-take-all society.

What has happened in recent years to bring about more winner-take-all markets and greater within-group income inequality? Frank and Cook identify two things: (1) developments in communications, manufacturing technology, and transportation costs that let top performers serve broader markets (a global marketplace); and (2) implicit and explicit rules that have led to more competition for top performers.

Let's look at the first cause identified by Frank and Cook. In a winner-take-all market, the demand for goods and services is focused on a small number of suppliers. This is not, as some may think, because government is limiting our choices. According to Frank and Cook, we are simply focusing on "the best" suppliers to a greater degree than before because of changes in technology, communications, and transportation costs.

For example, consumers today do not have to settle for buying tires, cars, clothes, books, or much of anything else from regional or national producers of these items. They can buy these items from the best producers in the world. As Frank notes, while once a firm that produced a good tire in northern Ohio could be assured of selling tires in its regional market, today it cannot. Consumers buy tires from a handful of the best tire producers in the world.

Let's consider another example, one in which technological development plays an important part. Before there were records, tapes, or CDs, a person had to go to a concert to hear music. After the technology was developed for producing records, tapes, and CDs, this was no longer necessary. The best singers and bands in the world could simply put their music on a record, tape, or CD and anyone in the world could listen to it. It was no longer necessary for a person living in a small town to go to a local concert to hear music performed by what may have been a very mediocre musician. Now that person could listen to music performed by the best musicians in the world. His demand for music, and that of others, became focused on a smaller pool of musicians. As a consequence, these top musicians began to witness large increases in their earnings.

Now consider the second cause identified by Frank and Cook for the increase in within-group income inequality. Frank and Cook argue that greater competition for top performers can be the result of a legal change. For example, consider the deregulation in airline, trucking, banking, brokerage, and other industries. Deregulation may have increased the salary competition for top performers, thus driving up their wages.

But why would this be an effect of deregulation? The answer is because in a deregulated environment, (market) competition comes to play a bigger role in determining outcomes—both "good" and "bad." Specifically, in a deregulated environment, the potential for both profits and losses is

---

3. This feature is based on Robert H. Frank, "Talent and the Winner-Take-All-Society," in *The American Prospect*, no. 17 (spring 1994): 97–107.

greater than in a regulated (less competitive) environment. To capture the higher potential profits and to guard against the increased likelihood of losses, talented professionals become more valuable to a firm.

Also, perhaps as a result of a less regulated, more fiercely competitive product market, the once widely accepted practice of companies promoting from within is today falling by the wayside. Increasingly, companies search for the top talent in other firms and industries and not just the top talent in their company pool. While once a top performer in a soft-drink company could expect only soft-drink companies to compete for his or her services, he or she can now expect to receive offers from soft-drink companies, computer companies, insurance companies, and more.

may practice discrimination—some white consumers may wish to deal only with white physicians and lawyers; some Asian Americans may wish to deal only with Asian-American physicians and lawyers.

INCOME DIFFERENCES: SOME ARE VOLUNTARY, SOME ARE NOT

Even in a world with no discrimination, differences in income would still exist. Other factors, which we have noted, account for this. Some individuals would have more marketable skills than others, some individuals would decide to work harder and longer hours than others, some individuals would take on more risk than others, and some individuals would undertake more schooling and training than others. Thus, some degree of income inequality occurs because individuals are innately different and make different choices. Of course, this also implies that some degree of income inequality is due to factors unrelated to innate ability or choices—such as discrimination or luck.

An interesting debate continues to be waged on the topic of discrimination-based income inequality. The opposing sides weight different factors differently. Some people argue that wage discrimination would be lessened if markets were allowed to be more competitive, more open, and more free. They believe that in an open and competitive market with few barriers to entry and no government protection of privileged groups, discrimination would have a high price. Firms that didn't hire the best and the brightest—regardless of a person's race, religion, or sex—would suffer. They would ultimately pay for their act of discrimination by having higher labor costs and lower profits. Individuals holding this view usually propose that government deregulate, reduce legal barriers to entry, and in general not hamper the workings of the free market mechanism.

Others contend that even if the government were to follow this script, much wage discrimination would still exist. They think government should play an active legislative role in reducing both wage discrimination and other types of discrimination that they believe ultimately result in wage discrimination. The latter include discrimination in education and discrimination in on-the-job training. Proponents of an active role for government usually believe that such policy programs as affirmative action, equal pay for equal work, and comparable worth (equal pay for comparable work) are beneficial in reducing both the amount of wage discrimination in the economy and the degree of income inequality.

Self-Test

1. Jack and Harry work for the same company, but Jack earns more than Harry. Is this evidence of wage discrimination? Explain your answer.

2. A person decides to assume a lot of risk in earning an income. How could this affect his or her income?

NORMATIVE STANDARDS OF INCOME DISTRIBUTION

Don't need to know!

For hundreds of years, economists, political philosophers, and political scientists, among others, have debated what constitutes a proper, just, or fair distribution of income and have proposed different normative standards. This section discusses three of the better known normative standards of income distribution: the marginal productivity normative standard, the absolute (complete) income equality normative standard, and the Rawlsian normative standard.

THE MARGINAL PRODUCTIVITY NORMATIVE STANDARD

The marginal productivity theory of factor prices states that in a competitive setting, people tend to be paid their marginal revenue products.[4] The marginal productivity normative standard of income distribution holds that people *should* be paid their marginal revenue products.

This idea is illustrated in Exhibit 8a. The first "income pie" in (a) represents the actual income shares of eight individuals, *A–H,* who work in a competitive setting and are paid their respective *MRP*s. The income distribution is unequal because the eight persons do not contribute equally to the productive process. Some individuals are more productive than others.

The second income pie in (a), which is the same as the first, is the income distribution that the proponents of the marginal productivity normative standard believe should exist. In short, individuals should be paid their marginal revenue products.

Proponents of this position argue that it is just for individuals to receive their contribution (high, low, or somewhere in between) to the productive process, no more and no less. Also, paying people according to their productivity gives them an incentive to become more productive. For example, individuals have an incentive to learn more and to become better trained if they know they will be paid more as a consequence. According to this argument, without such incentives, work effort would decrease, laziness would increase, and in time the entire society would feel the harmful effects. Critics respond that some persons are innately more productive than others and that rewarding them for innate qualities is unfair.

Q & A   **Q:** This discussion assumes a competitive setting where people are paid their *MRP*s. Suppose a person is in a monopsony setting and is not being paid his or her *MRP*. Would the proponents of the marginal productivity normative standard argue that he or she should be?

A: Yes, they would. People who propose normative standards think the marginal productivity standard should be applied regardless of the current situation. In other words, it is possible to be a proponent of the marginal productivity normative standard whether or not you believe people are currently being paid their marginal revenue products.

THE ABSOLUTE INCOME EQUALITY NORMATIVE STANDARD

Exhibit 8b illustrates the viewpoint of those persons who advocate the absolute income equality normative standard. The first income pie represents the income distribution that exists—in which there is income inequality. The second income pie represents the income distribution that the persons who argue for absolute income equality believe should exist. Notice that each individual receives an equal percentage of the income pie. No one has any more or any less than anyone else.

Proponents of this position hold that an equal distribution of income will lead to the maximization of total utility (in society). The argument is as follows: (1) Individuals are alike when it comes to how much satisfaction they receive from an added increase in income. (2) Receiving additional income is subject to the law of diminishing marginal utility; that is, each additional dollar is worth less to the recipient than the dollar that preceded it. (3) From points 1 and 2 it

---

4. Recall that in a competitive setting, value marginal product (*VMP*) equals marginal revenue product (*MRP*). Thus, the marginal productivity theory holds that in a competitive setting, people tend to be paid their *VMP*s, or *MRP*s.

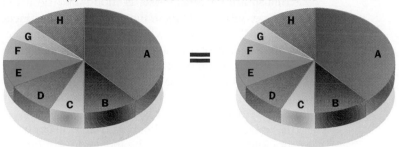

(a) MARGINAL PRODUCTIVITY NORMATIVE STANDARD

Income Distribution That Is   Income Distribution That Should Be

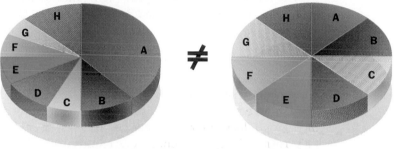

(b) ABSOLUTE INCOME EQUALITY NORMATIVE STANDARD

Income Distribution That Is   Income Distribution That Should Be

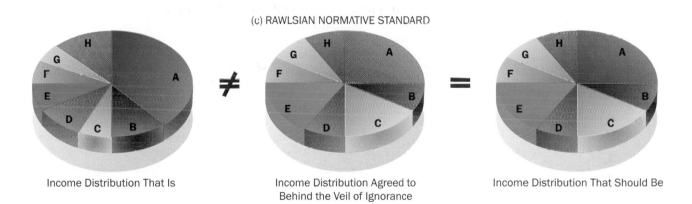

(c) RAWLSIAN NORMATIVE STANDARD

Income Distribution That Is   Income Distribution Agreed to   Income Distribution That Should Be
                                 Behind the Veil of Ignorance

follows that redistributing income from the rich to the poor will raise total utility. The rich will not lose as much utility from the redistribution as the poor will gain. Overall, total utility (of society) will rise through the redistribution of income from the rich to the poor. Total utility will be maximized when all persons receive the same income.

Opponents of this position hold that it is impossible to know if all individuals receive equal utility from an added dollar of income and that a rich person may receive far more utility from an added dollar of income than a poor person receives. If so, then redistributing income until it is equalized would not maximize total utility.

THE RAWLSIAN NORMATIVE STANDARD

In *A Theory of Justice,* philosopher John Rawls states that individuals will argue for a different income distribution if they know what their position is in the current

exhibit 8

Different Normative Standards of Income Distribution

(a) The marginal productivity, (b) the absolute, and (c) the Rawlsian normative standards of income distribution. Note that the income pies do not change as income distribution changes. In reality, the size of the income pies might depend on the income distribution. We are not concerned with this point here, but only with illustrating what different income distributions, based on different normative standards, look like at one point in time.

income distribution than if they don't know what their position is in the current income distribution.[5]

To illustrate, Patricia Jevons is thought to be a rich person. Her income is $500,000 per year, so she is in the top 5 percent of income earners. Furthermore, the income distribution in which she occupies this position is largely unequal. There are few rich people and many poor people. Given that Patricia knows her position in the income distribution and considers it a comfortable position to occupy, she is less likely to argue for a more equal income distribution (and the high taxes that will be needed to bring it about) than if she were placed behind John Rawls's fictional **veil of ignorance.**

The veil of ignorance is the imaginary veil or curtain behind which a person does not know her position in the income distribution; that is, a person does not know whether she will be rich or poor when the veil is removed. Rawls argues that the "average" person would be more likely to vote for a more equal income distribution behind the veil than she would vote for without the veil.

The full power of Rawls's veil of ignorance idea and its impact on the income distribution can be seen in the following scenario. On Monday, everyone knows his position in the income distribution. Some people are arguing for more income equality, but a sizable group do not want this. They are satisfied with the status quo income distribution.

On Tuesday, everyone is somehow magically transported behind Rawls's veil of ignorance. Behind it, no one knows his position on the other side of the veil. No one knows whether he is rich or poor, innately talented or not, lucky or unlucky. As a group, the persons behind the veil must decide on the income distribution they wish to have when the veil is removed. Rawls believes that individuals are largely risk avoiders and will not want to take the chance that when the veil is removed, they will be poor. They will opt for an income distribution that will assure them that if they are (relatively) poor, their standard of living is not too low.

The Rawlsian normative standard is illustrated in Exhibit 8c, which shows three income pies. The first represents the income distribution that currently exists. The second represents the income distribution that individuals behind the veil of ignorance would accept. The third and last income pie, which is the same as the second, represents the income distribution that Rawls holds should exist because it was agreed to in an environment where individuals were, in a sense, equal: No one knew how he or she would fare when the veil was removed.

Critics of the Rawlsian position argue that individuals behind the veil of ignorance might not reach a consensus on the income distribution that should exist and that they might not be risk avoiders to the degree Rawls assumes they will be.

Furthermore, the individuals behind the veil of ignorance will consider the tradeoff between less income inequality and more output. In a world where the income distribution is likely to be unequal due to unequal individual productivities (sharply different marginal revenue products), reducing income inequality requires higher taxes and a lower reward for productive effort. In the end, this will lead to less productive effort being expended and less output for consumption. In short, the size of the income pie might change given different income distributions. Some of Rawls's critics maintain that individuals are likely to consider this information to a greater degree than Rawls assumes they will.

Q & A   **Q:** To expand on the last point: In Exhibit 8, the income pies are drawn so that their size does not change no matter what the income distribution is. Isn't this unlikely? For example, isn't it possible that the income pie over time will be larger with an unequal income distribution than with an absolutely equal income distribution? After all, individuals may not work as hard if they know that government is determined to make all incomes the same.

---

5. John Rawls, *A Theory of Justice* (Cambridge: Harvard University Press, 1971).

A: That is correct. The income pies are drawn to illustrate what different income distributions, based on different normative standards, look like at one point in time, not over time. Over time the size of the pies might indeed change.

POVERTY

This section presents some facts about poverty and examines its causes.

WHAT IS POVERTY?

There are principally two views of poverty. One view holds that poverty should be defined in absolute terms; the other holds that poverty should be defined in relative terms.

In absolute terms, poverty might be defined as follows: Poverty exists when the income of a family of four is less than $10,000 per year. In relative terms, poverty might be defined as follows: Poverty exists when the income of a family of four places it in the lowest 10 percent of income recipients.

Viewing poverty in relative terms means that poverty will always exist—unless, of course, there is absolute income equality. Given any unequal income distribution, some persons will always occupy the bottom rung of the income ladder; thus, there will always be poverty. This holds no matter how high the absolute standard of living of the members of the society. For example, in a society of ten persons where nine earn $1 million per year and one earns $400,000 per year, the person earning $400,000 per year is in the bottom 10 percent of the income distribution. If poverty is defined in relative terms, this person is considered to be living in poverty.

The U.S. government defines poverty in absolute terms. The absolute poverty measure was developed in 1964 by the Social Security Administration, based on findings of the Department of Agriculture. Called the **poverty income threshold** or **poverty line,** this measure refers to the income below which people are considered to be living in poverty. Individuals or families with incomes below the poverty income threshold, or poverty line, are considered poor.

Poverty Income Threshold (Poverty Line)
Income level below which people are considered to be living in poverty.

In 2000, the poverty income threshold was $17,603 for a family of four. It was $8,959 for an individual under 65 years old. For an individual 65 years and older, it was $8,259.

The poverty threshold is updated yearly to reflect changes in the consumer price index. In 2000, 31.1 million people (in the United States), or 11.3 percent of the entire population, were living below the poverty line.

LIMITATIONS OF THE OFFICIAL POVERTY INCOME STATISTICS

The official poverty income statistics have certain limitations and shortcomings. First, the poverty figures are based solely on money incomes. Many money-poor persons receive in-kind benefits. For example, a family of four with a money income of $17,603 in 2000 was defined as poor, although it might have received in-kind benefits worth, say, $4,000. If the poverty figures are adjusted for in-kind benefits, the percentage of persons living in poverty drops.

Second, poverty figures are not adjusted for unreported income, leading to an overestimate of poverty. Third, poverty figures are not adjusted for regional differences in the cost of living, leading to both overestimates and underestimates of poverty.

Finally, government counters are unable to find some poor persons—such as some illegal aliens and some of the homeless—which leads to an underestimate of poverty.

WHO ARE THE POOR?

Although the poor are persons of all religions, colors, sexes, ages, and ethnic backgrounds, some groups are represented much more prominently in the

http://

Go to *http://www.odci.gov/cia/ publications/factbook/index.html*. Use "Country Listing" to find the per capita GDP, unemployment rate, and percentage of the population below the poverty line (poverty rate) for Algeria, Estonia, Honduras, and the United States. (Most of the data can be found in the "Economy" section for each country.) Are the poverty rates in each country about the same? Which country has the highest poverty rate? Do you think the poverty threshold is the same for each country? For example, if the poverty threshold is 30 percent of the median earnings in one country, do you think it is the same for all countries? Can a change in the poverty threshold change the poverty rate?

poverty figures than others. For example, a greater percentage of African Americans and Hispanics than whites are poor. In 2000, 19.1 percent of African Americans, 18.5 percent of Hispanics, and 6.9 percent of whites lived below the poverty line (see Exhibit 9).

A greater percentage of families headed by females than families headed by males are poor, and families with seven or more persons are much more likely to be poor than are families with fewer than seven persons. In addition, a greater percentage of young persons than others are poor, and the uneducated and poorly educated are more likely to be poor than are the educated. Overall, a disproportionate percentage of the poor are African American or Hispanic and live in large families headed by a female who is young and has little education.

If we look at poverty in terms of absolute numbers instead of percentages, then most poor persons are white, largely because there are more whites than other groups in the total population. In 2000, 14.5 million whites, 7.9 million African Americans, and 7.1 million Hispanics lived below the poverty line.

WHAT IS THE JUSTIFICATION FOR GOVERNMENT REDISTRIBUTING INCOME?

Is there some justification for government redistributing income from the rich to the poor? Some individuals say there is no justification for government welfare assistance. In their view, playing Robin Hood is not a proper role of government. Persons who make this argument say they are not against helping the poor (for instance, they are usually in favor of private charitable organizations) but are against government using its powers to take from some to give to others.

Some persons who believe in government welfare assistance usually present the *public good–free rider* justification or the *social insurance* justification. Proponents of the public good–free rider position make the following arguments, for instance.

1. Most individuals in society would feel better if there were little or no poverty. It is distressing to view the signs of poverty, such as slums, hungry and poorly clothed people, and the homeless. Therefore, there is a demand for reducing or eliminating poverty.

exhibit 9

Poverty in Different Groups of the Population. All data are for 2000.

Source: U.S. Bureau of the Census

Group	Percent of Group in Poverty
TOTAL POPULATION	11.3
BY RACE/ETHNIC GROUP	
White	6.9
African American	19.1
Hispanic	18.5
BY REGION OF COUNTRY	
Northeast	10.3
Midwest	9.5
South	12.5
West	11.9
BY AGE	
Under 18 years old	16.2
18–24 years old	14.4
25–34 years old	10.4
35–44 years old	8.2
45–54 years old	6.4
55–59 years old	8.8
60–64 years old	10.2
65 years old and older	10.2

ECONOMICS IN...

Monks, Blessings, and Free Riders

A chief way to deal with poverty and the inequality of income is through government redistribution programs. In essence, the government can tax people with relatively high incomes and redistribute the funds—either directly or in the form of goods and services—to people with relatively low or no incomes. For example, government may use tax revenue to provide food, shelter, and medical care for the poor.

Almost all countries redistribute income in other ways too. In the United States, for example, there are private (nonreligious) and religious charities. A private organization may collect voluntary donations and use the funds to provide shelter for the homeless. Or a religious organization may collect donations from its members and use the funds to provide food and clothes for the poor.

In Thailand, Buddhist monks often play an important role in redistributing income.[6] By 10 A.M. each day, hundreds of Buddhist believers wait for the Buddhist monk, Luang Poh Koon, to emerge from his residence at the Ban Rai Temple.

When he arrives, the believers raise their right hands, which are holding (paper) money. Luang Poh Koon circulates through the crowd, taking the money from their upraised hands. He keeps one of the bills from each person; the others are returned as good-luck charms. As each person files past him to leave, he blesses them by tapping them on the head with a wand of rolled-up paper.

The believers come to Luang Poh Koon, it is reported, for two reasons. First, they believe that he will use their donations for worthwhile purposes. Luang Poh Koon collects approximately $1,000 a day and there is strong evidence that he gives away most of the money to help build schools and hospitals. Speaking of the donors, he says, "The way I see it, they entrust it (their money) to me to do things that are useful for the country." The second reason donors give is to be blessed. Moreover, they believe that the better the person receiving the offering, the more merit they will get.

Other monks in Thailand collect donations from believers too. Not all of them allocate the funds the way Luang Poh Koon does, however. Some of them use the money to enrich their lives. For example, some monks use the donations to purchase expensive cars and to furnish their monastery cells with high-tech audio and video equipment.

Before we conclude, think of how the "monk system" of redistributing income (to benefit the needy) solves the public good–free rider problem. Recall that the reduction or elimination of poverty is a public good—that is, when poverty is reduced or eliminated, everyone can share in the benefits of not having to view and feel the upsetting sights of poverty. But it is the public good aspect of poverty reduction and elimination that produces free riders. If no one can be excluded from experiencing the benefits of poverty reduction, then individuals will not have any incentive to pay for what they can get for free.

How does the "monk system" deal with the public good-free rider problem? If a person doesn't give funds to the monk—funds that are to be used for worthwhile purposes—then he doesn't receive the monk's blessing. No donation, no blessing. In this way, the monks have tied something that people can receive only if they pay for it—the blessing—to a public good—the reduction or elimination of poverty.

---

2. The reduction or elimination of poverty is a (*nonexcludable*) *public good*—a good that if consumed by one person can be consumed by other persons to the same degree, and the consumption of which cannot be denied to anyone. That is, when poverty is reduced or eliminated, everyone will benefit from no longer viewing the ugly and upsetting sights of poverty, and no one can be excluded from such benefits.

3. If no one can be excluded from experiencing the benefits of poverty reduction, then individuals will not have any incentive to pay for what they can get

6. This feature is adapted from "Rich Are the Blessed," *Far Eastern Economic Review,* 4 May 1995.

for free. Thus, they will become free riders. The economist Milton Friedman sums up the force of the argument this way:

> *I am distressed by the sight of poverty. I am benefited by its alleviation; but I am benefited equally whether I or someone else pays for its alleviation; the benefits of other people's charity therefore partly accrue to me. To put it differently, we might all of us be willing to contribute to the relief of poverty, provided everyone else did it. We might not be willing to contribute the same amount without such assurance.*[7]

Accepting the public good–free rider argument means that government is justified in taxing all persons to pay for the welfare assistance of some.

The social-insurance justification is a different type of justification for government welfare assistance. It holds that individuals currently not receiving welfare think they might one day need welfare assistance and thus are willing to take out a form of insurance for themselves by supporting welfare programs (with their tax dollars and votes).

Self-Test

1. "Poor people will always exist." Comment.

2. What percentage of the U.S. population was living in poverty in 2000?

3. In 2000, what age category had the largest percentage of its group living in poverty?

A Reader Asks...
Are There Degrees of Poverty?

For a family of four, the poverty threshold or poverty line was $17,603 in 2000. This means that if a family of four earned less than $17,603 in 2000, it was living in poverty. But it seems that just setting a dollar figure below which someone is said to be living in poverty doesn't capture the severity or depth of poverty. After all, couldn't two four-person families have earned less than $17,603 in 2000, but still one family have earned much less than the other?

To focus in on the severity or depth of poverty, economists sometimes talk about the ratio of income to poverty.

$$\text{Ratio of income to poverty} = \frac{\text{Family's income}}{\text{Family's poverty income threshold}}$$

For example, consider two four-person families, *A* and *B*. In 2000, family *A* earned $16,000 and family *B* earned $9,000. The ratio of income to poverty for family *A* is:

$$\$16,000/\$17,603 = 0.91$$

The ratio of income to poverty for family *B* is:

$$\$9,000/\$17,603 = 0.51$$

In other words, while both families are poor, family *B* is poorer than family *A*. The depth or severity of family *B*'s poverty is greater than family *A*'s poverty.

Now suppose we consider family *C*, another four-person family, whose income was, say, $21,000 in 2000. The ratio of income to poverty for family *C* is:

$$\$21,000/\$17,603 = 1.19$$

Any time the ratio of income to poverty is greater than 1.00, a family is not considered to be living in poverty. However, if the ratio of income to poverty is between 1.00 and 1.25, the family is considered to be "near poor." Family C, therefore, is near poor.

As an aside, data show that one's chances of living in poverty decrease as one's educational level rises. To illustrate, 22.2 percent of the persons who did not have a high school diploma were living in poverty in 2000. This contrasts with 9.2 percent who had a high school diploma but no college, 5.9 percent who had some college but not a bachelor's degree, and 3.2 percent who had completed college and earned a bachelor's degree.

---

7. Milton Friedman, *Capitalism and Freedom* (Chicago: University of Chicago Press, 1962), p. 191.

Chapter Summary

The Distribution of Income

- The government can change the distribution of income through taxes and transfer payments. The evidence available shows that the ex post distribution of income is more equal than the ex ante distribution of income.
- Individual income = Labor income + Asset income + Transfer payments − Taxes. Government directly affects transfer payments and taxes.
- The Lorenz curve represents the income distribution. The Gini coefficient is a measure of the degree of inequality in the distribution of income. A Gini coefficient of 0 means perfect income equality; a Gini coefficient of 1 means complete income inequality.
- Income inequality exists because individuals differ in their innate abilities and attributes, their choices of work and leisure, their education and other training, their attitudes about risk taking, the luck they experience, and the amount of wage discrimination directed against them. Some income inequality is the result of voluntary choices, some is not.
- There are three major normative standards of income distribution: (1) The marginal productivity normative standard holds that the income distribution should be based on workers being paid their marginal revenue products. (2) The absolute income equality normative standard holds that there should be absolute or complete income equality. (3) The Rawlsian normative standard holds that the income distribution decided on behind the veil of ignorance (where individuals are equal) should exist in the real world.

Poverty

- The income poverty threshold, or poverty line, is the income level below which a family or person is considered poor and living in poverty.
- It is important to be aware of the limitations of poverty income statistics. The statistics are usually not adjusted for (1) in-kind benefits, (2) unreported and illegal income, and (3) regional differences in the cost of living. Furthermore, the statistics do not count the poor who exist but are out of sight, such as illegal aliens and some of the homeless.
- People who believe government should redistribute income from the rich to the poor usually base their argument on the public good–free rider justification or the social-insurance justification. The public good–free rider justification holds that many people are in favor of redistributing income from the rich to the poor and that the elimination of poverty is a public good. But, unfortunately, it is a public good that individuals cannot "produce" because of the incentive everyone has to free ride on the contributions of others. Consequently, government is justified in taxing all persons to pay for the welfare assistance of some. The social-insurance justification holds that individuals not currently receiving redistributed monies may one day find themselves in a position where they will need to, so they are willing to take out a form of insurance. In essence, they are willing to support redistribution programs today so that these programs exist if they should need them in the future.

Key Terms and Concepts

Ex Ante Distribution (of Income)
Ex Post Distribution (of Income)
Transfer Payments
In-Kind Transfer Payments

Lorenz Curve
Gini Coefficient
Human Capital
Wage Discrimination

Veil of Ignorance
Poverty Income Threshold
(Poverty Line)

Economic Connections to You

Economic facts, actions, and changes create ripples that move away from their point of origin. Eventually, these ripples can intersect your life and have an effect on you. Consider the following arguments.

Some people argue that there is a connection between the structure of a welfare system and the cultural cli-

mate. Some people say, "If we make welfare assistance more difficult to obtain, we will impart a sense of responsibility into our culture. This will pay high dividends. People will become responsible for themselves, they will work more, they will depend on others less, and they will slowly begin to feel better about themselves. This is what society needs." Other people disagree. They say, "If we make welfare assistance more difficult to obtain, we will become a less sensitive, harsher people. We will be creating a 'Darwinian world,' where only the strong and lucky survive. This is not what society needs. We do not need to become a harsher, colder people—a people who do not care about others."

Do you think the structure of the welfare system, or changes in a given welfare system, can permeate throughout society and change society in fundamental ways—ways that could affect you? Explain your answer.

Questions and Problems

1. The Gini coefficient for country *A* is 0.35, and the Gini coefficient for country *B* is 0.22. From this it follows that the bottom 10 percent of income recipients in country *B* have a greater percentage of the total income than the bottom 10 percent of the income recipients in country *A*. Do you agree or disagree? Why?

2. Would you expect greater income inequality in country *A*, where there is great disparity in age, or in country *B*, where there is little disparity in age? Explain your answer.

3. What is a major criticism of the absolute income equality normative standard?

4. In what ways does the Rawlsian technique of hypothesizing individuals behind a veil of ignorance help or not help us decide whether we should have a 55 mph speed limit or a higher one, a larger or smaller welfare system, and higher or lower taxes imposed on the rich?

5. Welfare recipients would rather receive cash benefits than in-kind benefits, but much of the welfare system provides in-kind benefits. Is there any reason for not giving recipients their welfare benefits the way they want to receive them? Would it be better to move to a welfare system that provides benefits only in cash?

6. What is the effect of age on the income distribution?

7. Can more people live in poverty at the same time that a smaller percentage of people live in poverty? Explain your answer.

8. Is the ex ante income distribution more equal or less equal than the ex post income distribution in the United States? What is the difference between the two income distributions?

9. Can luck partly explain income inequality? Explain your answer.

10. How would you determine whether the wage difference between two individuals is due to wage discrimination or not?

Working with Numbers and Graphs

1. The lowest fifth of income earners have a 10 percent income share, the second fifth a 17 percent income share, the third fifth a 22 percent income share, the fourth fifth a 24 percent income share, and the highest fifth a 27 percent income share. Draw the Lorenz curve.

2. In Exhibit 7, using Lorenz curve 2, approximately what percentage of income goes to the second-highest 20 percent of households?

3. Is it possible for real income for everyone in society to rise even though the income distribution has become more unequal? Prove your answer with a numerical example.

1. Go to *http://www.census.gov/hhes/www/poverty.html*, and select "Poverty Thresholds" for the most recent year. What is the poverty threshold for one person (under 65 years of age? for a family of seven? Would a 36-year-old single person who earns an annual income of $10,000 be considered poor by the federal government? Do you think the person is poor? Why or why not?

2. Go to *http://www.census.gov/hhes/poverty/histpov/hstpov4.html*. What is the poverty rate for all married-couple families in the most recent year? What is the poverty rate for white married-couple families in the most recent year? African-American married-couple families? Hispanic married-couple families? Generally, is the poverty rate higher for "all families" or for "married-couple families"? What is the poverty rate for a male householder (with no wife present) in the most recent year? What is the poverty rate for a female householder (with no husband present) in the most recent year? Why do you think the poverty rate for a male householder (with no wife present) is lower than the poverty rate for a female householder (with no husband present)?

Log on to the Arnold Xtra! Web site now (*http://arnoldxtra.swcollege.com*) for additional learning resources such as practice quizzes, help with graphing, video clips, and current event applications.

ch.16

INTEREST, RENT, AND PROFIT

From the time individuals decide to start a business until the day they open their door for the first time can seem like forever. The process of starting a business includes decisions and payments. Most likely, the entrepreneurs will need to obtain a loan, on which they will pay interest. They will need to find a suitable location and may need to pay rent on a piece of land. Finally, the grand opening day will arrive and the new owners can look forward to earning profit.

Interest, rent, and profit are the payments to capital, land, and entrepreneurship. A knowledge of these three resource payments is critical to understanding how markets operate and economies function.

Chapter Road Map

Economists talk about four resources, or factors of production—land, labor, capital, and entrepreneurship. We have already discussed the resource labor, including the labor market, the payments to labor (wages), and much more.

In this chapter, we discuss the payments to the three remaining resources—capital, land, and entrepreneurship. The payment to capital is interest; *the payment to land is* rent; *and the payment to entrepreneurship is* profit.

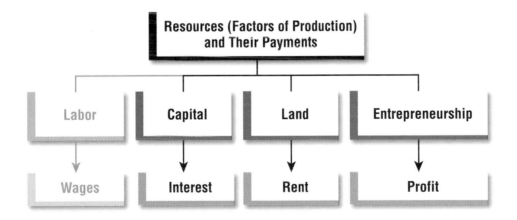

INTEREST

The word *interest* is used in two ways in economics. Sometimes it refers to the price for credit or **loanable funds.** For example, Lars borrows $100 from Rebecca and a year later pays her back $110. The interest is $10.

Interest can also refer to the return earned by capital as an input in the production process. A person who buys a machine (a capital good) for $1,000 and earns $100 a year by using the productive services of the machine is said to earn $100 interest, or a 10 percent interest rate, on the capital.

Economists refer to both the price for loanable funds and the return on capital goods as interest because there is a tendency for the two to become equal, as discussed later in this section.

Q: Is there a difference between interest and the interest rate?

A: Yes. Interest refers to an absolute dollar amount; the interest rate is the ratio of the annual interest to the principal amount. Suppose someone lends Maria $100 and she pays back $120 in a year. She pays $20 in interest. The ratio of the annual interest to the principal ($20/$100) gives us the interest as a percentage of the loan, or the interest rate; it is 20 percent.

LOANABLE FUNDS: DEMAND AND SUPPLY

The equilibrium interest rate, or the price for loanable funds (or credit), is determined by the demand for and supply of loanable funds (or credit). The demand for loanable funds is composed of the demand for consumption loans, the demand for investment loans, and government's demand for loanable funds. With respect to the latter, the U.S. Treasury may need to finance budget deficits by borrowing (demanding) loanable funds in the loanable funds market. This chapter focuses on the demand for consumption loans and the demand for investment loans.

The supply of loanable funds comes from people's saving and from newly created money. This chapter discusses only people's saving.

In summary, in our discussion in this chapter, the demand for loanable funds is composed of (1) the demand for consumption loans and (2) the demand for investment loans. The supply of loanable funds is composed of people's saving.

The Supply of Loanable Funds

Savers are people who consume less than their current income. Without savers, there would be no supply of loanable funds. Savers receive an interest rate for the use of their funds, and the amount of funds saved and loaned is directly related to the interest rate.[1] Specifically, the supply curve of loanable funds is upward-sloping: The higher the interest rate, the greater the quantity supplied of loanable funds; the lower the interest rate, the less the quantity supplied of loanable funds.

The Demand for Loanable Funds: Consumption Loans

Loanable funds are demanded by consumers because they have a **positive rate of time preference;** that is, consumers prefer earlier availability of goods to later availability. For example, most people would prefer to have a car today than a car five years from today.

There is nothing irrational about a positive rate of time preference—most, if not all, people have it. People differ, though, as to the degree of their preference for earlier, compared with later, availability. Some people have a high rate of time preference, signifying that they greatly prefer present to future consumption (I must

---

1. Because a higher interest rate may have both a substitution effect and an income effect, many economists argue that a higher interest rate can lead to either more saving or less saving, depending on which effect is stronger. We will ignore these complications at this level of analysis and hold that the supply curve of loanable funds (from savers) is upward-sloping.

Loanable Funds
Funds that someone borrows and another person lends, for which the borrower pays an interest rate to the lender.

Positive Rate of Time Preference
Preference for earlier availability of goods over later availability of goods.

have that new car today). Other people have a low rate, signifying that they prefer present to future consumption only slightly. (Who would be more likely to save, that is, postpone consumption—people with a high rate of time preference or people with a low rate? The answer is people with a low rate of time preference. People with a high rate of time preference have to have things now.)

Because consumers have a positive rate of time preference, there is a demand for consumption loans. Consumers borrow today in order to buy today; they will pay back the borrowed amount plus interest tomorrow. The interest payment is the price consumers-borrowers pay to obtain the earlier availability of goods.

The Demand for Loanable Funds: Investment Loans

Investors (or firms) demand loanable funds (or credit) so they can invest in capital goods and finance **roundabout methods of production.** A firm using a roundabout method of production first directs its efforts to producing capital goods and then uses those goods to produce consumer goods.

Roundabout Method of Production The production of capital goods that enhance productive capabilities in order to ultimately bring about increased consumption.

Let's consider the direct method and the roundabout method for catching fish. In the direct method, a person uses his hands to catch fish. In the roundabout method, the person weaves a net (which is a capital good) and then uses the net to catch fish. Let's suppose that by using the direct method, Charlie can catch 4 fish per day. Using the roundabout method, he can catch 10 fish per day.

Furthermore, let's suppose it takes Charlie 10 days to weave a net. If Charlie does not weave a net and instead catches fish by hand, he can catch 1,460 fish per year (4 fish per day times 365 days). If, however, Charlie spends 10 days weaving a net (during which time he catches no fish), he can catch 3,550 fish the first year (10 fish per day times 355 days). We conclude that the capital-intensive roundabout method of production is highly productive.

Because roundabout methods of production are so productive, investors are willing to borrow funds to invest in them. For example, Charlie might reason, "I'm more productive if I weave a fishing net, but to do so, I'll need to take 10 days off from catching fish and devote all my energies to weaving a net. What will I eat during the 10 days? Perhaps I can borrow some fish from my neighbor. I'll need to borrow 40 fish for the next 10 days. But, I must make it worthwhile for my neighbor to enter into this arrangement, so I will promise to pay her back 50 fish at the end of the year. Thus, my neighbor will lend me 40 fish today in exchange for 50 fish at the end of the year. I realize I'm paying an interest rate of 25 percent (the interest payment of 10 fish is 25 percent of the number of fish borrowed, 40), but still it will be worth it." The highly productive nature of the capital-intensive roundabout method of production is what makes it worthwhile.

The reasoning in our fish example is repeated whenever a firm makes a capital investment. Making computers on an assembly line is a roundabout method of production compared with making them one by one by hand. Making copies on a copying machine is a roundabout method of production compared with copying by hand. In both cases, firms are willing to borrow now, use the borrowed funds to invest in roundabout methods of production, and pay back the loan with interest later. If roundabout methods of production were not productive, firms would not be willing to do this.

The Loanable Funds Market

The sum of the demand for consumption loans and the demand for investment loans is the total demand for loanable funds. The demand curve for loanable funds is downward-sloping. As interest rates rise, consumers' cost of earlier availability of goods rises, and they curtail their borrowing. Also, as interest rates rise, some investment projects that would be profitable at a lower interest rate will no longer be profitable. We conclude that the interest rate and the quantity demanded of loanable funds are inversely related.

exhibit 1

Loanable Funds Market

The demand curve shows the different quantities of loanable funds demanded at different interest rates. The supply curve shows the different quantities of loanable funds supplied at different interest rates. Through the forces of supply and demand, the equilibrium interest rate and the quantity of loanable funds at that rate are established as i_1 and Q_1.

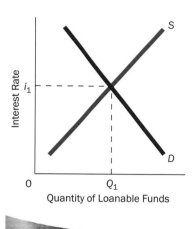

Exhibit 1 illustrates the demand for and supply of loanable funds. The equilibrium interest rate occurs where the quantity demanded of loanable funds equals the quantity supplied of loanable funds.

Q: When would a project be profitable at lower interest rates but not at higher interest rates?

A: Suppose a firm estimates that if it buys a particular capital good, the return next year will be 10 percent. The price of the loanable funds needed to buy the capital good is 8 percent. At this price, the firm will borrow the funds and buy the capital good. If, however, the price of the loanable funds rises to 10.5 percent, the firm will not buy the capital good.

THE PRICE FOR LOANABLE FUNDS AND THE RETURN ON CAPITAL GOODS TEND TO EQUALITY

As mentioned earlier, both the price for loanable funds and the return on capital are referred to as interest because they tend to equality. To illustrate, suppose the return on capital is 10 percent and the price for loanable funds is 8 percent. In this setting, firms will borrow in the loanable funds market and invest in capital goods. As they do this, the quantity of capital increases, and its return falls (capital is subject to diminishing marginal returns). In short, the return on capital and the price for loanable funds begin to approach each other.

Suppose, instead, that the percentages are reversed and the price for loanable funds is 10 percent and the return on capital is 8 percent. In this situation, no one will borrow loanable funds at 10 percent to invest at 8 percent. Over time, the capital stock will decrease (capital depreciates over time; it doesn't last forever), its marginal physical product will rise, and the return on capital and the price for loanable funds will eventually equal each other.

THINKING LIKE AN ECONOMIST

In economics, it is not uncommon for factors to converge. For example, in supply-and-demand analysis, the quantity demanded and the quantity supplied of a good tend to equality (through the equilibrating process). In consumer theory, the marginal utility-price ratios for different goods tend to equality. And, as just discussed, the price of loanable funds and the return on capital tend to equality.

But why do many things tend to equality in economics? It is because equality is often representative of equilibrium. When quantity demanded equals quantity supplied, a market is said to be in equilibrium. When the marginal utility-price ratio for all goods is the same, the consumer is said to be in equilibrium. Inequality, therefore, often signifies disequilibrium. When the price of loanable funds is greater than the return on capital, there is disequilibrium. The next logical question is, "So what happens now?"

The economist, knowing that equality often signifies equilibrium, looks for inequalities and then asks, "So what happens now?"

WHY DO INTEREST RATES DIFFER?

The supply-and-demand analysis in Exhibit 1 may suggest that there is only one interest rate in the economy. In reality, there are many. For example, a major business is not likely to pay the same interest rate for an investment loan to purchase new machinery as the person next door pays for a consumption loan to buy a car. Some of the factors that affect interest rates are discussed in the following paragraphs. In each case, the *ceteris paribus* condition holds.

Risk

Any time a lender makes a loan, there is a possibility that the borrower will not repay it. Some borrowers are better credit risks than others. A major corporation with a long and established history is probably a better credit risk than a person who has been unemployed three times in the last seven years. The more risk associated with a loan, the higher the interest rate; the less risk associated with a loan, the lower the interest rate.

Term of the Loan

In general, the longer the term of the loan, the higher the interest rate; the shorter the term of the loan, the lower the interest rate. Borrowers are usually more willing to pay higher interest rates for long-term loans because this gives them greater flexibility. Lenders require higher interest rates to part with funds for extended periods.

Cost of Making the Loan

A loan for $1,000 and a loan for $100,000 may require the same amount of record keeping, making the larger loan cheaper (per dollar) to process than the smaller loan. Also, some loans require frequent payments (such as payments for a car loan), whereas others do not. This difference is likely to be reflected in higher administrative costs for loans with more frequent payments. We conclude that loans that cost more to process and administer will have higher interest rates than loans that cost less to process and administer.

NOMINAL AND REAL INTEREST RATES

The **nominal interest rate** is the interest rate determined by the forces of supply and demand in the loanable funds market. It is the interest rate in current dollars. The nominal interest rate will change if the demand for or supply of loanable funds changes. Individuals' expectations of inflation are one of the factors that can change both the demand for and supply of loanable funds. Inflation occurs when the money prices of goods, on average, increase over time. To see exactly how this can affect the nominal interest rate, look at Exhibit 2.

We start with an interest rate of 8 percent and an actual and expected inflation rate of zero (actual inflation rate = expected inflation rate = 0 percent). Later, both the demanders and suppliers of loanable funds expect a 4 percent inflation rate. What will this 4 percent expected inflation rate do to the demand

Nominal Interest Rate
The interest rate determined by the forces of supply and demand in the loanable funds market.

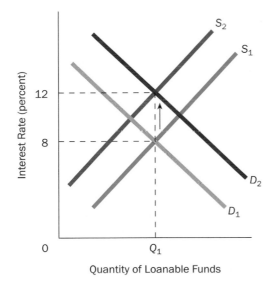

for and supply of loanable funds? Borrowers (demanders of loanable funds) will be willing to pay 4 percent more interest for their loans because they expect to be paying back the loans with dollars that have 4 percent less buying power than the dollars they are being lent. (Another way of looking at this is to say that if they wait to buy goods, the prices of the goods they want will have risen by 4 percent. To beat the price increase, they are willing to pay up to 4 percent more to borrow and purchase the goods now.) In effect, the demand for loanable funds curve shifts rightward, so that at Q_1, borrowers are willing to pay a 4 percent higher interest rate.

On the other side of the loanable funds market, the lenders (suppliers of loanable funds) require a 4 percent higher interest rate (that is, 12 percent) to compensate them for the 4 percent less valuable dollars in which the loan will be repaid. In effect, the supply of loanable funds curve shifts leftward, so that at Q_1, lenders will receive an interest rate of 12 percent.

Thus, an expected inflation rate of 4 percent increases the demand for loanable funds and decreases the supply of loanable funds, so that the interest rate is 4 percent higher than it was when there was a zero inflation rate. In this example, 12 percent is the nominal interest rate. It is the interest rate in current dollars and it includes the expected inflation rate.

If we adjust for the expected inflation rate, we have the **real interest rate.** The real interest rate is the nominal interest rate adjusted for the expected inflation rate; that is, it is the nominal interest rate minus the expected inflation rate. In the example, the real interest rate is 8 percent (real interest rate = nominal interest rate − expected inflation rate).

The real interest rate, not the nominal interest rate, matters to borrowers and lenders. Consider a lender who grants a $1,000 loan to a borrower at a 20 percent nominal interest rate at a time when the actual inflation rate is 15 percent. The amount repaid to the lender is $1,200, but $1,200 with a 15 percent inflation rate does not have the buying power that $1,200 with a zero inflation rate has. The 15 percent inflation rate wipes out much of the gain, and the lender's real return on the loan is not 20 percent, but rather only 5 percent. Thus, the rate lenders receive and borrowers pay (and therefore the rate they care about) is the real interest rate.

Real Interest Rate
The nominal interest rate adjusted for expected inflation; that is, the nominal interest rate minus the expected inflation rate.

Q: When a person calls a bank to find out the interest rate he or she would pay for a loan, which interest rate is quoted, the nominal or the real?

A: The bank will quote the nominal interest rate. Remember, the nominal interest rate is the interest rate that is determined by the current forces of supply and demand. It is the interest rate expressed in current dollars.

Q: Are the nominal interest rate and the real interest rate ever the same?

A: They are the same when the expected inflation rate is zero. The real interest rate = the nominal interest rate − the expected inflation rate. (Alternatively, this can be written as the nominal interest rate = the real interest rate + the expected inflation rate.) If the expected inflation rate is zero, the real interest rate = the nominal interest rate.

PRESENT VALUE: WHAT IS SOMETHING TOMORROW WORTH TODAY?

Because of people's positive rate of time preference, $100 today is worth more than $100 a year from now. (Don't you prefer $100 today to $100 in a year?) Thus, $100 a year from now must be worth less than $100 today. Can we be more specific and say just how much $100 a year from now is worth today?

This question introduces the concept of **present value.** Present value refers to the current worth of some future dollar amount (of receipts or income). In our example, present value refers to what $100 a year from now is worth today.

Present Value
The current worth of some future dollar amount of income or receipts.

Present value (PV) is computed by using the formula:

$$PV = A_n/(1 + i)^n$$

where A_n is the actual amount of income or receipts in a particular year in the future, i is the interest rate (expressed as a decimal), and n is the number of years in the future. The present value of $100 one year in the future at a 10 percent interest rate is $90.91:

$$PV = \$100/(1 + 0.10)^1$$
$$= \$90.91$$

This means that the right to receive $100 a year from now is worth $90.91 today. Another way to look at this is to realize that if $90.91 is put in a savings account paying a 10 percent interest rate, it would equal $100 in a year.

Now suppose we wanted to know what a particular future income stream was worth today. That is, instead of finding out what a particular future dollar amount is worth today, our objective is to find out what a series of future dollar amounts are worth today. The general formula is:

$$PV = \Sigma \, A_n/(1 + i)^n$$

where the Greek letter Σ stands for "sum of."

Suppose a firm buys a machine that will earn $100 a year for the next three years. What is this future income stream—$100 per year for three years—worth today? What is its present value? At a 10 percent interest rate, this income stream has a present value of $248.68:

$$PV = A_1/(1 + 0.10)^1 + A_2/(1 + 0.10)^2 + A_3/(1 + 0.10)^3$$
$$= \$100/1.10 + \$100/1.21 + \$100/1.331$$
$$= \$90.91 + \$82.64 + \$75.13$$
$$= \$248.68$$

DECIDING WHETHER TO PURCHASE A CAPITAL GOOD

Business firms often compute present values when trying to decide whether or not to buy a capital good. Let's look again at the machine that will earn $100 a year for the next three years. Suppose we assume that after the three-year period the machine must be scrapped and that it will have no scrap value. The firm will compare the present value of the future income generated by the machine ($248.68) with the cost of the machine. Suppose the cost of the machine is $250. The firm will decide not to buy the machine because the cost of the machine is greater than the present value of the income stream the machine will generate.

Would the business firm buy the machine if the interest rate had been 4 percent instead of 10 percent? The present value of $100 a year for three years at 4 percent interest is $278. Comparing this amount with the cost of the machine ($250), we see that the firm is likely to buy the machine. We conclude that as interest rates decrease, present values increase and firms will buy more capital goods; as interest rates increase, present values decrease and firms will buy fewer capital goods, all other things held constant.

Self-Test (Answers to Self-Test questions are in the Self-Test Appendix.)

1. Why does the price for loanable funds tend to equal the return on capital goods?
2. Why does the real interest rate, and not the nominal interest rate, matter to borrowers and lenders?

Lotteries, Art, and Old Age

Lotteries, art, and old age may not seem to be related. But, they have one thing in common—the present value of a future dollar amount.

What Would You Do If You Won the Lottery?

Suppose you buy a lottery ticket and win $5 million. Dollar winnings in a lottery are usually paid out to the winner over time. For example, you may receive $1 million each year for five years. Often, though, lottery winners can choose to receive less money but receive it all at once. For example, you might be able to choose between receiving $1 million a year for five years, or $3.5 million right now. Which would you choose?

One way to help you decide is discussed in this chapter. You can calculate the present value of each sum of money. The present value of $3.5 million today is, of course, $3.5 million. The present value of $1 million each year for five years at, say, an interest rate of 5 percent, is $4.3 million. The present value of $1 million each year for the next five years is greater than the present value of $3.5 million now, so it is better to take the $1 million each year for five years.

What might you do with your $1 million a year? Would you buy a Cezanne painting?

Interest Rates and the Price of a Cezanne Painting

There are two reasons why you might buy a Cezanne painting. The first reason is to enjoy the painting. Just as we get enjoyment from attending a baseball game, going to a concert, or jogging on a warm spring day, we also get enjoyment from viewing a great work of art. How much would you be willing and able to pay to have that enjoyment? Whatever the amount is, those are the "dividends" you would receive from viewing your Cezanne. The second reason you might purchase a Cezanne painting is because you think it will rise in value over time. In other words, it may be a good "investment."

Let's say you are contemplating the purchase of a Cezanne with your lottery winnings and (1) believe you will receive $1,000 worth of enjoyment each year from viewing it and (2) expect to be able to sell it in five years for $1 million. What would you be willing to pay for a Cezanne today if you believe you will receive $1,000 worth of benefits each year for five years and $1 million in five years when you sell the painting? Obviously, we need to find the present value of $1,000 each year for five years plus the present value of $1 million five years from now. Using an interest rate of 5 percent, this sum is approximately $787,853.

What will a decline in the interest rate do to the price of Cezannes? Obviously, a decline in the interest rate will raise the present value of a Cezanne. We would expect that Cezannes will rise in price as interest rates fall.

Old Age and the Price of a Cezanne Painting

If medical science makes it possible for people to live longer and healthier lives, how will this affect the price of your Cezanne painting? Suppose you buy the Cezanne painting simply for the benefits you will receive from viewing it. (You never intend to sell the painting.) If you receive, say, $2,000 a year in benefits, the price you would be willing to pay for the painting depends on the interest rate and the number of years you expect to benefit from viewing the painting. If you are 20 years old now, and expect to die when you are 73 years old, then you will have 53 years of benefits from the Cezanne. If you expect to live longer, say to 85 years old, then you will have 65 years of enjoying the Cezanne. The present value of a Cezanne that can be enjoyed for 65 years is greater than the present value of a Cezanne that can be enjoyed for 53 years. It follows that if medical science makes it possible to live longer and healthier lives, the prices of Cezannes are likely to rise along with age.

3. What is the present value of $1,000 two years from today if the interest rate is 5 percent?

4. A business firm is thinking of buying a capital good. The capital good will earn $2,000 a year for the next four years and it will cost $7,000. The interest rate is 8 percent. Should the firm buy the machine? Explain your answer.

RENT

Mention the word *rent,* and people naturally think of someone living in an apartment who makes monthly payments to a landlord. This is not the type of rent discussed here. To an economist, rent means **economic rent.** Economic rent is a payment in excess of opportunity costs. There is also a subset of economic rent called **pure economic rent.** This is a payment in excess of opportunity costs when opportunity costs are zero. Historically, the term *pure economic rent* was first used to describe the payment to the factor land, which is perfectly inelastic in supply.

In Exhibit 3, the total supply of land is fixed at Q_1 acres; there can be no more and no less than this amount of land. The payment for land is determined by the forces of supply and demand; this payment turns out to be R_1.

Notice that R_1 is more than sufficient to bring Q_1 acres into supply. In fact, we know by looking at the fixed supply of land (the supply curve is perfectly inelastic) that Q_1 acres would have been forthcoming at a payment of zero dollars. In short, this land has zero opportunity costs. Therefore, the full payment, all of R_1, is referred to as pure economic rent.

 **Q:** In other words, pure economic rent only exists if the supply curve of the factor is perfectly inelastic. Is this correct?

A: Yes, it is.

 **Q:** Can economic factors besides land receive pure economic rent?

A: Yes, they can, as long as the supply curve of these factors is perfectly inelastic.

DAVID RICARDO, THE PRICE OF GRAIN, AND LAND RENTS IN NEW YORK AND TOKYO

In nineteenth-century England, people were concerned about the rising price of grains, which were a staple in many English diets. Some argued that grain prices were rising because land rents were rising rapidly. Fingers began to be pointed at the landowners, as people maintained that the high rents the landowners received for their land made it more and more costly for farmers to raise grains. These higher costs, in turn, were passed on to consumers in the form of higher prices. According to this argument, the solution was to lower rents, which would lead to lower costs for farmers and eventually to lower prices for consumers.

The English economist David Ricardo thought this reasoning was faulty. He contended that grain prices weren't high because rents were high (as most individuals thought), but rather that rents were high because grain prices were high.

In current economic terminology, his argument was as follows: Land is a factor of production; therefore, the demand for it is derived. Also, land is in fixed supply; therefore, the only thing that will change the payment made to land is a change in the demand for land. (The supply curve isn't going to shift, and thus the only thing that can change price is a shift in the demand curve.) Landowners have no control over the demand for land. Demand comes from other persons who want to use it. In nineteenth-century England, the demand came from farmers who were raising grains and other foodstuffs. Therefore, landowners could not have pushed up land rents because they had no control over the demand for their land. It follows that if rents were high, this must have been because the demand for land was high, and the demand for land was high because grain prices were high.

The same confusion between high rents and high prices still exists today. For example, many people complain that prices in stores and restaurants in New York City and Tokyo are high. When they notice that land rents are also high, they reason that prices are high because land rents are high. But, as Ricardo pointed out,

Economic Rent
Payment in excess of opportunity costs.

Pure Economic Rent
A category of economic rent where the payment is to a factor that is in fixed supply, implying that it has zero opportunity costs.

exhibit 3

Pure Economic Rent and the Total Supply of Land
The total supply of land is fixed at Q_1. The payment for the services of this land is determined by the forces of supply and demand. Because the payment is for a factor in fixed supply, it is referred to as pure economic rent.

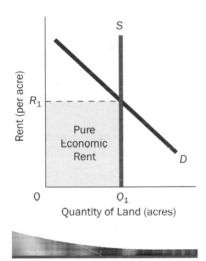

ECONOMICS IN...

What Does Present Value Have to Do with a Divorce?

Present values are important for many things besides the investment decisions of business firms. Lawyers, for example, often call on economists to calculate the present value of someone's future income. Accident cases involving personal injuries and divorce suits are examples of cases in which a lawyer might need to know the present value of a future income.

Consider a couple, Carol and Jack, who got married in 1989. Shortly after, Jack entered medical school, while Carol went to work to help pay Jack's medical school expenses.

In 2002, Jack and Carol realize that their marriage is in trouble. They seek professional help, but things don't work out. They both agree to a divorce and say they'll split the assets: the house, the cars, the furniture, the silverware, the paintings, the Persian rugs. There is one hitch, however. Carol claims that Jack's medical degree is an asset and that she has invested in it because she helped pay his way through medical school. Jack's lawyer object to this reasoning, and the case ultimately goes before a judge.

Before the case goes to trial, Carol's lawyer has to determine how much the medical degree is worth. After all, if Carol

is to get part of the value of the medical degree, it is important to know what that value is.

The lawyer consults an economist and asks him to determine the present value of the degree. The economist estimates that as a medical doctor, Jack will earn $100,000 more each year than if he had not gone to medical school. He also estimates that Jack will be practicing medicine for the next 25 years. Using an interest rate of 4 percent, the economist calculates the present value of $100,000 a year for 25 years. Of course, the economist's estimates will be subject to close scrutiny by Jack's lawyer ("How do you know my client will be practicing for 25 years or that he will be making $100,000 more a year?"), but our concern here is the role present value plays in the process, not the legal issues.

In any case, the economist calculates the present value of $100,000 a year for 25 years at 4 percent interest to be approximately $1.57 million. Now the court must decide if the medical degree is an asset whose proceeds should be divided between Carol and Jack and if so, what portion of the proceeds should to go Carol and over what period of time.

---

the reverse is true: land rents are high because prices are high. If the demand for living, visiting, and shopping in New York City and Tokyo were not as high as it is, prices for goods would not be as high. In turn, the demand for land would not be as high, and therefore the payments to land would not be as high. Economists put it this way: Land rents are price determined, not price determining.

THE SUPPLY CURVE OF LAND CAN BE UPWARD-SLOPING

Exhibit 3 depicts the supply of land as fixed. This is the case when the total supply of land is in question. For example, there are only so many acres of land in this country, and that amount is not likely to change.

Most subparcels of land, however, have competing uses. Consider 25 acres of land on the periphery of a major city. It can be used for farmland, a shopping mall, or a road. If a particular parcel of land (as opposed to all land, or the total supply of land) has competing uses, it follows that the parcel of land has opportunity costs. Land that is used for farming could have been used for a shopping mall. To reflect the opportunity cost of that land, we draw its supply curve as upward-sloping. This implies that if individuals want more land for a specific purpose—say, for a shopping mall—they must bid high enough to attract existing land away from other uses (farming, for example). This is illustrated in Exhibit 4, where the equilibrium payment to land is R_1. The shaded area indicates the economic rent.

ECONOMIC RENT AND OTHER FACTORS OF PRODUCTION

As mentioned earlier, the concept of economic rent applies to economic factors besides land. For example, it applies to labor. Suppose Hanson works for company X and is paid $40,000 a year. Furthermore, suppose that in his next best alternative job he would be earning $37,000. Is Hanson receiving economic rent working for company X? Yes, he is receiving a payment in excess of his opportunity costs; thus, he is receiving economic rent.

Or consider the local McDonald's that hires teenagers. It pays all its beginning employees the same wage. But not every beginning employee has the same opportunity costs as every other employee. Suppose two teenagers, Tracy and Paul, sign on to work at McDonald's for $6.00 an hour. Tracy's next best alternative wage is $6.00 an hour working for her mother's business, and Paul's next best alternative wage is $5.50 an hour. Tracy receives no economic rent in her McDonald's job, but Paul receives 50 cents an hour economic rent in the same job.

Over time, teenagers and other beginning employees usually find that their opportunity costs rise (owing to continued schooling and job experience) and that the McDonald's wage no longer covers their opportunity costs. When this happens, they quit their jobs.

ECONOMIC RENT AND BASEBALL PLAYERS: THE PERSPECTIVE FROM WHICH THE FACTOR IS VIEWED MATTERS

Economic rent differs depending on the perspective from which the factor is viewed. Let's look at a baseball star who earns $1 million a year playing baseball. Suppose that if he weren't playing baseball, he would be a coach at a high school. Therefore, the difference between what he is currently paid ($1 million a year) and what he would earn as a coach (say, $40,000 a year) is economic rent. This amounts to $960,000. In this case, economic rent is determined by identifying the alternative to the baseball star playing baseball.

However, a different alternative would be identified by asking: What is the alternative to the baseball star playing baseball for his present team? The answer is probably that he can play baseball for another team. For example, if he weren't playing for the Boston Red Sox, he might be playing for the Pittsburgh Pirates and earning $950,000 a year. His economic rent in this instance is only $50,000.

The baseball player's economic rent as a player for the Boston Red Sox is $50,000 a year (his next best alternative is playing for the Pittsburgh Pirates earning $950,000 a year). But his economic rent as a baseball player is $960,000 (his next best alternative is being a high school coach earning $40,000 a year).

COMPETING FOR ARTIFICIAL AND REAL RENTS

Individuals and firms will compete for both *artificial rents* and *real rents*. An artificial rent is an economic rent that is artificially contrived by government; it would not exist without government. Suppose government decides to award a monopoly right to one firm to produce good X. In so doing, it legally prohibits all other firms from producing good X. If the firm with the monopoly right receives a price for good X in excess of its opportunity costs, it receives a "rent" or "monopoly profit" because of government's supply restraint. Firms that compete for the monopoly right to produce good X expend resources in a socially wasteful manner.[2] They use resources to lobby politicians in the hope of getting the monopoly—resources that (from society's perspective) are better used to produce goods and services.

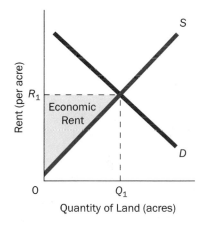

exhibit 4

Economic Rent and the Supply of Land (Competing Uses)
A particular parcel of land, as opposed to the total supply of land, has competing uses, or positive opportunity costs. For example, to obtain land to build a shopping mall, the developers must bid high enough to attract existing land away from competing uses. The supply curve is upward-sloping. At a payment of R_1, economic rent is identified as the payment in excess of (positive) opportunity costs.

---

2. This may sound familiar. The process described here where individuals expend resources lobbying government for a special privilege was described as rent seeking in the chapter about monopoly.

Is the Car Worth Buying?

Business firms often compute present values when trying to decide whether or not to buy capital goods. Should consumers do the same when they are thinking about buying a durable good (a good that will last for a few years), such as a car?

Suppose you are thinking about buying a car. The market price of the car is $15,500. Should you buy it? The answer depends on the value of the services you intend to get from the car and the length of time you expect to receive these services. For example, suppose you anticipate that you will receive $2,000 worth of services from the car each year for the next 10 years, after which time the car will have to be scrapped and will have no scrap value.

What is the question you should ask yourself? Ask the same question that the business firm asks when it considers buying a capital good. In your case ask, "Is the present value of the car more than, less than, or equal to the present market price of the car?"

What is the present value of the car in our discussion? A car that yields $2,000 worth of benefits each year for 10 years at a 4 percent interest rate has a present value of approximately $16,223:

$$PV = \$2,000/(1 + 0.04)^1 + \$2,000/(1 + 0.04)^2 + \ldots$$
$$+ \$2,000/(1 + 0.04)^{10}$$
$$= \$16,223 \text{ (approximately)}$$

The market price of the car ($15,500) is less than the present value of the car ($16,223), so it is worthwhile to purchase the car.

What will an increase in the interest rate do to the present value of the car? All other things remaining constant, an increase in the interest rate will lower the present value of the car. For example, at a 7 percent interest rate, the present value of the car is approximately $15,377. Now, the market price of the car ($15,500) is greater than the present value of the car ($15,377); it is not worthwhile to purchase this car. In other words, we would expect fewer cars to be sold when the interest rate rises and more cars to be sold when the interest rate falls. Why? A change in the interest rate changes the present value of cars.

http://

Go to *http://www.californiacu.org*. Click on "rates," and then select "Vehicle loans." Is the interest rate on a new auto loan the same as that on a used car loan? If not, which is higher? Why do you think the interest rate on a new car loan is not the same as the interest rate on a used car loan?

Competing for real rents is different, however. If the rent is real (it has not been artificially created) and there are no barriers to competing for it, resources are used in a way that is socially productive. For example, suppose firm Z currently receives economic rent in the production of good Z. Government does not prohibit other firms from competing with firm Z, so some do. These other firms also produce good Z, thus increasing the supply of the good and lowering its price. The lower price reduces the rent firm Z receives in its production of good Z. In the end, firm Z has less rent, while society has more of good Z and pays a lower price for it.

DO PEOPLE OVERESTIMATE THEIR WORTH TO OTHERS, OR ARE THEY SIMPLY SEEKING ECONOMIC RENT?

Johnson is an accountant with seven years' experience who is currently earning $75,000 annually. One day he walks into his employer's office and asks for a raise in salary to $85,000. His employer asks him why he thinks he deserves the $10,000 raise. Johnson says that he is sure he is worth that much. (If he is, he can leave his current company and receive an offer of $85,000 from another company. We don't know whether he can do this or not.)

His employer believes that Johnson is overestimating his worth to others. She thinks, "There is no way that Johnson is worth $10,000 more a year. He is simply overestimating his worth."

Is the employer correct? Is Johnson really overestimating his worth to others? Not necessarily. Johnson could believe his worth to others is $75,000—in other words, $75,000 is his opportunity cost—but he could be attempting to receive economic rent ($10,000 more than his opportunity cost) by getting his employer to believe his opportunity cost is really $85,000. In other words, a person who may appear to others to be overestimating his worth may be attempting to obtain economic rent.

Self-Test

1. Give an example that illustrates that land rents are price determined, not price determining.

2. Nick's salary is pure economic rent. What does this imply about Nick's "next best alternative salary"?

3. What are the social consequences of firms competing for artificial rents as opposed to competing for real rents (where there are no barriers to competing for real rents)?

PROFIT

The "profits" that appear in newspaper headlines are *accounting profits,* not economic profits. Economic profit is the difference between total revenue and total cost, where both explicit and implicit costs are included in total cost.

Economists emphasize economic profit over accounting profit because economic profit determines entry into and exit from an industry. For the most part, this is how economic profit figures in the discussion of market structures in earlier chapters.

This section goes beyond the entry-and-exit role of profit. First, we discuss the source of profits to find out why economic profit exists. Second, we examine why the full value of the product produced by firms is not divided among the factors land, labor, and capital.

THEORIES OF PROFIT

Several different theories address the question of where profit comes from, or the source of profit. One theory holds that profit would not exist in a world of certainty; hence, uncertainty is the source of profit. Another theory holds that profit is the return for alertness to (broadly defined) arbitrage opportunities. A third theory holds that profit is the return to the entrepreneur as innovator.

Profit and Uncertainty

Uncertainty exists when a potential occurrence is so unpredictable that a probability cannot be estimated. (For example, what is the probability that the United States will enter a world war in 2010? Who knows?) Risk, which many people mistake for uncertainty, exists when the probability of a given event can be estimated. (For example, there is a 50-50 chance that a toss of a coin will come up heads.) It follows that risks can be insured against, uncertainties cannot.

Anything that can be insured against can be treated as just another cost of doing business. Insurance coverage is an input in the production process. Only uncertain events can cause a firm's revenues to diverge from costs (including insurance costs). The investor-decision maker who is adept at making business decisions under conditions of uncertainty earns a profit. For example, based on experience and some insights, an entrepreneur may believe that 75 percent of college students will buy personal computers next year. This assessment, followed by the act of investing in a chain of retail computer stores near college campuses, will ultimately prove to be right or wrong. The essential point is that the entrepreneur's judgment is not something that can be insured against. If correct, the entrepreneur will earn a profit; if incorrect, a loss.

Profit and Arbitrage Opportunities

The way to make a profit, the advice goes, is to "buy low and sell high." Usually, what is bought (low) and sold (high) is the same item. For example, someone might buy an ounce of gold in New York for $390 and sell the same ounce of gold in London for $396. We might say that the person is alert to where she can buy low and sell high, thereby earning a profit. She is alert to an arbitrage opportunity.

Sometimes buying low and selling high does not refer to the same item. Sometimes it refers to buying factors in one set of markets at the lowest possible prices, combining the factors into a finished product, and then selling the product in another market for the highest possible price. An example of this would be buying oranges and sugar (in the oranges and sugar markets), combining the two, and selling an orange soft drink (in the soft-drink market). If doing this results in profit, we would then say that the person who undertook the act was alert to a (broadly defined) arbitrage opportunity. He saw that oranges and sugar together, in the form of an orange soft drink, would fetch more than the sum of oranges and sugar separately.

Profit and Innovation

In this theory, profit is the return to the entrepreneur as innovator—the person who creates new profit opportunities by devising a new product, production process, or marketing strategy. Viewed in this way, profit is the return to "innovative genius." People such as Thomas Edison, Henry Ford, and Richard Sears and Alvah Roebuck are said to have had innovative genius.

Q & A

Q: If profit is the "return" to entrepreneurship, what exactly is entrepreneurship, and how does it differ from the other factors of production?

A: An earlier chapter refers to entrepreneurship as "the particular talent that some people have for organizing the resources of land, labor, and capital to produce goods, seek new business opportunities, and develop new ways of doing things." More narrowly, an entrepreneur bears uncertainty, is alert to arbitrage opportunities, and exhibits innovative behavior. Most entrepreneurs probably exhibit different degrees of each. For example, Thomas Edison may have been more the innovator-entrepreneur than the arbitrager-entrepreneur.

Unlike the other factors of production (land, labor, capital), entrepreneurship cannot be measured. There are no entrepreneurial units, as there are labor, capital, and land units. Furthermore, an entrepreneur receives profit as a residual after the other factors of production have been paid.

WHAT DO A MICROWAVE OVEN AND AN ERRAND RUNNER HAVE IN COMMON?

The answer to the question in the title of this section is: They both economize on your time. Many people today complain that they don't have enough time to do all they want to do. Where these people see a problem, the entrepreneur sees a business opportunity. If people do not have enough time to do what they want to do, she reasons, then perhaps they will be willing to pay for a product or service that economizes on their time and frees some time for another use. Consider the microwave oven. The microwave oven reduces the time it takes to make a meal, thus freeing time for other activities—reading a book, working, sleeping, and so on.

Consider Charles Vaughn, who recently started a business that tries to economize on people's time. Vaughn started a company called Roving Oil Can. For $29.95 plus tax, he drives to a customer's car, whether it is at home or at work, and changes the oil, lubricates the chassis, and checks the engine. He says that he expects to do 90 jobs a day after his three vans are in operation.

Or consider the professional errand runner who will pick up the laundry, manage the house, feed the cat, pick up food for a party, and do other such things. In some large cities around the country, professional errand runners will do the things that a two-earner family or working single men and women would rather pay someone to do than take the time to do themselves.

MONOPOLY PROFITS

Monopolies can earn positive economic profits owing to the high barriers to entry. In contrast to the temporary profits that exist where barriers to entry are low or nonexistent, monopoly profits can exist for a long time. Remember, however, that monopoly profits may be competed for and may disappear altogether if the monopoly market is contestable.

PROFIT AND LOSS AS SIGNALS

Too often, profit and loss are viewed in terms of the benefit or hurt they bring to particular persons. However, profit and loss also signal how a market may be changing.

When a firm earns a profit, entrepreneurs in other industries view this as a signal that the profit-earning firm is producing and selling a good that buyers value more than the factors that go to make the good. The profit causes entrepreneurs to move resources into the production of the particular good to which the profit is linked. In short, resources follow profit.

On the other hand, if a firm is taking a loss, this is a signal to the entrepreneur that the firm is producing and selling a good that buyers value less than the factors that go to make the good. The loss causes resources to move out of the production of the particular good to which the loss is linked. Resources turn away from losses.

THINKING LIKE AN ECONOMIST

Throughout history, interest, land rent, and profits have often been attacked. For example, Henry George (1839–1897), who wrote the influential book Progress and Poverty, *believed that all land rents were pure economic rents and should be heavily taxed. Landowners benefited simply because they had the good fortune to own land. In George's view, landowners did nothing productive. He maintained that the early owners of land in the American West reaped high land rents, not because they had made their land more productive, but because individuals from the East began to move West, driving up the price of land. In arguing for a heavy tax on land rents, George said there would be no supply response in land owing to the tax because land was in fixed supply.*

Profits have also frequently come under attack. High profits are somehow thought to be evidence of corruption or manipulation. Those who earn profits are sometimes considered no better than thieves.

The economist thinks of interest, land rent, and profits differently from many laypersons. The economist understands that all are returns to resources, or factors of production. Most people find it easy to understand that labor is a factor of production and that wages are the return to this factor. But understanding that land, capital, and entrepreneurship are also genuine factors of production with returns that flow to them seems to be more difficult.

Another point that is overlooked is that interest exists largely because individuals naturally have a positive rate of time preference. Those who dislike interest are in fact criticizing individuals because of a natural characteristic. If these critics could change this natural trait and make individuals not weight present consumption higher than future consumption, interest would diminish.

A similar point can be made about profit. Some say profit is the consequence of living in a world of uncertainty. If those who do not like profit could make the world less uncertain, or bring certainty to it, then profit would disappear.

Self-Test

1. What is the difference between risk and uncertainty?
2. Why does profit exist?
3. "Profit is not simply a dollar amount, it is a signal." Comment.

A Reader Asks...
Are There Calculators to Help Me Plan My Life?

Present value is discussed in this chapter, and I know that the World Wide Web has calculators available for finding present value. Are there other calculators available—especially ones that will help me plan my life?

People often have questions about the financial aspects of their life that they would like to answer. For example, you might want to know how much you have to save each month (beginning now) in order to have a million dollars by the time you retire. Or you might want to know what your mortgage payments will be if you put a $50,000 down payment on a house that sells for $200,000. Or perhaps you want to know what a million dollars will be worth 10 years from now if the annual inflation rate over this time period is 4 percent.

With this in mind, here are some specific questions (yours may be similar) and their answers, along with the location of the online calculators we used.

1. I am planning on taking out a $200,000 mortgage loan to buy a house. The term of the loan will be 30 years and the interest rate will be 7 percent. What will my monthly mortgage payment be? Answer: $1,330.60

    Go to *http://www.bloomberg.com/money/loan/mtge_calc .html*, then fill in the information for loan amount, number of years, and interest rate.

2. If I save $200 a month at 5 percent interest (compounded monthly), how much will I have in savings in 30 years? Answer: $166,451

    Go to *http://www.interest.com/hugh/calc/*, and click on "Simple Savings Calculator." Fill in the information requested.

    By the way, just adding another $100 a month increases the total to approximately $250,000.

3. I am 20 years old and plan to retire when I am 65. I currently have $5,000 in my savings account. If I reap an annual return of 6 percent, how much do I need to save each year in order to retire with a million dollars? Answer: $4,377

    Go to *http://www.bloomberg.com/money/tools/retire .html*, and fill in the information.

4. I have a young child who will start college in the year 2020. The college I would like for her to attend currently charges $20,000 tuition per year. If tuition inflation is 2 percent, a 5 percent return on savings is reasonable, and I am paying a 28 percent marginal tax rate, what dollar amount must I save each week to pay my child's tuition in the future? Answer: $76.18

    Go to *http://www.bloomberg.com/money/tools/education .html*, and fill in the information.

5. I'm thinking of quitting smoking. Currently, I smoke a pack a day. If I take the money I spend on cigarettes and instead save it at an annual 5 percent interest rate, what dollar amount will I have at the end of 10 years? Answer: If we assume a pack of cigarettes is $3, you will have $13,772.

    Go to *http://www.interest.com/hugh/calc/smoking.cgi*, and fill in the information.

6. I currently have a $200,000 mortgage loan (30 years) at 8 percent. My monthly payment is $1,467. If I want to pay off the loan in half the time (15 years instead of 30 years), what should I increase my monthly mortgage payment to? Answer: $1,916

    Go to *http://www.interest.com/hugh/calc/duration.cgi*, and fill in the information.

    In other words, if you voluntarily increase your payment by $449 a month, you will pay off your loan 15 years early. By the way, this will save you approximately $183,000 in interest.

Interest

- Interest refers to (1) the price paid by borrowers for loanable funds and (2) the return on capital in the production process. There is a tendency for these two to become equal.

- The equilibrium interest rate (in terms of the price for loanable funds) is determined by the demand for and supply of loanable funds. The supply of loanable funds comes from savers, people who consume less than their current incomes. The demand for loanable funds comes from the demand for consumption and investment loans.

- Consumers demand loanable funds because they have a positive rate of time preference; they prefer earlier availability of goods to later availability. Investors (or firms) demand loanable funds so they can finance roundabout methods of production.

- The nominal interest rate is the interest rate determined by the forces of supply and demand in the loanable funds market. It is the interest rate in current dollars. The real interest rate is the nominal interest rate adjusted for expected inflation. Specifically, real interest rate = nominal interest rate − expected inflation rate (which means nominal interest rate = real interest rate + expected inflation rate).

Rent

- Economic rent is a payment in excess of opportunity costs. A subset of this is pure economic rent, which is a payment in excess of opportunity costs when opportunity costs are zero. Historically, the term *pure economic rent* was used to describe the payment to the factor land because land (in total) was assumed to be fixed in supply (perfectly inelastic). Today, the terms *economic rent* and *pure economic rent* are also used when speaking about economic factors other than land.

- David Ricardo argued that high land rents were an effect of high grain prices, not a cause of them (in contrast to many of his contemporaries who thought high rents caused the high grain prices). Land rents are price determined, not price determining.

- The amount of economic rent a factor receives depends on the perspective from which the factor is viewed. For example, a university librarian earning $50,000 a year receives $2,000 economic rent if his next best alternative income at another university is $48,000. The economic rent is $10,000 if his next best alternative is in a nonuniversity (nonlibrarian) position that pays $40,000.

Profit

- Several different theories of profit address the question of the source of profit. One theory holds that profit would not exist in a world of certainty; hence, uncertainty is the source of profit. Another theory holds that profit is the return for alertness to arbitrage opportunities. A third theory holds that profit is the return to the entrepreneur as innovator.

- Taking the three profit theories together, we can say that profit is the return to entrepreneurship, where entrepreneurship entails bearing uncertainty, being alert to arbitrage opportunities, and being innovative.

Loanable Funds	Nominal Interest Rate	Economic Rent
Positive Rate of Time Preference	Real Interest Rate	Pure Economic Rent
Roundabout Method of Production	Present Value	

Economic facts, actions, and changes create ripples that move away from their point of origin. Eventually, these ripples can intersect your life and have an effect on you. Consider the following example.

Interest rates fall, causing the present value of capital goods to rise and business firms to buy more capital goods. An increase in capital goods leads to a rise in the marginal productivity of labor. An increase in the marginal productivity of labor increases the demand for labor. And an increase in the demand for labor increases the wage rate that you will receive. Thus, there is a connection between the level of interest and your wage rate—an economic connection to you.

Based on the material in this chapter, identify other ways in which economic facts, actions, and changes create ripples that eventually affect you.

Questions and Problems

1. What type of people are most willing to pay high interest rates?
2. Some people have argued that in a moneyless (or barter) economy, interest would not exist. Is this true? Explain your answer.
3. In what ways are a baseball star who can do nothing but play baseball and a parcel of land similar?
4. What is the overall economic function of profits?
5. "The more economic rent a person receives in his job, the less likely he is to leave the job and the more content he will be on the job." Do you agree or disagree? Explain your answer.
6. It has been said that a society with a high savings rate is a society with a high standard of living. What is the link (if any) between saving and a relatively high standard of living?
7. Make an attempt to calculate the present value of your future income.
8. Describe the effect of each of the following events on individuals' rate of time preference, and thus on interest rates: (a) a technological advance that increases longevity; (b) an increased threat of war; (c) growing older.
9. "As the interest rate falls, firms are more inclined to buy capital goods." Do you agree or disagree? Explain your answer.

Working with Numbers and Graphs

1. Compute the following:
   a. The present value of $25,000 each year for 4 years at a 7 percent interest rate.
   b. The present value of $152,000 each year for 5 years at a 6 percent interest rate.
   c. The present value of $60,000 each year for 10 years at a 6.5 percent interest rate.
2. Bobby is a baseball player who earns $1 million a year playing for team X. If he weren't playing baseball for team X, he would be playing baseball for team Y and earning $800,000 a year. If he weren't playing baseball at all, he would be working as an accountant earning $120,000 a year. What is his economic rent as a baseball player playing for team X? What is his economic rent as a baseball player?
3. Diagrammatically represent pure economic rent.

Internet Activities

1. Go to *http://research.stlouisfed.org/fred*, and select "Interest Rates." For 1972.01, 1982.01, and 1992.01, identify each of the following: (a) Bank Prime Loan Rate, (b) 3-Month Treasury Bill—Auction Average, (c) 30-Year Treasury Constant Maturity Rate, and (d) 30-Year Conventional Mortgage Rate. Do the four interest rates rise and fall together? Are some interest rates always higher than other interest rates? If so, explain why. Would it matter which of the four interest rates you used to calculate the real interest rate?

Log on to the Arnold Xtra! Web site now (*http://arnoldxtra.swcollege.com*) for additional learning resources such as practice quizzes, help with graphing, video clips, and current event applications.

ch.17

MARKET FAILURE:
EXTERNALITIES, PUBLIC GOODS, AND
ASYMMETRIC INFORMATION

Market failure is a situation in which the market does not provide the ideal or optimal amount of a particular good. Economists want to know under what conditions market failure may occur. For example, consider a commercial airplane whose flight pattern takes it over a residential neighborhood. The airline is producing flights for its customers, but the people who live in the homes under the flight path are bothered by excessive noise. Does it follow that the market fails in this situation? Are there "too many" airline flights? This chapter's analysis of market failures provides answers to these and other thorny questions.

Chapter Road Map

Markets are a major topic of this book. We have analyzed how markets work, beginning with the simple supply-and-demand model. We have also examined various market structures—perfect competition, monopoly, and so on. As you know, goods and services are produced in markets. For example, cars are produced in car markets, houses are produced in housing markets, and computers are produced in computer markets. We now ask, Do these markets produce the "right amount" (optimal or ideal amount) of these various goods, and what does the "right amount" mean? For example, what is the "right amount" of houses to produce, and does the housing market actually produce this right amount?

When markets produce more or less than the right amount (yet to be defined), there is said to be market failure. This chapter discusses three topics in which market failure is a prominent part of the discussion: externalities, public goods, and asymmetric information.

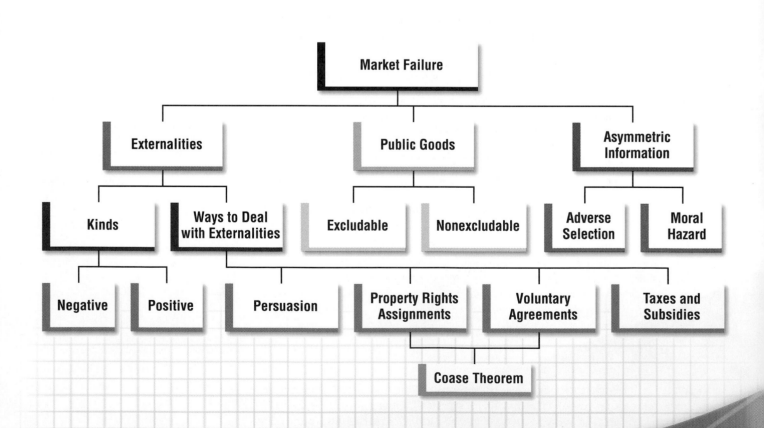

EXTERNALITIES

Sometimes, when goods are produced and consumed, side effects (spillover or third-party effects) occur that are felt by people who are not directly involved in the market exchanges. In general, these side effects are called **externalities** because the costs or benefits are external to the person(s) who caused them. Externalities may be negative or positive.

COSTS AND BENEFITS: PRIVATE AND EXTERNAL

Most activities in life have both costs and benefits. For example, when Jimmy sits downs to read a book, this activity has some benefits for Jimmy and some costs. These benefits and costs are private to him—they only affect him—hence, we call them *private benefits* and *private costs*.

Can Jimmy undertake some activity that has benefits and costs not only for him but also for others? Suppose Jimmy decides to smoke a cigarette in the general vicinity of Angelica. For Jimmy, there are both benefits and costs to smoking a cigarette—his private benefits and costs. But might Jimmy's smoking also affect Angelica in some way?

Suppose Angelica doesn't like the smell of cigarette smoke and develops a cough when she is around it. In this case, Jimmy's smoking might impose a cost on Angelica. Because the cost Jimmy imposes on Angelica is external to him, we call it an *external cost*. Stated differently, we might say that Jimmy's activity imposes a *negative externality* on Angelica, for which she incurs an external cost. A **negative externality** exists when a person's or group's actions cause a cost (or adverse side effect) to be felt by others.

Now let's consider a slightly different example. Suppose Jimmy lives across the street from Yvonne and beautifies his front yard (which Yvonne can clearly see from her house) by planting trees, flowers, and a new lawn. Obviously, Jimmy receives some benefits and costs by beautifying his yard, but might Yvonne receive some benefits too? Might Yvonne benefit when Jimmy beautifies his yard? Not only does she have a pretty yard to gaze at (in much the same way that someone might benefit by gazing at a beautiful painting), but Jimmy's beautification efforts may raise the market value of Yvonne's property.

Because the benefit that Jimmy generates for Yvonne is external to him, we call it an *external benefit*. Stated differently, we might say that Jimmy's activity generates a *positive externality* for Yvonne, for which she receives an external benefit. A **positive externality** exists when a person's or group's actions cause a benefit (or beneficial side effect) to be felt by others.

MARGINAL COSTS AND BENEFITS: BOTH PRIVATE AND EXTERNAL

When considering activities for which there are different degrees or amounts of costs and benefits (Does Jimmy smoke one cigarette an hour or two? Does Jimmy plant three trees or four?), it makes sense to speak in terms of marginal benefits and costs. More specifically, for Jimmy there are marginal private benefits (MPB) and marginal private costs (MPC) to various activities. If Jimmy's activities generate external benefits or costs for others, then it makes sense to speak in terms of marginal external benefits (MEB) and marginal external costs (MEC).

Because we want to know the total marginal costs and benefits, we sum these various benefits and costs. The sum of marginal private costs (MPC) and marginal external costs (MEC) is **marginal social costs (MSC).**

$$MSC = MPC + MEC$$

To illustrate, let's return to our example of Jimmy smoking a cigarette and imposing an external cost on Angelica. Suppose Jimmy's MPC of smoking a cigarette is $1 and Angelica's MEC of Jimmy smoking a cigarette is $2; it follows, then, that

Market Failure
A situation in which the market does not provide the ideal or optimal amount of a particular good.

Externality
A side effect of an action that affects the well-being of third parties.

Negative Externality
Exists when a person's or group's actions cause a cost (adverse side effect) to be felt by others.

Positive Externality
Exists when a person's or group's actions cause a benefit (beneficial side effect) to be felt by others.

Marginal Social Costs (MSC)
The sum of marginal private costs (MPC) and marginal external costs (MEC). $MSC = MPC + MEC$.

Marginal Social Benefits (*MSB*)
The sum of marginal private benefits (*MPB*) and marginal external benefits (*MEB*). *MSB* = *MPB* + *MEB*.

Socially Optimal Amount (Output)
An amount that takes into account and adjusts for all benefits (external and private) and all costs (external and private). The socially optimal amount is the amount at which *MSB* = *MSC*. Sometimes, the socially optimal amount is referred to as the efficient amount.

the *MSC* of Jimmy smoking a cigarette (taking into account both Jimmy's private costs and Angelica's external costs) is $3.

The sum of marginal private benefits (*MPB*) and marginal external benefits (*MEB*) is **marginal social benefits (*MSB*).**

$$MSB = MPB + MEB$$

To illustrate, let's return to our example of Jimmy beautifying his yard and causing an external benefit for Yvonne. Suppose Jimmy's *MPB* of beautifying his yard is $5 and Yvonne's *MEB* of Jimmy beautifying his yard is $3; it follows, then, that the *MSB* of Jimmy beautifying his yard (at a given level of beautification) is $8.

SOCIAL OPTIMALITY OR EFFICIENCY CONDITIONS

For an economist, there is always a right amount of something. There is a right amount of time to study for a test, a right amount of exercise, a right number of cars to be produced—there is even a right amount of pollution (as you will learn later in this chapter). The "right amount," for an economist, is the **socially optimal amount (output),** or the efficient amount (output).

But what is the socially optimal amount, or efficient amount? It is the amount at which a particular condition is met: *MSB* = *MSC*. In other words, the right amount of anything is the amount at which the *MSB* (of that thing) equals the *MSC* (of that thing). Later in this section, we illustrate this condition graphically.

THREE CATEGORIES

For the person who engages in an activity (whether producing a computer or studying for an exam), there are almost always benefits and costs. In other words, it is hard to think of any activities in life in which private benefits and private costs do not exist.

It is not so hard, however, to think of activities in life in which external benefits and external costs do not exist. For example, again consider reading a book. The person reading the book incurs benefits and costs, but probably no one else does. We can characterize this activity the following way: *MPB* > 0, *MPC* > 0, *MEB* = 0, *MEC* = 0. In other words, both marginal private benefits and costs are positive (greater than zero), but there are no marginal external benefits or costs. Another way of saying this is that there are no positive or negative externalities.

In other words, activities may be categorized according to whether negative or positive externalities exist, as shown in the following table.[1]

Category	Definition	Meaning in Terms of Marginal Benefits and Costs
1	No negative or positive externality	*MEC* = 0 and *MEB* = 0; it follows that *MSC* = *MPC* and *MSB* = *MPB*
2	Negative externality but no positive externality	*MEC* > 0 and *MEB* = 0; it follows that *MSC* > *MPC* and *MSB* = *MPB*
3	Positive externality but no negative externality	*MEB* > 0 and *MEC* = 0; it follows that *MSB* > *MPB* and *MSC* = *MPC*

EXTERNALITIES IN CONSUMPTION AND IN PRODUCTION

Externalities can arise because someone consumes something that has an external benefit or cost for others or because someone produces something that has an external benefit or cost for others. To illustrate, consider two examples. Sup-

---

1. Theoretically, there is a fourth category—where both a positive externality and a negative externality exist—but one would reasonably assume that this category has little, if any, practical relevance. For example, suppose Jimmy smokes a cigarette and cigarette smoke is a negative externality for Angelica but a positive externality for Bobby. It is possible that what is a "bad" for Angelica is a "good" for Bobby, but little is added to the discussion (at this time) of discussing such cases.

pose Barbara plays the radio in her car loudly, adversely affecting those drivers around her at the stoplight. Here Barbara is "consuming" music and creating a negative externality for others.

Now consider John, who produces cars in his factory. As a result of the production process, he emits some pollution into the air that adversely affects some people who live downwind from the factory. Here we have a negative externality that is the result of John producing a good.

DIAGRAM OF A NEGATIVE EXTERNALITY

Exhibit 1 shows the downward-sloping demand curve, D, for some good. (The demand curve represents the marginal private benefits received by the buyers of the good, so it is the same as the MPB curve. Because there are no positive externalities in this case, it follows that $MPB = MSB$. So the demand curve is also the MSB curve). The supply curve, S, represents the marginal private costs of the producers of the good. Equilibrium in this market setting is at E_1; Q_1 is the output—specifically, the market output.

Now assume that negative externalities arise as a result of the production of the good. (For example, suppose the good happens to be cars that are produced in a factory and, as a result of producing the cars, some air pollution results.) The marginal external costs that are linked to the negative externalities are taken into account by adding them (as best we can) to the marginal private costs. The result is the marginal social cost (MSC) curve shown in Exhibit 1. If all costs are taken into account (both external costs and private costs), equilibrium is at E_2 at the quantity Q_2. This, as we state earlier, is referred to as the socially optimal output (or efficient output).

Notice that the market output (Q_1) is greater than the socially optimal output (Q_2) when negative externalities exist. The market is said to "fail" (hence, market failure) because it *overproduces* the good connected with the negative externality. The triangle in Exhibit 1 is the visible manifestation of the market failure. It is the net social cost of producing the market output (Q_1) instead of the socially optimal output (Q_2), or of moving from the socially optimal output to the market output.

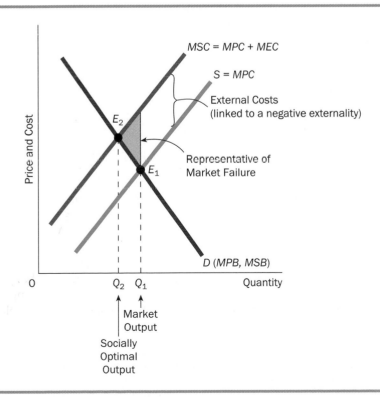

exhibit 1

The Negative Externality Case
Because of a negative externality, marginal social costs (MSC) are greater than marginal private costs (MPC) and the market output is greater than the socially optimal output. The market is said to fail in that it overproduces the good.

![Q & A]

Q: How exactly does the triangle in Exhibit 1 represent the net social cost of moving from the socially optimal output to the market output?

A: Look at Exhibit 2, where Q_2 is the socially optimal output and Q_1 is the market output. If "society" moves from Q_2 to Q_1, who specifically benefits and how do we represent these benefits? Buyers benefit (they are a part of society) because they will be able to buy more output at prices they are willing to pay. Thus, the area under the demand curve between Q_2 and Q_1 represents the benefits of moving from Q_2 to Q_1 (see the shaded area in Window 1 of Exhibit 2).

Next we ask, If society moves from Q_2 to Q_1, how can we illustrate the costs that are incurred? Both sellers and third parties incur costs. Sellers incur private costs and third parties incur external costs. The area under S only takes into account part of society—sellers— and ignores third parties. The area under the MSC curve between Q_2 and Q_1 represents the full costs of moving from Q_2 to Q_1 (see the shaded area in Window 2).

The shaded area in Window 2 is larger than the shaded area in Window 1, so the costs to sellers and third parties of moving from Q_2 to Q_1 outweigh the benefits to buyers of moving from Q_2 to Q_1. The difference between the shaded areas is the triangle shown in the main diagram. Thus, costs outweigh benefits by the triangle. In short, the triangle in this example represents the net social cost of moving from Q_2 to Q_1, or of producing Q_1 instead of Q_2.

THINKING LIKE AN ECONOMIST

Economists prefer to look at the complete picture instead only part of it. If there are both private costs and external costs, then economists will consider both—not just one or the other. Similarly, if there are both private benefits and external benefits, economists will consider both.

---

exhibit 2

The Triangle
Q_2 is the socially optimal output; Q_1 is the market output. If society moves from Q_2 to Q_1, buyers benefit by an amount represented by the shaded area in Window 1; but sellers and third parties together incur greater costs, represented by the shaded area in Window 2. The triangle (the difference between the two shaded areas) represents the net social cost to society of moving from Q_2 to Q_1, or of producing Q_1 instead of Q_2.

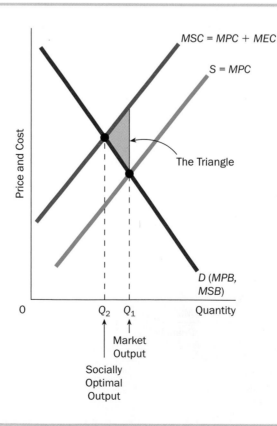

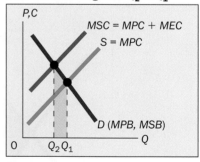

Window 1
Benefits of moving from Q_2 to Q_1

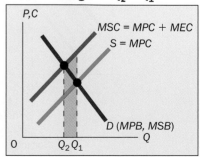

Window 2
Costs of moving from Q_2 to Q_1

422 Part 5 *Market Failure and Public Choice*

DIAGRAM OF A POSITIVE EXTERNALITY

Exhibit 3 shows the downward-sloping demand curve, D, for some good. (As earlier, the demand curve represents the marginal private benefits received by the buyers of the good, so it is the same as the MPB curve). The supply curve, S, represents the marginal private costs of the producers of the good. (The marginal social costs are the same as the marginal private costs—$MPC = MSC$—because there are no negative externalities in this case.) Equilibrium in this market setting is at E_1; Q_1 is the output—specifically, the market output.

Now assume that positive externalities arise as a result of the production of the good. (Suppose Erica is a beekeeper who produces honey. Erica lives near an apple orchard and her bees occasionally fly over to the orchard and pollinate the blossoms, in the process making the orchard more productive. Doesn't the orchard owner benefit from Erica's bees?) The marginal external benefits that are linked to the positive externality are taken into account by adding them (as best we can) to the marginal private benefits. The result is the marginal social benefit (MSB) curve shown in Exhibit 3. If all benefits are taken into account (both external benefits and private benefits), equilibrium is at E_2 at the quantity Q_2. This, as we state earlier, is referred to as the socially optimal output (or efficient output).

Notice that the market output (Q_1) is less than the socially optimal output (Q_2) when positive externalities exist (just the opposite was the case when negative externalities existed). The market is said to "fail" (hence, market failure) because it *underproduces* the good connected with the positive externality. The triangle in Exhibit 3 is the visible manifestation of the market failure. It is the net social benefit *that is lost* by producing the market output (Q_1) instead of the socially optimal output (Q_2). Stated differently, at the socially optimal output (Q_2), society realizes grater benefits than at the market output (Q_1). So by being at Q_1, society loses out on some net benefits it could obtain if it were at Q_2.

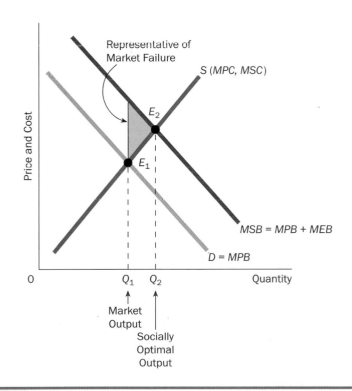

exhibit 3

The Positive Externality Case
Because of a positive externality, marginal social benefits (MSB) are greater than marginal private benefits (MPB) and the market output is less than the socially optimal output. The market is said to fail in that it underproduces the good.

Q&A

Q: Is it the case that the market output (the output at market equilibrium) always occurs where the supply and demand curves intersect and that the socially optimal output always occurs where $MSB = MSC$?

A: Yes. Think of it this way: Other names for supply and demand are MPC and MPB, respectively. In other words, the supply curve is the MPC curve and the demand curve is the MPB curve.

Now market participants—buyers and sellers—care about their costs and benefits. In other words, they care about their *private* costs and benefits. Market equilibrium is where these two parties consider their costs and benefits and nothing else.

However, sometimes costs and benefits exist that market participants (buyers and sellers) do not take into account. In other words, sometimes external costs and benefits exist that buyers and sellers do not care about. When these external costs and benefits exist, then the output at market equilibrium may be different than the socially optimal output (where all benefits and costs are considered, not only the private ones).

Q&A

Q: Under what condition will the market output and the socially optimal output be the same?

A: Under the condition that there are neither negative nor positive externalities. In this case, both MEC and MEB equal zero, so that $MSB = MPB$ and $MSC = MPC$. Obviously, the market output ($MPB = MPC$) is the same here as the socially optimal output ($MSB = MSC$) because $MSB = MPB$ and $MSC = MPC$.

THINKING LIKE AN ECONOMIST

From what we have said so far, it may be natural to conclude that the economist prefers the socially optimal output (where all benefits and costs are taken into account) to the market output (where only private benefits and costs are taken into account). But this is not necessarily true. An economist prefers the socially optimal output to the market output (assuming they are different) only when the benefits of moving from the market output to the socially optimal output are greater than the costs.

To illustrate, suppose $400 in benefits exists if we move from the market output to the socially optimal output, but the costs of making the move are $1,000. According to an economist, it wouldn't be worth trying to make the adjustment.

Self-Test *(Answers to Self-Test questions are in the Self-Test Appendix.)*

1. What is the major difference between the market output and the socially optimal output?

2. For an economist, is the socially optimal output preferred to the market output?

INTERNALIZING EXTERNALITIES

Internalizing Externalities
An externality is internalized if the persons or group that generated the externality incorporate into their own private or internal cost-benefit calculations the external benefits (in the case of a positive externality) or the external costs (in the case of a negative externality) that third parties bear.

An externality is **internalized** if the persons or group that generated the externality incorporate into their own private or *internal* cost-benefit calculations the external benefits (in the case of a positive externality) or the external costs (in the case of a negative externality) that third parties bear. Simply put, internalizing externalities is the same as adjusting for externalities. An externality has been internalized or adjusted for *completely* if, as a result, the socially optimal output emerges. A few of the numerous ways to adjust for, or internalize, externalities are presented in this section.

✕ PERSUASION

Many negative externalities arise partly because persons or groups do not consider other individuals when they decide to undertake an action. Consider the person who plays his CD player loudly at three o'clock in the morning. Perhaps if he considered the external cost his action imposes on his neighbors, he either would not play the CD player at all or would play it at low volume.

Trying to persuade those who impose external costs on us to adjust their behavior to take these costs into account is one way to make the imposers adjust for—or internalize—externalities. In today's world, such slogans as "Don't Drink and Drive" and "Don't Litter" are attempts to persuade individuals to take into account the fact that their actions affect others. The golden rule of ethical conduct, "Do unto others as you would have them do unto you," makes the same point.

TAXES AND SUBSIDIES

Taxes and subsidies are sometimes used as corrective devices for a market failure. A tax adjusts for a negative externality, a subsidy adjusts for a positive externality.

Consider the negative externality case in Exhibit 1. The objective of the corrective tax is to move the supply curve from S to the MSC curve (recall from earlier chapters that a tax can shift a supply curve), and therefore move from the market determined output, Q_1, to the socially optimal output, Q_2.

In the case of a positive externality, illustrated in Exhibit 3, the objective is to subsidize the demand side of the market so that the demand curve moves from D to the MSB curve and output moves from Q_1 to the socially optimal output, Q_2.

However, taxes and subsidies also involve costs and consequences. For example, suppose, as illustrated in Exhibit 4, government misjudges the external costs when it imposes a tax on the supplier of a good. Instead of the supply curve

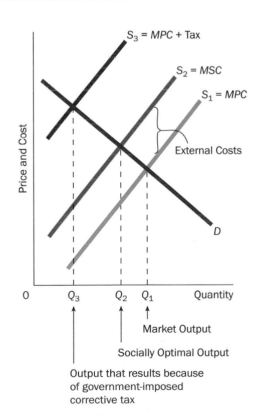

exhibit 4

A Corrective Tax Gone Wrong
Government may miscalculate external costs and impose a tax that moves the supply curve from S_1 to S_3 instead of from S_1 to S_2. As a result, the output level will be farther away from the socially optimal output than before the "corrective" tax was applied. Q_3 is farther away from Q_2 than Q_1 is from Q_2.

moving from S_1 to S_2 (the *MSC* curve), it moves from S_1 to S_3. As a result, the output level will be farther away from the socially optimal output than it was before the "corrective" tax was applied.

ASSIGNING PROPERTY RIGHTS

Consider the idea that air pollution and ocean pollution—both of which are examples of negative externalities—are the result of the air and oceans being unowned. No one owns the air, no one owns the oceans, and because no one does, many individuals feel free to emit wastes into them. If private property, or ownership, rights in air and oceans could be established, the negative externalities would likely become much less. If someone owns a resource, then actions that damage it have a price; namely, the resource owner can sue for damages.

For example, in the early West when grazing lands were open and unowned (common property), many cattle ranchers allowed their herds to overgraze. The reason for this was simple. No one owned the land, so no one could stop the overgrazing to preserve the value of the land. Even if one rancher decided not to allow his herd to graze, this simply meant there was more grazing land for other ranchers. As a consequence of overgrazing, a future generation inherited barren, wasted land. From the point of view of future generations, the cattle ranchers who allowed their herds to overgraze were generating negative externalities.

What would have happened if the western lands had been privately owned? In this case, there would not have been any overgrazing because the monetary interests of the owner of the land would not have permitted it. The landowner would have charged ranchers a fee to graze their cattle, and more grazing would have entailed additional fees. There would have been less grazing at a positive fee than at a zero fee (the case when the lands were open and unowned). The externalities would have been internalized.

Q & A

Q: In the example of grazing lands, assigning private property rights, or establishing ownership rights to unowned land, would have lessened the externality problem. Establishing ownership rights in land is possible, but how can this be done with the air and oceans? For example, the person who plays his CD player loudly at three o'clock in the morning would generate less of a negative externality (or none at all) if Amy Cohan, who lives next door, owned the air over her property. Then, she could charge him a fee for sending loud music through her air. By putting a price on his behavior, the externalities would be internalized. But is it possible to assign property rights in air?

A: It is very difficult and costly to establish ownership rights in air. Consequently, assigning property rights is not likely to be the method chosen to deal with externalities that arise as a consequence of unowned air or oceans. There are other ways of dealing with the problem, however.

VOLUNTARY AGREEMENTS

Externalities can sometimes be internalized through individual voluntary agreements. Consider two persons, Pete and Sean, living on a tiny deserted island. Pete and Sean have agreed between themselves that Pete owns the northern part of the island and Sean owns the southern part. Pete occasionally plays his drums in the morning, and the sound awakens Sean. Pete and Sean have a negative externality problem. Pete wants to be free to play his drums in the morning, and Sean would like to continue to sleep.

Suppose that Sean values his sleep in the morning by a maximum of 6 oranges—he would give up 6 oranges to be able to sleep without Pete playing his drums. On the other hand, Pete values drum playing in the morning by 3 oranges—he would give up a maximum of 3 oranges to be able to play his drums in the morning. Because Sean values his sleep by more than Pete values playing his drums, they have an opportunity to strike a deal. Sean can offer Pete some number of oranges greater than 3, but less than 6, to refrain from playing his drums in the morning. The deal will make both Pete and Sean better off.

In this example, the negative externality problem is successfully addressed through the individuals voluntarily entering into an agreement. The condition for this output is that the *transaction costs,* or costs associated with making and reaching the agreement, must be low relative to the expected benefits of the agreement.

COMBINING PROPERTY RIGHTS ASSIGNMENTS AND VOLUNTARY AGREEMENTS

The last two ways of internalizing externalities—property rights assignments and voluntary agreements—can be combined, as in the following example.[2] Suppose a rancher's cattle occasionally stray onto the adjacent farm and damage (or eat) some of the farmer's crops. The court assigns liability to the cattle rancher and orders him to prevent his cattle from straying, so a property rights assignment solves the externality problem. As a result, the rancher puts up a strong fence to prevent his cattle from damaging his neighbor's crops.

But, the court's property rights assignment may be undone by the farmer and the cattle rancher if they find it in their mutual interest to do so. Suppose the rancher is willing to pay $100 a month to the farmer for permission to allow his cattle to stray onto the farmer's land, and the farmer is willing to give permission for $70 a month. Assuming trivial or zero transaction costs, the farmer and the rancher will undo the court's property rights assignment. For a payment of $70 or more a month, the farmer will allow the rancher's cattle to stray onto his land.

X Coase Theorem

Suppose in our example, that the court, instead of assigning liability to the cattle rancher, had given him the property right to allow his cattle to stray. What would the resource allocative outcome have been in this case? With this (opposite) property rights assignment, the cattle would have been allowed to stray (which was exactly the outcome of the previous property rights assignment after the cattle rancher and farmer voluntarily agreed to undo it). We conclude that *in the case of trivial or zero transaction costs, the property rights assignment does not matter to the resource allocative outcome.* In a nutshell, this is the **Coase theorem.**

The Coase theorem can be expressed in other ways, two of which we mention here: (1) In the case of trivial or zero transaction costs, a property rights assignment will be undone (exchanged) if it benefits the relevant parties to undo it. (2) In the case of trivial or zero transaction costs, the resource allocative outcome will be the same no matter who is assigned the property right.

The Coase theorem is significant for two reasons: (1) It shows that under certain conditions the market can internalize externalities. (2) It provides a benchmark for analyzing externality problems—that is, it shows what will happen if transaction costs are trivial or zero.

Coase Theorem
In the case of trivial or zero transaction costs, the property rights assignment does not matter to the resource allocative outcome.

X Pigou versus Coase

The first editor of the *Journal of Law and Economics* was Aaron Director. In 1959, Director published an article by Ronald Coase entitled "The Federal Communications Commission." In the article, Coase took issue with economist A. C. Pigou, a trailblazer in the area of externalities and market failure, who had argued that government should use taxes and subsidies to adjust for negative and positive externalities, respectively. Coase argued that in the case of negative externalities, it is not clear that the state should tax the person imposing the negative externality. First, Coase stressed the reciprocal nature of externalities, pointing out that it takes two to make a negative externality (it is not always clear who is harming

---

2. See Ronald Coase, "The Problem of Social Cost," *Journal of Law and Economics* 3 (October 1960): 1–44.

Software, Switching Costs and Benefits, and Market Failure

Let's consider a series of events that some economists believe are occurring today. A company produces a good, say software X. It finds that its major costs of producing the software are "up front"—at the research and development stage. After it has produced one copy of the software program, it is relatively cheap to produce each additional copy. The company sells software X at a price that is likely to generate a large number of sales. As some people buy the software program, additional people find it worth buying because the good is important in terms of "networking" with others. (For example, if some people use the spreadsheet Excel, you may choose Excel as your spreadsheet.) Because of its "network externalities," good X becomes widely used in the industry. At some point, the good simply dominates the market. For example, it may have 90 percent of market sales.

At this point, some economists ask, "Is good X the best product, or is it inferior to the substitutes that exist for it?" For example, if softwares Y and Z are substitutes for X, is X superior to both Y and Z or is either Y or Z superior to X? A real-world example illustrates our point. Both Beta and VHS formats for VCRs came out at about the same time. VHS initially sold better than Beta, although Beta was a strong competitor. At some point, the higher percentage of VHS users in the market (relative to Beta users) seemed to matter to people who were considering buying a VCR. "Why not buy a VHS format?" they thought. "That way videotapes can be shared with more people." At this

point, the sales of VHS began to explode and before long, very few people were buying Beta. Some of the initial buyers of the Beta format even switched over to the VHS format.

In the race between VHS and Beta, VHS has won, not necessarily because it is superior to Beta, but simply because it got an early lead in the race. If network externalities are present, the early lead may be the only lead that is necessary to win the race for customers' dollars.

Some economists conclude that if it is only the early lead that counts and not the quality of the product, then it is possible for an inferior product that gets an early lead to outsell a superior product that doesn't get an early lead. To go back to our software example, if X outcompetes Y and Z not because it is superior but because it gets an early lead in the software market, then there is the possibility that the market has "chosen" the inferior product. Stated differently, there is market failure in the sense that the market has failed to choose a superior product over an inferior product.

But not all economists agree with this analysis. Some economists say that in order to justify market failure, it is not sufficient to have the market choose an inferior product over a superior product. There must also be net benefits to switching (from the inferior to the superior product) that are not being acted upon by market participants. To illustrate, suppose the market has chosen good X and that it is inferior to good Y. Furthermore, suppose the benefits of switching from X to Y are $30 and the costs of switching are $45. In this case, even if the market stays with good X, there is no market failure because it is not worth switching to the superior product. The market fails, argue these economists, only if the benefits of switching are, say, $30 and the costs are $10 (and therefore there are net benefits to switching)—yet the market doesn't switch. In short, when the benefits and costs of switching are considered, what may initially look like a market failure may turn out not to be.

whom). Second, Coase proposed a market solution to externality problems that was not implicit in Pigou's work.

Aaron Director and others believed that Coase was wrong and Pigou was right. Coase, who was teaching at the University of Virginia at the time, was invited to discuss his thesis with Director and a handful of well-known economists. The group included Martin Bailey, Milton Friedman, Arnold Harberger, Reuben Kessel, Gregg Lewis, John McGee, Lloyd Mints, George Stigler, and, of course, Director.

The group met at Aaron Director's house one night. Before Coase began to outline his thesis, the group took a vote and found that everyone (with the exception of Coase) sided with Pigou. Then the sparks began to fly. Friedman, it is reported, "opened fire" on Coase. Coase answered the intellectual attacks of his colleagues. At the end of the debate, another vote was taken. Everyone sided with Coase against Pigou. It is reported that as the members of the group left Director's home that night, they said to one another that they had witnessed history in the making. The Coase theorem had taken hold in economics.

BEYOND INTERNALIZING: SETTING REGULATIONS

One way to deal with externalities, in particular with negative externalities, is for government to apply regulations directly to the activities that generate the externalities. For example, factories producing goods also produce smoke that rises up through smokestacks. The smoke is often seen as a negative externality. Government may decide that the factory must install pollution-reducing equipment or that it can emit only a certain amount of smoke into the air per day or that it must move to a less populated area.

Critics of this approach often note that regulations, once instituted, are difficult to remove even if conditions warrant removal. Also, regulations are often applied across the board when circumstances dictate otherwise. For example, factories in relatively pollution-free cities might be required to install the same pollution control equipment as factories in smoggy, pollution-ridden cities.

Finally, regulation entails costs. If government imposes regulations, there must be regulators (whose salaries must be paid), offices (to house the regulators), word processors (to produce the regulations), and more. As previously noted, dealing with externalities successfully may offer benefits, but the costs need to be considered as well.

Q & A   **Q:** Is there any one best way of dealing with externalities? It is not clear whether it is better to use persuasion or to use, say, taxes and subsidies.

A: Almost all economists would agree that some methods of dealing with externalities are more effective in some situations than in others. For example, if the smoke from Vincent's neighbor's barbecue comes into his yard and bothers him, it is unlikely that any economist would think this negative externality situation warrants direct government involvement in the form of regulations or taxes. In this case, persuasion may be the best way to proceed. In the case of a factory emitting smoke into the air, however, persuasion might not be effective. Nor might voluntary agreements because the transaction costs of entering into an agreement would very likely be high (getting together all or most persons affected by the factory's smoke is difficult, for example). In this case, the inclination to propose taxes or regulations would be strong.

Self-Test

1. What does it mean to *internalize* an externality?
2. Are the transaction costs of buying a house higher or lower than the transaction costs of buying a hamburger at a fast-food restaurant? Explain your answer.
3. Does the property rights assignment a court makes matter to the resource allocative outcome?
4. What condition must be satisfied for a corrective tax to correctly adjust for a negative externality?

DEALING WITH A NEGATIVE EXTERNALITY IN THE ENVIRONMENT

The environment has become a major economic, political, and social issue. Environmental problems are manifold and include acid rain, the greenhouse effect, deforestation (including the destruction of the rain forests), solid waste (garbage) disposal, water pollution, air pollution, and many more. This section principally discusses air pollution.

Economists make three principal points about pollution. First, it is a negative externality. Second, and perhaps counterintuitively, no pollution is sometimes worse than some pollution. Third, the market can be used to deal with the problem of pollution.

IS NO POLLUTION WORSE THAN SOME POLLUTION?

When might some pollution be preferred to no pollution? The answer is, when all other things are not held constant—in short, most of the time.

Certainly, if all other things are held constant, less pollution is preferred to more pollution and, therefore, no pollution is preferred to some pollution. But the world would be different with no pollution—and not only because it would have cleaner air, rivers, and oceans. Pollution is a by-product of the production of many goods and services. For example, it is unlikely that steel could be produced without some pollution as a by-product. Given the current state of pollution technology, less pollution from steel production means less steel and fewer products made from steel.

Pollution is also a by-product of many of the goods we use daily, including our cars. We could certainly end the pollution caused by cars tomorrow, but to do so, we would have to give up driving cars. Are there any benefits to driving cars? If there are, then perhaps we wouldn't choose zero pollution. In short, zero pollution is not preferable to some positive amount of pollution when we realize that goods and services must be forfeited to have less pollution.

The same conclusion can be reached through Coasian-type analysis. Suppose there are two groups, polluters and nonpolluters. For certain units of pollution, the value of polluting to polluters might be greater than the value of a less-polluted environment to nonpolluters. In the presence of trivial or zero transaction costs, a deal will be struck. The outcome will be characterized by some positive amount of pollution.

TWO METHODS TO REDUCE AIR POLLUTION

One of the biggest movements of the early 1990s was market environmentalism: the use of market forces to clean up the environment. This was the idea behind the Clean Air Act amendments, which President Bush signed into law in November 1990. The amendments lowered the maximum allowable sulfur dioxide emissions (the major factor in acid rain) for 111 utilities, but gave the utilities the right to trade permits for sulfur dioxide emissions. In other words, the amendments to the Clean Air Act make it possible for the utilities to buy and sell the right to pollute.

"To buy and sell the right to pollute" may sound odd to people accustomed to thinking about dealing with pollution through government regulations or standards. Let's consider two methods of reducing pollution. In method 1, the government sets pollution standards. In method 2, the government allocates pollution permits and allows them to be traded.

Method 1: Government Sets Pollution Standards

Suppose three firms, *X, Y,* and *Z,* are located in the same area. Currently, each firm is spewing three units of pollution into the area under consideration, for a total of nine pollution units. The government wants to reduce the total pollution in the area to three units and, to accomplish this objective, sets pollution standards (or regulations) stating that each firm must reduce its pollution by two units.

Exhibit 5 shows the respective cost of eliminating each unit of pollution for the three firms. The costs are different because eliminating pollution is more difficult for some kinds of firms than for others. For example, the pollution that an

http://

Go to *http://www.unep.org/GEO/*. Under "News and Highlights," select the most recent press release regarding "The State of the Environment: Past, Present, Future?" According to the United Nations, is the environment improving? What choices do we have for the future?

exhibit 5

	Firm X	Firm Y	Firm Z
Cost of Eliminating:			
First unit of pollution	$ 50	$ 70	$ 500
Second unit of pollution	75	85	1,000
Third unit of pollution	100	200	2,000

The Cost of Reducing Pollution for Three Firms
These are hypothetical data showing the cost of reducing pollution for three firms. The text shows that it is cheaper to reduce pollution through market environmentalism than through government standards or regulations.

automobile manufacturer produces might be more costly to eliminate than the pollution a clothing manufacturer produces. Stated differently, we assume that the three firms eliminate pollution by installing antipollution devices in their factories, and the cost of the antipollution devices may be much higher for an automobile manufacturer than for a clothing manufacturer.

The cost to firm X of eliminating its first two units is $125 ($50 + $75 = $125); the cost to firm Y of eliminating its first two units is $155; and the cost to firm Z of eliminating its first two units is $1,500. Thus, the total cost of eliminating six units of pollution is $1,780 ($125 + $155 + $1,500).

$$\frac{\text{Total cost of eliminating six units of pollution}}{\text{through standards or regulations}} = \$1,780$$

Method 2: Market Environmentalism at Work: Government Allocates Pollution Permits and Then Allows Them to Be Bought and Sold

The objective of the government is still to reduce the pollution in the area of firms X, Y, and Z from nine units to three units, but this time the government issues one pollution permit (sometimes these permits are called allowances or credits) to each firm. The government tells each firm that it can emit one unit of pollution for each permit it has in its possession. Furthermore, the firms are allowed to buy and sell these permits.

Look at the situation from the perspective of firm X. It has one pollution permit in its possession, so it can emit one unit of pollution and must eliminate the other two units of pollution. But firm X does not have to keep its pollution permit and emit one unit of pollution. Instead, firm X can sell its permit. If it does so, the firm can emit no pollution. Might firm X be better off selling the permit and eliminating all three units of pollution?

Firm Y is in the same situation as firm X. This firm also has only one permit and must therefore eliminate two units of pollution. Firm Y also wonders if it might be better off selling the permit and eliminating three units of pollution.

But what about firm Z? Exhibit 5 shows that this firm has to pay $500 to eliminate its first unit of pollution and $1,000 to eliminate its second unit. Firm Z wonders if it might be better off buying the two permits in the possession of firms X and Y and not eliminating any pollution at all.

Suppose the owners of the three firms get together. The owner of firm Z says to the owners of the other firms, "I have to spend $500 to eliminate my first unit of pollution and $1,000 to eliminate my second unit. If either of you is willing to sell me your pollution permit for less than $500, I'm willing to buy it."

The owners of the three firms agree on a price of $330 for a permit, and both firms X and Y sell their permits to firm Z. This exchange benefits all three parties. Firm X receives $330 for its permit and then spends $100 to eliminate its third unit of pollution. Firm Y receives $330 for its permit and then spends $200 to eliminate its third unit of pollution. Firm Z spends $660 for the two pollution permits instead of spending $1,500 to eliminate its first two units of pollution.

Under this scheme, firm X and firm Y eliminate all their pollution (neither firm has a pollution permit). Firm X spends $225 ($50 + $75 + $100) to eliminate all three units of its pollution, and firm Y spends $355 to do the same. The two firms together spend $580 ($225 + $355) to eliminate six units of pollution.

$$\text{Total cost of eliminating six units of pollution through market environmentalism} = \$580$$

This cost is lower than the cost incurred by the three firms when government standards simply ordered each firm to eliminate two units of pollution (or six units for all three firms). The cost in that case was $1,780. In both cases, however, six pollution units were eliminated. We conclude that it is less costly for firms to eliminate pollution when the government allocates pollution permits that can be bought and sold than when it simply directs each firm to eliminate so many units of pollution.

Q & A

Q: What about the $660 that firm Z paid to buy the two pollution permits? This was not included in the cost of reducing pollution in the second method. Why not?

A: The $660 is a real cost of doing business for firm Z, but it is not a cost to society of eliminating pollution. The $660 was not actually used to eliminate pollution. It was simply a transfer from firm Z to firms X and Y. The distinction is between a resource cost, which signifies an expenditure of resources, and a *transfer,* which does not.

Q & A

Q: It is easy to see that it is cheaper to eliminate pollution through market environmentalism than through government standards. But why?

A: Under the method of selling and buying permits, the firms that can clean up pollution for the least cost are the ones that actually do so. This is not the case when standards are set. In that case, each firm must eliminate some pollution—no matter how much it costs.

Self-Test

1. The layperson finds it odd that economists often prefer some pollution to no pollution. Explain how the economist reaches this conclusion.

2. Why does reducing pollution cost less by using market environmentalism than by setting standards?

3. Under market environmentalism, the dollar amount firm Z has to pay to buy the pollution permits from firms X and Y is not counted as a cost to society. Why not?

PUBLIC GOODS: EXCLUDABLE AND NONEXCLUDABLE

Many economists maintain that the market fails to produce nonexcludable public goods. We discuss public goods in general, and nonexcludable public goods in particular in this section.

GOODS

Economists talk about two kinds of goods—private goods and public goods. A *private good* is a good the consumption of which by one person reduces the consumption for another person. For example, a sweater, an apple, and a computer are all private goods. If one person is wearing a sweater, another person cannot wear (consume) the same sweater. If one person takes a bite of an apple, there is that much less apple for someone else to consume. If someone is using a computer, someone else can't use the same computer. A private good is said to be **rivalrous in consumption.**

A **public good,** in contrast, is a good the consumption of which by one person does not reduce the consumption by another person. For example, a movie in a movie theater is a public good. If there are 200 seats in the theater, then 200 people can see the movie at the same time and no one person's viewing of the movie detracts from another person's viewing of the movie. An economics lecture is also a public good. If there are 30 seats in the classroom, then 30 people can consume the economics lecture at the same time and one person's consumption does not detract from any other person's consumption. The chief characteristic of a public good is that it is **nonrivalrous in consumption**—which means that its consumption by one person does not reduce its consumption by others.

While all public goods are nonrivalrous in consumption, they are not all the same. Some public goods are excludable and some are nonexcludable. A public good is **excludable** if it is possible, or not prohibitively costly, to exclude someone from obtaining the benefits of the good after it has been produced. For example, a movie in a movie theater is excludable, in that persons who do not pay to see the movie can be excluded from seeing it. The same holds for an economics lecture. If someone does not pay the tuition to obtain the lecture, he or she can be excluded from consuming it. We summarize by noting that both movies in movie theaters and economics lectures in classrooms are *excludable public goods.*

A public good is **nonexcludable** if it is impossible, or prohibitively costly, to exclude someone from obtaining the benefits of the good after it has been produced. Consider national defense. First, national defense is a public good in that it is nonrivalrous in consumption. For example, if the U.S. national defense system is protecting people in New Jersey from incoming missiles then it is automatically protecting people in New York as well. And just as important, protecting people in New Jersey does not reduce the degree of protection for the people in New York. Second, once national defense has been produced, it is impossible (or prohibitively costly) to exclude someone from consuming its services. In other words, national defense is a *nonexcludable public good.* The same holds for flood control or large-scale pest control. After the dam has been built or the pest spray has been sprayed, it is impossible to exclude persons from benefiting from it.

THE FREE RIDER

When a good is excludable (whether it is a private good or a public good), individuals can obtain the benefits of the good only if they pay for it. For example, no one can consume an apple (a private good) or a movie in a movie theater (a public good) without first paying for the good. This is not the case with a nonexcludable public good, though. Individuals can obtain the benefits of a nonexcludable public good without paying for it. Persons who do so are referred to as **free riders.** Because of the so-called *free rider problem,* most economists hold that the market will fail to produce nonexcludable public goods, or at least fail to produce them at a desired level.

To illustrate, consider someone contemplating the production of nonexcludable public good *X,* which because it is a public good, is also nonrivalrous in consumption. After good *X* has been produced and provided to one person, there is no incentive for others to pay for it (even if they demand it) because they can receive all of its benefits without paying. No one is likely to supply a good that people can consume without paying for it. The market, it is argued, will not produce nonexcludable public goods. The door then is opened to government involvement in the production of nonexcludable public goods. It is often stated that if the market will not produce nonexcludable public goods, although they are demanded, then the government must.

Rivalrous in Consumption
A good is rivalrous in consumption if its consumption by one person reduces its consumption by others.

Public Good
A good the consumption of which by one person does not reduce the consumption by another person— that is, a public good is characterized by nonrivalry in consumption. There are both excludable and nonexcludable public goods. An excludable public good is a good that while nonrivalrous in consumption can be denied to a person who does not pay for it. A nonexcludable public good is a good that is nonrivalrous in consumption and that cannot be denied to a person who does not pay for it.

Nonrivalrous in Consumption
A good is nonrivalrous in consumption if its consumption by one person does not reduce its consumption by others.

Excludability
A good is excludable if it is possible, or not prohibitively costly, to exclude someone from receiving the benefits of the good after it has been produced.

Nonexcludability
A good is nonexcludable if it is impossible, or prohibitively costly, to exclude someone from receiving the benefits of the good after it has been produced.

Free Rider
Anyone who receives the benefits of a good without paying for it.

ECONOMICS IN...

Free Riders and Charitable Giving

Some persons contend that charitable giving is a nonexcludable public good and subject to free riding. Consider Bill Jones, who receives utility when individuals less fortunate than he are being helped. When a homeless person is given a home, he feels good inside. When he learns that a rich entrepreneur in Houston has decided to pay the college tuition of 20 poor, college-age students, it makes his day. Notice that charitable giving appears to be a nonexcludable public good. It is nonrivalrous in consumption and nonexcludable. If the rich entrepreneur in Houston pays the tuition of 20 poor, college-age students, Bill Jones receives utility from the gesture as easily as the rich entrepreneur; and it is impossible to exclude him from receiving the utility after the rich entrepreneur's charity has been reported.

Is Bill Jones a free rider? Will he take a free ride on the charitable giving of others? Using the following line of reasoning, many persons argue that he will: (1) The average person's charitable contribution is a tiny percentage of total charitable contributions (say, $75 out of many millions). (2) Consequently, the average person realizes that even if he or she does not make a charitable contribution, charitable giving by others will not be much different (charitable giving will be less by only $75—a mere drop in the bucket). (3) A person has an incentive to become a free rider when the person realizes that his or her contribution will not affect total contributions by more than the tiniest amount and that he or she can benefit from the charitable giving of others. We conclude: When a person feels that his contribution is insignificant to the total contribution or that the benefits he receives from a good will not be appreciably different in the absence of his paying for it, then he has a strong incentive to become a free rider.

http://

Go to *http://w3.access.gpo.gov/ usbudget/*. Under the most recent Fiscal Year Budget, select "Searching and Viewing Documents On-line." Key "function" in the "Search Terms Box," and click "SUBMIT." Finally, select the "TXT" icon under "Outlays by Function and Subfunction." Look over the complete list of government functions. Identify those government functions that you believe are in the category of nonexcludable public goods.

The free rider argument is the basis for accepting government (the public or taxpayers) provision of nonexcludable public goods. We need remind ourselves, though, that a nonexcludable public good is not the same as a government-provided good. A nonexcludable public good is a good that is nonrivalrous in consumption and nonexcludable. A government-provided good is self-defined: it is a good that government provides. In some instances, a government-provided good is a nonexcludable public good, such as when the government furnishes national defense. But it need not be. The government furnishes mail delivery and education, two goods that are also provided privately and are excludable and thus not subject to free riding.

Q & A

Q: It seems that the market only fails to produce a demanded good when the good is nonexcludable because the free rider problem only arises if the good is nonexcludable. The rivalry vs. nonrivalry issue is not relevant to the issue of market failure; that is, a good can be rivalrous in consumption or nonrivalrous in consumption and still be produced by the market. Isn't this correct?

A: That is correct. As noted earlier, a movie may be nonrivalrous in consumption but be excludable too. And the market has no problem producing movies and movie theaters. The free rider problem occurs only with goods that are nonexcludable. Also relevant to the question is the case of "the lighthouse in economics." For a long time, a lighthouse was thought to have the two characteristics of a nonexcludable public good: (1) It is nonrivalrous in consumption—any ship can use the light from the lighthouse and one ship's use of the light does not detract from another's use. (2) It is nonexcludable—it is difficult to exclude any nonpaying ships from using the light. The lighthouse seemed to be a perfect good for government provision.

There is only one problem. Economist Ronald Coase found that in the eighteenth and early nineteenth centuries, many lighthouses were privately owned, which meant that the market had not failed to provide lighthouses. Economists were left to conclude either that the market could provide nonexcludable public goods or that the lighthouse wasn't a nonexcludable public good as had been thought. Closer examination showed that while the lighthouse was nonrivalrous in consumption (it was a public good), the costs of excluding others from using it were fairly low (so it was an excludable public good). Lighthouse owners knew that usually only one ship was near the lighthouse at a time and that they could turn off the light if a ship did not exhibit the flag of a paying vessel.

Self-Test

1. Why does the market fail to produce nonexcludable public goods?

2. Identify each of the following goods as a nonexcludable public good, an excludable public good, or a private good: (a) composition notebook used for writing, (b) Shakespearean play performed in a summer theater, (c) apple, (d) telephone in service, (e) sunshine.

3. Give an example, other than a movie in a movie theater or a play in a theater, of a good that is nonrivalrous and excludable.

ASYMMETRIC INFORMATION

Market failure is a situation in which the market does not provide the efficient or optimal amount of a particular good. This chapter has shown that both externalities and nonexcludable public goods can lead to market failure. Specifically, when externalities exist, the market output is different from the socially optimal output. In the case of negative externalities, the market produces "too much"; in the case of positive externalities, the market produces "too little." In the case of nonexcludable public goods, some economists maintain that the market "produces" zero output. Assuming that there is a demand for the nonexcludable public good, this is definitely "too little."

This section looks at another possible cause of market failure—asymmetric information. **Asymmetric information** exists when either the buyer or the seller in a market exchange has some information that the other does not have. In other words, some information is "hidden." For example, the seller of a house may have information about the house that the buyer does not have, such as that the roof leaks after a heavy rainfall.

The analysis of the effects of asymmetric information is similar to the analysis of externalities—with one important difference. The discussion of externalities considers buyers, sellers, and third parties; this discussion considers only buyers and sellers.

Asymmetric Information
Exists when either the buyer or the seller in a market exchange has some information that the other does not have.

ASYMMETRIC INFORMATION IN A PRODUCT MARKET

In the discussion of externalities, the demand for a good represents marginal private benefits and the supply of a good represents marginal private costs. This is also the case for the asymmetric information situation shown in Exhibit 6; that is, the demand curve, D_1, represents marginal private benefits (MPB) and the supply curve, S_1, represents marginal private costs (MPC). In Exhibit 6, D_1 and S_1 are the relevant curves when the seller has some information that the buyer does not have. It follows that Q_1 is the market output when there is asymmetric information.

Now suppose the buyer acquires the information she previously did not have (but which the seller did have). With the new information, buying this particular good does not seem as appealing. In other words, the information that the buyer has acquired causes her to lower her demand for the good. The relevant demand curve is now D_2. With symmetric information, the market output will be Q_2, which is less than Q_1.

Let's consider an example. Suppose the good is cigarettes. Furthermore, suppose the suppliers of cigarettes know that cigarette consumption can cause cancer,

exhibit 6

Asymmetric Information in a Product Market

Initially, the seller has some information that the buyer does not have; there is asymmetric information. As a result, D_1 represents the demand for the good and Q_1 is the equilibrium quantity. Then, the buyer acquires the information that she did not have earlier, and there is symmetric information. The information causes the buyer to lower her demand for the good so that now D_2 is the relevant demand curve and Q_2 is the equilibrium quantity. Conclusion: Fewer units of the good are bought and sold when there is symmetric information than when there is asymmetric information.

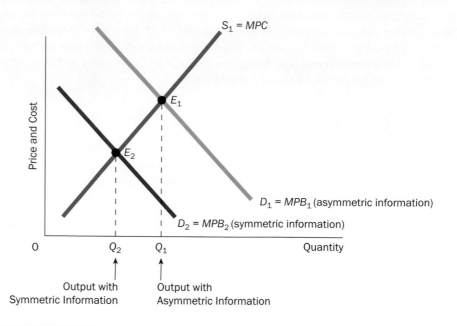

but do not release this information to potential buyers of cigarettes. Under this condition, suppliers of cigarettes have certain information about cigarettes that buyers don't have; there is asymmetric information. Without this information, the demand for cigarettes may be higher than it would be if buyers had the information. In Exhibit 6, demand is D_1 instead of D_2. It follows, then, that more cigarettes will be purchased and consumed (Q_1) when there is asymmetric information than when there is symmetric information (Q_2).

ASYMMETRIC INFORMATION IN A FACTOR MARKET

Now consider a resource or factor market, such as the labor market shown in Exhibit 7. In this case, the buyer has information that the seller does not have. Suppose a firm knows that its workers will be using a possibly toxic substance that may cause health problems in 20 to 30 years. Furthermore, suppose the company does not release this information to workers—that is, it is "hidden" from them. Without this information, the supply curve of labor is represented by S_1 and the quantity of labor will be Q_1 at a wage rate of W_1.

With the information, though, not as many people will be willing to work at the firm at the current wage. The supply curve of labor shifts left to S_2. The new equilibrium position shows that the quantity of labor falls to Q_2 and the wage rate rises to W_2.

IS THERE MARKET FAILURE?

Does asymmetric information cause markets to fail? That is, does it cause a situation in which the market does not provide the optimal output of a particular good? Certainly, in our examples, the output level of a good and the quantity of labor were lower when there was symmetric information than when there was asymmetric information. Stated differently, asymmetric information seemingly resulted in "too much" or "too many" of something—either too much of a good being consumed or too many workers working for a particular firm.

Some people argue that asymmetric information exists in nearly all exchanges. Rarely do buyers and sellers have the same information; each usually knows something the other doesn't.

This argument misses the point, however. The point is whether or not the asymmetric information fundamentally changes the outcome from what it would

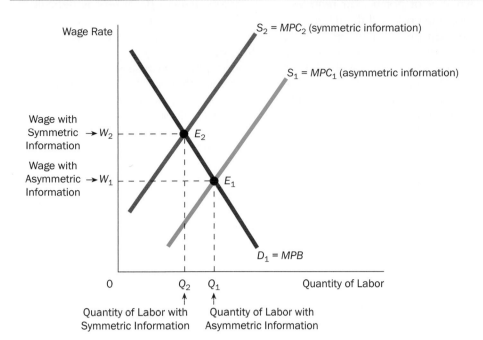

Wage Rate

$S_2 = MPC_2$ (symmetric information)

$S_1 = MPC_1$ (asymmetric information)

Wage with Symmetric Information → W_2

E_2

Wage with Asymmetric Information → W_1

E_1

$D_1 = MPB$

0   Q_2 Q_1 Quantity of Labor

Quantity of Labor with Symmetric Information

Quantity of Labor with Asymmetric Information

exhibit 7

Asymmetric Information in a Factor Market

Initially, the buyer (of the factor labor), or the firm, has some information that the seller (of the factor) does not have; there is asymmetric information. Consequently, S_1 is the relevant supply curve, W_1 is the equilibrium wage, and Q_1 is the equilibrium quantity of labor. Then, sellers acquire the information that they did not have earlier, and there is symmetric information. The information causes the sellers to reduce their supply of the factor so that now S_2 is the relevant supply curve, W_2 is the equilibrium wage, and Q_2 is the equilibrium quantity of labor. Conclusion: Fewer factor units are bought and sold and wages are higher when there is symmetric information than when there is asymmetric information.

be if there were symmetric information. For example, a buyer may know something that a seller doesn't know, but even if the seller knew what the buyer knows, it may not change the outcome.

To illustrate, suppose the waiter at a restaurant knows that the meal the buyer is ordering will cause a touch of heartburn. The buyer, however, does not know this, and later, she gets heartburn. Does asymmetric information matter here? Maybe not. It's possible the buyer would not have changed her behavior even if she had known the meal would cause a touch of heartburn. So there is asymmetric information, but it may not change the outcome.

But, of course, in another setting, the results may be different. Suppose the seller of a used car knows the car is a "lemon," but the buyer doesn't know this. The buyer buys the car because he doesn't have the information the seller has. Does asymmetric information matter to the outcome in this situation? It does if the buyer would not have bought the car or would not have bought the car at a given price had he known what the seller knew. In this setting, asymmetric information changes the outcome.

We conclude, then, that the presence of asymmetric information does not guarantee that the market fails. What matters is whether the asymmetric information brings about a different outcome than the outcome that would exist if there were symmetric information. If this occurs, then the case for market failure can be made.

ADVERSE SELECTION

Some economists argue that under certain conditions, information problems can eliminate markets (*missing markets*) or change the composition of markets (*incomplete markets*). To illustrate, let's return to our discussion of used cars.[3]

In the used car market, sellers know more than buyers about the cars they are offering to sell—there is asymmetric information. For example, a seller knows

---

3. The material here is based on the classic article by George Akerlof, "The Market for Lemons," *Quarterly Journal of Economics* (August 1970): 488–500.

whether or not his car requires a lot of maintenance. Because it is difficult for most buyers to tell the difference between good used cars and "lemons," a single used car price will emerge for a given model-make-year car that is a reflection of both lemons and good cars. Suppose this price is $10,000.

A lemon owner will think this is a good price because she will receive an average price for a below-average car. On the other hand, a person who owns an above-average car will find this price too low; he won't want to sell his above-average car for an average price. As a result of lemon owners liking the price and the owners of good cars not liking it, lemon owners will offer their cars for sale ("great price") and the owners of good used cars will not ("the price is too low").

This is called the problem of adverse selection. **Adverse selection** exists when the parties on one side of the market, who have information not known to others, self-select in a way that adversely affects the parties on the other side of the market. In the example, the owners of lemons offer their cars for sale—they select to sell their cars—because they know, and only they know, that the average price they are being offered for their below-average cars is a "good deal."

Through adverse selection, the supply of lemons on the market will rise and the supply of high-quality, or good, used cars will fall. The relatively greater number of lemons will lower the average quality of a used car. As a result, there will be a new average price for a given make-model-year used car that is lower than previously. Let's say it is $8,000.

The process repeats: People with above-average cars will think the average price of $8,000 is too low, and people with below-average cars will think this is a good price. The people with above-average cars will drop out of the used car market, leaving only those with below-average used cars. Again, this will lead to a decline in the average quality of a used car, and eventually the average price of a used car will drop.

Thus, asymmetric information leads to adverse selection, which in the used car market example, brings about a steady decline in the quality of used cars offered for sale. Theoretically, the adverse selection problem could lead to the total elimination of the good used car market. In other words, the lemons will "drive out" all the good cars.

What might prevent this outcome? Is there anything implicit in the way markets work that could solve the adverse selection problem? There are several possible solutions for adverse selection in the used car market. For example, a buyer could hire his own mechanic to check the car he is thinking about buying. By doing this, he would acquire almost as much, if not as much, information about the car as the seller has. Thus, there would no longer be asymmetric information.

Or the seller of a high-quality used car could offer a warranty on her car. Essentially, she could offer to fix any problems with the used car for a period of time after she sells it. The warranty offer would likely increase both the demand for the car and its price. (Lemon owners would not be likely to offer warranties, so their cars would sell for less than cars with warranties.)

In some cases, government has played a role in dealing with adverse selection problems. State governments can pass, and in some situations have passed, "lemon laws," stating that car dealers must take back any defective cars. Also, many states now require car dealers to openly state on used cars whether a warranty is included or a car is offered "as is."

MORAL HAZARD

In the used car example illustrating adverse selection, asymmetric information existed *prior* to an exchange. That is, before dollars changed hands, the seller of the used car had information about the car that the potential buyer did not have.

Asymmetric information can also exist *after* a transaction has been made. If it does, it can cause a moral hazard problem. **Moral hazard** occurs when one party

Adverse Selection
Exists when the parties on one side of the market, who have information not known to others, self-select in a way that adversely affects the parties on the other side of the market.

Go to *http://www.AutoNation.com*, and select "FIND A VEHICLE." Click on "FIND A PRE-OWNED VEHICLE." Choose a make and model, enter your zip code, and click "Go." Look over the list of vehicles. Is information provided on the condition of the various cars? Can you tell a "lemon" from a car that runs well? Click "Our Promise." Does the promise adjust or compensate for the fact that the sellers of used cars have more information than the buyers of used cars?

Moral Hazard
Exists when one party to a transaction changes his behavior in a way that is hidden from and costly to the other party.

Finding Economics in College Life

A series of young children's books, titled *Where's Waldo?*, present the character Waldo drawn among hundreds of people and things. While the objective, finding Waldo, may seem easy, finding Waldo is roughly similar to finding a needle in a haystack. If you look long and hard, you'll eventually find him; if you simply glance at the page, you won't.

Finding economics is similar to finding Waldo. If you simply glance at your daily life, you'll miss the economics; if you look long and hard, you'll often find it.

With this in mind, consider your life as a college student. On a typical day, you walk into a college classroom, sit down, listen to a lecture and take notes, enter into discussions, ask questions, answer questions, and then leave. Can you find the economics in this daily experience? Here are some places you might find economics lurking.

Arriving Late to Class

Class started five minutes ago. You are sitting at your desk, listening to the professor and taking notes. The professor is discussing an unusually challenging topic today and you are listening attentively. Then, the classroom door opens. You turn at the sound and see two of your classmates arriving late to class. For a few seconds, your attention is diverted from the lecture. When you refocus your attention on the professor, you realize that you have missed an essential point. You are mildly frustrated over this.

The scenario described is a negative externality. Your two classmates undertook an action—they arrived to class late—and you incurred a cost because of their action. Your two classmates considered only their private benefits and costs of arriving to class late. They did not consider your cost—the external cost—of their action.

What can be done to get students to internalize the cost to others of their being late? The professor could try to persuade students not to be late. She could say that lateness imposes a cost on those who arrive to class on time and are attentively listening to the lecture. Alternatively, the professor could impose a "corrective tax" on tardy students. In other words, she could try to set a tax equal to the external cost. The tax could take the form of a one-half to one point deduction from a student's test grade for each time he or she is late.

Grading on a Curve

Consider Alex, who is currently taking a sociology course. Ideally, he would like to get an "A" or a "B" in the class, but this can't be guaranteed. He believes it is likely that he will receive a "C" or a "D." Alex's situation is similar to that of a person who would like to be healthy every day for the rest of her life, but knows that she probably won't be.

What does a person do when she knows she probably won't be healthy for her entire life? She buys health insurance. And, as discussed in this chapter, after a person has purchased health insurance a moral hazard problem may arise. The person may not have so strong an incentive to remain healthy when she has health insurance as when she doesn't.

Will Alex react the same way if he can buy grade insurance? Suppose his sociology professor promises Alex that he will grade on a curve and that no one in the class will receive a grade lower than a "C−." With this assurance from his professor, will Alex have as strong an incentive to work hard to learn sociology? Does a moral hazard problem now arise? An economist is likely to answer the first question "no," and the second question "yes."

Studying Together for the Midterm

Consider two types of colleges: (1) a dormitory-based college in which many of the students live on campus in dormitories and (2) a commuter college in which the entire student body lives off campus.

Students usually study together if they think it will be mutually beneficial to them. That is, when two people agree to study together (say, for a midterm), they are usually entering into an exchange: I will help you learn more of the material so you can get a better grade if you do the same for me.

It is more common for students to study together on dormitory-based campuses than on commuter campuses. Why? The transaction costs of studying together—of entering into the aforementioned exchange—are relatively lower on a dormitory-based campus. If you live in a dormitory on campus, you incur relatively low transaction costs by studying with someone who also lives on campus (maybe a person living down the hall from you). But if everyone lives off campus, you incur relatively high transaction costs by studying with a fellow student. Do you drive over to that person's house or apartment, or does she drive over to your house or apartment? Do you meet at a local coffee bar?

to a transaction changes his behavior in a way that is hidden from and costly to the other party. For example, suppose Smith buys a health insurance policy. After she has the insurance, she may be less careful to maintain good health because the cost to her of future health problems is not so high as it would have been without the insurance. We are not implying that Smith sets out to make herself ill so she can collect on the insurance. We are simply saying that her incentive to be as careful about her health and physical well-being is not so strong as it once was.

Consider another example: A person who has automobile collision insurance may be more likely to try to drive on an icy road in December in Minneapolis than he would if he didn't have the insurance. Or a person who has earthquake insurance may be more likely to "forget" to do a few things that will minimize damage during an earthquake, such as attaching bookcases to the walls. In these examples, the moral hazard problem causes people to take "too few" precautionary actions.

Insurance companies try to control for moral hazard in different ways. One way is by specifying certain precautions that an insured person must take. For example, a company that insures your house from fire may require you to have smoke detectors and a fire extinguisher. Also, the insurance company may set a deductible so that you must pay part of the loss in case of a fire. This increases your cost of a fire and provides you with an added incentive to be careful.

Self-Test

1. Give an example that illustrates how asymmetric information can lead to more of a good being consumed than if there is symmetric information.
2. Adverse selection has the potential to eliminate some markets. How is this possible?
3. Give an example (not discussed in the text) that illustrates moral hazard.

A Reader Asks...
Are Houses and Shopping Centers a Sign of "Progress"?

I live in an area that used to have many trees, large parcels of empty land, creeks, and so on, but in the past two years, more and more houses, apartment buildings, and shopping centers have been built. What was once a nice place to live has become filled with people; the natural beauty of the place and the quality of life have suffered. Would an economist call what has happened "progress"?

The economist doesn't have a preconceived notion of the way the world should look—whether an area should have creeks, trees, and birds or houses and shopping centers. The economist wants resources to be allocated in a welfare-maximizing way. To illustrate, let's discuss the area in which you live. To keep things simple, let's suppose we are talking about an area of 5 square miles that we call area X. Now it sounds like you (and perhaps others) preferred area X the way it was. Let's say that you and others with similar preferences constitute group A. There may be other persons, though, who prefer area X the way it has become. We'll say these other persons

constitute group B. In some sense, then, we are talking about two groups of people—A and B—who want to do different things with area X.

Which group should get to do what it wants with area X? Should group A have the right to keep area X the way it wants—an area with few houses and shopping centers and with many trees, empty parcels of land, and so on? Or should group B have the right to change area X to what it wants—an area with many houses and shopping centers and with few trees, empty parcels of land, and so on?

Suppose group A values area X at a maximum of $40 million and group B values it at a maximum of $50 million. This means that even if group A owned area X, it would sell it to group B. If group B offered $45 million for area X, group A would sell it because area X is only worth a maximum of $40 million to group A. (If the dollar amounts were reversed, group A wouldn't sell area X.)

It is hard to tell how much group A valued area X the way it was. It is certainly possible that group A valued area X more than group B did but that the transaction costs of individuals in this group getting together and bidding the land away from group *B* were just too high to overcome. In this case, area *X* may have ended up in the hands of people who value it less than others.

It may also be the case that because certain things were "not priced," group *B* was able to buy area *X* for something less than a price that accounts for full costs. To illustrate, suppose some of the members of group *B* are developers who bought parcels of area *X* in order to put up houses. In building the houses, they create noise and congestion (on the roads) for the nearby residents. As far as the nearby residents are concerned, the noise and congestion are negative externalities. If the price of the land the developers purchased (for the purpose of building houses) did not fully reflect the external costs incurred by nearby residents, then it is very possible that more houses were built in area *X* than was socially optimal or efficient.

Chapter Summary

Externalities

- An externality is a side effect of an action that affects the well-being of third parties. There are two types of externalities: negative and positive. A negative externality exists when an individual's or group's actions cause a cost (adverse side effect) to be felt by others. A positive externality exists when an individual's or group's actions cause a benefit (beneficial side effect) to be felt by others.

- When either negative or positive externalities exist, the market output is different from the socially optimal output. In the case of a negative externality, the market is said to overproduce the good connected with the negative externality (the socially optimal output is less than the market output). In the case of a positive externality, the market is said to underproduce the good connected with the positive externality (the socially optimal output is greater than the market output). See Exhibits 1 and 3.

- Negative and positive externalities can be internalized or adjusted for in a number of different ways, including persuasion, the assignment of property rights, voluntary agreements, and taxes and subsidies. Also, regulations may be used to adjust for externalities directly.

The Coase Theorem

- The Coase theorem holds that in the case of trivial or zero transaction costs, the property rights assignment does not matter to the resource allocative outcome. To put it differently, a property rights assignment will be undone if it benefits the relevant parties to undo it. The Coase theorem is significant for two reasons: (1) It shows that under certain conditions the market can internalize externalities. (2) It provides a benchmark for analyzing externality problems—that is, it shows what would happen if transaction costs were trivial or zero.

The Environment

- Some pollution is likely to be a better situation than no pollution. The reason is that people derive utility from things that cause pollution, such as cars to drive.

- There is more than one way to tackle environmental problems. For example, both setting standards and selling pollution permits can be used to deal with pollution. The economist is interested in finding the cheapest way to solve environmental problems. Often, this tends to be through some measure of market environmentalism.

Public Goods

- A public good is a good characterized by nonrivalry in consumption. A public good can be excludable or nonexcludable. Excludable public goods are goods that while nonrivalrous in consumption can be denied to people if they do not pay for them. Nonexcludable public goods are goods that are nonrivalrous in consumption and cannot be denied to people who do not pay for them. The market is said to fail in the provision of nonexcludable public goods because of the free rider problem—that is, a supplier of the good would not be able to extract payment for the good because its benefits can be received without making payment.

Asymmetric Information

- Asymmetric information exists when either the buyer or the seller in a market exchange has some information that the other does not have. Outcomes based on asymmetric information may be different than outcomes based on symmetric information.

- Adverse selection exists when the parties on one side of the market, who have information not known to others, self-select in a way that adversely affects the parties on the other side of the market. Adverse selection can lead to missing or incomplete markets.

- Moral hazard occurs when one party to a transaction changes his behavior in a way that is hidden from and costly to the other party.

Key Terms and Concepts

Market Failure
Externality
Negative Externality
Positive Externality
Marginal Social Costs (*MSC*)
Marginal Social Benefits (*MSB*)

Socially Optimal Amount (Output)
Internalizing Externalities
Coase Theorem
Rivalrous in Consumption
Public Good
Nonrivalrous in Consumption

Excludability
Nonexcludability
Free Rider
Asymmetric Information
Adverse Selection
Moral Hazard

Questions and Problems

1. Give an example that illustrates the difference between private costs and social costs.

2. Consider two types of divorce laws. Law *A* allows either the husband or the wife to obtain a divorce without the other person's consent. Law *B* permits a divorce only if both parties agree to the divorce. Will there be more divorces under law *A* or law *B,* or will there be the same number of divorces under both laws? Why?

3. People have a demand for sweaters, and the market provides sweaters. There is evidence that people also have a demand for national defense, yet the market does not provide national defense. What is the reason the market does not provide national defense? Is it because government is providing national defense and therefore there is no need for the market to do so, or because the market won't provide national defense?

4. Education is often said to generate positive externalities. How might it do this?

5. Give an example of each of the following: (a) a good rivalrous in consumption and excludable; (b) a good nonrivalrous in consumption and excludable; (c) a good rivalrous in consumption and nonexcludable; (d) a good nonrivalrous in consumption and nonexcludable.

6. Some individuals argue that with increased population growth, negative externalities will become more common and there will be more instances of market failure and more need for government to solve externality problems. Other individuals believe that as time passes, technological advances will be used to solve negative externality problems. They conclude that over time there will be fewer instances of market failure and less need for government to deal with externality problems. What do you believe will happen? Give reasons to support your position.

7. Name at least five government-provided goods that are not nonexcludable public goods.

8. One view of life is that life is one big externality. Just about everything that someone does affects someone else either positively or negatively. To permit government to deal with externality problems is to permit government to tamper with everything in life. No clear line divides those externalities government should become involved in and those it should not. Do you support this position? Why?

9. Economists sometimes shock noneconomists by stating that they do not favor the complete elimination of pollution. Explain the rationale for this position.

10. Why is it cheaper to reduce, say, air pollution through market environmentalism than through government standards and regulations?

11. Identify each of the following as an adverse selection or a moral hazard problem.
    a. A person with car insurance fails to lock his car doors when he shops at a mall.
    b. A person with a family history of cancer purchases the most complete health coverage available.
    c. A person with health insurance takes more risks on the ski slopes of Aspen than he would otherwise.
    d. A college professor receives tenure (assurance of permanent employment) from her employer.
    e. A patient pays his surgeon before she performs the surgery.

1. Graphically portray (a) a negative externality and (b) a positive externality.
2. Graphically represent (a) a corrective tax that achieves the socially optimal output and (b) one that moves the market output further away from the socially optimum output than was the case before the tax was applied.
3. Using the data below, prove that pollution permits that can be bought and sold can reduce pollution from 12 units to 6 units at lower cost than a regulation that specifies each of the three firms must cut its pollution in half.

	Firm *X*	Firm *Y*	Firm *Z*
Cost of Eliminating:			
First unit of pollution	$200	$500	$1,000
Second unit of pollution	300	700	2,000
Third unit of pollution	400	800	2,900
Fourth unit of pollution	500	900	3,400

1. Go to *http://www.epa.gov/epahome/aboutepa.htm*, and read the Web page.
   a. What does EPA stand for? What is the EPA?
   b. What is the EPA's mission statement?
   c. What does the EPA do?
   d. Which EPA regional office is responsible for the area where you live?

2. Go to *http://org.eea.eu.int/documents/who_we_are*, and read the Web page. What is the core task of the European Environment Agency (EEA)? Are the objectives of the EPA different from those of the EEA? Explain your answer.

Log on to the Arnold Xtra! Web site now (*http://arnoldxtra.swcollege.com*) for additional learning resources such as practice quizzes, help with graphing, video clips, and current event applications.

ch.18

PUBLIC CHOICE: ECONOMIC THEORY APPLIED TO POLITICS

Economics is a powerful analytical tool. As you have already seen in this text, it can be used to analyze how markets and the economy work. Economics can also be used to analyze the behavior of politicians, voters, members of special interest groups, and bureaucrats. This is how economics is used in this chapter. Specifically, this chapter analyzes **public choice,** *the branch of economics that deals with the application of economic principles and tools to public-sector decision making.*

Chapter Road Map

Public choice is one branch on the tree of econom-

ics. A shorthand definition of public choice is "economics applied

to politics." Public choice economists use the tools of economics (usually

microeconomic tools) to analyze topics usually discussed in political science—topics

such as politicians, elections, voters, bureaucrats, and special interest groups. In this chapter,

we discuss the actions of four major players in the political world: politicians, voters, special interest

groups, and bureaucrats.

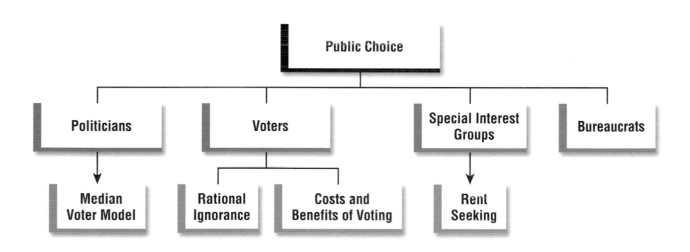

PUBLIC CHOICE THEORY

Public choice theorists reject the notion that people are like Dr. Jekyll and Mr. Hyde: exhibiting greed and selfishness in their transactions in the private (market) sector and altruism and public spirit in their actions in the public sector. The same people who are the employers, employees, and consumers in the market sector are the politicians, bureaucrats, members of special interest groups, and voters in the public sector. According to public choice theorists, people in the market sector and people in the public sector behave differently, not because they have different motives (or are different types of people), but because the two sectors have different institutional arrangements.

Consider a simple example. Erin Bloom currently works for a private, profit-seeking firm that makes radio components. Erin is cost-conscious, does her work on time, and generally works hard. She knows that she must exhibit this particular work behavior if she wants to keep her job and be promoted.

Time passes. Erin leaves her job at the radio components company and takes a job with the Department of Health and Human Services (HHS) in Washington, D.C. Is Erin a different person (with different motives) working for HHS than she was when she worked for the radio components company? Public choice theorists would say no.

But simply because Erin is the same person in and out of government, it does not necessarily follow that she will exhibit the same work behavior. The reason is that the costs and benefits of certain actions may be substantially different at HHS than at the radio components company. For example, perhaps the cost of being late for work is less in Erin's new job at HHS than at her old job. In her job at the radio components company, she had to work overtime if she came in late; in her new job, her boss doesn't say anything when she comes in late. We predict that Erin is more likely to be late in her new job than she was in her old one. She is simply responding to costs and benefits as they exist in her new work environment.

Q & A   **Q:** Some people talk as if government is made up exclusively of good and giving people who have only the public good in mind. Other people talk as if government is made up exclusively of bad and grabbing people who have only their own welfare at stake. Are public choice theorists saying that both are caricatures of the real people who work in government?

A: Yes, they are. One of the first public choice theorists, James Buchanan, said, "If men should cease and desist from their talk about and their search for evil men [and his sentiments include "purely good men" too] and commence to look instead at the institutions manned by ordinary people, wide avenues for genuine social reform might appear."[1]

THE POLITICAL MARKET

Economists who practice positive economics want to understand their world. They want to understand not only the production and pricing of goods, unemployment, inflation, and the firm but also political outcomes and political behavior. This section is an introduction to the political market.

MOVING TOWARD THE MIDDLE: THE MEDIAN VOTER MODEL

During political elections, voters often complain that the candidates for office are "too much alike." Some find this frustrating; they say they would prefer to have

---

1. James Buchanan, *The Limits of Liberty: Between Anarchy and Leviathan* (Chicago: University of Chicago Press, 1975), p. 149.

more choice. However, as the following discussion illustrates, two candidates running for the same office often sound alike because they are competing for votes.

In Exhibit 1, parts (a), (b), and (c) show a distribution of voters in which the political spectrum goes from the "Far Left" to the "Far Right." Note that (relatively) few voters hold positions in either of these two extreme wings. We assume that voters will vote for the candidate who comes closest to matching their ideological or political views. People whose views are in the Far Left of the political spectrum will vote for the candidate closest to the Far Left, and so on.

Our election process begins with two candidates, a Democrat and a Republican, occupying the positions D_1 and R_1 in part (a), respectively. If the election were held today, the Republican would receive more votes than his Democratic opponent. The Republican would receive all the votes of the voters who position themselves to the right of R_1, the Democrat would receive all the votes of the voters who position themselves to the left of D_1, and the voters between R_1 and D_1 would divide their votes between the two candidates. The Republican would receive more votes than the Democrat.

If, however, the election were not held today, the Democrat would likely notice (through polls and the like) that her opponent was doing better than she was. To offset this, she would move toward the center, or middle, of the political spectrum to pick up some votes. Part (b) in Exhibit 1 illustrates this move by the Democrat. Relative to her position in part (a), the Democrat is closer to the middle of the political spectrum, and as a result, she picks up votes. Voters to the left of D_2 vote for the Democrat, voters to the right of R_2 vote for the Republican, and the voters between the two positions divide their votes between the two candidates. If the election were held now, the Democrat would win the election.

In part (c), the candidates, in an attempt to get more votes than their opponent, have moved to positions D_3 and R_3—close to the middle of the political spectrum. At election time, the two candidates are likely to be positioned side by side at the political center or middle. Notice that in part (c), both candidates have become middle-of-the-roaders in their attempt to pick up votes. This tendency to move to a position at the center of the distribution—captured in the **median voter model**   is what causes many voters to complain that there is not much difference between the candidates for political office.

Median Voter Model
Suggests that candidates in a two-person political race will move toward matching the preferences of the median voter (that is, the person whose preferences are at the center, or in the middle, of the political spectrum).

exhibit 1

The Move toward the Middle
Political candidates tend to move toward the middle of the political spectrum. Starting with (a), the Republican receives more votes than the Democrat and would win the election if it were held today. To offset this, as shown in (b), the Democrat moves inward toward the middle of the political spectrum. The Republican tries to offset the Democrat's movement inward by also moving inward. As a result, both candidates move toward the political middle, getting closer to each other over time.

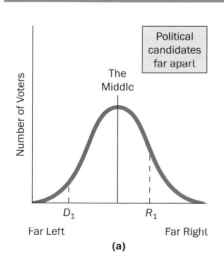

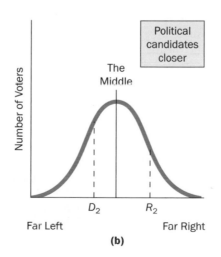

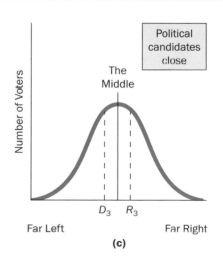

WHAT DOES THE THEORY PREDICT?

The theory we have just presented explains why politicians running for the same office often sound alike. But what does the theory predict? Here are a few of its predictions:

1. **Candidates will label their opponent as either "too far right" or "too far left."** The candidates know that whoever is closer to the middle of the political spectrum (in a two-person race) will win more votes and thus the election. As noted earlier, to accomplish this feat, they will move toward the political middle. At the same time, they will say that their opponent is a member of the political fringe (that is, a person far from the center). A Democrat may argue that his Republican opponent is "too conservative"; a Republican, that her Democratic opponent is "too liberal."

2. **Candidates will call themselves "middle-of-the-roaders," not right- or left-wingers.** In their move toward the political middle, candidates will try to portray themselves as moderates. In their speeches, they will assert that they represent the majority of voters and that they are practical, not ideological. They will not be likely to refer to themselves as "ultra-liberal" or "ultra-conservative" or as right- or left-wingers because to do so would send the wrong message to the voters.

3. **Candidates will take polls, and if they are not doing well in the polls and their opponent is, they will modify their positions to become more like their opponent.** Polls tell candidates who the likely winner of the election will be. A candidate who finds out that she would lose the election (she is down in the polls) is not likely to sit back and do nothing. The candidate will change her positions. Often this means becoming more like the winner of the poll; that is, becoming more like her opponent in the political race.

4. **Candidates will speak in general, instead of specific, terms.** Voters agree more on ends than on the means of accomplishing those ends. For example, voters of the left, right, and middle believe that a strong economy is better than a weak economy. However, they do not all agree on the best way to obtain a strong economy. The person on the right might advocate less government intervention as a way to strengthen the economy, while the person on the left might advocate more government intervention. Most political candidates soon learn that addressing the issues specifically requires them to discuss "means" and that doing so, increases the probability they will have an extreme-wing label attached to them.

   For example, a candidate who advocates less government intervention in the economy is more likely to be labeled a right-winger than a candidate who simply calls for a stronger national economy without discussing the specific means he would use to bring this about. In the candidate's desire to be perceived as a middle-of-the-roader, he is much more likely to talk about ends, on which voters agree, than about means, on which voters disagree.

THINKING LIKE AN ECONOMIST

An economist thinks about theories and then tests them. She is not content to have a theory—such as the one that says candidates in a two-person political race will gravitate toward the center of the political distribution—simply sound right. The economist asks herself, "If the theory is right, what should I expect to see in the real world? If the theory is wrong, what should I expect to see in the real world?" Such questions direct the economist to look at effects to see whether the theory has explanatory and predictive power. If we actually see the four predictions of the median voter theory occurring in the real world—candidates labeling themselves one way, speaking in general terms, and so on—then we can conclude that the evidence supports the theory. But suppose we see that candidates en masse do not speak in general terms and so on. What then? Then we would know to reject the theory.

VOTERS AND RATIONAL IGNORANCE

The preceding section explains something about the behavior of politicians, especially near or at election time. We turn now to a discussion of voters.

THE COSTS AND BENEFITS OF VOTING

Political commentators often remark that the voter turnout for a particular election was low. They might say, "Only 54 percent of registered voters actually voted." Are voter turnouts low because Americans are apathetic or because they do not care who wins an election? Are they uninterested in political issues? Public choice economists often explain low voter turnouts in terms of the costs and benefits of voting.

Consider Mark Quincy, who is thinking about voting in a presidential election. Mark may receive many benefits from voting. He may feel more involved in public affairs or think that he has met his civic responsibility. He may see himself as more patriotic. Or he may believe he has a greater right to criticize government if he takes an active part in it. In short, he may benefit from seeing himself as a doer instead of a talker. Ultimately, however, he will weigh these positive benefits against the costs of voting, which include driving to the polls, standing in line, and so on. If, in the end, Mark perceives the benefits of voting as greater than the costs, he will vote.

But, suppose Mark believes he receives only one benefit from voting—that his vote will have an impact on the election outcome. His benefits of voting equation may look like this:

$$\text{Mark's benefits of voting} = \text{Probability of Mark's vote affecting the outcome} \times \text{Additional benefits Mark receives if his candidate wins}$$

Let's analyze this equation. Suppose two candidates are running for office, A and B. If Mark votes, he will vote for A because he estimates that he benefits $100 if A is elected but only $40 if B is elected. The difference, $60, represents the additional benefits Mark receives if his candidate wins.

What is the probability of Mark's vote affecting the outcome? When there are many potential voters, such as in a senatorial or presidential election, the probability that one person's vote will affect the outcome is close to zero. To recognize this fact on an intuitive level, consider any presidential election. Say there are two major candidates running for office, X and Y. If you, as an individual voter, vote for X, the outcome of the election is likely to be the same as if you had voted for Y or as if you had not voted at all. In other words, whether you vote, vote for X, or vote for Y, the outcome is likely to be the same. In short, the probability of one person's vote changing the outcome of an election is close to zero.

In Mark's benefits of voting equation, $60 is multiplied by a probability so small that it might as well be zero. So $60 times zero is zero. In short, Mark receives no benefits from voting. But Mark may face certain costs. His costs of voting equation may look like this:

$$\text{Mark's costs of voting} = \text{Cost of driving to the polls} + \text{Cost of standing in line} + \text{Cost of filling out the ballot}$$

Obviously, Mark faces some positive costs of voting. Because his benefits of voting are zero and his costs of voting are positive, Mark makes the rational choice if he chooses not to vote.

Will everyone behave the same way Mark behaves and choose not to vote? Obviously not; some people do vote in elections. Probably what separates the Marks in the world from the people who vote is that the people who vote receive some benefits from voting that Mark does not. They might receive benefits from simply being part of the excitement of election day, or from doing what they perceive as their civic duty, or from some other reason.

Go to *http://www.infoplease.com/ history.html*. Click on "U.S. Elections," and select "Participation in Elections for President and U.S. Representatives, 1930–1998." Is the voter participation rate higher for presidential elections or for House elections? Are the differences in the voter participation rate (of different elections) consistent with rational economic behavior? Explain your answer. Is there a trend in the voter participation rate in presidential elections? What was the voter participation rate in the most recent presidential election?

ECONOMICS IN...

Are You Rationally Ignorant?

Rational ignorance is usually easier to see in others than in ourselves. We understand that most people are not well informed about politics and government, but we often fail to put ourselves into the same category, even when we deserve to be there. We can take a giant leap forward in understanding rational ignorance and special interest legislation if we see ourselves more clearly. With this in mind, try to answer the following questions about politics or government.

1. What is the name of your most recently elected U.S. senator, and what party does he or she belong to?
2. How has your congressional representative voted in any of the last 20 votes in Congress?
3. What is the approximate dollar amount of federal government spending? What is the approximate dollar amount of federal government tax revenues?
4. Which political party controls the House of Representatives?
5. What is the name of your representative in the state legislature?
6. Name just one special interest group and note how much it received in federal monies (within a broad range) in the last federal budget.
7. Explain an issue in the most recent local political controversy that did not have to do with someone's personality or personal life.
8. Approximately how many persons sit in your state's legislature?

9. What political positions (if any) did the governor of your state hold before becoming governor?
10. In what month and year will the next congressional elections in your state be held?

If you know the answers to only a few of the questions, then consider yourself rationally ignorant about politics and government. This is what we would expect.

Now ask yourself why you don't know the answers to the questions. Is it because they are too hard (and almost impossible) to answer or because you have not been interested in answering such questions?

Finally, ask yourself if you will now take the time to find the answers to the questions you couldn't answer. If you do not know the answer to question 6, for example, are you going to take the time to find the answer? We think not. If we're right, then you should now understand rational ignorance—on a personal level.

The point that public choice economists make is that if many individual voters will vote only if they perceive their vote as making a difference, then they probably will not vote because their vote is unlikely to make a difference. The low turnouts that appear to be a result of voter apathy may instead be a result of cost-benefit calculations.

RATIONAL IGNORANCE

"Democracy would be better served if voters would take more of an interest in and become better informed about politics and government. They don't know much about the issues." How often have you heard this?

The problem is not that voters are too stupid to learn about the issues. Many people who know little about politics and government are quite capable of learning about both, but they choose not to learn.

But why would many voter-citizens choose to be uninformed about politics and government? The answer is perhaps predictable: because the benefits of becoming informed are often outweighed by the costs of becoming informed. In short, many persons believe that becoming informed is simply not worth the effort. Hence, on an individual basis, it makes sense to be uninformed about politics and government, to be in a state of **rational ignorance.**

Rational Ignorance
The state of not acquiring information because the costs of acquiring the information are greater than the benefits.

Consider Shonia Tyler. Shonia has many things she could do with her time. She could read a good novel, watch a television program, or go out with friends. Shonia could also become better informed about the candidates and the issues in the upcoming U.S. Senate race.

Becoming informed, however, has costs. If Shonia stays home and reads about the issues, she can't go out with her friends. If she stays up late to watch a news program, she might be too tired to work efficiently the next day. These costs have to be weighed against the benefits of becoming better informed about the candidates and the issues. For Shonia, as for many people, the benefits are unlikely to be greater than the costs.

Many people see little personal benefit to becoming more knowledgeable about political candidates and issues. As with voting, the decision to remain uninformed may be linked to the small impact any single individual can have in a large-numbers setting.

Q & A

Q: Earlier it was said that politicians move toward the middle of the political spectrum to increase the probability that they will win an election. Now it turns out that the voter in the middle of the political spectrum, or any other voter for that matter, isn't likely to be knowledgeable about the issues. Doesn't this imply that politicians are trying to match the political preferences of a group of largely uninformed voters?

A: Yes, it does. Some people believe this is one of the deficiencies of representative democracy.

Self-Test *(Answers to Self-Test questions are in the Self-Test Appendix.)*

1. If a politician running for office does not speak in general terms, does not try to move to the middle of the political spectrum, and does not take polls, does it follow that the median voter model is wrong?

2. Voters often criticize politicians running for office who do not speak in specific terms (tell them what spending programs will be cut, whose taxes will be raised, and so on). If voters want politicians running for office to speak in specific terms, then why don't politicians do this?

3. An English literature professor comments that his students are apathetic because they don't seem to be informed about what's happening in the political realm. Comment.

MORE ABOUT VOTING

Voting is often the method used to make decisions in the public sector. In this section, we discuss some of the effects (some might say "problems") of voting as a decision-making method. We illustrate some of these effects in the context of two examples.

EXAMPLE 1: VOTING FOR A NONEXCLUDABLE PUBLIC GOOD

Suppose a community of seven persons, *A–G,* wants to produce or purchase nonexcludable public good *X.* Each person in the community wants a different number of units, as shown in the following table.

Person	Number of Units of *X* Desired
A	1
B	2
C	3
D	4
E	5
F	6
G	7

If the community of seven persons holds a simple majority vote, then all seven people will vote to produce or purchase at least 1 unit of X. Six people (B–G) will vote for at least 2 units. Five people (C–G) will vote for at least 3 units. Four people (D–G) will vote for at least 4 units. Three people (E–G) will vote for at least 5 units. Two people (F–G) will vote for at least 6 units. Only one person (G) will vote for 7 units.

The largest number of units that receives a simple majority vote (half the total number of voters plus 1, or 4 votes) is 4 units. In other words, the community will vote to produce or purchase 4 units of X.

What is interesting is that 4 units is the most preferred outcome of only one of the seven members of the community, person D, who is the median voter. Half the voters (A, B, and C) preferred fewer than 4 units, and half the voters (E, F, and G) preferred more than 4 units. In other words, our voting process has resulted in only the median voter obtaining his most preferred outcome.

The outcome would have been the same even if the numbers had looked the way they do in the following table.

Person	Number of Units of X Desired
A	0
B	0
C	0
D	4
E	7
F	7
G	7

In this case, four people (D–G) would have voted for at least 4 units and only three people would have voted for anything more than or less than 4 units. Again, 4 units would have been the outcome of the vote and only the median voter would have obtained his most preferred outcome.

EXAMPLE 2: VOTING AND EFFICIENCY

Let's suppose that three individuals have the marginal private benefits (MPB) shown in the following table for various units of nonexcludable public good Y.

Person	MPB of First Unit of Y	MPB of Second Unit of Y	MPB of Third Unit of Y
A	$400	$380	$190
B	150	110	90
C	100	90	80

If the cost of providing a unit of good Y is $360, what is the socially optimal, or efficient, amount of good Y? To answer this question, we need to review a few of the relationships from the last chapter:

1. The socially optimal, or efficient, amount of anything is the amount at which the marginal social benefits (MSB) equal the marginal social costs (MSC).
2. The sum of the marginal private benefits and the marginal external benefits equals the marginal social benefits: MPB + MEB = MSB.
3. The sum of the marginal private costs and the marginal external costs equals the marginal social costs: MPC + MEC = MSC.

In our example, the MSC for each unit is given as $360. We calculate the MSB for each unit by summing the MPB for each unit. For the first unit, the MSB is $650 ($400 + $150 + 100); for the second unit, it is $580; and for the third unit, it is $360. The socially optimal, or efficient, amount of good Y is 3 units because this is the amount at which MSB = MSC.

Simple Majority Rule: The Case of the Statue in the Public Square

Public questions are often decided by the simple majority decision rule. Most people think this is the fair and democratic way to do things. In certain instances, however, a simple majority vote leads to a project being undertaken whose costs are greater than its benefits.

Consider a community of ten people. The names of the individuals in the community are listed in column 1 of Exhibit 2. The community is considering whether or not to purchase a statue to put in the center of the public square. The cost of the statue is $1,000, and the community has previously agreed that if the statue is purchased, the ten individuals will share the cost equally—that is, each will pay $100 in taxes (see column 3).

Column 2 shows the dollar value of the benefits each individual will receive from the statue. For example, Applebaum places a dollar value of $150 on the statue, Browning places a dollar value of $140 on the statue, and so on. Column 4 notes the net benefit (+) or net cost (−) of the statue to each individual. There is a net benefit for an individual if the dollar value he or she places on the statue is greater than the tax (cost) he or she must incur. There is a net cost if the reverse holds true. Finally, column 5 indicates how each member of the community would vote. If an individual believes there is a net benefit to the statue, he or she will vote for it. If an individual believes there is a net cost to the statue, he or she will vote against it. Six individuals vote for the statue and four individuals vote against it. The majority rules, and the statue is purchased and placed in the center of the public square.

Notice, though, that the total dollar value of benefits to the community ($812) is less than the total tax cost to the community ($1,000). Using the simple majority decision rule has resulted in the purchase of the statue even though the benefits of the statue to the community are less than the costs of the statue to the community.

This outcome is not surprising when it is understood that the simple majority decision rule does not take into account the intensity of individuals' preferences. No matter how strongly a person feels about the issue, he or she simply registers one vote. For example, even though Emerson places a net benefit of $1 on the statue and Isley places a net cost of $90 on the statue, each individual has only one vote. There is no way for Isley to register that he does not want the statue more than Emerson wants it.

(1) Individuals	(2) Dollar Value of Benefits to Individual	(3) Tax Levied on Individual	(4) Net Benefit (+) or Net Cost (−)	(5) Vote For or Against
Applebaum	$150	$ 100	+$50	For
Browning	140	100	+ 40	For
Carson	130	100	+ 30	For
Davidson	110	100	+ 10	For
Emerson	101	100	+ 1	For
Finley	101	100	+ 1	For
Gunter	50	100	− 50	Against
Harrls	10	100	− 90	Against
Isley	10	100	− 90	Against
Janowitz	10	100	− 90	Against
Total	$812	$1,000		

exhibit 2

Simple Majority Voting and Inefficiency
The simple majority decision rule sometimes generates inefficient results. Here the statue is purchased even though the total dollar value of the benefits of the statue is less than the total dollar costs.

Now will voting give us efficiency? The answer largely depends on what tax each person, *A–C*, expects to pay. Suppose each person must pay an equal share of the price of a unit of good *Y*. In other words, the tax for each person is $120 ($360 per unit divided by 3 persons equals $120).

Person *A* will vote for 3 units because his *MPB* for each unit is greater than his tax of $120 per unit. Person *B* will vote for only 1 unit because his *MPB* for the first unit is greater than his tax of $120 per unit but his *MPB* is not greater for the second or third unit. Person *C* will not vote for any units because his *MPB* for each unit is less than his tax of $120 per unit. The outcome, using a simple majority vote, is only 1 unit. In other words, a process of voting where each voter pays an equal tax results in an inefficient outcome.

Now suppose instead of each person paying an equal tax (of $120), each person pays a tax equal to his *MPB* at the socially optimal, or efficient, outcome. The socially optimal, or efficient, outcome is 3 units of good *Y*, so person *A* would pay a tax of $190 (his *MPB* for the third unit is $190). Person *B* would pay a tax of $90, and person *C* would pay a tax of $80. (Keep in mind that the sum of the taxes paid is equal to the cost of the unit, or $360).

With this different tax structure, will voting generate efficiency? If each person casts a truthful vote, the answer is yes. Each person will vote for 3 units.[2] In other words, if everyone casts a truthful vote and everyone pays a tax equal to his or her *MPB* at the efficient outcome, then voting will generate efficiency.

Comparing the two tax structures—one where each person paid an equal tax and one where each person paid a tax equal to his *MPB*—we see that the tax structure makes the difference. In the case of equal tax shares, voting did not lead to efficiency; in the case of unequal tax shares, it did.

Self-Test

1. If the *MSC* in example 2 had been $580 instead of $360, what would the socially optimal, or efficient, outcome be?

2. In example 2 with equal taxes, did the outcome of the vote make anyone worse off? If so, who and by how much?

SPECIAL INTEREST GROUPS

Special Interest Groups
Subsets of the general population that hold (usually) intense preferences for or against a particular government service, activity, or policy. Often special interest groups gain from public policies that may not be in accord with the interests of the general public.

Special interest groups are subsets of the general population that hold (usually) intense preferences for or against a particular government service, activity, or policy. Often special interest groups gain from public policies that may not be in accord with the interests of the general public. In recent decades, they have played a major role in government.

INFORMATIONAL CONTENT AND LOBBYING EFFORTS

The general voter is usually uninformed about issues. The same does not hold for members of a special interest group. For example, it is likely that teachers will know a lot about government education policies, farmers will know about government farm policies, and union members will know about government union policies. When it comes to "their" issue, the members of a particular special interest group will know much more than will the general voter. The reason for this is simple: The more directly and intensely issues affect them, the greater the incentive of individuals to become informed about the issues.

Given an electorate composed of uninformed general voters and informed members of a special interest group, we often observe that the special interest group is able to sway politicians in its direction. This occurs even when the gen-

---

2. Look at the situation for person *A*: His *MPB* for the first unit is $400 and his tax is $190, so he votes for the first unit; his *MPB* for the second unit is $380 and his tax is $190, so he votes for the second unit; his *MPB* for the third unit is $190 and his tax is $190, so he votes for the third unit. With respect to the last unit for person *A*, we are assuming that if his *MPB* is equal to the tax, he will vote in favor of the unit. The same holds for the analysis of voting for persons *B* and *C*.

eral public will be made worse off by such actions (which, of course, is not always the case).

Suppose special interest group A, composed of 5,000 individuals, favors a policy that will result in the redistribution of $50 million from 100 million general taxpayers to the group. The dollar benefit for each member of the special interest group is $10,000. Given this substantial dollar amount, it is likely that the members of the special interest group (1) will have sponsored or proposed the legislation and (2) will lobby the politicians who will decide the issue.

But will the politicians also hear from the general voter (general taxpayer)? The general voter-taxpayer will be less informed about the legislation than the members of the special interest group, and even if he or she were informed, each person would have to calculate the benefits and the costs of lobbying against the proposed legislation. If the legislation passes, the average taxpayer will pay approximately 50 cents. The benefits of lobbying against the legislation are probably not greater than 50 cents. Therefore, we can reasonably conclude that even if the general taxpayer were informed about the legislation, he or she would not be likely to argue against it. The benefits just wouldn't be worth the time and effort. We predict that special interest bills have a good chance of being passed in our legislatures.

Q & A

Q: Is special interest legislation necessarily bad legislation? Can't legislation proposed and lobbied for by a special interest group benefit not only the special interest (directly) but also the public interest (perhaps indirectly)?

A: Special interest legislation is not necessarily bad legislation, and certainly such legislation can benefit the public interest. What we are saying is: The costs and benefits of being informed about particular issues and of lobbying for and against issues are different for the member of the special interest group and the member of the general public, and this can make a difference in the type of legislation that will be proposed, passed, and implemented.

CONGRESSIONAL DISTRICTS AS SPECIAL INTEREST GROUPS

Most people do not ordinarily think of congressional districts as special interest groups. (Special interest groups are commonly thought to include the ranks of public school teachers, steel manufacturers, automobile manufacturers, farmers, environmentalists, bankers, truck drivers, doctors, and so on.) For some issues, however, a particular congressional district may be a special interest group.

Suppose an air force base is located in a Texas congressional district. Then, a Pentagon study determines that the air force base is not needed and that Congress should close it down. The Pentagon study demonstrates that the cost to the taxpayers of keeping the base open is greater than the benefits to the country of maintaining the base.

But closing the air force base will hurt the pocketbooks of the people in the congressional district that houses the base. Their congressional representative knows as much; she also knows that if she can't keep the base open, she isn't as likely to be reelected to office.

Therefore, she speaks to other members of Congress about the proposed closing. In a way, she is a lobbyist for her congressional district. Will the majority of the members of Congress be willing to go along with the Texas representative? If they do, they know that their constituents will be paying more in taxes than the Pentagon has said is necessary to assure the national security of the country. But if they don't, when they need a vote on one of their own special interest (sometimes the term *pork barrel* is used) projects, the representative from Texas may not be forthcoming. In short, members of Congress sometimes trade votes: my vote on your air force base for your vote on subsidies to dairy farmers in my district. This type of vote trading—the exchange of votes to gain support for legislation—is commonly referred to as **logrolling.**

Logrolling
The exchange of votes to gain support for legislation.

PUBLIC INTEREST TALK, SPECIAL INTEREST LEGISLATION

Special interest legislation usually isn't called by that name by the special interest group lobbying for it. Instead, it is referred to as "legislation in the best interest of the general public." A number of examples, both past and present, come to mind.

In the early nineteenth century, the British Parliament passed the Factory Acts, which put restrictions on women and children working. Those who lobbied for the restrictions said they did so for humanitarian reasons; for example, to protect young children and women from difficult and hazardous work in the cotton mills. There is evidence, however, that men working in the factories were the main lobbyists for the Factory Acts and that a reduced supply of women and children directly benefited them by raising wages. The male factory workers appealed to individuals' higher sensibilities instead of letting it be known that they would benefit at the expense of others.

Today, those people calling for, say, economic protection from foreign competitors or greater federal subsidies rarely explain that they favor the measure because it will make them better off while someone else pays the bill. Instead, they usually voice the public interest argument. Economic protectionism isn't necessary to protect industry *X,* it is necessary to protect American jobs and the domestic economy. The special interest message often is "Help yourself by helping us."

Sometimes this message holds true, and sometimes it does not. But it is likely to be as forcefully voiced in the latter case as in the former.

SPECIAL INTEREST GROUPS AND RENT SEEKING

Special interest groups often engage in rent-seeking behavior, which has consequences for society as a whole. Although rent seeking is discussed in earlier chapters, we review the concept here and describe how it relates to special interest groups.

Rent versus Profit

The term *rent seeking* was first used by Anne Krueger in an article in 1974, but the theory behind rent seeking had already been put forth by Gordon Tullock in a 1969 article. Strictly speaking, the term *rent* refers to the part of the payment to an owner of resources over and above the amount those resources could command in any alternative use. In other words, rent is payment over and above opportunity cost.

Everyone would like to receive payment in excess of opportunity cost, so the motive to seek rent is strong. *When rent is the result of entrepreneurial activity designed to either satisfy a new demand or rearrange resources in an increasingly valuable way, then rent is usually called profit.* To illustrate, suppose Jack finds a way to rearrange resources *X, Y,* and *Z* to produce a new good, *A.* If Jack receives a price for *A* that is greater than the cost of the resources, he receives a payment in excess of opportunity cost. Thus, Jack receives some rent; but, in this setting, the rent is called profit.

In what setting is rent not referred to as profit? The answer is *in a setting where no new demand is satisfied or no additional value is created.* To illustrate, suppose Vernon lives and works as a taxi driver in a city in the Midwest. The city council licenses taxi drivers as long as they meet certain minimum requirements—such as having a valid driver's license and so on. Currently, Vernon receives a monthly income that is equal to his opportunity cost. In other words, he does not receive any rent. Then, one day, Vernon and the other taxi drivers in the city lobby the city council to stop issuing taxi licenses, and the city council grants this request. Over time, the demand for taxis is likely to rise, but the supply of taxis will not. As a result, the dollar price for a taxi ride will rise. In time, it is possible that Vernon will earn an income over and above his opportunity cost. In other words, he will receive some rent.

In this setting, Vernon and the other taxi drivers have neither satisfied a new demand nor rearranged resources in a way that increases value. They have simply lobbied the city government to bring about a change that results in their receiving higher taxi fares and higher incomes at the expense of the customers who must pay the higher fares. There has a been a transfer of income from taxi riders to taxi drivers. Notice that this transfer of income has a cost. Vernon and the other taxi drivers expended resources in order to bring about this pure transfer, which is referred to as rent seeking. In short, *rent seeking is the expenditure of scarce resources to capture a pure transfer.*

Rent Seeking Is Socially Wasteful

From society's perspective, the resources used in rent seeking are wasted and make society (but not necessarily all individuals in society) poorer as a result. To illustrate, suppose there are only two people in a society, Smith and Brown. The total amount of resources in this society, or the total income, is $10,000. We could (1) give all of the income to Smith, (2) give all of it to Brown, or (3) give some amount to each. Exhibit 3 shows a line, I_1, that represents the possible combinations of income the two persons may receive. Currently, Smith and Brown are located at point A on I_1, where each receives some income.[3]

Smith would prefer to be located at point B, where he would receive more income than he currently does at point A. To this end, Smith lobbies legislators to pass a law that effectively redistributes income from Brown to him. Smith is successful in his lobbying efforts and the law passes. Do Brown and Smith move from point A to point B as a result? No. This movement doesn't adjust for the resources that were used by Smith when he was rent seeking. If we take these

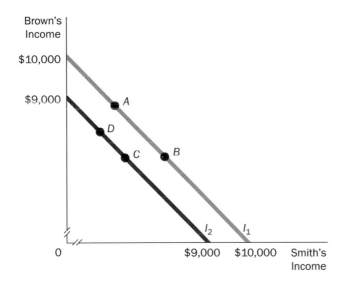

exhibit 3

Rent Seeking
Brown and Smith are the only two people in a society in which the total amount of resources, or the total income, is $10,000. Currently, Brown and Smith are located at point A on I_1, where each receives some of the $10,000. Smith wants to move to point B, where he would receive more income than he does at point A. To try to bring this outcome about, he lobbies legislators to pass a law that will transfer income away from Brown to him. In other words, he is rent seeking. Because rent seeking activity uses resources in a socially unproductive way, there are fewer resources, or less total income, to divide between Brown and Smith. Still, Smith may not mind this if he has moved from point A on I_1 to point C on I_2 as a result of his rent-seeking activities. Overall, Brown and Smith are worse off (sharing $9,000 instead of $10,000), but Smith is better off at point C than at point A.

---

3 The analysis here is based on Chapter 18: The Rent-Seeking Society in Richard McKenzie and Gordon Tullock, *The New World of Economics* (New York: McGraw Hill, 1994).

Inheritance, Heirs, and Why the Firstborn Became King or Queen

Some economists have said that rent-seeking activity often goes on within families, especially when an inheritance is involved. We present their argument in the form of a short story.

An elderly widow with three children has an estate worth $10 million. It is understood that she will leave her $10 million to her children upon her death. But, of course, there are different ways to leave $10 million to three adult children. She can split the $10 million into three equal parts, leaving $3.333 million to each. Or she can divide the $10 million unequally, perhaps leaving $9 million to A, $500,000 to B, and $500,000 to C. Furthermore, she can either tell each child how much he or she will inherit or she can keep the dollar amount secret (until after her death). In other words, the elderly woman has two major decisions to make. The first relates to how much money she will give to each child. The second relates to whether or not she will tell each child what he or she will receive upon her death.

If the woman is the type of person who craves attention and wants her children to fawn over her, can she use her inheritance to bring this about? She certainly can. All she has to do is (1) tell her children that she will not divide her estate equally among the three of them and (2) say that she hasn't yet decided on the amount each will receive. If she promises unequal inheritances that are yet to be determined, she almost guarantees that her children will engage in a rent-seeking battle for the bulk of her inheritance. This rent-seeking battle is likely to take the form of each child fawning over the mother in order to curry favor.

Let's look at the situation from the perspective of any one child, say A. He knows there is a fixed inheritance, $10 million, and what goes to one of his siblings will not go to him. For example, if $3 million goes to sibling B or to sibling C, this is $3 million less for him (A). The widow has effectively set up an arrangement where her three children will invest resources (to fawn over her) in order to effect a pure transfer. This is rent seeking.

The situation is different if the woman tells her children what she plans to leave each and then guarantees that under no circumstances will she change her mind. For example, if she tells child A that he will receive $2 million, child B that she will receive $7 million, and child C that he will receive $1 million, then there is no reason for any of the children to invest resources in rent seeking. The $10 million has already been split up. Alternatively, the mother can simply tell her children that she plans to divide her inheritance equally and nothing on earth can get her to do differently. Once again, if the children know how things are guaranteed to turn out and that any resources they use to change the results will be wasted, they will decide against trying to change the outcome. No child will seek rents, in other words.

Now, let's consider the concept of rent seeking in a slightly different context. In the days when kings and queens ruled, the firstborn of a king or queen usually inherited the throne. But why the first? Couldn't the third child be more capable than the first to be king or queen? Was every first child more capable of being king or queen than every second, third, or fourth child?

Before you answer these questions, consider what might have happened if it was not predetermined that the first child inherited the throne. The king's or queen's children would have engaged in a rent-seeking battle for the throne. In and of itself, the queen or king may not have had anything against this. In fact, they may have liked it.

But what they wouldn't have liked is their children engaged in such an intense rent-seeking battle that each might have tried to kill the others. From the child's perspective, there would be two ways to get the throne. The first would be to have the queen or king choose you from among all your brothers and sisters to ascend to the throne. The second would be to kill your brothers and sisters so that you were the only one left to ascend to the throne. One way to cut down on sibling killings was to simply have a rule that stated that the firstborn would become king or queen. This rule didn't eliminate sibling murders completely because it was still possible for the second child to try to kill the first and therefore inherit the throne, but it certainly reduced sibling murders over and above what might happen if any of the many children could ascend to the throne.

resources into account, there is now less total income for Smith and Brown to share. If $1,000 worth of resources were expended in effecting the transfer, income is now $9,000 instead of $10,000. In other words, I_1 is no longer relevant, I_2 is. The result of Smith's rent seeking is that he and Brown move from point A to point C. At point C, Smith receives more income than he did at point A and Brown receives less.

One effect of Smith's rent seeking is that he is made better off and Brown is made worse off. The other effect is that society as a whole (that is, the sum of Smith and Brown) is poorer than it was when there was no rent seeking. In short, rent seeking may be rational from an individual's perspective (after all, Smith does make himself better off through rent seeking), but it is harmful to society.

Now consider a slight modification to our analysis. Suppose Brown is aware that Smith is lobbying legislators in an attempt to transfer income from her to him. Brown may try to lobby defensively—that is, to lobby against Smith. Brown's lobbying efforts are not costless; resources are expended in trying to defend the status quo income distribution. While Brown may not be seeking rent, she is using resources in order to prevent someone else from obtaining rent. The resources she uses are wasted as far as society is concerned because they do not go to build bridges, educate children, or do any number of other things. These resources are used to prevent a pure transfer. In other words, because of Brown's defensive lobbying efforts, society may move from I_1 to I_2. If Brown is successful at preventing Smith from effecting a pure transfer, then Brown and Smith may end up moving from point A to point D. The relative income shares of the two individuals may not be any different at point D than at point A, but both Brown and Smith receive less income at point D than at point A. The combination of offensive lobbying (for rent) by Smith and defensive lobbying (to prevent Smith from getting rent) by Brown results in both individuals being made worse off.

http://

Go to *http://www.house.gov/cha/*, and click "Committee Business." Read the transcript of a hearing that deals with campaign reform. Is a bill being proposed? If so, what is the objective of the bill? Does the bill have anything to do with rent seeking? If so, what?

Self-Test

1. The "average" farmer is likely to be better informed about federal agricultural policy than the "average" food consumer. Why?

2. Consider a piece of special interest legislation that will transfer $40 million from group A to group B, where group B includes 10,000 persons. Is this piece of special interest legislation more likely to pass (a) when group A includes 10,000 persons or (b) when group A includes 10 million persons? Explain your answer.

3. Give an example of public interest talk spoken by a special interest group.

4. Why is rent-seeking activity socially wasteful?

GOVERNMENT BUREAUCRACY

A discussion of politics and government is not complete without mention of the government bureau and bureaucrat. A **government bureaucrat** is an unelected person who works in a government bureau and is assigned a special task that relates to a law or program passed by the legislature.

Government Bureaucrat
An unelected person who works in a government bureau and is assigned a special task that relates to a law or program passed by the legislature.

GOVERNMENT BUREAUS: SOME FACTS AND THEIR CONSEQUENCES
Consider a few facts about government bureaus:

1. A government bureau receives its funding from the legislature. Often, its funding in future years depends on how much it spends carrying out its specified duties in the current year.
2. A government bureau does not maximize profits.
3. There are no transferable ownership rights in a government bureau. There are no stockholders in a government bureau.

4. Many government bureaus provide services for which there is no competition. For example, if a person wants a driver's license, there is usually only one place to go—the Department of Motor Vehicles.
5. If the legislation that established the government bureau in the first place is repealed, there is little need for the government bureau.

These five facts about government bureaus have corresponding consequences. Many economists see these consequences as follows:

1. Government bureaus are not likely to end the current year with surplus funds. If they do, their funding for the following year is likely to be less than it was for the current year. The motto is "spend the money, or lose it."
2. Because a government bureau does not attempt to maximize profits the way a private firm would, it does not watch its costs as carefully. Combining points 1 and 2, we conclude that government bureau costs are likely to remain constant or rise but are not likely to fall.
3. No one has a monetary incentive to monitor the government bureau because no one "owns" the government bureau and no one can sell an "ownership right" in the bureau. Stockholders in private firms have a monetary incentive to ensure that the managers of the firms do an efficient job. Because there is no analog to stockholders in a government bureau, there is no one to ensure that the bureau managers operate the bureau efficiently.
4. Government bureaus and bureaucrats are not so likely to try to please the "customer" as private firms are because (in most cases) they have no competition and are not threatened by any in the future. If the lines are long at the Department of Motor Vehicles, the bureaucrats do not care. Customers cannot go anywhere else to get what they need.
5. Government bureaucrats are likely to lobby for the continued existence and expansion of the programs they administer. To behave differently would go against their best interests. To argue for the repeal of a program, for example, is to argue for the abolition of their jobs.

Q & A   **Q:** This description makes it sound as if government bureaucrats are petty, selfish people. Aren't many government bureaucrats nice, considerate people who work hard at their jobs?

A: The point is not that government bureaucrats are bad people set on taking advantage of the general public. The point is that ordinary people will behave in certain predictable ways in a government bureau that is funded by the legislature, does not maximize profits, has no analog to private-sector stockholders, has little (if any) competition, and depends on the continuance of certain legislation for its existence.

A VIEW OF GOVERNMENT

The view of government presented in this chapter is perhaps much different from the view presented by your elementary school social studies teacher. He may have described government as made up of people who were kind, charitable, altruistic, generous, and, above all, dedicated to serving the public good. No doubt some will say that the view of government in this chapter is cynical and exaggerated. It may very well be. But remember, it is based on a theory, and most theories are not descriptively accurate. The real question is whether the theory of public-sector decision making presented here meets the test that any theory must meet. It must explain and predict real-world events. Numerous economists and political scientists have concluded that it does.

A Reader Asks...
What Is the Significance of Public Choice?

Public choice hits on some interesting topics—such as the median voter model, special interests, and rational ignorance—but why is it studied in economics? Why isn't it studied in political science?

According to public choice economists, public choice fills a gap that existed in economics. They often say that before public choice came along, too many economists simply assumed that if "markets failed," government would and could step up and fix the problem. For example, if a negative externality caused the market to "fail"—and the market overproduced a good—then government officials could be relied on to set the right tax and correct the problem. If individuals demanded a nonexcludable public good and the market didn't provide it, then government would. In the area of macroeconomics, if the self-regulating properties of the economy were not working and the unemployment rate rose too high, then government would step forward and stimulate the economy in just the right way to reduce the unemployment rate to an acceptable level.

What all this assumed, say public choice economists, is that government would work flawlessly to correct the failures of the market. Public choice theory questions whether government works as flawlessly and as unselfishly as many people assume. Just as there is "market failure," say public choice economists, there is "government failure," or "political failure," too.

Here is what James Buchanan, one of the founders of public choice, has to say about the subject:

Lest we forget, it is useful to remind ourselves in the 1990s that the predominant emphasis of the theoretical welfare economics of the 1950s and 1960s was placed on the identification of "market failure," with the accompanying normative argument for politicized correction. In retrospect, it seems naïve in the extreme to advance institutional comparisons between the workings of an observed and idealized alternative. Despite Wicksell's early criticism, however, economists continued to assume, implicitly, that politics would work ideally in the corrective adjustments to market failures that analysis enabled them to identify.

The lasting contribution of public choice theory has been to correct this obvious imbalance in analysis. Any institutional comparison that is worthy of serious considerations must compare relevant alternatives; if market organization is to be replaced by politicized order, or vice versa, the two institutional structures must be evaluated on the basis of predictions as to how they will actually work. Political failure, as well as market failure, must become central to the comprehensive analysis that precedes normative judgment.[4]

Chapter Summary

Politicians and the Middle

- In a two-person race, candidates for the same office will gravitate toward the middle of the political spectrum to pick up votes. If a candidate does not do this and her opponent does, the opponent will win the election. Candidates do a number of things during campaigns that indicate they understand where they are headed—toward the middle. For example, candidates attempt to label their opponents as either "too far right" or "too far left." Candidates usually pick labels for themselves that represent the middle of the political spectrum, they speak in general terms, and they take polls and adjust their positions accordingly.

Voting and Rational Ignorance

- There are both costs and benefits to voting. Many potential voters will not vote because the costs of

voting—in terms of time spent going to the polls and so on—outweigh the benefits of voting, measured as the probability of their single vote affecting the election outcome.

- There is a difference between being unable to learn certain information and choosing not to learn certain information. Most voters choose not to be informed about political and governmental issues because the costs of becoming informed outweigh the benefits of becoming informed. They choose to be rationally ignorant.

More about Voting

- In a simple majority vote where there are several options from which to choose, the voting outcome is the same as the most preferred outcome of the median voter.

---

4. James M. Buchanan, *Better Than Plowing and Other Personal Essays* (Chicago: University of Chicago Press, 1992), p. 99.

- Simple majority voting and equal tax shares can generate a different result than simple majority voting and unequal tax shares.

Special Interest Groups
- Special interest groups are usually well informed about their issues. Individuals have a greater incentive to become informed about issues the more directly and intensely the issue affects them.
- Legislation that concentrates the benefits on a few and disperses the costs over many is likely to pass because the beneficiaries will have an incentive to lobby for it, whereas those who pay the bill will not lobby against it because each of them pays such a small part of the bill.
- Special interest groups often engage in rent seeking, which is the expenditure of scarce resources to cap-

ture a pure transfer. Rent seeking is a socially wasteful activity because resources that are used to effect transfers are not used to produce goods and services.

Bureaucracy
- Public choice economists do not believe government bureaucrats are bad people set on taking advantage of the general public. They believe bureaucrats are ordinary people (just like our friends and neighbors) who behave in predictable ways in a government bureau that is funded by the legislature, does not maximize profits, has no analog to private-sector stockholders, has little (if any) competition, and depends on the continuance of certain legislation for its existence.

Key Terms and Concepts

Public Choice	Rational Ignorance	Logrolling
Median Voter Model	Special Interest Groups	Government Bureaucrat

Questions and Problems

1. Some observers maintain that not all politicians move toward the middle of the political spectrum to obtain votes. They often cite Barry Goldwater in the 1964 presidential election and George McGovern in the 1972 presidential election as examples. Are these exceptions to the theory developed in this chapter?

2. Would voters have a greater incentive to vote in an election in which there were only a few registered voters or in one in which there were many registered voters? Why?

3. Many individuals learn more about the car they are thinking of buying than about the candidates running for the presidency of the United States. Explain why.

4. If the model of politics and government presented in this chapter is true, what are some of the things we would expect to see?

5. It has often been remarked that Democratic candidates are more liberal in the Democratic primaries and Republican candidates are more conservative in

the Republican primaries than either is in the general election, respectively. Explain why.

6. What are some ways of reducing the cost of voting to voters?

7. Provide a numerical example that shows simple majority voting may be consistent with efficiency. Next, provide a numerical example that shows simple majority voting may be inconsistent with efficiency.

8. What are some ways of making government bureaucrats and bureaus more cost-conscious?

9. Some individuals see national defense spending as benefiting special interests—in particular, the defense industry. Others see it as directly benefiting not only the defense industry but the general public as well. Does this same difference in view exist for issues other than national defense? Name a few.

10. Evaluate each of the following proposals for reform in terms of the material discussed in this chapter: (a) linking all spending programs to visible tax hikes; (b) a balanced budget amendment that stipulates that Con-

gress cannot spend more than total tax revenues; (c) a budgetary referenda process whereby the voters actually vote on the distribution of federal dollars to the different categories of spending (*X* percentage to agriculture, *Y* percentage to national defense, and so on), instead of the elected representatives deciding.

11. Rent seeking may be rational from the individual's perspective, but it is not from society's perspective. Do you agree or disagree? Explain your answer.

Working with Numbers and Graphs

1. Suppose there are three major candidates, *A*, *B*, and *C*, running for the presidency of the United States and the distribution of voters is the same as evidenced in Exhibit 1. Two of the candidates, *A* and *B*, are currently viewed as right of the median, and *C* is viewed as left of the median. Is it possible to predict which candidate is most likely to win?

2. Look back at Exhibit 2. Suppose net benefits and net costs for each person are known a week before election day and it is legal to buy and sell votes. Furthermore, suppose there is no conscious cost to either

buying or selling votes. Would the outcome of the election be the same? Explain your answer.

3. In part (a) of the following figure, the distribution of voters is skewed to the left; in part (b), the distribution of voters is skewed neither left nor right; and in part (c), the distribution of voters is skewed right. Assuming a two person race for each distribution, will the candidate who wins the election in (a) hold different positions than the candidates who win the elections in (b) and (c)? Explain your answer.

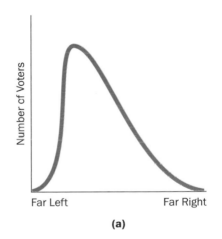

(a)

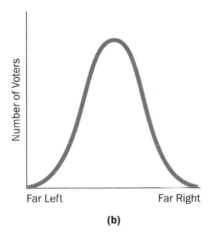

(b)

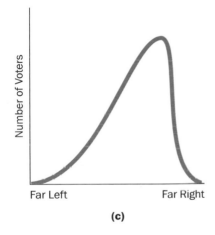

(c)

Internet Activities

1. Go to *http://www.fec.gov*. Click on "Campaign Finance Reports and Data," and then on "House Campaign Summaries by State" (for the most recent year). Choose a state with numerous House elections (such as California, New York, or Texas).

  a. Look at the "Gen Result" column (W = won and L = lost) and the "Net Receipts" column. In what

percentage of House elections did the candidate who spent the lesser amount of money win?

  b. Look at the "Inc/Chl/Open" column. "Inc" stands for incumbent (an incumbent is running for reelection), "chl" stands for challenger (to the incumbent), and "open" signifies that an incumbent is not running for reelection. Identify three House races with an incumbent. Next, look at the "Contrib from Other Cmtes" column. The dollar amounts in this column represent money contributed to the candidates by political action committees (PACs). Who received more PAC money, the incumbent or the challenger? Why do you think there is a difference between the amount of money contributed to an incumbent and the amount contributed to a challenger?

c. Look at PAC contributions in open races. Is the dollar difference in PAC contributions smaller between candidates in an open race than in a race in which there is an incumbent? If so, why might this be the case? Do you think some PACs give to both candidates in a two-person open race?

2. Use your "Back" button to return to the "Campaign Finance Reports and Data" page. Select "PAC Activity" for the most recent period.

a. For the most recent period shown, did PACs contribute more to Republicans or to Democrats running for the House of Representatives? running for the U.S. Senate?

b. For the earliest period shown, did PACs contribute more to Republicans or to Democrats running for the House of Representatives? running for the U.S. Senate?

c. In the most recent period shown, how much did PACs contribute to incumbents? to challengers?

d. Select "Top 50 PACs by Contributions to Candidates." Which political action committee contributed the most money to candidates in the period shown? What percentage of the Top 50 PACs are labor unions? professional employee associations? corporations?

Log on to the Arnold Xtra! Web site now (*http://arnoldxtra.swcollege.com*) for additional learning resources such as practice quizzes, help with graphing, video clips, and current event applications.

ch.19

INTERNATIONAL TRADE

*Economics is about trade, and trade crosses boundaries. People do not trade exclu-
sively with people who live in their city, state, or country. They trade with people in
other countries, too. No doubt, many of the goods you consume are produced in
other countries. This chapter examines international trade and the prohibitions that
are sometimes placed on it.*

*We state in an early chapter that economics is largely
about trade, and we have discussed the various aspects of trade and
its economic implications. But mainly, we have examined domestic trade—trade
between people who live within the United States. In this chapter, we extend our discussion
of trade to the rest of the world. We discuss international trade.*

*As shown in the chapter road map, we examine two main topics in international trade. First, we answer
the question of why people in different countries trade, which leads us to the law of comparative advantage. Second, we discuss the effects of tariffs and quotas, two of the major restrictions sometimes placed on international trade.*

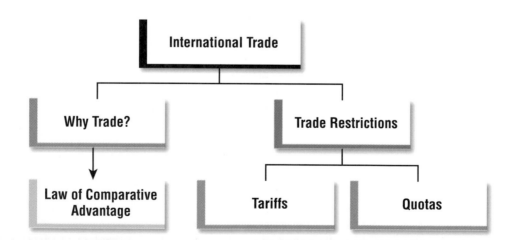

INTERNATIONAL TRADE THEORY

International trade exists for the same reasons that trade at any level exists. Individuals trade to make themselves better off. Pat and Zach, both of whom live in Cincinnati, Ohio, trade because they both value something the other has more than they value some of their own possessions. On an international scale, Elaine in the United States trades with Cho in China because Cho has something that Elaine wants and Elaine has something that Cho wants.

Obviously, different countries have different terrains, climates, resources, skills, and so on. It follows that some countries will be able to produce some goods that other countries cannot produce or can produce only at extremely high costs.

For example, Hong Kong has no oil, and Saudi Arabia has a large supply. Bananas do not grow easily in the United States, but they flourish in Honduras. Americans could grow bananas if they used hothouses, but it is cheaper for Americans to buy bananas from Hondurans than to produce bananas themselves.

Major U.S. exports include automobiles, computers, aircraft, corn, wheat, soybeans, scientific instruments, coal, and plastic materials. Major imports include petroleum, automobiles, clothing, iron and steel, office machines, footwear, fish, coffee, and diamonds. Some of the countries of the world that are major exporters are the United States, Germany, Japan, France, and the United Kingdom. These same countries are some of the major importers in the world too.

HOW DO COUNTRIES KNOW WHAT TO TRADE?

To explain how countries know what to trade, we need to discuss the concept of *comparative advantage,* an economic concept first discussed in Chapter 2. Here is a simple model.

Comparative Advantage

Assume a two country–two good world. The countries are the United States and Japan, and the goods are food and clothing. Both countries can produce the two goods in the four different combinations listed in Exhibit 1. For example, the United States can produce 90 units of food and 0 units of clothing, or 60 units of food and 10 units of clothing, or another combination. Japan can produce 15 units of food and 0 units of clothing, or 10 units of food and 5 units of clothing, or another combination.

Suppose the United States is producing and consuming the two goods in the combination represented by point *B* on its production possibilities frontier, and Japan is producing and consuming the combination of the two goods represented by point *B'* on its production possibilities frontier. In other words, in this case, neither of the two countries is specializing in the production of one of the two goods, nor are the two countries trading with each other. We call this the *no specialization–no trade (NS-NT) case.* (See column 1 in Exhibit 2.)

Now suppose the United States and Japan decide to specialize in the production of a specific good and to trade with each other, called the *specialization–trade (S-T) case.* Will the two countries be made better off through specialization and trade? A numerical example will help answer this question. But, first, we need to find the answers to two other questions: What good should the United States specialize in producing? What good should Japan specialize in producing?

The general answer to both these questions is the same: *Countries specialize in the production of the good in which they have a comparative advantage.* A country has a **comparative advantage** in the production of a good when it can produce the good at lower opportunity cost than another country can.

For example, in the United States, the opportunity cost of producing 1 unit of clothing is 3 units of food (for every 10 units of clothing it produces, it forfeits 30 units of food). So the opportunity cost of producing 1 unit of food is $\frac{1}{3}$ unit of clothing. In Japan, the opportunity cost of producing 1 unit of clothing is 1 unit of food (for every 5 units of clothing it produces, it forfeits 5 units of food). To

Comparative Advantage
The situation where a country can produce a good at lower opportunity cost than another country can.

exhibit 1

Production Possibilities in Two Countries

The United States and Japan can produce the two goods in the combinations shown. Initially, the United States is at point B on its PPF and Japan is at point B' on its PPF. Both countries can be made better off by specializing in and trading the good in which each has a comparative advantage.

United States			Japan		
Points on Production Possibilities Frontier	Food	Clothing	Points on Production Possibilities Frontier	Food	Clothing
A	90	0	A'	15	0
B	60	10	B'	10	5
C	30	20	C'	5	10
D	0	30	D'	0	15

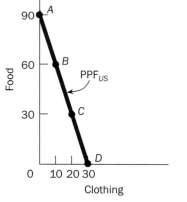

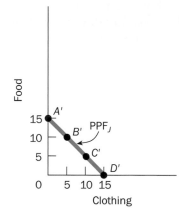

recap, in the United States, the situation is $1C = 3F$, or $1F = \frac{1}{3}C$; in Japan the situation is $1C = 1F$, or $1F = 1C$.

The United States can produce food at a lower opportunity cost ($\frac{1}{3}C$ as opposed to $1C$ in Japan), whereas Japan can produce clothing at a lower opportunity cost ($1F$ as opposed to $3F$ in the United States). Thus, the United States has a comparative advantage in food, and Japan has a comparative advantage in clothing.

Suppose the two countries specialize in the production of the good in which they have a comparative advantage. In other words, the United States specializes in the production of food (producing 90 units), and Japan specializes in the production of clothing (producing 15 units). In Exhibit 1, the United States locates at point A on its PPF, and Japan locates at point D' on its PPF. (See column 2 in Exhibit 2.)

Settling on the Terms of Trade

After they have determined which good to specialize in producing, the two countries must settle on the terms of trade, that is, how much food to trade for how much clothing. Recall that the United States faces the following situation: For every 30 units of food it does not produce, it can produce 10 units of clothing, as shown in Exhibit 1. Thus, 3 units of food have an opportunity cost of 1 unit of clothing ($3F = 1C$), or 1 unit of food has a cost of $\frac{1}{3}$ unit of clothing ($1F = \frac{1}{3}C$). Meanwhile, Japan faces the following situation: For every 5 units of food it does not produce, it can produce 5 units of clothing. Thus, 1 unit of food has an opportunity cost of 1 unit of clothing ($1F = 1C$). Recapping, for the United States, $3F = 1C$, and for Japan, $1F = 1C$.

With these cost ratios, it would seem likely that both countries could agree on terms of trade that specify $2F = 1C$. The United States would prefer to give up 2 units of food instead of 3 units for 1 unit of clothing, whereas Japan would prefer to give up 1 unit of clothing and get 2 units of food instead of only 1 unit.

Country	No Specialization–No Trade (*NS-NT*) Case (1) Production and Consumption in the *NS-NT* Case		Specialization-Trade (*S-T*) Case (2) Production in the *S-T* Case		(3) Exports (−) Imports (+) Terms of Trade Are 2*F* = 1*C*	(4) Consumption in the *S-T* Case (2) + (3)	(5) Gains from Specialization and Trade (4) − (1)
United States							
Food	60	Point *B* in	90	Point *A* in	−20	70	10
Clothing	10	Exhibit 1	0	Exhibit 1	+10	10	0
Japan							
Food	10	Point *B'* in	0	Point *D'* in	+20	20	10
Clothing	5	Exhibit 1	15	Exhibit 1	−10	5	0

Suppose the two countries agree to the terms of trade of $2F = 1C$ and trade, in absolute amounts, 20 units of food for 10 units of clothing. (See column 3 in Exhibit 2.)

Results of the Specialization-Trade (*S-T*) Case

Now the United States produces 90 units of food and trades 20 units to Japan, receiving 10 units of clothing in exchange. It consumes 70 units of food and 10 units of clothing. Japan produces 15 units of clothing and trades 10 to the United States, receiving 20 units of food in exchange. It consumes 5 units of clothing and 20 units of food. (See column 4 in Exhibit 2.)

Comparing the consumption levels in both countries in the two cases, the United States and Japan each consume 10 more units of food and no less clothing in the specialization-trade case than in the no specialization–no trade case (column 5 in Exhibit 2). We conclude that a country gains by specializing in producing and trading the good in which it has a comparative advantage.

Q&A

Q: Specialization and trade appear to allow a country's inhabitants to consume at a level beyond its production possibilities frontier. Is this correct?

A: Yes, that is correct. To see this, look at the PPF for the United States in Exhibit 1. In the *NS-NT* case, the United States consumes 60 units of food and 10 units of clothing—that is, the United States consumes at point *B* on its PPF. In the *S-T* case, however, it consumes 70 units of food and 10 units of clothing. A point that represents this combination of the two goods is beyond the country's PPF.

HOW DO COUNTRIES KNOW WHEN THEY HAVE A COMPARATIVE ADVANTAGE?

Government officials of a country do not analyze pages of cost data to determine what their country should specialize in producing and then trade. Countries do not plot production possibilities frontiers on graph paper or calculate opportunity costs. Instead, it is individuals' desire to earn a dollar, a peso, or a euro that determines the pattern of international trade. The desire to earn a profit determines what a country specializes in and trades.

Take the case of Henri, an enterprising Frenchman who visits the United States. Henri observes that beef is relatively cheap in the United States (compared with the price in France) and perfume is relatively expensive. Noticing the price differences for beef and perfume between his country and the United States, he decides to buy some perfume in France, bring it to the United States, and sell it for the relatively higher U.S. price. With his profits from the perfume transaction,

exhibit 2

Both Countries Gain from Specialization and Trade
Column 1: Both the United States and Japan operate independently of each other. The United States produces and consumes 60 units of food and 10 units of clothing. Japan produces and consumes 10 units of food and 5 units of clothing. Column 2: The United States specializes in the production of food; Japan specializes in the production of clothing. Column 3: The United States and Japan agree to the terms of trade of 2 units of food for 1 unit of clothing. They actually trade 20 units of food for 10 units of clothing. Column 4: Overall, the United States consumes 70 units of food and 10 units of clothing. Japan consumes 20 units of food and 5 units of clothing. Column 5: Consumption levels are higher for both the United States and Japan in the *S-T* case than in the *NS-NT* case.

ECONOMICS IN...

Dividing Up the Work

John and Veronica, husband and wife, have divided up their household tasks the following way: John usually does all the lawn work, fixes the cars, and does the dinner dishes, while Veronica cleans the house, cooks the meals, and does the laundry. Why have John and Veronica divided up the household tasks the way they have? Some sociologists might suggest that John and Veronica have divided up the tasks along gender lines—men have for years done the lawn work, fixed the cars, and so on, and women have for years cleaned the house, cooked the meals, and so on. In other words, John is doing "man's work," and Veronica is doing "woman's work."

Well, maybe, but that leaves unanswered the question of why certain work became "man's work" and other work became "woman's work." Moreover, it doesn't explain why John and Veronica don't split every task evenly. In other words, why doesn't John clean half the house and Veronica clean half the house? Why doesn't Veronica mow the lawn on the second and fourth week of every month and John mow the lawn every first and third week of the month?

The law of comparative advantage may be the answer to all our questions. To illustrate, suppose we consider two tasks, cleaning the house and mowing the lawn. The following table shows how long John and Veronica take to complete the two tasks individually.

	Time to Clean the House	Time to Mow the Lawn
John	120 minutes	50 minutes
Veronica	60 minutes	100 minutes

Here is the opportunity cost of each task for each person.

	Opportunity Cost of Cleaning the House	Opportunity Cost of Mowing the Lawn
John	2.40 mowed lawns	0.42 clean houses
Veronica	0.60 mowed lawns	1.67 clean houses

In other words, John has a comparative advantage in mowing the lawn and Veronica has a comparative advantage in cleaning the house.

Now let's compare two settings. In setting 1, John and Veronica each do half of each task. In setting 2, John only mows the lawn and Veronica only cleans the house.

In setting 1, John spends 60 minutes cleaning half of the house and 25 minutes mowing half of the lawn for a total of 85 minutes; Veronica spends 30 minutes cleaning half of the house and 50 minutes mowing half of the lawn for a total of 80 minutes. The total time spent by Veronica and John cleaning the house and mowing the lawn is 165 minutes.

In setting 2, John spends 50 minutes mowing the lawn and Veronica spends 60 minutes cleaning the house. The total time spent by Veronica and John cleaning the house and mowing the lawn is 110 minutes.

In which setting, 1 or 2, are Veronica and John better off? John works 85 minutes in setting 1 and 50 minutes in setting 2, so he is better off in setting 2. Veronica works 80 minutes in setting 1 and 60 minutes in setting 2, so Veronica is better off in setting 2. Together, John and Veronica spend 55 fewer minutes in setting 2 than in setting 1. Getting the job done in 55 fewer minutes is the benefit of specializing in various duties around the house. Given our numbers, we would expect that John will mow the lawn (and nothing else) and Veronica will clean the house (and nothing else).

he buys beef in the United States, ships it to France, and sells it for the relatively higher French price. Obviously, Henri is buying low and selling high. He buys a good in the country where it is cheap and sells it in the country where the good is expensive.

What are the consequences of Henri's activities? First, he is earning a profit. The larger the price differences in the two goods between the two countries and the more he reshuffles goods between countries, the more profit Henri earns.

Second, Henri's activities are moving each country toward its comparative advantage. The United States ends up exporting beef to France, and France ends up exporting perfume to the United States. Just as the pure theory predicts, individuals in the two countries specialize in and trade the good in which they have a comparative advantage. The outcome is brought about spontaneously through the actions of individuals trying to make themselves better off; they are simply trying to gain through trade.

Self-Test *(Answers to Self-Test questions are in the Self-Test Appendix.)*

1. Suppose the United States can produce 120 units of X at an opportunity cost of 20 units of Y, and Great Britain can produce 40 units of X at an opportunity cost of 80 units of Y. Identify favorable terms of trade for the two countries.

2. If a country can produce more of all goods than any other country, would it benefit from specializing and trading? Explain your answer.

3. Do government officials analyze data to determine what their country can produce at a comparative advantage?

TRADE RESTRICTIONS

International trade theory shows that countries gain from free international trade, that is, from specializing in the production of the goods in which they have a comparative advantage and trading these goods for other goods. In the real world, however, there are numerous types of trade restrictions, which raises the question: If countries gain from international trade, why are there trade restrictions?

WHY ARE THERE TRADE RESTRICTIONS IN THE REAL WORLD?

The previous section explains that specialization and international trade benefit individuals in different countries. But this benefit occurs on net. Every individual person may not gain. Suppose Pam Dickson lives and works in the United States making clock radios. She produces and sells 12,000 clock radios per year at a price of $40 each. As the situation stands, there is no international trade. Individuals in other countries who make clock radios do not sell their clock radios in the United States.

Then one day, the U.S. market is opened to clock radios from Japan. It appears that the Japanese manufacturers have a comparative advantage in the production of clock radios. They sell their clock radios in the United States for $25 each. Pam realizes that she cannot compete at this price. Her sales drop to such a degree that she goes out of business. Thus, the introduction of international trade in this instance has harmed Pam personally. This example raises the issue of the distributional effects of trade. Using the tools of supply and demand, we concentrate on two groups: U.S. consumers and U.S. producers. But first let's consider consumers' and producers' surplus.

CONSUMERS' AND PRODUCERS' SURPLUS

The concepts of consumers' and producers' surplus are first discussed in Chapter 2. These two concepts can help determine the effects of trade restrictions on consumers and producers. Let's start with a brief review.

Consumers' surplus is the difference between the maximum price a buyer is willing and able to pay for a good or service and the price actually paid.

Consumers' surplus = Maximum buying price − Price paid

Consumers' surplus is a dollar measure of the benefit gained by being able to purchase a unit of a good for less than one is willing to pay for it. For example, if Yakov would have paid $10 to see the movie at the Cinemax but paid only $4, his consumer surplus is $6. Consumers' surplus is the consumers' net gain from trade.

Producers' surplus (or sellers' surplus) is the difference between the price sellers receive for a good and the minimum or lowest price for which they would have sold the good.

Producers' surplus = Price received − Minimum selling price

Producers' surplus is a dollar measure of the benefit gained by being able to sell a unit of output for more than one is willing to sell it. For example, if Joan sold her knit sweaters for $24 each but would have sold them for as low as (but no lower than) $14 each, her producer surplus is $10 per sweater. Producers' surplus is the producers' net gain from trade.

Both consumers' and producers' surplus are represented in Exhibit 3. In part (a), consumers' surplus is represented by the shaded triangle. This triangle includes the area under the demand curve and above the equilibrium price. In part (b), producers' surplus is represented by the shaded triangle. This triangle includes the area above the supply curve and under the equilibrium price.

HOW IS TRADE RESTRICTED?

There are numerous ways to restrict free trade. Tariffs and quotas are two of the more commonly used methods.

Tariffs

A **tariff** is a tax on imports. The primary effect of a tariff is to raise the price of the imported good for the domestic consumer. Exhibit 4 illustrates the effects of a tariff.

The world price for cars is P_W, as shown in Exhibit 4a. At this price in the domestic (U.S.) market, U.S. consumers buy Q_2 cars, as shown in part (b). They buy Q_1 from U.S. producers and the difference between Q_2 and Q_1 ($Q_2 − Q_1$) from foreign producers. In other words, U.S. imports at P_W are $Q_2 − Q_1$.

What are consumers' and producers' surplus in this situation? Consumers' surplus is the area under the demand curve and above the world price, P_W. This is areas $1 + 2 + 3 + 4 + 5 + 6$. Producers' surplus is the area above the supply curve and below the world price, P_W. This is area 7. (See Exhibit 4b.)

Consumers' and Producers' Surplus
(a) Consumers' surplus. As the shaded area indicates, the difference between the maximum or highest amount consumers would be willing to pay and the price they actually pay is consumers' surplus. (b) Producers' surplus. As the shaded area indicates, the difference between the price sellers receive for the good and the minimum or lowest price they would be willing to sell the good for is producers' surplus.

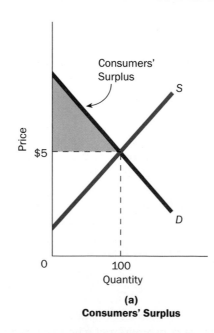

(a)
Consumers' Surplus

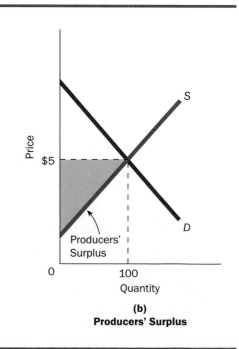

(b)
Producers' Surplus

	Consumers' Surplus	Producers' Surplus	Government Tariff Revenue
Free Trade (No tariff)	$1 + 2 + 3 + 4 + 5 + 6$	7	None
Tariff	$1 + 2$	$3 + 7$	5
Loss or Gain	$-(3 + 4 + 5 + 6)$	$+3$	$+5$

Result of Tariff	=	Loss to consumers	+ Gain to producers	+ Tariff revenue
	=	$-(3 + 4 + 5 + 6)$	$+3$	$+5$
	=	$-(4 + 6)$		

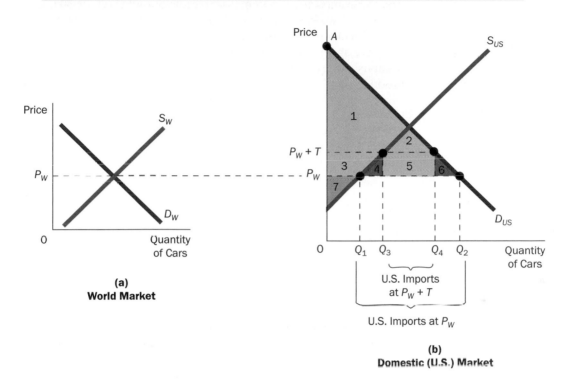

(a)
World Market

(b)
Domestic (U.S.) Market

exhibit 4

The Effects of a Tariff
A tariff raises the price of cars from P_W to $P_W + T$, decreases consumers' surplus, increases producers' surplus, and generates tariff revenue. Because consumers lose more than producers and government gain, there is a net loss due to the tariff.

Now suppose a tariff is imposed. The price for imported cars in the U.S. market rises to $P_W + T$ (the world price plus the tariff). At this price, U.S. consumers buy Q_4 cars: Q_3 from U.S. producers and $Q_4 - Q_3$ from foreign producers. U.S. imports are $Q_4 - Q_3$, which is a smaller number of imports than at the pretariff price. An effect of tariffs, then, is to reduce imports. What are consumers' and producers' surplus equal to after the tariff has been imposed? At price $P_W + T$, consumers' surplus is areas $1 + 2$ and producers' surplus is areas $3 + 7$.

Notice that consumers receive more consumers' surplus when tariffs do not exist and less when they do exist. In our example, consumers received areas $1 + 2 + 3 + 4 + 5 + 6$ in consumers' surplus when the tariff did not exist but only areas $1 + 2$ when the tariff did exist. Because of the tariff, consumers' surplus was reduced by an amount equal to areas $3 + 4 + 5 + 6$.

Producers, though, receive less producers' surplus when tariffs do not exist, and more when they do exist. In our example, producers received producers' surplus equal to area 7 when the tariff did not exist, but they received producers' surplus equal to areas $3 + 7$ with the tariff. Because of the tariff, producers' surplus increased by an amount equal to area 3.

The government collects tariff revenue equal to area 5. This area is obtained by multiplying the number of imports ($Q_4 - Q_3$) times the tariff, which is the difference between $P_W + T$ and P_W.[1]

---

1. For example, if the tariff is $100 and the number of imports is 50,000, then the tariff revenue is $5 million.

In conclusion, the effects of the tariff are a decrease in consumers' surplus, an increase in producers' surplus, and tariff revenue for government. Because the loss to consumers (areas $3 + 4 + 5 + 6$) is greater than the gain to producers (area 3) plus the gain to government (area 5), it follows that *a tariff results in a net loss*. The net loss is areas $4 + 6$.

Quotas

A **quota** is a legal limit on the amount of a good that may be imported. For example, the government may decide to allow no more than 100,000 foreign cars to be imported, or 10 million barrels of OPEC oil, or 30,000 Japanese television sets. A quota reduces the supply of a good and raises the price of imported goods for domestic consumers (Exhibit 5).

Once again, we consider the situation in the U.S. car market. At a price of P_W (established in the world market for cars), U.S. consumers buy Q_1 cars from U.S. producers and $Q_2 - Q_1$ cars from foreign producers. Consumers' surplus is equal to areas $1 + 2 + 3 + 4 + 5 + 6$. Producers' surplus is equal to area 7.

Suppose now that the U.S. government sets a quota equal to $Q_4 - Q_3$. Because this is the number of foreign cars U.S. consumers imported when the tariff was imposed (see Exhibit 4), the price of cars rises to P_Q in Exhibit 5 (which is equal to $P_W + T$ in Exhibit 4). At P_Q, consumers' surplus is equal to areas $1 + 2$

Quota
A legal limit on the amount of a good that may be imported.

exhibit 5

The Effects of a Quota
A quota that sets the legal limit of imports at $Q_4 - Q_3$ causes the price of cars to increase from P_W to P_Q. A quota raises price, decreases consumers' surplus, increases producers' surplus, and increases the total revenue importers earn. Because consumers lose more than producers and importers gain, there is a net loss due to the quota.

	Consumers' Surplus	Producers' Surplus	Revenue of Importers
Free Trade (No quota)	$1 + 2 + 3 + 4 + 5 + 6$	7	8
Quota	$1 + 2$	$3 + 7$	$5 + 8$
Loss or Gain	$-(3 + 4 + 5 + 6)$	$+3$	$+5$

Result of quota	=	Loss to consumers	+ Gain to producers	+ Gain to importers
	=	$-(3 + 4 + 5 + 6)$	$+3$	$+5$
	=	$-(4 + 6)$		

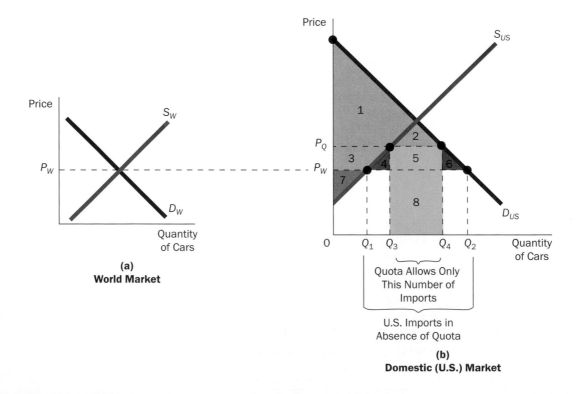

(a)
World Market

(b)
Domestic (U.S.) Market

and producers' surplus is areas $3 + 7$. The decrease in consumers' surplus due to the quota is equal to areas $3 + 4 + 5 + 6$; the increase in producers' surplus is equal to area 3.

But what about area 5? Is this area transferred to government, as was the case when a tariff was imposed? No, it isn't. This area represents the additional revenue earned by the importers (and sellers) of $Q_4 - Q_3$. Look at it this way: Before the quota, importers were importing $Q_2 - Q_1$, but only part of this total amount—$Q_4 - Q_3$—is relevant here. The reason only $Q_4 - Q_3$ is relevant is because this is the amount of imports now that the quota has been established. So, what dollar amount did the importers receive for $Q_4 - Q_3$ before the quota was established? The answer is $P_W \times (Q_4 - Q_3)$ or area 8. Because of the quota, the price rises to P_Q and they now receive $P_Q \times (Q_4 - Q_3)$ or areas $5 + 8$. The difference between the total revenues on $Q_4 - Q_3$ with a quota and without a quota is area 5.

In conclusion, the effects of a quota are a decrease in consumers' surplus, an increase in producers' surplus, and an increase in total revenue for the importers who sell the allowed number of imported units. Because the loss to consumers (areas $3 + 4 + 5 + 6$) is greater than the increase in producers' surplus (area 3) plus the gain to importers (area 5), there is a *net loss as a result of the quota*. The net loss is equal to areas $4 + 6$.[2]

THINKING LIKE AN
ECONOMIST

International trade often becomes a battleground between economics and politics. The simple tools of supply and demand and consumers' and producers' surplus show that there are net gains from free trade. On the whole, tariffs and quotas make living standards lower than they would be if free trade were permitted.

On the other side, though, are the realities of business and politics. Domestic producers may advocate quotas and tariffs to make themselves better off, giving little thought to the negative effects felt by foreign producers or domestic consumers.

Perhaps the battle over international trade comes down to this: Policies are largely advocated, argued, and lobbied for based more on their distributional effects than on their aggregate or overall effects. On an aggregate level, free trade produces a net gain for society, whereas restricted trade produces a net loss. But economists understand that just because free trade in the aggregate produces a net gain, it does not necessarily follow that every single person benefits more from free trade than from restricted trade. We have just shown how a subset of the population (producers) gains more, in a particular instance, from restricted trade than from free trade. In short, economists realize that the crucial question in determining real-world policies is more often "How does it affect me?" than "How does it affect us?"

IF FREE TRADE RESULTS IN NET GAIN, WHY DO NATIONS SOMETIMES RESTRICT TRADE?

Based on the analysis in this chapter so far, the case for free trade (no tariffs or quotas) appears to be a strong one. The case for free trade has not gone unchallenged, however. Some persons maintain that at certain times, free trade should be restricted or suspended. In almost all cases, they argue that it is in the best interest of the public or country as a whole to do so. In short, they advance a

---

2. It is perhaps incorrect to imply that government receives nothing from a quota. Although it receives nothing directly, it may gain indirectly. Economists generally argue that because government officials are likely to be the persons who will decide which importers will get to satisfy the quota, they will naturally be lobbied by importers. Thus, government officials will likely receive something, if only dinner at an expensive restaurant while the lobbyist makes his or her pitch. In short, in the course of the lobbying, resources will be spent by lobbyists as they curry favor with those government officials or politicians who have the power to decide who gets to sell the limited number of imported goods. In economics, lobbyists' activities geared toward obtaining a special privilege are referred to as rent seeking.

http://

Go to *http://www.ustr.gov/*, and click on "About USTR." Select "USTR's Role." What is the official U.S. trade policy? Click on the "Back" button and then on "Press Releases." Select the most recent month and year. Find a press release that deals with a specific country and click the "HTML" link. Does the press release deal with a trade restriction? If so, what kind of trade restriction? What is the content of the press release?

public interest argument. Other persons contend that the public interest argument is only superficial; down deep, they say, it is a special interest argument clothed in pretty words. As you might guess, the debate between the two groups is often heated.

The following paragraphs describe some arguments that have been advanced for trade restrictions.

The National-Defense Argument

It is often stated that certain industries—such as aircraft, petroleum, chemicals, and weapons—are necessary to the national defense. Suppose the United States has a comparative advantage in the production of wheat and country X has a comparative advantage in the production of weapons. Should the United States specialize in the production of wheat and then trade wheat to country X in exchange for weapons? Many Americans would answer no. It is too dangerous, they maintain, to leave weapons production to another country.

The national-defense argument may have some validity. But even valid arguments may be abused. Industries that are not really necessary to the national defense may maintain otherwise. In the past, the national-defense argument has been used by some firms in the following industries: pens, pottery, peanuts, papers, candles, thumbtacks, tuna fishing, and pencils.

The Infant-Industry Argument

Alexander Hamilton, the first U.S. secretary of the treasury, argued that "infant" or new industries often need to be protected from older, established foreign competitors until they are mature enough to compete on an equal basis. Today, some persons voice the same argument. The infant-industry argument is clearly an argument for temporary protection. Critics charge, however, that after an industry is protected from foreign competition, removing the protection is almost impossible. The once infant industry will continue to maintain that it isn't old enough to go it alone. Critics of the infant-industry argument say that political realities make it unlikely that a benefit once bestowed will be removed.

Finally, the infant-industry argument, like the national-defense argument, may be abused. It may well be that all new industries, whether they could currently compete successfully with foreign producers or not, would argue for protection on infant-industry grounds.

The Antidumping Argument

Dumping is the sale of goods abroad at a price below their cost and below the price charged in the domestic market. If a French firm sells wine in the United States for a price below the cost of producing the wine and below the price charged in France, it is said to be dumping wine in the United States. Critics of dumping maintain that it is an unfair trade practice that puts domestic producers of substitute goods at a disadvantage.

In addition, critics charge that dumpers seek only to penetrate a market and drive out domestic competitors; then they will raise prices. However, some economists point to the infeasibility of this strategy. After the dumpers have driven out their competition and raised prices, their competition is likely to return. The dumpers, in turn, would have obtained only a string of losses (owing to their selling below cost) for their efforts. Opponents of the antidumping argument also point out that domestic consumers benefit from dumping because they pay lower prices.

The Foreign-Export-Subsidies Argument

Some governments subsidize the firms that export goods. If a country offers a below-market (interest rate) loan to a company, it is often argued that the government subsidizes the production of the good the firm produces. If, in turn, the

Dumping
The sale of goods abroad at a price below their cost and below the price charged in the domestic market.

firm exports the good to a foreign country, that country's producers of substitute goods call foul. They complain that the foreign firm has been given an unfair advantage that they should be protected against.[3]

Others say that one should not turn one's back on a gift (in the form of lower prices). If foreign governments want to subsidize their exports, and thus give a gift to foreign consumers at the expense of their own taxpayers, then the recipients should not complain. Of course, the recipients are usually not the ones who are complaining. Usually, the ones complaining are the domestic producers who can't sell their goods at as high a price because of the gift domestic consumers are receiving from foreign governments.

The Low-Foreign-Wages Argument

It is sometimes argued that American producers can't compete with foreign producers because American producers pay high wages to their workers and foreign producers pay low wages to their workers. The American producers insist that free trade must be restricted or they will be ruined. However, the argument overlooks the reason American wages are high and foreign wages are low in the first place: productivity. High productivity and high wages are usually linked, as are low productivity and low wages. If an American worker, who receives $20 per hour, can produce (on average) 100 units of X per hour, working with numerous capital goods, then the cost per unit may be lower than when a foreign worker, who receives $2 per hour, produces (on average) 5 units of X per hour, working by hand. In short, a country's high-wage disadvantage may be offset by its productivity advantage; a country's low-wage advantage may be offset by its productivity disadvantage. High wages do not necessarily mean high costs when productivity (and the costs of nonlabor resources) is included.

The Saving-Domestic-Jobs Argument

Sometimes the argument against completely free trade is made in terms of saving domestic jobs. Actually, we have already discussed this argument in its different guises. For example, the low-foreign-wages argument is one form of it. That argument continues along this line: If domestic producers cannot compete with foreign producers because foreign producers pay low wages and domestic producers pay high wages, domestic producers will go out of business and domestic jobs will be lost. The foreign-export-subsidies argument is another form of this argument. Its proponents generally state that if foreign-government subsidies give a competitive edge to foreign producers, not only will domestic producers fail but as a result of their failure, domestic jobs will be lost. Critics of the saving-domestic-jobs argument (in all its guises) often argue that if a domestic producer is being outcompeted by foreign producers and domestic jobs in a particular industry are being lost as a result, the world market is signaling that those labor resources could be put to better use in an industry in which the country holds a comparative advantage.

WHAT PRICE JOBS?

Suppose the U.S. government imposes a tariff on imported good X. As a result, the domestic producers of good X sell their goods for higher prices, receive higher producers' surplus, and are generally better off. Some of the domestic workers who produce good X are better off too. Perhaps without the tariff on imports of good X, some of them would have lost their jobs.

Such scenarios raise two important questions: How many domestic jobs in the firms that produce good X are saved because of the tariff? How much do

---

3. Words are important in this debate. For example, domestic producers who claim that foreign governments have subsidized foreign firms say that they are not asking for *economic protectionism*, but only for *retaliation*, or *reciprocity*, or simply *tit-for-tat*—words that have less negative connotation than the words their opponents use.

ECONOMICS IN...

The World   Popular Culture   Technology   Everyday Life

Immigration and Wages

Many immigrants come to the United States each year. Immigrants who have the permission of the U.S. government to come to the country are officially referred to as documented immigrants. Immigrants who do not have the permission of the U.S. government are officially referred to as undocumented immigrants. During the 1990s, more than 9 million documented immigrants were admitted into the country and the undocumented immigrant population increased by about 5 million. Demographers expect the number of both documented and undocumented immigrants to the United States to rise in the near future.

Some residents of the United States argue that increased immigration will cause wages in the United States to decline. Their argument is based on simple supply and demand analysis: increased immigration leads to a greater supply of workers and lower wages.

There is little doubt that increased immigration will affect the supply of labor in the country. But it will affect the demand for labor too. The demand for labor is a derived demand—derived from the demand for the product that labor produces. With increased immigration, there will be more people living in the United States. A larger population translates into higher demand for food, housing, clothes, entertainment services, and so on. A higher demand for these goods translates into a higher demand for the workers who produce these goods.

In summary, increased immigration will affect both the supply of and demand for labor. What will be the effect on wages? It depends on whether the increase in the demand is greater than, less than, or equal to the increase in supply. If demand increases by more than supply, wages will rise; if supply increases by more than demand, wages will fall; if demand rises by the same amount as supply rises, wages will not change.

---

consumers have to pay in higher prices to save these jobs? Economists are interested in answering such questions. Here are a few answers for different industries at different times:

"Voluntary" Export Restraint (VER)
An agreement between two countries in which the exporting country "voluntarily" agrees to limit its exports to the importing country.

- In 1977, tariffs and quotas were imposed on imports of foreign footwear. An estimated 21,000 domestic jobs were protected in the domestic footwear industry as a result. The average worker in the industry earned $8,340 (in 1980 dollars). However, it cost domestic consumers $77,714 for each domestic footwear job protected.

- In 1981, **"voluntary" export restraints (VERs),** which work the way quotas do, were placed on Japanese car imports. The U.S. International Trade Commission estimated that 44,000 domestic jobs were protected—at a cost of $193,000 per job.

- In 1988, the consumer cost of VERs on machine tools was $48 million, while the gain to U.S. machine tool manufacturers was $11 million. The consumer cost per job saved turned out to be $120,000.

- In 1994, tariffs are said to have protected 190,000 jobs in 21 U.S. industries at a cost of $170,000 per job.

- In 1989, tariffs in Japan are said to have saved 180,000 jobs at a cost of $600,000 per job.

THE WORLD TRADE ORGANIZATION (WTO)

The international trade organization, the *World Trade Organization (WTO),* came into existence on January 1, 1995. It is the successor to the General Agreement on Tariffs and Trade (GATT), which was set up in 1947. In early 2002, 144 countries in the world were members of the WTO.

According to the WTO, its "overriding objective is to help trade flow smoothly, freely, fairly, and predictably." It does this by administering trade agreements, acting as a forum for trade negotiations, settling trade disputes, reviewing national trade policies, assisting developing countries in trade policy issues, and cooperating with other international organizations. Perhaps its most useful and controversial role is adjudicating trade disputes. For example, suppose the United States claims that the Canadian government is preventing U.S. producers from openly selling their goods in Canada. The WTO will look at the matter, consult with trade experts, and then decide the issue. A country that is found engaging in unfair trade can either desist from this practice or face appropriate retaliation from the injured country.

In theory, at least, the WTO is supposed to lead to freer international trade, and there is some evidence that it has done just this. The critics of the WTO often say that it has achieved this objective at some cost to a nation's sovereignty. For example, in the past, some of the trade disputes between the United States and other countries have been decided against the United States.

http://

Go to *http://www.wto.org/*, and select "TRADE TOPICS." Under "Dispute settlement," choose "Dispute settlement gateway page." Identify some of the current disputes. How does the WTO settle disputes?

Self-Test

1. Who benefits and who loses from tariffs? Explain your answer.

2. Identify the directional change in consumers' surplus and producers' surplus when we move from free trade to tariffs. Is the change in consumers' surplus greater than, less than, or equal to the change in producers' surplus?

3. What is a major difference between the effects of a quota and the effects of a tariff?

4. Outline the details of the infant-industry argument for trade restriction.

A Reader Asks...

Why Does the Government Impose Tariffs and Quotas?

If tariffs and quotas result in higher prices for U.S. consumers, then why does the government impose them?

The answer is that government is sometimes more responsive to producer interests than to consumer interests. But, then, we have to wonder why. To try to explain why, consider the following example.

Suppose there are 100 U.S. producers of good X and 20 million U.S. consumers of good X. The producers want to protect themselves from foreign competition, so they lobby for and receive a quota on foreign goods that compete with good X. As a result, consumers must pay higher prices. For simplicity's sake, let's say that consumers must pay $40 million more. Thus, producers receive $40 million more for good X than they would have if the quota had not been imposed.

If the $40 million received is divided equally among the 100 producers, each producer receives $400,000 more as a result of the quota. If the additional $40 million paid is divided equally among the 20 million consumers, each customer pays $2 more as a result of the quota.

A producer is likely to think, "I should lobby for the quota because if I'm effective, I'll receive $400,000." A consumer is likely to think, "Why should I lobby against the quota? If I'm effective, I'll only save $2. Saving $2 isn't worth the time and trouble my lobbying would take."

In short, the benefits of quotas are concentrated on relatively few producers, and the costs of quotas are spread out over relatively many consumers. This makes each producer's gain relatively large compared with each consumer's loss. We predict that producers will lobby government to obtain the relatively large gains from quotas but that consumers will not lobby government to keep from paying the small additional cost due to quotas.

Politicians are in the awkward position of hearing from those people who want the quotas but not hearing from those people who are against them. It is likely the politicians will respond to the vocal interests. Politicians may mistakenly assume that consumers' silence means that the consumers accept the quota policy, when in fact they may not. Consumers may simply not find it worthwhile to do anything to fight the policy.

Specialization and Trade

- A country has a comparative advantage in the production of a good if it can produce the good at a lower opportunity cost than another country can.
- Individuals in countries that specialize and trade have a higher standard of living than would be the case if their countries did not specialize and trade.
- Government officials do not analyze cost data to determine what their country should specialize in and trade. Instead, the desire to earn a dollar, peso, or euro guides individuals' actions and produces the unintended consequence that countries specialize in and trade the good(s) in which they have a comparative advantage. However, trade restrictions can change this outcome.

Tariffs and Quotas

- A tariff is a tax on imports. A quota is a legal limit on the amount of a good that may be imported.
- Both tariffs and quotas raise the price of imports.
- Tariffs lead to a decrease in consumers' surplus, an increase in producers' surplus, and tariff revenue for the government. Consumers lose more through tariffs than producers and government (together) gain.
- Quotas lead to a decrease in consumers' surplus, an increase in producers' surplus, and additional revenue for the importers that sell the quota. Consumers lose more through quotas than producers and importers (together) gain.

Arguments for Trade Restrictions

- The national-defense argument states that certain goods—such as aircraft, petroleum, chemicals, and weapons—are necessary to the national defense and should be produced domestically whether the country has a comparative advantage in their production or not.
- The infant-industry argument states that "infant" or new industries should be protected from free (foreign) trade so that they may have time to develop and compete on an equal basis with older, more established foreign industries.
- The antidumping argument states that domestic producers should not have to compete (on an unequal basis) with foreign producers that sell products below cost and below the prices they charge in their domestic markets.
- The foreign-export-subsidies argument states that domestic producers should not have to compete (on an unequal basis) with foreign producers that have been subsidized by their governments.
- The low-foreign-wages argument states that domestic producers cannot compete with foreign producers that pay low wages to their employees when domestic producers pay high wages to their employees. For high-paying domestic firms to survive, limits on free trade are proposed.
- The saving-domestic-jobs argument states that through low foreign wages or government subsidies (or dumping, and so forth), foreign producers will be able to outcompete domestic producers, and therefore domestic jobs will be lost. For domestic firms to survive and domestic jobs not be lost, limits on free trade are proposed.
- Everyone does not accept the arguments for trade restrictions as valid. Critics often maintain that the arguments can be and are abused and, in most cases, are motivated by self-interest.

Key Terms and Concepts

Comparative Advantage
Tariff

Quota
Dumping

"Voluntary" Export Restraint (VER)

Economic Connections to You

Economic facts, actions, and changes create ripples that move away from their point of origin. Eventually, these ripples can intersect your life and have an effect on you. Consider the following example.

The federal government, in response to protectionism policies in a foreign country, imposes a quota on cars imported from that country. Consequently, car prices rise in the United States. You must pay a higher price for your new car than you would have had the quota not been imposed. Thus, there is a connection between protectionism policies in a foreign country and in the United States and the price you pay for a car—an economic connection to you.

Based on the material in this chapter, identify other ways in which economic facts, actions, and changes create ripples that eventually affect you.

Questions and Problems

1. Although a production possibilities frontier is usually drawn for a country, one could be drawn for the world. Picture the world's production possibilities frontier. Is the world positioned at a point on the curve or below the frontier? Give a reason for your answer.
2. "Whatever can be done by a tariff can be done by a quota." Discuss.
3. Consider two groups of domestic producers: those that compete with imports and those that export goods. Suppose the domestic producers that compete with imports convince the legislature to impose a high tariff on imports, so high, in fact, that almost all imports are eliminated. Does this policy in any way adversely affect domestic producers that export goods? How?
4. Suppose the U.S. government wants to curtail imports; would it be likely to favor a tariff or a quota to accomplish its objective? Why?
5. Suppose the landmass known to you as the United States of America had been composed, since the nation's founding, of separate countries instead of separate states. Would you expect the standard of living of the people who inhabit this landmass to be higher, lower, or equal to what it is today? Why?
6. Even though Jeremy is a better gardener and novelist than Bill is, Jeremy still hires Bill as his gardener. Why?
7. Suppose that tomorrow, a constitutional convention were called and you were chosen as one of the delegates from your state. You and the other delegates must decide whether it will be constitutional or unconstitutional for the federal government to impose tariffs and quotas or restrict international trade in any way. What would be your position?
8. Some economists have argued that because domestic consumers gain more from free trade than domestic producers gain from (import) tariffs and quotas, consumers should buy out domestic producers and rid themselves of costly tariffs and quotas. For example, if consumers save $400 million from free trade (through paying lower prices) and producers gain $100 million from tariffs and quotas, consumers can pay producers something more than $100 million but less than $400 million and get producers to favor free trade too. Assuming this scheme were feasible, what do you think of it?
9. If there is a net loss to society from tariffs, why do tariffs exist?

Working with Numbers and Graphs

1. Using the data in the table, answer the following questions: (a) For which good does Canada have a comparative advantage? (b) For which good does Italy have a comparative advantage? (c) What might be a set of favorable terms of trade for the two countries? (d) Prove that both countries would be better off in the specialization-trade case than in the no specialization–no trade case.

Points on Production Possibilities Frontier	Canada		Italy	
	Good X	Good Y	Good X	Good Y
A	150	0	90	0
B	100	25	60	60
C	50	50	30	120
D	0	75	0	180

2. In the following figure, P_W is the world price and $P_W + T$ is the world price plus a tariff. Identify the following:

a. The level of imports at P_W
b. The level of imports at $P_W + T$
c. The loss in consumers' surplus as a result of a tariff
d. The gain in producers' surplus as a result of a tariff
e. The tariff revenue as the result of a tariff
f. The net loss to society as a result of a tariff
g. The net benefit to society of moving from a tariff situation to a no-tariff situation

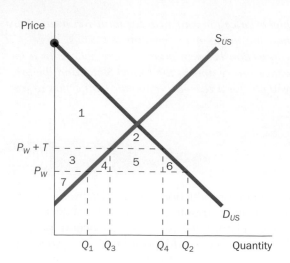

Internet Activities

1. Go to *http://www.wto.org*, and select "What is the WTO?" Under "The WTO in Brief," click "Browse html version online." What is the objective of the WTO? How many countries are members of the WTO? Do you think the WTO is producer-oriented or consumer-oriented? Explain your answer.

2. Click on the "Back" button, and under "10 Benefits of the WTO Trading System," select "Browse html version online," and then select "Incomes." What evidence does the WTO present to prove that trade raises incomes? Click on the "Back" button, and review the top 10 benefits of WTO trade. One of the benefits listed is "peace." Do you think that the WTO trading system promotes peace? Explain your answer.

3. Click on the "Back" button, and under "10 common misunderstandings about the WTO," select "Browse html version online." Select and read "Anti-Green" and "Small left out." What is the WTO position on both issues?

Log on to the Arnold Xtra! Web site now (*http://arnoldxtra.swcollege.com*) for additional learning resources such as practice quizzes, help with graphing, video clips, and current event applications.

ch.20

INTERNATIONAL FINANCE

When people travel to a foreign country, they buy various goods and services in the country. The prices of the goods and services are quoted in yen, euros, francs, pesos, or some other currency. For example, a tourist in Japan might want to buy a pair of shoes priced in yen. What would the shoes cost in U.S. currency? The answer depends on the current exchange rate between the dollar and the yen. But, what determines the exchange rate? This is just one of the many questions answered in this chapter.

Our two major topics in international finance are the balance of payments and exchange rates. Think of the balance of payments as a statement of the money value of the transactions between residents of different countries. In other words, Americans buy things from and sell things to people all over the world. The balance of payments tells us how much buying and selling is going on, among other things.

An exchange rate is the price of one currency in terms of another currency—for example, the price of U.S. dollars in terms of Japanese yen. In this chapter, we explain why exchange rates are what they are (why is 1 dollar equal to 130 yen and not 120 yen?) and discuss two types of exchange rate structures—flexible and fixed.

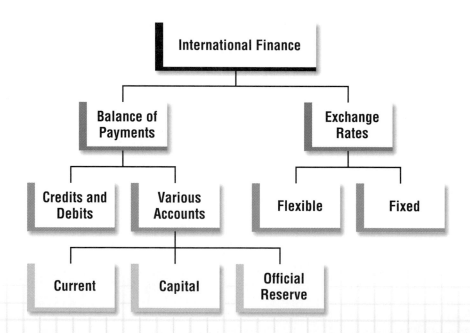

THE BALANCE OF PAYMENTS

Countries keep track of their domestic level of production by calculating their gross domestic product (GDP). Similarly, they keep track of the flow of their international trade (receipts and expenditures) by calculating their balance of payments.

The **balance of payments** is a periodic statement (usually annual) of the money value of all transactions between residents of one country and residents of all other countries. The balance of payments provides information about a nation's imports and exports, domestic residents' earnings on assets located abroad, foreign earnings on domestic assets, gifts to and from foreign countries (including foreign aid), and official transactions by governments and central banks.

Balance of payments accounts record both debits and credits. A debit is indicated by a minus (−) sign, and a credit is indicated by a plus (+) sign. *Any transaction that supplies the country's currency in the foreign exchange market is recorded as a* **debit.** (The **foreign exchange market** is the market in which currencies of different countries are exchanged.) For example, suppose a U.S. retailer wants to buy Japanese television sets so that he can sell them in his stores in the United States. In order to buy the TV sets from the Japanese, the retailer first has to supply U.S. dollars (in the foreign exchange market) in return for Japanese yen. Then he will turn over the yen to the Japanese in exchange for the television sets.

Any transaction that creates a demand for the country's currency in the foreign exchange market is recorded as a **credit.** For example, suppose a Russian retailer wants to buy computers from U.S. computer producers. Can she pay the U.S. producers in Russian rubles? Probably not; U.S. producers want U.S. dollars. So the Russian retailer must supply rubles (in the foreign exchange market) in return for dollars. Then she will turn over the dollars to the U.S. producers in exchange for the computers. See Exhibit 1 for a summary of debits and credits.

The international transactions that occur, and that are summarized in the balance of payments, can be grouped into three categories, or three accounts—the current account, the capital account, and the official reserve account—and a statistical discrepancy. Exhibit 2 illustrates a U.S. balance of payments account for year Z. The data in the exhibit are hypothetical (to make the calculations simpler), but not unrealistic.

Q & A

Q: When Americans buy Japanese goods, they supply dollars and demand yen. When the Japanese buy American goods, they supply yen and demand dollars. Thus, the first transaction is recorded as a debit (it supplies U.S. currency) and the second transaction is recorded as a credit (it increases demand for U.S. currency) in the U.S. balance of payments. Is this correct?

A: Yes, that is correct.

Item	Definition	Example
Debit (−)	Any transaction that supplies the country's currency.	Jim, an American, supplies dollars in exchange for yen so that he can use the yen to buy Japanese goods.
Credit (+)	Any transaction that creates a demand for the country's currency.	Svetlana, who is Russian and living in Russia, supplies rubles in order to demand dollars so that she can use the dollars to buy U.S. goods.

exhibit 1

Debits and Credits

exhibit 2

U.S. Balance of Payments, Year Z
The data in this exhibit are hypothetical, but not unrealistic. All numbers are in billions of dollars. The plus and minus signs in the exhibit should be viewed as operational signs.

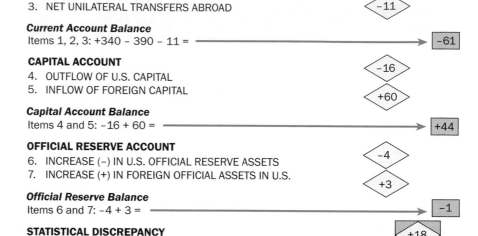

CURRENT ACCOUNT

1. EXPORTS OF GOODS AND SERVICES   +340
   a. Merchandise exports (including military sales)   +220
   b. Services   +30
   c. Income from U.S. assets abroad   +90
2. IMPORTS OF GOODS AND SERVICES   −390
   a. Merchandise imports (including military purchases)   −300
   b. Services   −40
   c. Income from foreign assets in U.S.   −50

Merchandise Trade Balance
Difference between value of merchandise exports (item 1a)
and value of merchandise imports (item 2a): +220 − 300 = −80

3. NET UNILATERAL TRANSFERS ABROAD   −11

Current Account Balance
Items 1, 2, 3: +340 − 390 − 11 =   → **−61**

CAPITAL ACCOUNT
4. OUTFLOW OF U.S. CAPITAL   −16
5. INFLOW OF FOREIGN CAPITAL   +60

Capital Account Balance
Items 4 and 5: −16 + 60 =   → **+44**

OFFICIAL RESERVE ACCOUNT
6. INCREASE (−) IN U.S. OFFICIAL RESERVE ASSETS   −4
7. INCREASE (+) IN FOREIGN OFFICIAL ASSETS IN U.S.   +3

Official Reserve Balance
Items 6 and 7: −4 + 3 =   → **−1**

STATISTICAL DISCREPANCY   +18

TOTAL $0 $0
                                  (always zero)

Balance of Payments =

Summary statistic of all ◇ items (items 1 − 7 and the statistical discrepancy)

+$340 − $390 − $11 − $16 + $60 − $4 + $3 + $18 = $0

or

Summary statistic of all ▢ items (current account balance, capital account balance, official reserve balance, and the statistical discrepancy)

−$61 + $44 − $1 + $18 = $0

Note: The pluses (+) and the minuses (−) in the exhibit serve two purposes. First, they distinguish between credits and debits. A plus is always placed before a credit, and a minus is always placed before a debit. Second, in terms of the calculations, the pluses and minuses are viewed as operational signs. In other words, if a number has a plus in front of it, it is added to the total. If a number has a minus in front of it, it is subtracted from the total.

Current Account
Includes all payments related to the purchase and sale of goods and services. Components of the account include exports, imports, and net unilateral transfers abroad.

CURRENT ACCOUNT

The **current account** includes all payments related to the purchase and sale of goods and services. The current account has three major components: exports of goods and services, imports of goods and services, and net unilateral transfers abroad.

1. **Exports of goods and services.** Americans export goods (say, cars), they export services (such as insurance, banking, transportation, and tourism), and they receive income on assets they own abroad. All three activities increase the demand for U.S. dollars at the same time that they increase the supply of foreign currencies; thus, they are recorded as credits (+). For example, if a foreigner buys a U.S. computer, payment must ultimately be made in U.S. dollars. Thus, she is required to supply her country's currency when she demands U.S. dollars. (We use foreigner in this chapter to refer to a resident of a foreign country.)

2. **Imports of goods and services.** Americans import goods and services, and foreigners receive income on assets they own in the United States. These activities increase the demand for foreign currencies at the same time that they increase the supply of U.S. dollars to the foreign exchange market; thus, they are recorded as debits (−). For example, if an American buys a Japanese car, payment must ultimately be made in Japanese yen. Thus, he is required to supply U.S. dollars when he demands Japanese yen.

In Exhibit 2, exports of goods and services total +$340 billion in year *Z*, and imports of goods and services total −$390 billion.[1]

Before discussing the third component of the current account—net unilateral transfers abroad—we define some important relationships between exports and imports. Look at the difference between the *value of merchandise exports* (1a in Exhibit 2) and the *value of merchandise imports* (2a in the exhibit). This difference is the merchandise trade balance or the balance of trade. Specifically, the **merchandise trade balance** is the difference between the value of merchandise exports and the value of merchandise imports. In year *Z*, this is −$80 billion.

$$\text{Merchandise trade balance} = \frac{\text{Value of}}{\text{merchandise exports}} - \frac{\text{Value of}}{\text{merchandise imports}}$$

If the value of a country's merchandise exports is less than the value of its merchandise imports, it is said to have a **merchandise trade deficit.**

Merchandise trade deficit: Value of merchandise exports < Value of merchandise imports

If the value of a country's merchandise exports is greater than the value of its merchandise imports, it is said to have a **merchandise trade surplus.**

Merchandise trade surplus: Value of merchandise exports > Value of merchandise imports

Exhibit 3 shows the U.S. merchandise trade balance from 1990–2001. Notice that there has been a merchandise trade deficit in each of these years. As an aside, the merchandise trade deficit for the period January–June 2002 (not shown in the exhibit) was $229 billion.

Go to *http://www.bea.doc.gov/bea/di/ trans1.htm*. What are exports in the most recent quarter? What are imports in the most recent quarter?

Merchandise Trade Balance
The difference between the value of merchandise exports and the value of merchandise imports.

Merchandise Trade Deficit
The situation where the value of merchandise exports is less than the value of merchandise imports.

Merchandise Trade Surplus
The situation where the value of merchandise exports is greater than the value of merchandise imports.

---

1. In everyday language, people do not say, "Exports are a positive $*X* billion and imports are a negative $*Y* billion." Placing a plus sign (+) in front of exports and a minus sign (−) in front of imports simply reinforces the essential point that exports are credits and imports are debits. This will be useful later when we calculate certain account balances.

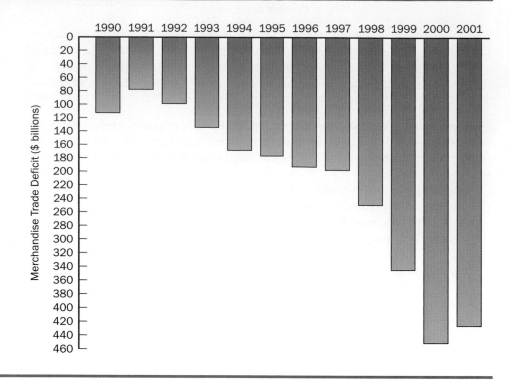

exhibit 3

U.S. Merchandise Trade Balance
In each of the years shown, 1990–2001, a merchandise trade deficit has existed.

Source: U.S. Department of Commerce, Bureau of Economic Analysis

Q & A

Q: In Exhibit 2, merchandise exports are +$220 billion (item 1a) and merchandise imports are −$300 billion (item 2a). Can't the merchandise trade balance be calculated simply by subtracting the merchandise imports from the merchandise exports? Why does the definition use the "value of" exports and imports?

A: The merchandise trade balance can be calculated by subtracting merchandise imports from merchandise exports. But, you must be careful not to make the mistake of subtracting a negative $300 billion from a positive $220 billion. In other words, the merchandise trade balance does not equal $220 billion minus (negative $300 billion), or $520 billion. The merchandise trade balance is found by subtracting the *value of* the merchandise imports, $300 billion, from the *value of* the merchandise exports, $220 billion. In other words, balance of trade = $220 billion − $300 billion = −$80 billion.

In terms of calculations, the positive and negative signs in Exhibit 2 are operational signs. When a negative sign (−) appears in front of a number, subtract that number from the total. When a positive sign (+) appears in front of a number, add that number to the total.

3. **Net unilateral transfers abroad.** Unilateral transfers are one-way money payments. They can go from Americans or the U.S. government to foreigners or foreign governments. If an American sends money to a relative in a foreign country, or the U.S. government gives money to a foreign country as a gift or grant, or an American retires in a foreign country and receives a Social Security check there, all these transactions are referred to as unilateral transfers. If an American makes a unilateral transfer abroad, this gives rise to a demand for foreign currency and a supply of U.S. dollars; thus, it is entered as a debit item in the U.S. balance of payments accounts.

   Unilateral transfers can also go from foreigners or foreign governments to Americans or to the U.S. government. If a foreign citizen sends money to a relative living in the United States, this is a unilateral transfer. If a foreigner makes a unilateral transfer to an American, this gives rise to a supply of foreign currency and a demand for U.S. dollars; thus, it is entered as a credit item in the U.S. balance of payments accounts.

Net unilateral transfers abroad include both types of transfers—from the United States to foreign countries and from foreign countries to the United States. The dollar amount of net unilateral transfers is negative if U.S. transfers are greater than foreign transfers. It is positive if foreign transfers are greater than U.S. transfers.

For year Z in Exhibit 2, we have assumed that unilateral transfers made by Americans to foreign citizens are greater than unilateral transfers made by foreign citizens to Americans. Thus, there is a *negative* net dollar amount, −$11 billion, in this case.

Items 1, 2, and 3 in Exhibit 2—exports of goods and services, imports of goods and services, and net unilateral transfers abroad—are known as the current account. The **current account balance** is the summary statistic for these three items. In year Z, it is −$61 billion. The news media sometimes call the current account balance the balance of payments. To an economist, this is incorrect; the balance of payments includes several more items.

http://

Go to *http://www.bea.doc.gov/bea/di/trans1.htm*. What is the current account balance in the most recent quarter? What are net unilateral transfers in the most recent quarter? What is the statistical discrepancy in the most recent quarter? What is the value of net exports?

Current Account Balance
The summary statistic for exports of goods and services, imports of goods and services, and net unilateral transfers abroad.

CAPITAL ACCOUNT

The **capital account** includes all payments related to the purchase and sale of assets and to borrowing and lending activities. Its major components are outflow of U.S. capital and inflow of foreign capital.

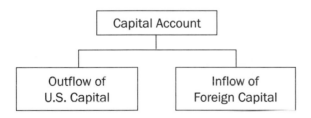

Capital Account
Includes all payments related to the purchase and sale of assets and to borrowing and lending activities. Components include outflow of U.S. capital and inflow of foreign capital.

1. **Outflow of U.S. capital.** American purchases of foreign assets and U.S. loans to foreigners are outflows of U.S. capital. As such, they give rise to a demand for foreign currency and a supply of U.S. dollars on the foreign exchange market. Hence, they are considered a debit. For example, if an American wants to buy land in Japan, U.S. dollars must be supplied to purchase (demand) Japanese yen.

2. **Inflow of foreign capital.** Foreign purchases of U.S. assets and foreign loans to Americans are inflows of foreign capital. As such, they give rise to a demand for U.S. dollars and to a supply of foreign currency on the foreign exchange market. Hence, they are considered a credit. For example, if a Japanese citizen buys a U.S. Treasury bill, Japanese yen must be supplied to purchase (demand) U.S. dollars.

Items 4 and 5 in Exhibit 2—outflow of U.S. capital and inflow of foreign capital—comprise the capital account. The **capital account balance** is the summary statistic for these two items. It is equal to the difference between the outflow of U.S. capital and the inflow of foreign capital. In year Z, it is $44 billion.

Capital Account Balance
The summary statistic for the outflow of U.S. capital and the inflow of foreign capital. It is equal to the difference between the outflow of U.S. capital and the inflow of foreign capital.

International Monetary Fund (IMF)
An international organization created to oversee the international monetary system. The IMF does not control the world's money supply, but it does hold currency reserves for member nations and make loans to central banks.

Special Drawing Right (SDR)
An international money, created by the IMF, in the form of bookkeeping entries; like gold and currencies, they can be used by nations to settle international accounts.

OFFICIAL RESERVE ACCOUNT

A government possesses official reserve balances in the form of foreign currencies, gold, its reserve position in the **International Monetary Fund,** and **special drawing rights (SDR).** Countries that have a deficit in their combined current and capital accounts can draw on their reserves. For example, if the United States has a combined deficit in its current and capital accounts of $5 billion, it can draw down its official reserves to meet this combined deficit.

Item 6 in Exhibit 2 shows that the United States increased its reserve assets by $4 billion in year Z. This is a debit item because if the United States acquires official reserves (say, through the purchase of a foreign currency), it has increased the demand for the foreign currency and supplied dollars. Thus, an increase in official reserves is like an outflow of capital in the capital account and appears as a payment with a negative sign. It follows that an increase in foreign official assets in the United States is a credit item.

STATISTICAL DISCREPANCY

If someone buys a U.S. dollar with, say, Japanese yen, someone must sell a U.S. dollar. Thus, dollars purchased = dollars sold.

In all the transactions discussed earlier—exporting goods, importing goods, sending money to relatives in foreign countries, buying land in foreign countries—dollars were bought and sold. The total number of dollars sold must always equal the total number of dollars purchased. However, balance of payments accountants do not have complete information; they can record only credits and debits that they observe. There may be more debits or credits than those observed in a given year.

Suppose in year Z, all debits are observed and recorded, but not all credits are observed and recorded—perhaps because of smuggling activities, secret bank accounts, people living in more than one country, and so on. To adjust for this, balance of payments accountants use the *statistical discrepancy,* which is that part of the balance of payments that adjusts for missing information. In Exhibit 2, the statistical discrepancy is +$18 billion. This means that $18 billion worth of credits (+) went unobserved in year Z. There may have been some hidden exports and unrecorded capital inflows that year.

WHAT THE BALANCE OF PAYMENTS EQUALS

The balance of payments is the summary statistic for the following:

- Exports of goods and services (item 1 in Exhibit 2)
- Imports of goods and services (item 2)
- Net unilateral transfers abroad (item 3)
- Outflow of U.S. capital (item 4)
- Inflow of foreign capital (item 5)
- Increase in U.S. official reserve assets (item 6)
- Increase in foreign official assets in the United States (item 7)
- Statistical discrepancy

Calculating the balance of payments using these items, we have (in billions of dollars) $+340 - 390 - 11 - 16 + 60 - 4 + 3 + 18 = 0$.

Alternatively, the balance of payments is the summary statistic for the following:

- Current account balance
- Capital account balance
- Official reserve balance
- Statistical discrepancy

Calculating the balance of payments using these items, we have (in billions of dollars) $-61 + 44 - 1 + 18 = 0$. The balance of payments for the United States in year Z equals zero. The balance of payments *always* equals zero.

Q: Why does the balance of payments always equal zero?

A: The reason the balance of payments always equals zero is that the three accounts that comprise the balance of payments, when taken together, plus the statistical discrepancy, include all of the *sources* and all of the *uses* of dollars in international transactions. And because every dollar used must have a source, adding the sources (+) to the uses (−) necessarily gives us zero.

Self-Test *(Answers to Self-Test questions are in the Self-Test Appendix.)*

1. If an American retailer buys Japanese cars from a Japanese manufacturer, is this transaction recorded as a debit or a credit? Explain your answer.

2. Exports of goods and services equal $200 billion and imports of goods and services equal $300 billion. What is the merchandise trade balance?

3. What is the difference between the merchandise trade balance and the current account balance?

4. A newspaper reports that the U.S. balance of payments is −$100 billion. Can this be correct?

FLEXIBLE EXCHANGE RATES

If a U.S. buyer wants to purchase a good from a U.S. seller, the buyer simply gives the required number of U.S. dollars to the seller. If, however, a U.S. buyer wants to purchase a good from a seller in Mexico, the U.S. buyer must first exchange her U.S. dollars for Mexican pesos. Then, with the pesos, she buys the good from the Mexican seller.

As mentioned earlier, the market in which currencies of different countries are exchanged is the foreign exchange market. In the foreign exchange market, currencies are bought and sold for a price; an **exchange rate** exists. For instance, it might take 96 cents to buy a euro, 10 cents to buy a Mexican peso, and 13 cents to buy a Danish krone.

Exchange Rate
The price of one currency in terms of another currency.

In this section, we discuss how exchange rates are determined in the foreign exchange market when the forces of supply and demand are allowed to rule. Economists refer to this as a **flexible exchange rate system.** In the next section, we discuss how exchange rates are determined under a fixed exchange rate system.

Flexible Exchange Rate System
The system whereby exchange rates are determined by the forces of supply and demand for a currency.

THE DEMAND AND SUPPLY OF CURRENCIES

To simplify our analysis, we assume that there are only two countries in the world, the United States and Mexico. This, then, means there are only two currencies in the world, the U.S. dollar (USD) and the Mexican peso (MXP).[2] We want to answer the following two questions:

1. What creates the demand for and supply of dollars on the foreign exchange market?
2. What creates the demand for and supply of pesos on the foreign exchange market?

Suppose an American wants to buy a couch from a Mexican producer. Before he can purchase the couch, the American must buy Mexican pesos—hence, Mexican pesos are demanded. But the American buys Mexican pesos with U.S. dollars; that is, he supplies U.S. dollars to the foreign exchange market in order to demand Mexican pesos. We conclude that *the U.S. demand for Mexican goods leads to (1) a demand for Mexican pesos and (2) a supply of U.S. dollars on the foreign exchange market* (see Exhibit 4a). Thus, the demand for pounds and the supply of dollars are linked:

Demand for pesos ↔ Supply of dollars

---

2. Sometimes the abbreviation MXN instead of MXP is used for the Mexican peso.

exhibit 4

The Demand for Goods and the Supply of Currencies

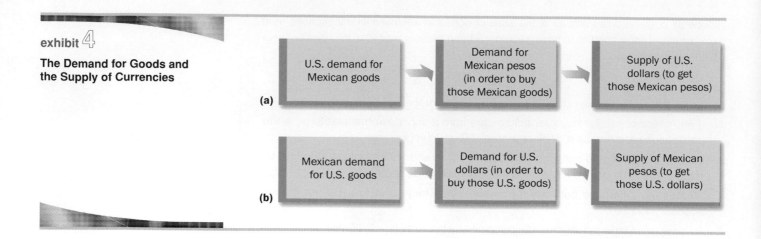

(a)

| U.S. demand for Mexican goods | → | Demand for Mexican pesos (in order to buy those Mexican goods) | → | Supply of U.S. dollars (to get those Mexican pesos) |

(b)

| Mexican demand for U.S. goods | → | Demand for U.S. dollars (in order to buy those U.S. goods) | → | Supply of Mexican pesos (to get those U.S. dollars) |

The result is similar for a Mexican who wants to buy a computer from a U.S. producer. Before she can purchase the computer, the Mexican must buy U.S. dollars—hence, U.S. dollars are demanded. The Mexican buys the U.S. dollars with Mexican pesos. We conclude that *the Mexican demand for U.S. goods leads to (1) a demand for U.S. dollars and (2) a supply of Mexican pesos on the foreign exchange market* (see Exhibit 4b). Thus, the demand for dollars and the supply of pesos are linked:

Demand for dollars ↔ Supply of pesos

Now let's look at Exhibit 5 to see the markets for pesos and dollars. Part (a) shows the market for Mexican pesos. The quantity of pesos is on the horizontal axis, and the exchange rate—stated in terms of the dollar price per peso—is on the vertical axis. Exhibit 5b shows the market for U.S. dollars, which mirrors what is happening in the market for Mexican pesos. Notice that the exchange rates in (a) and (b) are reciprocals of each other. If 0.10 USD = 1 MXP, then 10 MXP = 1 USD.

In Exhibit 5a, the demand curve for pesos is downward-sloping, indicating that as the dollar price per peso increases, Americans buy fewer pesos, and as the dollar price per peso decreases, Americans buy more pesos.

Dollar price per peso↑   Americans buy fewer pesos
Dollar price per peso↓   Americans buy more pesos

For example, if it takes 0.10 dollars to buy a peso, Americans will buy more pesos than they would if it takes 0.20 dollars to buy a peso. (It is analogous to buyers purchasing more soft drinks at 3 dollars a six-pack than at 5 dollars a six-pack.) Simply put, the higher the dollar price per peso, the more expensive Mexican goods are for Americans and the fewer Mexican goods Americans will buy. Thus, a smaller quantity of pesos are demanded.

The supply curve for pesos in Exhibit 5a is upward-sloping. It is easy to understand why if we recall that the supply of Mexican pesos is linked to the Mexican demand for U.S. goods and U.S. dollars. Consider a price of 0.20 dollars for 1 peso compared with a price of 0.10 dollars for 1 peso. At 0.10 USD = 1 MXP, a Mexican buyer gives up 1 peso and receives 10 cents in return. But at 0.20 USD = 1 MXP, a Mexican buyer gives up 1 peso and receives 20 cents in return. At which exchange rate are U.S. goods cheaper for Mexicans? The answer is at the exchange rate of 0.20 USD = 1 MXP.

To illustrate, suppose a U.S. computer has a price tag of 1,000 dollars. At an exchange rate of 0.20 USD = 1 MXP, a Mexican will have to pay 5,000 pesos to buy the American computer (1,000 USD/0.20 USD = 5,000 MXP). But at an

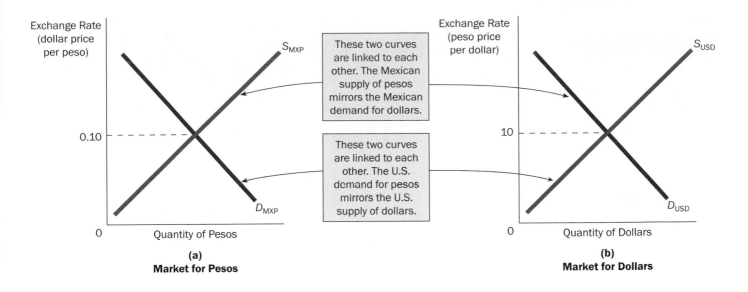

Exchange Rate (dollar price per peso)

S_{MXP}

These two curves are linked to each other. The Mexican supply of pesos mirrors the Mexican demand for dollars.

0.10

These two curves are linked to each other. The U.S. demand for pesos mirrors the U.S. supply of dollars.

D_{MXP}

0   Quantity of Pesos

(a)
Market for Pesos

Exchange Rate (peso price per dollar)

S_{USD}

10

D_{USD}

0   Quantity of Dollars

(b)
Market for Dollars

exchange rate of 0.10 USD = 1 MXP, a Mexican will have to pay 10,000 pesos for the computer (1,000 USD/0.10 USD = 10,000 MXP). To a Mexican buyer, the American computer is cheaper at the exchange rate of 0.20 dollars per peso than at 0.10 dollars per peso.

Exchange Rate	Dollar Price	Peso Price
0.20 USD = 1 MXP	1,000 USD	5,000 MXP (1,000 USD/0.20 USD)
0.10 USD = 1 MXP	1,000 USD	10,000 MXP (1,000 USD/0.10 USD)

It follows, then, that the higher the dollar price per peso, the greater the quantity demanded of dollars by Mexicans (because U.S. goods will be cheaper), and therefore the greater the quantity supplied of pesos to the foreign exchange market. The upward sloping supply curve for pesos illustrates this.

THINKING LIKE AN
ECONOMIST

The demand for dollars is linked to the supply of pesos and the demand for pesos is linked to the supply of dollars. Economists often think in terms of one activity being linked to another because economics, after all, is about exchange. In an exchange, one gives (supply) and gets (demand): John "supplies" $25 in order to demand the new book from the shopkeeper; the shopkeeper supplies the new book in order that he may "demand" the $25. In such a transaction, we usually diagrammatically represent the demand for and supply of the new book—but we could also diagrammatically represent the demand for and supply of money. Of course, in international exchange, where monies are bought and sold before goods are bought and sold, this is exactly what we do.

THE EQUILIBRIUM EXCHANGE RATE

In a completely flexible exchange rate system, the forces of supply and demand are allowed to rule. Suppose in this situation that the equilibrium exchange rate (dollar price per peso) is 0.10 USD = 1 MXP, as shown in Exhibit 6. At this dollar price per peso, the quantity demanded of pesos equals the quantity supplied of pesos. There are no shortages or surpluses of pesos. At any other exchange rate, however, either an excess demand for pesos or an excess supply of pesos exists.

Let's look at the exchange rate of 0.12 USD = 1 MXP. At this exchange rate, a surplus of pesos exists. As a result, downward pressure will be placed on the

exhibit 5

Translating U.S. Demand for Pesos into U.S. Supply of Dollars and Mexican Demand for Dollars into Mexican Supply of Pesos
(a) The market for pesos. (b) The market for dollars. The demand for pesos in (a) is linked to the supply of dollars in (b). When Americans demand pesos, they supply dollars. The supply of pesos in (a) is linked to the demand for dollars in (b): When Mexicans demand dollars, they supply pesos. In (a), the exchange rate is $0.10 USD = 1 MXP, which is equal to 10 MXP = 1 USD in (b). Exchange rates are reciprocals of each other.

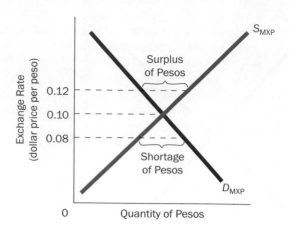

The Foreign Exchange Market
The demand curve for pesos is downward-sloping. The higher the dollar price for pesos, the fewer pesos will be demanded; the lower the dollar price for pesos, the more pesos will be demanded. At 0.12 USD = 1 MXP, there is a surplus of pesos, placing downward pressure on the exchange rate. At 0.08 USD = 1 MXP, there is a shortage of pesos, placing upward pressure on the exchange rate. At the equilibrium exchange rate, 0.10 USD = 1 MXP, the quantity demanded of pesos equals the quantity supplied of pesos.

dollar price of a peso (just as downward pressure will be placed on the dollar price of an apple if there is a surplus of apples). At the exchange rate of 0.08 USD = 1 MXP, there is a shortage of pesos, and upward pressure will be placed on the dollar price of a peso.

Q & A

Q: Are the demand and supply curves in Exhibit 6 related in any way to the U.S. balance of payments in Exhibit 2?

A: Yes, they are. For example, U.S. exports represent a demand for U.S. dollars by foreigners (and therefore constitute the supply of foreign currencies), while U.S. imports represent the U.S. demand for foreign currencies (and therefore constitute the supply of U.S. dollars). In fact, any dollar amount with a plus sign (+) in front of it in Exhibit 2 represents a demand for U.S. dollars and a supply of foreign currencies, and any dollar amount with a minus sign (−) in front of it represents a demand for foreign currencies and a supply of U.S. dollars.

CHANGES IN THE EQUILIBRIUM EXCHANGE RATE

Chapter 3 explains that a change in the demand for a good, or in the supply of a good, or in both will change the equilibrium price of the good. The same holds true for the price of currencies. A change in the demand for pesos, or in the supply of pesos, or in both will change the equilibrium dollar price per peso. If the dollar price per peso rises—say, from 0.10 USD = 1 MXP to 0.12 USD = 1 MXP—the peso is said to have **appreciated** and the dollar to have **depreciated.**

A currency has appreciated in value if it takes more of a foreign currency to buy it. A currency has depreciated in value if it takes more of it to buy a foreign currency. For example, a movement in the exchange rate from 0.10 USD = 1 MXP to 0.12 USD = 1 MXP means that it now takes 12 cents instead of 10 cents to buy a peso, so the dollar has depreciated. The other side of the "coin," so to speak, is that it takes fewer pesos to buy a dollar, so the peso has appreciated. That is, at an exchange rate of 0.10 USD = 1 MXP it takes 10 pesos to buy 1 dollar, but at an exchange rate of 0.12 USD = 1 MXP, it takes only 8.33 pesos to buy 1 dollar.

If the equilibrium exchange rate can change owing to a change in the demand for and supply of a currency, then it is important to understand what factors can change the demand for and supply of a currency. Three are presented here.

Appreciation
An increase in the value of one currency relative to other currencies.

Depreciation
A decrease in the value of one currency relative to other currencies.

A Difference in Income Growth Rates

An increase in a nation's income will usually cause the nation's residents to buy more of both domestic and foreign goods. The increased demand for imports will result in an increased demand for foreign currency.

Suppose U.S. residents experience an increase in income, but Mexican residents do not. As a result, the demand curve for pesos shifts rightward, as illustrated in Exhibit 7. This causes the equilibrium exchange rate to rise from 0.10 USD = 1 MXP to 0.12 USD = 1 MXP. *Ceteris paribus*, if one nation's income grows and another's lags behind, the currency of the higher-growth-rate country *depreciates* and the currency of the lower-growth-rate country *appreciates*. To many persons this seems paradoxical; nevertheless, it is true.

Differences in Relative Inflation Rates

Suppose the U.S. price level rises 10 percent at a time when Mexico experiences stable prices. An increase in the U.S. price level will make Mexican goods relatively less expensive for Americans and U.S. goods relatively more expensive for Mexicans. As a result, the U.S. demand for Mexican goods will increase and the Mexican demand for U.S. goods will decrease.

How will this affect the demand for and supply of Mexican pesos? As shown in Exhibit 8, the demand for Mexican pesos will increase (Mexican goods are relatively cheaper than they were before the U.S. price level rose), and the supply of Mexican pesos will decrease (American goods are relatively more expensive, so Mexicans will buy fewer American goods; thus, they demand fewer U.S. dollars and supply fewer Mexican pesos).

As Exhibit 8 shows, the result of an increase in the demand for Mexican pesos and a decrease in the supply of Mexican pesos is an *appreciation* in the peso and a *depreciation* in the dollar. It takes 11 cents instead of 10 cents to buy 1 peso (dollar depreciation); it takes 9.09 pesos instead of 10 pesos to buy 1 dollar (peso appreciation).

An important question is: How much will the U.S. dollar depreciate as a result of the 10 percent rise in the U.S. price level? (Recall that there is no change in Mexico's price level.) The **purchasing power parity (PPP) theory** predicts that the U.S. dollar will depreciate by 10 percent. This requires the dollar price of a peso to rise to 11 cents (10 percent of 10 cents is 1 cent, and 10 cents + 1 cent = 11 cents). A 10 percent depreciation in the dollar restores the *original relative prices of American goods to Mexican customers.*

http://

Go to *http://research.stlouisfed.org/fred/data/exchange.html*. Under "Exchange Rates," find "U.S. Dollars to One Euro," and click "Monthly." What was the dollar-euro exchange rate in the earliest month and year specified? the most recent month and year specified? Has the dollar appreciated or depreciated (relative to the euro) over the time period reported?

Purchasing Power Parity (PPP) Theory
States that exchange rates between any two currencies will adjust to reflect changes in the relative price levels of the two countries.

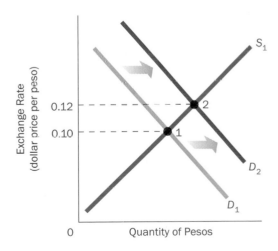

exhibit 7

The Growth Rate of Income and the Exchange Rate
If U.S. residents experience a growth in income but Mexican residents do not, U.S. demand for Mexican goods will increase, and with it, the demand for pesos. As a result, the exchange rate will change; the dollar price of pesos will rise. The dollar depreciates, the peso appreciates.

exhibit 8

Inflation, Exchange Rates, and Purchasing Power Parity (PPP)

If the price level in the United States increases by 10 percent while the price level in Mexico remains constant, then the U.S. demand for Mexican goods (and therefore pesos) will increase and the supply of pesos will decrease. As a result, the exchange rate will change; the dollar price of pesos will rise. The dollar depreciates, and the peso appreciates. PPP theory predicts that the dollar will depreciate in the foreign exchange market until the original price (in pesos) of American goods to Mexican customers is restored. In this example, this requires the dollar to depreciate 10 percent.

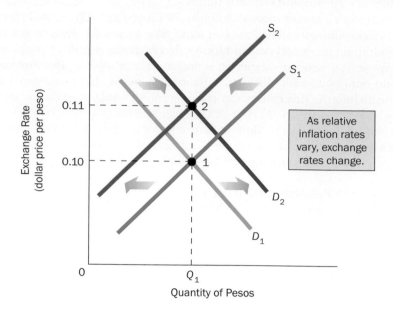

As relative inflation rates vary, exchange rates change.

Consider a U.S. car with a price tag of 20,000 dollars. If the exchange rate is 0.10 USD = 1 MXP, a Mexican buyer of the car will pay 200,000 pesos. If the car price increases by 10 percent to 22,000 dollars and the dollar depreciates 10 percent (to 0.11 USD = 1 MXP), the Mexican buyer of the car will still pay only 200,000 pesos.

Exchange Rate	Dollar Price	Peso Price
0.10 USD = 1 MXP	20,000 USD	200,000 MXP (20,000 USD/0.10 USD)
0.11 USD = 1 MXP	22,000 USD	200,000 MXP (22,000 USD/0.11 USD)

In short, the PPP theory predicts that *changes in the relative price levels of two countries will affect the exchange rate in such a way that one unit of a country's currency will continue to buy the same amount of foreign goods* as it did before the change in the relative price levels. In our example, the higher U.S. inflation rate causes a change in the equilibrium exchange rate and leads to a depreciated dollar, but one peso continues to have the same purchasing power it previously did.

On some occasions, the PPP theory of exchange rates has predicted accurately, but on others, it has not. Many economists suggest that the theory does not always predict accurately because the demand for and supply of a currency are affected *by more than the difference in inflation rates between countries.* For example, we have already noted that different income growth rates affect the demand for a currency and therefore the exchange rate. In the *long run,* however, and in particular, when there is a *large difference in inflation rates across countries,* the PPP theory does predict exchange rates accurately.

Changes in Real Interest Rates

As shown in the U.S. balance of payments in Exhibit 2, more than goods flow between countries. Financial capital also moves between countries. The flow of financial capital depends on different countries' *real interest rates*—interest rates adjusted for inflation. To illustrate, suppose, initially, that the real interest rate is 3 percent in both the United States and Mexico. Then the real interest rate in the

United States increases to 4.5 percent. What will happen? Mexicans will want to purchase financial assets in the United States that pay a higher real interest rate than financial assets in Mexico. The Mexican demand for dollars will increase, and therefore Mexicans will supply more pesos. As the supply of pesos increases on the foreign exchange market, the exchange rate (dollar price per peso) will change; fewer dollars will be needed to buy pesos. In short, the dollar will appreciate and the peso will depreciate.

Self-Test

1. In the foreign exchange market, how is the demand for dollars linked to the supply of pesos?

2. What could cause the U.S. dollar to appreciate against the Mexican peso on the foreign exchange market?

3. Suppose the U.S. economy grows while the Swiss economy does not. How will this affect the exchange rate between the dollar and the Swiss franc? Why?

4. What does the purchasing power parity theory say? Give an example to illustrate your answer.

FIXED EXCHANGE RATES

The major alternative to the flexible exchange rate system is the **fixed exchange rate system.** This system works the way it sounds. Exchange rates are fixed; they are not allowed to fluctuate freely in response to the forces of supply and demand. Central banks buy and sell currencies to maintain agreed-on exchange rates. The workings of the fixed exchange rate system are described in this section.

Fixed Exchange Rate System
The system where a nation's currency is set at a fixed rate relative to all other currencies, and central banks intervene in the foreign exchange market to maintain the fixed rate.

FIXED EXCHANGE RATES AND OVERVALUED/UNDERVALUED CURRENCY

Once again, we assume a two country–two currency world. Suppose this time, the United States and Mexico agree to fix the exchange rate of their currencies. Instead of letting the dollar depreciate or appreciate relative to the peso, the two countries agree to set the price of 1 peso at 0.12 dollars; that is, they agree to the exchange rate of 0.12 USD = 1 MXP. Generally, we call this the fixed exchange rate or the *official price* of a peso.[3] We will be dealing with more than one official price in our discussion, so we refer to 0.12 USD = 1 MXP as official price 1 (Exhibit 9).

If the dollar price of pesos is above its equilibrium level (which is the case at official price 1), a surplus of pesos exists. Also, the peso is said to be **overvalued.** This means that the peso is fetching more dollars than it would at equilibrium. For example, if in equilibrium, 1 peso trades for 0.10 dollars but at the official exchange rate, 1 peso trades for 0.12 dollars, then the peso is said to be overvalued.

It follows that if the peso is overvalued, the dollar is undervalued, which means it is fetching fewer pesos than it would at equilibrium. For example if in equilibrium, 1 dollar trades for 10 pesos but at the official exchange rate, 1 dollar trades for 8.33 pesos, then the dollar is undervalued.

Similarly, if the dollar price of pesos is below its equilibrium level (which is the case at official price 2 in Exhibit 9), a shortage of pesos exists. Also, the peso is **undervalued.** This means that the peso is not fetching as many dollars as it would at equilibrium. It follows that if the peso is undervalued, the dollar must be overvalued.

Overvaluation
A currency is overvalued if its price in terms of other currencies is above the equilibrium price.

Undervaluation
A currency is undervalued if its price in terms of other currencies is below the equilibrium price.

Overvalued peso ↔ Undervalued dollar
Undervalued peso ↔ Overvalued dollar

---

3. If the price of 1 peso is 0.12 dollars, it follows that the price of 1 dollar is approximately 8.33 pesos. Thus setting the official price of a peso in terms of dollars automatically sets the official price of a dollar in terms of pesos.

exhibit 9

A Fixed Exchange Rate System
In a fixed exchange rate system, the exchange rate is fixed—and it may not be fixed at the equilibrium exchange rate. The exhibit shows two cases. (1) If the exchange rate is fixed at official price 1, the peso is overvalued, the dollar is undervalued, and a surplus of pesos exists. (2) If the exchange rate is fixed at official price 2, the peso is undervalued, the dollar is overvalued, and a shortage of pesos exists.

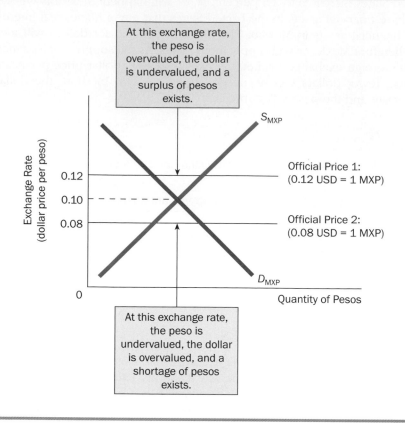

At this exchange rate, the peso is overvalued, the dollar is undervalued, and a surplus of pesos exists.

Official Price 1: (0.12 USD = 1 MXP)

Official Price 2: (0.08 USD = 1 MXP)

At this exchange rate, the peso is undervalued, the dollar is overvalued, and a shortage of pesos exists.

WHAT IS SO BAD ABOUT AN OVERVALUED DOLLAR?

Suppose you read in the newspaper that the dollar is overvalued. You also read that economists are concerned about the overvalued dollar. "But why are economists concerned?" you ask.

They are concerned because the exchange rate—and hence the value of the dollar in terms of other currencies—affects the amount of U.S. exports and imports. Because it affects exports and imports, it naturally affects the merchandise trade balance. To illustrate, suppose the demand for and supply of pesos are represented by D_1 and S_1 in Exhibit 10. With this demand curve and supply curve, the equilibrium exchange rate is 0.10 USD = 1 MXP. Let's also suppose the exchange rate is fixed at this exchange rate. In other words, the equilibrium exchange rate and the fixed exchange rate are initially the same.

Time passes and eventually the demand curve for pesos shifts to the right, from D_1 to D_2. Under a flexible exchange rate system, the exchange rate would rise to 0.12 USD = 1 MXP. But a flexible exchange rate is not operating here—a fixed one is. In other words, the exchange rate stays fixed at 0.10 USD = 1 MXP. This means the fixed exchange rate (0.10 USD = 1 MXP) is below the new equilibrium exchange rate (0.12 USD = 1 MXP).

Recall that if the dollar price per peso is below its equilibrium level (which is the case here), the peso is undervalued and the dollar is overvalued. In other words, in equilibrium (at point 2 in Exhibit 10), 1 peso would trade for 0.12 dollars but at its fixed rate (at point 1), it trades for only 0.10 dollars—so the peso is undervalued. In equilibrium (at point 2), 1 dollar would trade for 8.33 pesos but at its fixed rate (at point 1), it trades for 10 pesos—so the dollar is overvalued.

But what is so bad about the dollar being overvalued? The answer is that it makes U.S. goods more expensive (for foreigners to buy), which in turn can affect the U.S. merchandise trade balance.

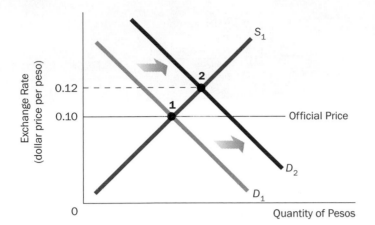

exhibit 10

Fixed Exchange Rates and an Overvalued Dollar
Initially, the demand for and supply of pesos are represented by D_1 and S_1, respectively. The equilibrium exchange rate is 0.10 USD = 1 MXP, which also happens to be the official (fixed) exchange rate. In time, the demand for pesos rises to D_2, and the equilibrium exchange rate rises to 0.12 USD = 1 MXP. The official exchange rate is fixed, however, so the dollar will be overvalued. As explained in the text, this can lead to a trade deficit.

For example, suppose a U.S. good costs 100 dollars. At the equilibrium exchange rate (0.12 USD = 1 MXP), a Mexican would pay 833 pesos for the good; but at the fixed exchange rate (0.10 USD = 1 MXP), he will pay 1,000 pesos.

Exchange Rate	Dollar Price	Peso Price
0.12 USD = 1 MXP (equilibrium)	100 USD	833 MXP (100 USD/0.12 USD)
0.10 USD = 1 MXP (fixed)	100 USD	1,000 MXP (100 USD/0.10 USD)

The higher the prices of U.S. goods (exports), the fewer of those goods Mexicans will buy, and, as just shown, an overvalued dollar makes U.S. export goods higher in price.

Ultimately, an overvalued dollar can affect the U.S. merchandise trade balance. As U.S. exports become more expensive for Mexicans, they buy fewer U.S. exports. If exports fall below imports, the result is a U.S. trade deficit.[4]

GOVERNMENT INVOLVEMENT IN A FIXED EXCHANGE RATE SYSTEM

Look back at Exhibit 9. Suppose the governments of Mexico and the United States agree to fix the exchange rate at 0.12 USD = 1 MXP. At this exchange rate, a surplus of pesos exists. What becomes of the surplus of pesos?

To maintain the exchange rate at 0.12 USD = 1 MXP, the Federal Reserve System (the Fed) could buy the surplus of pesos. But what would it use to buy the pesos? The Fed would buy the surplus of pesos with dollars. Consequently, the demand for pesos will increase and the demand curve will shift to the right, one hopes by enough to raise the equilibrium rate to the current fixed exchange rate.

Alternatively, instead of the Fed buying pesos (to mop up the excess supply of pesos), the Banco de Mexico (the central bank of Mexico) could buy pesos with some of its reserve dollars. (Why doesn't it buy pesos with pesos? Using pesos would not reduce the surplus of pesos on the market.) This action by the Banco de Mexico will also increase the demand for pesos and raise the equilibrium rate.

---

4. The other side of the coin, so to speak, is that if the dollar is overvalued, the peso must be undervalued. An undervalued peso makes Mexican goods cheaper for Americans. So while the overvalued dollar is causing Mexicans to buy fewer U.S. exports, the undervalued peso is causing Americans to import more goods from Mexico. In conclusion, U.S. exports fall, U.S. imports rise, and we move closer to a trade deficit, or if one already exists, it becomes larger.

The Nobel Prize in Economics and Foreign Exchange Markets

Do winners of the Nobel Prize in Economics care what is happening on foreign exchange markets? Because the prize money they win is paid in Swedish kronor, should they care?[5]

Consider the case of Robert Mundell, the 1999 winner of the prize. Mundell received a prize of 7.9 million Swedish kronor. In mid-October, when he was informed that he had won the prize, the prize money was worth nearly 1 million dollars. Mundell, however, decided not to take the prize money in kronor and then exchange it for dollars. Instead, he asked the Nobel Foundation to deposit the funds in his bank account in euros because he expected that over the next few months the euro would appreciate relative to the dollar.

Gary Becker was the 1992 winner of the Nobel Prize in Economics. Like all winners, he was notified of his winning the coveted prize in mid-October. He would not actually collect the prize money, however, until late December. In mid-October, the prize money (at current exchange rates) was worth 1.2 million dollars. Becker thought that the Swedish kronor was likely to depreciate in the near future, and so intended to buy dollars on the futures market. He never got around to it, though. Two weeks after he had been notified that he had won the Nobel Prize, there was a currency crisis in Sweden. As a result, his prize money shrank to 900,000 dollars.

Ronald Coase, who won the Nobel Prize in Economics in 1991, was to be paid his prize money at the end of 1991. Coase suspected that the kronor was about to appreciate in value relative to the dollar, so he asked the Foundation to pay him part of his prize money in January, 1992, to which the Foundation agreed. In January, the kronor appreciated in value, giving Coase more dollars per kronor.

Finally, the two actions could be combined; that is, both the Fed and the Banco de Mexico could buy pesos.

Q & A

Q: Why does the Fed play a much larger role under a fixed exchange rate system than under a flexible exchange rate system?

A: To support or maintain a fixed exchange rate, someone or something has to do the supporting or the maintaining. Central banks play this role. Under a flexible exchange rate system, there is no exchange rate to support or maintain; exchange rates simply respond to the forces of supply and demand.

OPTIONS UNDER A FIXED EXCHANGE RATE SYSTEM

Suppose there is a surplus of pesos in the foreign exchange market—indicating that the peso is overvalued and the dollar is undervalued. The Fed and the Banco de Mexico each attempt to rectify this situation by buying pesos. But suppose this combined action is not successful. The surplus of pesos persists for weeks, along with an overvalued peso and an undervalued dollar. What is there left to do? There are a few options.

Devaluation and Revaluation

Mexico and the United States could agree to reset the official price of the dollar and the peso. This entails *devaluation* and *revaluation*.

A **devaluation** occurs when the official price of a currency is lowered. A **revaluation** occurs when the official price of a currency is raised. For example, suppose the first official price of a peso is 0.10 USD = 1 MXP. It follows that the first official price of 1 dollar is 10 pesos.

Devaluation
A government act that changes the exchange rate by lowering the official price of a currency.

Revaluation
A government act that changes the exchange rate by raising the official price of a currency.

---

5. This feature is based on Sylvia Nasar, "Nobel Economics: Spending the Check," *New York Times*, 5 December 1999.

Now suppose Mexico and the U.S. agree to change the official price of their currencies. The second official price is 0.12 USD = 1 MXP. This means, then, that the second official price of 1 dollar is 8.33 pesos.

Moving from the first official price to the second, the peso has been revalued. That's because it takes *more dollars to buy a peso* (12 cents instead of 10 cents). Of course, moving from the first official price to the second means the dollar has been devalued. That's because it takes *fewer pesos to buy a dollar* (8.33 pesos instead of 10 pesos).

Might one country want to devalue its currency but another country not want to revalue its currency? For example, suppose Mexico wants to devalue its currency relative to the U.S. dollar. Would U.S. authorities always willingly comply? Not necessarily.

To see why, we have to understand that the United States will not sell as many goods to Mexico if the dollar is revalued. That's because, as we stated earlier, revaluing the dollar means Mexicans have to pay more for it—instead of paying, say, 8.33 pesos for 1 dollar, Mexicans might have to pay 10 pesos for 1 dollar. At a revalued dollar (higher peso price for a dollar), Mexicans will find U.S. goods more expensive and not want to buy as many. Americans who produce goods to sell to Mexico may see that a revalued dollar will hurt their pocketbooks and so they will argue against it.

Protectionist Trade Policy (Quotas and Tariffs)

Recall that an overvalued dollar can bring on or widen a trade deficit. How can a country deal with both the trade deficit and the overvalued dollar at once? Some say it can impose quotas and tariffs to reduce domestic consumption of foreign goods. (The previous chapter explains how both tariffs and quotas meet this objective.) A drop in the domestic consumption of foreign goods goes hand in hand with a decrease in the demand for foreign currencies. In turn, this can affect the value of the country's currency on the foreign exchange market. In this case, it can get rid of an overvalued dollar.

Economists are quick to point out, though, that trade deficits and overvalued currencies are sometimes used as an excuse to promote trade restrictions—many of which simply benefit special interests (such as U.S. producers that compete for sales with foreign producers in the U.S. market).

Changes in Monetary Policy

Sometimes a nation can use monetary policy to support the exchange rate or the official price of its currency. Suppose the United States is continually running a merchandise trade deficit; year after year, imports are outstripping exports. To remedy this, the United States might enact a tight monetary policy to retard inflation and drive up interest rates (at least in the short run). The tight monetary policy will reduce the U.S. rate of inflation and thereby lower U.S. prices relative to prices in other nations. This will make U.S. goods relatively cheaper than they were before (assuming other nations didn't also enact a tight monetary policy) and promote U.S. exports and discourage foreign imports, as well as generate a flow of investment funds into the United States in search of higher real interest rates.

Some economists argue against fixed exchange rates because they think it unwise for a nation to adopt a particular monetary policy simply to maintain an international exchange rate. Instead, they believe domestic monetary policies should be used to meet domestic economic goals—such as price stability, low unemployment, low and stable interest rates, and so forth.

THE GOLD STANDARD

If nations adopt the gold standard, they *automatically fix* their exchange rates. Suppose the United States defines a dollar as equal to 1/10 of an ounce of gold and Mexico defines a peso as equal to 1/100 of an ounce of gold. This means that one ounce of gold could be bought with either 10 dollars or 100 pesos. What, then, is the exchange rate between dollars and pesos? It is 10 MXP = 1 USD or 0.10 USD = 1 MXP. This is the fixed exchange rate between dollars and pesos.

To have an international gold standard, countries must do the following:

1. Define their currencies in terms of gold.
2. Stand ready and willing to convert gold into paper money and paper money into gold at the rate specified (for example, the United States would buy and sell gold at 10 dollars an ounce).
3. Link their money supplies to their holdings of gold.

With this last point in mind, consider how a gold standard would work. Let's again look at Mexico and the United States, and initially assume that the gold-standard (fixed) exchange rate of 0.10 USD = 1 MXP is the equilibrium exchange rate. Then, a change occurs: Inflation in Mexico raises prices there by 100 percent. A Mexican table that was priced at 2,000 pesos before the inflation is now priced at 4,000 pesos. At the gold-standard (fixed) exchange rate, Americans now have to pay 400 dollars (4,000 pesos/10 pesos per dollar) to buy the table, whereas before the inflation Americans had to pay only 200 dollars (2,000 pesos/ 10 pesos per dollar) for the table. As a result, Americans buy fewer Mexican tables; Americans import less from Mexico.

At the same time, Mexicans import more from the U.S. because American prices are now relatively lower than before inflation hit Mexico. A quick example illustrates our point. Suppose that before inflation hit Mexico, an American pair of shoes cost 200 dollars and, as before, a Mexican table cost 2,000 pesos. At 0.10 USD = 1 MXP, the 200-dollar American shoes cost 2,000 pesos and the 2,000-peso Mexican table cost 200 dollars. In other words, 1 pair of American shoes traded for (or equaled) 1 Mexican table.

Now look at things after inflation has raised the price of the Mexican table to 4,000 pesos, or 400 dollars. Because the American shoes are still 200 dollars (there has been no inflation in the United States), and the exchange rate is still fixed at 0.10 USD = 1 MXP, 1 pair of American shoes no longer equals 1 Mexican table; instead, it equals 1/2 of a Mexican table. In short, the inflation in Mexico has made U.S. goods *relatively cheaper* for Mexicans. As a result, Mexicans buy more U.S. goods; Mexicans import more from the United States.

To summarize: The inflation in Mexico has caused Americans to buy fewer goods from Mexico and Mexicans to buy more goods from the United States. What does this mean in terms of the merchandise trade balance for each country? In the United States, imports decline (Americans are buying less from Mexico) and exports rise (Mexicans are buying more from the United States), so the U.S. trade balance is likely to move into surplus. Contrarily, in Mexico, exports decline (Americans are buying less from Mexico) and imports rise (Mexicans are buying more from the United States), so Mexico's trade balance is likely to move into deficit.

On a gold standard, Mexicans have to pay for the difference between their imports and exports with gold. Gold is therefore shipped to the United States. An increase in the supply of gold in the United States expands the U.S. money supply. A decrease in the supply of gold in Mexico contracts the Mexican money supply. Prices are affected in both countries. In the United States, prices begin to rise; in Mexico, prices begin to fall.

As U.S. prices go up and Mexican prices go down, the earlier situation begins to reverse itself. American goods look more expensive to Mexicans, and they begin to buy less, whereas Mexican goods look cheaper to Americans, and they begin to buy more. Consequently, American imports begin to rise and exports begin to fall; Mexican imports begin to fall and exports begin to rise. Thus, by changing domestic money supplies and price levels, the gold standard begins to correct the initial trade balance disequilibrium.

The change in the money supply that the gold standard sometimes requires has prompted some economists to voice the same argument against the gold standard that is often heard against the fixed exchange rate system; that is, it subjects domestic monetary policy to international instead of domestic considerations. In fact, many economists cite this as part of the reason many nations abandoned the gold standard in the 1930s. At a time when unemployment was unusually high, many nations with trade deficits felt that matters would only get worse if they contracted their money supplies to live by the edicts of the gold standard. We explore this question in greater detail in a later section.

Self-Test

1. Under a fixed exchange rate system, if one currency is overvalued, then another currency must be undervalued. Explain why this is true.

2. How does an overvalued dollar affect U.S. exports and imports?

3. In each case, identify whether the U.S. dollar is overvalued or undervalued.
   a. The fixed exchange rate is 2 dollars = 1 pound and the equilibrium exchange rate is 3 dollars = 1 pound.
   b. The fixed exchange rate is 1.25 dollars = 1 euro and the equilibrium exchange rate is 1.10 dollars = 1 euro.
   c. The fixed exchange rate is 1 dollar = 10 pesos and the equilibrium exchange rate is 1 dollar = 14 pesos.

4. Under a fixed exchange rate system, why might the United States want to devalue its currency?

FIXED EXCHANGE RATES VERSUS FLEXIBLE EXCHANGE RATES

As is the case in many economic situations, there are both costs and benefits to any exchange rate system. This section discusses some of the arguments and issues surrounding fixed exchange rates and flexible exchange rates.

PROMOTING INTERNATIONAL TRADE

Which are better at promoting international trade, fixed or flexible exchange rates? This section presents the case for each.

The Case for Fixed Exchange Rates

Proponents of a fixed exchange rate system often argue that fixed exchange rates promote international trade, whereas flexible exchange rates stifle it. A major advantage of fixed exchange rates is certainty. Individuals in different countries know from day to day the value of their nation's currency. With flexible exchange rates, individuals are less likely to engage in international trade because of the added risk of not knowing from one day to the next how many dollars or euros or yen they will have to trade for other currencies. Certainty is a necessary ingredient in international trade; flexible exchange rates promote uncertainty, which hampers international trade.

Economist Charles Kindleberger, a proponent of fixed exchange rates, believes that having fixed exchange rates is analogous to having a single currency for the entire United States instead of having a different currency for each of the 50 states. One currency in the United States promotes trade, whereas 50 different currencies would hamper it. In Kindleberger's view:

> The main case against flexible exchange rates is that they break up the world market. . . . Imagine trying to conduct interstate trade in the USA if there were fifty different state monies, none of which was dominant. This is akin to barter, the inefficiency of which is explained time and again by textbooks.[6]

---

6. Charles Kindleberger, *International Money* (London: Allen and Unwin, 1981), p. 174.

The Case for Flexible Exchange Rates

Advocates of flexible exchange rates, as we have noted, maintain that it is better for a nation to adopt policies to meet domestic economic goals than to sacrifice domestic economic goals to maintain an exchange rate. They also say that there is too great a chance that the fixed exchange rate will diverge greatly from the equilibrium exchange rate, creating persistent balance of trade problems. This leads deficit nations to impose trade restrictions (tariffs and quotas) that hinder international trade.

OPTIMAL CURRENCY AREAS

As of 2002, the European Union (EU) consists of 15 member states—Austria, Belgium, Denmark, Finland, France, Germany, Greece, Ireland, Italy, Luxembourg, The Netherlands, Portugal, Spain, Sweden, and the United Kingdom. According to the European Union, its ultimate goal is "an ever close union among the peoples of Europe, in which decisions are taken as closely as possible to the citizen." As part of meeting this goal, the EU established its own currency—the euro—on January 1, 1999.[7] Although euro notes and coins were not issued until January 1, 2002, certain business transactions were made in euros beginning in January 1, 1999.

The issue of the European Union and the euro is relevant to a discussion of an **optimal currency area.** An optimal currency area is a geographic area in which exchange rates can be fixed or a *common currency* used without sacrificing domestic economic goals—such as low unemployment. The concept of an optimal currency area originated in the debate over whether fixed or flexible exchange rates are better. Most of the pioneering work on optimal currency areas was done by Robert Mundell, the winner of the 1999 Nobel Prize in Economics.

Before discussing an optimal currency area, we need to look at the relationships among labor mobility, trade, and exchange rates. Labor mobility means that it is easy for the residents of one country to move to another country.

Optimal Currency Area
A geographic area in which exchange rates can be fixed or a common currency used without sacrificing domestic economic goals—such as low unemployment.

Trade and Labor Mobility

Suppose there are only two countries, the United States and Canada. The United States produces calculators and soft drinks and Canada produces bread and muffins. Currently, the two countries trade with each other and there is complete labor mobility between the two countries.

One day, the residents of both countries reduce their demand for bread and muffins and increase their demand for calculators and soft drinks. In other words, there is a change in relative demand. Demand increases for U.S. goods and falls for Canadian goods. Business firms in Canada lay off employees because their sales have plummeted. Incomes in Canada begin to fall and the unemployment rate begins to rise. In the United States, prices initially rise because of the increased demand for calculators and soft drinks. In response to the higher demand for their products, U.S. business firms begin to hire more workers and increase their production. Their efforts to hire more workers drive wages up and reduce the unemployment rate.

Because labor is mobile, some of the newly unemployed Canadian workers move to the United States to find work. This will ease the economic situation in both countries. It will reduce some of the unemployment problems in Canada, and with more workers in the United States, more output will be produced, thus dampening upward price pressures on calculators and soft drinks. Thus, changes in relative demand pose no major economic problems for either country if labor is mobile.

---

7. So far, only 11 of the 15 member states have adopted the euro as their official currency.

ECONOMICS IN...

Back to the Futures

Meet (the fictional) Bill Whatley, owner of a Toyota dealership in Tulsa, Oklahoma. It is currently May, and Bill is thinking about a shipment of Toyotas he plans to buy in August. He knows that he must buy the Toyotas from Japan with yen, but he has a problem. At the present time, the price of 1 yen is 0.008 dollars. Bill wonders what the dollar price of a yen will be in August when he plans to make his purchase. Suppose the price of 1 yen rises to 0.010 dollars. If this happens, then instead of paying 20,000 dollars for a Toyota priced at 2.5 million yen, he would have to pay 25,000 dollars.[8] This difference of 5,000 dollars may be enough to erase his profit on the sale of the Toyotas.

What is Bill to do? He could purchase a futures contract today for the needed quantity of yen in August. A futures contract is a contract in which the seller agrees to provide a particular good (in this example, a particular currency) to the buyer on a specified future date at an agreed-on price. In short, Bill can buy yen today at a specified dollar price and take delivery of the yen at a later date (in August).

But suppose the price of 1 yen falls to 0.007 dollars in August. If this happens, Bill would have to pay only 17,500 dollars (instead of 20,000 dollars) for a Toyota priced at 2.5 million yen. Although he could increase his profit in this case, Bill, like other car dealers, might not be interested in assuming the risk associated with changes in exchange rates. He may prefer to lock in a sure thing.

Who would sell yen to Bill? The answer is someone who is willing to assume the risk of changes in the value of currencies—for example, Julie Jackson. Julie thinks to herself, "I think the dollar price of a yen will go down between now and August. Therefore, I'll enter into a contract with Bill stating that I'll give him 2.5 million yen in August for 20,000 dollars—the exchange rate specified in the contract being 1 JPY = 0.008 USD. If I'm right, and the actual exchange rate in August is 1 JPY = 0.007 USD, then I can purchase the 2.5 million yen for 17,500 dollars, and fulfill my contract with Bill by turning the yen over to him for 20,000 dollars. I walk away with 2,500 dollars in profit."

Many economists argue that futures contracts offer people a way of dealing with the risk associated with a flexible exchange rate system. If a person doesn't know what next month's exchange rate will be and doesn't want to take the risk of waiting to see, then he or she can enter into a futures contract and effectively shift the risk to someone who voluntarily assumes it.

Trade and Labor Immobility

Now let's change things. Suppose that relative demand has changed but this time labor is not mobile between the United States and Canada (labor immobility). There are either political or cultural barriers to people moving between the two countries. What happens in the economics of the two countries if people cannot move? The answer depends largely on whether exchange rates are fixed or flexible.

If exchange rates are flexible, the value of U.S. currency changes vis-à-vis Canadian currency. If Canadians want to buy more U.S. goods, they will have to exchange their domestic currency for U.S. currency. This increases the demand for U.S. currency on the foreign exchange market at the same time that it increases the supply of Canadian currency. Consequently, U.S. currency appreciates and Canadian currency depreciates. Because Canadian currency depreciates, U.S. goods become relatively more expensive for Canadians, so they buy fewer. And because U.S. currency appreciates, Canadian goods become relatively cheaper for Americans, so they buy more. Canadian business firms begin to sell more goods, so they

---

8. If 1 yen equals 0.008 dollars, then a Toyota with a price of 2.5 million yen costs 20,000 dollars because 2.5 million × 0.008 dollars = 20,000 dollars. If 1 yen equals 0.010 dollars, then a Toyota with a price of 2.5 million yen costs 25,000 dollars because 2.5 million × 0.010 dollars equals 25,000 dollars.

hire more workers, the unemployment rate drops, and the bad economic times in Canada begin to disappear.

If exchange rates are fixed, however, U.S. goods will not become relatively more expensive for Canadians and Canadian goods will not become relatively cheaper for Americans. Consequently, the bad economic times in Canada (high unemployment) might last for a long time indeed instead of beginning to reverse. Thus, if labor is immobile, changes in relative demand may pose major economic problems when exchange rates are fixed but not when they are flexible.

Costs, Benefits, and Optimal Currency Areas

There are both costs and benefits to flexible exchange rates. The benefits we have just discussed. The costs include the cost of exchanging one currency for another (there is a charge to exchange, say, U.S. dollars for Canadian dollars or U.S. dollars for Japanese yen) and the added risk of not knowing what the value of one's currency will be on the foreign exchange market on any given day. For many countries, the benefits outweigh the costs, and so they have flexible exchange rate regimes.

Suppose some of the costs of flexible exchange rates could be eliminated, while the benefits were maintained. Under what conditions could two countries have a fixed exchange rate or adopt a common currency and retain the benefits of flexible exchange rates? The answer is when labor is mobile between the two countries. Then, there is no reason to have separate currencies that float against each other because resources (labor) can move easily and quickly in response to changes in relative demand. There is no reason why the two countries cannot fix exchange rates or adopt the same currency.

When labor in countries within a certain geographic area is mobile enough to move easily and quickly in response to changes in relative demand, the countries are said to constitute an *optimal currency area*. Countries in an optimal currency area can either fix their currencies or adopt the same currency and thus keep all the benefits of flexible exchange rates without any of the costs.

It is commonly argued that the states within the United States constitute an optimal currency area. Labor can move easily and quickly between, say, North Carolina and South Carolina in response to relative demand changes. Some economists argue that the countries that compose the European Union are within an optimal currency area and that adopting a common currency—the euro—will benefit these countries. Other economists disagree. They argue that while labor is somewhat more mobile in Europe today than in the past, there are still certain language and cultural differences that make labor mobility less than sufficient to truly constitute an optimal currency area.

THE CURRENT INTERNATIONAL MONETARY SYSTEM

Today's international monetary system is best described as a managed flexible exchange rate system, sometimes referred to more casually as a **managed float.** In a way, this system is a rough compromise between the fixed and flexible exchange rate systems. The current system operates under flexible exchange rates, but not completely. Nations now and then intervene to adjust their official reserve holdings to moderate major swings in exchange rates.

Proponents of the managed float system stress the following advantages:

1. **It allows nations to pursue independent monetary policies.** Under a (strictly) fixed exchange rate system, fixed either by agreement or by gold, a nation with a merchandise trade deficit might have to enact a tight monetary policy in order to retard inflation and promote its exports. This would not be the case with the managed float. Its proponents argue that it is better to adjust one price—the exchange rate—than to adjust the price level to solve trade imbalances.

Managed Float
A managed flexible exchange rate system, under which nations now and then intervene to adjust their official reserve holdings to moderate major swings in exchange rates.

2. **It solves trade problems without trade restrictions.** As stated earlier, under a fixed exchange rate system, nations sometimes impose tariffs and quotas to solve trade imbalances. For example, a deficit nation might impose import quotas so that exports and imports of goods will be more in line. Under the current system, trade imbalances are usually solved through changes in exchange rates.

3. **It is flexible and therefore can easily adjust to shocks.** In 1973–1974, the OPEC nations dramatically raised the price of oil, which resulted in many oil-importing nations running trade deficits. A fixed exchange rate system would have had a hard time accommodating such a major change in oil prices. The current system had little trouble, however. Exchange rates took much of the shock (there were large changes in exchange rates) and thus allowed most nations' economies to weather the storm with a minimum of difficulty.

Opponents of the current international monetary system stress the following disadvantages:

1. **It promotes exchange rate volatility and uncertainty and results in less international trade than would be the case under fixed exchange rates.** Under a flexible exchange rate system, volatile exchange rates make it riskier for importers and exporters to conduct business. As a result, there is less international trade than there would be under a fixed exchange rate system.

   Proponents respond that the futures market in currencies allows importers and exporters to shift the risk of fluctuations in exchange rates to others. For example, if an American company wants to buy a certain quantity of a good from a Japanese company three months from today, it can contract today for the desired quantity of yen it will need, at a specified price. It will not have to worry about a change in the dollar price of yen during the next three months. There is, of course, a cost to purchasing a futures contract, but it is usually modest.

2. **It promotes inflation.** As we have seen, the monetary policies of different nations are not independent of one another under a fixed exchange rate system. For example, a nation with a merchandise trade deficit is somewhat restrained from inflating its currency because this will worsen the deficit problem. It will make the nation's goods more expensive relative to foreign goods and promote the purchase of imports. In its attempt to maintain the exchange rate, a nation with a merchandise trade deficit would have to enact a tight monetary policy.

   Under the current system, a nation with a merchandise trade deficit does not have to maintain exchange rates or try to solve its deficit problem through changes in its money supply. Opponents of the current system argue that this frees nations to inflate. They predict more inflation will result than would occur under a fixed exchange rate system.

3. **Changes in exchange rates alter trade balances in the desired direction only after a long time; in the short run, a depreciation in a currency can make the situation worse instead of better.** It is often argued that soon after a depreciation in a trade-deficit nation's currency, the trade deficit will increase (not decrease, as was hoped). The reason is that import demand is inelastic in the short run: Imports are not very responsive to a change in price.

   Suppose Mexico is running a trade deficit with the United States at the present exchange rate of 0.12 USD = 1 MXP. At this exchange rate, the peso is overvalued. Mexico buys 2,000 television sets from the United States, each with a price tag of 500 dollars. Assume Mexico therefore spends 8.33 million pesos on imports of American television sets.

   Now suppose the overvalued peso begins to depreciate, say, to 0.11 USD = 1 MXP. Furthermore, in the short run, Mexican customers buy only 100 fewer American television sets; that is, they import 1,900 television sets. At a price of 500 dollars each and an exchange rate of 0.11 USD = 1 MXP, Mexicans now spend 8.63 million pesos on imports of American television sets.

In the short run, then, a depreciation in the peso has widened the trade deficit because imports fell by only 5 percent while the price of imports (in terms of pesos) increased by 9.09 percent. As time passes, imports will fall off more (it takes time for Mexican buyers to shift from higher-priced American goods to lower-priced Mexican goods), and the deficit will shrink.

Q & A

Q: Does the discussion here imply that a system of flexible exchange rates is undesirable?

A: Some economists say yes. They argue that if import demand is inelastic, then changes in exchange rates are a rather crude way of solving a trade imbalance because in the short run they make things worse.

Self-Test

1. What is an optimal currency area?

2. Country 1 produces good *X* and country 2 produces good *Y*. People in both countries begin to demand more of good *X* and less of good *Y*. Assume there is no labor mobility between the two countries and that a flexible exchange rate system exists. What will happen to the unemployment rate in country 2? Explain your answer.

3. How important is labor mobility in determining whether or not an area is an optimal currency area?

A Reader Asks...
How Do I Convert Currencies?

I plan to travel to several different countries in the summer. How do I convert prices of products in other countries into dollars?

Here is the general formula you would use:

Price of the product in dollars = Price of the product in foreign currency × Price of the foreign currency in dollars

For example, suppose you travel to Mexico and see something priced at 100 pesos. You'd change the general formula into a specific one:

Price of the product in dollars = Price of the product in pesos × Price of a peso in dollars

If the dollar price of a peso is, say, 0.12 dollars, then the dollar price of the product is 12 dollars. Here is the calculation:

Price of the product in dollars = 100 × 0.12
= 12

Or suppose you are in Tokyo and you see a product for 10,000 yen. What is the price in dollars? At the exchange rate of 0.008 USD = 1 JPY, it is 80 dollars.

Price of the product in dollars = 10,000 × 0.008
= 80

Now let's suppose you are in Russia and you don't know what the exchange rate is between dollars and rubles. You pick up a newspaper to find out (often exchange rates are quoted in the newspaper). But instead of finding the exchange rate quoted in terms of the dollar price of a ruble (for example, 0.0318 dollars for 1 ruble), you find the ruble price of a dollar (31.4190 rubles for 1 dollar). What do you do now?

Perhaps the easiest thing to do is first convert rubles per dollar into dollars per ruble, and then use the earlier formula to find the price of the Russian product in dollars. Recall that exchange rates are reciprocals, so:

$$\text{Dollars per ruble} = \frac{1}{\text{Rubles per dollar}}$$

To illustrate, if it takes 31.4190 rubles to purchase 1 dollar, then it takes 0.0318 dollars to buy 1 ruble. Here is the computation:

$$\text{Dollars per ruble} = \frac{1}{31.4190}$$
$$= 0.0318$$

Now because you know that 0.0318 dollars = 1 ruble, it follows that, say, a Russian coat that costs 10,000 rubles costs 318 dollars:

$$\text{Price of the product in dollars} = 10{,}000 \times 0.0318$$
$$= 318$$

Chapter Summary

Balance of Payments

- The balance of payments provides information about a nation's imports and exports, domestic residents' earnings on assets located abroad, foreign earnings on domestic assets, gifts to and from foreign countries, and official transactions by governments and central banks.
- In a nation's balance of payments, any transaction that supplies the country's currency in the foreign exchange market is recorded as a debit ($-$). Any transaction that creates a demand for the country's currency is recorded as a credit ($+$).
- The three main accounts of the balance of payments are the current account, capital account, and official reserve account.
- The current account includes all payments related to the purchase and sale of goods and services. The three major components of the account are exports of goods and services, imports of goods and services, and net unilateral transfers abroad.
- The capital account includes all payments related to the purchase and sale of assets and to borrowing and lending activities. The major components are outflow of U.S. capital and inflow of foreign capital.
- The official reserve account includes transactions by the central banks of various countries.
- The merchandise trade balance is the difference between the value of merchandise exports and the value of merchandise imports. If exports are greater than imports, a nation has a trade surplus; if imports are greater than exports, a nation has a trade deficit. The balance of payments equals current account balance + capital account balance + official reserve balance + statistical discrepancy.

The Foreign Exchange Market and Flexible and Fixed Exchange Rates

- The market in which currencies of different countries are exchanged is called the foreign exchange market. In this market, currencies are bought and sold for a price; an exchange rate exists.
- If Americans demand Mexican goods, they also demand Mexican pesos and supply U.S. dollars. If Mexicans demand American goods, they also demand U.S. dollars and supply Mexican pesos. When the residents of a nation demand a foreign currency, they must supply their own currency.
- Under flexible exchange rates, the foreign exchange market will equilibrate at the exchange rate where the quantity demanded of a currency equals the quantity supplied of the currency; for example, the quantity demanded of U.S. dollars equals the quantity supplied of U.S. dollars.
- If the price of a nation's currency increases relative to a foreign currency, the nation's currency is said to have appreciated. For example, if the price of a peso rises from 0.10 USD = 1 MXP to 0.15 USD = 1 MXP, the peso has appreciated. If the price of a nation's currency decreases relative to a foreign currency, the nation's currency is said to have depreciated. For example, if the price of a dollar falls from 10 MXP = 1 USD to 8 MXP = 1 USD, the dollar has depreciated.
- Under a flexible exchange rate system, the equilibrium exchange rate is affected by a difference in income growth rates between countries, a difference in inflation rates between countries, and a change in (real) interest rates between countries.
- Under a fixed exchange rate system, countries agree to fix the price of their currencies. The central banks of the countries must then buy and sell currencies to maintain the agreed-on exchange rate. If a persistent deficit or surplus in a nation's combined current and capital account exists at a fixed exchange rate, the nation has a few options to deal with the problem: devalue or revalue its currency, enact protectionist trade policies (in the case of a deficit), or change its monetary policy.

The Gold Standard

- To have an international gold standard, nations must do the following: (1) define their currencies in terms of gold; (2) stand ready and willing to convert gold into paper money and paper money into gold at a specified rate; and (3) link their money supplies to their holdings of gold. The change in the money supply that the gold standard sometimes requires has prompted some economists to voice the same argument against the gold standard that is often heard against the fixed exchange rate system: It subjects domestic monetary policy to international instead of domestic considerations.

The Current International Monetary System

- Today's international monetary system is described as a managed flexible exchange rate system, or managed float. For the most part, the exchange rate system is flexible, although nations do periodically intervene in the foreign exchange market to adjust exchange rates. Because it is a managed float system, it is difficult to tell if nations will emphasize the "float" part or the "managed" part in the future.

- Proponents of the managed flexible exchange rate system believe it offers several advantages: (1) It allows nations to pursue independent monetary policies. (2) It solves trade problems without trade restrictions. (3) It is flexible and therefore can easily adjust to shocks. Opponents of the managed flexible exchange rate system believe it has several disadvantages: (1) It promotes exchange rate volatility and uncertainty and results in less international trade than would be the case under fixed exchange rates. (2) It promotes inflation. (3) It corrects trade deficits only a long time after a depreciation in the currency; in the interim, it can make matters worse.

Key Terms and Concepts

Balance of Payments
Debit
Foreign Exchange Market
Credit
Current Account
Merchandise Trade Balance
Merchandise Trade Deficit
Merchandise Trade Surplus
Current Account Balance

Capital Account
Capital Account Balance
Exchange Rate
Flexible Exchange Rate System
Appreciation
Depreciation
Purchasing Power Parity (PPP)
  Theory
Fixed Exchange Rate System

Overvaluation
Undervaluation
Devaluation
Revaluation
Optimal Currency Area
International Monetary Fund
  (IMF)
Special Drawing Right (SDR)
Managed Float

Economic Connections to You

Economic facts, actions, and changes create ripples that move away from their point of origin. Eventually, these ripples can intersect your life and have an effect on you. Consider the following example.

The Fed increases the money supply in the United States by a larger percentage than Banco de Mexico (the central bank of Mexico) increases the money supply in Mexico. As a result, the inflation rate in the United States rises relative to the inflation rate in Mexico. This changes the demand for and supply of dollars and pesos on foreign exchange markets. Con-

sequently, the dollar depreciates and the peso appreciates. Just as the dollar is depreciating and the peso is appreciating, you take a trip to Mexico. You must pay higher prices for the goods and services you buy in Mexico. Thus, there is a connection between a change in the money supply and the prices you pay on a trip abroad—an economic connection to you.

Based on the material in this chapter, identify other ways in which economic facts, actions, and changes create ripples that eventually affect you.

1. Suppose the United States and Japan have a flexible exchange rate system. Explain whether each of the following events will lead to an appreciation or depreciation in the U.S. dollar and Japanese yen. (a) U.S. real interest rates rise above Japanese real interest rates. (b) The Japanese inflation rate rises relative to the U.S. inflation rate. (c) Japan imposes a quota on imports of American radios.

2. Give an example that illustrates how a change in the exchange rate changes the relative price of domestic goods in terms of foreign goods.

3. Suppose the media report that the United States has a deficit in its current account. What does this imply about the U.S. capital account balance and official reserve account balance?

4. Suppose Canada has a merchandise trade deficit and Mexico has a merchandise trade surplus. The two countries have a flexible exchange rate system, so the Mexican peso appreciates and the Canadian dollar depreciates. It is noticed, however, that soon after the depreciation of the Canadian dollar, Canada's trade deficit grows instead of shrinks. Why might this occur?

5. What are the strong and weak points of the flexible exchange rate system? What are the strong and weak points of the fixed exchange rate system?

6. Individuals do not keep a written account of their balance of trade with other individuals. For example, John doesn't keep an account of how much he sells to Alice and how much he buys from her. In addition, neither cities nor any of the 50 states calculate their balance of trade with all other cities and states. However, nations do calculate their merchandise trade balance with other nations. If nations do it, should individuals, cities, and states do it? Why or why not?

7. Every nation's balance of payments equals zero. Does it follow that each nation is on an equal footing in international trade and finance with every other nation? Explain your answer.

8. Suppose your objective is to predict whether the euro (the currency of the European Union) and the U.S. dollar will appreciate or depreciate on the foreign exchange market in the next two months. What information would you need to help you make your prediction? Specifically, how would this information help you predict the direction of the foreign exchange value of the euro and dollar? Next, explain how a person who could accurately predict exchange rates could become extremely rich in a short time.

9. Suppose the price of a Big Mac always rises by the percentage rise in the price level of the country in which it is sold. According to the purchasing power parity (PPP) theory, we would expect the price of a Big Mac to be the same everywhere in the world. Why?

10. If everyone in the world spoke the same language, would the world be closer to or further from being an optimal currency area? Explain your answer.

1. The following foreign exchange information appeared in a newspaper:

	U.S. Dollar Equivalent		Currency per U.S. Dollar	
	THURS.	FRI.	THURS.	FRI.
Russia (ruble)	0.0318	0.0317	31.4190	31.5290
Brazil (real)	0.3569	0.3623	2.8020	2.7601
India (rupee)	0.0204	0.0208	48.9100	47.8521

a. Between Thursday and Friday, did the U.S. dollar appreciate or depreciate against the Russian ruble?

b. Between Thursday and Friday, did the U.S. dollar appreciate or depreciate against the Brazilian real?

c. Between Thursday and Friday, did the U.S. dollar appreciate or depreciate against the Indian rupee?

2. If 1 dollar equals 0.0093 yen, then what does 1 yen equal?

3. If 1 dollar equals 7.7 krone (Danish), then what does 1 krone equal?

4. If 1 dollar equals 31 rubles, then what does 1 ruble equal?

5. If the current account is −$45 billion, the capital account is +$55 billion, and the official reserve balance is −$1 billion, what does the statistical discrepancy equal?

6. Why does the balance of payments always equal zero?

1. Go to *http://www.imf.org*, click on "About the IMF," and then select "IMF at a Glance." How many countries are members of the IMF? When did the IMF come into existence? What are the objectives of the IMF? What is the most recent amount of loans outstanding (in billions of SDRs)?

2. Click on the "Back" button to return to the "About the IMF" page. Click on "Frequently asked questions," and select "Where does the IMF get its money?" Where does the IMF get its money? Which country is the largest contributor to the IMF?

3. Click on the "Back" button to return to the home page. Click on "Country Information," and select "Latvia." Read one of the notices, press releases, or statements about Latvia and the IMF. What is the extent of IMF involvement in Latvia?

4. Go to *http://www.worldbank.org/*, and choose "Countries & Regions." Scroll down the Web page, and select "El Salvador." Under "Our Work in El Salvador," select "IFC in El Salvador." Read the Web page.
   a. What does IFC stand for? What does it do? What is its relationship with the World Bank?
   b. What is the World Bank Group's current strategy for El Salvador's economic development?
   c. Is El Salvador's current account balance positive or negative? What could explain this fact?

Log on to the Arnold Xtra! Web site now (*http://arnoldxtra.swcollege.com*) for additional learning resources such as practice quizzes, help with graphing, video clips, and current event applications.

CHAPTER 1

Chapter 1, page 5

1. False. It takes two things for scarcity to exist: finite resources and infinite wants. If peoples' wants were equal to or less than the finite resources available to satisfy their wants, there would be no scarcity. Scarcity exists only because peoples' wants are greater than the resources available to satisfy their wants. Scarcity is the condition of infinite wants clashing with finite resources.

2. Both define economics as having to do with ends and means, which implicitly brings up the concept of scarcity. In short, both Friedman and Robbins emphasize the concept of scarcity in their definitions.

3. Positive economics deals with what is; normative economics, with what should be. Macroeconomics deals with human behavior and choices as they relate to an entire economy. Microeconomics deals with human behavior and choices as they relate to relatively small units—an individual, a firm, an industry, a single market.

Chapter 1, page 15

1. Because of scarcity, there is a need for a rationing device. People will compete for the rationing device. For example, if dollar price is the rationing device, people will compete for dollars.

2. Every time a person is late to history class, the instructor subtracts one-tenth of a point from the person's final grade. If the instructor raised the opportunity cost of being late to class—by subtracting one point from the person's final grade—economists predict there would be fewer persons late to class. In summary, the higher the opportunity cost of being late to class, the less likely people will be late to class.

3. Yes. To illustrate, suppose the marginal benefits and marginal costs (in dollars) are as follows for various hours of studying.

Hours	Marginal Benefits	Marginal Costs
First hour	$20.00	$10.00
Second hour	$14.00	$11.00
Third hour	$13.00	$12.00
Fourth hour	$12.10	$12.09
Fifth hour	$11.00	$13.00

Clearly you will study the first hour because the marginal benefits are greater than the marginal costs. Stated differently, there is a net benefit of $10 (the difference between the marginal benefits of $20 and the marginal costs of $10) for studying the first hour. If you stop studying after the first hour and do not proceed to the second, then you will forfeit the net benefit of $3 for the second hour. To maximize your net benefits of studying, you must proceed until the marginal benefits are as close to equal to the marginal costs as possible. (In the extreme, this is an epsilon away from equality. However, economists simply speak of "equality" between the two for convenience.) In this case, you will study through the fourth hour. You will not study the fifth hour because it is not worth it; the marginal benefits of studying the fifth hour are less than the marginal costs. In short, there is a net cost to studying the fifth hour.

4. An example is a politician who says: "My opponent has been in office for the past two years and during this time, interest rates have gone up and bankruptcies have gone up. We don't need any more bad economics. Don't cast your vote for my opponent. Vote for me." The politician implies that his opponent caused the dismal economic record when this is probably not the case.

5. Unless stated otherwise, when economics instructors identify the relationship between two variables they implicitly make the *ceteris paribus* assumption. In other words, the instructor is really saying, "If the price of going to the movies goes down, people will go to the movies more often—assuming that nothing else changes, such as the quality of movies, etc." Instructors don't always state *"ceteris paribus"* because if they did, they would be using the term every minute of a lecture. So the instructor is right, although a student new to economics might not know what the instructor is assuming but not saying.

Chapter 1, page 20

1. The purpose of building a theory is to explain something that is not obvious. For example, the cause of changes in the unemployment rate is not obvious, and so the economist would build a theory to explain changes in the unemployment rate.

2. A theory of the economy would seek to explain why certain things in the economy happen. For example, a theory of the economy might try to explain why prices rise or why output falls. A description of the economy is simply a statement of what exists in the economy. For example, we could say the economy is growing, or the economy is contracting, or more jobs are available this month than last month. A description doesn't answer questions; it simply tells us what is. A theory tries to answer a "why" question, such as: Why are more jobs available this month than last month?

3. If you do not test a theory, you will never know if you have accomplished your objective in building the theory in the first place. That is, you will not know if you have accurately explained something. We do not simply accept a theory if it "sounds right" because what sounds right may actually be wrong. For example, no doubt during the time of Columbus, the theory that the earth was flat sounded right to many people and the theory that the earth was round sounded ridiculous. The right-sounding theory turned out to be wrong, though, and the ridiculous-sounding theory turned out to be right.

CHAPTER 2

Chapter 2, page 48

1. A straight-line PPF represents constant opportunity costs between two goods. For example, for every unit of X produced, one unit of Y is forfeited. A bowed-outward PPF represents increasing opportunity costs. For example, we may have to forfeit 1 unit of X to produce the eleventh unit of Y, but we have to forfeit 2 units of X to produce the one hundredth unit of Y.

2. Political battles are most often waged when one political party can have more of what it wants only if another political party gets less of what it wants. This condition exists when the economy is on its PPF and stagnant (not growing). More of X means less of Y. In a growing economy, it is possible to get more of X without getting any less of Y, or to get more of both X and Y.

3. The first condition is that the economy is currently operating *below* the PPF. It is possible to move from a point below the PPF to a point on the PPF and get more of all goods. The second condition is that the economy's PPF shifts outward.

4. False. Take a look at Exhibit 5. There are numerous efficient points, all of which lie on the PPF.

Chapter 2, page 54

1. The producers' surplus is $3,000; the consumers' surplus is $8,000.

2. Transaction costs are the costs associated with the time and effort needed to search out, negotiate, and consummate a trade. The transaction costs are likely to be higher for buying a house than for buying a car because buying a house is a more detailed and complex process.

3. Not necessarily. Cynthia may simply be expressing her discontent over the terms of trade. Stated differently, she may wish she could have obtained more consumers' surplus than she obtained.

4. Answers will vary. Sample answer: John buys a magazine and reads it. There is no third-party effect. Sally asks a rock band to play at a party. Sally's next-door neighbor (a third party) is disturbed by the loud music.

Chapter 2, page 56

1. If George goes from producing $5X$ to $10X$, he gives up $5Y$. This means the opportunity cost of 5 more X is 5 fewer Y. It follows that the opportunity cost of $1X$ is $1Y$. Conclusion: the opportunity cost of $1X$ is $1Y$.

2. If Harriet produces 10 more X she gives up $15Y$. It follows that the opportunity cost of $1X$ is $1.5Y$ and the opportunity cost of $1Y$ is $0.67X$. If Bill produces 10 more X he gives up $20Y$. It follows that the opportunity cost of $1X$ is $2Y$ and the opportunity cost of $1Y$ is $0.5X$. Harriet is the lower-cost producer of X and Bill is the lower-cost producer of Y. In short, Harriet has the comparative advantage in the production of X; Bill has the comparative advantage in the production of Y.

Chapter 2, page 60

1. What goods will be produced? How will the goods be produced? For whom will the goods be produced?

2. Trade benefits the traders. If George buys a book for $40, both George and the bookseller have been made better off. George would not have traded $40 for the book unless he expected to be made better off. Similarly, the seller would not have sold the book unless she expected to be made better off.

3. One of the questions every society must answer is *What goods will be produced?* In a way, this is no different than *Where on its PPF will an economy operate?* In other words, what combination of goods will be produced? Under capitalism, where on its PPF the economy operates is largely decided by the market (buyers and sellers). Under socialism, where on its PPF the economy operates is largely decided by government.

CHAPTER 3

Chapter 3, page 76

1. Popcorn is a normal good for Sandi. Prepaid telephone cards are an inferior good for Mark.

2. Asking why demand curves are downward-sloping is the same as asking why price and quantity demanded are inversely related (as one rises, the other falls). There are two reasons mentioned in this section: (1) As price rises, people substitute lower-priced goods for higher-priced goods. (2) Because individuals receive less utility from an additional unit of a good they consume, they are only willing to pay less for the additional unit. The second reason is a reflection of the law of diminishing marginal utility.

3. Suppose only two people, Bob and Alice, have a demand for good X. At a price of $7, Bob buys 10 units and Alice buys 3 units; at a price of $6, Bob buys 12 units and Alice buys 5 units. One point on the market demand curve represents a price of $7 and a quantity demanded of 13 units; another point represents $6 and 17 units. A market demand curve is derived by adding the quantities demanded at each price.

4. A change in income, preferences, prices of related goods, number of buyers, and expectations of future price can change demand. A change in the price of the good changes the quantity demanded of the good. For example, a change in *income* can change the *demand* for oranges, but only a change in the *price* of oranges can directly change the *quantity demanded* of oranges.

Chapter 3, page 81

1. It would be difficult to increase the quantity supplied of houses over the next 10 hours, so the supply curve in (a) is vertical, as in Exhibit 8. It is possible to increase the quantity supplied of houses over the next 3 months, however, so the supply curve in (b) is upward-sloping.

2. **a.** The supply curve shifts to the left.
   b. The supply curve shifts to the left.
   c. The supply curve shifts to the right.

3. The upward-sloping supply curve illustrates that a rising price of a good brings about an increase in the quantity supplied of the good. This occurs because in most instances, a higher price acts as an incentive for producers to produce more of the good.

Chapter 3, page 88

1. Disagree. In the text, we plainly saw how supply and demand work at an auction. Supply and demand are at work in the grocery store, too, although there is no auctioneer present. The essence of the auction example is the auctioneer raising the price when there was a shortage and lowering the price when there was a surplus. The same thing happens at the grocery store.

For example, if there is a surplus of corn flakes, the manager of the store is likely to have a sale (lower prices) on corn flakes. Many markets without auctioneers act as if there are auctioneers raising and lowering prices in response to shortages and surpluses.

2. No. It could be the result of a higher supply of computers. Either a decrease in demand or an increase in supply will lower price.

3. **a.** Lower price and quantity
   b. Lower price and higher quantity
   c. Higher price and lower quantity
   d. Lower price and quantity

Chapter 3, page 91

1. Yes, if nothing else changes—that is, yes, *ceteris paribus*. If some other things change, though, they may not. For example, if the government imposes an effective price ceiling on gasoline, Jamie may pay lower gas prices at the pump but have to wait in line to buy the gas (due to first-come-first-served trying to ration the shortage). It is not clear if Jamie is better off paying a higher price and not waiting in line or paying a lower price and having to wait in line. The point, however, is that buyers don't necessarily prefer lower prices to higher prices unless everything else (quality, wait, service, etc.) stays the same.

2. Disagree. Both long-lasting shortages and long lines are caused by price ceilings. First the price ceiling is imposed, creating the shortage; then the rationing device first-come-first-served (FCFS) emerges because price isn't permitted to fully ration the good. There are shortages every day that don't cause long lines to form. Instead, buyers bid up price, output and price move to equilibrium, and there is no shortage.

3. Buyers might argue for price ceilings on the goods they buy—especially if they don't know that price ceilings have some effects they may not like (such as fewer exchanges, FCFS used as a rationing device, and so on.) Sellers might argue for price floors on the goods they sell—especially if they expect their profits to rise. Employees might argue for a wage floor on the labor services they sell—especially if they don't know that they may lose their jobs or have their hours cut back as a result.

CHAPTER 4

Chapter 4, page 99

1. If supply and tuition are constant and demand rises, the shortage of openings at the university will become greater. The university will continue to use its non-price rationing devices (GPA, SAT scores, ACT scores) but will have to raise the standards of admission. Instead of requiring a GPA of, say, 3.5 for admission, it may raise the requirement to 3.8.

2. Not likely. A university that didn't make admission easier in the face of a surplus of openings might not be around much longer. When tuition cannot be adjusted directly—in other words, when the rationing device of price cannot be adjusted—it is likely that the nonprice rationing device (standards) will be.

Chapter 4, page 100

1. In the section, we say "Because the workers in groups *B* and *C* are equally productive and because employers show no preference for hiring one group of workers over the other, the demand for group *B* workers is the same as the demand for group *C* workers." It follows, then, that if some workers are more productive than other workers or if employers show a preference for hiring one group of workers over the other (and that preference is unrelated to differences in productivity), then the demand for workers will be different. Bottom line: If *B* workers are more productive than *C* workers, the demand for *B* workers will be higher than the demand for *C* workers, *ceteris paribus*.

2. If two groups of people are equally productive and a discriminator employer decides not to hire one group, the demand for that group's services is less. Lower demand translates into lower wages and lower costs for nondiscriminator employers. In turn, lower costs will give nondiscriminator employers the ability to underprice their discriminator competitors.

Chapter 4, pages 100–101

1. Price will fall.
2. Quantity will rise.

Chapter 4, page 102

1. Yes. At the equilibrium wage rate, the quantity demanded of labor equals the quantity supplied. At a higher wage (the minimum wage), the quantity supplied stays constant (given the vertical supply curve) but the quantity demanded falls. Thus, a surplus results.

2. The person is assuming that the labor demand curve is vertical (no matter what the wage rate is, the quantity demanded of labor is always the same).

Chapter 4, page 104

1. Agree. At any price below equilibrium price, a shortage exists: the quantity demanded of kidneys is greater than the quantity supplied of kidneys. As price rises toward its equilibrium level, quantity supplied rises and quantity demanded falls until the two are equal.

2. It depends on whether or not $0 is the equilibrium price of kidneys. If it is—that is, if the kidney demand and supply curves intersect at $0—then there is no shortage of kidneys. But if, at $0, the quantity demanded of kidneys is greater than the quantity supplied, then a shortage exists.

Chapter 4, page 106

1. The wholesale price of electricity rises. Because of this, the supply curve of electricity in the retail market shifts leftward. The retail price is prevented from rising, so there is now a shortage of electricity in the retail market.

2. No, not if, say, demand for electricity had risen in the retail market. Specifically, if demand had risen in the retail market and price was prevented from rising, there would still be a shortage of electricity and blackouts in the retail market. There would also be shortages in the wholesale market. Higher demand in the wholesale market and no change in price would result in a shortage.

Chapter 4, page 107

1. The answer can be either "the shifting supply of gold" or "the attempt to earn profit." Consider the first answer. If the price of gold is higher in one location than another, the supply of gold shifts from the lower-priced location to the higher-priced location. In the process, the gold prices in the two locations converge. Now, if we want to know what causes the shifting supply of gold, the answer is the attempt to earn profit. Specifically, it is the attempt to earn profit that prompts people to buy gold in the lower-priced location and sell it in the higher-priced location.

2. You can move a Camry from one place to another in response to a rising price. What holds for gold holds for Camrys too.

Chapter 4, page 108

1. Prices go up at some times, down at other times. If greed explains higher prices, does altruism explain lower prices? Is the person who is greedy in June and raises prices the same person who is altruistic in July and lowers prices? If so, what caused him to be greedy one month and altruistic the next? The greed explanation of higher prices seems incapable of answering this question. Economists do not assume that people are greedy one month and not greedy the next month. They assume that sellers are always greedy and want to receive the highest price possible for what they sell, and they assume that buyers are always greedy and want to pay the lowest price possible for what they buy.

2. Expectations of future price. To illustrate, suppose there is an earthquake in southern California. Consequently, some people, rightly or wrongly, think that the price of bottled water will rise due to interruption or contamination of piped water. Because they expect a higher price for bottled water in the future, their current demand for bottled water rises. When the current demand for bottled water rises, the current price of bottled water rises, *ceteris paribus*.

Chapter 4, page 110

1. Moving from a system where patients cannot sue their HMOs to one where they can gives patients something they didn't have before (the right to sue) at a higher price (higher charges for health care coverage). The "free lunch"—the right to sue—isn't free after all.

2. If the students get the extra week and nothing else changes, then the students will probably say they are better off. In other words, more of one thing (time) and no less of anything else makes one better off. But if because of the extra week, the professor grades their papers harder than she would have otherwise, then some or all of the students may say that they weren't made better off by the extra week.

Chapter 4, page 111

1. One possible answer is: There are two cities, one with clean air and the other with dirty air. The demand to live in the clean-air city is higher than the demand to live in the dirty-air city. As a result, housing prices are higher in the clean-air city than in the dirty-air city.

2. Ultimately, the person who owns the land in the good-weather city receives the payment. Look at it this way: People have a higher demand for houses in good-weather cities than in bad-weather cities. As a result, house builders receive higher prices for houses built and sold in good-weather cities. Because of the higher house prices in good-weather cities, house builders have a higher demand for land in good-weather cities. In the end, higher demand for land translates into higher land prices or land rents for landowners.

Chapter 4, page 112

1. The shortage is greater in computer science. If supply in each field is the same, the wage rate is the same, and demand is greater in computer science than in biology, then the horizontal difference (which measures the degree of shortage) between the demand curve and supply curve in computer science is greater than in biology. Draw this and see.

2. Under the condition that demand and supply are the same in all fields. Stated differently, under the condition that the equilibrium wage in each field is the same.

Chapter 4, page 113

1. They may not. Because of the tax, the demand for the new houses may be lower than it would be if there were no special tax. As a result of lower demand, the price of the houses may be lower than it would be without the tax. This is similar to the new car–used car example. Because people can resell the cars they buy, their demand for new cars is higher than it would be if they couldn't resell their old cars.

Similarly, because people who buy the new houses dislike the tax, their demand for the houses is lower than it would be without the tax.

2. Yes, being able to sell your old car is like getting a rebate. You pay a certain price for a new car (say, $15,000), use the car for a few years, and then sell it on the used car market (for, say, $10,000). The price you paid for the car, some would say, was $5,000, not $15,000.

Chapter 4, page 114

1. Any price above 70 cents.

2. Assuming that tolls are not used, freeway congestion will worsen. An increase in driving population simply shifts the demand curve for driving to the right.

Chapter 4, page 115

1. A person's time is worth something. For example, if a person spends one hour doing something instead of working and has a wage rate of $10 an hour, then one hour of her time is worth $10. When we know a person's wage rate, we can convert "time spent" into "dollars forfeited."

2. If demand rises more than supply and price is held constant, there will be a shortage of parking. Some nonprice rationing device will emerge to allocate parking spaces along with dollar price. It will probably be first-come-first-served (whoever gets to an empty parking spot first gets to park).

Chapter 4, page 116

1. All other things equal—such as the number of people on a flight, and so on—lines will be longer for a Southwest flight because all seats are rationed on a first-come-first-served basis on the day of the flight. On other airlines, seats are rationed on a first-come-first-served basis starting one month before the flight. Lines are shorter on the day of the flight because many seats have already been rationed.

2. On flight A. The shortage of aisle seats is greater on flight A than flight B, which means that more seats must be rationed by first-come-first-served on that flight.

3. In both cases there are submarkets within markets. Specifically, demand and supply intersect at a different equilibrium price for some airline seats than for other airline seats just as demand and supply intersect at a different equilibrium wage for professors in some fields than for professors in other fields. Equilibrium price (or wage) in one submarket is likely to be different than equilibrium price (or wage) in another submarket.

Chapter 4, page 117

1. Answers will vary. Students sometimes say that it is "fairer" if everyone is charged the same price. Is it unfair then that moviegoers pay less if they go to the 2 P.M. movie than if they go to the 8 P.M. movie?

2. Both analyses deal with an equilibrium price being charged in one submarket and a disequilibrium price being charged in another submarket. Both deal with the effects of a disequilibrium price.

Chapter 4, page 119

1. Broadway doesn't have any need to have people line up early for the show. There are no slot machines in the playhouse.

2. It depends on two things: the equilibrium price for a good seat and the price that is charged for a good seat. The higher the equilibrium price, all other things equal, the greater the tip. The lower the price charged, all other things equal, the greater the tip. We would expect that those persons who do the seating and receive the tips would argue to keep show prices down.

Chapter 4, page 120

1. Disagree. The demand for romance novels may be greater than the demand for classic novels, but this is not necessarily the case. In fact, the demand for classic novels may be greater than the demand for romance novels, but if the price of romance novels is lower than the price of classic novels, the quantity demanded of romance novels may be greater.

2. This is really the same question as number 1. If popularity is equated with "quantity demanded," then popularity is a function of both demand and price. The greater the demand, for a given price, the greater the quantity demanded; the lower the price, for a given demand, the greater the quantity demanded.

Chapter 4, page 122

1. If there is a "speed trap," the probability of being apprehended for speeding rises, and, for a given speeding ticket price, the price of speeding rises. If you slow down, you are responding to a change in the price of speeding the way that the law of demand predicts you will respond.

2. As police officers earn more, the costs (to taxpayers) of a police force increase. Taxpayers (or the public) may want to reduce the number of police officers, but not at the expense of more speeders. To prevent people from speeding more often with fewer officers working, the price of a speeding ticket will have to increase.

Chapter 4, page 123

1. Oil that is owned is more likely to be conserved than oil that is not owned. If it is not owned, then the first person to the oil gets to sell it. Leaving it in the ground (conserving it) increases the probability that someone will get to it before you do. Individuals will rush to get to the oil first and sell it immediately (before someone else does). Conclusion: Private property is critical to conservation.

2. If he expects to die, and he has no children (no heirs), then Tex is less likely to conserve oil for the future because he won't be around to receive payment for the oil. He may think that it is better to sell the oil now. If Tex has children, he may conserve the oil and not sell it now. He may benefit by leaving a more valuable resource to his children.

CHAPTER 5

Chapter 5, page 139

1. $E_d = 1.44$

2. It means that if there is a change in price, quantity demanded will change (in the opposite direction) by 0.39 times the percentage change in price. For example, if price rises 10 percent, then quantity demanded will fall 3.9 percent. If price rises 20 percent, then quantity demanded will fall 7.8 percent.

3. **a.** Total revenue falls.
   b. Total revenue falls.
   c. Total revenue remains constant.
   d. Total revenue rises.
   e. Total revenue rises.

4. She is implicitly assuming that demand is inelastic. If, however, Alexi is wrong and demand is elastic, then a rise in price will actually lower total revenue.

Chapter 5, page 143

1. No. Moving from 7 to 9 substitutes doesn't necessarily change demand from being inelastic to elastic. It simply leads to a rise in price elasticity of demand, *ceteris paribus*. For example, if price elasticity of demand is 0.45 when there are 7 substitutes, it will be higher than this when there are 9 substitutes, *ceteris paribus*. Higher could be 0.67. If this is the case, demand is still inelastic (but less so than before).

2. **a.** Compaq computers
   b. Heinz ketchup
   c. Perrier water
   In all three cases, the good with the higher price elasticity of demand is the more specific of the two goods; therefore it has more substitutes.

Chapter 5, page 152

1. It means that the good (in question) is a normal good and that it is income elastic—that is, as income rises, the quantity demanded rises by a greater percentage. In this case, quantity demanded rises by 1.33 times the percentage change in income. If income rises by 10 percent, the quantity demanded of the good will rise by 13.3 percent.

2. A change in price does not change quantity supplied.

3. Tax revenue is equal to the tax times the quantity sold. If demand is inelastic, there will be a smaller cutback in quantity sold due to the higher price brought about by the tax.

4. Under the condition that the demand for computers is perfectly inelastic or that the supply of computers is perfectly elastic.

CHAPTER 6

Chapter 6, page 164

1. The paradox is that water, which is essential to life, is cheap and diamonds, which are not essential to life, are expensive. The solution to the paradox depends on knowing the difference between total and marginal utility and the law of diminishing marginal utility. By saying that water is essential to life and diamonds are not essential to life, we signify that water gives us high total utility relative to diamonds. But then someone asks, "Well, if water gives us greater total utility than diamonds do, why isn't the price of water greater than the price of diamonds?" The answer is, "Price isn't a reflection of total utility; it is a reflection of marginal utility. The marginal utility of water is less than the marginal utility of diamonds." This answer raises another question, "How can the total utility of water be greater than the total utility of diamonds, but the marginal utility of water be less than the marginal utility of diamonds?" The answer is based on the fact that water is plentiful and diamonds are not and on the law of diminishing marginal utility. There is so much more water relative to diamonds that the next (additional) unit of water gives us less utility (lower marginal utility) than the next unit of diamonds.

2. If total utility declines, marginal utility must be negative. For example, if total utility is 30 utils when Lydia consumes 3 apples and 25 utils when she consumes 4 apples, it must be because the fourth apple had a marginal utility of minus 5 utils. Chapter 1 explains that something that takes utility away from us (or gives us disutility) is called a bad. For Lydia, the fourth apple is a bad, not a good.

3. The total and marginal utility of a good are the same for the first unit of the good consumed. For example, before Tomas eats his first apple, he receives no utility or disutility from apples. Eating the first apple, he receives 15 utils. So, the total utility (TU) for one apple is 15 utils and the marginal utility (MU) for the first apple is 15 utils. Exhibit 1 shows that TU and MU are the same for the first unit of good X.

Chapter 6, page 169

1. Alesandro is not in consumer equilibrium because the marginal utility-per-dollar of X is 16 utils and the marginal utility-per-dollar of Y is 13.14 utils. To be in equilibrium, a consumer has to receive the same marginal utility per dollar for each good consumed.

2. For a normal good, the substitution and income effects reinforce each other; for an inferior good, they do not. To illustrate, if good A is a normal good

and the absolute price of A declines, two things happen: (1) the relative price of good A declines, which leads the consumer to buy more of good A, and (2) real income rises, which, because the good is a normal good, also causes the consumer to buy more of the good. If good A is an inferior good, the increase in real income will cause the consumer to buy less, not more, of the good.

Chapter 6, pages 172–173

1. Yes, Brandon is compartmentalizing. He is treating $100 that comes from his grandmother differently than $100 that comes from his father.

2. The endowment effect relates to individuals valuing X more highly when they possess it than when they don't have it but are thinking of acquiring it. Friedman argues that if we go back in time to a hunter-gatherer society when there were no well-established property rights (no rules as to what is "mine and thine"), individuals who would fight hard to keep what they possessed, but wouldn't fight as hard to acquire what they did not possess, would have a higher probability of surviving than those individuals who would fight hard at both times. Thus, those who would fight hard only to keep what they possessed would have a higher probability of reproductive success. The characteristic of "holding on to what you have" has been passed down from generation to generation and, although it may not be as important today as it was in a hunter-gatherer society, it still influences behavior.

CHAPTER 7

Chapter 7, page 191

1. He spoke of an invisible hand that leads individuals to an end that was not part of their intention. The market does this; it guides and coordinates peoples' actions even when people can't see what the market is doing.

2. No. According to Alchian and Demsetz, teams (firms) are formed only when a certain condition exists: when the sum of what individuals can produce as a team is greater than the sum of what they can produce alone. If this condition does not exist—if the sum of team production is less than the sum of individual production—then there would be no reason to form a team.

3. The costs of shirking are lower when working in a team than they are when working alone. For example, if one person shirks in a team of 100 persons, the effect of his shirking is spread over 100 persons. He "pays" 1/100 of the cost of his shirking. When working alone, he pays 100 percent of the cost of his shirking. Economists predict that people will shirk more as the cost of shirking falls.

4. The monitor monitors herself because she is a residual claimant of the firm. If she shirks and, as a result, profits fall, then she receives less income.

Chapter 7, page 197

1. Corporations
2. There are three advantages: (1) the owners of the corporation are not personally liable for the debts of the corporation; (2) corporations continue to exist even when owners of the corporation sell their shares or die; and (3) corporations are usually able to raise large sums of financial capital for investment purposes.
3. General partners have unlimited liability; limited partners have limited liability.
4. Separation of ownership from control refers to the fact that the owners of many large corporations are not the managers of the corporations. This presents the owners with a problem if the objectives of the managers and the owners are not the same. Owners can solve this problem by issuing stock to managers. When managers become stockholders (owners), they will likely want the same thing that other owners want—an increase in the value of their stock.

   Owners can also monitor the price of their stock. If the price continues to go down, owners can reason that the present management is not doing what is necessary to meet the objectives of the owners. The owners can then simply fire the current managers and replace them with new managers. Over time, you would expect managers to learn that if they do not earn profits for the owners of the corporation, they will lose their jobs.

CHAPTER 8

Chapter 8, page 209

1. The person earning the low salary has lower implicit costs and so is more likely to start his or her own business. He or she gives up less to go into business.
2. Accounting profit is larger. Only explicit costs are subtracted from total revenue in computing accounting profit, but both explicit and implicit costs are subtracted from total revenue in computing economic profit. If implicit costs are zero, then accounting profit and economic profit are the same. Economic profit is never greater than accounting profit.
3. When he is earning (positive) accounting profit but his total revenue does not cover the sum of his explicit and implicit costs. For example, suppose Brad earns total revenue of $100,000 and has explicit costs of $40,000 and implicit costs of $70,000. His accounting profit is $60,000, but his total revenue of $100,000 is not large enough to cover the sum of his explicit and implicit costs ($110,000). Brad's economic profit is a negative $10,000. In other words,

while Brad earns an accounting profit, he takes an economic loss.

Chapter 8, page 215

1. No. The short run and the long run are not "lengths of time." The short run is that period of time when some inputs are fixed and, therefore, the firm has fixed costs. The long run is that period of time when no inputs are fixed (that is, all inputs are variable) and, thus, all costs are variable costs. It's possible for the short run to be, say, six months, and the long run to be a much shorter period of time. In other words, the time period when there are no fixed inputs can be shorter than the time period when there are fixed inputs.
2. The law of diminishing marginal returns holds only when we add more of one input to a given (fixed) quantity of another input. The statement does not identify one input as fixed (it says that both increase), and so the law of diminishing marginal returns is not relevant in this situation.
3. When MC is declining, MPP is rising; when MC is constant, MPP is constant; and when MC is rising, MPP is falling.

Chapter 8, page 223

1. $ATC = TC/Q$ and $ATC = AFC + AVC$
2. Yes. Suppose a business incurs a cost of $10 to produce a product. Before it can sell the product, though, the demand for the product falls and moves the market price from $15 to $6. Does the owner of the business say, "I can't sell the product for $6 because I'd be taking a loss"? If she does, she chooses to let a sunk cost affect her current decision. Instead, she should ask herself, "Do I think the market price of the product will rise or fall?" If she thinks it will fall, she should sell the product today for $6.
3. Unit costs are another name for average total costs (ATC), so the question is: What happens to ATC as MC rises? You might be inclined to say that as MC rises, so does ATC—but this is not necessarily so. (See Region 1 in Exhibit 5b.) What matters is whether or not MC is greater than ATC. If it is, then ATC will rise. If it is not, then ATC will decline.

   This is a trick question of sorts. There is a tendency to misinterpret the average-marginal rule and to believe that as marginal cost rises, average total cost rises; and as marginal cost falls, average total cost falls. But this is not what the average-marginal rule says. The rule says that when MC is above ATC, ATC rises; and when MC is below ATC, ATC falls.
4. Yes. As marginal physical product (MPP) rises, marginal cost (MC) falls. If MC falls enough to move below unit cost (which is the same as average total cost), then unit cost declines. Similarly, as MPP falls, MC rises. If MC rises enough to move above unit cost, then unit cost rises.

Chapter 8, page 228

1. It currently takes 10 units of *X* and 10 units of *Y* to produce 50 units of good *Z*. Let both *X* and *Y* double to 20 units each. As a result, the output of *Z* more than doubles—say, to 150 units. When inputs are increased by some percentage and output increases by a greater percentage, then economies of scale are said to exist. When economies of scale exist, unit costs fall. And another name for unit costs is average total costs.

2. It would be horizontal. When there are constant returns to scale, output doubles if inputs double. If this happens, unit costs stay constant. In other words, they don't rise and they don't fall, so the *LRATC* curve is horizontal.

3. Unit costs must have been lower when it produced 200 units than when it produced 100 units. In other words, there were economies of scale between 100 units and 200 units.

   To explain further: Profit per unit is the difference between price per unit and cost per unit (or unit costs): profit per unit = price per unit − cost per unit. Suppose the unit cost is $3 when the price is $4—giving a profit per unit of $1. Next, there are economies of scale as the firm raises output from 100 units to 200 units. It follows that unit costs fall—let's say to $2 per unit. If price is $3, then there is still a $1 per-unit profit.

CHAPTER 9

Chapter 9, page 237

1. It means the firm cannot change the price of the product it sells by its actions. For example, if firm *A* cuts back on the supply of what it produces and the price of its product does not change, then we'd say that firm *A* cannot control the price of the product it sells. In other words, if price is independent of a firm's actions, that firm does not have any control over price.

2. The easy, and incomplete, answer is that a perfectly competitive firm is a price taker because it is in a market where it cannot control the price of the product it sells. But this simply leads to the question: Why can't it control the price of the product it sells? The answer is because it is in a market where its supply is small relative to the total market supply, it sells a homogeneous good, and all buyers and sellers have all relevant information.

3. If a perfectly competitive firm tries to charge a price higher than equilibrium price, all buyers will know this (assumption 3). These buyers will then simply buy from another firm that sells the same (homogeneous) product (assumption 2).

4. No. A market doesn't have to perfectly match all assumptions of the theory of perfect competition for it to be labeled a perfectly competitive market. What is important is whether or not it acts *as if* it is perfectly competitive. You know the old saying, "If it walks like a duck and it quacks like a duck, it's a duck." Well, if it acts like a perfectly competitive market, it's a perfectly competitive market.

Chapter 9, page 243

1. No. Whether a firm earns profit or not depends on the relationship between price (*P*) and average total cost (*ATC*). If *P* > *ATC*, then the firm earns profits. To understand this, remember that profits exist when total revenue (*TR*) minus total cost (*TC*) is a positive number. Total revenue is simply price times quantity (*TR* = *P* × *Q*), and total cost is average total cost times quantity (*TC* = *ATC* × *Q*). Because quantity (*Q*) is common to both *TR* and *TC*, if *P* > *ATC*, then *TR* > *TC* and the firm earns profits.

2. In the short run, whether or not a firm should shut down operations depends on the relationship between price and average variable cost (*AVC*). It depends on whether price is greater than or less than average variable cost. If *P* > *AVC*, the firm should continue to produce; if *P* < *AVC*, it should shut down.

3. As long as *MR* > *MC*—for example, *MR* = $6 and *MC* = $4—the firm should produce and sell additional units of a good because this adds more to *TR* than it does to *TC*. It's adding $6 to *TR* and $4 to *TC*. Whenever you add more to *TR* than you do to *TC*, the gap between the two becomes larger.

4. We start with the upward-sloping market supply curve and work backward. First, market supply curves are upward-sloping because they are the "addition" of individual firms' supply curves—which are upward-sloping. Second, individual firms' supply curves are upward-sloping because they are that portion of their marginal cost curves above their average variable cost curves and this portion of the *MC* curve is upward-sloping. Third, marginal cost curves have upward-sloping portions to them because of the law of diminishing marginal returns. In conclusion, market supply curves are upward-sloping because of the law of diminishing marginal returns.

Chapter 9, page 252

1. According to the theory of perfect competition, the profits will draw new firms into the market. As these new firms enter the market, the market supply curve will shift to the right. As a result of a larger supply, price will fall. As price declines, profit will decline until firms in the market are earning (only) normal (or zero) profit. When there is zero economic profit, there is no longer an incentive for firms to enter the market.

2. No. The market is only in long-run competitive equilibrium when (1) there is no incentive for firms to enter or exit the industry, (2) there is no incentive for

firms to produce more or less output, and (3) there is no incentive for firms to change their plant size. If any of these conditions is not met, then the market is not in long-run equilibrium.

3. Initially, price will rise. Recall from Chapter 3 that when demand increases, *ceteris paribus,* price rises. In time, though, price will drop because new firms will enter the industry due to the positive economic profits generated by the higher price. How far the price drops depends on whether the firms are in a constant-cost, an increasing-cost, or a decreasing-cost industry. In a constant-cost industry, price will return to its original level; in an increasing-cost industry, price will return to a level above its original level; and in a decreasing-cost industry, price will return to a level below its original level.

4. Maybe initially, but probably not after certain adjustments are made. If firm *A* really has a genius on its payroll and, as a result, earns higher profits than firm *B,* the implicit costs of the genius will rise in time. For instance, firm *B* might try to hire the genius away from firm *A* by offering the genius a higher income. In order to keep the genius, firm *A* will have to match the offer. As a result, the costs of firm *A* will rise and, if nothing else changes, its profits will decline.

Chapter 9, page 253

1. It depends on how many firms in the market witness higher costs. If it is only one, then it is doubtful that the market supply curve will shift enough to bring about a higher price. If, however, many of the firms in the market witness higher costs, then the market supply curve will shift left, and price will rise.

2. No. Perfectly competitive firms that sell homogeneous products won't individually advertise, but this doesn't mean that the industry won't advertise in the hope of pushing the market (industry) demand curve (for their product) to the right.

CHAPTER 10

Chapter 10, page 262

1. Let's assume that John is right when he says that there are always some close substitutes for the product a firm sells. The question, however, is: How close does the substitute have to be before the theory of monopoly is not useful? For example, a "slightly close" substitute for a seller's product may not be close enough to matter. The theory of monopoly may still be useful in predicting a firm's behavior.

2. Economies of scale exist when a firm doubles inputs and its output more than doubles, lowering its unit costs (average total costs) in the process. If economies of scale exist only when a firm produces a large quantity of output and one firm is already producing

this output, then new firms (that start off producing less output) will have higher unit costs than those of the established firm. Some economists argue that this will make the new firms uncompetitive when compared to the established firm. In other words, economies of scale will act as a barrier to entry, effectively preventing firms from entering the industry and competing with the established firm.

3. In a monopoly, there is a single seller of a good for which there are no close substitutes and there are extremely high barriers to competing with the single seller. If a movie superstar has so much talent that the moviegoing public puts her in a class by herself, she might be considered a monopolist. Can anyone compete with her? They can try, but she may have such great talent (relative to everyone else) that no one will be able to effectively compete with her. In other words, her immense talent acts as a barrier to entry in the sense that even if someone does try to compete with her, they won't be a close substitute for her.

Chapter 10, page 267

1. The single-price monopolist has to lower price in order to sell an additional unit of its good (this is what a downward-sloping demand curve necessitates). As long as it has to lower price to sell an additional unit, its marginal revenue will be below its price. A demand curve plots price (P) and quantity (Q), and a marginal revenue curve plots marginal revenue (MR) and quantity (Q). Because $P > MR$ for a monopolist, its demand curve will lie above its marginal revenue curve.

2. No. Profit depends on whether or not price is greater than average total cost. It is possible for a monopolist to produce the quantity of output at which $MR = MC$, charge the highest price per unit possible for the output, and still have its unit costs (ATC) greater than price. If this is the case, the monopolist takes losses; it does not earn profits.

3. No. The last chapter explains that a firm is resource allocative efficient when it charges a price equal to its marginal cost ($P = MC$). The monopolist does not do this; it charges a price above marginal cost. Profit maximization ($MR = MC$) does not lead to resource allocative efficiency ($P = MC$) because for the monopolist $P > MR$. This is not the case for the perfectly competitive firm, where $P = MR$.

4. A monopolist is searching for the highest price at which it can sell its product. In contrast, the perfectly competitive firm doesn't have to search; it simply takes the equilibrium price established in the market. For example, suppose Nancy is a wheat farmer. She gets up one morning and wants to know at what price she should sell her wheat. She simply turns on the radio, listens to the farm report, and finds out that the equilibrium price per bushel of

wheat is, say, $5. Being a price taker, she knows she can't sell her wheat for a penny more than this ($5 is the highest price), and she won't want to sell her wheat for a penny less than this.

The monopolist firm doesn't know what the highest price is for the product it sells. It has to search for it; it has to experiment with different prices before it finds the "highest" price.

Chapter 10, page 273

1. There are three in particular:
   a. A monopoly firm produces too little output relative to a perfectly competitive firm; this causes the deadweight loss of monopoly.
   b. The profits of the monopoly are sometimes subject to rent-seeking behavior. Rent seeking, while rational for an individual firm, wastes society's resources. What good does society receive if one firm expends resources to take over the monopoly position of another firm? Answer: none. Resources that could have been used to produce goods (computers, software, shoes, houses, and so on) are instead used to transfer profits from one firm to another.
   c. A monopolist may not produce its products at the lowest possible cost. Again, this wastes society's resources.
2. An example helps to illustrate this concept. Suppose that a perfectly competitive firm would produce 100 units of good X, but that a monopoly firm would produce only 70 units of good X. This is a difference of 30 units. Buyers value these 30 units by more than it would cost the monopoly firm to produce them, yet the monopoly firm chooses not to produce the units. The net benefit (benefits to buyers minus costs to the monopolist) of producing these 30 units is said to be the deadweight loss of monopoly. It represents how much buyers lose because the monopolist chooses to produce less than the perfectly competitive firm.
3. If a seller is not a price searcher, then he is a price taker. A price taker can sell his product at only one price, the market equilibrium price.

CHAPTER 11

Chapter 11, page 283

1. It is like a monopolist in that it faces a downward-sloping demand curve, it is a price searcher, $P > MR$, and it is not resource allocative efficient. It is like a perfect competitor in that it sells to many buyers and competes with many sellers and there is easy entry into and exit from the market.
2. Essentially, because they face downward-sloping demand curves. Because the demand curve is downward-sloping, it cannot be tangent to the lowest point on a U-shaped ATC curve. See Exhibit 3.

Chapter 11, page 290

1. The incentive in both cases is the same: profit. Firms have an incentive to form a cartel in order to increase their profits. After the cartel is formed, however, each firm has an incentive to break the cartel to increase its profits even further. This is illustrated in Exhibit 5. If there is no cartel agreement, the firm is earning zero profits producing q_1. After the cartel is formed, it earns CP_CAB in profits by producing q_C. But it can earn even higher profits (FP_CDE) by cheating on the cartel and producing q_{CC}.
2. There is a kink because the demand curve for an oligopolist is more elastic above the kink than it is below the kink. The difference in elasticity is based on the assumption that rival (oligopoly) firms will not match a price hike but will match a price decline. Thus, if a given oligopolist raises product price, it is assumed that its quantity demanded will fall a lot; but if it lowers price, its quantity demanded will not rise much.
3. The dominant firm tries to figure out the price that would exist if it were not in the market. Suppose this price is $10. Then it figures out how much it would supply at this price (the answer is zero) and at all prices less than this. For example, suppose the firm supplies 0 units at $10, 20 units at $9, and 30 units at $8. These, then, are three points on the dominant firm's demand curve—sometimes called the residual demand curve. Next, the dominant firm produces the level of output at which $MR = MC$ and charges the highest price per unit consistent with this output.

CHAPTER 12

Chapter 12, page 318

1. The way a market is defined will help determine whether or not a particular firm is considered a monopoly. If a market is defined broadly, it will include more substitute goods and so the firm is less likely to be considered a monopolist. If a market is defined narrowly, it will include fewer substitute goods, and so the firm is more likely to be considered a monopolist.
2. The four-firm concentration ratio is 20 percent; the Herfindahl index is 500. The formulas in Exhibit 1 show how each is computed.
3. The Herfindahl index provides information about the dispersion of firm size in an industry. For example, suppose the top four firms in an industry have 15 percent, 10 percent, 9 percent, and 8 percent market shares. The four-firm concentration ratio will be the same for an industry with 15 firms as it is for an industry with 150 firms. The Herfindahl index will be different in the two situations.

Chapter 12, page 326

1. Average cost pricing is the same as profit regulation. The regulators state that the natural monopolist must charge a price equal to its average total costs ($P = ATC$). Under this pricing scheme, there is no incentive for the natural monopolist to keep costs down. In fact, there may be an incentive to deliberately push costs up. Higher costs—in the form of higher salaries or more luxurious offices—simply mean higher prices to cover the higher costs.

2. No matter what the motive for initially regulating an industry, eventually the regulating agency will be "captured" by the special interests (the firms) in the industry. In the end, the regulatory body will not so much regulate the industry as serve the interests of the firms in the industry.

3. According to the capture theory, the outcomes of the regulatory process will favor the regulated firms. According to the public choice theory, the outcomes of the regulatory process will favor the regulators.

4. Sometimes they favor regulation and at other times they do not. Economists make the point that regulation involves both costs and benefits and whether the particular regulation in question is worthwhile depends on whether the costs are greater than or less than the benefits.

CHAPTER 13

Chapter 13, page 339

1. $MRP = MR \times MPP$. For a perfectly competitive firm, $MR = P$, so MR is $10. MPP in the example is 19 units. It follows that $MRP = 190.

2. There is no difference between MRP and VMP if the firm is perfectly competitive. In this situation, $P = MR$, and because $MRP = MR \times MPP$ and $VMP = P \times MPP$, the two are the same. If the firm is a price searcher—monopolist, monopolistic competitor, or oligopolist—$P > MR$; therefore $VMP > MRP$.

3. It can buy all it wants of a factor at the equilibrium price and it will not cause factor price to rise. For example, if firm X is a factor price taker in the labor market, it can buy all the labor it wants at the equilibrium wage and it will not cause this wage to rise.

4. It should buy that quantity at which MRP of labor = MFC of labor.

Chapter 13, page 349

1. The MRP curve is the firm's factor demand curve. $MRP = P \times MPP$ for a perfectly competitive firm, so if either the price of the product that labor produces rises or the MPP of labor rises (reflected in a shift in the MPP curve), the factor demand curve shifts rightward.

2. It means that for every 1 percent change in the wage rate, the quantity demanded of labor changes by three times this percentage. For example, if wage

rates rise 10 percent, then the quantity demanded of labor falls 30 percent.

3. The short answer is because supply and demand conditions differ among markets. But this raises the question: Why do supply and demand conditions differ? This question is answered in Exhibit 11.

4. We can't answer this question specifically without more information. We know that under four conditions, wage rates would not differ. These conditions are: (1) the demand for every type of labor is the same; (2) there are no special nonpecuniary aspects to any job; (3) all labor is ultimately homogeneous and can costlessly be trained for different types of employment; and (4) all labor is mobile at zero cost. For wage rates to differ, one or more of these conditions is not being met. For example, perhaps labor is not mobile at zero cost.

CHAPTER 14

Chapter 14, page 364

1. The demand for union labor is lowered by (a) a decline in the demand for the product union labor produces, (b) a decline in the price of substitute factors, and (c) a decline in the marginal physical product of union labor.

2. A closed shop requires an employee to be a member of the union before he or she can be hired; a union shop does not. The union shop does require employees to join the union within a certain period of time after becoming employed.

3. To prove to management that union members will not work for a wage rate that is lower than the rate specified by the union. In terms of Exhibit 3, it is to prove that union members will not work for less than W_2.

Chapter 14, page 369

1. A monopsonist cannot buy additional units of a factor without increasing the price it pays for the factor. A factor price taker can.

2. Under the following conditions: (1) the firm hiring the labor is a monopsonist and (2) the minimum wage is above the wage it is already paying and below the wage that corresponds to the point where $MFC = MRP$. To understand this completely, look at Exhibit 4c. Suppose the firm is currently purchasing Q_1 labor and paying W_1. Then, W_3 becomes the minimum wage the monopsonist can pay to workers. Now it hires Q_3 workers. Notice however, that if the monopsonist had to pay a wage higher than the wage that equates MFC and MRP, it would employ fewer workers than Q_1.

3. If the higher wage rate reduces the number of people working in the unionized sector and the people who lose their jobs in the unionized sector move to

the nonunionized sector, then the supply of labor will increase in the nonunionized sector and wage rates will fall. This is illustrated in Exhibit 6.

CHAPTER 15

Chapter 15, page 380

1. It can change the distribution of income through transfer payments and taxes. Look at this equation: Individual income = Labor income + Asset income + Transfer payments − Taxes. By increasing one person's taxes and increasing another person's transfer payments, government can change peoples' incomes.

2. The statement is true. For example, two people can have unequal incomes at any one point in time and still earn the same incomes over time. For example, in year 1, John earns $40,000 and Francine earns $20,000. In year 2, Francine earns $40,000 and John earns $20,000. In each year, there is income inequality, but over the two years, John and Francine earn the same income ($60,000).

3. No. Individual income = Labor income + Asset income + Transfer payments − Taxes. It is possible for Smith's income to come entirely from labor income and Jones's income to come entirely from asset income. The same dollar income does not necessitate the same source of income.

Chapter 15, page 383

1. No, the income shares total 105 percent.

2. A Gini coefficient of 0 represents perfect income equality and a Gini coefficient of 1 represents complete income inequality, so we are sure that country *A* has neither perfect income equality nor complete income inequality. Beyond this, it is difficult to say anything. Usually, the Gini coefficient is used as a comparative measure. For example, if country *A*'s Gini coefficient is 0.45 and country *B*'s coefficient is 0.60, we could then conclude that country *A* has a more equal (less unequal) distribution of income than country *B* has.

Chapter 15, page 387

1. The simple fact that Jack earns more than Harry is not evidence of wage discrimination. We lack the information necessary to know whether wage discrimination exists. For example, we don't know if Jack and Harry work the same job, we don't know how productive each person is, and so on.

2. It could affect it negatively or positively. There is a higher probability of both higher and lower income if a person assumes a lot of risk than if a person simply plays it safe. To illustrate, Nancy has decided she wants to be an actor although her parents want her to be an accountant. The chances of her being successful in acting are small, but if she is successful, she will earn a much higher income than if she had been an accountant (a top actor earns more than a top accountant). Of course if she isn't successful, she will earn less income as an actor than she would have as an accountant (the "average" actor earns less than the "average" accountant).

Chapter 15, page 394

1. Whether poor people always exist or not depends on how we define poor. If we define poor in relative terms and we assume that there is not absolute income equality, then there must be some people who fall into, say, the lowest 10 percent of income earners. We could refer to these persons as poor. Remember, though, these persons are relatively poor—they earn less than a large percentage of the income earners in the country—but we do not know anything about their absolute incomes. In a world of multimillion-dollar income-earners, a person who earns $100,000 might be considered poor.

2. 11.3 percent

3. Under 18 years old

CHAPTER 16

Chapter 16, pages 405–406

1. Because there is a monetary incentive for them to be equal. To illustrate, suppose the return on capital is 12 percent and the price for loanable funds is 10 percent. In this case, a person could borrow loanable funds at 10 percent and invest in capital goods to earn the 12 percent return. As this happens, though, the amount of capital increases and its return falls. If the interest rates are reversed and the return on capital is lower than the price for a loanable fund, no one will borrow to invest in capital goods. Over time, then, the stock of capital will diminish and its return will rise.

2. Because the real interest rate is the rate paid by borrowers and received by lenders. For example, if a borrower borrows funds at a 12 percent interest rate and the inflation rate is 4 percent, he will be paying only an 8 percent (real) interest rate to the lender. Stated differently, the lender has 8 percent, not 12 percent, more buying power because he made the loan.

3. $907.03. The formula is $PV = \$1,000/(1 + 0.05)^2$.

4. No. The present value of $2,000 a year for four years at an 8 percent interest rate is $6,624.25. [$PV = \$2,000/(1 + 0.08)^1 + \$2,000/(1 + 0.08)^2 + \$2,000/(1 + 0.08)^3 + \$2,000/(1 + 0.08)^4$]. The present value is less than the cost of the machine, so it is not worth purchasing.

Chapter 16, page 411

1. A person has dinner at a restaurant in New York City (Manhattan). When she gets the bill, she exclaims about how expensive the meal was. The owner of

the restaurant explains that the rent for his restaurant is high and high rent leads to high dinner prices. But the owner's explanation is wrong. The high demand for meals in Manhattan is the reason meals are expensive and is the reason owners of restaurants are willing and able to pay high rents.

2. It is zero dollars.

3. When a firm competes for artificial rents, it expends resources to simply transfer economic rent from another firm to itself. In other words, resources are used to bring about a transfer only. There are no additional goods and services produced as a part of the process. But when a firm competes for real rents, resources are used to produce additional goods and services.

Chapter 16, page 414

1. A probability cannot be assigned to uncertainty; a probability can be assigned to risk.

2. There are many different theories that purport to explain profit. One theory states that profit exists because uncertainty exists. No uncertainty, no profit. Another theory states that profit exists because arbitrage opportunities exist (the opportunities to buy low and sell high) and some people are alert to these opportunities. Still another theory states that profit exists because some people (called entrepreneurs) are capable of creating profit opportunities by devising a new product, production process, or marketing strategy. Finally, monopoly profit exists because there is some high barrier to entering a market.

3. Profit can be a signal, especially if the profit is earned in a competitive market. Specifically, profit signals that buyers value a good (as evidenced by the price they are willing and able to pay for the good) by more than the factors that go to make the good.

CHAPTER 17

Chapter 17, page 424

1. The market output does not reflect or adjust for either external costs (in the case of a negative externality) or external benefits (in the case of a positive externality). The socially optimal output does.

2. Certainly, if there are no costs incurred by moving from the market output to the socially optimal output, the answer is yes. But this isn't likely to be the case. The economist considers whether the benefits of moving to the socially optimal output are greater than or less than the costs of moving to the socially optimal output. If the benefits are greater than the costs, then yes; if the benefits are less than the costs, then no.

Chapter 17, page 429

1. It means to adjust the private cost by the external cost. To illustrate, suppose someone's private cost is $10 and the external cost is $2. If the person internalizes the externality, the external cost becomes his cost. In other words, his cost is now $12.

2. Transaction costs are the costs associated with the time and effort needed to search out, negotiate, and consummate an exchange. These costs are higher for buying a house than they are for buying a hamburger. It takes more time and effort to search out a house to buy, negotiate a price, and consummate the deal than it takes to search out and buy a hamburger.

3. Under certain conditions, no. Specifically, if transaction costs are zero or trivial, the property rights assignment that a court makes is irrelevant to the resource allocative outcome. Of course, if transaction costs are not zero or trivial, then the property rights assignment a court makes does matter.

4. If there is a negative externality, there is a marginal external cost. The marginal external cost (MEC) plus the marginal private cost (MPC) equals the marginal social cost (MSC): $MSC = MPC + MEC$. If a corrective tax (t) is to correctly adjust for the marginal external cost associated with the negative externality, it must be equal to the marginal external cost—in other words, $t = MEC$. With this condition fulfilled, $MPC + \text{tax} = MSC = MPC + MEC$.

Chapter 17, page 432

1. All other things held constant, less pollution is preferable to more pollution. Zero pollution is the least amount of pollution possible; therefore, zero pollution is best. But, in reality, all other things are not held constant. Sometimes, when we reduce pollution, we also eliminate some of the things we want. Remember the car example? We can eliminate all the pollution from cars tomorrow, but we'd have to give up driving cars. Is it worth it?

The economist wants to eliminate pollution as long as the benefits of eliminating pollution are greater than the costs. When the benefits equal the costs, the economist would stop eliminating pollution. If society has eliminated so much pollution that the costs of eliminating it are greater than the benefits, then society has gone too far. It has eliminated too much pollution. Some units of pollution were simply not worth eliminating.

2. Under market environmentalism, the entities that can eliminate pollution at least cost are the ones that eliminate the pollution. This is not the case under standards, where both the low-cost and high-cost eliminators of pollution must reduce pollution.

3. The dollar price of the pollution permits is a cost for firm Z, but it is not a cost to society. As far as society is concerned, firm Z simply paid $660 to firms X and Y. Firm Z ended up with $660 less and firms X and

Y ended up with $660 more; the amounts offset. Only when resources are used in eliminating pollution is the dollar cost of those resources counted as a cost to society of eliminating pollution.

Chapter 17, page 435

1. Because after a nonexcludable public good is produced, the individual or firm that produced it wouldn't be able to collect payment for it. When a nonexcludable public good is provided to one person, it is provided to everyone. Because an individual can consume the good without paying for it, he is likely to take a free ride. Another way of answering this question is to simply say, "The market fails to produce nonexcludable public goods because of the free rider problem."

2. (a) A composition notebook is a private good. It is rivalrous in consumption; if one person is using it, someone else cannot. (b) A Shakespearean play performed in a summer theater is an excludable public good. It is nonrivalrous in consumption (everyone in the theater can see the play), but excludable (a person must pay to get into the theater). (c) An apple is a private good. It is rivalrous in consumption; if one person eats it, someone else cannot. (d) A telephone is a private good. One person using the phone (in, say, your house) prevents someone else from using it. (e) Sunshine is a nonexcludable public good. It is nonrivalrous in consumption (one person's consumption of it doesn't reduce its consumption by others) and nonexcludable (it is impossible to exclude free people from consuming the sunshine).

3. A concert is an example. If one person consumes the concert, this does not take away from others consuming it to the same degree. However, people can be excluded from consuming it.

Chapter 17, page 440

1. Consider a fictional product, X. The sellers of X know that the good could, under certain conditions, cause health problems, but they do not release this information to the buyers. Consequently, the demand for good X is likely to be greater than it would be if there were symmetric information. The quantity consumed of good X is likely to be higher when there is asymmetric information than when there is symmetric information.

2. To illustrate, consider again the used car market discussed in the text. If there are two types of used cars—good used cars and "lemons"—and asymmetric information, the market price for a used car may understate the value of a good used car and overstate the value of a lemon. This will induce sellers of lemons to enter the market and sellers of good cars to leave it. (The owners of good used cars will not want to sell their cars for less than their cars are worth.) In theory, the used car market may consist of nothing but lemons. In other words, a used car market for good cars does not exist.

3. A college professor tells her students that she does not believe in giving grades of "D" or "F." As a result, her students do not take as many "precautionary" measures to guard against receiving low grades. Does your example have the characteristic of this example—namely, one person's assurance affects another person's incentive?

CHAPTER 18

Chapter 18, page 451

1. No. The model doesn't say every politician has to do these things; it simply predicts that politicians who do these things have an increased chance of winning the election in a two-person race.

2. Voters may want more information from politicians, but supplying that information is not always in the best interests of politicians. When they speak in specific terms, politicians are often labeled as being at one end or the other of the political spectrum. But politicians don't win elections by being in the right wing or left wing; they win elections by being in the middle.

3. The students might not be apathetic at all; they may simply be rationally ignorant. In other words, they may have concluded that the benefits of becoming informed about politics are less than the costs, and so they choose to be uninformed. By the way, while the professor may be informed about politics, it is doubtful that he is informed about everything in life. If he is not informed about biochemistry, then why isn't he? The answer may be that he is rationally ignorant of biochemistry just as his students are rationally ignorant of politics. Everyone is rationally ignorant of something.

Chapter 18, page 454

1. 2 units

2. In example 2 with equal taxes, 1 unit received a simple majority of the votes. Person C was made worse off because his MPB for the first unit of good Y was $100 but he ended up paying a tax of $120. In other words, he was worse off by $20.

Chapter 18, page 459

1. Both farmers and consumers are affected by federal agricultural policy—but not in the same way and not to the same degree. Federal agricultural policy directly affects farmers' incomes, usually by a large amount. It indirectly affects consumers' costs, but not so much as it affects farmers' incomes. Simply put, farmers have more at stake than consumers when it comes to federal agricultural policy. People tend to be better informed about matters that mean more to them.

2. The legislation is more likely to pass when group A includes 10 million persons because the wider the dispersal of the costs of the legislation, the greater the likelihood of passage. When costs are widely dispersed, the cost to any one individual is so small that she or he is unlikely to lobby against the legislation.

3. Examples include teachers saying that more money for education will help the country compete in the global marketplace; domestic car manufacturers saying that tariffs on foreign imports will save American jobs and U.S. manufacturing; farmers saying that subsidies to farmers will preserve the "American" farm and a way of life that Americans cherish. Whether any of these groups is right or wrong is not the point. The point is that special interest groups are likely to advance their arguments (good or bad) with public interest talk.

4. Rent seeking is socially wasteful because the resources that are used to seek rent could instead be used to produce goods and services.

CHAPTER 19

Chapter 19, page 471

1. For the United States, $1X = 1/6Y$ or $1Y = 6X$. For England, $1X = 2Y$ or $1Y = 1/2X$. Let's focus on the opportunity cost of $1X$ in each country. In the United States $1X = 1/6Y$ and in Great Britain $1X = 2Y$. Terms of trade that are between these two endpoints would be favorable for the two countries. For example, suppose we choose $1X=1Y$. This is good for the United States because it would prefer to give up $1X$ and get $1Y$ in trade than to give up $1X$ and only get $1/6Y$ (without trade). Similarly, Great Britain would prefer to give up $1Y$ and get $1X$ in trade than to give up $1Y$ and get only $1/2X$ (without trade). Any terms of trade between $1X = 1/6Y$ and $1X = 2Y$ will be favorable to the two countries.

2. Yes; this is what the theory of comparative advantage shows. Exhibit 1 shows that the United States could produce more of both food and clothing than Japan. Still, the United States benefits from specialization and trade, as shown in Exhibit 2. In column 5 of this exhibit, the United States can consume 10 more units of food by specializing and trading.

3. No. It is the desire to buy low and sell high (earn a profit) that pushes countries into producing and trading at a comparative advantage. Government officials do not collect cost data and then issue orders to firms in the country to produce X, Y, or Z. We have not drawn the PPFs in this chapter and identified the cost differences between countries to show what countries actually do in the real world. We described things technically to simply show how countries benefit from specialization and trade.

1. Domestic producers benefit because producers' surplus rises; domestic consumers lose because consumers' surplus falls. Also, government benefits in that it receives the tariff revenue. Moreover, consumers lose more than producers and government gain, so that there is a net loss resulting from tariffs.

2. Consumers' surplus falls by more than producers' surplus rises.

3. With a tariff, the government receives tariff revenue. With a quota, it does not. In the latter case, the revenue that would have gone to government goes, instead, to the importers who get to satisfy the quota.

4. Infant or new domestic industries need to be protected from older, more established competitors until they are mature enough to compete on an equal basis. Tariffs and quotas provide these infant industries the time they need.

CHAPTER 20

Chapter 20, page 491

1. A debit. When an American enters into a transaction in which he has to supply U.S. dollars in the foreign exchange market (in order to demand a foreign currency), the transaction is recorded as a debit.

2. We do not have enough information to answer this question. The merchandise trade balance is the difference between the value of merchandise exports and merchandise imports. The question gives only the value of exports and imports. Exports is a more inclusive term than merchandise exports. Exports include (a) merchandise exports, (b) services, and (c) income from U.S. assets abroad. See Exhibit 2. Similarly, imports is a more inclusive term than merchandise imports. It includes (a) merchandise imports, (b) services, and (c) income from foreign assets in the United States.

3. The merchandise trade balance includes fewer transactions than are included in the current account balance. The merchandise trade balance is the summary statistic for merchandise exports and merchandise imports. The current account balance is the summary statistic for exports of goods and services (which includes merchandise exports), imports of goods and services (which includes merchandise imports), and net unilateral transfers abroad. See Exhibit 2.

4. No. The balance of payments always equals zero. It is possible that the journalist who wrote the story is reporting something other than the balance of payments (although he or she uses this term). Often, the news media use the term *balance of payments* when they are actually referring to the current account balance.

Chapter 20, page 497

1. As the demand for dollars increases, the supply of pesos increases. For example, suppose someone in Mexico wants to buy something produced in the United States. The American wants to be paid in dollars, but the Mexican doesn't have any dollars—she has pesos. So, she has to buy dollars with pesos; in other words, she has to supply pesos to buy dollars. Thus, as she demands more dollars, she will necessarily have to supply more pesos.

2. The dollar is said to have appreciated (against the peso) when it takes more pesos to buy a dollar and fewer dollars to buy a peso. For this to occur, either the demand for dollars must increase (which means the supply of pesos increases) or the supply of dollars must decrease (which means the demand for pesos decreases). To see this graphically, look at Exhibit 5b. The only way for the peso price per dollar to rise (on the vertical axis) is for either the demand curve for dollars to shift to the right or the supply curve of dollars to shift to the left. Each of these occurrences is mirrored in the market for pesos in part (a) of the exhibit.

3. *Ceteris paribus,* the dollar will depreciate relative to the franc. As incomes for Americans rise, the demand for Swiss goods rises. This increases the demand for francs and the supply of dollars on the foreign exchange market. In turn, this leads to a depreciated dollar and an appreciated franc.

4. The theory states that the exchange rate between any two currencies will adjust to reflect changes in the relative price levels of the two countries. For example, suppose the U.S. price level rises 5 percent and Mexico's price level remains constant. According to the PPP theory, the U.S. dollar will depreciate 5 percent relative to the Mexican peso.

Chapter 20, page 503

1. The terms *overvalued* and *undervalued* refer to the equilibrium exchange rate: the exchange rate at which the quantity demanded and quantity supplied of a currency are the same in the foreign exchange market. Let's suppose the equilibrium exchange rate is 0.10 USD = 1 MXP. This is the same as saying that 10 pesos = 1 dollar. If the exchange rate is fixed at 0.12 USD = 1 MXP (which is the same as 8.33 pesos = 1 dollar), the peso is overvalued and the dollar is undervalued. Specifically, a currency is overvalued if 1 unit of it fetches more of another currency than it

would in equilibrium; a currency is undervalued if 1 unit of it fetches less of another currency than it would in equilibrium. In equilibrium, 1 peso would fetch 0.10 dollars and at the current exchange rate it fetches 0.12 dollars—so the peso is overvalued. In equilibrium, 1 dollar would fetch 10 pesos and at the current exchange rate it fetches only 8.33 pesos—so the dollar is undervalued.

2. An overvalued dollar means some other currency is undervalued—let's say it is the Japanese yen. An overvalued dollar makes U.S. goods more expensive for the Japanese, so they buy fewer U.S. goods. This reduces U.S. exports. On the other hand, an undervalued yen makes Japanese goods cheaper for Americans, so they buy more Japanese goods; the U.S. imports more. Thus, an overvalued dollar reduces U.S. exports and raises U.S. imports.

3. **a.** Dollar is overvalued.
   b. Dollar is undervalued
   c. Dollar is undervalued.

4. When a country devalues its currency, it makes it cheaper for foreigners to buy its products.

Chapter 20, page 508

1. An optimal currency area is a geographic area in which exchange rates can be fixed or a common currency used without sacrificing any domestic economic goals.

2. As the demand for good Y falls, the unemployment rate in country 2 will rise. This increase in the unemployment rate is likely to be temporary, though. The increased demand for good X (produced by country 1) will increase the demand for country 1's currency, leading to an appreciation in country 1's currency and a depreciation in country 2's currency. Country 1's good (good X) will become more expensive for the residents of country 2, and they will buy less. Country 2's good (good Y) will become less expensive for the residents of country 1, and they will buy more. As a result of the additional purchases of good Y, country 2's unemployment rate will begin to decline.

3. Labor mobility is very important to determining whether or not an area is an optimal currency area. If there is little or no labor mobility, an area is not likely to be an optimal currency area. If there is labor mobility, an area is likely to be an optimal currency area.

Glossary

Absolute (Money) Price The price of a good in money terms. (Chapter 3)

Abstract The process (used in building a theory) of focusing on a limited number of variables to explain or predict an event. (Chapter 1)

Accounting Profit The difference between total revenue and explicit costs. (Chapter 8)

Adverse Selection Exists when the parties on one side of the market, who have information not known to others, self select in a way that adversely affects the parties on the other side of the market. (Chapter 17)

Antitrust Law Legislation passed for the stated purpose of controlling monopoly power and preserving and promoting competition. (Chapter 12)

Appreciation An increase in the value of one currency relative to other currencies. (Chapter 20)

Arbitrage Buying a good in a market where its price is low and selling the good in another market where its price is higher. (Chapter 10)

Assets Anything of value to which the firm has a legal claim. (Chapter 7)

Asymmetric Information Exists when either the buyer or the seller in a market exchange has some information that the other does not have. (Chapter 17)

Average Fixed Cost (*AFC*) Total fixed cost divided by quantity of output: $AFC = TFC/Q$. (Chapter 8)

Average Total Cost (*ATC*), or Unit Cost Total cost divided by quantity of output: $ATC = TC/Q$. (Chapter 8)

Average Variable Cost (*AVC*) Total variable cost divided by quantity of output: $ATC = TVC/Q$. (Chapter 8)

Average-Marginal Rule When the marginal magnitude is above the average magnitude, the average magnitude rises; when the marginal magnitude is below the average magnitude, the average magnitude falls. (Chapter 8)

Bad Anything from which individuals receive disutility or dissatisfaction. (Chapter 1)

Balance of Payments A periodic statement (usually annual) of the money value of all transactions between residents of one country and residents of all other countries. (Chapter 20)

Balance Sheet An accounting of the assets, liabilities, and net worth of a business firm. (Chapter 7)

Bond A debt obligation to repay a certain sum of money (the principal) at maturity and also to pay periodic fixed sums until that date. (Chapter 7)

Budget Constraint All the combinations or bundles of two goods a person can purchase given a certain money income and prices for the two goods. (Chapter 6 Appendix)

Business Firm An entity that employs factors of production (resources) to produce goods and services to be sold to consumers, other firms, or the government. (Chapter 7)

Capital Produced goods that can be used as inputs for further production, such as factories, machinery, tools, computers, and buildings. (Chapter 1)

Capital Account Includes all payments related to the purchase and sale of assets and to borrowing and lending activities. Components include outflow of U.S. capital and inflow of foreign capital. (Chapter 20)

Capital Account Balance The summary statistic for the outflow of U.S. capital and the inflow of foreign capital. It is equal to the difference between the outflow of U.S. capital and the inflow of foreign capital. (Chapter 20)

Capture Theory of Regulation Holds that no matter what the motive is for the initial regulation and the establishment of the regulatory agency, eventually the agency will be "captured" (controlled) by the special interests of the industry that is being regulated. (Chapter 12)

Cartel An organization of firms that reduces output and increases price in an effort to increase joint profits. (Chapter 11)

Cartel Theory In this theory of oligopoly, oligopolistic firms act as if there were only one firm in the industry. (Chapter 11)

Ceteris Paribus A Latin term meaning "all other things held constant." (Chapter 1)

Closed Shop An organization in which an employee must belong to the union before he or she can be hired. (Chapter 14)

Coase Theorem In the case of trivial or zero transaction costs, the property rights assignment does not matter to the resource allocative outcome. (Chapter 17)

Collective Bargaining The process whereby wage rates and other issues are determined by a union bargaining with management on behalf of all union members. (Chapter 14)

Comparative Advantage The situation where an individual or country can produce a good at lower opportunity cost than another individual or country can. (Chapters 2, 19)

Complements Two goods that are used jointly in consumption. If two goods are complements, the demand for one rises as the price of the other falls (or the demand for one falls as the price of the other rises). (Chapter 3)

Concentration Ratio The percentage of industry sales (or assets, output, labor force, or some other factor) accounted for by x number of firms in the industry. (Chapter 11)

Conglomerate Merger A merger between companies in different industries. (Chapter 12)

Constant Returns to Scale Exist when inputs are increased by some percentage and output increases by an equal percentage, causing unit costs to remain constant. (Chapter 8)

Constant-Cost Industry An industry in which average total costs do not change as (industry) output increases or decreases when firms enter or exit the industry, respectively. (Chapter 9)

Consumer Equilibrium Occurs when the consumer has spent all income and the marginal utilities per dollar spent on each good purchased are equal: $MUA/PA = MUB/PB = MUC/PC = \ldots = MUZ/PZ$, where the letters A-Z represent all the goods a person buys. (Chapter 6)

Consumers' Surplus (CS) The difference between the maximum price a buyer is willing and able to pay for a good or service and the price actually paid. $CS =$ Maximum buying price $-$ Price paid. (Chapter 2)

Contestable Market A market in which entry is easy and exit is costless, new firms can produce the product at the same cost as current firms, and exiting firms can easily dispose of their fixed assets by selling them. (Chapter 11)

Corporation A legal entity that can conduct business in its own name the way an individual does; ownership of the corporation resides with stockholders who have limited liability in the debts of the corporation. (Chapter 7)

Coupon Rate The percentage of the face value of a bond that is paid out regularly (usually quarterly or annually) to the holder of the bond. (Chapter 7)

Craft (Trade) Union A union whose membership is made up of individuals who practice the same craft or trade. (Chapter 14)

Credit In the balance of payments, any transaction that creates a demand for the country's currency in the foreign exchange market. (Chapter 20)

Cross Elasticity of Demand Measures the responsiveness in quantity demanded of one good to changes in the price of another good. (Chapter 5)

Current Account Includes all payments related to the purchase and sale of goods and services. Components of the account include exports, imports, and net unilateral transfers abroad. (Chapter 20)

Current Account Balance The summary statistic for exports of goods and services, imports of goods and services, and net unilateral transfers abroad. (Chapter 20)

Deadweight Loss of Monopoly The net value (value to buyers over and above costs to suppliers) of the difference between the monopoly quantity of output (where $P > MC$) and the competitive quantity of output (where $P = MC$). The loss of not producing the competitive quantity of output. (Chapter 10)

Debit In the balance of payments, any transaction that supplies the country's currency in the foreign exchange market. (Chapter 20)

Decisions at the Margin Decision making characterized by weighing additional (marginal) benefits of a change against the additional (marginal) costs of a change with respect to current conditions. (Chapter 1)

Decreasing-Cost Industry An industry in which average total costs decrease as output increases and increase as output decreases when firms enter and exit the industry, respectively. (Chapter 9)

Demand The willingness and ability of buyers to purchase different quantities of a good at different prices during a specific time period. (Chapter 3)

Demand Schedule The numerical tabulation of the quantity demanded of a good at different prices. (Chapter 3)

Depreciation A decrease in the value of one currency relative to other currencies. (Chapter 20)

Derived Demand Demand that is the result of some other demand. For example, factor demand is the result of the demand for the products that the factors go to produce. (Chapter 13)

Devaluation A government act that changes the exchange rate by lowering the official price of a currency. (Chapter 20)

Diamond-Water Paradox The observation that those things that have the greatest value in use sometimes have little value in exchange and those things that have little value in use sometimes have the greatest value in exchange. (Chapter 6)

Diseconomies of Scale Exist when inputs are increased by some percentage and output increases by a smaller percentage, causing unit costs to rise. (Chapter 8)

Disequilibrium A state of either surplus or shortage in a market. (Chapter 3)

Disequilibrium Price A price other than equilibrium price. A price at which quantity demanded does not equal quantity supplied. (Chapter 3)

Disutility The dissatisfaction one receives from a bad. (Chapter 1)

Dividends A share of profits distributed to stockholders. (Chapter 7)

(Downward-sloping) Demand Curve The graphical representation of the law of demand. (Chapter 3)

Dumping The sale of goods abroad at a price below their cost and below the price charged in the domestic market. (Chapter 19)

Economic Profit The difference between total revenue and total cost, including both explicit and implicit costs. (Chapter 8)

Economic Rent Payment in excess of opportunity costs. (Chapter 16)

Economic System The way in which society decides to answer key economic questions—in particular those questions that relate to production and trade. (Chapter 2)

Economics The science of scarcity: the science of how individuals and societies deal with the fact that wants are greater than the limited resources available to satisfy those wants. (Chapter 1)

Economies of Scale Exist when inputs are increased by some percentage and output increases by a greater percentage, causing unit costs to fall. (Chapter 8)

Efficiency Exists when marginal benefits equal marginal costs. In terms of production, the condition where the maximum output is produced with given resources and technology. Efficiency implies the impossibility of gains in one area without losses in another. (Chapters 1, 2)

Elastic Demand The percentage change in quantity demanded is greater than the percentage change in price. Quantity demanded changes proportionately more than price changes. (Chapter 5)

Elasticity of Demand for Labor The percentage change in the quantity demanded of labor divided by the percentage change in the wage rate. (Chapter 13)

Employee Association An organization whose members belong to a particular profession. (Chapter 14)

Entrepreneurship The particular talent that some people have for organizing the resources of land, labor, and capital to produce goods, seek new business opportunities, and develop new ways of doing things. (Chapter 1)

Equilibrium Equilibrium means "at rest"; it is descriptive of a natural resting place. Equilibrium in a market is the price-quantity combination from which there is no tendency for buyers or sellers to move away. Graphically, equilibrium is the intersection point of the supply and demand curves. (Chapters 1, 3)

Equilibrium Price (Market-Clearing Price) The price at which quantity demanded of the good equals quantity supplied. (Chapter 3)

Equilibrium Quantity The quantity that corresponds to equilibrium price. The quantity at which the amount of the good that buyers are willing and able to buy equals the amount that sellers are willing and able to sell, and both equal the amount actually bought and sold. (Chapter 3)

Ex Ante Phrase that means "before," as in before a trade. (Chapter 2)

Ex Ante Distribution (of Income) The before-tax-and-transfer-payment distribution of income. (Chapter 15)

Ex Post Phrase that means "after," as in after a trade. (Chapter 2)

Ex Post Distribution (of Income) The after-tax-and-transfer-payment distribution of income. (Chapter 15)

Excess Capacity Theorem States that a monopolistic competitor in equilibrium produces an output smaller than the one that would minimize its costs of production. (Chapter 11)

Exchange Rate The price of one currency in terms of another currency. (Chapter 20)

Excludability A good is excludable if it is possible, or not prohibitively costly, to exclude someone from receiving the benefits of the good after it has been produced. (Chapter 17)

Explicit Cost A cost that is incurred when an actual (monetary) payment is made. (Chapter 8)

Externality A side effect of an action that affects the well-being of third parties. (Chapter 17)

Face Value (Par Value) Dollar amount specified on a bond. (Chapter 7)

Factor Price Taker A firm that can buy all of a factor it wants at the equilibrium price. It faces a horizontal (flat, perfectly elastic) supply curve of factors. (Chapter 13)

Fallacy of Composition The erroneous view that what is good or true for the individual is necessarily good or true for the group. (Chapter 1)

Fixed Costs Costs that do not vary with output; the costs associated with fixed inputs. (Chapter 8)

Fixed Exchange Rate System The system where a nation's currency is set at a fixed rate relative to all other currencies, and central banks intervene in the foreign exchange market to maintain the fixed rate. (Chapter 20)

Fixed Input An input whose quantity cannot be changed as output changes. (Chapter 8)

Flexible Exchange Rate System The system whereby exchange rates are determined by the forces of supply and demand for a currency. (Chapter 20)

Foreign Exchange Market The market in which currencies of different countries are exchanged. (Chapter 20)

Free Rider Anyone who receives the benefits of a good without paying for it. (Chapter 17)

Game Theory A mathematical technique used to analyze the behavior of decision makers who try to reach an optimal position for themselves through game playing or the use of strategic behavior, are fully aware of the interactive nature of the process at hand, and anticipate the moves of other decision makers. (Chapter 11)

Gini Coefficient A measure of the degree of inequality in the income distribution. (Chapter 15)

Good Anything from which individuals receive utility or satisfaction. (Chapter 1)

Government Bureaucrat An unelected person who works in a government bureau and is assigned a special task that relates to a law or program passed by the legislature. (Chapter 18)

Herfindahl Index Measures the degree of concentration in an industry. It is equal to the sum of the squares of the market shares of each firm in the industry. (Chapter 12)

Horizontal Merger A merger between firms that are selling similar products in the same market. (Chapter 12)

Human Capital Education, development of skills, and anything else that is particular to the individual and increases his or her productivity. (Chapter 15)

Implicit Cost A cost that represents the value of resources used in production for which no actual (monetary) payment is made. (Chapter 8)

Income Effect In microeconomics, the portion of the change in the quantity demanded of a good that is attributable to a change in real income (brought about by a change in absolute price). (Chapter 6)

Income Elastic The percentage change in quantity demanded of a good is greater than the percentage change in income. (Chapter 5)

Income Elasticity of Demand Measures the responsiveness of quantity demanded to changes in income. (Chapter 5)

Income Inelastic The percentage change in quantity demanded of a good is less than the percentage change in income. (Chapter 5)

Income Unit Elastic The percentage change in quantity demanded of a good is equal to the percentage change in income. (Chapter 5)

Increasing-Cost Industry An industry in which average total costs increase as output increases and decrease as output decreases when firms enter and exit the industry, respectively. (Chapter 9)

Indifference Curve Represents an indifference set. A curve that shows all the bundles of two goods that give an individual equal total utility. (Chapter 6 Appendix)

Indifference Curve Map Represents a number of indifference curves for a given individual with reference to two goods. (Chapter 6 Appendix)

Indifference Set Group of bundles of two goods that give an individual equal total utility. (Chapter 6 Appendix)

Industrial Union A union whose membership is made up of individuals who work in the same firm or industry but do not all practice the same craft or trade. (Chapter 14)

Inefficiency In terms of production, the condition where less than the maximum output is produced with given resources and technology. Inefficiency implies the possibility of gains in one area without losses in another. (Chapter 2)

Inelastic Demand The percentage change in quantity demanded is less than the percentage change in price. Quantity demanded changes proportionately less than price changes. (Chapter 5)

Inferior Good A good the demand for which falls (rises) as income rises (falls). (Chapter 3)

In-Kind Transfer Payments Transfer payments, such as food stamps, medical assistance, and subsidized housing, that are made in a specific good or service rather than in cash. (Chapter 15)

Internalizing Externalities An externality is internalized if the persons or group that generated the externality incorporate into their own private or internal cost-benefit calculations the external benefits (in the case of a positive externality) or the external costs (in the case of a negative externality) that third parties bear. (Chapter 17)

International Monetary Fund (IMF) An international organization created to oversee the international monetary system. The IMF does not control the world's money supply, but it does hold currency reserves for member nations and make loans to central banks. (Chapter 20)

Interpersonal Utility Comparison Comparing the utility one person receives from a good, service, or activity with the utility another person receives from the same good, service, or activity. (Chapter 6)

Kinked Demand Curve Theory A theory of oligopoly that assumes that if a single firm in the industry cuts price, other firms will do likewise, but if it raises price, other firms will not follow suit. The theory predicts price stickiness or rigidity. (Chapter 11)

Labor The physical and mental talents people contribute to the production process. (Chapter 1)

Land All natural resources, such as minerals, forests, water, and unimproved land. (Chapter 1)

Law of Demand As the price of a good rises, the quantity demanded of the good falls, and as the price of a good falls, the quantity demanded of the good rises, ceteris paribus. (Chapter 3)

Law of Diminishing Marginal Returns As ever-larger amounts of a variable input are combined with fixed inputs, eventually the marginal physical product of the variable input will decline. (Chapter 8)

Law of Diminishing Marginal Utility For a given time period, the marginal (additional) utility or satisfaction gained by consuming equal successive units of a good will decline as the amount consumed increases. (Chapters 3, 6)

Law of Increasing Opportunity Costs As more of a good is produced, the opportunity costs of producing that good increase. (Chapter 2)

Law of Supply As the price of a good rises, the quantity supplied of the good rises, and as the price of a good falls, the quantity supplied of the good falls, ceteris paribus. (Chapter 3)

Least-Cost Rule Specifies the combination of factors that minimizes costs. This requires that the following condition be met: $MPP_1/P_1 = MPP_2/P_2 = \ldots = MPP_n/P_n$, where the numbers stand for the different factors. (Chapter 13)

Liabilities Debts of the business firm. (Chapter 7)

Limited Liability A legal term that signifies that the owners (stockholders) of a corporation cannot be sued for the corporation's failure to pay its debts. (Chapter 7)

Limited Partnership A form of business that is organized as a partnership but that gives some of the partners the legal protection of limited liability. (Chapter 7)

Loanable Funds Funds that someone borrows and another person lends, for which the borrower pays an interest rate to the lender. (Chapter 16)

Lock-In Effect Descriptive of the situation where a particular product or technology becomes settled upon as the standard and is difficult or impossible to dislodge as the standard. (Chapter 12)

Logrolling The exchange of votes to gain support for legislation. (Chapter 18)

Long Run A period of time in which all inputs in the production process can be varied (no inputs are fixed). (Chapter 8)

Long-Run Average Total Cost (LRATC) Curve A curve that shows the lowest (unit) cost at which the firm can produce any given level of output. (Chapter 8)

Long-Run Competitive Equilibrium The condition where $P = MC = SRATC = LRATC$. There are zero economic profits, firms are producing the quantity of output at which price is equal to marginal cost, and no firm has an incentive to change its plant size. (Chapter 9)

Long-Run (Industry) Supply (LRS) Curve Graphic representation of the quantities of output that the industry is prepared to supply at different prices after the entry and exit of firms is completed. (Chapter 9)

Lorenz Curve A graph of the income distribution. It expresses the relationship between cumulative percentage of households and cumulative percentage of income. (Chapter 15)

Macroeconomics The branch of economics that deals with human behavior and choices as they relate to highly aggregate markets (such as the goods and services market) or to the entire economy. (Chapter 1)

Managed Float A managed flexible exchange rate system, under which nations now and then intervene to adjust

their official reserve holdings to moderate major swings in exchange rates. (Chapter 20)

Managerial Coordination The process in which managers direct employees to perform certain tasks. (Chapter 7)

Marginal Cost (MC) The change in total cost that results from a change in output: $MC = \Delta TC/\Delta Q$. (Chapter 8)

Marginal Factor Cost (MFC) The additional cost incurred by employing an additional factor unit. (Chapter 13)

Marginal Physical Product (MPP) The change in output that results from changing the variable input by one unit, holding all other inputs fixed. (Chapter 8)

Marginal Productivity Theory States that firms in competitive or perfect product and factor markets pay factors their marginal revenue products. (Chapter 13)

Marginal Rate of Substitution The amount of one good an individual is willing to give up to obtain an additional unit of another good and maintain equal total utility. (Chapter 6 Appendix)

Marginal Revenue (MR) The change in total revenue that results from selling one additional unit of output. (Chapter 9)

Marginal Revenue Product (MRP) The additional revenue generated by employing an additional factor unit. (Chapter 13)

Marginal Social Benefits (MSB) The sum of marginal private benefits (MPB) and marginal external benefits (MEB). $MSB = MPB + MEB$. (Chapter 17)

Marginal Social Costs (MSC) The sum of marginal private costs (MPC) and marginal external costs (MEC). $MSC = MPC + MEC$. (Chapter 17)

Marginal Utility The additional utility a person receives from consuming an additional unit of a particular good. (Chapter 6)

Market Coordination The process in which individuals perform tasks, such as producing certain quantities of goods, based on changes in market forces, such as supply, demand, and price. (Chapter 7)

Market Failure A situation in which the market does not provide the ideal or

optimal amount of a particular good. (Chapter 17)

Market Structure The particular environment of a firm, the characteristics of which influence the firm's pricing and output decisions. (Chapter 9)

Median Voter Model Suggests that candidates in a two-person political race will move toward matching the preferences of the median voter (that is, the person whose preferences are at the center, or in the middle, of the political spectrum). (Chapter 18)

Merchandise Trade Balance The difference between the value of merchandise exports and the value of merchandise imports. (Chapter 20)

Merchandise Trade Deficit The situation where the value of merchandise exports is less than the value of merchandise imports. (Chapter 20)

Merchandise Trade Surplus The situation where the value of merchandise exports is greater than the value of merchandise imports. (Chapter 20)

Microeconomics The branch of economics that deals with human behavior and choices as they relate to relatively small units—an individual, a firm, an industry, a single market. (Chapter 1)

Minimum Efficient Scale The lowest output level at which average total costs are minimized. (Chapter 8)

Mixed Capitalism An economic system characterized by largely private ownership of the factors of production, market allocation of resources, and decentralized decision making. Most economic activities take place in the private sector in this system, but government plays a substantial economic and regulatory role. (Chapter 2)

Monitor Person in a business firm who coordinates team production and reduces shirking. (Chapter 7)

Monopolistic Competition A theory of market structure based on three assumptions: many sellers and buyers, firms producing and selling slightly differentiated products, and easy entry and exit. (Chapter 11)

Monopoly A theory of market structure based on three assumptions: There is one seller, it sells a product for which no close substitutes exist, and there are extremely high barriers to entry. (Chapter 10)

Monopsony A single buyer in a factor market. (Chapter 14)

Moral Hazard Exists when one party to a transaction changes his behavior in a way that is hidden from and costly to the other party. (Chapter 17)

Natural Monopoly The condition where economies of scale are so pronounced in an industry that only one firm can survive. (Chapter 10)

Negative Externality Exists when a person's or group's actions cause a cost (adverse side effect) to be felt by others. (Chapter 17)

Net Worth (Equity or Capital Stock) Value of the business firm to its owners; it is determined by subtracting liabilities from assets. (Chapter 7)

Network Good A good whose value increases as the expected number of units sold increases. (Chapter 12)

Neutral Good A good the demand for which does not change as income rises or falls. (Chapter 3)

Nominal Interest Rate The interest rate determined by the forces of supply and demand in the loanable funds market. (Chapter 16)

Nonexcludability A good is nonexcludable if it is impossible, or prohibitively costly, to exclude someone from receiving the benefits of the good after it has been produced. (Chapter 17)

Nonprofit Firm A firm in which there are no residual claimants; any revenues over costs must be reinvested in the firm so that "what comes in" equals "what goes out." (Chapter 7)

Nonrivalrous in Consumption A good is nonrivalrous in consumption if its consumption by one person does not reduce its consumption by others. (Chapter 17)

Normal Good A good the demand for which rises (falls) as income rises (falls). (Chapter 3)

Normal Profit Zero economic profit. A firm that earns normal profit is earning

revenue equal to its total costs (explicit plus implicit costs). This is the level of profit necessary to keep resources employed in that particular firm. (Chapter 8)

Normative Economics The study of "what should be" in economic matters. (Chapter 1)

Oligopoly A theory of market structure based on three assumptions: few sellers and many buyers, firms producing either homogeneous or differentiated products, and significant barriers to entry. (Chapter 11)

Opportunity Cost The most highly valued opportunity or alternative forfeited when a choice is made. (Chapter 1)

Optimal Currency Area A geographic area in which exchange rates can be fixed or a common currency used without sacrificing domestic economic goals—such as low unemployment. (Chapter 20)

Overvaluation A currency is overvalued if its price in terms of other currencies is above the equilibrium price. (Chapter 20)

Own Price The price of a good. For example, if the price of oranges is $1, this is (its) own price. (Chapter 3)

Partnership A form of business that is owned by two or more co-owners (partners) who share any profits the business earns; each of the partners is legally responsible for all debts incurred by the firm. (Chapter 7)

Perfect Competition A theory of market structure based on four assumptions: there are many sellers and buyers, sellers sell a homogeneous good, buyers and sellers have all relevant information, and there is easy entry into and exit from the market. (Chapter 9)

Perfect Price Discrimination Occurs when the seller charges the highest price each consumer would be willing to pay for the product rather than go without it. (Chapter 10)

Perfectly Elastic Demand A small percentage change in price causes an extremely large percentage change in

quantity demanded (from buying all to buying nothing). (Chapter 5)

Perfectly Inelastic Demand Quantity demanded does not change as price changes. (Chapter 5)

Positive Economics The study of "what is" in economic matters. (Chapter 1)

Positive Externality Exists when a person's or group's actions cause a benefit (beneficial side effect) to be felt by others. (Chapter 17)

Positive Rate of Time Preference Preference for earlier availability of goods over later availability of goods. (Chapter 16)

Poverty Income Threshold (Poverty Line) Income level below which people are considered to be living in poverty. (Chapter 15)

Present Value The current worth of some future dollar amount of income or receipts. (Chapter 16)

Price Ceiling A government-mandated maximum price above which legal trades cannot be made. (Chapter 3)

Price Discrimination Occurs when the seller charges different prices for the product it sells, and the price differences do not reflect cost differences. (Chapter 10)

Price Elasticity of Demand A measure of the responsiveness of quantity demanded to changes in price. (Chapter 5)

Price Elasticity of Supply Measures the responsiveness of quantity supplied to changes in price. (Chapter 5)

Price Floor A government-mandated minimum price below which legal trades cannot be made. (Chapter 3)

Price Leadership Theory In this theory of oligopoly, the dominant firm in the industry determines price and all other firms take their price as given. (Chapter 11)

Price Searcher A seller that has the ability to control to some degree the price of the product it sells. (Chapter 10)

Price Taker A seller that does not have the ability to control the price of the product it sells; it takes the price determined in the market. (Chapter 9)

Producers' (Sellers') Surplus (PS) The difference between the price sellers receive for a good and the minimum or lowest price for which they would have sold the good. PS = Price received − Minimum selling price. (Chapter 2)

Production Possibilities Frontier (PPF) Represents the possible combinations of two goods that can be produced in a certain period of time, under the conditions of a given state of technology and fully employed resources. (Chapter 2)

(Production) Subsidy A monetary payment by government to a producer of a good or service. (Chapter 3)

Productive Efficiency The situation that exists when a firm produces its output at the lowest possible per unit cost (lowest *ATC*). (Chapter 9)

Profit The difference between total revenue and total cost. (Chapter 8)

Profit-Maximization Rule Profit is maximized by producing the quantity of output at which *MR = MC*. (Chapter 9)

Proprietorship A form of business that is owned by one individual who makes all the business decisions, receives the entire profits, and is legally responsible for the debts of the firm. (Chapter 7)

Public Choice The branch of economics that deals with the application of economic principles and tools to public-sector decision making. (Chapter 18)

Public Choice Theory of Regulation Holds that regulators are seeking to do, and will do through regulation, what is in their best interest (specifically to enhance their power and the size and budget of their regulatory agencies). (Chapter 12)

Public Employee Union A union whose membership is made up of individuals who work for the local, state, or federal government. (Chapter 14)

Public Franchise A right granted to a firm by government that permits the firm to provide a particular good or service and excludes all others from doing the same. (Chapter 10)

Public Good A good the consumption of which by one person does not reduce the consumption by another person-that is, a public good is characterized by nonrivalry in consumption. There are both excludable and nonexcludable public goods. An excludable public good is a good that while nonrivalrous in consumption can be denied to a person who does not pay for it. A nonexcludable public good is a good that is nonrivalrous in consumption and that cannot be denied to a person who does not pay for it. (Chapter 17)

Public Interest Theory of Regulation Holds that regulators are seeking to do, and will do through regulation, what is in the best interest of the public or society at large. (Chapter 12)

Purchasing Power Parity (PPP) Theory States that exchange rates between any two currencies will adjust to reflect changes in the relative price levels of the two countries. (Chapter 20)

Pure Economic Rent A category of economic rent where the payment is to a factor that is in fixed supply, implying that it has zero opportunity costs. (Chapter 16)

Quota A legal limit on the amount of a good that may be imported. (Chapter 19)

Rational Ignorance The state of not acquiring information because the costs of acquiring the information are greater than the benefits. (Chapter 18)

Rationing Device A means for deciding who gets what of available resources and goods. (Chapter 1)

Real Income Income adjusted for price changes. A person has more (less) real income as the price of a good falls (rises), *ceteris paribus.* (Chapter 6)

Real Interest Rate The nominal interest rate adjusted for expected inflation; that is, the nominal interest rate minus the expected inflation rate. (Chapter 16)

Regulatory Lag The time period between when a natural monopoly's costs change and when the regulatory agency adjusts prices for the natural monopoly. (Chapter 12)

Relative Price The price of a good in terms of another good. (Chapter 3)

Rent Seeking Actions of individuals and groups who spend resources to influence public policy in the hope of redistributing (transferring) income to themselves from others. (Chapter 10)

Residual Claimants Persons who share in the profits of a business firm. (Chapter 7)

Resource Allocative Efficiency The situation that exists when firms produce the quantity of output at which price equals marginal cost: *P = MC*. (Chapter 9)

Revaluation A government act that changes the exchange rate by raising the official price of a currency. (Chapter 20)

Rivalrous in Consumption A good is rivalrous in consumption if its consumption by one person reduces its consumption by others. (Chapter 17)

Roundabout Method of Production The production of capital goods that enhance productive capabilities in order to ultimately bring about increased consumption. (Chapter 16)

Satisficing Behavior Behavior directed to meeting some satisfactory (not maximum) profit target. (Chapter 7)

Scarcity The condition in which our wants are greater than the limited resources available to satisfy those wants. (Chapter 1)

Screening The process used by employers to increase the probability of choosing "good" employees based on certain criteria. (Chapter 13)

Second-Degree Price Discrimination Occurs when the seller charges a uniform price per unit for one specific quantity, a lower price for an additional quantity, and so on. (Chapter 10)

Separation of Ownership from Control (or Management) Refers to the division of interests between owners and managers that may occur in large business firms. (Chapter 7)

Share of Stock A claim on the assets of a corporation that gives the purchaser a share of the ownership of the corporation. (Chapter 7)

Shirking The behavior of a worker who is putting forth less than the agreed-to effort. (Chapter 7)

Short Run A period of time in which some inputs in the production process are fixed. (Chapter 8)

Short-Run (Firm) Supply Curve The portion of the firm's marginal cost curve that lies above the average variable cost curve. (Chapter 9)

Short-Run Market (Industry) Supply Curve The horizontal "addition" of all existing firms' short-run supply curves. (Chapter 9)

Shortage (Excess Demand) A condition in which quantity demanded is greater than quantity supplied. Shortages occur only at prices below equilibrium price. (Chapter 3)

Socially Optimal Amount (Output) An amount that takes into account and adjusts for all benefits (external and private) and all costs (external and private). The socially optimal amount is the amount at which $MSB = MSC$. Sometimes, the socially optimal amount is referred to as the efficient amount. (Chapter 17)

Special Drawing Right (SDR) An international money, created by the IMF, in the form of bookkeeping entries; like gold and currencies, they can be used by nations to settle international accounts. (Chapter 20)

Special Interest Groups Subsets of the general population that hold (usually) intense preferences for or against a particular government service, activity, or policy. Often special interest groups gain from public policies that may not be in accord with the interests of the general public. (Chapter 18)

Strike The situation in which union employees refuse to work at a certain wage or under certain conditions. (Chapter 14)

Substitutes Two goods that satisfy similar needs or desires. If two goods are substitutes, the demand for one rises as the price of the other rises (or the demand for one falls as the price of the other falls). (Chapter 3)

Substitution Effect The portion of the change in the quantity demanded of a good that is attributable to a change in its relative price. (Chapter 6)

Sunk Cost A cost incurred in the past that cannot be changed by current decisions and therefore cannot be recovered. (Chapter 8)

Supply The willingness and ability of sellers to produce and offer to sell different quantities of a good at different prices during a specific time period. (Chapter 3)

Supply Schedule The numerical tabulation of the quantity supplied of a good at different prices. (Chapter 3)

Surplus (Excess Supply) A condition in which quantity supplied is greater than quantity demanded. Surpluses occur only at prices above equilibrium price. (Chapter 3)

Tariff A tax on imports. (Chapter 19)

Technology The body of skills and knowledge concerning the use of resources in production. An advance in technology commonly refers to the ability to produce more output with a fixed amount of resources or the ability to produce the same output with fewer resources. (Chapter 2)

Terms of Trade How much of one thing is given up for how much of something else. (Chapter 2)

Theory An abstract representation of the real world designed with the intent to better understand that world. (Chapter 1)

Third-Degree Price Discrimination Occurs when the seller charges different prices in different markets or charges a different price to different segments of the buying population. (Chapter 10)

Tie-in Sale A sale whereby one good can be purchased only if another good is also purchased. (Chapter 3)

Total Cost (*TC*) The sum of fixed costs and variable costs. (Chapter 8)

Total Revenue Price times quantity sold. (Chapter 5)

Total Utility The total satisfaction a person receives from consuming a particular quantity of a good. (Chapter 6)

Trade (Exchange) The process of giving up one thing for something else. (Chapter 2)

Tradeoff More of one good means less of another good. (Chapter 2)

Transaction Costs The costs associated with the time and effort needed to search out, negotiate, and consummate an exchange. (Chapter 2)

Transfer Payments Payments to persons that are not made in return for goods and services currently supplied. (Chapter 15)

Transitivity The principle whereby if *A* is preferred to *B,* and *B* is preferred to *C,* then *A* is preferred to *C*. (Chapter 6 Appendix)

Trust A combination of firms that come together to act as a monopolist. (Chapter 12)

Undervaluation A currency is undervalued if its price in terms of other currencies is below the equilibrium price. (Chapter 20)

Union Shop An organization in which a worker is not required to be a member of the union to be hired, but must become a member within a certain period of time after being employed. (Chapter 14)

Unit Elastic Demand The percentage change in quantity demanded is equal to the percentage change in price. Quantity demanded changes proportionately to price changes. (Chapter 5)

Unlimited Liability A legal term that signifies that the personal assets of the owner(s) of a firm may be used to settle the debts of the firm. (Chapter 7)

(Upward-sloping) Supply Curve The graphical representation of the law of supply. (Chapter 3)

Util An artificial construct used to measure utility. (Chapter 6)

Utility A measure of the satisfaction, happiness, or benefit that results from the consumption of a good. (Chapters 1, 6)

Value Marginal Product (*VMP*) The price of the good multiplied by the marginal physical product of the factor: $VMP = P \times MPP$. (Chapter 13)

Variable Costs Costs that vary with output; the costs associated with variable inputs. (Chapter 8)

Variable Input An input whose quantity can be changed as output changes. (Chapter 8)

Veil of Ignorance The imaginary veil or curtain behind which a person does not know his or her position in the income distribution. (Chapter 15)

Vertical Merger A merger between companies in the same industry but at different stages of the production process. (Chapter 12)

"Voluntary" Export Restraint (VER) An agreement between two countries in which the exporting country "voluntarily" agrees to limit its exports to the importing country. (Chapter 19)

Wage Discrimination The situation that exists when individuals of equal ability and productivity (as measured by their contribution to output) are paid different wage rates. (Chapter 15)

X-Inefficiency The increase in costs and organizational slack in a monopoly resulting from the lack of competitive pressure to push costs down to their lowest possible level. (Chapter 10)

Photo Credits